Securities Industry Association

CAPITAL
MARKETS
HANDBOOK
Second Edition

edited by

John C. Burch, Jr.
and Bruce S. Foerster

Securities Industry Association

CAPITAL MARKETS HANDBOOK
Second Edition

edited by

John C. Burch, Jr.
and Bruce S. Foerster

ASPEN LAW & BUSINESS
A Division of Aspen Publishers, Inc.
Gaithersburg   New York

This publication is designed to provide accurate and authoritative information in regard to the subject matter covered. It is sold with the understanding that the publisher is not engaged in rendering legal, accounting, or other professional services. If legal advice or other professional advice is required, the services of a competent professional person should be sought.

—From a *Declaration of Principles* jointly adopted by
a Committee of the American Bar Association and a
Committee of Publishers and Associations

1 2 3 4 5 6 7 8 9 0

About Aspen Law & Business

Aspen Law & Business — comprising the former Prentice Hall Law & Business, Little, Brown and Company's Professional Division, and Wiley Law Publications — is a leading publisher of authoritative treatises, practice manuals, services, and journals for attorneys, financial and tax advisors, corporate and bank directors, and other business professionals. Our mission is to provide practical solution-based how-to information keyed to the latest legislative, judicial, and regulatory developments.

We offer publications in the areas of banking and finance; bankruptcy; business and commercial law; construction law; corporate law; pensions, benefits, and labor; insurance law; securities; taxation; intellectual property; government and administrative law; real estate law; matrimonial and family law; environmental and health law; international law; legal practice and litigation; and criminal law.

Other Aspen Law & Business products treating securities law issues include:

Corporate Finance and the Securities Laws
Securities Regulation
U.S. Regulation of the International Securities and Derivatives Markets
U.S. Securities Regulation of Foreign Issuers: Financial Reporting and Disclosure Practice
INSIGHTS: The Corporate & Securities Law Advisor
The Investment Lawyer: Covering Legal and Regulatory Issues of Asset Management
Broker-Dealer Law and Regulation
Fundamentals of Securities Regulation
The Regulation of Money Managers
A Practical Guide to SEC Proxy and Compensation Rules
A Practical Guide to Section 16: Reporting and Compliance
EDGAR Filer Handbook: A Guide for Electronic Filing with the SEC
Meetings of Stockholders
Securities Activities of Banks
Raising Capital
Securitization of Financial Assets

ASPEN LAW & BUSINESS
A Division of Aspen Publishers, Inc.
A Wolters Kluwer Company
www.aspenpublishers.com

SUBSCRIPTION NOTICE

This Aspen Law & Business product is updated on a periodic basis with supplements to reflect important changes in the subject matter. If you purchased this product directly from Aspen Law & Business, we have already recorded your subscription for the update service.

If, however, you purchased this product from a bookstore and wish to receive future updates and revised or related volumes billed separately with a 30-day examination review, please contact our Customer Service Department at 1-800-234-1660, or send your name, company name (if applicable), address, and the title of the product to:

ASPEN LAW & BUSINESS
A Division of Aspen Publishers, Inc.
7201 McKinney Circle
Frederick, MD 21704

ABOUT THE EDITORS

John C. Burch, Jr., born and educated in Nashville, Tennessee, graduated from Vanderbilt University in 1966 after service in the U.S. Army. He began his business career that year with the Bank of New York. He entered the investment banking business with Loeb Rhoades & Co. in 1970. In 1976 he returned to Nashville to accept a position with J. C. Bradford & Co. He joined Equitable Securities in 1982 and headed its Equity Syndicate Department for sixteen years.

He is active in the Securities Industry Association, chairs its Syndicate Committee and is Chairman-elect of the Southern/South Central District. He is also a NASDR arbitrator and a member of the Nashville Securities Dealers Association and the Association for Investment Management and Research. For thirty years he has been involved in all aspects of capital markets including institutional sales, trading and research and investment banking for natural gas utilities. He is listed in Who's Who in America and Who's Who in Finance and Industry. John is currently a Managing Director with SunTrust Equitable Securities Corporation.

John and his wife Susan live in Nashville and raised three children—Frances (1970), Christina (1972) and John (1977).

Bruce S. Foerster, a midwesterner by birth and upbringing, earned an AB in English at Haverford College and an MBA in Management Information and Control at the University of Pennsylvania's Wharton School. Sandwiched between these academic pursuits were seven years of active duty as a commissioned officer in the U.S. Navy (followed by twenty years in the Naval Reserve with retirement as a Captain).

Bruce spent twenty-three years with five different Wall Street firms from 1972–1994, in increasingly senior positions in equity and fixed income capital markets. In 1995, he founded South Beach Capital as a corporate financial advisory firm and served as an independent director

of a group of mutual funds, a non-industry governor of the Philadelphia Stock Exchange and a director of several public and private
companies. In April 1999, his firm merged with a Milwaukee broker-
dealer, Collopy & Company, to become South Beach Capital Markets
Incorporated—an investment bank—headquartered in downtown
Miami.

   Bruce and his second wife Gail live in Miami Beach and are raising two children—Otto (1982) and Lucy (1984). Bruce's oldest child
from his first marriage, Samantha (1975), lives in San Francisco, and
her mother, Suzanne, lives in Charleston, South Carolina.

SUMMARY OF CONTENTS

TABLE OF CONTENTS

Chapter 1

INTRODUCTION TO THE SECURITIES AND EXCHANGE COMMISSION AND COMPILATION OF THE FEDERAL SECURITIES LAWS AND THE GLASS-STEAGALL ACT

Chapter 2

UNDERWRITING DOCUMENTATION

Chapter 3

UNDERWRITING AND NEW ISSUE
MARKETING PROCESSES

Chapter 4

DEAL PRICING

Chapter 5

FORMS OF NEW ISSUE DISTRIBUTION
AND AFTERMARKET TRADING

Chapter 6

SETTLEMENT AND DELIVERY

Chapter 7

COMPLIANCE

Chapter 8

SELF-REGULATION CONCEPT—MAJOR DOMESTIC AND SELECTED INTERNATIONAL SECURITIES MARKETS AND OTHER ENTITIES INTERFACING WITH THE SECURITIES INDUSTRY

APPENDICES

FOREWORD TO THE SECOND EDITION

Technology, globalization, competition, consolidation and demographics are reshaping the securities industry's role in the global economy. Information technology enables securities professionals to provide more services and more complex financial strategies to issuers and investors as the intermediary roles that firms and markets play are redefined. Financial markets throughout the world are increasingly linked to each other. U.S. holdings, for example, of foreign securities continue to reach new highs as foreign holdings of U.S. stocks also set records. Meanwhile, the "baby boomers," within 12 years of starting to retire at age 65, are moving away from being spenders to being savers and investors. In 1990, one in five American families held stocks, bonds, mutual funds or other securities; by 1995, that ratio had dropped to one in three; by 2000, the ratio was one in two.

Our industry is on the leading edge of these changes, raising capital to help finance growth and innovation. Our success and global preeminence result from the high level of trust and confidence that the public has in the U.S. capital markets. Enhancing the public's trust and confidence continues to be the Securities Industry Association's most important goal. Our initiatives include "best practices" to guide securities professionals in their relationships with customers, investor education materials, and industry education programs.

The *Capital Markets Handbook* is one of the latest Securities Industry Association initiatives. It is designed to help firms train their capital markets professionals and to be used as a desk reference manual. It addresses a need that has been left unserved until now.

The industry's response to the First Edition was very positive, and we hope you find this Second Edition even more useful. As always, we welcome your comments.

Marc E. Lackritz
President
Securities Industry Association
Washington D.C.
October 2000

PREFACE TO THE SECOND EDITION

When our publisher proposed accelerating the time schedule for this edition, Bruce quickly realized that the only way to cope with the enormity of the editing task and the short time frame for completion of it would be to take on a co-editor. John Burch was the logical choice given his significant contributions to the First Edition and his infectious enthusiasm for the project dating from inception. Our partnership melds disparate abilities, a shared love for the business and a common goal – helping investment bankers, both in corporate finance and in capital markets, become ever more skilled practitioners.

We have many people to thank, most of whose names already appear in the Acknowledgements to the First Edition. Specifically, we owe deep gratitude to the many talented people at our publisher, Aspen Law & Business. This opus never would have come to fruition without the enthusiastic support and vision of Richard H. Kravitz, Publisher and Senior Vice President and the understated but firm leadership of Ronald V. Sinesio, Group Editorial Director—"thank you, Rick and Ron." Additionally, we thank the other members of the Aspen staff with whom we worked directly: Ramona C. Baxter, Marketing Manager; Laurel Binder-Arain, Editor; Betsey Cohen, Managing Editor; Marc P. Gallant, Director of New Product Development; and Larry Teator, Bulk Sales Manager.

The continued support of Marc Lackritz, Don Kittell and George Monahan of SIA has been gratifying and invaluable—"thank you" again. Lastly, we both thank our families for their support and encouragement. Friends and business acquaintances readily provide kudos when one experiences success, but it is to family where one always goes for nurturing and psychic replenishment in times of stress.

Lastly, we repeat the close of the Preface to the First Edition, modified slightly to reflect our partnership. As editors, we were fortunate enough to work with many talented people who deserve the bulk of whatever credit users of this handbook bestow on its creators. With regard to mistakes, errors and omissions, all editors must absorb full responsibility, and we do so readily. Revisions will speak to the users' criticisms. This handbook is for your use to help enable you to become more professional participants in an exciting business.

John C. Burch, Jr.   Bruce S. Foerster
Nashville, Tennessee   Miami, Florida

October 2000

PREFACE TO THE FIRST EDITION

The securities industry has been good to my family and me, providing a livelihood for most of my adult years. Those years have been intellectually and financially both challenging and rewarding. Editorship of this handbook allows me the opportunity to give back something to the business and to the next generation of investment banking professionals.

In the Acknowledgements section, the reader will find the names of all who helped me either in fostering my fascination for the many legal, regulatory, and procedural nuances of the securities business or in putting together this opus. However, special thanks go to the Securities Industry Association—Marc Lackritz and Don Kittell, who patiently believed in the project, and George Monahan, who provided me with administrative backup, encouragement, insightful criticism, and unflagging support over the two-year production process—and to my wife, Gail, and our children Samantha, Otto, and Lucy—who all have been indelibly affected by the time I devoted to the business of investment banking at their expense. Their understanding and unconditional love for me takes my breath away.

As editor, I was fortunate enough to work with many talented people who deserve the bulk of whatever credit users of this handbook bestow on its creators. With regard to mistakes, errors and omissions, all editors must absorb full responsibility, and I do so readily. Revisions will speak to the users' criticisms. This handbook is for your use to help enable you to become more professional participants in an exciting business.

Bruce S. Foerster
Miami Beach, Florida
May 1999

ACKNOWLEDGEMENTS TO THE FIRST EDITION

The Editor thanks the people listed below who were instrumental in bringing this project to fruition—particularly Charles L. Bennett, John C. Burch, Jr. and William H. Dowson, all of whom did heavy lifting in manuscript adaptation, production and editing.

Also, Michael T. Ott for his early support and consistent encouragement; SunTrust Equitable Securities for its gracious hospitality, cooperation and technical support in hosting drafting sessions, printing and binding drafts and Laurie Ford Hinkle and Ray Ryan of its capital markets group for editing and research; Edmund J. Cashman and Charles R. Treuhold for early document review; Richard B. duBusc for review with regard to the fixed income side of the business; Ross M. Langill for trial draft review; and J. Scott Coburn, under whose chairmanship of the SIA's Syndicate Committee this opus came to life.

SIA
Linda Connelly
Lenore C. Dittmar
Doreen Giletto
Andrea D. Kennedy

South Beach Capital
Pamela J. Moran-Walcutt
Susan L. Walcutt

Thanks also to all the people listed below who at one time or another helped fuel my interest in either the technical, procedural or legal aspects of the investment banking business; encouraged me to teach elements of this business to the next generation; or contributed directly to the completion of this Handbook. My sincere apology to all whom I neglected to mention.

Industry
Silas R. Anthony, Jr.
Andrew M. Blum

Howard L. Blum Jr.
Ruth Braun

T. Anthony Brooks
Jeffrey H. Bunzel
James F. Burns III
James Carlucci
Richard C. Casey
Theodore J. Coburn
William Cockrum
Andrew J. Cooley
Judith Cutler
Justin C. Day
Carl H. Doerge, Jr.
John E. Eckleberry
Jason M. Elsas Jr.
Roger D. Elsas
Thomas A. Fleming
Archibald McG. Foster
Timothy H. Ganahl
Gary L. Gastineau
Robert J. Glenn
Thomas E. Goss
John H. Gutfreund
Randy Harris
Emmett J. Harty
Gate H. Hawn
Oliver C. Hazard
Fred Hessinger
Fred L. Heyes
William Hinners
John C. Kallop
Robert J. Kase
Byron D. Klapper

Robert A. Kleinert
Erica Levitt
Andrew J. Macchia
Adrian M. Massie, Jr.
Jill G. Monroe
Frederick C. Moss
William M. Osborne III
Norman H. Pessin
Rodney A. Plaskett
Stephen R. Pierce
Jeffrey Posner
Humbert B. Powell
Peter S. Rawlings
Barbara Russo
Gregory E. Sacco Jr.
James H. Scott
Thomas G. Shea
Craig S. Sim
Philip M. Skidmore
Patrick Stevenson
James M. Stewart
David C. Strauss
Sabin C. Streeter
Charles H. Symington
Peter Taussig
Milton J. Walters
Mark E. Waxman
David Weild IV
Frederick B. Whittemore
John A. Wing

SIA
Edward I. O'Brien
Jack O'Neill
Jeffrey M. Schaeffer

Harvard University
Samuel L. Hayes III

University of Florida
David T. Brown
W. Andrew McCollough
John Kraft
Alan S. Pareira
Jay R. Ritter
Michael D. Ryngaert

Michigan State University
James R. Ledinsky

DTC
Edward J. McGuire Jr.
Anthony P. Reres

Legal Profession
Joseph M. Armbrust
Richard Chase
Robert E. Dineen
Charles J. Johnson, Jr.
Richard M. Leisner
Robert C. Lewis
Richard T. Prins
Jeffrey S. Puretz
E. Thomas Unterman

New York University
Jules Bachman
Ernest C. Bloch

University of Miami School of Law
C. Raymond Langston III
Soia Mentschikoff
Hugh Sowards

New York Times
Peter Truell

Financial Journalist
John Rothchild

NASD
Frank J. Formica
Richard J. Fortwengler
Joseph R. Hardiman
Suzanne E. Rothwell
Carl R. Sperapani

NYSE
Stephen Wheeler

ACKNOWLEDGEMENTS TO THE SECOND EDITION

The Editors thank the people listed below who were helpful in preparing the Second Edition.

Industry
David Krell
James J. Jockle
Gina Penix

INTRODUCTION

The Securities Industry Association (SIA) was established in 1972 through the merger of The Association of Stock Exchange Firms, which was founded in 1913 and represented retail brokerage firms, and the Investment Bankers Association of America which was founded in 1912 and represented investment banks.

The SIA works with its more than 750 member firms throughout North America to foster an effective capital raising and investment process; to present member firm views to legislative and regulatory bodies at the federal and state level; to serve as a forum for addressing key industry issues; to act as a source of information and a catalyst for ideas; and to offer a broad range of services to assist member firm executives in their management responsibilities.

SIA member firms—including investment banks, broker-dealers, and mutual fund companies—account for approximately 90 percent, or $270 billion, of securities firms' revenues and employ more than 400,000 individuals as of year end 1999. Such firms handle or manage the accounts of more than 50 million investors directly and tens of millions of investors indirectly through corporate, thrift, and pension plans. Each day, billions of dollars in transactions clear and settle on the stock and bond markets based on a handshake, a nod, a hand signal, a keystroke, a click of a mouse or a phone call. Any lapse in professionalism by a firm or its employees can undermine the public's trust and confidence not only in the firm itself but in the capital markets generally. Enhancing the public trust and confidence in capital markets is the SIA's highest strategic goal.

The SIA Syndicate Committee is one of more than 30 SIA committees made up of individuals from various member firms that serve as forums for key industry issues. Among recent topics addressed by this committee are syndicate settlements, prospectus delivery under T+3, and DTC electronic tracking. This *Capital Markets Handbook* (Handbook) is published under the auspices of the SIA Syndicate

Committee in furtherance of maintaining public trust and confidence through the education of industry participants to achieve and maintain a high level of professionalism.

The SIA respects and encourages the individuality of each member firm's unique approach to the business of capital raising for its issuer clients. How often have you heard the phrase "pricing a deal is an art not a science . . ." enunciated by a senior industry professional? The answer is "often" because creativity and individuality are integral to the very essence of deal making. As such, The Board of Directors of the SIA has no interest in instructing its individual member firms in the "how-to's" of deal making. It is not SIA's place or mandate. SIA is an industry trade group not a Self-Regulatory Organization. Nonetheless, the Board believes that setting high standards of professional conduct and encouraging adherence to just and equitable principles of fair trade will inure to the benefit of the industry's issuer and investor clients alike. Thus, this Handbook is designed and intended to be a user friendly, desk reference source and training manual for capital markets, syndicate and corporate finance practitioners.[1]

Feedback is both necessary and welcome to help keep this handbook relevant and current for you the user, since both securities laws and investment banking industry practices will most likely continue to evolve. Please address comments, feedback, suggestions for additions, deletions, and changes to either editor:

John C. Burch, Jr.
SunTrust Equitable Securities
800 Nashville City Center
8th Floor
Nashville, TN 37219
615-780-9380/4171 fax
JOHN.BURCH@suntrust.com

Bruce S. Foerster
South Beach Capital Markets
150 Southeast Second Avenue
Suite 1007
Miami FL 33131-1577
305-358-3232/8606 fax
bsf@sbcmkts.com

---

1. By its very nature, publication of a manual such as this one requires an end or cut-off date for text. However, since the nation's securities laws and the rules of all securities Self-Regulatory Organizations are ever changing, the SIA and the editors caution the reader/user to consult appropriate counsel whenever or wherever necessary to ensure compliance with the most current and applicable portions of the rule or regulation in question.

Chapter 1

INTRODUCTION TO THE SECURITIES AND EXCHANGE COMMISSION AND COMPILATION OF THE FEDERAL SECURITIES LAWS AND THE GLASS-STEAGALL ACT

§ 1.01 INTRODUCTION TO THE SECURITIES AND EXCHANGE COMMISSION

[A] Background and Overview

Early in President Franklin Delano Roosevelt's first term in office, there was vigorous public debate and outcry over perceived and real abuses that occurred in the sale of new issue securities during the period leading up to the stock market crash of October 1929. In response, the United States Congress drafted and passed, and the President signed into law over time, significant legislation impacting the securities industry.

The United States Securities and Exchange Commission (SEC or the Commission) became an independent, nonpartisan, quasi-judicial regulatory agency on June 6, 1934. The SEC's mission is to administer federal securities laws, to issue rules and regulations to provide protection for investors, and to ensure that the securities markets are fair and honest—primarily by promoting adequate and effective disclosure of information to the investing public. The laws administered by the Commission are the

- Securities Act of 1933;
- Securities Exchange Act of 1934;

- Public Utility Holding Company Act of 1935;

- Trust Indenture Act of 1939;

- Investment Advisers Act of 1940;

- Investment Company Act of 1940;

- Securities Investment Protection Act of 1970;

- National Securities Improvement Act of 1996; and

- Financial Services Modernization Act of 1999.

The SEC reports annually to Congress on administration of these laws and also serves as adviser to federal courts in corporate reorganization proceedings under Chapter 11 of the Bankruptcy Reform Act of 1978.[1]

The Commission is composed of five members appointed by the President of the United States, with the advice and consent of the Senate, for fixed five-year terms. The original appointees were Joseph P. Kennedy (a Democrat and father of John F. Kennedy, the nation's thirty-fifth President); two other Democrats—James F. Landis (a New York attorney who, along with Benjamin V. Cohen, largely wrote the Securities Act of 1933) and Ferdinand Pecora (counsel to the 1932 Senate subcommittee examining stock market and investment banking practices); and two Republicans from the Federal Trade Commission—George C. Matthews (a former state securities law administrator in Wisconsin) and Robert E. Healy (from Vermont and formerly in charge of a 1928 congressional investigation of the public utility industry of Vermont).[2]

---

1. Large portions of this chapter have been adapted initially from *The Work of the SEC*, 1997, and *The Investor Advocate: How the SEC Protects Investors and Maintains Market Integrity*, 2000. http://www.sec.gov/asec/wet.htm. Washington D.C. 1997. The SEC Web site is a public document and therefore without copyright. (Editor conversation with the Director of the Office of Investor Education and Assistance—July 15, 1997.) Readers should know that the laws, regulations, and practices cited herein are subject to continuous change and/or modification, and thus certain portions of this handbook may become outmoded or obsolete prior to publisher revision.

2. Vincent P. Carosso, *Investment Banking in America* (Cambridge, MA: Harvard University Press, 1970), pp. 376–381.

The Chairman is designated by the President. Terms are staggered, expiring annually on June 5, with not more than three members having the same political party affiliation. A deliberative collegial body, the Commission meets numerous times monthly to debate and decide upon regulatory issues. Like other regulatory agencies, the Commission has two types of meetings. As prescribed under the Government in Sunshine Act of 1973, federal governmental agency meetings must be open to the public and to members of the press.[3] However, if necessary to protect the Commission's ability to conduct investigations and/or protect the rights of individuals and entities, which may be the subject of Commission inquiries, certain individual meetings may be closed.

Commission meetings are generally held to deliberate on and resolve issues the SEC staff brings before the Commissioners. Issues may include interpretations of federal securities laws, amendments to existing rules under the laws, new rules (often to reflect changed conditions in the marketplace), actions to enforce the laws or to discipline those subject to direct regulation, legislation to be proposed by the SEC, and matters concerning administration of the Commission itself. Matters not requiring joint deliberation may be resolved by procedures set forth in the Code of Federal Regulations. Resolution of issues brought before the SEC may take the form of new rules or amendments to existing ones, enforcement actions, or disciplinary actions. The most common activity is rulemaking, generally the result of staff recommendations made to the Commissioners.

The SEC's staff is composed of lawyers, accountants, financial analysts and examiners, engineers, investigators, economists, and other professionals. Under the direction of the Commission, the staff attempts to assure that publicly held companies, broker-dealers in securities, investment companies and advisers, and other participants in the securities markets comply with federal securities laws and that securities markets are fair, honest, and in compliance with federal securities laws, rules, and regulations. The Commission's work is remedial, not punitive, and so it also works closely with criminal authorities in matters of mutual interest. The staff is separated into divisions with regional and district offices, each directed by officials appointed by the Chairman. Brief descriptions of the duties and responsibilities of the staff follow.

---

3. Chief sponsor of this legislation was then Senator (D-FL) Lawton M. Chiles, Jr. (*New York Times,* December 13, 1998).

[B]   Divisions and Offices

[1]   Division of Corporation Finance

Corporation Finance has overall responsibility for ensuring that disclosure requirements are met by publicly held companies registered with the SEC. Its work includes reviewing registration statements for new securities, proxy materials, annual reports the SEC requires from publicly held companies, documents concerning tender offers, and mergers and acquisitions.

This division renders administrative interpretations of the Securities Act, the Securities Exchange Act, and regulations thereunder to registrants, prospective registrants, and others. It is also responsible for certain statutes and regulations pertaining to small businesses and for the Trust Indenture Act of 1939. Applications for qualification of trust indentures are examined for compliance with the applicable requirements of the law and the Commission's rules. Corporation Finance works closely with the Office of the Chief Accountant in drafting rules and regulations that prescribe requirements for financial statements.

[2]   Division of Market Regulation

Market Regulation is responsible for oversight of activity in the secondary markets—registration and regulation of broker-dealers, oversight of Self-Regulatory Organizations (SROs), and oversight of other participants in the secondary markets such as transfer agents and clearing organizations.

Financial responsibility of these entities, trading and sale practices, policies affecting operation of the securities markets, and surveillance all fall under the purview of this division. In addition, Market Regulation carries out activities aimed at achieving the goal of a national market system as set forth in the Securities Act Amendments of 1975.[4] Market Regulation develops and presents market structure issues to the Commissioners for their consideration and oversees both the Securities Investor Protection Corporation (SIPC) and the Municipal Securities Rulemaking Board (MSRB).

---

4. 89 Stat. 97, P.L. 94-29 (1975).

[3]   Division of Investment Management

Investment Management has basic responsibility for administering the Investment Company Act of 1940 (40 Act),[5] the Investment Advisers Act of 1940,[6] and the Public Utility Holding Company Act of 1935 (35 Act).[7] This division attempts to assure compliance with regulations regarding the registration, sales practices, and advertising of mutual funds and investment advisers. Investment Management drafts rules and regulations and also processes investment company registration statements, proxy statements, periodic reports, applications for exemptive relief, requests for interpretation, and requests for no-action relief.

The division oversees the activities of all active, registered, public utility holding company systems, ensuring that their corporate structures and financings are permissible according to certain tests set forth in the 35 Act. Investment Management analyzes legal, financial, accounting, and engineering issues arising under the 35 Act. It participates in hearings to develop factual records when necessary, files briefs and participates in oral arguments before the SEC, and makes recommendations regarding the Commission's findings and decisions in cases that arise in administration of the law. All hearings are conducted in accordance with the SEC's Rules of Practice.

[4]   Division of Enforcement

This division is charged with enforcing federal securities laws, rules, and regulations. The division's responsibilities include investigating possible violations of federal securities laws and recommending appropriate remedies for consideration by the Commission. Possible violations may be discovered through the division's own inquiries; through referrals from other divisions or from outside sources such as self-regulatory organizations; or by other means including review of investor complaints and inquiries.

When potential securities violations warrant further investigation by the staff, the Commission is consulted before proceeding. The SEC

---

5. 54 Stat. 789, P.L. 76-768 (1940) (codified as amended at 15 U.S.C. § 80a-1 (1998)).

6. 54 Stat. 789, P.L. 76-768 (1940) (codified as amended at 15 U.S.C. § 80b-1 (1998)).

7. 49 Stat. 803, P.L. 74-333 (1935) (codified as amended at 15 U.S.C. § 79 (1998)).

may issue a formal order of investigation, which allows the staff to issue subpoenas and take other investigative action. At the conclusion of an investigation, the Commission may authorize the staff to seek injunctions or other court-ordered remedies, institute administrative proceedings against entities directly regulated by the SEC, or pursue other action as appropriate.

[5] Office of Administrative Law Judges

Pursuant to the Administrative Procedure Act of 1946 and the federal securities laws, administrative law judges preside at evidentiary hearings where the Commission has determined that public hearings are appropriate, in the public interest, and necessary for the protection of investors. The hearings, governed by the SEC's Rules of Practice, are conducted in a manner similar to a non-jury trial in federal district court. After notice is given, the parties appear at a hearing and present evidence as to the allegations in the Commission's Order Instituting Proceedings.

[6] Office of Administration and Personnel Management

This office develops, implements, and evaluates the Commission's programs for human resource and personnel management. In addition, it develops and executes programs for office services, such as procurement and contracting, property management, space acquisition and management, security, mail, and publications, printing, and desktop publishing.

[7] Office of the Chief Accountant

The Chief Accountant is the principal adviser to the SEC on accounting and auditing matters arising from the administration of the securities laws. Primary Commission activities designed to achieve compliance with the accounting and financial disclosure requirements of the federal securities laws include:

- rulemaking and interpretation that supplement private-sector accounting standards, implement financial disclosure requirements, and establish independence criteria for accountants;
- review and comment processes for agency filings directed to improving disclosures in filings, identifying emerging accounting

issues (which may result in rulemaking or private-sector standard setting), and identifying problems that may warrant enforcement actions;

- enforcement actions that impose sanctions and serve to deter
  improper financial reporting by enhancing the care with which
  registrants and their accountants analyze accounting issues;
  and

- oversight of private-sector efforts, principally by the Financial
  Accounting Standards Board (FASB) and the American Institute of Certified Public Accountants (AICPA), the two bodies
  charged with establishing accounting and auditing standards
  designed to improve financial accounting and reporting and the
  quality of audit practices.

[8]   Office of Compliance Inspections and Examinations (OCIE)

This office examines SROs, broker-dealers, transfer agents, clearing firms, investment companies, and investment advisers to foster
compliance with the securities laws, detect violative conduct, and keep
the SEC informed of developments in the regulated community. OCIE
determines policies and procedures with respect to the examination
program, and both OCIE and the SEC's regional offices conduct such
examinations.

The SEC conducts four types of inspections and examinations: (1)
compliance examinations of investment companies and investment
advisers; (2) inspections of SROs; (3) oversight examinations of broker-dealers; and (4) special purpose, sweep, and cause examinations.

Examinations of investment companies and investment advisers
test and evaluate such firms' compliance with securities laws and
applicable regulations. Inspections of SROs test and evaluate how
these organizations are performing their regulatory responsibilities.
Oversight examinations of broker-dealers test and evaluate the quality
of the examination oversight being exercised by broker-dealer SROs
and look for undiscovered violations or deficiencies. Special purpose,
sweep, and cause examinations provide a variety of techniques for
addressing matters of particular interest or concern. In special purpose
examinations, the staff conducts a series of limited examinations in a
carefully focused area of regulatory interest. In sweep examinations,

several teams conduct simultaneous examinations to provide regulatory oversight for particular geographic areas or segments of the industry. Finally, in cause examinations, the staff has reason to believe something is wrong and focuses on the transactions or events giving rise to such concern.

Among the more important goals of the examination program is quick and informal correction of compliance problems. When the staff finds deficiencies, it provides the registrant with a letter (known as a deficiency letter), identifying the problem(s) needing correction. Such letters are generally sent to the registrant within 90 days of the end of the examination. If the staff discovers violations that appear too serious for informal correction, the matter is referred to the Division of Enforcement for further investigation and possible enforcement action. The staff also lets the registrant know when it finds no violations.

[9]   Office of the Comptroller

This office administers the financial management and budget function. It assists the Executive Director in formulating budget and authorization requests, monitors the utilization of agency resources, and develops, oversees, and maintains SEC financial systems.

[10]   Office of Economic Analysis

This office deals with the economic and empirical issues that are inextricably associated with the SEC's regulatory activities. It analyzes the impacts and benefits of proposed regulations, conducts studies on specific rules, engages in long-term research and policy planning, and analyzes potentially significant developments in the marketplace.

[11]   Office of Equal Employment Opportunity (EEO)

The EEO develops and recommends policies designed to promote equal opportunity in all aspects of the agency's recruitment, selection, training, advancement, compensation, and supervision of employees. In its capacity as liaison between the Commission and the securities industry on diversity issues, this office sponsors roundtables and symposiums to encourage greater employment diversity in the securities industry.

[12]   Office of Executive Director

The Executive Director develops and executes the overall management policies of the Commission for all operating divisions and offices.

[13]   Office of Filings and Information Technologies

This office is responsible for receipt and initial handling of all public documents filed with the Commission. It also is responsible for custody and control of the SEC's official records, development and implementation of the records management program, and authentication of all documents produced for administrative or judicial proceedings.

Through this office's Public Reference Branch, the public may obtain a wide range of information from quarterly and annual reports, registration statements, proxy material, and other reports submitted by SEC filers. All corporate filings made after May 6, 1996, are available on the SEC Internet Web site <www.sec.gov>. All public documents are available for inspection in the Public Reference Room of the Commission's headquarters office in Washington, D.C., and in the Northeast and Midwest regional offices in New York City and Chicago, respectively. Copies of documents may be obtained for a nominal charge.

[14]   Office of the General Counsel

The General Counsel is the chief legal officer of the Commission. The office is the focal point for handling all appellate and other litigation brought by the SEC, either in connection with securities laws or against the Commission or its staff.

Duties of this office include representing the Commission in judicial proceedings; handling multidivisional legal matters; and acting in disciplinary proceedings under the Rules of Practice and providing independent advice and assistance to the SEC, its operating divisions, and offices. Advice may cover such matters as statutory interpretation, regulatory, and legislative matters, public or private investigations, and congressional hearings and investigations. The General Counsel directs and supervises all contested civil litigation and SEC responsibilities under the Bankruptcy Code and all related litigation. It also represents the Commission in all cases in appellate courts, filing briefs and presenting oral arguments. In private litigation involving the statutes

the Commission administers, this office represents the SEC as an ami-
cus curiae (friend of the court) on legal issues of general importance.

The Commission also recommends revisions in the statutes it
administers. In addition, it prepares comments on proposed legislation
that might affect its work or when asked for its views by Congress.
The Office of the General Counsel, together with the Office of Legislative Affairs and the division affected by such legislation, prepares
this legislative material.

[15]   Office of Information Technology

This office organizes and implements an integrated information
technology program to support the Commission and the staff. This
office operates the Electronic Data Gathering and Retrieval (EDGAR)
system, which electronically receives, processes, and disseminates
more than 500,000 public filings every year. It also maintains a very
active Web site containing a wealth of information about the Commission and the securities industry and hosts the entire EDGAR financial database for free public access.

[16]   Office of the Inspector General

This office conducts internal audits and internal investigations of
agency programs and operations, reviews existing and proposed legislation and regulations related to agency programs and operations,
and recommends policies to promote economy and efficiency and prevent fraud and abuse in agency programs and operations.

[17]   Office of International Affairs (OIA)

OIA has primary responsibility for negotiation and implementation of information-sharing arrangements and development of other
initiatives to facilitate international enforcement and regulatory cooperation. These arrangements provide for cooperation in investigations
of suspected unlawful conduct, market surveillance, and in the oversight of operations of regulated entities involved in cross-border activities.

[18]   Office of Investor Education and Assistance (formerly Office of Consumer Affairs)

The SEC created this office specifically to serve individual investors. The office makes sure that the concerns and problems encoun-
tered by individual investors are known throughout the SEC and

considered when the agency takes action. While investor assistance specialists are available to answer questions and analyze complaints, the office cannot act as lawyer or force a broker, brokerage firm, or company to resolve complaints.

[19]   Office of Legislative Affairs (OLA)

This office coordinates the legislative efforts of the Commission and communication between the SEC and Congress, including preparation of congressional testimony. OLA facilitates liaison with members of Congress and their committees and staffs, responds to congressional requests, and disseminates information about Commission legislative proposals and actions to Congress.

[20]   Office of Municipal Securities

This office acts as a clearinghouse and point of coordination for the SEC's municipal securities activities.

[21]   Office of Public Affairs, Policy Evaluation and Research

This office administers internal and external Commission information programs, coordinates press relations, manages the foreign visitors program, and monitors press coverage of issues related to the SEC and the securities industry.

[22]   Office of the Secretary

This office schedules Commission meetings, prepares and maintains records of its actions, and reviews documents submitted to the SEC for action.

[C]   General SEC Information[8]

Main Office
United States Securities and Exchange Commission
450 Fifth Street NW
Washington DC 20549
SEC Web site   <www.sec.gov>

Regional and district offices are maintained primarily to conduct broker-dealer and SRO examinations.

8. <http://www.sec.gov/asec/phones.htm> Last Update: 9/8/00.

Useful Telephone Numbers

Investor Information Service
1-800-SEC-0330   1-800-732-0330

Information Line (general SEC information)
202-942-8088/7114 TTY

Personnel Locator
202-942-4150/4095 TTY

Public Affairs (for press inquiries)
202-942-0020

Public Reference Room (for copies of public SEC records,
    filed documents, and notices of action)
202-942-8090/8092 TTY

Division of Corporation Finance, Office of Chief Counsel
202-942-2900

**Division of Market Regulation, Office of Interpretation
    and Guidance**
202-942-0069

Electronic Data Gathering and Retrieval (EDGAR)
    (Office of Filings and Information Services)
202-942-8900
     Web site address for Search EDGAR Archives Index <http://www.
sec.gov/egi-bin/srch-edgar>. The index is a full-text, WAIS searchable
index of the header information contained in each document.

EDGAR Filing Fee Information
    (Office of Filings and Information Services)
202-942-8989

Office of Filings and Information Services
    (Filing Desk for Paper Filings)
202-942-8050

Office of Investor Education and Assistance
    (Investor Assistance and Complaints)
202-942-7040/7065 TTY

Office of Municipal Securities
202-942-7300

Publications and Blank Forms Unit
202-942-4040

Office of Filings and Information Services
  (Branch of Registrations and Examinations)
202-942-8980

Office of the Secretary
202-942-7070

Office of Small Business—Small Business Ombudsman;
  Division of Corporation Finance
202-942-2950

(Editors' note—the SEC cannot accept collect calls.)

[D]   Compilation of Federal Securities Laws

[1]   Securities Act of 1933

The first piece of what today are the country's seven major securities statutes is the Securities Act of 1933 (33 Act).[9] The 33 Act marked a shift in oversight of new issue—primary market—securities activities from an individual state's merit review to federal government oversight and was modeled on the British system of full disclosure. This change was so profound that President Roosevelt, when signing the legislation into law, proclaimed that "securities law was to be changed from a system of *caveat emptor* (buyer beware) to one of *caveat vendor* (seller beware) . . ."[10]

The 33 Act was an attempt by the federal government to restore the public's confidence in the nation's securities markets, particularly with respect to the sale of new issues by providing "full and fair disclosure of the character of securities sold in interstate and foreign commerce and through the mails, and to prevent frauds in the sale thereof, and for other purposes."[11]

---

9. 48 Stat. 74, P.L. 73-22 (1933) (codified as amended at 15 U.S.C. § 77a (1998)).

10. Elizabeth L. Still and David E. Strongin, *The Securities Industry Briefing Book—A Partnership with America,* p. 32, Securities Industry Association, 1994.

11. *Id.*

The 33 Act stands to this day as the bedrock foundation upon which the new issue securities business rests. The concept of a regulator, the United States Securities and Exchange Commission, reviewing an offering document to ensure full disclosure of all aspects of the issuer/registrant's business helped to level the new issue playing field and left merit review—*i.e.,* the investment decision—mostly in the hands of the investor. Some individual state securities commissions continued to require merit review, a practice that has all but died out today.

It is important to understand that the SEC does not guarantee the value or merit of any particular investment, and it cannot bar the sale of securities of questionable value. The investor must make the ultimate judgment of the worth of securities offered for sale.[12] Additionally, the requirement that all corporate officers and directors sign the registration document puts real teeth into the government's determination to make the process fair and equitable.

The 33 Act defines industry terms. It also covers exempted securities and transactions and prohibitions relating to interstate commerce and the mails; registration of securities with the SEC; signing of the registration statement (by the issuer's officers and directors) and information required in it; declaration of effectiveness of registration statements; cease-and-desist proceedings; court review of orders; information required in prospectuses and civil liability relating to false registration statements, prospectuses, and communication; limitations of actions; liability of controlling persons; fraudulent interstate transactions; state control of securities; special powers of the SEC; injunctions and prosecution of offenses; SEC hearings; jurisdictions of offenses and lawsuits; unlawful representations; penalties; and jurisdiction of other government agencies over securities. It is a far-reaching statute.

Often called the "truth in securities" law, the 33 Act has two basic objectives: (1) to ensure that investors have access to material information about securities offered for public sale; and (2) to prevent misrepresentation, deceit, and other fraud in the sale of securities. The SEC attempts to accomplish these objectives through its requirement for the registration of public offers and sales of securities. Most offerings of debt and equity securities issued by corporations, limited

---

12. *The Work of the SEC.*

partnerships, trusts, and other issuers must be registered with the SEC. Federal and most domestic government debt securities are exempt, as are certain other transactions identified later in this section.

[a]   *Purpose of Registration.* Registration[13] is intended to provide adequate and accurate disclosure of all material facts concerning the issuing company and the securities it proposes to sell. Investors then have the information necessary to make a realistic appraisal of the merit of the securities and exercise informed judgment in determining whether or not to purchase.

Disclosure in and of itself does not guarantee the accuracy of the facts represented in the registration statement and prospectus. However, the law does prohibit false and misleading statements and nondisclosure of material facts under penalty of fine, imprisonment, or both. Investors who purchase securities and suffer losses have important recovery rights under the law if they can prove there was incomplete or inaccurate disclosure of material facts in the registration statement or prospectus. These rights must be asserted in an appropriate federal or state court, not before the SEC, which has no power to award damages.

[b]   *The Registration Process.* Registration of securities does not preclude the sale of securities by risky, poorly managed, or unprofitable companies. In fact, it is unlawful to represent that the SEC approves or disapproves of securities on their merits. The SEC has promulgated disclosure rules and registration forms for different types of companies. These forms require essential facts while minimizing the burden and expense of complying with the law. In general, registration forms call for:

- description of the company's properties and business;
- description of the security to be offered for sale and its relationship to the company's other securities;
- information about the management of the company; and
- financial statements certified by independent public accountants.

---

13. Most of the balance of this chapter has been adapted directly from *The Work of the SEC.*

Registration statements and preliminary prospectuses (red herring) covering securities become publicly available immediately after filing with the SEC. However, registration statements are subject to examination by SEC staff attorneys and accountants for compliance with disclosure requirements. It is unlawful to sell the securities until the staff gives the company and its underwriter(s) an "effective" date.

If a registration statement appears to be incomplete or inaccurate, the company usually is informed by letter and given an opportunity to file correcting or clarifying amendments. However, the SEC may conclude that material deficiencies in some registration statements appear to stem from a deliberate attempt to conceal or mislead, or that the deficiencies do not lend themselves to correction through the informal letter process. In these cases, the Commission may decide that it is in the public interest to conduct a hearing to develop the facts by evidence and determine if a "stop order" should be issued to refuse or suspend effectiveness of the registration statement. The Commission also may issue a stop order after a sale of securities has been commenced or completed. A stop order is not a permanent bar to the effectiveness of a registration statement or to the sale of securities. If the registrant files an amendment(s) correcting the statement in accordance with the stop order decision, the SEC must lift the stop order and declare the registration statement effective.

As of October 1, 1998, the SEC adopted new rules that require all public and first-time filing companies to use "plain English" in all offering documents.[14]

  [c] *Exemptions from Registration.* In general, the requirement to register securities of both U.S. and foreign companies or governments sold to public investors in U.S. securities markets is broad and inclusive. However, there are certain exemptions, including:

- private offerings to a limited number of persons or institutions who have access to the kind of information that registration would disclose and who do not plan to redistribute the securities;

---

14. Securities Act Rel. No. 7497 (1998).

- offerings restricted to residents of the state in which the issuing company is organized and doing business;

- securities of municipal, state, federal, and other domestic governmental instrumentalities as well as charitable institutions and banks;

- small issues not exceeding certain specified amounts made in compliance with SEC regulations; and

- offerings of small business investment companies made in accordance with SEC regulations.

Whether or not the securities are registered, antifraud provisions apply to all sales of securities involving interstate commerce or the mails.

Exemptions are also available when certain specified conditions are met. These conditions include use of an offering circular containing certain basic information in the sale of the securities. For a more complete discussion of these and other special provisions adopted by the Commission to facilitate capital formation by small business, obtain a copy of the small business packet from the SEC Publication's Branch or consult the Small Business Information page on the SEC Web site <www.sec.gov>.

[d]   Capital Formation Alternatives. In the years that have passed since 1933, issuers and underwriters have sought to expand the availability and uses of transactions exempt from the registration provisions of the 33 Act, in part to avoid the onerous application of the liability apportionment provided in Section 11 of the 33 Act. The following chart and preliminary notes presents a quick way to open a discussion on the options available to first-time issuers of securities and is included here in its entirety with the gracious permission of its authors.[15] Users should note that the continuing evolution of the nation's securities laws may make portions of this chart outdated. For instance, see pages 47 and 48 of this chapter with regard to the outcome of the SEC's mammoth 1998 "Aircraft Carrier" release.

---

15. Stanley Keller and Richard M. Leisner, *Capital Formation Alternatives,* 1995 (Revised 4/30/99).

CAPITAL FORMATION ALTERNATIVES

By

Jean E. Harris	**Stanley Keller**	**Richard M. Leisner**
O'Connor, Cavanagh,	Palmer & Dodge,	Trenam, Kemker,
Anderson,	LLP	Scharf
Killingsworth		Barkin, Frye, O'Neill
& Beshears, P.A.		& Mullis, P.A.

Preliminary Notes

The chart that follows is intended for use as a tool to aid business lawyers generally familiar with federal and state securities laws make threshold analyses and decisions concerning various alternatives to full S-1 registration for capital formation. It should be used with the following limitations and assumptions in mind:

1. Descriptions of various federal and state securities registration requirements and exemptions are of necessity summaries and must not be relied upon as complete and accurate statements of all the conditions required to comply with applicable law. Practitioners should consult the actual law, regulations and forms to refine the threshold analyses made with the assistance of the chart.

2. The chart does not address compliance with the antifraud rules. All securities transactions are subject to various antifraud rules that generally operate to prohibit persons engaged in the offer and sale of securities from making materially misleading statements or omissions or engaging in conduct that tends to work a fraud on purchasers or sellers of securities. A securities transaction may comply with applicable registration exemptions or registration requirements and nevertheless still violate one or more antifraud rules.

3. The chart does not address compliance with the specific requirements of applicable state securities registration or exemption provisions. Compliance with individual state securities law can be assured only by reference to the specific state statutes and rules that apply to a particular transaction. The capital formation alternatives described in the chart relate principally to federal securities registration procedures and exemptions. For comparison purposes, information is provided with respect to certain provisions of the Uniform Securities Act and certain statements or policy positions of the North

American Securities Administrators Association (NASAA). **The National Securities Markets Improvement Act of 1996 has made state blue sky registration requirements generally inapplicable to "covered securities," which include major stock exchange and Nasdaq National Market listed securities and securities sold under Rule 506 or to "qualified purchasers" as defined by the SEC.**

4. The chart does not address federal or state regulatory requirements applicable to persons engaged in the business of effecting purchases and sales of securities. These persons may be required to register federally and in various states as securities broker-dealers or agents. In some cases, the involvement of an unregistered person in the purchase and sales process may jeopardize the availability of a securities registration exemption. In others, a transaction that otherwise complies with the securities registration or exemption requirements of applicable federal and state law may nevertheless fail to comply with federal or state law governing the conduct of persons involved in the purchase and sales process. This failure may give rise to its own violation of law.

5. The chart is not intended to cover all securities registration alternatives and exemptions. The alternatives are intended primarily for capital formation activities for start-up, newly formed or relatively small businesses. Accordingly, for example, the securities registration exemptions provided by Section 3(a)(2), Section 3(a)(9) and Section 3(a)(10) of the Securities Act of 1933 are not covered in the chart because we do not view these exemptions as generally being used in the foregoing capital formation activities. For simplicity, the chart also does not include the Regulation S exemption for offshore offerings.

6. Except where specifically noted, the chart does not address alternatives for resales. Where references are to securities being "freely resalable," these relate only to the restrictions imposed by the specific offering alternative. Other limitations may affect resales, such as those applicable to resales by affiliates or statutory underwriters and those imposed by state securities laws.

7. The chart does not deal with the SEC's proposals to revise the securities offering process set forth in Rel. No. 33-7606 (1998). These include revisions that would increase the size of small business issuers and provide other relief.

8. The chart was last revised on April 30, 1999, and does not reflect changes in the law occurring after that date.

Note: The National Securites Market Improvement Act of 1996 has made state blue sky registration requirements generally inapplicable to "covered securities," which include major stock exchange and Nasdaq National Market listed securities and securities shold under Rule 506 or to "qualified purchasers" as defined by the SEC.

[e]　Filing Fees. SEC Registration Fee[16]—payable by issuer/seller(s) at filing, nonrefundable and calculated as follows:

For an IPO—the product of the total number of shares, including any over-allotment option, multiplied by the high end of the filing price range times the number .000295.[17]

For an already publicly traded security—the product of the total number of shares, including any over-allotment option, multiplied by the average of the high and low sale prices of the security as reported on the day prior to filing, times the number .000295.

NASD Corporate Financing Filing Fee[18]—payable by issuer/seller(s) at filing and calculated as follows:

For an IPO—same product calculation as above times the number .0001 + $500, not to exceed $30,500.[19]

For an already publicly traded security—same product calculation as above times the number .0001 + $500, not to exceed $30,500.

The NASD fee is generally not refundable. However, if the NASD Corporate Financing Department has not issued its initial comment letter, the department may entertain a refund request if the offering is withdrawn. Also, if the ultimate dollar proceeds of the offering are larger than the initial filing fee computation, the issuer/seller(s) must

---

16. Formulae for SEC calculations are accurate as of October 1998 but are subject to change or revision.

17. 17 CFR 230.457.

18. Formulae for NASD calculations are accurate as of October 1998 but are subject to change or revision.

19. NASD (CCH) IP 2710 (1998).

Capital Formation Alternatives Comparison Chart

Type of Offering	Nature of Issuer	Limit on Amount	Manner of Offering	Offeree and Purchaser Requirements
Section 4(2)	No limitation, but nature of issuer may be relevant factor.	None.	Limit to manner designed to assure qualified offerees and purchasers, including no general solicitation or advertising. Resales permitted under like circumstances (Section "4(1½) Exemption").	All offerees and purchasers must meet sophistication and access to information test so as not to need protection of registration. Number not determinative; has been used as rule-of-thumb.
Section 4(6)	No limitation.	Section 3(b) limit ($5,000,000).	No general solicitation or advertising.	"Accredited investors" only (defined in Section 2(15) and Rule 215); similar to Rule 501(a) under Regulation D. No limitation on number.
Rule 504 Regulation D	Not available to 1934 Act reporting companies, investment companies or "blank check" companies.	$1,000,000 within prior 12 months (including all Section 3(b) sales and sales in violation of Section 5).	No general solicitation or advertising unless registered in a state requiring use of a substantive disclosure document or sold under state exemption for sales to accredited investors with general solicitation.	No requirements.

21

Capital Formation Alternatives Comparison Chart *(continued)*

Type of Offering	Nature of Issuer	Limit on Amount	Manner of Offering	Offeree and Purchaser Requirements
Rule 505 Regulation D	Not available to investment companies or issuers disqualified under "bad boy" provisions of Rule 262 of Regulation A.	$5,000,000 within prior 12 months (including all Section 3(b) sales and sales in violation of Section 5).	No general solicitation or advertising.	No limitation on offerees. Unlimited accredited investors and 35 non-accredited investors. "Accredited investors" include certain institutions; directors, executive officers and general partners of issuer; natural persons who with spouse meet $1 million net worth or $300,000 income test, or alone meet $200,000 income test; and entities with over $5,000,000 total assets or owned solely by accredited investors. No qualifications for purchasers under Rule 505; all non-accredited investors under Rule 506 must be sophisticated alone or with purchaser representatives.
Rule 506 Regulation D	No limitation.	None.	No general solicitation or advertising.	

Capital Formation Alternatives Comparison Chart (continued)

Rule 144A	Any issuer but securities being offered may not be fungible with publicly traded securities. Covers only resales but can be combined with private offering to permit institutional distribution by issuers.	None.	Resales to "qualified institutional buyers" (institutions with $100 million portfolios). Not an issuer exemption per se.	Offerees and purchasers must be "QIBs." No limitation on number.
Regulation A	Domestic or Canadian issuers not subject to 1934 Act reporting requirements or disqualification under "bad boy" provisions of Rule 262. Not available to investment companies, blank check companies or issuers of oil, gas or mineral rights.	$5,000,000 within prior 12 months, but no more than $1,500,000 by selling security holders (no affiliate sales unless issuer had net income in one of the last two fiscal years).	"Testing the waters" permitted before filing Form 1-A (but no funds or commitments to purchase may be accepted). Sales permitted after Form 1-A qualified. Resales permitted (if not disqualified under "bad boy" provisions of Rule 262). Test the waters documents not a "prospectus."	No requirements.
Form SB-1	Transitional "small business issuers" (not registered more than $10 million in prior 12 months or elected to graduate to non-transitional forms).	$10,000,000 within prior 12 months (including all registered offerings, except offerings on Form S-8).	Normal registered offering requirements. Resales permitted. Limited to cash offerings.	No requirements.

Capital Formation Alternatives Comparison Chart (*continued*)

Type of Offering	Nature of Issuer	Limit on Amount	Manner of Offering	Offeree and Purchaser Requirements
Form SB-2	"Small business issuer" defined as domestic or Canadian issuer with revenues and a public float (using estimated offering price for an IPO) less than $25,000,000. Not available to investment companies or subsidiaries of non-small business issuers.	None (but must be a "small business issuer").	Normal registered offering requirements. Resales permitted. Limited to cash offerings.	No requirements.
Section 3(a)(11)	Issuer must be organized and doing business within the state (interpreted to mean substantial operations and use of proceeds for intrastate purposes).	None.	No limitation other than to maintain intrastate character. Includes resales.	All offerees and purchasers must be resident in state (interpreted as domicile). No limitation on number.
Rule 147	Issuer must be organized and doing business in state (80% of gross revenues and assets and net proceeds used, and principal office).	None.	No limitation other than to maintain intrastate character.	All offerees and purchasers must be resident in state (principal office, if business, or principal residence, if individual). No limitation on number.

Capital Formation Alternatives Comparison Chart *(continued)*

| Rule 701 | Not available to 1934 Act reporting companies or investment companies. (Form S-8 available to reporting companies.) | Greater of 15% of total assets, 15% of outstanding securities of that class or $1,000,000 within 12 months. Options counted at time of grant. Must count value of consultant and employee services. | Pursuant to a written compensatory plan or contract, including stock options. Not available for non-compensatory (i.e., capital raising) offerings. | Employees, directors, officers, and employee-type consultants (including family members receiving securities by gift or domestic relations order) providing bona fide services other than in connection with a securities offering. Consultants as defined for Form S-8. No limitation on number. |

Capital Formation Alternatives Comparison Chart

Type of Offering	Information Required	Filing Requirement	Restriction on Resale	Blue Sky Aspects	Other Factors
Section 4(2)	No requirements, but authority that nature and availability of information is element of exemption.	None.	Restricted securities (resales limited to registration or exemption such as Rules 144 or 144A). Use investment letters, legends, stop orders and disclosure of resale restrictions to police.	Uniform Securities Act §§ 402(b)(8) and (9) may be available. § 402(b)(9) limits number of offerees and payment of commissions.	Uncertain standards. Issuer's burden to prove exemption available as to all offerees.
Section 4(6)	No requirements.	File Form D with SEC as under Regulation D.	Restricted securities. Take steps as under Section 4(2) to police resales.	USA § 402(b)(8) may be available for institutional investors. There may be "accredited investor exemption."	Similar to Rule 505 offerings solely to accredited investors.
Rule 504 Regulation D	Delivery of substantive disclosure document required for unrestricted securities status. Form U-7 meets requirement.	File Form D with SEC not later than 15 days after first sale. Filing not a condition of the exemption.	Restricted unless registered in a state requiring use of a substantive disclosure document or sold under state exemption for sale to accredited investors with general solicitation.	Need to comply with state blue sky law by registration (Form U-7 may be available) or state exemption.	Represents substantial federal delegation to states adopted under Section 3(b). Safe harbor on integration.

Capital Formation Alternatives Comparison Chart (*continued*)

Rule 505 Regulation D	None if all purchasers are accredited investors. For any non-accredited investors, (a) if 1934 Act reporting company, certain reports or filings or (b) non-reporting, company, (1) Regulation A narrative information for eligible issuers and otherwise narrative information required by	File Form D with SEC not later than 15 days after first sale. Filing not a condition of the exemption.	Restricted securities; take reasonable care to limit resales as provided in Rule 502(d).	Coordinates with state Uniform Limited Offering Exemption (ULOE).	All conditions must be met but subject to Rule 508 substantial compliance relief. Adopted under Section 3(b). Safe harbor on integration.
Rule 506 Regulation D	Part I of available registration form and (2) *the following audited financials:* (i) up to $2,000,000, a current balance sheet, (ii) up to $7,500,000, the financial information required by Part I of Form SB-2 and (iii) over $7,500,000, the financial information required by the available form (with some relief possible); also, a description of resale restrictions. Make available certain other information and opportunity to ask questions.	File Form D with SEC not later than 15 days after first sale. Filing not a condition of exemption.	Restricted securities; take reasonable care to limit resales as provided in Rule 502(d).	Exempt as "covered security" under NSMIA.	All conditions must be met but subject to Rule 508 substantial compliance relief. Adopted as safe harbor under Section 4(2). Safe harbor on integration.

Capital Formation Alternatives Comparison Chart (*continued*)

Type of Offering	Information Required	Filing Requirement	Restriction on Resale	Blue Sky Aspects	Other Factors
Rule 144A	If not 1934 Act reporting company, purchasers able to get summary information about issuer and "reasonably current" financials (*audited if available*).	None.	Restricted Securities. Seller must disclose reliance on this exemption.	USA § 402b(8) and resale exemptions.	NASD has established PORTAL to facilitate market. Sometimes tied to Form S-3 registration for resales or Exxon-Capital exchange offer. No integration with other offerings.
Regulation A	Simplified disclosure with choice for corporate issuers of Q&A (Model A) or narrative (Model B) formats of Form 1-A or narrative format of Part I of Form SB-2. Current balance sheet and 2 years' other financials, plus interims, complying with GAAP *but need not be audited unless audit is available.*	File test the waters documents, Form 1-A, any sales material and Form 2-A report of sales and use of proceeds with SEC. Filing of test the waters documents and Form 2-A not conditions of the exemption.	None; freely resalable.	May have to register by qualification since registration by coordination may be unavailable. Form U-7 may be available. States may allow "testing the waters" with added requirements, including filing before first use.	Adopted under Section 3(b). Issuer does not become subject to 1934 Act reporting unless Section 12(g) applies. Generally, no integration with other offerings. Substantial compliance relief. No Section 11 liability.

Capital Formation Alternatives Comparison Chart *(continued)*

	Disclosure	Filing	Resale	State Law	Notes
Form SB-1	Regulation A type disclosure, except financials must be *audited*.	File with SEC Form SB-1.	None; freely resalable.	Registration by coordination.	Traditional disclosure form patterned after Regulation A. Not limited to IPOs. Issuer becomes subject to 1934 Act reporting with transitional small business issuer relief. Section 11 liability.
Form SB-2	Simplified Regulation S-B disclosure; *audited* recent balance sheet and 2 years' other financials, plus unaudited interims, complying with GAAP (not S-X).	File with SEC Form SB-2.	None; freely resalable.	Registration by coordination.	Not limited to IPOs. Issuer becomes subject to 1934 Act reporting, but with relief for small business issuers. Section 11 liability.
Section 3(a)(11)	No requirements.	None.	Coming to rest within the state (generally a one year period for resales within state). Take steps to police resales.	Need to comply with state blue sky law by registration or exemption.	Exemption interpreted narrowly and difficult to maintain. Possible integration of transactions.

Capital Formation Alternatives Comparison Chart (*continued*)

Type of Offering	Information Required	Filing Requirement	Restriction on Resale	Blue Sky Aspects	Other Factors
Rule 147	No requirements.	None.	Resales limited for 9 months to residents of state; take steps to limit interstate resales (including letter as to residence, legending, stop order and disclosure).	Need to comply with state blue sky law by registration or exemption.	All conditions must be met (no substantial compliance relief). Safe harbor on integration.
Rule 701	No requirements for sales of less than $5 million, except for delivery of a copy of the written plan or contract. More than $5 million requires specific disclosure including risks and financial statements.	None.	Restricted securities; restricted nature ceases, however, 90 days after the issuer becomes a reporting company (except for manner of sale requirement under Rule 144).	USA § 402(a)(11) or state rules may provide an exemption.	Exemption adopted under Section 3(b) and 28 for compensatory plans for employees and consultants. Exemption remains available for exercise of options outstanding when issuer becomes reporting company. No integration or aggregation.

pay the incremental additional fees to both the SEC and NASD; if smaller, no refunds are available.

Additional issuer/seller(s) expenses associated with an underwritten transaction, and payable as incurred, will include at a minimum:

- exchange or dealer market listing fee
- blue sky filing fees and preparatory expenses
- printing and engraving expenses
- legal fees and expenses
- auditor fees and expenses
- transfer agent and registrar fees and expenses
- underwriting gross spread (only if transaction is completed)

These fees and expenses are detailed in Part II of the registration statement but are not required in the actual prospectus itself.

[2]   Banking Act of 1933 (Glass-Steagall Act)

The passage of the Banking Act of 1933 (not part of the Securities Laws per se), also known as the Glass-Steagall Act (Glass-Steagall) and named for the two legislative sponsors of the bill—Senator Carter Glass (D-Virginia and a former Secretary of the Treasury) and Congressman Henry Bascom Steagall (D-Alabama)—was another of President Roosevelt's initiatives to restore public confidence in the nation's financial system in the wake of the post-Depression failure or forced merger of over 11,000 banks.[20]

Again, a perception existed in the country at large, whether true in part or in whole, that self-dealing at less than arm's length by the large banks that underwrote new issues, accepted customer time and demand deposits, and acted as investment adviser/fiduciary for their trust clients was at the heart of the collapse in prices on the nation's securities exchanges that fateful Tuesday, October 29, 1929. The President and Congress wisely perceived that a distrustful and frightened American public needed strong encouragement to place and keep its hard-earned/saved money in the U.S. banking system. Depositors needed to believe that their ability to withdraw cash was not in any way imperiled, in truth or in perception, by securities underwriting activities.

---

20. Glass-Steagall Act, 12 U.S.C. 335.

To address this perception head-on, Glass-Steagall mandated the separation of commercial and investment banking and insurance underwriting. Financial institutions had to make a choice: (1) to pursue the traditional commercial banking business of accepting demand (checking) deposits and time (savings) deposits for use in making commercial and individual mortgage loans; (2) to make at-risk underwriting commitments to issuers of common stock, preferred stock, and term debt securities; or (3) to pursue insurance underwriting. As a result of this legislation, new firms appeared. For example, the old house of Morgan continued on as a commercial bank and trust operation, while certain former partners resigned to create Morgan Stanley & Co., which opened its doors on September 16, 1935, as an investment bank.[21]

To be totally accurate, commercial banks were not completely out of the securities business per se, since Glass-Steagall neither addresses nor prohibits banks dealing in U.S. Government, U.S. Government Agency, and state and local municipal tax-exempt general obligation backed securities. Presumably, in the eyes of the framers of Glass-Steagall, such securities carried little to no risk of default. Default on corporate debt and loss of most or all principal in equity securities of failed business enterprises or of companies still operating but whose stock prices had been ravaged by the crash of 1929 and subsequent market sell-offs in the 1930s were at the heart of the then existing investor paranoia.

This congressionally mandated division of the financial services industry held into the 1970s before serious cracks started to develop in the so-called Chinese Wall separating deposit taking and new issue risk taking. With the passage of time and ongoing consolidation within both commercial and investment banking, the toeholds established by commercial banks in the 1970s became footholds in the early 1980s, beachheads in the late 1980s, and fully fortified, congressionally and Federal Reserve sanctioned strongholds in the mid-1990s.

Members of Congress mounted at least 11 separate efforts to abolish Glass-Steagall before succeeding with the passage of the Financial Services Modernization Act of 1999, better know as the Gramm-Leach-Bliley Act, which President William Jefferson Clinton signed

21. For a detailed and fascinating description of this era, *see* the Vincent Carosso treatise, particularly chapters 13-18 (*see* Bibliography/Selected Reference Sources).

into law on November 12, 1999.[22] The act allows banks, securities firms, and insurance companies to affiliate under a one-holding-company structure in the United States for the first time since 1933. Non-U.S.-headquartered financial services holding companies, so-called banc assurance entities, were already free to act in this manner, and some have done so, particularly in Europe (*e.g.,* Credit Suisse and ING).

[3]   Securities Exchange Act of 1934

The second major piece of legislation enacted after the 1929 crash was the Securities Exchange Act of 1934 (34 Act).[23] Like the 33 Act, the 34 Act was also an attempt to restore the public's trust and confidence, in this case, to restore confidence in the operation and oversight of the nation's secondary securities markets, the aftermarket trading arena for new issues (new issues themselves take place in the primary market). Specifically, the 34 Act was passed: "To provide for the regulation of securities exchanges and of over-the-counter markets operating in interstate and foreign commerce and through the mails (and) to prevent inequitable and unfair practices on such exchanges and markets . . ."[24]

The 34 Act specifically defines all the major components and participants in the securities industry. It formally established the United States Securities and Exchange Commission (SEC) and laid out rules for governing all national securities exchanges. Other important concepts covered include margin lending, borrowing activities of securities firms for their own account, market manipulation, trading practices, securities information processing and dissemination, securities registration, reporting procedures, proxy rules, and registration of securities broker-dealers and their trade group(s). The legislation and its amendments also speak to related broker-dealer/underwriter activity in both municipal and government securities. It gives corporate governance guidance to directors, officers, and principal stockholders of companies; discusses the topics of accounts and records, reports, and examinations of exchanges, members, and other (entities); covers a national system for clearance and settlement of securities transactions (a 1975 amendment); deals with penny stocks; and treats liability for

---

22. Section 509(4) P.L. 106-102, 113 Stat. 1338 (1999).

23. 48 Stat. 881, P.L. 73-291 (1934) (codified as amended at 15 U.S.C. 78a (1998)).

24. *Id.*

misleading statements. It also sets forth rules with regard to registration, responsibilities, and oversight of self-regulatory organizations.

By the 34 Act, Congress extended the disclosure doctrine of investor protection to securities listed and registered for public trading on our national securities exchanges. Thirty years later, the Securities Act Amendments of 1964 extended disclosure and reporting provisions to equity securities in the over-the-counter market, thereby including hundreds of companies with assets exceeding $10 million and shareholders numbering 500 and more. Today, securities of thousands of companies are traded over-the-counter. The 34 Act seeks to assure fair and orderly securities markets by prohibiting certain types of activities and setting forth rules regarding the operations of the markets and its participants.

[a] *Corporate Reporting.* Companies whose securities are registered and listed for public trading on an exchange must file periodic reports with the exchange and the SEC. Companies whose equities securities are traded over-the-counter must file similar reports if meeting certain size tests. SEC rules prescribe the nature and content of these reports and require certified financial statements. Annual, quarterly, and periodic filings are submitted on Forms 10-K, 10-Q, and 8-K (10-KSB, 10-QSB, and 8-KSB for small businesses), respectively. The reports' contents are generally comparable to, but less extensive than, the disclosure required in 33 Act registration statements. Reports may be read at the SEC's public reference rooms, copied there at nominal cost, or obtained at reasonable rates from a copying service under contract to the SEC. Also, since May 16, 1996, all corporate filings are available electronically on the SEC's Web site <www.sec.gov>.

[b] *Proxy Solicitations.* Another provision of this law governs soliciting proxies (votes) from holders of registered securities, both listed and over-the-counter, for the election of directors and/or for approval of other corporate action. Solicitations, whether by management or shareholder groups, must disclose all material facts concerning matters on which holders are asked to vote, and holders must be given an opportunity to vote "yes" or "no" on each matter. When a contest for control of corporate management is involved, the rules require disclosure of the names and interests of all participants in the proxy contest. Thus, holders are enabled to vote intelligently on corporate actions requiring their approval.

[c]   Tender Offer Solicitations. In 1968, Congress amended the 34 Act to extend its reporting and disclosure provisions to situations where control of a company is sought through tender offer or other planned stock acquisition of over 10 percent of the target company's equity securities.[25] Commonly called the Williams Act, this amendment was further amended in 1970 to reduce the stock acquisition threshold to 5 percent.[26] These amendments, and SEC rules under the 34 Act, require disclosure of pertinent information by anyone seeking to acquire over 5 percent of a company's securities by direct purchase or by tender offer. This disclosure also is required of anyone soliciting shareholders to accept or reject a tender offer. Thus, as with the proxy rules, public investors holding stock in such a targeted corporation may make more informed decisions on how to react to a takeover bid.

[d]   Insider Trading. Insider trading prohibitions are designed to curb misuse of material confidential information not available to the general public. Examples of such misuse are buying or selling securities to make profits or avoid losses based on possession of material nonpublic information, or telling others of such information so that they may buy or sell securities before such information is generally available to the public. The SEC has brought numerous civil actions in federal court against persons whose use of material nonpublic information constituted fraud under the securities laws. The Insider Trading Sanctions Act (ITSA), signed into law on August 10, 1984, amended the 34 Act by allowing imposition of fines up to three times the profit gained or loss avoided by use of material nonpublic information.[27] Subsequently, Congress enacted new legislation, the Insider Trading and Securities Fraud Enforcement Act of 1988 (ITSFEA).[28] This law granted the SEC expanded authority to deal with a person(s) profiting from the use of material, nonpublic information.

ITSFEA added Section 15(f) to the 34 Act as an amendment in 1987, which requires every broker or dealer to establish, maintain, and enforce written policies and procedures designed to erect so-called

---

25. Williams Act, 82 Stat. 454, P.L. 90-439 (1968).

26. 84 Stat. 1435, P.L. 91-547 (1970).

27. 98 Stat. 1264 (1984) (repealed 1988).

28. 102 Stat. 4677 (1988) (codified as amended at 15 U.S.C. 78u-1 (1998)).

Chinese walls within the firm to prohibit the misuse of material, non-public information. For example, "Chinese walls" must prevent the merger and acquisition group or research analysts or investment bankers from passing information on prospective business transactions "over the wall" to trading or sales people. In fact, in recognition of the extremely sensitive nature of merger and acquisition engagements, most firms completely segregate physically that group from the rest of the firm and severely restrict its client information flow.

      [e]   Short Swing Profits. Section 16 of the 34 Act requires all officers and directors of a company and beneficial owners of more than 10 percent of its registered equity securities to file an initial report with the SEC, and with the exchange on which the stock may be listed (or the NASD for Nasdaq issues), showing their holdings of each of the company's equity securities. Thereafter, such persons must file reports for any month during which there was any change in their holdings. In addition, the law provides that profits obtained from purchases and sales of such equity securities within any six-month period (so-called short swing profits) may be recovered by the company or by any security holder on its behalf. This recovery right must be asserted in the appropriate U.S. District Court. Such "insiders" are also prohibited from making short sales of their company's equity securities.

      [f]   Margin Trading. Margin trading in securities also falls under certain provisions of the 34 Act. Congress authorized the Board of Governors of the Federal Reserve System (the Fed) to set limitations on the amount of credit that may be extended for the purpose of purchasing or carrying securities. The Fed periodically reviews these limitations, which are promulgated in Regulations T, U, X, and G.[29] The objective here is to prevent the excessive use of credit for the purchase or carrying of securities. (Editors' note—many observers and chroniclers of the 1929 stock market crash attribute much of the cause of this event to excessive speculation fueled by liberal margin lending.) While credit restrictions are set by the Fed's Board, the SEC retains responsibility for investigation and enforcement of the rules. However, individual firms are free to set more restrictive margin lending parameters.

---

    29. *See* Section [12] of this chapter for a brief glossary of all Federal Reserve Regulations.

[g]   *Trading and Sales Practices.* Securities trading and sales practices on exchanges and in over-the-counter markets are subject to provisions designed to protect the interests of the investing public. These provisions seek to curb misrepresentations and deceit, market manipulation, and other fraudulent acts and practices, and strive to establish and maintain just and equitable principles of trade conducive to maintaining open, fair, and orderly markets.

These provisions of the law establish the general regulatory pattern. The SEC is responsible for promulgating specific rules and regulations for its implementation and thus has adopted regulations that, among other things:

- define acts or practices that constitute a manipulative or deceptive device or contrivance prohibited by the statute;

- regulate short selling, stabilizing transactions, and similar matters;

- regulate hypothecation (use of customer's securities as collateral for loans); and

- provide safeguards with respect to the financial responsibility of brokers and dealers.

[h]   *Corporate Reorganization.* Reorganization proceedings in the U.S. courts under the various chapters of the Federal Bankruptcy Code are begun by a debtor (voluntarily) or by its creditors (involuntarily). Federal bankruptcy law allows a debtor in reorganization to continue operating under a bankruptcy court's protection while it attempts to rehabilitate its business and work out a plan to pay its debts. If a debtor corporation has publicly issued securities outstanding, the reorganization process may raise many issues that materially affect the rights of public investors.

Chapter 11 of the Bankruptcy Code authorizes the SEC to appear in any reorganization case and to present its views on any issue. Although Chapter 11 covers all types of business reorganizations, the Commission generally limits its participation to proceedings involving significant public investor interest—protecting public investors holding the debtor's securities and participating in legal and policy issues of concern to public investors. The SEC also addresses matters of traditional Commission expertise and interest relating to securities. When appropriate, it comments on the adequacy of reorganization plan disclosure statements and participates when there is SEC law enforcement interest.

Under Chapter 11, the debtor, official committees, and institutional creditors negotiate the terms of a reorganization plan filed with the appropriate federal bankruptcy court. The jurisdictional court can confirm such a reorganization plan if it is accepted by creditors for:

- at least two-thirds of the amounts of allowed claims;

- more than one-half of the number of allowed claims; or

- at least two-thirds of the amount of the allowed shareholder interest.

The principal safeguard for public investors is the requirement that the debtor or plan proponent transmit a disclosure statement containing adequate information in connection with soliciting votes on the plan. In addition, reorganization plans involving publicly held debt usually provide for issuing new securities to creditors and shareholders which may be exempt from registration under Section 5 of the 33 Act.

[4] Public Utility Holding Company Act of 1935

The Public Utility Holding Company Act of 1935 (35 Act) was passed in response to fears that a major consolidation of the many state and local public utility companies providing electricity and gas to industrial and individual consumers into a few large and powerful holding companies would have an adverse effect on the pricing of utility services to the general public.[30]

Interstate holding companies engaged, through subsidiaries, in the electric utility business or in the retail distribution of natural or manufactured gas are subject to regulation under this act. These systems must register with the SEC and file initial and periodic reports containing the organization, financial structure, and operations of the holding company and its subsidiaries. However, if a holding company

---

30. 49 Stat. 803, P.L. 74-333 (1935) (codified as amended at 15 U.S.C. § 79 (1998)). *See also* Carosso for a discussion of the trials and tribulations of the Chicago utility magnate Samuel Insull, who was the target of significant public and congressional venom.

or its subsidiaries meet certain specifications, the SEC may exempt it from part or all of the duties and obligations otherwise imposed by statute. Holding companies are also subject to SEC regulations on such matters as structure of the system, acquisitions, combinations, and the issue and sale of new securities.

[a]   *Integration and Simplification.* The most important provisions of the 35 Act are the requirements for physical integration and corporate simplification of holding company systems. Integration standards restrict a holding company's operations to an "integrated utility system." Such a system is defined as one:

- capable of economical operation as a single coordinated system;

- confined to a single area or region in one or more states; and

- not so large that it negates the advantages of localized management, efficient operation, and effective regulation.

The capital structure and continued existence of any company in a holding company system must not unnecessarily complicate its corporate structure or distribute voting power inequitably among its security holders.

[b]   *Acquisitions.* The SEC must authorize the acquisition of securities and utility assets by holding companies and their subsidiaries according to the following standards:

- the acquisition must not tend toward interlocking relations or concentrating control to an extent detrimental to investors or the public interest;

- consideration paid for the acquisition (including fees, commissions, and other remuneration) must not be unreasonable;

- the acquisition must not complicate the capital structure of the holding company system or have a detrimental effect on system functions; and

- the acquisition must tend toward economical, efficient development of an integrated public utility system.

[c]   *Issuance and Sale of Securities.* The staff must analyze and evaluate, and the Commission must approve, any proposed

security issue by a holding company to ensure that the issue(s) meets the following tests under prescribed standards of the law:

- the security must be reasonably adapted to the security structure of the issuer and of other companies in the same holding company system;

- the security must be reasonably adapted to the earning power of the company;

- the proposed issue must be necessary and appropriate to the economical and efficient operation of the company's business;

- fees, commissions, and other remuneration paid in connection with the issue must not be unreasonable; and

- the terms and conditions of the issue or sale of the security must not be detrimental to the public or investor interest.

Subject to satisfaction of certain conditions, issuances of securities by subsidiaries of registered holding companies are, for the most part, exempt from the requirement of prior Commission approval.

[d]   *Other Regulatory Provisions.* Changes in the utility industry, its structure, and regulation are causing the 35 Act to be out of step, in many cases, with the realities of operation of the industry it regulates. Recognizing this situation, in 1994 the Commission staff undertook a study of the future of public utility holding company regulation, culminating in a June 1995 report. The report concluded that, because of the increased role of state and federal regulators and current federal securities laws and the efficiency of financial markets, many provisions of the 35 Act are no longer essential. The report's primary recommendation was repeal of the act, conditioned on preservation of some aspects that continue to provide needed consumer protections, such as transfer of audit functions and jurisdiction over transactions among affiliated companies in holding company systems to the Federal Energy Regulatory Commission (FERC) and of access to the books and records of companies in holding company systems to state utility commissions. The report also recommended, pending legislative action, administrative measures to streamline and modernize regulation.

Of particular interest to the securities industry for many years was old Rule 50 of the 35 Act (repealed in 1994), which required that all sales of new securities by either a holding company or any of its operating subsidiaries must take place through sealed competitive bidding. (*See* pages 71 through 74 of Chapter 2 for a historical explanation of the competitive bidding process and its evolution into today's world of Rule 415 bidding.)

[5]   Trust Indenture Act of 1939

The Trust Indenture Act of 1939 (39 Act) was also a result of administrative and congressional response to the aftermath of the Crash of 1929.[31] According to a congressional report, during the decade following World War I, some $50 billion of new securities had been floated in the United States, of which fully half had proved to be worthless.[32]

The 39 Act supplements the 33 Act when a distribution consists of debt securities. A trust indenture must be filed and qualified with the SEC, and conforms to a mass of specified provisions that are designed to impose appropriate obligations on the trustee, particularly in the event of default. Also, there must be a corporate trustee that satisfies a batch of stringent tests to assure its independence from both the obligor and every underwriter.[33]

The 39 Act applies to bonds, debentures, notes, and similar debt securities offered for public sale and issued under trust indentures with more than $7.5 million of securities outstanding at any one time. Even though such securities may be registered under the 33 Act, the securities may not be offered for sale to the public unless the trust indenture conforms to statutory standards of this act. Designed to safeguard the rights and interests of the purchasers, the 39 Act also:

- prohibits the indenture trustee from conflicting interests that might interfere with exercising its duties on behalf of securities purchasers;

---

31. 53 Stat. 1149, P.L. 76-253 (1939) (codified as amended at 15 U.S.C. 77 aaa (1998)).

32. Charles J. Johnson, Jr., *Corporate Finance and the Securities Laws,* p. 2 H.R. Rep. No. 85, 73d Cong., 1st Sess. 2 (1933) (1991).

33. Louis Loss, *Fundamentals of Securities Regulation,* p. 40 (1983).

- requires the trustee to be a corporation with a minimum combined capital and surplus;

- imposes high standards of conduct and responsibility on the trustee;

- precludes, in the event of default, preferential collection of certain claims owing to the trustee by the issuer;

- provides that the issuer supply to the trustee evidence of compliance with indenture terms and conditions (such as those relating to the release or substitution of mortgaged property, issue of new securities, or satisfaction of the indenture); and

- requires the trustee to provide reports and notices to security holders.

Other provisions of the 39 Act prohibit impairing the security holder's right to sue individually for principal and interest, except under certain circumstances. It also requires maintenance of a list of security holders for their use in communicating with each other regarding their rights as security holders. Applications for qualification of trust indentures are examined by the SEC's Division of Corporation Finance for compliance with the law and the Commission's rules.

In 1987, the Commission sent a legislative proposal to Congress to modernize procedures under the act to meet the public's needs in view of the introduction of novel debt instruments and modern financing techniques. This legislative proposal was adopted and enacted into law in 1990.[34]

[6]   Investment Advisers Act of 1940

This law regulates the activities of investment advisers, including advisers to investment companies, private money managers, and most financial planners.[35] With certain exceptions, it requires persons or firms that are compensated for providing advice about investing in securities to register with the SEC and to conform to statutory requirements designed to protect their clients' financial interests.

---

34. Trust Indenture Reform Act of 1990. 104 Stat. 2713, P.L. 101-550 (1990) (codified as amended at 15 U.S.C. aaa (1998)).

35. 54 Stat. 789, P.L. 76-768 (1940) (codified as amended at 15 U.S.C. § 80 b-1 (1998)).

The most significant of the statutory provisions is a broad prohibition against fraudulent conduct, which has been interpreted by the U.S. Supreme Court as prohibiting violation of the fiduciary duties of an investment adviser to its clients. Among other things, this act requires an adviser to:

- disclose to clients material facts concerning any conflict of interest the adviser may have with the client;
- refrain from taking advantage of the position of trust the adviser occupies without the client's informed consent; and
- comply with the specific prohibitions the SEC has adopted by rule designed to prevent fraudulent conduct.

The act requires investment advisers registered with the SEC to maintain books and records according to SEC rules. The Commission conducts periodic examinations to review these books and records to determine whether the adviser is in compliance with the act as well as other federal securities laws.

The SEC has the authority under this act to deny, suspend, or revoke investment adviser registration based on a violation by the adviser of the act or of any other laws prohibiting fraud, theft, or other kinds of financial misconduct. In addition, the SEC may impose various forms of sanctions on an investment adviser, including substantial fines, and it may issue a cease and desist order or seek an injunction in federal court prohibiting further violation of the law. The SEC may also recommend criminal prosecution by the U.S. Department of Justice for a violation of the Investment Advisers Act.

[7]   Investment Company Act of 1940

The 35 Act required Congress to direct the SEC to study the activities of investment companies and investment advisers.[36] The study results were sent to Congress in a series of reports filed in 1938, 1939, and 1940, causing the creation of the Investment Company Act of 1940 (the 40 Act) and the Investment Advisers Act of 1940. The legislation was supported by both the Commission and the investment company industry.

---

36. 54 Stat. 789, P.L. 76-768 (1940) (codified as amended at 15 U.S.C. § 80 a-1 (1998)).

Activities of companies engaged primarily in investing, reinvesting, and trading in securities, and whose own securities are offered to the investing public, are subject to certain statutory prohibitions and to Commission regulation under this act. Also, public offerings of investment company securities must be registered under the 33 Act. However, the Commission does not supervise the actual day-to-day activities of these companies, and regulation by the SEC does not imply the safety of any investment recommended by an adviser.

The 40 Act requires that investment companies disclose their financial condition and investment policies to provide investors complete information about their activities. This act also:

- prohibits such companies from substantially changing the nature of their business or investment policies without stockholder approval;

- bars persons guilty of securities fraud from serving as officers and/or directors;

- prevents underwriters, investment bankers, or brokers from constituting more than a minority of the directors of such companies;

- requires that security holders approve management contracts and any material changes thereto;

- prohibits transactions between such companies and their directors, officers, or affiliated companies or persons, except as approved by the SEC;

- forbids issuance of senior securities except under specified terms and conditions; and

- prohibits pyramiding of such companies and cross-ownership of their respective securities.

Other provisions of this act relate to advisory fees, adviser's fiduciary duties, sales and repurchases of securities issued by investment companies, exchange offers, and other activities of investment companies, including special provisions for periodic payment plans and face-amount certificate companies.

In addition to enforcing the requirements described above, the SEC may institute court action to remove management officials who have engaged in personal misconduct constituting a breach of fiduciary duty. Investment companies also must file periodic reports and are subject to the SEC's proxy and insider trading rules.

[8]   Securities Investor Protection Act of 1970

The Securities Investor Protection Act of 1970 (70 Act) was enacted in large measure to shore up the public's confidence in the securities industry's ability to make good on individual investor accounts held in custody at failed firms.[37] An extraordinary surge of stock market trading volume in the mid-to-late 1960s, particularly on the part of individuals, temporarily overwhelmed the industry's ability to process (clear and settle) such transactions—a task largely performed manually at that time—and caused a large number of securities firms to merge or fail financially.

Passage of the 70 Act led to the creation of the Securities Investor Protection Corporation (SIPC). This quasi-government institution operates under the oversight of public directors and was originally funded by securities firms according to a revenue-based formula. Today its management reviews funding needs and the financial adequacy of SIPC on an ongoing basis. Due to a strong growth in assets, since 1996 the fund has been maintained via an annual assessment of $150 per member firm. As of December 31, 1999, the fund stood at $1.30 billion, with a $1 billion bank consortium backup credit line and an ability to borrow up to an additional $1 billion from the SEC. If necessary, the SEC itself has the authority to borrow from the United States Treasury.[38]

Current SIPC coverage provides for protection of investor customer cash and securities up to $500,000 in total, of which no more than $100,000 of cash claims are covered in the event of a broker-dealer bankruptcy. The combination of strong finances, the implied

---

37. 84 Stat. 1653, P.L. 91-958 (1970). SIPC was the brainchild of Edmund S. Muskie, the former Democratic senator from Maine, who "introduced a bill in 1969 to create a Federal Broker-Dealer Insurance Corporation that would insure brokerage firm customers against losses, as the F.D.I.C. does with bank depositors." "Many Holes Weaken Safety Net for Victims of Failed Brokerages," Gretchen Morgenson, *New York Times,* September 25, 2000.

38. Editor interview with Joseph S. Furr, Jr., Assistant Vice President, Finance, at SIPC on May 21, 1999.

full faith and credit of the United States government, and carefully honed procedures that permit timely restitution to a failed firm's customers, within the fund's specified limits, have all helped to restore and build the public's confidence in leaving securities on deposit in a firm.

As an aside, the private casualty insurance industry also responded to the set of circumstances that led to SIPC's creation by offering so-called excess SIPC coverage to securities firms that allows for additional coverage for customer accounts beyond SIPC coverage, in amounts typically up to $100 million or more.

[9] National Securities Markets Improvement Act of 1996

The National Securities Markets Improvement Act (NSMIA)[39] of 1996 was passed in an effort to streamline duplicative regulatory efforts of federal and state authorities. Under NSMIA, federal law generally preempts state disclosure and merit standards and laws for companies that have covered securities. Generally, covered securities (in this context) are securities of a company that are listed and traded on the New York Stock Exchange, the American Stock Exchange, or the Nasdaq National Market System.

NSMIA charges the SEC to oversee markets, improve market efficiency, foster competition in the securities industry, enable capital formation, and eliminate regulations that no longer serve the public interest. NSMIA also requires investment advisers with $25 million or more in assets under management, as well as advisers in states that do not require registration, to register with the SEC. Investment advisers with less than $25 million in assets under management must register on a state basis only. Investment advisers that solicit fewer than six clients in a state within one year are entirely exempt from registration. Broker-dealers are exempt from registration in a state with regard to any client who has less than 30 days of temporary residence in such state.

Under NSMIA, investment management companies are now exempt from state registration and regulation, overseen by the SEC, and permitted to use performance figures in advertising campaigns (subject to SEC reporting requirements). In addition, registered investment

---

39. 110 Stat. 3416, P.L. 104-290 (1996).

companies are no longer required to file quarterly or semiannual reports with the SEC.

Private investment companies formed to raise capital for business ventures are an unregistered form of an investment company. Participation in such funds may be sold to qualified purchasers categorized as follows:

1. individuals with $5 million in investments

2. trusts sponsored by qualified purchasers

3. family businesses with $5 million or more invested

4. businesses with no less than $25 million invested

Also, advisers may receive performance-based fees in addition to traditional management fees.

[a]   Recent Development. On October 15, 1998, the SEC announced details of its long-anticipated "Aircraft Carrier" release (so nicknamed because of its size and importance) designed to "bring SEC rules into line with the era of instantaneous information and internet investing."[40] According to the SEC, the proposed rules, released in full in November 1998, would accomplish the following objectives:

- larger companies would no longer be subject to a months-long review process after filing with the SEC to sell securities;

- companies would have fewer restrictions in communicating with potential investors;

- underwriters would have increased due-diligence responsibilities;

- companies would have to file quarterly and annual reports more quickly and include more information; and

- investors would get more timely and better information.[41]

---

40. "SEC Proposes New Rules to Streamline Stock Offerings by Public Companies," *Wall Street Journal,* October 16, 1998.

41. *Id.*

The "Aircraft Carrier" effort proved to be far too ambitious, but key parts of it will probably emerge in specific rule proposals, NASD interpretative releases, and SEC "no action" letters. For example, on November 12, 1999, the SEC responded with a "no action" letter to a request from Charles Schwab and Company proposing to make road show meetings available in a password-protected Internet environment to customers who meet certain financial criteria. Subsequently, in an interpretive release dated April 28, 2000, the SEC provided guidance on the use of electronic media by issuers and capital markets intermediaries (i.e., investment banking underwriters and distributing broker-dealers). The guidance addresses three areas: (1) document delivery under federal securities law, (2) issuer liability for Web site content, and (3) basic legal principles that issuers and underwriters/broker-dealers should consider in conducting on-line underwritten offerings. The SEC also has requested comment regarding all issues pertaining to electronic delivery of deal-related information and electronic-only offerings.

[10] Financial Services Modernization Act of 1999 (Gramm-Leach-Bliley Act)

In response to years of pressure supplied initially by commercial banks (the late 1970s), later by federal legislators (the late 1980s) and lastly by certain investment banking and financial services corporate interests, notably Citigroup (the late 1990s), the Gramm-Leach-Bliley Act of 1999 repealed parts of the Banking Act of 1933 (Glass-Steagall Act) and the 1956 Bank Holding Company Act. These latter two acts, among many other things, prevented commercial banks from entering into the insurance and the corporate securities underwriting businesses. In addition the Gramm-Leach-Bliley Act

- requires financial institutions to disclose in writing to their customers the entity's policies on collecting, using, and protecting personal financial information;

- prohibits nonfinancial firms from moving into commercial banking by setting up or acquiring federal savings and loan institutions; and

- allows the Federal Reserve and the Treasury Department to split oversight over commercial banks entering new financial activities.

The new bill permits the convergence of commercial banks, investment banks, and insurance companies into all-encompassing financial holding companies, the first of which in the United States is Citigroup.

Over the past 67 years, the nation's securities laws have seen many proposals and undergone many amendments and modifications. The most recent enactments and proposals will no doubt not be the last. What is most important for capital markets practitioners is to respond in a timely manner to the SEC's request for comments regarding all new securities rules proposals, a traditional but often ignored participative feature. However complicated, our securities laws have been and still are the very bedrock upon which rest our new issue and secondary capital markets, both of which have long been the envy of issuers and investors worldwide.

[11] Federal Reserve System

President Woodrow Wilson signed into law the Federal Reserve Act on December 23, 1913, creating the Federal Reserve System (the Fed)—our nation's central bank. This legislation was the result of, and an attempt to deal with, a series of liquidity crises (panics) that plagued the United States periodically throughout the nineteenth and early twentieth centuries.[42]

The President of the United States appoints, and the Senate confirms, each member of the Fed's Board of Governors to a 14-year term (with one term expiring every two years). This structure and makeup have given the Fed a large degree of political independence over the years (often frustrating both presidents and members of Congress alike) to pursue its original stated goals: ". . . to give the country an elastic currency, to provide facilities for discounting commercial paper, and to improve the supervision of banking."[43]

---

42. *See* Richard Sylla, J. P. Morgan to the Rescue? *New York Times,* October 4, 1998, and Jean Strouse, "The Brillant Bailout," *New Yorker,* November 23, 1998, for interesting descriptions of the events surrounding each of these panics.

43. *The Federal Reserve System—Purposes and Functions,* 5th ed. (Washington, D.C.: Board of Governors of the Federal Reserve System, 1963), p. 1.

As the U.S. economy grew and its financial system expanded, so did the role of the Fed. Today, the Federal Reserve's duties fall into four general areas:

- conducting the nation's monetary policy by influencing the money and credit conditions in the economy in pursuit of full employment and stable prices;

- supervising and regulating banking institutions to ensure the safety and soundness of the nation's banking and financial system and to protect the credit rights of consumers;

- maintaining the stability of the financial system and containing systemic risk that may arise in financial markets; and

- providing certain financial services to the U.S. government, to the public, to financial institutions, and to foreign official institutions, including playing a major role in operating the nation's payments system.

Most developed countries have a central bank whose functions are broadly similar to those of the Federal Reserve. The Bank of England has existed since the end of the seventeenth century. Napoleon I established the Banque de France in 1800, and the Bank of Canada began operations in 1935. The German central bank was reestablished after World War II and is loosely modeled on the Federal Reserve.[44]

Contact information for the Board and the 12 district banks follows.

Board of Governors of the Federal Reserve System
20th and Constitution Avenue, NW
Washington, DC 20551
202-452-3000
www.federalreserve.gov

---

44. *Id.*

Federal Reserve District Banks servicing the 50 states and all U.S. commonwealths and territories.

Federal Reserve Bank of Atlanta
104 Marietta Street NW
Atlanta, GA 30303-2713
404-521-8500/8050 fax—
Public Affairs
www.frbatlanta.org

Federal Reserve Bank of Boston
600 Atlantic Avenue
Boston, MA 02106
617-973-3000/5918 fax
www.bos.frb.org

Federal Reserve Bank of Chicago
230 South LaSalle Street
Chicago, IL 60604
312-322-5322/5515 fax
www.frbchi.org

Federal Reserve Bank of Cleveland
1455 East Sixth Street
Cleveland, OH 44114
216-579-2000/2477 fax
www.clev.frb.org

Federal Reserve Bank of Dallas
2200 North Pearl Street
Dallas, TX 75201-2272
214-922-6000/5268 fax
www.dallasfed.org

Federal Reserve Bank of Kansas City
925 Grand Boulevard
Kansas City, MO 64198
816-881-2000/2569 fax
www.kc.frb.org

Federal Reserve Bank of Minneapolis
90 Hennepin Avenue
Minneapolis, MN 55480
612-204-5000/5273 fax
www.minneapolisfed.org

Federal Reserve Bank of New York
33 Liberty Street
New York, NY 10045
212-720-5000/7459 fax
212-720-6130 Public
Information
www.ny.frb.org

Federal Reserve Bank of Philadelphia
Ten Independence Mall
Philadelphia, PA 19106
215-574-6000/4114 fax
www.phil.frb.org

Federal Reserve Bank of Richmond
701 East Byrd Street
Richmond, VA 23219
804-697-8000/8123 fax
www.rich.frb.org

Federal Reserve Bank of St. Louis	Federal Reserve Bank of San Francisco
411 Locust Street St. Louis, MO 63102 314-444-8444/8503 fax www.stls.frb.org	P.O. Box 7702 101 Market Street San Francisco, CA 94120 415-974-2000/3430 fax www.frbsf.org

In addition, the Fed maintains an operations center in East Rutherford, New Jersey, and 25 branches and 10 offices (serving only as regional check processing centers) throughout the continental United States.[45]

To learn more about the Fed and to order any of its brochures and publications, write to:

PUBLICATIONS SERVICES MS-127
Board of Governors of the Federal Reserve System
Washington, DC 20551
202-452-3244/728-5886 fax
<www.bog.frb.fed.us>

[12]   Federal Reserve Regulations[46]

Regulation	Subject	Purpose
A	Extensions of credit by Federal Reserve Banks	Governs borrowing by depository institutions at the Federal Reserve discount window
B	Equal credit opportunity	Prohibits lenders from discriminating against credit applicants, establishes guidelines for gathering and evaluating credit information, and requires written notification when credit is denied

---

45. Branch and office numbers accurate as of October 1998.

46. *The Federal Reserve System—Purposes and Functions,* 8th ed. (Washington, D.C.: Board of Governors of the Federal Reserve System, 1994), Appendix B.

Regulation	Subject	Purpose
C	Home mortgage disclosure	Requires certain mortgage lenders to disclose data regarding their lending patterns
D	Reserve requirements of depository institutions	Sets uniform requirements for all depository institutions to maintain reserve balances either with their Federal Reserve Bank or as cash in their vaults
E	Electronic funds transfer	Established the rights, liabilities, and responsibilities of parties in electronic funds transfers and protects consumers when they use such systems
F	Limitations on interbank liabilities	Prescribes standards to limit the risks posed by obligations of insured depository institutions to other depository institutions
G	Securities credit by persons other than banks, brokers or dealers	Governs extension of credit by parties other than banks, brokers, or dealers to finance the purchase or the carrying of margin securities; *see also* regulations T, U, and X
H	Membership of state banking institutions in the Federal Reserve System	Defines the requirements for membership by state-chartered banks in the Federal Reserve System and establishes minimum levels for the ratio of capital to assets to be maintained by state member banks
I	Issue and cancellation of capital stock of Federal Reserve Banks	Sets forth stock-subscription requirements for all banks joining the Federal Reserve System
J	Collection of checks and other items by Federal Reserve Banks and funds transfers through the Fedwire	Establishes procedures, duties and responsibilities among (1) Federal Reserve Banks (2) senders and payors of checks and other items (3) senders and recipients of wire transfer of funds

Regulation	Subject	Purpose
K	International banking operations	Governs the international banking operations of U.S. banking organizations and the operations of foreign banks in the United States
L	Management official interlocks	Restricts the management relationships that an official in one depository institution may have with other depository institutions
M	Consumer leasing	Implements the consumer leasing provisions of the Truth in Lending Act by requiring meaningful disclosure of leasing terms
N	Relations with foreign banks and bankers	Govern relationships and transactions between Federal Reserve Banks and foreign banks, bankers, or governments
O	Loans to executive officers, directors, and principal shareholders of member banks	Restricts credit that a member bank may extend to its executive officers, directors, and principal shareholders and their related interests
P	Minimum security devices and procedures for Federal Reserve Banks and state member banks	Sets requirements for a security program that state-chartered member banks must establish to discourage robberies, burglaries, and larcenies
Q	Prohibition against payment of interest on demand deposits	Prohibits member banks from paying interest on demand deposits (for example, checking accounts)
R	Relationships with dealers in securities under Section 32 of the Banking Act of 1933	Restricts employment relations between securities dealers and member banks to avoid conflict of interest, collusion, or undue influence on member bank investment policies or advice to customers
S	Reimbursement to financial institutions for assembling or providing financial records	Establishes rates and conditions for reimbursement to financial institutions for providing customer records to a government authority

Regulation	Subject	Purpose
T	Credit by brokers and dealers	Governs extension of credit by securities brokers and dealers, including all members of national securities exchanges; *see also* regulations G, U, and X
U	Credit by banks for purchasing or carrying margin stocks	Governs extension of credit by banks to finance the purchase or the carrying of margin securities; *see also* regulations G, T, and X
V	Loan guarantees for defense production (dormant)	Facilitates the financing of contracts deemed necessary to national defense production
W	Vacant	
X	Borrowers of securities credit	Extends to borrowers who are subject to U.S. laws the provisions of regulations G, T, and U for obtaining credit within or outside the United States for the purpose of purchasing securities
Y	Bank holding companies and change in bank control	Governs the bank and nonbank expansion of bank holding companies, the divestiture of impermissible nonbank interests, and the acquisition of a bank by individuals
Z	Truth in lending	Prescribes uniform methods for computing the cost of credit, for disclosing credit terms, and for resolving errors on certain types of credit accounts
AA	Unfair or deceptive acts or practices	Establishes consumer complaint procedures and defines unfair or deceptive practices in extending credit to consumers
BB	Community reinvestment	Implements the Community Reinvestment Act and encourages banks to help meet the credit needs of their communities
CC	Availability of funds and collection of checks	Governs the availability of funds deposited in checking accounts and the collection and return of checks

Regulation	Subject	Purpose
DD	Truth in savings	Requires depository institutions to provide disclosures to enable consumers to make meaningful comparisons of deposit accounts
EE	Netting eligibility for financial institutions	Defines financial institutions to be covered by statutory provisions regarding netting contracts—that is, contracts in which the parties agree to pay or receive the net, rather than the gross, payment due

Organization of the Federal Reserve System[47]
Washington, D.C. 20551

---

47. Excerpted from an 8-page looseleaf public handout obtained by one of the editors at the publication office of the Fed in October 1998.

Organization

BOARD OF GOVERNORS		FEDERAL RESERVE BANKS	MEMBER BANKS
7 Members appointed by the President of the United States and confirmed by the Senate	**FEDERAL OPEN MARKET COMMITTEE** 12 Members: The Board of Governors and 5 Presidents of F.R. Banks	**Appoints** (top) 12 Banks operating 25 Branches and 9 additional Offices for processing checks EACH BANK WITH 9 DIRECTORS 3 Class A–Banking 3 Class B–Business 3 Class C–Public DIRECTORS at each F.R. Bank appoint President First Vice President and other Officers and Employees	Contribute capital About 5400 Large about 400 Medium about 1600 Small about 3,400 Each group elects one Class A and one Class B Director in each F.R. District
	FEDERAL ADVISORY COUNCIL 12 Members Approves appointments and salaries Approves salaries	Elect	Elect

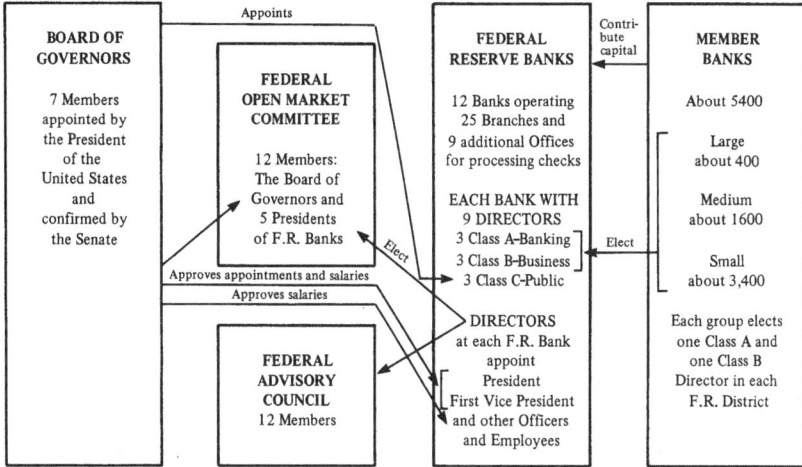

Relationship to Instruments of Credit Policy

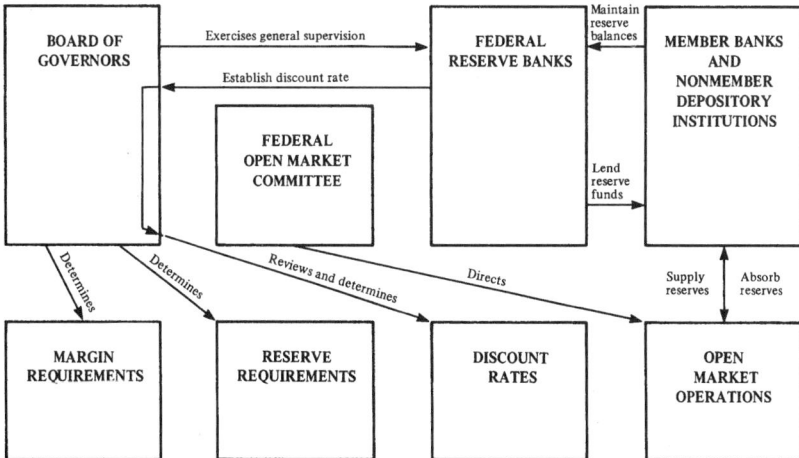

BOARD OF GOVERNORS — Exercises general supervision → FEDERAL RESERVE BANKS — Maintain reserve balances → MEMBER BANKS AND NONMEMBER DEPOSITORY INSTITUTIONS

Establish discount rate

FEDERAL OPEN MARKET COMMITTEE

Lend reserve funds

Determines → MARGIN REQUIREMENTS

Determines → RESERVE REQUIREMENTS

Reviews and determines

Directs → DISCOUNT RATES

Supply reserves / Absorb reserves → OPEN MARKET OPERATIONS

THE FEDERAL RESERVE SYSTEM

The basic function of the Federal Reserve System is to make possible a flow of credit and money that will foster orderly economic growth and a stable dollar, encourage business and employment, and facilitate long-run balance in our international payments. The System was created by the Federal Reserve Act which became law on December 23, 1913. The statute provides for a Board of Governors in Washington, the 12 Federal Reserve Banks and their branches, the Federal Open Market Committee, the Federal Advisory Council, and the member banks. The relationships of those groups are indicated below. Solid lines indicate statutory relationships; broken lines, an informal relationship.

BOARD OF GOVERNORS OF THE FEDERAL RESERVE SYSTEM

The Board is comprised of seven members, each appointed by the President and confirmed by the Senate for a term of 14 years. It is an independent agency of the Federal Government, reporting directly to the Congress. The Board's primary responsibilities include the formulation of appropriate credit and monetary policies to carry out the basic function of the Federal Reserve System. It also has certain supervisory responsibilities with respect to the Reserve Banks, bank holding companies, and banks belonging to the System.

- - Information - -

FEDERAL OPEN MARKET COMMITTEE

This Committee is comprised of the seven members of the Board of Governors, the President of the Federal Reserve Bank of New York and four other Reserve Bank presidents who serve on a rotating basis. The Committee meets in Washington at frequent intervals to determine System open market policy. To carry out its policies, the Committee directs the purchase or sale of Government securities in the open market for the purpose of influencing the supply and availability of money and credit. The Committee has annually designated the New York Reserve Bank to act as agent in executing transactions for the System open market account.

Advice and recommendation

Consultation and recommendation

FEDERAL ADVISORY COUNCIL

The Council is comprised of one banker from each Federal Reserve District selected annually by the board of directors of the Federal Reserve Bank. It meets four times a year in Washington and confers with the Board of Governors on business conditions, credit and monetary policies, and other System matters.

Directions re open market operations

Consultation and recommendation

Information

CHAIRMEN'S CONFERENCE

An informal organization of the Chairmen of the 12 Federal Reserve Banks, the Conference meets at least once a year, generally in Washington. Matters of interest to the System are discussed from the standpoint of the Chairmen in their dual capacity as Chairmen of the boards of directors of the Reserve Banks and as statutory agents of the Board of Governors at the Reserve Banks.

Supervisory and regulatory relations

PRESIDENTS' CONFERENCE

An informal organization of the Presidents of the 12 Federal Reserve Banks, the Conference meets at least quarterly, primarily for the purpose of helping to coordinate System operations. The Conference considers a wide variety of System policies and makes recommendations to the Banks and to the Board. It has many committees, consisting of the Presidents and other officers of Reserve Banks, to study and make reports and recommendations on problems arising in System operations. There is also a Conference of the 12 First Vice Presidents which is organized and operates in a similar manner.

Consultation and recommendation

Consultation and recommendation

THE TWELVE FEDERAL RESERVE BANKS

For the purpose of administering the Federal Reserve System, the United States has been divided into 12 Federal Reserve Districts with one Reserve Bank in each District. The Reserve Banks differ from commercial banks in that profits are not the objective of their operations; and their stockholders, which are the member banks of the Federal Reserve System, do not have the powers and privileges that customarily belong to stockholders of private corporations.

Each Bank is under the immediate supervision and control of a board of nine directors. Under law, three Class A directors, who represent the member banks, and three Class B directors, who are engaged in pursuits other than banking, are elected by the member banks in each District. The three Class C directors are appointed by the Board of Governors; one is designated chairman and another deputy chairman. The chief executive officer of each Bank is its President. He and the First Vice President are each appointed by the board of directors, with approval of the Board of Governors, for a term of five years.

The Reserve Banks are the principal medium through which the monetary and credit policies and general supervisory powers of the System are executed. They perform many of the services which depository institutions perform for the public. In addition, they are fiscal agents, depositaries, and custodians for the United States Treasury and certain other Government agencies.

The Reserve Banks maintain 25 branches and 9 additional offices for check processing in principal cities of the United States. The branches perform for their territories most of the functions performed at the head office. Subject to the regulations of the Board of Governors and general supervision by its parent Reserve Bank, each branch is under the immediate supervision of a board of either five or seven directors, a majority being appointed by the Reserve Bank and the remainder by the Board of Governors.

The locations of the twelve Federal Reserve Banks and their branches and other offices are shown below.

Federal Reserve Bank of:											
Boston	New York	Philadelphia	Cleveland	Richmond	Atlanta	Chicago	St. Louis	Minneapolis	Kansas City	Dallas	San Francisco
Offices:	Branch:		Branches:	Branches:	Branches:	Branch:	Branches:	Branch:	Branches:	Branches:	Branches:
Lewiston	Buffalo		Cincinnati	Baltimore	Birmingham	Detroit	Little Rock	Helena	Denver	El Paso	Los Angeles
Windsor Locks	Offices:		Pittsburgh	Charlotte	Jacksonville	Offices:	Louisville		Oklahoma City	Houston	Portland
	Cranford		Office:	Communications	Miami	Des Moines	Memphis		Omaha	San Antonio	Salt Lake City
	Jericho		Columbus	Center:	Nashville	Indianapolis					Seattle
				Culpeper	New Orleans	Milwaukee					
				Office:							
				Columbia							

MEMBER BANKS

All national banks are required by law to be members of the System. Banks with State charters may voluntarily join the System, if qualified for membership, upon approval by the Board of Governors. Somewhat less than half of all banks in the United States belong to the System but these banks hold about 71 per cent of the country's total bank deposits.

Each member bank is required to hold stock in its Federal Reserve Bank in an amount equal to 3 per cent of the member's capital and surplus. Under the Monetary Control Act of 1980, member banks are subject to a uniform structure of reserve requirements applicable also to nonmember depository institutions. Access to Federal Reserve credit facilities and to Federal Reserve services for which an explicit fee schedule is established – including check clearance and transfers of funds – is accorded to both member and nonmember depository institutions.

Supervision

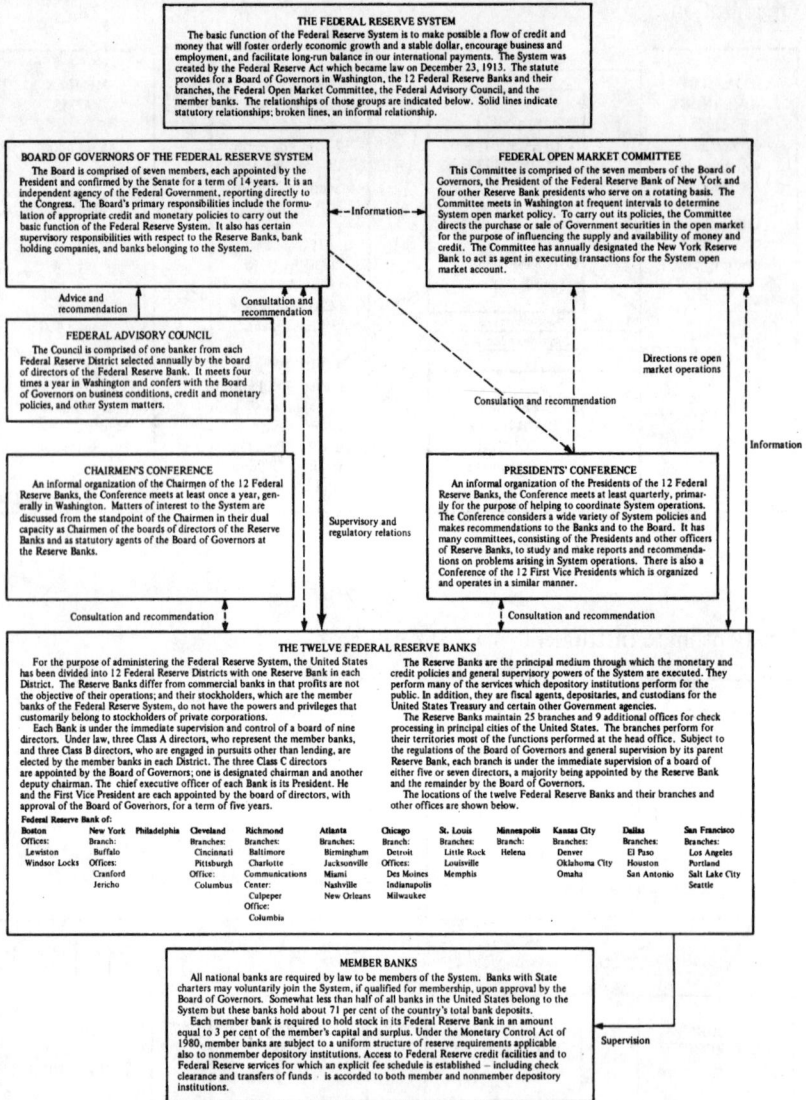

For a more readable version of this organizational chart of the Federal Reserve System, see the foldout in this chapter.

Chapter 2

UNDERWRITING DOCUMENTATION

§ 2.01   UNDERWRITING DOCUMENTS

The basic documents that define the rights and obligations of participants in a public distribution of securities are the Letter of Intent (LOI), the Underwriting Agreement (UA), the Agreement Among Underwriters (AAU), and the Selected Dealer Agreement (SDA).[1] These agreements contain provisions designed to assure that the registration statement and accompanying prospectus relating to the offering contain full disclosure of the issuer's financial and business condition and provisions designed to protect the underwriter(s) if certain conditions are not satisfied. These documents also define the framework under which underwriters conduct the offering and set forth the relative rights and responsibilities of underwriters and selected dealers participating in the selling of the securities.

§ 2.02   DISTINCTION BETWEEN FIRM UNDERWRITING AND BEST-EFFORTS OFFERING

In a firm underwriting, the underwriter(s) purchase the securities from the issuer or selling security holder(s) as principal; once the underwriting agreement is signed, the underwriter(s) are at risk—they own the securities. In a best-efforts offering, a securities firm acts as

---

1. Much of this chapter has been adapted from Charles J. Johnson, Jr., and Joseph McLaughlin, *Corporate Finance and the Securities Laws,* 2d ed. (Aspen Law and Business, 1997), with the generous permission of the

an agent for the issuer or selling security holder(s), promising an earnest sales effort, but the firm is not at risk. In an underwritten offering, the principal underwriter often forms an underwriting syndicate in order to share the underwriting risk. In a best-efforts offering, there may or may not be more than one firm involved, and the proceeds from selling the securities are placed temporarily in an escrow account. Such proceeds must be returned to investors if all (in the case of an "all-or-none" offering) or a specified minimum (in the case of a "minimum-maximum" offering) of the proceeds are not obtained by a specified date.

§ 2.03   LETTER OF INTENT

Some firms enter into an agreement in principle (Letter of Intent) with the issuer early in the process, usually well before the filing of a registration statement. Such letters are nonbinding agreements, except to the extent that they authorize the conduct of due diligence on the issuer by the lead manager and its counsel and spell out provisions for the reimbursement of the lead manager's expenses related to its conduct of due diligence if the transaction does not close.

[A]   Due Diligence Examination

The SEC and NASD both have acknowledged that attempts to define or standardize the elements of underwriters' due diligence obligations have not been successful. The appropriate due diligence process will depend on the nature of the issuer, the level of the risk involved in the offering, and the investment banker's knowledge of the issuer.

The goal of due diligence is to understand fully the business of the issuer, to identify the risks and problems it will face, and to assure that the registration statement is complete and accurate.[2] Thoughtful analysis concerning a particular issuer as well as the experience, knowledge, and care of the underwriters and their counsel in this process represent the critical ingredients of due diligence. A checklist of topics and procedures merely serves as an aid in the due diligence process

---

publisher and the encouragement of the authors. Select portions of this chapter have been adapted from Samuel N. Allen, *A Lawyer's Guide to the Operation of Underwriting Syndicates,* 26 New England Law Review 319 (Winter 1991), with the generous permission of the publisher and the author.

2. *Going Public,* The Nasdaq Stock Market, p. 59 (1998).

and should be used in conjunction with thoughtful analysis and the review of applicable registration forms, rules, and guides promulgated by the SEC.

However, it is not possible to develop a boilerplate questionnaire that will cover all issues or all offerings. Due diligence is not a mechanical process. The use or absence of a checklist does not indicate the quality of due diligence. Conversely, deviation from any checklist used does not taint a due diligence review any more than the following of a checklist validates such a review.

Nonetheless, the due diligence process is a critical element in the preparation of the registration statement as each participant is potentially liable for any material misstatements or omissions in the document (unless such participant can establish that it conducted a reasonable investigation to determine the accuracy of the information presented—the so-called due diligence defense).[3]

§ 2.04   UNDERWRITING AGREEMENT

The UA or purchase agreement, as it is occasionally called, is the written agreement pursuant to which an underwriter, or group of underwriters, commits to purchase a particular security at a specified price or at a price to be determined by an agreed-upon formula. The UA is signed immediately before or shortly after the SEC declares the registration statement effective. The effective date of the registration statement depends upon the completion of the review process by the Commission's staff. The SEC may declare a discrete registration effective (the formality of granting permission for the offering to proceed) shortly after filing (two to three days), the review process may take as long as four to six weeks, or the SEC may declare a shelf registration effective. When the lead manager believes that all aspects of pre-price activity have been completed satisfactorily and when the price negotiation is complete, then (and only then) does it execute the UA on behalf of all members of the underwriting group, thus legally committing the participants to the purchase of the securities.

---

3. Excellent legal references for the subject of due diligence are, with regard to underwriters: *Sanders v. John Nuveen & Co.,* 619 F.2d 1222 (7th Cir. 1980); and with regard to issuers: *Escott v. BarChris Constr. Corp.,* 285 F. Supp. 643 (S.D.N.Y. 1968).

The UA specifies the price the underwriters will pay for the securities, usually the public offering price less an underwriting discount (gross spread). The UA also specifies the date of the closing, normally the third business day after the day of pricing, and usually provides for payment in same day (Federal) funds. If any portion of an over-allotment option is exercised after the closing date, a second closing is scheduled.[4] To minimize physical handling of certificates, the securities of underwritings are delivered to underwriters through the Depository Trust Company (DTC).[5]

[A]   Delayed Delivery Contracts

In offerings of preferred stock or nonconvertible debt securities, the underwriter(s) may elect to satisfy some portion of the distribution obligation to investors through delayed delivery contracts. Under such a contract, an investor (usually an institution) agrees to purchase a specified amount of the securities being offered at the initial public offering price on a specified date after the first closing. Such an arrangement may facilitate the marketing of the securities to institutions that wish to purchase, do not currently have funds available, but know that such funds will become available at a specified future date.

Delayed delivery contracts, although rarely employed, allow institutions to make investments in a forthcoming calendar quarter or the next calendar year. The issuer must approve each purchaser, and once a delayed delivery contract has been delivered to the issuer at the first closing, the underwriter's distribution obligation has been met and it has no liability with respect to the contract's ultimate fulfillment. A delayed delivery contract is not an arrangement of credit in violation of Federal Reserve Regulation T because the security itself is not formally issued until the specified future closing date.[6]

In addition to the basic purchase and sale commitment, the UA contains certain conditions, representations and warranties, indemnification provisions, and other terms governing the relationship between the issuer and/or the selling securityholders and the underwriters.

---

4. Editors' note: Occasionally, exercise of an over-allotment option may occur over the full life of the option, thus creating the need for multiple closings after the initial one.

5. *See* Glossary for description of DTC's functions.

6. *See* Glossary for expanded definition of Reg T.

[B] Representations and Warranties

Underwriting agreements traditionally contain representations and warranties from the issuer (and in some cases selling security holders) to the underwriter(s) that the registration statement complies in all material respects with the requirement of the 33 Act and does not contain any untrue statement of a material fact or omit to state any material fact required or necessary to ensure that no statements in the registration statement are misleading.

If an offering includes any selling security holders, each one must represent that he/she/it has the authority to enter into the underwriting agreement and has good title to the securities being sold. If there are a large number of selling security holders, it is often customary for administrative purposes for each of them to enter into a custody agreement and grant a power-of-attorney to a single designated party—an attorney-in-fact. The attorney-in-fact signs the underwriting agreement on behalf of all selling security holders and delivers the securities to the underwriter(s) at closing. The closing is the date, time, and place at which securities are exchanged for monies.

[C] Underwriting Agreement Covenants

The issuer customarily pledges to notify the lead manager of any communications received by it from the SEC with respect to the registration statement. The issuer should agree not to file any amendment or supplement to the registration statement to which the lead manager shall reasonably object. Additionally, it is customary for the issuer to pledge that if any material event shall occur as a result of which, in the opinion of counsel for the underwriters, it is necessary to amend the registration statement or supplement the prospectus, the issuer will in fact prepare and furnish to the underwriters the requisite amended or supplemental prospectus.

The underwriting agreement should include a covenant that the issuer will make available an earnings statement covering the 12-month period beginning no later than the first day of the fiscal quarter next following the effective date of the registration statement.

[D] Underwriter's Commitment and Default

The underwriter's individual underwriting commitments are several and not joint. In other words, each underwriter is committed to purchase a specified amount of securities (its statutory underwriting commitment as disclosed in the prospectus section "Underwriting") and its proportionate share of any securities purchased pursuant to the exercise of any part or all of an over-allotment option if existent (the so-called green shoe).[7] Hence, each underwriter is only liable for the specified securities it has agreed to purchase and is not responsible for any other underwriter(s) who default on their commitment. However, there is generally a provision in the underwriting agreement that if one or more of the underwriters fails at the closing to purchase the securities which it or they are obligated to purchase, then the lead manager has the right to substitute another underwriter or to make arrangements for one or more of the nondefaulting underwriters to purchase the defaulted securities. Alternatively, if the amount of defaulted securities does not exceed 10 percent of the total issue, the nondefaulting underwriters are obligated to purchase the defaulted securities in the same proportion that their respective underwriting commitments bear to the underwriting commitments of all nondefaulting underwriters. If the amount of defaulted securities exceeds 10 percent of the total, the underwriting agreement terminates without liability on the part of any nondefaulting underwriter. The defaulting underwriter has a liability to the other members of the underwriting group to the extent that the group purchases the defaulting member's securities. If the agreement is terminated due to the defaulting underwriter, the defaulting underwriter has a liability to the issuer and/or selling security holders as well.

[E]   Issuance of Additional Securities and Lock-Up Agreements

In the case of an offering of equity securities, underwriters normally require that the issuer, as well as its officers, directors, and principal stockholders, enter into agreements (lock-ups) promising not to sell any additional securities of the same class, or any securities convertible or exchangeable into the same class, for a specified period of time after the date of the prospectus. Time periods most frequently seen are 180 to 270 days for initial public offerings and 90 or 120 days

---

7. *See* Glossary, Sections 5.02 and 5.09, and Guidelines for Stabilization on pp. 130–131.

for follow-on offerings. This prohibition is designed to facilitate the distribution of the newly issued securities at the stated fixed price by preventing the issuance and/or offering of large blocks of additional securities, a process that may depress the price of the securities in the secondary market while the underwritten distribution is in process. The managing underwriter has the right to exempt any sales that it judges would not disrupt the distribution or have an adverse effect on the after-market for the securities being distributed.

In the aftermath of the hot IPO market for technology and Internet-related stocks (1998-1999), many market observers have come to believe that the expiration of the lock-up period for entrepreneur founders, venture capitalists, and "insiders" often coincided with sharp price declines in the company's common stock. In response to this phenomenon, be it real or imagined, the financial media has begun publishing lock-up expiration dates. In an attempt to manage better the volume of shares that will inevitably hit the market upon such expiration, underwriters appear more willing to let "insiders" out of a portion or all of their locked-up securities early if the underwriter perceives strong market demand for the securities. Alternatively, there appears to be growing evidence of follow-on offerings that permit individuals restricted by lock-up agreements to "piggyback" their shares on to a second or third underwritten offering occurring increasingly close to completion of the IPO.

[F]   Conditions in the Underwriting Agreement and Comfort Letters

The underwriting agreement specifies certain conditions that the issuer and/or selling security holder(s) must meet before the obligation of the underwriters to purchase the securities at closing becomes final. For example, the underwriters must receive an opinion (comfort) from the company's general counsel on the validity of incorporation of the company and its subsidiaries and on the significance of material contracts and litigation. The company's outside counsel must opine on the validity of the issuance of the securities, the effectiveness of the registration statement, and its compliance as to form with the requirements of the 33 Act. Both general counsel and outside counsel for the issuer are required to give assurance that "nothing has come to their attention" that would lead them to believe that the registration statement is false or misleading in any material respect.

The underwriter(s) also receives a comfort letter from the company's independent auditors stating that: (1) the certified financial statements comply as to form in all material respects with the applicable accounting requirements of the 33 Act; and (2) that nothing has come to the auditor's attention that causes it to believe that any unaudited financial statements included in the registration statement do not comply as to form with SEC requirements or are not presented in conformity with generally accepted accounting principles and are substantially consistent with the certified financial statements.

Another customary condition to closing found in the UA is the delivery by an officer of the company of an "officer's certificate" stating that there has been, since the signing of the underwriting agreement, no material adverse change in the circumstance or business of the company or its subsidiaries.

[G]   Underwriter's Indemnification

The issuer and, in appropriate cases, the selling security holder(s) customarily agree to indemnify each underwriter against liabilities and expenses arising out of any alleged material misstatements or omissions in the registration statement and prospectus. The UA usually includes contribution clauses which state that if indemnification is for any reason held to be unavailable to the underwriters, the issuer and the selling security holder(s), if any, and the underwriters shall contribute to the aggregate losses in such proportions as each is responsible.

[H]   Termination of the Underwriting Agreement

A critical provision found in UAs allows the lead manager to terminate the obligations of the underwriting syndicate if there has been a material adverse change (MAC) in the condition, financial or otherwise, of the company or its subsidiaries, or to its earnings, business affairs, or business prospects. It is also customary to permit the lead manager to terminate underwriter obligations "if there have occurred any calamity or crisis or any new outbreak of hostilities, the effect of which on the financial markets of the United States is such as to make it, in the judgment of the managing underwriter(s), impracticable to market the securities or enforce contracts for the sale of the securities." This provision is commonly called the "calamity out" clause. The UA may also provide a "market out" (or MAC out) clause permitting the lead manager to terminate the agreement if there is a material adverse change in market conditions such as the suspension of trading on the stock exchange where the securities are listed or the existence of a nationwide bank moratorium or the occurrence of any other extraordinary event rendering it impracticable to market the securities. (Editors' note—a calamity out is not a market out.)

The SEC and NASD have both indicated that the term "material adverse change" is deemed to be a decline in a general market index (*i.e.,* Dow, NYSE, Nasdaq NMS) of greater than 15 percent as measured from the commencement of the offering through closing (*i.e.,* three business days). The term does not include or cover an inability on the part of the underwriters to market the securities.[8]

§ 2.05   AGREEMENT AMONG UNDERWRITERS

The AAU defines the rights and obligations of the underwriters among and between themselves. The AAU empowers the lead manager (the manager) to act in a leadership role on behalf of the underwriting syndicate with respect to all aspects of the distribution of the securities. The manager's authority is broad and sweeping. The AAU authorizes the manager: to select the form and negotiate the terms of the UA; to take such action as it deems necessary to carry out the provisions of the UA; to execute the purchase, on behalf of all underwriters, and carry out the distribution and sale of the securities; to waive or modify any provision in the UA; and to execute the UA on behalf of all the underwriters. The manager has the authority to negotiate the public offering price, and the discounted price at which the underwriters will acquire the securities (the difference being the gross spread—the compensation to the underwriters and dealers that distribute the securities), and all other terms of the relationship between the issuer and/or selling security holder(s) and the underwriters.

The AAU authorizes the lead manager to over-allot for the account of the syndicate and to make stabilizing bids and purchases for the syndicate account; to determine the amount of securities available for sale by each underwriter; and to reserve some securities for sale to

---

8. *See* SEC No Action Letter to William Williams Esq. of Sullivan & Cromwell, representing The First Boston Corporation, August 2, 1985; and NASD Corporate Finance Reminder to Members, November 1996. *See also* Section 6.02 Market Outs/Calamity Outs.

selected dealers and to institutional investors that prefer to purchase from the institutional pot. The AAU provides that, at the close of any business day, an underwriter's net commitment for either long or short account resulting from over-allotment and/or stabilization purchases may not exceed a specified percentage, usually 15 or 20 percent, of its underwriting commitment. The actual post-deal accounting for all such actions is proportional to the respective underwriting commitments of each firm listed in the UA.

Most AAUs also contain a "penalty" clause permitting the lead manager either to require an underwriter to repurchase at the syndicate cost any securities allotted to that underwriter that are purchased by the syndicate in the open market or otherwise or to charge that underwriter's account an amount equal to the selling concession on any and all securities repurchased.

[A] Price Maintenance

The AAU contains an agreement that all underwriters will offer the securities to the public in conformity with the terms of the offering as set forth in the prospectus—so-called price and trading restrictions. The most important offering term is the public offering price specified on the cover of the prospectus. In almost all underwritten offerings, all underwriters and selected dealers are obligated initially to offer the securities to the public at the specified public offering price until the lead manager deems the distribution complete or determines that, given prevailing market conditions, investors will no longer effect purchases at that price. However, until the lead manager terminates price and trading restrictions, all underwriters and selected dealers must adhere to the initial fixed price offering.

There have been rare instances of public offerings at varying prices based on the prevailing market or on terms negotiated with individual purchasers. In some cases, underwriters may offer volume discounts for purchases of large amounts. If the offering is at a fixed price, the manager has the sole authority to lower the offering price or to terminate "price and trading restrictions."[9] If the offering is not at a fixed price, the underwriters must offer the securities to the public in conformity with the terms set forth in the prospectus.

---

9. *See* Chapter 5 for an additional discussion of distribution.

[B]   Claims Against Underwriters

The AAU normally contains a provision authorizing the lead manager to settle any claims, litigation, or governmental proceedings involving the syndicate arising out of alleged material misstatements or omissions in the registration statement or prospectus. It specifies that each underwriter will pay its proportionate share of all expenses, including legal fees, incurred in defending against any claim as well as its proportionate share of any judgment or settlement rendered by competent jurisdictional authority. Traditionally and customarily, such payments are based on each underwriter's individual underwriting commitment as a percentage of the total size of the offering.

[C]   NASD and SEC Provisions

The AAU contains a number of representations by each member of the underwriting syndicate such as: (1) the firm is a member in good standing of the NASD or, if a foreign dealer, that it agrees to comply with all SEC rules and NASD requirements relating to the subject distribution; (2) the firm is familiar with the prospectus delivery requirements of the 34 Act, Rule 15c2-8(b); and (3) the firm is in compliance with the SEC net capital Rule 15c3-1 under the 34 Act. The AAU also makes reference to the obligation of the underwriters to increase their underwriting commitment, to the extent provided in the UA, in the event of a default of one or more of the underwriters. In addition, the AAU contains a provision that underwriters will indemnify each other to the extent that, and on the terms upon which, the underwriters indemnify the issuer and other specified persons as outlined in the UA.

[D]   Termination of the Agreement
Among Underwriters

Limitations specified in the AAU on the price at which the securities may be sold, the time that the penalty clause remains in operation, the authorization to stabilize, and the enforcement of price and trading restrictions all terminate automatically at a specified time (usually 30 days) after commencement of the offering.[10] However, the manager may terminate any and all of these provisions upon formal

---

10. For discussion of an underwriter's/selected dealer's responsibility with regard to distribution of a new issue, *see* Chapter 5.

notice to the underwriters at any time after the lead manager declares the offering "all sold." In practice, price and trading restrictions often terminate very shortly after the offering has been officially released for sale to the public or coincident with such release.

The historical practice of requiring each underwriter to sign an AAU for each specific issue in which it participates has all but disappeared, as most major investment banks have adopted master AAUs which are pre-signed by potential underwriters and used for all of that particular investment bank's lead managed issues.

§ 2.06   SELECTED DEALER AGREEMENT

The SDA covers the behavior of both underwriters whose net takedown exceeds their underwriting commitment and securities dealers who are not members of the underwriting syndicate but who nevertheless participate in the distribution of the securities. The selected dealer becomes a member of the selling group at the invitation of the lead manager. As with AAUs, the historical practice of requiring dealers to sign specific SDAs in connection with each transaction has also all but disappeared, as most major investment banks have adopted master SDAs. In many offerings there are no selected dealers, in which case members of the underwriting syndicate distribute all the securities.

Dealers participating in the selling group agree to offer the securities to the public at the same stated public offering price as underwriters. Such dealers (and underwriters) also may make sales to other dealers at the public offering price less a discount no larger than the dealer re-allowance. Selected dealers must be either members of the NASD or foreign dealers who agree to comply with NASD regulations and must confirm their familiarity with SEC prospectus delivery requirements. Like the AAU, the SDA contains a penalty clause permitting the lead manager to recapture the selling concession attached to any securities allotted to a dealer that are purchased by the manager in after-market stabilizing or short covering transactions.

§ 2.07   INTERNATIONAL TRANCHES

If a portion of an issue is to be offered to investors outside the United States, the manager must engage expert legal counsel to ensure compliance with all laws and regulations in applicable non-U.S.

jurisdictions. Typically, this effort may involve Canadian, European, or Asian counsel, if securities are to be offered in these areas. Most securities offered to international investors are offered on the basis of a private placement or institutional investor exemption. If there is more than one underwriting tranche, the lead manager usually acts as "global coordinator" and oversees the preparation of: (1) an international prospectus (in substantially the same form as the U.S. prospectus except for certain tax and liability claims); (2) an international UA; (3) an international AAU; (4) an international SDA; and, most important, (5) an agreement between U.S. and international underwriters.[11] These agreements all conform with their U.S. counterpart agreements, and the agreement between U.S. and international underwriters gives the global coordinator the authority to manage all distribution activities and to treat the separate offerings as one. For example, the global manager will have authority to execute stabilizing transactions wherever appropriate and to transfer securities from one tranche to another and to allocate securities among the various underwriting groups, as it deems appropriate to complete the distribution.

§ 2.08   COMPETITIVE BIDDING

Rule 50 under the Public Utility Holding Company Act of 1935 (rescinded in 1994) required utility holding companies and their operating subsidiaries to sell new securities via sealed competitive bidding, and the public utility laws of many states also required competitive bidding for such securities. The SEC and state public utility regulatory commissions could grant exemption to such requirements if competitive bidding was deemed not to be in the public interest, for example, if market or industry conditions were so uncertain or turbulent that the risk existed that no bids would be forthcoming. Such exemptions were routinely granted during the early-to-mid 1970s.

In competitive bidding, the agreement between the issuer and the underwriting firm(s) is usually called the purchase agreement and is quite similar in purpose and function to a UA. If two or more securities firms join together to form a bidding group, the lead manager may utilize its existing master AAU or devise a simple ad hoc form called

---

11. *See* Glossary for a definition of tranche.

an Agreement Among Purchasers to govern the behavior of the bidding group.

Time-honored traditions and procedures with regard to the competitive bidding process developed and evolved over time. Prior to the advent of the SEC Shelf Registration Rule 415 in 1982, competitive bidding was utilized only by public utility and railroad issuers. Over the years, underwriters and issuers developed an informal but Street-wide accepted set of procedures. Individual issuers sought space on a calendar published by the Irving Trust Company (now part of the Bank of New York). Most bids took place on Tuesday, Wednesday, and Thursday at 11:00 A.M. or 12:00 noon eastern time for bonds, preferred stock, and equipment trust certificates, and one half hour after the close of NYSE trading for common stock.

Issuer's counsel prepared a bidding prospectus without any underwriters listed, and issuers advertised publicly the date, time, and place for acceptance of sealed bids and the nonmoney terms of the issue. Securities firms formed syndicates or bidding groups that met, initially both the day before (preliminary price meeting) and the day of (final price meeting) the bid to review market terms, arrange underwriting commitments, and produce the actual bid to submit to the issuer.

Underwriting syndicates were customarily required to put up 3 percent of the gross principal or par amount of the securities being offered as a good faith deposit (refundable for nonwinning bids). At or prior to the stated time of receipt for bids, each syndicate submitted a sealed bid specifying the price to be paid to the issuer for common stock and the price plus the interest rate coupon (for bonds) or the dividend rate (for preferred stock). For bonds and preferred stock, the winning bid was the one that produced the lowest net interest (or net dividend) cost for the issuer. For common stock, the winning bid was the one with the highest price per share to be paid to the issuer. The announcement of results for fixed income securities was an often-confusing mixture of phraseologies to the outside observer, since the winning (highest) bidder was the one offering the lowest net interest/dividend cost to the issuer.

Under the practice of forming syndicates to amass the capital then necessary to underwrite transactions, a pattern of behavior developed whereby so-called historical bidding accounts, that contained the same securities firms (or the surviving entity resulting from a merger of two firms) as the prior account bidding for similar securities of that particular issuer, bid for securities of specific issuers year after year. Some remnants of this practice exist today in the makeup of syndicates bidding for fixed income securities of certain issuers. This pattern of behavior that developed during the 1935-1981 period set the early tone for competitive bidding procedures for non-public-utility securities offerings that have proliferated since the introduction of the shelf registration process. From this rather casual yet formalized process evolved the procedures in place today when issuers offer securities in a competitive environment under Rule 415.[12] Gone are requirements for a good faith deposit and a sealed bid delivered in person. Instead, underwriters are often given little notice (*e.g.*, 15 minutes) and only a telephone number to call a bid into an issuer that may or may not be accepted even if it is the best (highest). Disclosure of the identity of other bidders may or may not be made, and bids may occur at almost any time of the day or night.

Rule 415 bidding illustrates the essence of transactional investment banking today—the ability of an investment bank(s) to commit firm capital in size with little or no advance notice (and thus no premarketing) to an issuing company with all paperwork to be completed ex post facto. Thus, relationships between issuers and investment banks may be more critical than ever with regard to the need for ongoing conduct of due diligence and the offer and acceptance of a telephonic contract between parties reached via a Rule 415 competitive bid or even a negotiated offering coming off a shelf registration (the primary vehicle today for investment grade issuers, as opposed to a discrete filing).

In the first five to eight years after the shelf registration process took effect, many industrial and finance company issuers offered fixed income securities at competitive bid. However, frequent issuers increasingly became more concerned with initial market reception and aftermarket price performance of their issues in the 1990s, so much so that, by 1998, fixed income primary capital markets professionals estimate that more than nine of every 10 new issues are offered on a negotiated rather than a competitive bid basis.[13] The theory is that the lead

---

12. The so-called Shelf Registration Rule 17 CFR 230.415 (1998). *See* Glossary for a definition of Rule 415.

13. Editor interviews with Gary W. James, CommScan LLC, and Richard B. duBusc, CS First Boston, December 1998.

manager has the ability to test reoffering terms, prepricing, in a negotiated environment—a task that is virtually impossible in an unexpected but suddenly announced competitive offering—and the issuer
has an opportunity to reward (pay) investment banks for other services
performed via the underwriting spread. The elimination of most of the
risk-taking function ensures the payment.

§ 2.09   CANADIAN WRAPPER

The offering of securities in Canada is regulated by the individual
provincial securities commissions.

[A]   Ontario

To comply with Ontario Securities laws, U.S. firms may offer new
issue securities pursuant to a private placement memorandum composed of the U.S. prospectus and a wrapper (a four-page document
attached to or "wrapped" around the U.S. prospectus) dealing with matters relevant to the private placement and containing:

- language required to exempt the issuer from providing Ontario
  purchasers with a contractual right of action as remedy for misrepresentation in the offering memorandum; and

- other language Canadian counsel may require such as the private placement exemption for purchases of not less than Cdn
  $150,000.

U.S. securities firms registered in Ontario as an "International
Dealer" are permitted to trade only in foreign securities (securities of
non-Canadian corporations and governments) and only with designated institutions (such as banks, insurance companies, loan and trust
companies, and certain pension and mutual funds).

To purchase securities of a U.S. new issue, a designated institution
in Ontario almost always relies on one of three exemptions under the
Securities Act of Ontario:

1. Institutional Purchaser Exemption—available to financial
   institutions such as banks, trust companies and federal, provincial, or municipal governments. There is no minimum Cdn dollar amount for such exemption.

2. Exempt Purchaser Exemption—available to exempt purchasers recognized by the Ontario Securities Commission (OSC). There is no minimum Cdn dollar amount for such exemption.

3. Private Placement Exemption—available where the designated institution is ineligible for either of the above exemptions, in which case the acquisition cost of securities to the designated institution must not be less than Cdn $150,000 and not less than Cdn $150,000 for each account where a portfolio manager is purchasing for more than one fully managed account.

An issuer of securities making an offering in Ontario must file a report with the OSC within 10 days after a sale made under each of the three exemptions listed above and pay a fee of the greater of Cdn $100 or 0.02 percent of the gross proceeds realized in sales made in Ontario.

U.S. issuers are exempt from providing a contractual right of action for misrepresentation to Ontario purchasers under a blanket ruling of the OSC dated December 1, 1995, and entitled "International Offerings by Private Placement in Ontario."

[B]   Quebec

A U.S. firm is not required to register as a dealer in Quebec provided it sells only to sophisticated purchasers similar but not identical to the classes of designated institutions identified in Ontario provisions, and there is no requirement to provide Quebec purchasers with an offering memorandum or a contractual right of action. An issuer of securities must file a notice with the Quebec Securities Commission within 10 days after a sale made under the sophisticated purchaser exemption. The filing fee payable is the greater of Cdn $250 or 0.02 percent of the gross proceeds realized in sales made in Quebec.

Chapter 3

UNDERWRITING AND NEW ISSUE MARKETING PROCESSES

Underwriting securities is a dynamic process that involves a financial intermediary (investment bankers and capital markets professionals working with syndicate, sales, trading, and research people) raising money from investors for the benefit of an issuer who will use the proceeds to implement or expand upon its business plan (if a primary offering). An underwriter competing for lead managed business commits enormous amounts of human, intellectual, and financial capital to a process designed to find companies that will be viewed as outstanding investment opportunities and successfully introduce the securities of those companies to the public trading markets.

Competition is fierce for lead managed mandates. In the face of opportunities to skirt the law in order to win all, or a large portion, of an underwritten mandate, investment bankers and capital markets personnel must be cognizant of the federal antitrust laws and avoid anticompetitive practices, particularly when an issuer is negotiating on the basis of underwriting compensation. Investment banks have been censored and fined over allegations centered on efforts by a firm to avoid price competition with other underwriters competing for a mandate.

§ 3.01   UNDERWRITING PROCESS

The underwriting process involves many interrelated activities.[1]

---

1. Most of the particular steps or events that follow relate to an equity offering. The process for a fixed income offering is more often akin to the

1. Selection by the issuer of the managing underwriter(s), company's outside counsel, company's independent auditors, special patent counsel or professional engineers/consultants (if needed), a registrar, and transfer agent to administer issuance of the new securities and a financial printer.

2. The preparation of the registration statement (of which the prospectus is the major component) under the leadership of company counsel, and performance of due diligence by the lead manager and its counsel to ensure the accuracy and completeness of the issuing company's business description presented in the documents prepared for the SEC filing. The names of each of these law firms appear in the "Experts" section of the prospectus along with that of the auditor.

3. Advice on the structure, size, and timing of the offering and on the presentation of the company's business in the prospectus will come from the lead manager and co-manager(s). Company counsel assists in issuer compliance with the technical laws that govern disclosure in the prospectus and in negotiating the Underwriting Agreement (UA) with the lead manager. The company's auditor's primary role is to advise on how to conform the financial statements in the registration statement to SEC requirements and to deliver an audited report of the company's financial condition.

4. Registration or filing of the company's securities for sale with the SEC pursuant to the Securities Act of 1933. Filing under the securities laws (blue sky laws) of the various states in which the securities shall be offered, if necessary, and with the NASD; and notification/application to list the securities on an exchange or market.

5. Most public offerings are made through investment banking firms that act as firm commitment underwriters for the company's securities. In this structure, the company does not sell its securities directly to the public, but rather sells the securities to the investment bank(s) at a negotiated discount (gross spread) to the public offering price. The investment bank(s) in

---

competitive bidding process described in Chapter 2 but retains elements of what follows here.

turn sells the securities to its (their) institutional and retail customers at the marked-up, fixed re-offering price, retaining the difference (gross spread) as compensation for structuring, conducting due diligence, underwriting (with its attendant liability), and distributing the securities. To help ensure a successful distribution of securities, the lead investment bank may form an underwriting syndicate in order to spread the financial risk of purchasing (*i.e.,* underwriting) the securities and to achieve a balanced, widespread, or targeted distribution to investors. Underwriting syndicates have been employed to share financial risk in this manner since the seventeenth century in Europe and after the Civil War in the United States.[2] The lead manager (also known as "managing underwriter," "book running manager," or the firm with the "books") selects participating underwriters based upon a variety of qualifications that might include: (a) financial capability; (b) ability to distribute the security to a particular type of investor or in a particular geographic location or area; (c) research expertise on the company or the industry; (d) market making strength; and perhaps (e) geographic location of the firm itself.

In reality, the marketing process begins when the issuer selects a lead or book running manager. At the first "All Hands" organizational meeting and subsequent drafting sessions prior to filing a registration statement, marketing issues may be more fully discussed. At the lead manager's commitment committee and/or marketing committee meetings, the marketing plan begins to take form.

The manager's investment banking group (or corporate finance department), sometimes in conjunction with its research analyst, if she/he is brought "over the wall," drafts an internal selling memorandum to inform the manager's sales force of the investment merits of the proposed issue.[3] Extreme care must be taken to ensure that this

---

2. Vincent Carosso, *Investment Banking in America—A History,* 1970, p. 51. *See* Chapter 3 in its entirety for a more extensive discussion of the development of syndicates.

3. The term "over the wall" refers to the Chinese Wall, a SEC-mandated separation of research from investment banking client inside information. (*See also* Chapter 1.)

document does not receive distribution outside the firm as it can be deemed a prospectus.

Once a registration statement is filed with the SEC, the lead and co-manager's (if any) sales force(s) is (are) informed of the issue and its expected timing. The printing of the preliminary prospectus (red herring) typically does not occur until a determination is made that there will be an SEC review of the registration statement, for securities of an already public company, or that SEC comments have been received and the resultant necessary changes made in the registration statement for an IPO. To facilitate rapid, widespread distribution of the red herring, syndicate members have historically sent mailing labels preaddressed to their branch offices, marked with the appropriate denomination of prospectuses, directly to the financial printer. In 1998 the SEC authorized the electronic delivery of prospectuses, either through posting on an investment bank Web site or via a third-party service provider.[4] In an interpretive release dated April 28, 2000 (www.sec.gov/rules/concept/34-42728.htm/), the SEC provided further guidance on the use of electronic media. (See also page 48.)

Lead and co-managers normally schedule "in-house" (internal) teach-ins for their sales forces using a sales memorandum printed with a hedge clause (*e.g.,* "internal use only—not for distribution") and circulate a tentative roadshow schedule. Typically, an equity roadshow consists of a management presentation at the lead manager's and co-manager's offices followed by trips to major financial centers with group presentations to institutions at breakfast or lunch meetings and as many "one-on-one" (individual) meetings with qualified institutions (and sometimes underwriters) at their offices as can be fit into the schedule. Large offerings may involve roadshows in the United Kingdom, continental Europe, and on other continents if appropriate. The roadshows last one to two weeks but rarely more than three weeks as investor attention span and issuer management stamina may begin to wane.

More than 75 percent of investment grade fixed income offerings now occur via shelf registration.[5] If the issuer is offering debt or preferred stock for the first time or its ratings are less than investment

---

4. An early entrant in this area of service is Thomson Prospectus, a division of Thomson Financial Services. *See* <www.thomsonprospectus.com>.

5. CommScan LLC data.

grade, the lead manager will more than likely put together a modest two- or three-day roadshow along with an investor call-in meeting for potential purchasers located in areas not covered by the roadshow. If the issuer is a frequent visitor to the fixed income marketplace, there will most likely be no formal roadshow.

To augment the preliminary prospectus, the typical roadshow involves an overhead display, slide show, or computer-driven, screen-based presentation that describes the industry in which the company operates, the company business, financial operating characteristics, and results. This presentation usually lasts 20 to 30 minutes, followed by a question-and-answer period. One-on-one presentations more often rely on bound, flip-through books similar in character to the roadshow slide show. Care must be taken not to leave any of this material with the institution as it may be deemed a prospectus. If the company's securities are already trading in the public market, the issuer often brings copies of its most recent annual report and SEC 10-Q filing.

Increasingly, investment banks supplement the roadshow with presentations by the company's senior management on the Internet (*e.g.,* via NetRoadshow, Inc.) or via the Bloomberg Financial Marketing Service. The SEC has approved this new process as long as the lead manager carefully controls access and documents participation. In a "no action" letter dated November 12, 1999, the SEC responded to a request by Charles Schwab and Company to make "roadshow" meetings available in a password-protected Internet environment to customers who meet certain financial criteria.

In the case of a closed-end fund or for securities of an issuer with a strong geographic identity, placement of a pre-effective tombstone advertisement announcing the availability of a preliminary prospectus may be appropriate in select local newspapers. If the offering is weighted more toward retail buyers, the roadshow might involve more meetings in the lead manager's branch offices, and receptions may be held in various cities for all brokers in that particular market whose firms are members of the underwriting syndicate.

Research plays an important part in soliciting investment banking business, and the opinions of respected analysts are solicited by those interested in purchasing a public offering. The lead manager's analyst (and co-manager('s)) will be barraged with requests for internal memos, research reports, and earnings models/projections—all of which can be construed as a prospectus, an offer to sell, or an offer for sale and historically have been tightly controlled by participants in a distribution and prohibited during the restricted period.

§ 3.02   QUIET PERIOD

SEC anti-gun-jumping rules limit both the timing and the nature of disclosures, both written and oral, that may be made once a company has decided to effect a public offering. The most restrictive rules apply to the period commencing when the issuer first decides to effect a public offering and ending when the registration statement is filed with the SEC and a preliminary prospectus is available.

During an initial public offering, there should be no written announcement of new developments occurring within the company, except as filed by amendment to the registration statement, from the time of the signing of a letter of intent through the underwriting period, and for 25 days after pricing. This restriction extends to 40 days after an offering for a publicly traded company that does not file periodic reports with the SEC. This rule generally does not apply to offerings of already traded companies whose stock is currently listed on a national exchange or on the Nasdaq National Market System.

For IPOs, sell-side research reports may not be published or distributed by underwriters and selected dealers involved in the offering during the registration period or for 25 days following the completion of the distribution. For companies whose securities are already publicly traded, Rule 101 of Regulation M exempts actively traded securities with average daily trading volume of $1 million and a public float of at least $150 million from a restricted period.[6] Written information, opinions, or recommendations that satisfy Rule 138 or Rule 139 (such as "normal course of business" research reports about issuers using a Form S-3 registration statement) of the 33 Act can be published or distributed by a distribution participant during the restricted period.

In April 1988, the SEC amended Rule 174 under the 33 Act to reduce the aftermarket prospectus delivery period (quiet period) with respect to initial public offerings listed on either national exchange-

---

6. *See* Chapters 4 and 5 for a more detailed explanation of activity permitted under Regulation M.

listed or Nasdaq NMS-listed securities to 25 calendar days. Previously, Rule 174 required a quiet period of 40 to 90 days. Pursuant to amended Rule 174, during the 25-day quiet period, broker-dealers, whether or not they participated in the distribution of covered securities, must deliver a final prospectus when effecting most secondary market transactions in national exchange or Nasdaq NMS-listed securities that are the subject of a registration statement filed under the 33 Act (and whose issuers were not reporting companies before filing the registration statement). This 25-day period runs from the later of the effective date of the registration statement or the first date on which the underwriter(s) effects a bona fide offer of the securities to the public. The amendment to Rule 174 does not alter the prospectus deliver requirement for a dealer acting as an underwriter or effecting transactions in an unsold allotment of securities.

§ 3.03   UNDERWRITING CUSTOM, TRADITION, AND HISTORY

Philadelphia financier Jay Cooke is credited with first using the syndicate method of distribution in an 1870 underwriting of Pennsylvania Railroad bonds.[7] Prior to the late nineteenth century, issuers commonly offered their securities directly to potential investors, and underwriters stood by with commitments to purchase any securities not subscribed as a result of the issuers' own efforts.

The vast amount of capital required to build railroads and finance the growth of American industry after the Civil War strained the risk-bearing capacity of individual investment banks. Thus, firms joined together to form syndicates to share the underwriting risk.[8] Many of these arrangements grew out of friendship and fostered close business relationships. For example, in 1906 Henry Goldman of Goldman Sachs & Co. prevailed on his friend Philip Lehman of Lehman Brothers to direct some capital from Lehman's commodity business to participate in the underwriting of United Cigar Manufacturers, an underwriting commitment Goldman Sachs was unable to take on alone. Later that year, when Goldman Sachs had the opportunity to underwrite the

---

7. Louis Loss, *Securities Regulation,* p. 164 (2d ed. 1961), citing Larson, *Jay Cooke* 314 (1936).

8. Carosso, *supra* note 2, Chapter 3.

initial public financing for Sears, Roebuck & Co., the firm again turned to Lehman Brothers and continued to do so on a regular basis for other issuers as well until 1924.[9]

In the period prior to World War I, the originating banker or "house of issuance" would purchase an entire issue of securities directly from the issuer and immediately resell the securities at a "step up" in price to a relatively small number of firms, comprising a "purchase syndicate" in which the originating banker would customarily join as manager. A second group, known as the "banking syndicate," would then buy the securities at a further step up in price. The members of the purchase syndicate could become members of the banking syndicate, and the originating banker acted as manager. The banking syndicate would then distribute the securities to the investing public.[10]

Following World War I, an additional group called the "selling group syndicate" came into existence, initially performing an underwriting function by assuming the obligation to purchase pro rata any securities that the members of the selling syndicate were unable to sell, a technique sometimes referred to as an "unlimited liability selling syndicate." Subsequently, a second type of syndicate developed known as a "limited liability syndicate," in which the obligation of each member was limited to the amount of its individual underwriting commitment. Out of this progression also evolved the selling group of today in which the financial liability of each member is restricted to the amount of securities for which it subscribes.[11]

The Revenue Act of 1932 imposed a federal transfer tax on bonds and increased the transfer tax on stocks. Passage of the 33 Act limited the liability of underwriters to the offering price of securities underwritten by it. In reaction to this legislation, the old purchase and banking syndicates, with successive sales at increasing prices, gave way to a new single underwriting syndicate in which each underwriter would severally agree to purchase from the issuer a specified amount of securities. This structure, originally known as a "Western Account," remains in use today.

---

9. *United States v. Henry S. Morgan et al.,* 118 F. Supp. 621 (S.D.N.Y. 1953); and Carosso, Chapter 4, pp. 82–83.

10. Allen, New England Law Review.

11. *United States v. Henry S. Morgan et al.,* 118 F. Supp. 621 (S.D.N.Y. 1953).

After Glass-Steagall and up to the late 1960s, the structure and makeup of underwriting accounts—syndicates—was relatively static. Most issues were sole-managed with a "tiering" of underwriting commitments (brackets), with all members of each bracket underwriting equal amounts and appearing alphabetically within that bracket, both in the prospectus and in any tombstone ad(s).

The individual brackets had generic names, and firms took very seriously their position in this underwriting hierarchy—Wall Street's social pecking order—so much so that if a firm truly wanted to be in an offering but was unsatisfied with its position (bracket), it could elect not to appear in the tombstone ad announcing the deal, thereby saving face but still generating revenue. Movement up this status ladder was difficult and usually occurred only after the blessing of Morgan Stanley, the generally acknowledged, albeit unofficial, final arbitrator of bracketing status and keeper of Wall Street social standing during this period.

Many unwritten but well-known, hard-and-fast rules existed to govern the behavior of underwriters with respect to bracketing. For example, two typical 1960s offering syndicates might have looked as below:

	Fixed Income Security	*Equity Security*
	Manager	Manager
	Bulge/Special	Major
	Major	Mezzanine
Brackets	Mezzanine	Sub Major
	Sub Major	First Regional alkla First
	First Regional alkla First	out-of-town
	out-of-town	Second Regional
	Second Regional	Third Regional
	etc.	Fourth Regional
		etc.

Note that there was no bulge or special bracket in equity offerings. Also, the most prominent and prestigious underwriters of that era had conditions that other originating firms had to meet if these heavyweights were to participate (*e.g.,* Morgan Stanley had to appear first after the managers in any equity tombstone or it would not appear at all; First Boston would never accept "worse" than second in appearance in an ad; Blyth had to be on the first line of a tombstone)—quirky perhaps, when viewed today, but taken very seriously at that time.

As the business became more competitive in the 1970s, it became more difficult for firms to obtain sole-managed mandates. Many industry observers look to the $1 billion, 2 tranche (notes and debentures) IBM offering of October 1979 as a critical event in the long march to multiple managers of underwritten issues. In this deal, Morgan Stanley (IBM's historical investment banker) was offered the books with Salomon Brothers as a co-manager. Morgan declined to lead manage under those terms (although it ended up participating in a "special" special bracket all by itself), Salomon became the lead manager, and Merrill Lynch was added as a co-manager.

Increasingly, issuers have opted for two or three managers in equity transactions, with smaller syndicates underneath both in terms of number of brackets and number of firms within each bracket (*e.g.,* by 1997 the average equity deal had three brackets—managers, majors, and regionals). In 1998 a new electronic bracket (e-bracket) briefly came into use in response to early developments in the distribution of underwritten offerings via the Internet. By late 1999 or early 2000, the use of a specific e-bracket had all but disappeared as most underwriters by then either possessed internal e-distribution capability or inserted e-distribution firms in the deal without carving out a specified e-bracket or e-tranche.

In fixed income deals, the advent of Rule 415 shelf registration, the growth of capital of major firms, and the passage of Rule 144A have all helped narrow the syndication process to an all-manager or an all-manager plus one to fewer than 10 underwriters in bond deals. Occasionally, large syndicates are still assembled to distribute (more than to underwrite) retail-oriented preferred stocks (and closed-end funds).

Other developments worth noting and watching are the growing use of "co-lead" managers instead of a single book runner; the creation, in the mid-to-late 1980s, of the term "global coordinator" to reflect the leadership of a multi-tranche, cross-border offering sometimes having different lead managers in each tranche; and the use of the term "co-global" coordinator, which inevitably came into use in the early 1990s to mirror the term "co-lead" manager, however oxymoronic both terms are. In the opinion of the editors, the trend toward "co-lead/co-book/co-global/co-everything" is the direct result of both

the incredibly intense competition among underwriters for lead mandates and the overwhelming reluctance of issuers to make a very difficult, and always controversial, decision: to wit, naming only *one* firm
to act as lead. The result surely must confuse dedicated etymologists
and without question dilutes the relevance of the industry's league
tables.[12]

---

12. *See* Glossary for a definition of league tables.

Chapter 4

DEAL PRICING

The raising of debt or equity capital from investors is fundamental to the investment banking business—the bank(s) acting as intermediary(ies) between the user of capital (the client issuer) and the provider(s) of capital (the client investor(s)).

Pricing an underwritten public offering is the very essence of the art of deal making and the culmination of the entire process from beauty contest to soliciting potential buyers under a prospectus. The intellectual focus and attention to detail required of the capital markets team of the lead manager at this critical juncture are intense. However, whether underlying conditions in the secondary markets permit an easy or difficult pricing, from an emotional and creative point of view, one thing is certain—the need for attention to detail never goes away. Even the most experienced capital markets practitioner has learned that checklists are useful, particularly at periods of high stress such as a pricing meeting. Thus, this chapter attempts to address and identify some of the major items requiring attention.

§ 4.01   PRE-PRICING LEAD MANAGER HOUSEKEEPING ITEMS

[A]   Underwriting Account

Have all invitees:

1. responded to their invitation wire?

2. properly completed their underwriting papers (underwriters' questionnaire and power of attorney)?

3. executed the Master Agreement Among Underwriters?

4. been sent a Regulation M wire on the day prior to pricing?

[B]   Tombstone Advertising

It is helpful to have a proof created—vendors will also provide a quote sheet/menu of newspaper and slick cover publications that may be appropriate, thereby allowing the lead manager to budget this expense. If the deal has co-lead managers and requires a "neutral" tombstone ad, ask the vendor to provide at least two proofs that employ typefaces not associated with either co-lead. (Editors' note—Times Roman seems to have become a popular compromise choice.) (*See* Appendix 3 for a more detailed discussion of this subject.)

[C]   Compliance Items for Initial Public Offerings

1. Assure that issuer's counsel has obtained SEC effectiveness.

2. Assure that underwriter's counsel obtains an NASD "No Objections" letter.[1]

3. Assure that the listing process with applicable stock market(s) is (are) complete and the security is covered under NSMIA so that no blue sky clearances are necessary.

4. If the issue is not listed on the New York or American Stock Exchange or Nasdaq NMS, assure that underwriter's counsel has obtained individual state blue sky clearances.

5. Determine whether or not to impose a penalty bid or to purchase in the open market to cover any short position created in the syndicate account. If a penalty bid or short covering activity will take place, notify the SRO of the primary listing market prior to engaging in such activity.

6. Formally release the securities for sale to the public.

7. Determine that the distribution is complete (all sold) and send an all-sold wire removing price and trading restrictions.

---

1. *See* Chapter 4, Section 5, "Corporate Financing Rule."

8. If the issue is Nasdaq listed, assure that your trading desk has notified Nasdaq of the time to commence "IPO window" and secondary market trading.

[D]   Additional Items to Consider for Follow-On or Secondary Offerings of Equity Securities

1. Advise your firm's senior financial principal of timing for underwriting commitment/net capital computation purposes.

2. Determine if the security is subject to Regulation M or exempt.

3. If the security is subject to Regulation M, determine if it is a zero-, one-, or five-day security.[2]

	$Value of Avg Daily Trading Volume	*$Value of Public Float*	*Trading Restrictions (days)*
A.	≥ $1 million	+ ≥ $150 million	0
B.	≥ $100 K but < $1 million	+ ≥ $25 million	1
C.	All securities not meeting A or B[3]		5

4. If the security is Nasdaq listed, decide about engagement of Passive Market Making.[4] If Passive Market Making is planned, distribute 30 percent average daily trading volume (ADTV) information to syndicate participants. ADTV information is included in the Underwriting Activity Report.[5]

------

2. The security must meet both trading volume and float standards in categories A or B in the table to qualify for zero- or one-day status. For more detail, *see* Chapter 5, Trading Restrictions—Regulation M.

3. If the security is Nasdaq listed, request an "Underwriting Activity Report" from the NASD Regulation Corporate Financing Department (report may be requested electronically via CommScan Compliance Desk). The report will identify the restricted period, and firms may rely on it for compliance purposes.

4. *See* Chapter 5 for an explanation of Passive Market Making.

5. *See* Appendix 10, Regulation M.

5. Identify dealers who will conduct Passive Market Making and dealers who will withdraw their quotes from the market, and so notify Nasdaq.

6. Send trading notice to the SRO of primary exchange or Nasdaq market advising of time and date when the lead manager will first engage in short covering, impose a penalty bid, and/or stabilize after market trading.

[E] Important Pricing Day Details

1. time of pricing call;

2. location of principal parties (lead manager, co-manager(s), counsel for underwriters, issuer management/board members and/or pricing committee, issuer counsel); and

3. phone numbers (working party list helpful here).[6]

4. In preparation for aftermarket trading, if exchange listed, contact appropriate exchange official(s) and/or specialist firm assigned the issue. If Nasdaq traded, contact an NASD Corporate Financing analyst and Nasdaq Market operations to double-check Passive Market Making procedures. For an IPO, three registered and active market makers are required. Set Small Order Execution System (SOES) parameters at either 500 or 1,000 shares and up to five executions.

5. Looking ahead to settlement day—obtain Committee on Uniform Securities Identification Procedures (CUSIP) number, develop settlement details: wiring instructions for issuer's bank(s), custodian, selling shareholders as well as names, telephone numbers, and fax numbers for appropriate bank officers/transfer agent, issuer CFO, company, and underwriter counsel. If an IPO, decide if Depository Trust Company (DTC) tracking will be used (DTC closing department 212-898-3752).

---

6. *See* Glossary for definition of working party list.

§ 4.02   PRICING UNDER RULE 430A

For securities that already have a public trading market, Regulation C of the 33 Act permits the SEC to declare effective a registration that does not yet include information concerning the public offering price, the makeup of an underwriting syndicate, and certain price-related information. The issuer must supply the omitted information by filing an amendment under Rule 424(b) no later than the second business day after the earlier of the date the offering price was determined or the date of the first post-effective use of the final prospectus. An increase or decrease in the aggregate offering size does not trigger the need for a post-effective amendment as long as the net effect of the change represents less than a 20 percent deviation in the maximum aggregate offering price of the securities covered under the registration statement at the time of effectiveness.

Pricing under Rule 430A permits flexibility as to the time and date, since the SEC declares the registration effective prior to actual pricing. Then the issuer and lead-manager/co-manager(s) have 15 business days to execute a pricing agreement. If these two parties cannot agree within that time period, the underwriting agreement automatically terminates.

The compliance items listed at the beginning of this section are also applicable here. In addition, under Rule 430A, the lead manager must or may (as appropriate):

- ensure the issuer files an acceleration request two days before offering;
- commence restricted period (if applicable);
- begin passive market making (if desired);
- notify the NASD of intention to engage in stabilizing, short covering, or penalty bid invocation; and
- consider a request to halt trading in nonprimary market(s) (*e.g.*, the Pacific Exchange) after the close of trading in the security's primary market.

As pricing day approaches, the syndicate manager inevitably finds him- or herself evaluating current market conditions and relating such information to the indications of interest in the book for the deal. A daily diary of market and other pertinent developments, including those affecting comparable companies, can be a helpful tool. Alternatively, capital markets personnel can retrieve data periodically from one or more of many third-party securities markets service providers. Among the numerous items to consider might be:

1. **Economic calendar**—Bond market events invariably effect the price of stocks and equity deal pricing. Are there any economic news releases that may coincide with pricing the deal?

2. **Government bond market**—Price action producing changes in U.S. Treasury yields and/or the shape of the yield curve may be pertinent.

3. **Option expiration dates**—"Triple witching" dates (options and futures expiration) in March, June, September, and December (the third Friday) often bear watching.

4. **Comparable companies**—Earnings releases, short-term price charts, institutional holder lists, short interest ratio, and significant news releases of the comparables may be worth monitoring.

5. **Recent deal pricings**—It may be helpful to check deals done by comparable companies/industry groups or of similar size, for pricing relative to the filing range, increase/decrease in the offering size, gross spread, and after-market performance.

6. **Major secondary market indexes**—Which one(s) is (are) relevant to the deal at hand? Dow Jones, S&P, Nasdaq, RUSSELL 2000, country index, etc.?

7. **Issuer**—Indicators/information to review might include most recent open short interest, institutional holders, recent news, dividend dates, earnings estimates, and changes thereto.

8. **New issue calendar**—How much competition is there for investor attention? Generally? In the relevant industry sector?

9. **Industry conferences**—Are any scheduled on or around pricing day that include one or more presentations by comparable companies?

§ 4.03   DISCUSSION POINTS/NEGOTIATING STRATEGY

Determining the offering price for a client issuer is the most important and delicate task the syndicate manager faces.[7] The price performance of the offering in the immediate aftermarket is at stake as well as the lead manager's reputation for achieving issuers' goals.

Since equity represents ownership, it is the very soul of a corporation. Thus, it should not come as a surprise that entrepreneur founders/owners, venture capital investors, and the corporation's board of directors all will have very strong opinions about the valuation of the company. Therefore, pricing an equity offering is inevitably a significant emotional experience for all participants and represents the very essence of the art of investment banking. Pricing is the culmination of the so-called book-building process of soliciting indications of interest from various investor constituencies most often including but not limited to three main components:

1. Institutional domestic—mutual funds and private asset managers for defined benefit pension plans (corporate or public employee) and individual trusts, estates, etc.;

2. Individual domestic—retail investors typically defined by a value of assets or income; and

3. International—domiciled outside home country of issuer, institutional or retail.

Pricewise, indications of interest focus on the filing range included in the issuer's registration statement filed with the SEC, while sizewise, indications of interest rarely exceed 10 percent of the size of the entire offering. Where a public market already exists for the securities being offered, the public offering price is usually based, for exchange-listed stocks, on the closing price/last sale before pricing, and for Nasdaq stocks, on the closing high bid.

When an already traded security comes under price pressure, the lead manager has the option of entering a pre-effective stabilizing bid prior to the effectiveness of an offering or prior to pricing an offering

---

7. Underwriting Syndicates N.E. Law Review, p. 346.

already declared effective. However, pre-effective stabilization has historically not been widely used for two reasons: (1) potential buyers may balk at de facto pre-close pricing, especially if pre-price volume is substantial; and (2) short sellers may sense an overpriced or underdistributed deal, or both, and begin offering short in size.

Reasons for such price action are many, but two that often surface are (1) a reflection of the increased supply of securities to be outstanding and (2) the implicit message to the market that current price levels are advantageous to the issuer. Not surprisingly, it is not uncommon for issuers, especially those who are infrequent visitors to the capital markets, to be upset by this fall in price and insist that the lead manager do something to arrest the price erosion. In these circumstances, syndicate managers and capital markets people need to be familiar with sections 9 and 10 of the 34 Act, specifically Rule 10b-5 and Regulation M. Section 9 prohibits the manipulation of security prices for the purpose of inducing the purchase of a security by others (section 2) or of effecting alone or with one or more other persons any series of transactions for the purpose of pegging, fixing, or stabilizing the price. Section 10 regulates the use of certain manipulative and deceptive devices. Periodic review of the specifics of Rule 10b-5 and Regulation M is advisable.

Rule 10b-5 of the 34 Act makes it unlawful for any person, directly or indirectly, by the use of any means or instrumentality of intrastate commerce, or of the mails, or of a national securities exchange: (1) to employ any device, scheme, or artifice to defraud; (2) to make any untrue statement of a material fact or to omit to state a material fact necessary in order to make the statement made, in the light of the circumstances under which made, not misleading; or (3) to engage in any act, practice, or course of business that operates or would operate as a fraud or deceit upon any person, in connection with the purchase or sale of any securities.[8] Penalties for violations of the 34 Act are included in the Act and, upon conviction, may include fines of not more than $1 million or imprisonment of not more than 10 years or both. Very serious stuff indeed!

Regulation M, adopted by the SEC on March 4, 1997, replaced old SEC Rules 10b-6, 10b-6A, 10b-7, and 10b-21 under the 34 Act. The provisions of Regulation M that are analogous to old Rule 10b-6 are

---

8. 17 CFR 240.10b-5 (1998).

contained in new Rules 101 and 102, which cover distribution participants, issuers, and selling security holders, respectively. New Rule
103 replaces old Rule 10b-6A and expands the scope of Nasdaq Passive Market Making. New Rule 104 replaces old Rule 10b-7 and regulates stabilization and other activities related to a distribution, while
new Rule 105 recodifies old Rule 10b-21 governing short selling
activity of already trading securities subject to a public offering.

Rule 101 prohibits a distribution participant and its affiliated purchasers from bidding for, purchasing, or attempting to induce any person to bid for or purchase a covered security during a specified
restricted period, which generally commences one to five business
days (depending on ADTV and public float) before the pricing of the
offered security and continues until completion of the distribution.
Certain securities are exempt from Rule 101, including those with
$1 million minimum ADTV and a public float of $150 million. Rule
101 permits transactions that comply with Rule 103 (Passive Market
Making) or Rule 104 (stabilization, penalty bid, and syndicate short
covering transactions).

Rule 105 is designed to prevent manipulative short selling prior to
a public offering by market participants who intend to cover their short
sales by purchasing newly issued shares in the public offering (see
NASD Notice to Members 97-10).

The following data hopefully give the capital markets professional
some insight into prior pricing behavior and the level of activity of
equity offerings in recent years.

Relative Pricing History
Common Stock Offerings (Excludes Public Utilities, REITs,
and Closed-End Funds)[9]
IPOs (1990–10/31/2000)

	# of deals	% of deals
Within original filing range	2,488	53.7%
Above the range	1,128	24.3%
Below the range	1,018	22.0%
Total	4,634	100.0%
# of IPOs withdrawn or postponed	1,002	
% of total filings	18%	

---

9. Source: CommScan EquiDesk. Last update: November 2000.

Follow-ons (1990–10/31/2000)

	# of deals	% of deals
At last sale (bid) prior to filing	162	3.6%
Above last sale (bid) prior to filing	1,551	34.8%
Below last sale (bid) prior to filing	2,748	61.6%
Total	4,461	100.0%
# of Follow-ons withdrawn or postponed	466	
% of total filings	9%	

NASDAQ Listed Follow-ons (1990–10/31/00)

	# of deals	% of deals
At the closing bid	122	4.0%
Above the closing bid	1,056	34.6%
Below the closing bid	1,873	61.4%
Total	3,051	100.0%

Exchange Listed Follow-ons (1990–10/31/00)

	# of deals	% of deals
At the last sale	40	2.8%
Above the last sale	495	35.1%
Below the last sale	875	62.1%
Total	1,410	100.0%

Follow-ons (1990–10/31/00)

Final price terms (as a % from reported last sale (bid) prior to filing)	# of deals	% of deals
20+ premium	322	7.2%
10-20	365	8.2%
5-10	338	7.6%
0-5	526	11.8%
0	162	3.6%
0-5 discount	726	16.3%
5-10	650	14.6%
10-20	800	17.9%
20+	572	12.8%
Total	4,461	100.0%

The *pricing meeting/call* usually occurs or originates at the offices of the lead manager, more often than not via a telephonic conference. Attendees usually include for the underwriters—the syndicate manager/capital markets person and investment banker(s) from lead and co-manager(s) (underwriters' counsel rarely attends); for the issuer— executive management, usually the CEO and CFO, and the pricing committee of the board of directors, issuer counsel, and major selling shareholder(s) (if involved).

Items to determine include:

1. Issue size;

2. Public offering price;

3. Gross spread and breakdown (details of which are not usually of interest to the issuer); and

4. Trade (transaction) date and settlement date.

Price and size—The concern here centers on the possible need for prospectus recirculation should a reduction in either element significantly alter the "Use of Proceeds" (not applicable if offering is all selling shareholders).

Decimal pricing—Syndicate managers and capital markets people need to be aware that the SEC has ordered major U.S. exchanges and the Nasdaq market to implement decimal pricing for equities in four phases. The first phase began August 28, 2000, and the last phase will end with full implementation of decimal pricing for all equities and their underlying options on or before April 9, 2001. The SEC recommends employing minimal pricing variations (MPVs) of $.01 for all equities.

While issuers and investment banks were always free to price equity deals in decimals, historically few deals in fact were. Given the tradition to price follow-on offerings at the "reported last sale," it seems logical to expect more and more equity offerings to carry decimal pricings.

§ 4.04   UNDERWRITING COMPENSATION

While the NASD offers underwriters broad guidelines, no strict regulatory standard exists to guide issuers and investment banks with regard to underwriting compensation per se. However, third-party industry service providers produce exhaustive tables tabulating and recounting all the details of prior offerings, *i.e.,* offering price relative to last sale or closing bid (for equity) or spread off comparable U.S. Treasuries (for fixed income); gross spread as a percentage of offering price; and breakdown of the gross spread into its three components—management fee, underwriting fee, and selling concession.

Inevitably, issuers ask for and underwriters produce relevant benchmarks derived from the above data to use in the price negotiation process. Other factors influencing underwriting compensation are overall secondary market conditions and prevailing investor sentiment. Historically, there has been more uniformity in gross spreads for fixed income securities, due to their commodity-like characteristics—the similarity of securities carrying the same investment ratings, maturity, and other nonmoney terms. Equities, by their very nature (representing ownership interest in the issuer), are far more difficult to categorize, and gross spread statistics for follow-on equity offerings reflect this lack of homogeneity.

However, gross spreads for IPOs of more than $30 million and less than $75 million in size have tended to center on 7 percent, particularly in the post-1992 period. As the volume of IPOs soared in the 1990s, the focus of outside observers on the 7 percent gross spread issue intensified. Perhaps the seminal academic piece examining this subject was written by Hsuan-Chi Chen and Jay R. Ritter, Cordell Professor of Finance at the University of Florida.[10] According to this article, over 90 percent of the deals studied that raised between $20 and 80 million carried a gross spread of exactly 7.00 percent.

On March 9, 2000, NASD Regulation, Inc. (NASDR) announced that it had censured and fined Prudential Securities Inc. for violation of NASD Rule 2110 in that the firm's attempts to justify a 7 percent gross spread on an IPO did not "adhere to high standards of commercial honor and just and equitable principles of trade."[11]

On August 3, 2000, CHS Electronics, Inc., a Miami, Florida, international retailer of consumer electronic equipment (that was publicly

---

10. *The Seven Percent Solution.* Journal of Finance. vol. LV. no. 3. June 2000.

11. NASD Regulation, Inc. CRD Number BD-7471 and NASDR Press Release on this subject dated March 9, 2000.

traded since 1994 and filed for Chapter XI bankruptcy protection from its creditors in April 2000), filed suit against 18 investment banks and their alleged "co-conspirators" for collusion in the setting of IPO fees.[12]

Capital markets professionals might find it helpful to review NASD Notice to Members 98-88 on a regular basis in order to help them avoid any behavior that may, in hindsight, appear collusive or anticompetitive.[13]

The numerical difference between the offering price public investors pay and the net price the issuer (and/or selling shareholder(s)) receives is the *gross spread,* also known as the underwriting discount (or simply the spread). The Agreement Among Underwriters breaks the gross spread into three major components. The *management fee,* paid only to the lead and any co-manager(s), is typically and traditionally 20 percent of the gross spread (until the late 1960s it was 15 percent), almost always rounded up if a fractional number.

The *selling concession* usually varies between 50 and 60 percent of the gross spread. Each underwriter purchases its retention from the underwriting account at the public offering price less the selling concession and then reoffers those securities at the fixed public offering price. Institutional investors typically purchase their shares directly from the institutional pot rather than from individual underwriters and direct the manager to credit the selling concession for the shares they purchase to firms the institutions choose to designate—usually members of the underwriting account, occasionally to selling group members or to firms that did not participate in the underwriting pre-designation.

The remainder, 20 to 30 percent, is paid to the underwriters as an *underwriting fee* for making a capital commitment (taking an underwriting risk) and for bearing due diligence risk. The lead manager remits this fee, net of the expenses of the offering, at syndicate settlement with all underwriters on a pro rata basis of securities underwritten.

---

12. CHS Electronics, Inc. v. Credit Suisse First Boston, et al. (S.D. Fla. 2000) (Complaint).

13. NASD Notice to Members 98-88, Underwriting Compensation in Public Offerings, October 1998.

Of note, the NASD requires the lead manager to affect a final settlement, including a full and complete accounting of all deal-related expenses, with all underwriters no later than 90 days after termination of syndicate price and trading restrictions. Failure to meet this deadline subjects the lead manager to formal NASD sanction. Deal expenses can include legal fees, roadshow costs, interest on syndicate borrowings, stabilization and/or short covering costs, tombstone advertising, third-party communication services, telephone and cyberspace communications, due diligence, and any other (*e.g.,* closing dinner and deal mementos) expenses related to the specific deal (including legal expenses related to any post-offering litigation defense). If deal expenses exceed the amount of the underwriting fee, the lead manager may, according to the terms of its AAU, send out bills to all underwriters to pro-rate the underwriting loss to each underwriter's statutory commitment as a percentage of the deal size.

The selling concession may be broken down further into a *dealer reallowance* to facilitate sales by one firm to another. As set forth in the AAU, this dealer reallowance is the largest discount at which inter-dealer trading may occur; actual discounts may be less than the maximum amount and as small as zero, but no underwriter or selected dealer may effect transactions at higher than the issue price while price and trading restrictions are still in effect. Typically, firms set the dealer reallowance at 10 cents per share of stock and .250 percent of par per bond.

Lastly, the lead manager must establish a *trade date* and a *settlement date.* If the registration statement is already effective, the trade date may coincide with the pricing date. If pricing occurs before 4:30 P.M. eastern time, settlement is three business days later (T+3). If pricing occurs after 4:30 P.M. eastern time, then after-hours settlement standards obtain and settlement is T+4. The SEC has mandated a T+1 settlement by the year 2002. An oft-used negotiating ploy is to offer an issuer good money a day early if it comes to agreement quickly on offering terms, especially for Tuesday pricings where settlement on Friday is a definite advantage to the issuer over waiting until the next Monday to receive the funds.

§ 4.05   CORPORATE FINANCING RULE

NASD Conduct Rule 2710, generally known as the Corporate Financing Rule, is the successor rule to a highly effective interpretation

of the NASD Board of Governors—Review of Corporate Financing—
which was adapted in the early 1970s to preclude broker-dealers from
taking excessive amounts of underwriting compensation from issuers
whose securities they distributed.[14] The premise of Rule 2710 is the
concept that members are entitled to receive fair and reasonable compensation for public underwritings as set forth in confidential guidelines administered by the staff of NASD Regulation, Inc.'s
(NASDR) Corporate Financing Department. This rule also prohibits
a member from participating in a public underwriting until the lead
manager has filed its offering documents with the Corporate Financing Department and received an opinion from its staff. More significantly, the SEC has consistently refused to grant acceleration of
effectiveness to any registration statement if, under SEC Rule 461
(b)(6), the NASD has not yet issued an opinion that it has "no objections" to the underwriting compensation and other terms and agreements of the public offering. In June 1999 the NASD deployed a new
electronic filing system for underwritten offerings—Corporate Offerings Business Regulatory System (COBRA).

For some time now, the NASDR Corporate Financing Division has
been struggling with how to react to the aggressive manner with which
some securities law firms push their issuing clients' way to the front
of the line awaiting NASDR's formal approval of underwriter compensation—an approval that is necessary before the SEC will declare
an issue effective. Law firms that have not made the necessary filings
with NASDR on behalf of an issuer client in a timely manner often
create a crisis atmosphere by abruptly stating the intention of their
client to seek SEC effectiveness (and thus are in need of immediate
approval from NASDR). Lead managers can avoid this disruptive and
unnecessary expenditure of emotional energy by making an early
check to see that timely filings have been made. Unanticipated delays
in the going effective process inevitably happen, so any prevention of
events liable to disrupt the momentum of a deal will be helpful to all
parties.

During 2000, NASDR proposed amendments to the Corporate
Financing Rule regarding underwriter compensation in recognition of
the expanded services NASD members provide to their clients. Such
services may include venture capital investment, consulting, commercial

---

14. *NASD Manual* (CCH), p. 4051 (1998).

lending and banking, or all of the aforementioned. The proposed amendments also reflect the accelerated pace of financing and the shortened time period between a private round(s) of funding and an initial public offering(s). The proposed changes set an objective standard under which all items of value (*i.e.,* fees, securities, options, warrants) acquired by an underwriter during the 180-day period immediately preceding the filing date of a registration statement and the time of the actual public offering will constitute underwriting compensation, and the proposed changes provide safe harbor from the presumption of compensation during the 180-day period for:

- certain entities that regularly make venture capital investments;
- acquisition of issuers with significant institutional investor involvement in their corporate governance; and
- acquisitions that occur from the exercise of preemptive rights to purchase.

§ 4.06   INTRADAY PRICING

Most equity deals are priced after the close of trading in their primary market. On occasion, it is necessary to price intraday. Intraday pricing adds an additional element of risk to the transaction because of the possibility that indicated buyers may not accept the offering price if there is a change in the security's underlying market price before the transaction is confirmed. For NYSE-listed companies that have an effective registration, including a Rule 415 Shelf registration, and that are considered 19-c-3 eligible (company shares listed subsequent to April 26, 1979, may be traded off-board), Regulation M notification may be submitted simultaneously with the pricing of the new shares, and there is no need to halt trading. For exchange-listed companies that are not 19-c-3 eligible, the NYSE will decide if a trading halt is required.

§ 4.07   POST-PRICING HOUSEKEEPING ITEMS

The following is a checklist of items to consider post-pricing:

1. Underwriting account

- send effectiveness/terms wire with final underwriting commitment and retention;

- send release wire (noting penalty bid, if contemplated, and blue sky information);

- pace short covering (*e.g.,* uncovered balance) orders and keep status of such activity (rough P&L) current;

- send termination of price and trading restrictions wire;

- send MBD and designation wire prior to settlement;

- send payment wire;

- send green shoe wire, if appropriate; and

- send lifting of penalty bid wire, when appropriate.

2. Institutional pot

- advise institutions of pot allocations; and

- solicit aftermarket orders, particularly from those pot buyers who have unsatisfied demand.

3. Compliance

- send NASD effective wire with distribution information. If not effective, pre-effective stabilization is an option (on T+3 send NASD final retention for each participant for hot deal response);

- if exchange listed, advise exchange officials of termination of price and trading restrictions; and

- establish opening of secondary market trading time.

4. Co-manager(s)

- advise prior to release of issue for sale (the opening).

5. Co-manager(s) and participants

- inform of any directed orders and final retention (note— current practice varies widely with regard to timing of release of this information).

6. Tombstone

- advise advertising agency of final deal size, offering price, and underwriting participants; and

- select media for tombstone placement.

§ 4.08   DEAL PRICING IN AN AFTER-HOURS TRADING ENVIRONMENT AND T+1 SETTLEMENT

Proposals by exchanges and the Nasdaq market to establish after-hours trading sessions, the advent of after-hours trading on Electronic Communications Networks (ECNs) and the SEC's mandate for establishing T+1 settlement by 2002 all present major new challenges to capital markets professionals.

Historically the pricing of new issues of securities for already public companies, and of issues that derive their value from already publicly traded securities, took place (in compliance with then existing rules) after the close of the issue's primary market, and pricing was based on the last sale or the closing bid, for exchange- or Nasdaq-listed securities, respectively. After the SEC declared the registration statement effective, the lead manager then confirmed allotments to investors who had submitted indications of interest. Since most pricings occur after the close of trading, confirmation/allocation is typically not completed until just prior to market opening the following morning. After-hours trading could put underwriters' offering securities at a fixed price (a long and time-honored practice) at enormous risk if the securities traded lower in an after-hours session because investors might not then accept the higher fixed price of the deal. One solution might be for the issuer, in conjunction with the lead manager, to request a trading halt in all ancillary markets after the close of the primary market solely for the purpose of pricing the new issue securities and disseminating the terms of the deal.

Another alternative might be to delay pricing until after the close of the after-hours session, but this approach increases the difficulty of printing a final prospectus in time to deliver with the printed confirmation as current regulations require and would be impossible in a T+1 environment without significant regulatory change.

Chapter 5

FORMS OF NEW ISSUE DISTRIBUTION AND AFTERMARKET TRADING

§ 5.01 ALLOCATION AND CONFIRMATION OF UNDERWRITTEN SECURITIES

The lead manager of an underwriting syndicate has historically had absolute discretion as to the amount of securities to make available for direct sale by each of the underwriters—their retention. The syndicate manager also has the option to reserve securities for sale to selected dealers that are not members of the underwriting syndicate. These distributing firms are referred to as selected, or selling group, dealers. The syndicate manager also often reserves a portion of the offering for sale to institutional investors. Institutional investors who purchase in large amounts usually prefer to deal directly with the lead manager, rather than with several underwriters or dealers. Securities reserved by the lead manager, on behalf of the underwriters, for purchase by institutional investors in such a manner are held in a syndicate account known as the "institutional pot." The institutional pot not only facilitates the purchase of securities by institutional buyers, enabling them to buy large amounts from one firm, but also assists the lead manager in controlling the placement of securities by allowing allocation to whomever the lead manager deems most appropriate, however defined. In any event, in making its allocations, the lead manager has the obligation to attempt to assure that a bona fide distribution has occurred—*i.e.,* that all the underwritten securities have been placed with end investors—thereby allowing the lead manager to declare the deal "all sold."

Occasionally, a lead manager, co-manager, and/or participant may misjudge its/their actual demand for an underwritten security. Secondary market conditions sometimes soften, an investor account may reduce or cancel its indication of interest, or an error in communication may occur between a syndicate desk and salespeople or end investors. To cope with such an event(s), the lead manager may elect to reallocate unsold securities (pre-pricing/pre-termination of price and trading restrictions) or absorb them in the syndicate short (*see* Glossary), if one exists (post-pricing). Participants should consider that the applicable AAU obligates them to notify the lead manager of any retained but unsold securities. For securities not exempt from Rule 101 of Regulation M, a participant cannot make a market or solicit orders in such security until it has completed the distribution of its free retention (and/or any delivered pot liability).

Underwriting participants are often loath to admit an inability to complete distribution of their portion (retention) of an offering. Caught with an uncomfortable (and likely unprofitable) long position, the temptation (and opportunity) inevitably arises to confirm an unsold allotment temporarily ("park") with an investor account or another broker-dealer, with the understanding that the underwriter/ selected dealer will repurchase the security at a later date at the same price or make the purchaser whole on any loss incurred. Not surprisingly, securities law views parking as a "manipulative, deceptive or other fraudulent device or contrivance" under applicable provisions of the 34 Act including Section 9-1-A, and violators may be subject to severe sanctions including a significant fine and/or imprisonment.

A number of legal options exist to deal with unsold positions: (1) purchase the securities for firm investment account (the holding period for securities so purchased is subject to wide interpretation, and participants pursuing this course of action should seek opinion of counsel); (2) liquidate the position in the secondary market (securities law prohibits a firm long a new issue security from making a two-sided market in such security until the long position is eliminated); or (3) if a listed equity, dispose of it via sale(s) to an investor client(s) in an off-board net transaction(s) not reportable on the consolidated tape.

Section 5(a) of the 34 Act prohibits confirmation (allocation) of sales prior to the SEC declaring the registration statement effective.

Investment bankers have traditionally priced an offering under Rule 430A after the close of trading in its primary market, and the SEC declared the registration effective and then confirmed allocations to investors from whom they had received indications of interest. Both of these actions occurred before termination of the price and trading restrictions contained in the applicable AAU and the opening of trading in the secondary market the next day. This practice suddenly collided with the appearance of new "on-line" investors who had to wait by their computers the night a deal was scheduled to price in order to reconfirm or cancel their indications of interest. The on-line investment bank Wit Capital (now WitSoundview) developed a procedure to deal with this thorny issue by taking an investor's "conditional offer to buy" and allocating stock and accepting the offer to buy, post-pricing and post-effectiveness, electronically. The SEC responded to Wit's practice and new procedure with a "no action letter" dated July 14, 1999, but limited its no action position to registered IPOs underwritten on a "firm commitment" basis.

§ 5.02   OVER-ALLOTMENT AND PENALTY BID

Almost all AAUs authorize the managing underwriter, acting for the account of the entire syndicate, to over-allot or to sell more securities than advertised on the face of the prospectus. Any over-allotment necessarily creates a short position in the syndicate account and therefore potential after-market buying power. The purpose here is to assist and facilitate the distribution of a fixed price security by permitting the manager to maintain (or peg) the secondary market price at the issue price for a reasonable period of time.

The AAU provides that an underwriter's net commitment, either for long or short account and resulting from over-allotments, may not exceed a specified percentage, usually 15 to 20 percent of its underwriting commitment (including any over-allotment exercise). After completion of the distribution and termination of syndicate price and trading restrictions, the lead manager may cover any syndicate short position through (1) open market purchases; (2) order cancellations that occur in the institutional pot or in underwriter or selected dealer takedowns; or (3) the exercise of part or all of the over-allotment option, if one is so granted to the underwriters by the issuer or the

selling security holder(s), or both, in either proportionate or disproportionate amounts to the number of securities being offered.

The development of screen-based trading in over-the-counter
(where new issues are offered) equity securities in 1971 (Nasdaq), a
move that brought sunshine into the theretofore dark world of the tele-
phone-based dealer market, and the passage of the ERISA legislation
in 1974 both combined to increase trading volume and volatility dramatically. The requirement to distribute fully a new issue, customarily done at a fixed price based on the market price of the existing
shares, made the over-allotment procedure a necessary and vital part
of the new issue process. Creation of a syndicate short position—*i.e.,*
allocating more shares to underwriters (and ultimately end investors)
than the syndicate purchases from the issuer/seller(s)—gives the lead
manager the purchasing power it may need to bid for shares (cover the
short) in the secondary trading market and thereby facilitate orderly
commencement of secondary market trading for an initial public offering, or in the case of an already public security, accommodate the one-
time extraordinary supply of shares that an underwriting brings into
the market without overly disrupting normal trading.

The over-allotment option, or "green shoe" (or simply "the shoe"),
was first used in a 1963 underwritten secondary offering for certain
shareholders of the Green Shoe Manufacturing Company of Boston,
Massachusetts, lead managed by Paine, Webber, Jackson & Curtis (as
a historical note, the underwriters exercised the entire over-allotment
option). In employing this technique, the issuer or selling share-
holder(s) or both grant(s) the underwriters an option (usually 30 days,
but it can be of any length) to purchase from the seller(s) an amount
of securities (usually 15 percent, the maximum permitted amount, but
occasionally less) on the same terms as the actual offering (*i.e.,* at the
public offering price less the gross spread) solely for the purpose of
covering over-allotments. The 15 percent maximum (10 percent until
the early 1980s) green shoe is calculated solely on the securities
offered for sale, not on the securities registered. This limitation is contained in the Conduct Rules of the NASD.[1]

The green shoe option makes it possible for the lead manager to
help cover a syndicate short position through exercise of the over-
allotment option, in whole or in part. If the offering is successful and

---

1. NASD Conduct Rule 2710 (c)(6)(x).

trades to an aftermarket premium, the lead manager may exercise the entire option to help cover the syndicate short. If the issue fails to trade up in price, the lead manager can cover the syndicate short position in the open market and allow the green shoe to lapse.

Extreme care must be taken to segregate short covering activity conducted for the syndicate account from any secondary market-making activity conducted by the lead manager's own trading desk. Shorts initiated by the lead manager's secondary market trading desk must not be inadvertently covered by green shoe shares purchased through the exercise of the over-allotment option. Additionally, syndicate managers should be aware that short covering through open market purchases or cancellations reduces their ability to exercise fully the green shoe, since any portion of the shoe exercised to acquire more shares than the syndicate account is actually short is viewed as continuing the distribution or "refreshing" the green shoe and thus a violation of Regulation M.

§ 5.03   NAKED SHORT POSITION

As discussed earlier, the AAU typically grants the lead manager authority to over-allot (go short) an amount up to 15 percent of the deal size (some AAUs authorize an amount up to 20 percent) unprotected by any over-allotment option. This technique is known as a naked short, since the underwriters are totally at risk if the issue rises above the offering price, and any covering transactions must occur solely in the secondary market.

No SEC requirements exist that limit an underwriter's net commitment to a certain percentage of the offering. Rather, it is a contractual provision designed to limit the risk of the several individual underwriters. The size of the over-allotment option, however, is limited by the rules of the NASD to 15 percent of the firm commitment securities (although occasional exceptions have been granted).[2] While no rule exists specifying the maximum duration of an over-allotment

---

2. The so-called Borden's "extra width" green shoe, granted by the SEC to First Boston, as lead manager of a Borden's master limited partnership offering in the mid-1980s. First Boston successfully petitioned, ex post facto, to expand in effect, the size of the deal's over-allotment option by having Borden's register additional primary units to cover a syndicate naked

option, most are 30 days in length from the date of the final prospectus. However, many offerings of yield product aimed exclusively at retail investors carry 45-day duration options. Syndicate managers should note, however, that there is a greater risk of buy-ins against a syndicate short position if short covering extends beyond 30 days. Extending short covering beyond 30 days also creates potential problems for the lead manager with regard to its obligation to settle the syndicate books with the underwriting account within 90 days of issuer settlement as required by Rule 11880 of the NASD Uniform Practice Code.

In July 2000, the SEC proposed adding a new disclosure item in the "Plan of Distribution" section of a prospectus relating to the potential use of a syndicate short position(s) by the lead manager.[3] The proposed disclosure must describe both a covered and a naked short position and the ways in which the lead manager may cover either or both of them (*e.g.,* open market purchase, order cancellation(s), or over-allotment exercise). It is important to remember that syndicate "short" securities, covered or naked, are indistinguishable (fungible) from all other deal shares and are governed by the same confirmation rules, prospectus delivery rules, and antifraud and civil liability provisions of federal security laws as are the firm securities of an offering.

§ 5.04   TRADING RESTRICTIONS—REGULATION M

SEC Regulation M (*see* Appendix 10) governs the trading activities permitted during the public offering of securities registered under the 33 Act.[4] Rule 101 of Regulation M regulates the activities of underwriters, prospective underwriters, brokers, dealers, and other distribution participants.

---

short that was, in retrospect, way too large. The Commission evidently responded to what it must have considered extraordinary circumstances.

3. *Syndicate Short Sales.* Current Issues and Rulemaking Projects, p. 40, Division of Corporation Finance, United States Securities and Exchange Commission, Washington, D.C., revised July 25, 2000, originally posted to the SEC Web site April 13, 2000.

4. Regulation M replaced the old trading practice rules (Rule 10b-6, -7, -8, -18, and -21) in 1997. *See* Appendix 10, Regulation M and Appendix 11, NASD Notice to Members 97-10.

There is an exemption from Rule 101 for actively traded securities. Rule 101 defines "actively-traded securities" as those with a worldwide average daily trading volume (ADTV) of at least $1 million and whose issuers have outstanding common equity securities with a public float of at least $150 million. The ADTV measuring period is the two full calendar months preceding—or the 60 consecutive calendar days ending within the 10 calendar days preceding—the filing of the registration statement or preceding the determination of the offering price, in the case of shelf registration statements or unregistered offerings.

Offerings involving investment grade nonconvertible debt, preferred stock and asset-backed securities, government securities, and other securities exempt from SEC registration requirements do not have to adhere to Rule 101. All the outstanding securities of an issuer are exempt from trading restrictions unless they are identical or convertible, or have similar features to the security being distributed. For distributions of all other securities, the restrictions of Rule 101 apply. There is a one-business-day restricted period for the distribution of securities with an ADTV of at least $100,000 and whose issuer has outstanding common equity securities with a public float of at least $25 million. All other securities not exempt from Rule 101 are subject to a five-business-day restricted period.

The restricted period begins on the later of (1) one business day (or five business days) prior to the determination of the offering price or (2) upon a firm becoming a distribution participant, and ends on the completion of participation in the distribution and the lifting of price and trading restrictions. During the restricted period, an underwriter, prospective underwriter, broker, dealer, or other distribution participant cannot bid for, purchase, or induce others to bid for or purchase the security that is the subject of the distribution or that is convertible or exchangeable into securities that are the subject of the distribution.

Rule 103 of Regulation M permits Passive Market Making in all Nasdaq-listed securities throughout the restricted period. A passive market maker's bids and purchases may not exceed the highest current independent bid, which is the highest current bid from a market maker not involved in the subject distribution. In addition, a passive market maker's net purchase (total purchases minus total sales) on any day cannot exceed the greater of 30 percent of ADTV or 200 shares.

Rule 104 of Regulation M regulates stabilizing activities. There is no exemption from the provisions of Rule 104 for actively traded securities. According to Rule 104: (1) a stabilizing bid may be made in the principal market wherever located; (2) bids may be carried over to another market if the stabilizing bid has not been discontinued; and (3) bids may be raised to match higher independent bids in the market. No stabilizing bid may be initiated, maintained, or otherwise adjusted at a price higher than the stabilizing bid in the principal market or the security's actual offering price.

§ 5.05   PENALTY CLAUSE IN THE AGREEMENT AMONG UNDERWRITERS

In recognition of the importance of selling securities to bona fide investors, AAUs customarily provide that if any securities sold by an underwriter or selected dealer are purchased by the syndicate manager in stabilizing transactions in the after-market during a reasonable period of time, the underwriter must repurchase the securities at the syndicate's cost, or alternately and more customarily, the lead manager will charge the underwriter's account with an amount equal to the selling concession times the number of securities repurchased plus any purchasing cost. The theory is that under these circumstances, the penalized underwriter/distributor has not earned the selling concession on such securities because these securities were not placed in firm investor hands.

§ 5.06   OFFERING DISTRIBUTION

The AAU gives the lead manager broad authority to coordinate the selling effort by determining the underwriting commitments of each underwriter, the number of securities reserved for sale through the institutional pot, the amount of securities to be sold by selected dealers, and the amount of securities each underwriter will retain for direct sales to its customers. Over recent years, the book running manager has generally allowed underwriters initially to retain an amount equal to 10 percent of their underwriting participation in equity offerings. However, selected underwriters may often receive larger retentions because their sales force may have local interest in the security, the firm may have made a commitment to Nasdaq market marking or to research coverage of the company (if an equity), or the issuer may simply request special treatment for an underwriter. It is important to understand that there are no hard-and-fast rules with respect to retentions. Traditionally, the lead manager has enjoyed wide discretion in making allocation decisions.

In allocating stock, the lead manager may want to keep in mind the listing requirements of the exchange on, or market in, which the offering will trade. Current initial distribution requirements (in abbreviated form) are:[5]

	NYSE	*AMEX*	*Nasdaq NMS*	*Nasdaq Small Cap*
Round lot shareholders	2,000	400-800	400	300
Public float (in shares)	1,100,000	500,000-1,000,000	1,100,000	1,000,000
(in market value)	$40MM	$3MM-15MM	$8MM-20MM	$5MM

Regional exchanges have very few primary listings of common stock. Thus, their listing requirements do not appear here (*see* footnote 5).

If the lead manager wants total control of the distribution, it may elect to employ a "group sale." In such a sale, the manager makes no allocations to underwriters but instead arranges to pay each one a selling concession equal to a set percentage of its individual underwriting participation (usually 10 percent). All securities are placed in the institutional pot, resulting in a narrower, completely institutional distribution, with attendant aftermarket liquidity ramifications.

§ 5.07   DEAL ALLOCATION

Normally, the lead manager allocates a large portion (50 percent or more) of the total offering to the institutional pot, although certain

---

5. Requirements are accurate as of October 1998 but are subject to change or revision. Consult the relevant SRO's Constitution and Rules (NYSE, AMEX, and regional exchanges), Manual (NASD), or Web site for a full description of both original listing and maintenance requirements.

types of offerings with very strong individual investor affinity may have much smaller institutional pots or even no institutional pot at all. Again, the lead manager has total discretion here.

One of the major decision-making tasks facing the lead manager is the determination of why any investor, but particularly an institutional investor, is buying the security being distributed. An institution that has had a private or group meeting or participated in a conference call discussing the merits of the issuer with the lead manager's analyst may be presumed to have a longer investment time horizon and potential aftermarket interest than an institution interested only in a quick trade ("flip") that may be soft-dollar driven. Making most of these allocation decisions correctly is at the heart of deal making. There are no shortcuts to this process.

The allocation process has always been a difficult one for capital markets professionals, fraught with emotion resulting from, among other things, the deliberate creation of excess demand to help ensure a successful deal. In this regard, the SEC has a long history of examining industry allocation practices that dates to 1961. More recently, the Commission again put the underwriting community on notice that tieing new issue allocations directly to investor promises of aftermarket purchase is in direct violation of Rules 101 and 102 of Regulation M and may also violate other antifraud and antimanipulative provisions of the federal securities laws.[6]

To help ensure a complete and successful distribution of an equity issue, the lead manager may allocate the total amount of the offering plus the over-allotment or green shoe option plus additional shares (up to an amount not to exceed the percentage specified in its AAU—usually a maximum of 15 percent) prior to the opening of secondary market trading. If followed, this strategy creates a short position in the syndicate account, thereby giving the lead manager potential buying power (*i.e.,* stabilization ability) to help effect the distribution.

6. United States Securities and Exchange Commission, Division of Market Regulation: Staff Legal Bulletin No. 10 dated August 25, 2000, and entitled *Prohibited Solicitations and "Tie-in" Agreement for Aftermarket Purchases.*

§ 5.08   INSTITUTIONAL POT

The institutional pot has evolved over time as a mechanism to assist institutions whose size requirements could not be met by any one underwriter and who were often forced to call all of the underwriters in the account and process multiple trade confirmations. These multiple indication calls were cumbersome and often served to inflate the actual demand for the issue. The pot provides a mechanism whereby institutions may call the lead manager and attempt to fulfill their needs with minimal processing requirements. Additionally, this procedure gives the manager a truer picture of total institutional demand. The pot may also serve a marketing purpose in that the manager can adjust its size and allocations so that institutions do not get all their needs fulfilled, thus keeping overall interest in the deal high and hopefully generating aftermarket orders which are essential to a successful offering.

Institutions that purchase securities from the pot may attempt to designate underwriters or selling group members to receive selling concessions tied to the particular institution's purchase. Such orders are known as "designated," "directed," or "manager bill and deliver" orders. The lead manager typically receives a substantial portion of the selling concessions available in the pot primarily because the lead manager's securities analyst(s) and sales personnel usually do the heavy lifting in terms of convincing institutions to purchase the offering and because the lead manager has historically had sole discretion to allocate the pot among institutions. Additionally, the lead manager schedules the institutional one-on-one roadshow meetings that are so important to the institutional pot process.

[A]   Types of Institutional Pot—Equity Offering

[1]   Jump Ball or Competitive Pot[7]

What is it?

- It is designed to maximize the creation of pot orders by permitting/encouraging competition for sales credits among co-managers.

---

7. SIA Syndicate Committee handout, Syndicate Breakfast, SIA National convention, Boca Raton, FL, November 1996.

- Sales credits are supposed to be directed/allocated by the purchaser to the manager(s) according to the level of contribution to the consummation of an actual order.

- Jump ball portions generally vary between 60 and 70 percent of the total pot. The balance, or fixed portion, is usually split evenly among all managers, but it also may be split unevenly according to issuer wishes (*e.g.,* pro rata equal to the management fee split arrangement).

Positives:

- Creates competition among co-managers.

- Some co-managers may not sell anyway, so the lead manager deserves the majority of the pot for doing the work.

Negatives:

- Dilutes team effort.

- Co-manager salespeople may make fewer calls due to their concern about not receiving a significant amount of the pot because
  — there exists normal gravitation to the book manager, especially for larger, more active underwriters;
  — the book runner hogs orders by controlling allocations and attempting to limit designations away from its own sales force;
  — the purchaser does not want to irritate the book manager by attempting to interfere with the allocation process.

- Salespeople focus inordinate amounts of time on accounts that might favor their firm allocation wise, as opposed to a broader list of potential investors that may have a fundamental interest in owning the securities.

[2]   Capped Jump Ball
What is it?

- A recent development, believed to have been started by management of Occidental Petroleum in a large equity deal in 1988, is one where the issuer caps the lead manager's percentage of individual pot orders that the lead manager may receive, *e.g.,* 60 percent of the order, with the balance (40 percent) going to other managers (and/or underwriters/selected dealers).

- There may or may not be a limitation on the maximum percentage that an institutional account can designate away from the management group.

[3]   Open Pot

What is it?

- 100 percent of the pot is typically "jump ball," and there may be no guaranteed minimum to any individual co-manager.

Positives:

- Major incentive for institutional salespeople of co-manager(s) who recognize the potential to receive a significant piece of the order—*i.e.,* work performed will be rewarded.
- In the case of a sole-managed transaction, it could allow the book runner to provide incentives to secure research and market making from syndicate members.

Negatives:

- Designations may go to a dealer(s) as soft dollar payment for work not done on the deal itself.
- May increase infighting between book runner and co-managers.

[4]   Fixed Compensation Pot

What is it?

- Sales credit compensation is predetermined as a fixed percentage of the institutional pot.

Positives:

- May encourage team work in some instances.

- May reduce infighting between book runner and co-managers.

Negatives:

- May encourage co-managers' institutional sales forces to coast and do very little actual selling. This drawback is especially true in the case of a busy calendar environment where a firm's first priority will be to its own lead-managed business or business where focus and effort will knowingly result in incremental sales credits.

- Individual managers can do no better or worse than their fixed percentage.

[5]   Incentive or Performance Pot

What is it?

- An innovation often used in deals with numerous co-managers. The issuer controls a percentage of the sales credit attached to securities in the pot and "awards" them to co-managers on an ad hoc basis according to the issuer's perception of the performance and the contribution of each co-manager toward the distribution of the issue.

Positives:

- Encourages co-managers not to coast through a transaction when a number (three or more) of the non-book-running co-managers must split a relatively small portion of the sales credits attached to pot securities.

- Reduces the competitive advantage(s) larger firms may have in securing designations from institutional investors and puts smaller firms on a more equal footing, all other things being equal.

Negatives:

- Potentially rewards co-managers with the strongest relationships with issuer senior management, not necessarily those firms that perform well in the actual distribution.

§ 5.09   STABILIZATION

The rationale for stabilization is straightforward. New issue securities are almost always offered on a fixed price basis. If the secondary market price dips below the new issue fixed price, distribution of the new shares becomes difficult. Thus, stabilization is an SEC-sanctioned (via a series of no-action letters culminating in old Rule 10b-7, now Rule 104) form of pegging the secondary market price solely to facilitate distribution of the new issue shares. However, lead managers seldom employ stabilization in today's markets, due to the advent and now widespread use of syndicate short positions and over-allotment options.

Pre-effective, pre-pricing stabilization is also an option for the lead manager. However, this technique is tricky and likewise seldom employed because buyers may not accept a pegged or artificially derived offering price for a new issue resulting from pre-price stabilization of the existing shares rather than solely from secondary market price action resulting from the forces of supply and demand for the new issue.

The major change in stabilization activity from old Rule 10b-7 to new Rule 104 under Regulation M is the ability of the lead manager to increase a stabilizing bid to the level of the highest independent bid existent in the principal market. Rule 104 requires a new legend in the offering document, referenced to a discussion in the "plan of distribution" section of the prospectus, regarding stabilizing activities and aftermarket activities and its potential effects on the aftermarket price of the security being offered.

The Nasdaq market maker that intends to stabilize a security under Rule 104 (normally the lead manager of the offering) must submit a request to Nasdaq Market Operations for entry of a one-sided market (bid only, no offer, volume reported only on purchases) that is identified on Nasdaq with the acronym SYN, signifying a stabilizing bid. Securities purchased as a result of employing a stabilizing bid may be reoffered again at the public offering price via the same or other underwriters, at the sole discretion of the lead manager. Only one market maker can enter a stabilizing bid in an issue, and at least one other market maker must be registered in the security being stabilized and be entering quotes that are considered independent under Regulation M, Rule 104.

The stabilizing bid must be available for all freely tradable outstanding securities of the same class being offered. When initiating a pre-effective stabilizing bid, the market maker shall provide Nasdaq with formal notice including the name of the security, its Nasdaq symbol, contemplated effective date of the offering, a copy of the preliminary prospectus for the transaction, and whether the lead manager contemplates converting a pre-effective stabilizing bid into a post-effective stabilizing bid, and if so, whether the stabilizing bid will be penalty-free. This notice must be given to Nasdaq Market Operations verbally, confirmed in writing, and made in a fashion timely enough (allow $1\frac{1}{2}$ hours minimum) for Nasdaq to enter the stabilizing bid into its quote system.

Rule 104 replaces Rule 10b-7 to regulate stabilization activities during a distribution.[8] Rule 104 retains the requirement that only one stabilizing bid is permitted in any one market at the same price at the same time. The new rule permits the lead manager to institute, maintain, reduce, or raise its stabilized bid based on the current price in the principal market for the security (domestic or foreign), as long as the bid does not exceed the actual offering price of the deal. The rule stipulates that the appropriate price level for initiating a stabilizing bid is the price extant in the principal market for the securities being offered, with certain variations for different market situations.

As a reminder, any stabilization activity must cease prior to termination of price and trading restrictions.

§ 5.10   PASSIVE MARKET MAKING

New Rule 103 of Regulation M replaces old Rule 10b-6A and permits Passive Market Making activity in Nasdaq stocks in connection with distributions during the restricted period. Rule 103 generally limits a market maker's bids and purchases to the highest current independent bid (a bid from a market maker that is not participating in the distribution) and limits the amount of net purchases a passive market maker can make on any day to 30 percent of its ADTV. An initial ADTV limit of 200 shares is available for less active market makers—

---

8. Disclosure of the possibility of such activity occurring must appear on both the inside cover and the "Underwriting" section of the prospectus.

those with an ADTV between 1 and 199. Block trades or purchases and sales of a security are permitted as long as the two transactions are reported within 30 seconds of each other.

The lead manager has primary responsibility to obtain an excused withdrawal and/or the identification of quotes as those of a passive market maker (Passive Market Making quotes are identified with the letters PSMM).

Pursuant to Passive Market Making, NASD Corporate Financing Rule 2710 requires the manager of a distribution subject to SEC Rule 101 to submit a request to the NASD Corporate Financing Department for an Underwriting Activity Report (*see* Appendix 11, NASD Notice to Members 97-10, p. 802). The Underwriting Activity Report will inform the lead manager of the 30 percent ADTV of each market maker and define the restricted period as one or five days. The lead manager must provide a completed Underwriting Activity Report submitted through the CommScan (an NASD vendor/service provider) "Compliance Desk" to NASD Market Operations no later than the business day prior to the one- or five-day restricted period. This report identifies market makers who are distribution participants, indicates whether their quotes should be identified as those of passive market makers or if such participants wish an excused withdrawal from market making, and includes the time of the commencement of the restricted period. The lead manager is also required to advise each market maker participant that it has been identified to Nasdaq Market Operations as a distribution participant and that its quotations will be automatically withdrawn or identified as Passive Market Making quotations.

A passive market maker's bid may not exceed the highest independent bid for the covered security. If all of the independent bids fall below the passive market maker's bid, the passive market maker must lower its bid, subject to the following exceptions: (1) the passive market maker's original bid may be maintained at its original level until the passive market maker purchases an amount of securities that equals or exceeds the lesser of two times the minimum quotation size for the security as determined by Nasdaq rules; or (2) the passive market maker's remaining purchasing capacity (30 percent of its ADTV or 200 shares).

The prospectus must disclose the lead manager's intention to engage in Passive Market Making in a legend found on the inside cover or under the heading "Distribution" in the document itself.

§ 5.11   PRIVATE PLACEMENTS UNDER RULE 144A

One of the fastest growing segments of the capital markets is private placements conducted under Rule 144A involving primarily debt instruments sold to qualified institutional buyers (QIBs) that can certify at least $100 million in assets under management. Rule 144A exempts the issuer from registration under the 33 Act, thus permitting rapid access to the institutional market. Actual solicitation, pricing, and distribution activities occur in the same manner as in a registered underwritten public offering. The rule requires broker-dealers to keep a file of the certifications of its QIB clients eligible to purchase Rule 144A securities. Domestic institutions must update such certification every 16 months (18 months for foreign institutions).

Of note, on February 3, 1999, the SEC issued a no action letter in response to third-party service provider CommScan LLC's notice of intent to create an Internet Web site containing a QIB list that investment banks can rely upon to establish reasonable belief that a prospective purchaser is indeed a certified QIB.

The private placement market has become so large that the NASD established the PORTAL Market for foreign and domestic securities that meet the requirements of Rule 144 and comply with PORTAL rules. PORTAL provides regulatory review of such securities as well as clearance and settlement via the Depository Trust Company (DTC). Information on the PORTAL market can be found at www.nasdq-trader.com under "Trading Services" or by calling the NASD at 202-728-8479/81.

Private Investment in Public Equity (PIPES)

A PIPE is a private placement of equity securities of a publicly traded company purchased by accredited investors (usually institutions). Such investors enter into an agreement committing them to purchase a specified number of shares at a specified price with closing conditioned upon, among other things, the SEC's preparedness to declare effective a registration statement covering the resale from time to time of the shares purchased in the private placement. The private placement memorandum under which an investment bank offers these shares is usually a "wrapper" fitted around the issuer's latest public filing (Q or K). The issuer names the purchasers of the private placement as "Selling Shareholders" in the resale registration statement. The purchasers/investors must deliver to the issuer, and the issuer's transfer agent, a certificate of compliance with prospectus delivery requirements before obtaining unlegended stock certificates. Closing must take place before the SEC will declare the resale registration effective, the declaration of which usually occurs on the same day as the closing itself.

§ 5.12   RULE 144—THE SALE OF UNREGISTERED SECURITIES

Compliance with Rule 144 often falls under syndicate or capital markets purview. This rule provides investors a means for reselling restricted securities without registration. Stated simply, the rule permits officers and directors of an issuer, and persons who have acquired unregistered stock in an issue that has registered under the 34 Act, that has filed for at least 90 days and that is current in its filings, to sell unregistered shares. Such sales must take place as broker's transactions (where the broker does no more than execute the order as agent, receives no more than the usual and customary commission, and does not solicit or arrange for solicitation of customer orders to buy securities of the same class in anticipation of or in connection with the restricted transaction) or in transactions directly with a market maker. The seller must also have held such securities for a minimum of two years after paying the full purchase price. The seller may sell an amount every three months that does not exceed the greater of (1) 1 percent of the shares outstanding as shown by the most recent report or statement of the issuer or (2) the average weekly trading volume of the issuer during the four calendar weeks preceding the filing with the SEC of a notice to sell on Form 144 (three copies).

The rule requires the broker to make "reasonable inquiry" of the seller and states that such reasonable inquiry should discover

1. the length of time the securities have been held by the person for whose account they are sold. If practicable, the inquiry should include physical inspection of the securities;

2. the nature of the transaction in which the securities were acquired;

3. the amount of securities of the same class sold during the past three months by all persons whose sales are required to be taken into consideration;

4. whether such person intends to sell additional securities of the same class through any other means;

5. whether such person has solicited or made any arrangements for the solicitation of buy orders in securities of the same class in connection with the proposed sale of securities;

6. whether such person has made any payment to any other person in connection with the proposed sale of the securities; and

7. the number of shares or other units of the class outstanding or the relevant trading volume.

The executing broker can meet most of these affirmative inquiry requirements through receipt of a seller's formal representation letter. The executing broker should also obtain a completed copy of Form 144 for its own files. As an added compliance measure, many firms insist that the seller provide the three copies of Form 144 to the firm, which the firm then sends to the SEC with a return envelope for receipt purposes as evidence of proper filing. Before execution of a 144 transaction, capital markets professionals may consider taking the additional steps of providing issuer's counsel with copies of the securities to be sold, a representation letter(s), and the applicable Form 144, and requesting verbal assurance that issuer's counsel will issue a letter to the transfer agent authorizing the transfer of securities bearing a restrictive legend.

Any sale under Rule 144 that exceeds 500 shares or $10,000.00 must make use of From 144. The person filing the notice must have a bona fide intention to sell within a reasonable period of time after filing the notice.

Many of the requirements of the rule (*e.g.,* paragraphs c, e, f, and h) do not apply to restricted securities sold for the account of a person who is not an affiliate of the issuer at the time of the sale, or three months prior to the sale, and who has held his or her securities for three years or more.

For persons who acquire restricted stock in public companies as the result of a reclassification, merger consolidation, or acquisition of assets and who have held their securities at least three years, there are specific resale provisions under Rule 145.

§ 5.13 CORPORATE REPURCHASE OF EQUITY SECURITIES

Since the severe equity market correction of October 1987, many corporations have increasingly found it advantageous to repurchase their shares in the open market. This activity is regulated primarily by Rule 10b-18, which provides a safe harbor from Sections 9(a)(2) of the 34 Act or Rule 10b-5 under the 34 Act. This safe harbor is provided to facilitate corporate repurchase activities yet prevent companies from manipulating their share price through the use of such open market purchases. There are four major elements of the rule.

1. Agent limitation—The company may designate only one agent per day to repurchase its share in the open market. This limitation does not apply to unsolicited purchases by the issuer.

2. Price limitation—A company may not buy shares on an uptick in its share price, and the company may not be the party that actually moves up the price. The company may be the second purchaser after the price has been bid up by another market participant.

3. Time limitation—A company may not buy its own shares on the opening trade or during the first half hour of trading on any given day.

4. Volume limitation—On any given day, a company's purchase(s) may not exceed 25 percent of the average daily trading volume over the prior four weeks. "Block" purchases are exempted—shares purchased in blocks are not included in the 25 percent volume limitation. For purposes of this rule, a block is defined as a trade of $200,000 or more or 5,000 shares or more with an aggregate value of at least $50,000, or at least 20 round lots (generally 100 shares) whose total shares exceed 150 percent of trading volume.

Under Rule 13e-1, an issuer subject to a tender offer is restricted from continuing to repurchase additional securities until it has made the filings required in a Going Private Transaction. Of note, one of the disadvantages of a corporate buyback is that it creates "tainted" shares for "pooling of interest" purposes if a merger is undertaken within two years of the repurchase of shares.

§ 5.14   ON-LINE DUTCH AUCTIONS

On April 9, 1999, the investment bank W. R. Hambrecht & Co. completed an IPO for Ravenswood Winery using an on-line modified Dutch auction system to price the offering and allocate shares. Under this system, potential investors who maintain an account with W. R. Hambrecht, or with a broker-dealer that is a member of Hambrecht's "Open IPO Network," may submit a private bid(s) listing the number of shares they want to buy and the specific price they are willing to pay. At the expiration of the auction, the lead manager allocates shares starting with the highest bid as measured by price and continuing down until all the offered shares have been allocated. All shares are then "priced" at the lowest bid that clears the market (*i.e.,* fills the auction).

The U.S. Treasury Department adopted the Dutch auction procedure for use in public auctions of United States government obligations, first in 1992 as an experiment and then in 1998 for all its auctions. Prior to 1992, the U.S. Treasury sold its securities via English auction procedures whereby securities were awarded at varying prices, starting with the highest price submitted and moving down in price to the last lot that filled the auction.

Since completing the Ravenswood IPO, W. R. Hambrecht has done three more IPOs using its modified Dutch auction system. However, at this writing there does not appear to be widespread market acceptance of the modified Dutch auction for IPOs. Nonetheless, the Dutch auction process and the cost-cutting advantages offered by Internet connectivity may prove more advantageous in new issue fixed income transactions, especially for investment grade corporate bonds, U.S. agency securities, AAA-rated mortgage-backed securities, and U.S. Treasuries. On August 15, 2000, Bear Stearns joined with W. R. Hambrecht to place $300 million of the Dow Chemical Company five-year notes via a modified Dutch auction; Bear Stearns also placed over $600 million of seven-year notes for its parent company on August 10, 2000, using a proprietary Dutch auction Internet Syndication System (DAISS).

W. R. Hambrecht's "Open Book" modified fixed income Dutch auction permits the bidder to enter two competitive bids within a predetermined spread to a comparable U.S. Treasury issue. One of these bids, the initial bid, is displayed to the market in a demand curve showing the number of bids and aggregate dollar amount at each level.

The other bid, known as the final bid, can be in a 5 basis point range of the initial bid and is kept secret. The system also permits the bidder to enter a noncompetitive bid, or market order, similar to the procedure used for U.S. Treasury auctions. All these noncompetitive bids are included in the demand curve display. Bids can be changed during the bidding period up until a specified time. As in the equity procedure, the bonds are priced at the lowest price that clears the market.

Dutch auctions have also been used in corporate tender offers, and it is easy to envision the tender process going on-line also.

Guidelines for Initiating Stabilization[9]

Principal Market Open	Principal Market Closed	When There Is No Market	Stabilization Discontinued	Stabilization Outside U.S. During U.S. Offering
1) a) No higher than the last independent transaction in the principal market; and b) current ask is equal to or greater than the last independent transaction; or 2) if both a and b above are not satisfied, stabilization may begin in any market at a price no higher than the highest current independent bid in the principal market.	No higher than: 1) the price at which stabilization could be initiated in the principal market at the close, or if *prior to the opening* of the market where stabilizing will be initiated; 2) the most recent price at which an independent transaction has been effected in any market since close of the principal market; 3) if *after the opening of the market* where stabilization will be initiated, the last independent transaction price for the security in that market if:	No higher than the offering price or if *before offering price is determined*, stabilizing continued after determination of the offering price only at the price stabilizing could then be initiated.	May not be resumed at a price higher than the price at which stabilization could be initiated.	May be initiated if: 1) there is no stabilization in the United States; or 2) if it is made in a jurisdiction with provisions governing stabilization comparable to rule 104; and 3) no stabilizing at a price above the offering price in the United States. Bids may be expressed in a foreign market's currency and adjusted to reflect changes in exchange rates between the principal market and the foreign market.

a) the security has traded that day or prior business day;

b) the current asked price is equal to or greater than the last independent transaction; and

c) if a and b are not satisfied, only at a price no higher than the highest current independent bid in that market.

9. Managing underwriters are required by amendments to SEC Rule 17a-2 to keep records of syndicate short covering transactions, penalty bids, and all related stabilizing information for three years. The principal market is generally the market with the largest reported trading volume for the 12 months preceding the filing of the registration statement or, in the case of shelf (Rule 415) registrations, the 12 months preceding the determination of the offering price. Rule 144A securities, best-efforts offerings, and at-the-market offerings are exempt from Regulation M, and stabilization is not permitted in such distributions.

Chapter 6

SETTLEMENT AND DELIVERY

§ 6.01   PAYMENT, DELIVERY, AND AUTHORITY TO BORROW[1]

The Agreement Among Underwriters (AAU) provides that payment for underwritten securities must be made on such date as the lead manager specifies, normally the morning of the closing date. The closing is usually scheduled for the third business day after the date of the offering to conform to current practice of a three-business-day settlement period between brokers, dealers, and their investor customers for secondary market transactions. There are two exceptions to this practice. Underwriters often employ a four-business-day settlement date if: (1) the offering price is determined after 4:30 P.M. eastern time; or (2) the company and/or selling security holder(s) and the managing underwriter agree to a different settlement date for extenuating circumstances such as the undertaking of a global offering with multiple underwriting tranches.

The U.S. dollar amount that each underwriter agrees to pay the lead manager for its individual retention is usually the public offering price less the selling concession times the number of securities freely retained. The effect of this practice is that an underwriter will not receive its share of the net underwriting portion of the gross spread

---

1. Much of this chapter has been adapted from Samuel N. Allen, *A Lawyer's Guide to the Operation of Underwriting Syndicates,* 26 New England Law Review 319 (Winter 1991), with the generous permission of the publisher and the author.

until final settlement of the syndicate account, an event that must occur no later than 90 days after the closing. Failure to meet this deadline exposes the lead manager to NASD sanction.[2] The underwriting portion of the gross spread is subject to the expenses occasioned by the operation of the syndicate. Such expenses usually include underwriter counsel's fee, stabilization losses (if incurred), information meeting expenses, tombstone advertising, and so forth (*see* Chapter 4 for a more exhaustive list). The AAU also empowers the lead manager to arrange for loans to the syndicate account for the purchase, carry, sale, and distribution of the security if deemed necessary, with the interest on such a loan becoming a syndicate expense.

§ 6.02   MARKET OUTS/CALAMITY OUTS

Typically, fixed price equity offerings are priced and underwriting agreements are signed after the close of the underlying secondary market. Price and trading restrictions of the new issue are typically (but not necessarily) terminated prior to the opening the next morning. This period between pricing and termination is that of greatest risk for the underwriters, since on occasion events may occur that create adverse market conditions. The underwriting agreement should anticipate such a possibility, however remote, and contain specified provisions for dealing with any unusual or calamitous event.

The SEC indicated in a 1985 no action letter ". . . that a market-out provision of an underwriting agreement may be exercised appropriately in the context of a firm commitment underwriting only upon the occurrence of a 'material adverse event affecting the issuer that materially impairs the investment quality of the offered securities; and that, in any event, a market-out clause in a firm commitment underwriting may not permit the underwriter to abrogate its obligation to purchase the offered securities from the issuer based upon an inability

---

2. In 1985, the National Association of Securities Dealers (NASD) set forth a rule (known informally as the "Blum-Cashman Rule" after its two most ardent proponents) relating to this process, including a requirement to settle all accounts in 120 days, a procedure modeled after a similar one initially created by the Municipal Securities Rulemaking Board (MSRB Rule 39). As of this writing, the NASD rule specifies a 90-day requirement.

to market the securities.'"[3] In other words, the SEC does not view the inability of the underwriter(s) to redistribute the securities at the issue price as a factor or an appropriate reason for a syndicate or underwriter to fail to deliver the proceeds of the offering to the seller(s) at closing. An example of conditions that may warrant a market out is the so-called Castro Convertibles, a 1960s offering by American and Foreign Power, a company that did substantial business in Cuba. Cuban Premier Fidel Castro announced the imposition of a new confiscatory tax between the time of the signing of the Underwriting Agreement and the deal closing.

A calamity-out clause that looks to an outbreak of hostilities, a major devastation event, bankruptcy of a state or major city, imposition of a trading suspension in the securities being distributed, bank moratoriums, or other calamitous events for its trigger should be carefully specified in the underwriting agreement.[4]

An NASD member firm that fails to complete an offering may be found in violation of its obligation to comply with just and equitable principles of trade under NASD Rule 2110.[5] In November 1996, the NASD issued a *Reminder to Members* focused on the importance of fulfilling the firm commitment underwriting obligation after execution of the UA. During the months preceding this *Reminder*, six firm commitment underwritings failed to close for reasons not contemplated by the terms and language of the related underwriting agreement. Prior to issuance of the *Reminder*, the Corporate Finance Committee of the NASD examined 31 public offerings between 1983 and November 1996 where NASD members terminated firm commitment underwritings. A number of these terminations resulted from bona fide actions taken to protect the investing public where material adverse events had occurred or defects in the offering document were discovered that called into question the integrity of the disclosures and thus the distribution itself. Adverse market conditions were often cited by underwriters in the terminations examined, but such conditions mostly

---

3. NASD Corporate Finance *Reminder to Members*, November 1996, citing an SEC Division of Market Regulation letter to William J. Williams, Jr., Esq., partner of Sullivan & Cromwell—counsel to First Boston Corporation—August 2, 1985.

4. Johnson, *Corporate Finance*, First Edition, pp. 89–90.

5. *NASD Manual* (CCH) p. 4111 (1998).

surrounded the newly issued security itself, which had fallen below the public offering price, rather than overall market conditions that adversely impacted all trading securities.

§ 6.03   TERMINATION

Limitations in the AAU on the price at which securities may be sold; the length of time the penalty clause will remain in operation; and authorization to stabilize, over-allot, and invoke price and trading restrictions all terminate automatically by the terms of the AAU at a specified time (usually 30 to 45 days) after the commencement of the offering. The lead manager may terminate any or all of these provisions sooner than specified in the AAU or at any time upon formal notice to the underwriters. In current practice, price and trading restrictions are most often terminated prior to opening the issue for trading. The AAU should specify an automatic termination date to avoid a charge that the price maintenance provision of the AAU constitutes a violation of the Sherman Act.[6]

§ 6.04   DEFAULT

Underwriting commitments are several and not joint. If, at closing, one or more underwriters fail to purchase the securities which it/they are obligated to purchase, the lead manager has the right within 24 hours to make arrangements for one or more of the nondefaulting underwriters to purchase all, but not less than all, of the defaulted securities. If such arrangements have not been completed within that time period or if the amount of defaulted securities does not exceed 10 percent of the total, the nondefaulting underwriters shall be obligated to purchase the full amount pro rata to their individual underwriting commitments.

Such a default is a very rare occurrence. For example, in May 1973, Weis Voisin Securities found itself in liquidation under the Securities Investor Protection Act between the signing of the underwriting agreement and the closing of a public offering of 6.5 million shares of Consolidated Edison Company. Weis Voisin failed to make payment for its securities, and the nondefaulting underwriters purchased pro

---

6. Johnson, *id.* pp. 70–71.

rata the shares that Weis Voisin had contracted to purchase. Today most underwriting agreements permit substitution of underwriters and not merely an across-the-board step-up as occurred in the Weis Voisin/ Consolidated Edison situation.[7]

§ 6.05   SETTLEMENT WITH THE ISSUER

As of this writing, rules provide for T+3 settlement with an after-hours settlement option of T+4. Most firms use the SEC effective date as the deal trade date. Since most deals are priced after hours, a T+4 settlement is most common. Some firms, however, use the next day as trade date and settle on T+3. Thus, settlement occurs on the same day using either method. Prior to settlement date, attorneys for both the issuer and the underwriters review the documents that each party to the transaction has agreed to provide—e.g., certificate of incorporation, accountant's comfort letters, certificate of good standing, lock-up agreements—update or bring current due diligence items, and schedule a preclosing meeting to resolve any outstanding issue so that there are no hitches at actual settlement.

Once both sets of attorneys representing issuer/seller and underwriters are satisfied that the underwriting is properly documented, they will call the lead manager, the transfer agent, and DTC closing. When all parties are on line, DTC closing will ask the transfer agent the amount of securities being released to DTC and ask the managing underwriter the amount of securities being received into the underwriting account versus how much money is due the issuer/seller.

DTC settles transactions in federal funds. Most larger transfer agents access DTC through its proprietary FAST system and deliver securities electronically. Some smaller transfer agents still deliver physical certificates for each underwriter; if so, these certificates are then sent to DTC prior to settlement for immobilization. Once the lead manager releases securities to DTC, they are placed as per instructions from the lead manager into the accounts of the underwriters who are charged the appropriate funds. These funds are then credited to the lead manager's account for further credit to the issuer(s)/seller(s). These funds are then available for wire through the Federal Reserve System to the issuer's/seller'(s') bank(s).

---

7. *Id.* pp. 90–92.

In an equity offering, the lead manager has the option to make arrangements with DTC, prior to settlement, for DTC to track the distribution of shares electronically to allow identification of the original distributing firm with regard to any shares repurchased by the lead manager in the after-market. Accordingly, distributing firms may be subject to reversal of sales credits attached to any of their free retention shares so repurchased (regardless of price and of whether or not such shares were directly purchased by the lead manager) during stabilization/short covering activities. In addition, participants should be aware that any shares delivered out by one firm may be used by an agent/custodian to satisfy the settlement of another unrelated sales transaction by a third party or other firm. If a new issue settles via physical delivery instead of through the facilities of DTC, certificates will be registered in each underwriter's name. The lead manager always retains the right to monitor and trace the sale of these securities, and to assess a penalty on the original distributor related to any subsequent repurchase under the same circumstances outlined above.

Through this tracking, the lead manager can identify firms on which to assess a penalty (the cancellation of selling concessions attached to shares repurchased) to combat the so-called flipping process.[8] Once a penalty bid has been lifted, the lead manager should advise each underwriter of the number of shares bought back that were originally retained by that underwriter. Currently, there is near-uniform industry-wide agreement that the lead manager must also penalize itself and assess and allocate penalties for all institutional pot shares so repurchased. Any selling concessions so recovered through a penalty bid should be credited to the underwriting account under a heading such as "Penalty Recovery." If done in this manner, these recoveries are allocated to underwriters in proportion to their underwriting participation/commitment just as are expenses and losses on over-sale.

The SEC has mandated full implementation of T+1 settlement for all secondary market transactions by 2002. Among the many issues for underwriters to resolve in a T+1 environment are:

a. What constitutes satisfactory prospectus delivery?

---

8. The AAU grants the lead manager such authority, the disclosure of which appears in the "Underwriting" section of a prospectus.

    b. When can a firm require an individual investor to deposit a credit balance in his or her account to cover purchase of a new issue?

    c. How can an underwriter deal with an institutional account settling through DTC that fails to affirm an allocation, is tardy transmitting account breakdowns for its allocation, or is tardy in transmitting information to prime broker accounts?

Fails resulting from events described in (b) or (c) above will inevitably result in increased interest expense to underwriters. In addition, there are a number of additional unresolved issues regarding international purchases where time differences do not permit settlement through existing clearance systems and different settlement cycles prevailing in certain offshore jurisdictions do not jibe with a T+1 settlement environment.

§ 6.06   SETTLEMENT WITH UNDERWRITERS

Although underwriters are obligated to pay for securities at the closing, they may have open short positions, or the lead manager may own securities purchased long in stabilizing transactions. Additionally, the lead manager may have incurred interest costs to cover the financing of any open short position as well as paying for securities billed and delivered for various underwriters via the institutional pot. Rule 11880 of the Uniform Practice Code of the NASD, page 7987 (July 1997), requires the managing underwriter to settle all syndicate accounts within 90 days of the syndicate settlement date with the issuer/seller(s). The lead manager must provide each syndicate member with an itemized statement of syndicate expenses, including legal fees, tombstone and other advertising costs, due diligence and roadshow travel and entertainment, loss on over-sale, telephone, day or overnight loan interest, postage, computer, third-party service provider fees, and other miscellaneous expenses as well as any penalty recoveries. As mentioned earlier, failure to comply with this requirement subjects the firm to the possibility of formal NASD sanction.

To satisfy this requirement, most firms send a statement that credits each underwriter with its portion of the management fee (managers only); its underwriting fee based on final underwriting participation multiplied by the underwriting portion of the gross spread less the underwriter's percentage of underwriting expenses and any loss on over-sale. Payment of sales credits both for directed orders and for shares from the underwriter's retention billed and delivered by the manager and/or group sale credits are also included. If the sum of all these debits and credits is positive, the lead manager includes a check for the balance. If expenses exceed the underwriter's credit, the lead manager may include a bill for the balance due.

The SIA Syndicate Committee has addressed the question of what constitutes legitimate deal expenses on more than one occasion. For example, can the lead manager reasonably charge the expenses related to an investment banking visit made two years ago to the underwriting account? Should a banker calling on several prospective issuers in the same city as the issuer of the deal charge all his expenses to the offering in question? Should sales travel be charged to the underwriting account?

In most cases, the answers to these questions are no, but firms may argue that special circumstances create an exception. Many lead managers are reluctant to send bills to an underwriting account and will vigorously examine their own costs and those of their co-managers before sending one, or will even absorb the excess themselves or just among co-managers. Such practices vary considerably among firms depending on their own individual style and approach to the business of underwriting securities. It is important to note that the underwriting community has traditionally placed great faith in the lead manager to conduct itself and manage the affairs of the underwriting account in a way consistent with just and equitable principles of fair trade.

Since current industry practice provides notification of group sale sales credits via designated orders, the retention wire should include language to that effect—e.g., "All underwriters whose retention after designations is less than 10 percent [an often-used percentage for this technique] will receive a group sale check at final settlement for the difference between that amount and 10 percent." The lead manager may handle special arrangements for research coverage or other distribution-related services provided by a firm(s) either through a debit to "underwriting expenses" of the related sales credits or through the inclusion of such firm(s) in a group sale. When the lead manager elects to "charge" related sales credits as an underwriting expense, the underwriting component of the gross spread often increases proportionally, with the result that the sales credit must decrease, since the management fee component has steadfastly remained at 20 percent of the total gross spread.

In the case of a global offering with more than one tranche, each tranche usually has its own accounting statement, prepared on a basis consistent with all other tranches.

Chapter 7

COMPLIANCE

§ 7.01   FREE RIDING AND WITHHOLDING

On November 7, 1970, the Board of Governors of the NASD adopted an Interpretation to its Standards of Commercial Honor and Principles of Trade, known as the Free Riding and Withholding Interpretation (Interpretation).[1] This Interpretation was designed to protect the integrity of the public offering system by ensuring that all NASD members make a bona fide distribution of a Hot Issue security and not retain any of the securities for the members' own benefit or use the allocation of securities to induce reciprocal business or reward persons for the direction of future business, whatever the form that direction may take.

The Interpretation defines a "Hot Issue" as any distribution of a security that commences trading in the immediate aftermarket at a premium to the offer price, whenever such secondary market activity begins. The NASD has consistently taken the position that any premium, no matter how small, that is sustained in immediate secondary market trading satisfies the definition and triggers the application of the Interpretation. This definition places the normal desire of a lead manager to see a new issue trade to a slight premium into conflict with its natural desire to avoid triggering a request from the NASD to submit a free-riding questionnaire. Conversely, if a premium in immediate aftermarket trading is not sustained, the distribution does not meet the criteria of a Hot Issue and is generally referred to as a "Cold Issue."

---

1. *See* NASD Manual (1998)—NASD Conduct Rule IM-2110.

The following parties are prohibited from buying Hot Issues:

- NASD members who may hold the securities in any firm account;

- NASD firm employees (employees of limited business firms, *e.g.,* investment companies, direct participation, and variable product securities distributors are exempt);

- an account in which any of the above or a close relative (*i.e.,* parent, mother- or father-in-law, husband or wife, brother or sister, brother- or sister-in-law, son- or daughter-in-law, or child) has a beneficial interest. However, this restriction does not apply if the immediate family member does not receive support, directly or indirectly, to a material extent from the associated person and the sale occurs away from the family member.

The following parties are conditionally restricted from buying Hot Issues:

- Senior officers of commercial banks, savings and loans, insurance companies, registered investment advisers, institutional account(s), or persons in any securities department or trading position for an account or a finder in respect to the offering or fiduciary (lawyer/accountant).

If Hot Issue securities are sold to an investment partnership or an investment corporation (domestic or foreign) including, but not limited to, hedge funds and investment clubs, the distributing firm must have on file a current list (not more than 18 months old) of the participants (partners or shareholders) and their business affiliations, and none of these participants should be a restricted person under the definitions provided above. Alternatively, a current (not more than 18 months old) opinion of legal counsel or a certified public accountant, in a form specified by the NASD, must be on file.[2] Carve-out provisions are permitted if restricted persons have a beneficial interest in the account.

---

2. *See* Appendix 11, NASD Notice to Members, 95-7, Investment Partnerships and Corporations, pp. 733–734.

For sales to an undisclosed principal of a domestic bank/trust company, broker-dealer, or other conduit, the distributing firm must obtain certain assurances from the account that the account is familiar with the Free Riding and Withholding rule and that no restricted persons are beneficiaries of the account purchasing the Hot Issue. The name and title of the person giving the assurance must appear on the order ticket along with the nature of the assurances given.

For sales to similar foreign accounts, the distributing firm should have on file an NASD Form FR-1, or alternatively, the name and title of the person giving assurances must appear on the order ticket.

Special provisions exist for purchases by restricted persons, for issuer-directed securities, and for venture capital investors who wish to maintain their percentage ownership (if locked up for 90 days). Stand-by underwriting arrangements (if disclosed) are also subject to a 90-day lockup.

In January 2000, the SEC published for comment a proposal by NASDR to establish Rule 2790, Trading in Hot Equity Offerings, to replace the Free Riding and Withholding Interpretation, IM-2110-1, in an effort to focus and streamline this Interpretation. Among the many changes in the proposed new rule are (1) the creation of a formula to determine whether a new issue is a "hot issue," (2) the exclusion of fixed income securities, (3) the elimination of the category of conditionally restricted persons, (4) the insertion of a requirement that affiliates of broker-dealers would become "restricted persons," thus clearly articulating that term, and (5) the obligation of distributing dealers to obtain "documenting evidence" in the form of a written current certification from all public customers regarding their restricted person status. After the lapse of the comment period, it seems to have become clear that few, if any, of the proposed provisions minimize the complexity of the Interpretation, and thus most observers anticipate additional modifications in the form of yet another new rule proposal. It is quite possible that the next iteration forthcoming will make all IPOs subject to the rule and exclude all follow-on equity offerings, convertible offerings, preferred offerings, and straight debt issues.

(Readers should see Appendix 11, NASD Notice to Members 95-7, 95-27, 97-91, and 98-48 for an in-depth understanding of the evolution of Free Riding regulation.)

§ 7.02   FIRM COMPLIANCE—COMPLIANCE DESK AND THE SAFE HARBOR CANCELLATION RULE

The multitude of restricted persons, accounts, and entities enumerated in the Interpretation and the uncertainty surrounding allocation to such parties when it is not clear whether an offering will trade to a premium prompted the industry to demand a process that would give members certainty regarding when the NASD deems a distribution to be a Hot Issue. The industry also urged amendment of the Interpretation to contain relief from inadvertent sales that violated the Interpretation's provisions.

On December 7, 1994, the NASD adopted new provisions to the Interpretation, the most significant of which is called the "safe-harbor cancellation" provision. Under its terms, a member may break a sale in a Hot Issue made to a restricted account and reallocate the trade to a nonrestricted party, so long as this action occurs by the close of business on T+1. The NASD made formal announcement of this adoption in Notice to Members 95-7, February 1995.[3]

The initiation of the safe-harbor also intensified pressure on the NASD to publish prompt notice of offerings it deemed to be Hot Issues. Prior to 1994, lead managers did not receive notice until approximately 30 days after the offering, and syndicate and selling group members did not receive notice for as long as 120 days. Therefore, the NASD, in a cooperative effort with CommScan LLC, initiated a regulatory service called Compliance Desk in 1996. Compliance Desk allows the lead manager, co-managers, all underwriters, and selected dealers to receive prompt notice of each IPO that the NASD has declared a Hot Issue on trade date. Such timely notice facilitates the use of the safe-harbor cancellation provision and aids completion of free-riding questionnaires.

Compliance Desk has several preformatted wires that it electronically transmits between firms and the Corporate Financing Depart-

---

3. The NASD and SEC cautioned broker-dealers that breaking and reallocating too many trades could result in violations of Rule 101 of Regulation M because the offering might be deemed to be continuing. Thus, firms may elect to use the safe-harbor in a sparing fashion. *See* Appendix 11, NASD Notice to Members 95-7 Cancellation Provision, p. 724.

ment of NASD Regulation, Inc., the two most important of which are known as the "Hot Issue wire" and the "Free-Riding Request wire." The Hot Issue wire informs all firms that Corporate Financing has deemed the distribution to be subject to the provisions of the Interpretation. The Free-Riding Request wire should trigger a review by each participant firm's Compliance Department that concludes with electronic submission of a free-riding questionnaire transmitted to Corporate Financing within 45 days. The NASD also sends a Cold Issue wire that provides comfort to participating firms that a decision has been made by the Corporate Financing Department regarding the free-riding status of each and every IPO. (Editors' note—Publication and eventual ratification of a new "Trading in Hot Equity Offerings" proposal [as discussed above] may eliminate the need for the safe harbor cancellation rule.)

§ 7.03   QUALIFIED INDEPENDENT UNDERWRITER

An investor protection provision exists under schedule E of the NASD bylaws and is triggered when an underwriter owns more than 10 percent of the stock of an issue it is underwriting, or the issuer owns more than 10 percent of the stock of an underwriter of its issue. The provision creates certain safeguards to assure an arm's-length transaction. Usually, the securities firm affiliated with the issuer retains a qualified independent underwriter (QIU) to conduct independent due diligence and act as an independent pricer of the securities to be sold in the underwriting.

§ 7.04   CONFLICTS RULE

When a member proposes to participate in the distribution of a public offering of its own or an affiliate's securities, or of securities of a company with which it otherwise has a conflict of interest, NASD Rule 2720 requires that the price at which an equity issue or the yield at which a debt issue is to be distributed to the public must be established at a price no higher or a yield no lower than that recommended by a member acting as a QIU. The QIU must also participate in the preparation of the offering document and exercise the usual standards of due diligence in respect thereto. The participation of a QIU offers the public assurance of the independence of both the pricing and the due diligence functions in a situation containing a potential conflict of interest.

Because of the important investor protections provided by QIUs, they must meet certain standards as prescribed in Rule 2720 of the Conduct Rules. QIUs must possess a certain level of experience as demonstrated by having been engaged in the investment banking and securities business for at least five years; by a majority of its directors (or general partners) having been actively engaged in the investment banking and securities business for at least five years; and by acting as manager or co-manager in an underwriting of a similar size and type within a five-year period prior to the offering in question. Further, QIUs may not be affiliates or own more than 5 percent of certain securities of the issuing company; are subject to provisions ensuring that associated persons of the firm have not been convicted, suspended, barred, or otherwise disciplined for actions related to an offering; and must agree to accept the legal responsibilities and liabilities of an underwriter under Section 11 of the 33 Act.

Rule 2720 places additional requirements on sales forces designed to protect investors from conflicts by generally prohibiting sales to an investor account(s) over which any underwriter or selling group member has discretionary authority. It also imposes on any underwriter that is in conflict with the issuer an affirmative obligation to determine that an investment in the underwritten security is suitable for any/all investor customers of that underwriter and to record and retain that determination in its file for that transaction.

§ 7.05   REGULATION OF THE ALLOCATION PROCESS

Financial media exposure of IPO Spinning, and other highly visible allocation practices that may appear to favor certain classes of investors, has raised the issue of whether additional regulation of the syndicate allocation process is needed or appropriate. IPO Spinning was brought to the attention of the investing public through a series of press articles in 1997 and 1998, which alleged that IPO shares were withheld from public offerings and subsequently allocated to personal brokerage accounts of venture capitalists and corporate executives of potential investment banking clients of the lead manager. Authors of such articles further alleged that underwriting firms then sold or "spun" out these allocations, thereby capturing a quick profit for the beneficial owners in an effort to lure his or her investment banking business.

Earlier in the 1990s, similar press articles alleged that federal and state government elected officials were being allocated Hot Issue IPOs. Both of these situations highlight the tension that exists between the lead manager's desire to allocate new issues efficiently and its ability to compete effectively for new issue mandates. All the while, many members of the financial media continue to advocate that new issue securities should be more readily available and more broadly distributed to the general public.

Historically, instances like those cited above always cause regulatory authorities to consider whether to implement additional restrictions on syndicate allocation practices or make changes to the NASD's Free-Riding and Withholding Interpretation. Elimination of the perception of abuse and maintenance of the public's confidence in its ability to access the new issue market are objectives of paramount importance to both regulators and industry participants. Public policy has traditionally tilted strongly toward investors taking the risks and enjoying the rewards of the new issue market.

Chapter 8

SELF-REGULATION CONCEPT — MAJOR DOMESTIC AND SELECTED INTERNATIONAL SECURITIES MARKETS AND OTHER ENTITIES INTERFACING WITH THE SECURITIES INDUSTRY

The Securities Exchange Act of 1934 (34 Act) provides for the registration and oversight of self-regulatory organizations (SROs). In June 1938, Congress adopted the Maloney Act, which amended the 34 Act to provide the framework necessary to implement self-regulation.[1] The Maloney Act, introduced and named after Senator Francis T. Maloney of Connecticut, provided for the creation and registration with the SEC of national securities associations to regulate brokers and dealers doing business in the over-the-counter (OTC) markets. The only such association in existence is the National Association of Securities Dealers (NASD), which, as part of its role, requires membership by all broker-dealers engaged in interstate commerce. The NASD is responsible for preventing fraudulent and manipulative acts and practices and for promoting just and equitable trade principles among OTC brokers and dealers. The establishment, maintenance, and enforcement of a code of business ethics by the NASD are among the principal features of this provision of the law.

---

1. 52 Stat. 1070, P.L. 74-261 (1936) (codified as amended at 15 U.S.C. 78a (1998)).

§ 8.01   INDUSTRY-WIDE CONTINUING EDUCATION

In recognition of the importance of satisfied and confident investors, the securities industry supported a Securities Industry Institute Task Force recommendation regarding the value of continuing education standards for industry professionals and brokers and is working with SROs to implement ongoing professional training. Also, at the request of the industry and in a desire to keep the few bad apples (or so-called rogue brokers) out of the industry, the NASD is considering amending its broker-dealer Form U-5, which provides detailed explanations about circumstances surrounding a broker termination, to enlarge such detail and to gain immunity from defamation and libel lawsuits filed by terminated brokers based on incomplete or cursory information contained in a Form U-5. In late 1998, the NASD announced its intention to create a formal, professional training program for the securities industry—the NASD Institute for Professional Development. In the summer of 1999, the Securities Industry Association (SIA) introduced another in its series of initiatives designed to enhance the public's trust and confidence in the securities industry—the Capital Markets Program. The first course will be held in January 2001 in a conference center site, allowing for an intensive three-day, two-evening curriculum taught by experienced industry professionals and focused on capital markets personnel with two to three years of experience.

§ 8.02   INSIDER TRADING

In the 1980s, the temporary collapse of certain markets (such as the one for high-yield bonds), episodes of sharp price gyration in secondary markets, and several highly publicized cases of insider trading resulted in congressional passage of legislation to attempt to address actual and perceived abusive practices and market volatility. In 1988, Congress enacted the Insider Trading and Securities Fraud Enforcement Act (ITSFEA).[2] ITSFEA increased civil and criminal penalties for persons convicted of illegally trading securities while in possession

---

2. 102 Stat. 4677 (1988) (codified as amended at 15 U.S.C. 78u-1 (1998)).

of material, nonpublic information. It also supplemented SEC resources and placed additional obligations on broker-dealers, investment advisers, publicly held companies, law firms, and other controlling persons and employers to take steps to prevent insider trading. Broker-dealers and investment advisers are now required to "establish, adopt, maintain and enforce" written policies and procedures relating to the misuse of material, nonpublic information.

§ 8.03   REGISTRATION OF EXCHANGES, NATIONAL SECURITIES ASSOCIATIONS, AND OTHER ENTITIES

As amended, the 34 Act requires registration with the SEC of:

- national securities exchanges (unless the SEC grants a limited securities trading volume exemption);
- brokers and dealers who conduct securities business in interstate commerce;
- transfer agents;
- clearing agencies;
- government and municipal brokers and dealers; and
- securities information processors.

To obtain registration, exchanges must show that they are organized to comply with the provisions of the statute as well as the rules and regulations of the Commission. The registering exchanges must also show that their rules contain just and adequate provisions to ensure fair dealing and investor protection.

Each exchange or national securities association is an SRO. Its rules must provide for the expulsion, suspension, or other disciplinary action of member broker-dealers for conduct inconsistent with just and equitable principles of trade. The law intends that SROs shall have full opportunity to establish self-regulatory measures ensuring fair dealing and investor protection. The SEC must approve all proposed SRO rule changes to ensure that they are consistent with these and the other standards under the 34 Act. In addition, the SEC has the authority, by rule, to amend the rules of SROs, if necessary, to effectuate the purposes of the 34 Act. However, in practice, most rule changes are proposed by the SROs and generally reach their final form after discussion between representatives of both bodies and with an opportunity period for the public to submit comments.

[A] Broker-Dealer Registration

The registration of brokers and dealers engaged in soliciting and executing securities transactions is an important part of the regulatory plan of the 34 Act. Broker-dealers must apply for registration with the SEC and amend their registrations to show significant changes in financial conditions or other important facts. Applications and amendments are examined by the Commission. Brokers and dealers must conform their business practices to: the standards prescribed by the law; the SEC's regulations for protecting investors; and the rules of fair trade practices of the NASD. Additionally, brokers and dealers violating these regulations risk suspension or loss of registration with the Commission (and thus the right to continue conducting an interstate securities business) or of suspension or expulsion from an SRO.

At the second level of regulation, SROs (including the exchanges and the NASD) must verify that securities firms have systems and procedures in place to manage themselves properly. SROs require broker-dealers to create compliance systems by which organizations and individuals engaging in the buying and selling of securities can police their own activities. In addition, the SROs may discipline their members for violations of securities laws and their own regulations. In most cases, SROs take the first steps in detecting violations of securities laws, and even in major civil and criminal proceedings against industry personnel, SROs often handle the initial stages. SROs, including all of the registered exchanges, the NASD and the Municipal Securities Rulemaking Board (MSRB), operate in conjunction with the SEC, the Commodity Futures Trading Commission (CFTC), the Federal Reserve Board (Fed), the Office of the Comptroller of Currency (OCC), and the United States Treasury Department.

Exchanges have responsibilities concerning all matters and activities that involve securities listed on their respective trading floors. Apart from SEC rules and regulations, each exchange is free to establish separate requirements for listing of issuers' securities.

The exchanges establish rules for their members, and the NASD establishes and enforces rules concerning all OTC transactions.[3] The best-known and largest OTC market for stocks is the National Association of Securities Dealers Automated Quotation (Nasdaq) market, owned and operated by the NASD. It is a negotiated market in which buyers and sellers work out prices acceptable to both. Since many securities firms are members of one or more exchanges and engage in OTC transactions, these firms are thereby subject to overlapping jurisdiction of all relevant SROs. A third level of regulation occurs at the SEC, which is charged with preserving the integrity, efficiency, and fairness of the securities markets by administering and enforcing the federal securities laws.

Each of the SROs is required to register with the SEC under the 34 Act, and as part of that process, the SEC ensures that the rules of the SROs "are designed to prevent fraudulent and manipulative acts and practices [and] to promote just and equitable principles of trade." Due to its role in overseeing the SEC, Congress represents the final regulatory tier. In that vein, Congress must ensure that the SEC fulfills its own responsibilities as specified in the 34 Act.

The considerable degree of self-regulation within the securities industry and an equally strong commitment to cooperation between the members of the industry and the regulatory bodies that oversee the industry have helped create capital markets that have drawn investors and issuers from all over the world. Every day billions of dollars of transactions clear and settle in our fixed income and equity markets based on a handshake, a nod, a hand signal, or a phone call. This extraordinary reliance on word of mouth would not be possible without the public's confidence in the U.S. capital markets and securities industry. Confidence depends on the belief that our markets operate fairly and with complete transparency, so that every participant has access to the same information and plays by the same rules.

The NASD, through its two subsidiaries, NASD Regulation, Inc. and the Nasdaq Stock Market, Inc., provides regulatory and marketplace services and conducts disciplinary proceedings of members

---

3. Most of the material in this and the following four paragraphs has been adapted from the *NASD Manual* (CCH), pp. 151–160 (1998) with the generous permission of the NASD.

who do not comply with SEC or NASD rules and regulations. As of 1998, the NASD oversees some 5,400 securities firms that operate more than 58,000 branch offices and employ over 505,000 registered representatives.

NASD Regulation, Inc. is governed by a board of directors that has established nine standing committees to advise it in all deliberations pertaining to regulatory policy and rule making. One committee, Corporate Financing, is specifically charged with responsibility to advise the board on matters pertaining to underwriting of new issues, appropriate levels of acceptable underwriting compensation, regulation of conflicts and control issues arising when members own 10 percent or more of an issuing company's class of securities, sales practices directly related to new issue distributions (such as Free-Riding and Withholding), and designation and allocation of soft dollars.

The staff of NASD Regulation, Inc.'s Corporate Financing Department reviews registration statements for underwriter compliance with NASD Conduct Rules that regulate underwriting compensation (Conduct Rule 2710, the Corporate Financing Rule), Conflicts and Controlled Underwritings (Rule 2720), and Free-Riding and Withholding (IM-2110).

The United States is the only major country in the world to have more than one significant and successful secondary equity trading market for investors. This happenstance occurred through the confluence of two factors: (1) the Securities and Exchange Commission has consistently interpreted its mandate under the federal securities acts to encourage competitive markets as the best way to offer investors constant innovation and efficiency at the lowest possible cost; and (2) the automation and evolution of the old OTC market into the Nasdaq Stock Market. Thus, the United States hosts the world's largest auction market (the New York Stock Exchange) and the world's largest dealer market (the Nasdaq Stock Market).

As of 2000, distinctions between national stock exchanges and the Nasdaq Stock Market are becoming less marked. Actions by the SEC to increase the efficiency of investor customer pricing in secondary trading markets through adoption of its order-handling rules and the introduction of decimal trading so far seem to favor agency orders over principal or dealer activities. Graphic evidence supporting this observation is the 1998 NASD acquisition of the American Stock Exchange—

the creation of a "market of markets." A number of regional exchanges have announced or engaged in preliminary merger or joint venture discussions as well—*e.g.,* the Chicago Board Options Exchange, the Pacific Exchange, and the Philadelphia Stock Exchange—all in an effort to deal with increasing capital investment requirements necessary to stay current technologically, to help participants cope with ever-narrowing dealer/specialist spreads and with trading the same stocks and options in multiple locations, and to meet the competitive challenges posed by the proliferation of electronic communication networks (ECNs) in the late 1990s. Indeed, both the speed with which overseas securities exchanges have combined in the last five years and the rapidity with which customers have migrated to totally electronic exchanges challenge the very notion of a physical trading floor, with its reliance on an open outcry system that traces its roots to the Middle Ages.

What follows is a very brief synopsis of domestic stock and options markets, along with contact information for these markets and other selected entities.

[B]   American Stock Exchange

The American Stock Exchange (AMEX), also known as the "Curb," traces its origins to 1793 and is the nation's second-largest national auction market. In the 1980s and 1990s, the Curb became known for its aggressive, innovative, and sophisticated origination, listing, and trading of equity derivative issues. On October 30, 1998, the AMEX became a wholly owned subsidiary of the National Association of Securities Dealers. The AMEX is located at 86 Trinity Place, New York, NY 10006-1881. Telephone: 212-306-1000/8376 fax. Web site address: www.amex.com.

[C]   Arizona Stock Exchange

The Arizona Stock Exchange (AZX) was formed in 1990 to operate an electronic, single-price, auction trading system. AZX uses state-of-the-art telecommunications and computers located in Phoenix, Arizona, to execute trades at the same time in a single-price call auction. Participants can utilize AZX's "Open Book" to place limit-or-better orders and the "Reserve Book" for orders with limits in size or price. Web site address: www.azx.com.

[D]   Boston Stock Exchange

The Boston Stock Exchange (BSE) was founded in 1834 and currently is the only U.S. exchange permitting more than one specialist to compete in the same stock. The BSE is located at 100 Franklin Street, Boston, MA 02110. Telephone: 617-235-2000/2200 fax. Web site address: www.bostonstock.com.

[E]   Chicago Board Options Exchange

The Chicago Board Options Exchange (CBOE) was founded in 1973 to create liquidity in the then over-the-counter dealer market for equity puts and calls and is now the world leader in option volume. The CBOE is located at 400 South LaSalle Street, Chicago, IL 60605-1023. Telephone: 312-786-5600/7409 fax. Web site address: www. cboe.com.

[F]   Chicago Stock Exchange

Founded in 1882 and formerly known as the Midwest Stock Exchange (MSE, or the "Middie"), it enjoys the reputation of being the only fully automated market in the world as computers match and execute all transactions processed. The Middie is located at One Financial Plaza South, 440 LaSalle Street, Suite 3200, Chicago, IL 60605-1070. Telephone: 312-663-2222/2819 fax. Web site address: www.chicagostockex.com.

[G]   Cincinnati Stock Exchange

Established in 1885, the Cincinnati Stock Exchange ("Cincy") is the first U.S. exchange to abandon totally its physical trading floor. It is a computer system affiliated with the CBOE, with its hardware in Chicago and its trades taking place in cyberspace. The Cincinnati Stock Exchange is located at 440 South LaSalle Street, Suite 2600, Chicago, IL 60605. Telephone: 312-786-8803/939-7239 fax. Web site address: www.cincinnati.com.

[H]   International Securities Exchange

Conceived in 1998 and opened for trading on May 26, 2000, the International Securities Exchange (ISE) is the first de novo, full-fledged exchange formed in the United States since the creation of the

CBOE in 1973. The ISE is owned by a consortium of securities firms and initially plans to operate a totally electronic trading platform for options contracts. The ISE is located at 60 Broad Street, New York, NY 10004. Telephone: 212-943-2400/635-0210 fax. Web site address: www.iseoptions.com.

[I]   Nasdaq Stock Market

Nasdaq is the largest electronic, screen-based market in the world. It differs from national securities exchanges in that its members act as independent dealers, compete for order flow, and commit capital in the stocks in which they make markets. Beginning as a quotation-only service in 1971, Nasdaq has evolved into an almost totally electronic environment. As of 2000, over 5,000 companies were listed in two tiers: the National Market System and the Small Cap Market. It also maintains the PORTAL System to facilitate secondary market trading in Rule 144A securities. Nasdaq is located at 1735 K Street NW, Washington, DC 20006. Telephone: 202-728-8840/496-2699 fax. Web site address: www.nasdaq.com.

[J]   New York Stock Exchange

The New York Stock Exchange (NYSE) is the largest auction trading market in the world. Tracing its history to 1792, the "Big Board" currently lists over 2,500 companies, many of which are among the oldest, most venerable companies in the world. The NYSE is located at 11 Wall Street, New York, NY 10005. Telephone: 212-656-3000/2126 fax. Web site address: www.nyse.com.

[K]   Pacific Exchange

The Pacific (PCX, or the "PCoast") is the only domestic market with trading floors in two cities—San Francisco and Los Angeles. Its strength is execution of retail order flow and trading of technology-related issues on its options floor. In the spring of 2000, the PCX announced the creation of a partnership with Archipelago, a Chicago ECN. As of this writing, the combination was still awaiting SEC approval. The PCoast is headquartered at 301 Pine Street, San Francisco, CA 94104. Telephone: 415-393-4000/4018 fax. Web site address: www.pacificex.com.

[L]   Philadelphia Stock Exchange

The Philadelphia Stock Exchange (PHLX) is the nation's oldest (1790) exchange and currently the fastest-growing options trading exchange in the country. The PHLX is located at 1900 Market Street, Philadelphia, PA 19103-3584. Telephone: 212-496-5102/5653 fax. Web site address: www.phlx.com.

[M]   Third Market

An informal dealer market in exchange-listed shares. Non-exchange-member firms make ad hoc one- or two-sided markets in exchange-listed stocks and must report all such transactions effected on the consolidated tape.

[N]   Fourth Market

An informal market in exchange or Nasdaq listed shares, where transactions occur directly between two institutional investors without a broker-dealer intermediary but facilitated by Instinet.

Contact information for additional markets and entities follows.

American Association of
  Individual Investors
625 North Michigan Avenue
Chicago, IL 60611
800-428-2244
312-280-0170/9883 fax
www.aaii.com

American Finance Association
  c/o Prof. David Pyle
Haas School of Business
University of California
Berkeley, CA 94720-1900
510-642-2397 phone and fax
pyle@haas.berkeley.edu

American Institute of Certified
  Public Accountants
1211 Avenue of the Americas
New York, NY 10036-8775
212-596-6200/6213 fax
www.aicpa.org

American Stock Exchange
86 Trinity Place
New York, NY 10006-1881
212-306-1000/8376 fax
www.amex.com

Association for Investment
  Management & Research
Post Office Box 3668
560 Ray C. Hunt Drive
Charlottesville, VA 22903-0668

800-247-8132/804-951-5499
804-951-5262 fax
www.aimr.org

Bank Securities Association
303 West Lancaster Avenue,
    Suite 1C
Wayne, PA 19087
610-989-9047/9102 fax
www.bsanet.org

The Bond Market Association
40 Broad Street, 12th Floor
New York, NY 10004-2373
212-809-7000/440-5260 fax
www.bondmarkets.com

Boston Stock Exchange
100 Franklin Street
Boston, MA 02110
617-235-2000/2200 fax
www.bostonstock.com

The Canadian Depository for
    Securities Limited
85 Richmond Street West
Toronto, Ontario M5H 2C9
    Canada
416-365-8400/0843 fax
www.cds.ca

Canadian Venture Exchange
300 Fifth Avenue SW, 10th Floor
Calgary, Alberta T2P 3C4
    Canada
403-974-7400/237-0450 fax
www.cdnx.ca

The Chicago Board of Trade
141 West Jackson Boulevard
Chicago, IL 60604-2994
312-435-3500/341-3312/13
    communications fax
www.cbot.com

Chicago Board Options
    Exchange
400 South LaSalle Street
Chicago, IL 60605-1023
877-992-2263
312-786-5600/7409 fax
www.cboe.com

Chicago Mercantile Exchange
30 South Wacker Drive
Chicago, IL 60606-7499
312-930-1000/3219
    administration fax
www.cme.com

Chicago Stock Exchange, Inc.
One Financial Plaza South
440 South LaSalle Street
Chicago, IL 60605
312-663-2980/2396 fax
www.chicagostockex.com

Cincinnati Stock Exchange
440 South LaSalle Street,
    Suite 2600
Chicago, IL 60605
312-786-8803/939-7239 fax
www.cincinnatistock.com

Commodity Futures Trading
    Commission
Three LaFayette Centre
1155 21st Street NW
Washington, DC 20581
202-418-5000/5525 public
    affairs fax
www.cftc.gov

Consolidated Tape Association
11 Wall Street, 21st Floor
New York, NY 10005
212-656-2014/5848 fax
cta@nyse.com

The Depository Trust Company
55 Water Street
New York, NY 10041
212-855-1200/8331
    communications fax
www.dtc.org

European Association of
    Securities Dealers
56 Rue des Colonies Box 15
1000 Brussels, Belgium
+32-2-227-6565/6524
www.easd.com

Federal Reserve Bank of
    New York
33 Liberty Street
New York, NY 10045
212-720-5000/6628 public
    information fax
www.ny.frb.org

Financial Accounting Standards
    Board
401 Merritt 7
Post Office Box 5116
Norwalk, CT 06856-5116
203-847-0700/849-9714 fax
www.fasb.org

Financial Communications
    Society
Post Office Box 6748
FDR Station
New York, NY 10150
800-327-2927/718-237-4481 fax
mliebovitz@cg-ny.com

Financial Women's Association
    of New York
215 Park Avenue South,
    Suite 1713
New York, NY 10003
212-533-2141/982-3008 fax
www.fwa.org

International Banks and
    Securities Association of
    Australia
Level 12/2 Bligh Street
Sydney 2000 Australia
+61-02-9221-8144/8156 fax
www.ibsa.asn.au

International Primary Market
    Association
36-38 Cornhill
London EC3V 3NG UK
+44-207-623-9353/9356 fax

International Securities Market
  Association
Rigistrasse 60
Post Office Box 2772
CH-8033 Zurich Switzerland
+41-1-363-4222/7772 fax
www.isma.org

International Swaps and
  Derivatives Association
600 Fifth Avenue, 27th Floor
Rockefeller Center
New York, NY 10020-2302
212-332-1200/1212 fax
www.isda.org

Investment Company Institute
1401 H Street NW, Suite 1200
Washington, DC 20005-2148
202-326-5800/5874 public
  information fax
www.ici.org

Investment Dealers Association
  of Canada
121 King Street West, Suite
  1600
Toronto, Ontario M5H 3T9
  Canada
416-364-6133/0753 fax
www.ida.com

Japan Securities Dealers
  Association
1-5-8 Kayabacho
Nihonbashi Chuo-ku
Tokyo 103-0025 Japan
+81-3-3667-8451/3249-3020 fax
www.jsda.or.jp

The Korea Securities Dealers
  Association
34 Youido-Dong
  Yongdeungpo-Gu
Seoul 150-010 Korea
+82-2767-2601/2782-2149 fax
+82-2782-2149 fax
www.ksda.or.kr

London International Financial
  Futures and Options
  Exchange
One Exchange Plaza, Suite 2602
55 Broadway
New York, NY 10006
800-647-9979/212-482-3000
212-482-1100 fax
email: us.office@liffe.com

London Investment Banking
  Association
6 Frederick's Place
London EC2R 8BT UK
44-020-7796-3606
44-020-7796-4345 fax
www.martex.net/taf/0484.htm

The London Stock Exchange,
  plc
Old Broad Street
London EC2N 1HP UK
44-207-797-1000/334-8916
  corporate affairs
www.londonstockex.co.uk

Montreal Exchange
Tour de la Bourse
800 Victoria Square
Post Office Box 61
Montreal Quebec H4Z 1A9
  Canada
514-871-2424/3553
  communications fax
www.me.org

Municipal Securities
  Rulemaking Board
1150 18th Street NW, Suite 400
Washington, DC 20036-3816
202-223-9347/872-0347 fax
www.msrb.org

National Association of
  Securities Dealers, Inc.
1735 K Street NW
Washington, DC 20006
202-728-8000/293-6260
www.nasd.com

National Investor Relations
  Institute
8045 Leesburg Pike, Suite 600
Vienna, VA 22182
703-506-3570/3571 fax
www.niri.org

National Securities Clearing
  Corporation
55 Water Street, 22nd Floor
New York, NY 10041-0082
212-412-8400/363-6035 fax
www.nscc.com

New York Clearing House
  Association LLC
100 Broad Street
New York, NY 10004
212-612-9200/9253 fax
www.theclearinghouse.org

New York Institute of Finance
Two World Trade Center,
  17th Floor
New York, NY 10048
800-227-6943
212-390-5000/344-3469 fax
www.nyif.com

New York Society of Security
  Analysts, Inc.
One World Trade Center,
  Suite 4447
New York, NY 10048
212-912-9249/9310 fax
www.nyssa.org

New York Stock Exchange, Inc.
11 Wall Street
New York, NY 10005
212-656-3000/2126 fax
www.nyse.com

North American Securities
Administrators Association
10 G Street NE, Suite 710
Washington, DC 20002
202-737-0900/783-3571 fax
www.nasaa.org

The Options Clearing
Corporation
440 South LaSalle Street,
Suite 2400
Chicago, IL 60605
312-322-6200/6215 fax
www.optionsclearing.com

The Pacific Exchange
301 Pine Street
San Francisco, CA 94104
415-393-4000/4018 fax
www.pacificex.com

Philadelphia Stock Exchange,
Inc.
1900 Market Street
Philadelphia, PA 19103-3584
215-496-5000/5460 fax
1-800-THE-PHLX
www.phlx.com

Regional Investment Bankers
Association
171 Church Street, Suite 260
Charleston, SC 29401
843-577-2000/8952 fax
www.ribanet.org

Securities Industry Association
120 Broadway, 35th Floor
New York, NY 10271-0080
212-608-1500/1604 fax

Securities Industry Association
1401 Eye Street NW, 10th Floor
Washington, D.C. 20005-2225
(202) 296-9410/9775 fax
www.sia.com

Security Traders Association,
Inc.
One World Trade Center,
Suite 4511
New York, NY 10048
212-524-0484/321-3449 fax
www.securitytraders.org

Securities Industry Automation
Corporation
55 Water Street
New York, NY 10041
212-383-4800/479-3755 fax
2 Metro Tech Center
Brooklyn NY 11201
www.siac.com

Securities Investor Protection
Corporation
805 Fifteenth Street NW,
Suite 800
Washington, DC 20005-2215
202-371-8300/6728 fax
www.sipc.org

Taipei Securities Dealers
Association
Chinese Securities Association
6FL Number 268 Fu-Shin
South Road Section 2
Taipei, Taiwan ROC
+886-22-737-4721/732-1404
fax
www.tsda.org.tw
www.csa.org.tw

Toronto Stock Exchange
The Exchange Tower
130 King Street West
Toronto, Ontario M5X 1J2
  Canada
416-947-4700/4662 fax
www.tse.com

United States Securities and
  Exchange Commission
450 Fifth Street NW
Washington, DC 20549
202-942-7040/9525 corporate
  finance fax
www.sec.gov

Vancouver Stock Exchange
Post Office Box 103333
609 Granville Street
Vancouver, British Columbia
V7Y 1H1 Canada
604-689-3334
www.vse.ca
postmaster@vse.ca

For additional information regarding SIA member firms, *see* its *Securities Industry Yearbook,* published annually since 1978 and available in hardcover or CD-ROM. It includes information with regard to firm rankings by capital, number of branch offices, number of employees, specific department head names, underwriting statistics, etc. In addition, its "Sources: The Securities Executive's Guide to Products and Services" is a very useful compendium. To order, call 212-608-1500.

For a comprehensive listing of NASD member firms, *see Standard & Poors Security Dealers of North America* (a/k/a the S&P Red Book), published semiannually since 1922 by Standard and Poors. It includes information on the location, address, phone number, and key personnel of firms' headquarters and branch offices; SROs and associations; individual state NASAA's; major foreign stock exchanges and associations; a general locator index; and a business services guide. To order, call 212-208-8278.

For a comprehensive listing of international securities firms, *see* the *Euromoney Directory,* published annually since 1972 by Euromoney Publications PLC and available in hardcover, CD-ROM, or online at www.euromoney directory.com. It includes information on the location, address, phone number, and key personnel of firms' headquarters and branch offices and is cross-indexed by country. To order, call +44-1-41-779-8888/8815 fax.

For a comprehensive, concise compilation of industry facts and statistics, *see* SIA's annual *Securities Industry Fact Book.* To order, call 212-608-1500.

To obtain the name, address, phone number, etc. on key syndicate/capital markets personnel, conveniently cross-indexed by firm and city, *see Corporate Syndicate Personnel,* published semiannually since 1971 by Securities Data Publishing, 40 West 57th Street, 11th floor, New York, NY 10019. To order, call 212-765-5311 or e-mail sdp@tfn.com.

The editors recommend senior capital markets professionals keep a current copy of each of the major SRO constitution and rules manuals on the desk for ready reference:

- American Stock Exchange CONSTITUTION and RULES

- New York Stock Exchange CONSTITUTION and RULES

- National Association of Securities Dealers, Inc. MANUAL

All three publications, along with comparable ones for regional exchanges, are published annually for the SROs by CCH INCORPORATED. To order, call 800-835-5224.

Appendices

Appendix 1

SECURITIES INDUSTRY
THIRD-PARTY SERVICE PROVIDERS
AND PUBLICATIONS

The following is a list of securities industry third-party service providers and publications. (Editors' note—The SIA neither endorses any or all of the entities listed below nor denigrates any entities inadvertently omitted.)

American Banker*
One State Street Plaza
New York, NY 10004
212-803-8200/843-9600
　fax
800-221-1809 customer service
www.americanbanker.com

Barron's
Dow Jones & Co., Inc.
200 Liberty Street
New York, NY 10281
212-416-2000/2829 fax
www.barrons.com

Bloomberg L.P.
499 Park Avenue
New York, NY 10022

212-318-2000/917-369-5000 fax
www.bloomberg.com

Bridge Information System,
Inc.
Technology & Trading Center
717 Office Parkway
St. Louis, MO 63141-7115
800-325-2734
314-468-8300/432-5391 fax
www@bridge.com

Corporate Headquarters
3 World Financial Center
New York, NY 10281
800-927-2734
212-372-7100/7115 fax
www.bridge.com

---

* Owned by Thomson Financial Media Inc.

The Bridge**
(f lkla Dow Jones Telerate)
2 World Trade Center, 58th
   Floor
New York, NY 10048
Ph. 212-390-6000
Fx: 212-390-6958
www.bridge.com

CNBC
2200 Fletcher Avenue
Fort Lee, NJ 07024
201-585-2622/346-6527 fax
www.cnbc.com
www.cnbcdowjones.com

Euromoney Publications PLC
Nestor House
Playhouse Yard
London EC4V 5EX England
+44-207-779-8888/8815 fax
www.euromoney.com

Financial Times
U.S. Customer Service
1330 Avenue of the Americas,
   8th Floor
New York, NY 10019
Ph. 212-641-6500
Fx: 212-641-6479
www.ft.com

Institutional Investor, Inc.***
488 Madison Avenue
New York, NY 10022
212-224-3300/224-3368
   advertising fax
800-437-9997
www.iimagazine.com

International Herald Tribune
850 Third Avenue
New York, NY 10022
212-752-3890/755-8785 fax
www.iht.com

**Investment Dealers
   Digest******
40 West 57th Street, 11th Floor
New York, NY 10019
212-765-5311/8189 fax
Web site under construction

CNN/FN
5 Penn Plaza
New York, NY 10001
212-714-7800/no main fax
www.cnnfn.com

CCH Incorporated
Customer Service and
   Operations
4025 West Peterson Avenue
Chicago, IL 60646-6085
800-835-5244
773-866-6000/3895 fax
www.cch.com

** Now called The Bridge, owned by Bridge Information System.
*** Owned by Euromoney Publications PLC.
**** Part of Thomson Financial.

CCH Washington Service Bureau
655 15th Street NW
Washington, DC 20005
800-955-5219
202-508-0694
www.wsb.com

CommScan LLC
120 Broadway, 11th Floor
New York, NY 10271
800-221-3277
212-577-4400/4545 fax
www.commscan.com

Dow Jones
World Financial Center,
   12th Floor
New York, NY 10281
212-416-2000/2658 fax
www.dowjones.com

FirstCall Corporation*
22 Thomson Place
Boston, MA 02210
617-856-2000/330-1460
   support fax
www.firstcall.com

I|B|E|S International, Inc.
Institutional Brokers Estimate
   System
One World Trade Center
   18th Floor
New York, NY 10048-1818
212-437-8200/390-1701 fax
www.ibes.com

Instinet Corporation
875 Third Avenue
New York, NY 10022
212-310-9500/750-2569 fax
www.instinet.com

International Securities Regulation Report
747 Dresher Road, Suite 500
Post Office Box 980
Horsham, PA 19044-0980
215-784-0860/9639 fax
www.lrp.com

Investor's Business Daily Inc.
12655 Beatrice Street
Los Angeles, CA 90066
310-448-6000
310-577-7350 newsroom fax
www.investors.com

The IPO Reporter
1290 Avenue of the Americas,
   36th Floor
New York, NY 10104
Ph: 800-455-5844
Fx: 212-582-2471
www.sdponline.com

MULTEX.com, Inc.
33 Maiden Lane, 5th Floor
New York, NY 10038
Ph: 800-721-2225/
   212-859-9800
Fx: 212-859-9810
www.multex.com

---

*Owned by Thomson Financial Services.

**Nelson Information +
Thomson Financial**
One Gateway Plaza
Post Office Box 591
Port Chester, NY 10573
914-937-8400/8590 fax
800-333-6357
www.nelnet.com
   TFRINFO.com

The New York Times
229 West 43rd Street
New York, NY 10036-3959
212-556-1234/1448 financial
  news fax
www.nytimes.com

Opti Mark, Inc.
10 Exchange Place, 24th Floor
Jersey City, NJ 07302-3905
201-536-7000/7070 fax
www.optimark.com

Practicing Law Institute
810 Seventh Avenue
New York, NY 10019-5818
212-824-5700
800-260-4754
800-321-0093 fax
www.pli.edu

Prism CDA Spectrum
Securities Data Company
2 Gateway Center
Newark, NJ 07102
Ph: 973-622-3100
Fx: 973-733-2882
www.tfsd.com

**Research Bank Web
(Investext)**
Securities Data Company
2 Gateway Center
Newark, NJ 07102
Ph: 973-622-3100
Fx: 973-733-2882
www.tfsd.com

Reuters News Service
199 Water Street, 10th Floor
New York, NY 10038
Ph: 212-859-1660
Fx: 212-859-1669 (financial
  news)
www.reuters.com

SDC Platinum
Securities Data Company
2 Gateway Center
Newark, NJ 07102
Ph: 973-622-3100
Fx: 973-733-2882
www.tfsd.com

Shareworld
Securities Data Company
2 Gateway Center
Newark, NJ 07102
Ph: 973-622-3100
Fx: 973-733-2882
www.tfsd.com

Securities Data Publishing is
  part of Thomson Financial
  Media
Pratt's Guide
Thomson Direct
Venture Expert Web
www.tfsd.com

SNL Securities, LC
321 East Main Street
Charlottesville, VA 22902
804-977-1600/4466 fax
www.snlnet.com

Standard & Poors
  Headquarters
55 Water Street
New York, NY 10041
Ph: 212-438-2000
www.standardpoor.com

Stone & McCarthy Research
  Associates
101 Business Park Drive
Princeton, NJ 08542-0845
609-683-5237/9580 fax
www.smra.com

Thomson Financial
  Corporate Communications
22 Thomson Place, 11F2
Boston, MA 02210
Ph: 617-345-2000
Fx: 617-737-3177
www.thomsonfinancial.com

Thomson Prospectus
395 Hudson Street, 3rd Floor
New York, NY 10014
Ph: 212-806-8376
Fx: 212-989-6594
www.thomsonprospectus.com

Thomson Syndicator
40 West 57th Street, 10th Floor
Suite 1000
New York, NY 10019
212-484-4700/4740 fax
www.thomsonfinancial.com

Tradeline.com
Sales, Client Services, Web
  Production
29 John Street, Suite 1505
New York, NY 10038
Ph: 212-267-0094
Fx: 212-267-0291
www.tradeline.com

Value Line
220 East 42nd Street
New York, NY 10017
212-907-1500
212-818-9747 research fax
www.valueline.com

The Wall Street Journal
200 Liberty Street
New York, NY 10281
800-832-1234/212-416-2000
www.wsj.com

Wall Street Transcript
67 Wall Street, 16th Floor
New York, NY 10005
212-952-7400
212-668-9842 fax
www.twst.com

Zacks Investment Research
155 North Wacker Drive
Suite 300
Chicago, IL 60606
800-399-6659
312-630-0954 fax
www.myzacks.com

Editors' note—*See* John Downes and John Elliot Goodman's helpful publication for an exhaustive listing of over 350 additional finance and investment publications (Part V, Section 1.)[1]

Editors' note—CommScan LLC provides almost the entire investment banking community with new issue message processing and communications (wires), database tracking of capital markets transactions (EquiDesk/DebtDesk, etc.), and deal management software and services (SynDesk). Descriptions of its major component services follow.

Compliance Desk®

Under a mandate authorized by the SEC, dealers engaged in the public offering of securities must perform certain compliance record keeping functions and transmit Free Riding and Withholding information and Regulation M information to NASD Regulation via Compliance Desk.

CompsDesk®

Syndicate personnel involved in book building collate investor demand and make allocations. Among many factors influencing the allocation process are investor roadshow attendance, pre-pricing comments, demand, prior deal behavior, and current holdings of comparable companies. CompsDesk permits synthesizing this information with publicly available information on institutional holdings.

1. Downes, John and John Elliot Goodman, *Finance and Investment Handbook,* Fourth Edition, Hauppauge, NY: Barron's Educational Series, Inc., 1995.

EdgarDesk®

Capital markets personnel often need rapid access to SEC filings. These filings are directly linked to relevant deals in SynDesk, EquiDesk, DebtDesk, and M&A Desk to provide quick, seamless access to source documentation.

EquiDesk,® DebtDesk,® M&A Desk,® QIB Desk®

Capital markets and investment banking personnel involved in solicitation and structuring of transactions have a continuous business need for current information on new issue filings and offerings, M&A transactions, and common stock buyback announcements.

- EquiDesk tracks each public and private equity and equity linked offering from announcement through its life providing deal calendar, pricing notification, and aftermarket performance monitoring. EquiDesk Version 3.1 embraces the Internet and adds a host of new fields, features, and functions with DealCal. DealCal provides a browser-based calendar view of all Filed, Expected, Revised, Priced, and Withdrawn/Postponed issues.

- DebtDesk tracks each public and private fixed income offering of preferred stock, corporate bonds (investment grade and high yield, yankee and global), agency, asset-backed and mortgage-backed bond through its life providing deal calendar and pricing notification.

- M&A Desk tracks public and private merger activity and common stock buybacks, and its database includes deal valuations, consideration paid, advisor roles, fees, and tactics.

- QIB Desk tracks each 144A transaction providing information on registration rights, SEC effectiveness of the registration of underlying securities (if publicly traded), and Qualified Institutional Buyer (QIB) ownership.

EventDesk®

An enterprise-wide Web-based calendar containing all roadshow meetings and marketing events, EventDesk allows for seamless communication between Syndicate, Roadshow, Marketing, Research, Sales, and Trading. The Salesforce can request 1-on-1 meetings for their clients and add attendees to group meetings. Additionally, they can communicate client feedback to Syndicate, view their clients' orders and allocations for new issues, and maintain their client contact information. EventDesk, powered by SynDesk, the industry-standard in deal management systems, provides unparalleled event management capability.

iTicket®

iTicket is a Web-based business-to-business portal linking Institutional and Retail Investors to the Bookrunner for equity and fixed income offerings. iTicket provides the Investor with information on all new offerings as well as allowing them to submit data directly to their brokers desktop in SynTicket. Meeting Requests, Feedback, Orders, Designations, and Ticketing can be entered electronically, allowing straight through processing from the Roadshow through Delivery.

Penalty Bid Tracker®

Provides automated interface between underwriters and the Depository Trust Company with regard to syndicate penalty bid notification and documentation.

QIBList®

The SEC has authorized CommScan to be the central repository of all QIB letters removing the burden of each brokerage firm soliciting letters from every client that is a Qualified Institutional Buyer. QIBList enables institutions seeking inclusion to submit a certification questionnaire via the Internet. QIBList allows broker/dealers that distribute private placements and trade them in the secondary market to confirm whether a prospective investor is registered as a qualified institutional buyer (QIB).

SynDesk®

SynDesk enables capital markets personnel to: form a syndicate; coordinate a roadshow; track indications of interest, allocations, retentions, underwriting income, and expenses; and produce management reports on client and deal activity. Modules of SynDesk include SynWire (interdealer communication), SynTicket (paperless information flow between sales force and syndicate with automated ticketing), and Penalty Bid Tracker (an interface to DTC to provide dealer and investor flipping information). Additionally, SynDesk interfaces with EdgarDesk to provide direct access to SEC-filed source documents, with EquiDesk and DebtDesk to provide access to publicly available information on each deal in registration and with CompsDesk to provide information on institutional account names, addresses, and investment holdings.

Analytics

A monthly recap of activity in capital markets (equity and fixed income), mergers and acquisitions, and syndicated loans.

Appendix 2

FINANCIAL PRINTERS

The business of printing and delivering/distributing financial documents to assist reporting companies' compliance with applicable provisions of the securities laws has evolved from one of hand crafting and setting hot lead type in the 1930s, to offset printing, to today's computer assisted electronic digital document preparation and electronic filing. Financial printers help reporting companies comply with mandatory electronic delivery of quarterly, annual, and ad hoc information to the SEC via its Electronic Data Gathering and Retrieval (EDGAR) system.

Traditionally, the basic business of financial printers has been printing all the documents necessary to complete a public offering, *e.g.,* the registration statement (parts I and II); preliminary (amended preliminary(ies)) and final prospectus; preliminary and final blue sky survey; preliminary and final legal survey (for fixed income offerings); preliminary and final UA and AAU; preliminary and final bond indentures.

This work naturally led to the printing of other documents as the field of investment banking expanded, *e.g.,* tender offer and exchange offer material; required SEC filing documents—quarterly, annual, and ad hoc; and mergers, acquisitions, and divestitures.

Major financial printing firms also have developed extensive libraries of in-depth, for-public-sale brochures and pamphlets authored by current industry practitioners covering almost every facet of domestic and international securities law and the public offering process. In addition, each major financial printer offers sophisticated, comprehensive subscription services to keep investment banking and capital markets professionals up to date on developments/changes in securities law and a whole host of other securities markets related activities.

In days past, financial printing was not unlike the securities business—primarily a cottage industry of local "mom and pop" shops with
very few large players. However, like many other service industries,
financial printing has undergone significant consolidation. While a number of first-rate regional and local financial printers are still active, there
are three major financial printers with national and international branch
office presence and a capability to disseminate information/documents
globally via electronic means. Contact data for them follows.

Bowne & Co., Inc.
345 Hudson Street, 10th Floor
New York, NY 10014-4502
212-924-5500/229-3400 fax
www.bowne.com

RR Donnelley Financial
75 Park Place
New York, NY 10007-2161
212-341-7777/7798 fax and
  7799
www.rrdfin.com

Merrill Corporation
Financial Documents Services,
  11th Floor
Investment Company Services,
  12th Floor
225 Varick Street
New York, NY 10014
Ph: 800-888-2677/
  212-620-5600
Fx: 212-675-2805 (FDS)
Fx: 212-367-5900 (ICS)
www.merrillcorp.com

Appendix 3

TOMBSTONE ADVERTISING
AND SERVICE PROVIDERS

Tombstone advertising announcing the offering of new issue securities or the completion of other investment banking transactions such as private placements, syndicated loans, letters of credit, bridge loans, divestitures, mergers and acquisitions, etc. has long been used by investment banking firms for a variety of purposes.[1] SEC Rule 134, "Communications Not Deemed a Prospectus," of the Securities Act of 1933 gives securities underwriters relief under that Act by deeming a tombstone ad not to be a prospectus and delineating what may appear in it. Therefore, a tombstone, with its very limited information and almost no sales pitch, may appear in interstate communications with no latent culpability for material misstatement, omission, or over-statement of facts. The following observations hopefully shed some light on this somewhat arcane world.

A tombstone ad for an underwritten transaction basically identifies the issuer, the securities being offered, their price and the dollar

---

1. Perhaps named due to its drab similarity to a graveyard tombstone; with a gray uninspiring look and stelar (sic) shape with simple horizontal lines of traditional type styles; also, usually appears only after a deal is "dead and buried." For an extensive discussion of the importance of the order of dealer appearance in tombstones announcing underwritten transactions, *see U.S. v. Henry S. Morgan et al.,* "Transcript of Trial: Defendants' Opening — Mr. [William Dwight] Whitney" (February 15, 1951, 3164-3165). This piece may help the capital markets practitioner understand the derivation of certain current industry practice and custom with regard to the topic of placement/appearance in a tombstone ad.

amount of bonds (and perhaps certain bond covenants) or number of shares of stock, and the underwriters. Thus, the primary function of a tombstone ad historically has been to proclaim an underwritten issue and announce, via a hedge clause, the availability of prospectuses and therefore, perhaps, securities from those participants listed in the ad.

With regard to tombstone style, each securities firm has historically adopted a distinctive (although not proprietary) typeface; an individual border design; unique placement of firm names with regard to center, left, or right justification; use of firm logo(s) or trademarks (*e.g.*, the old Smith Barney "radiator" logo that used to appear in the upper left hand corner of that firm's tombstones or the current Morgan Stanley Dean Witter global mercator projection super-imposed—screened—across the top of its ads) and/or issuer client logo; varying sizes of type (although the same size for all underwriters) and placement of SEC mandated hedge clauses—all in an understated effort to catch the eye of the reader and hopefully enhance the lead manager and issuer firms' name recognition and franchise value.

As the terms "co-lead" and "co-global coordinator" came into more common use in the late 1990s (*see Chapter 3, Underwriting Custom, Tradition, and History*), some changes in tombstone style and typeface also appeared. The most noticeable was the use of a "neutral" typeface/font in the ad, different from that historically associated with either of the co-leads. Additionally, in a "neutral" tombstone there are no corporate logos or background screens in evidence—a rather bland solution to an otherwise intensely inflammatory debate between the two co-leads over what the outside world must see as insignificant minutiae.

Tombstone advertising costs, both production and placement, have historically been paid for by the underwriter(s) on a pro-rata basis based on underwriting commitment as a percentage of total deal size, and the lead manager normally selects the media placement—*e.g.*, national and/or international business newspapers, securities industry oriented magazines and/or newsletters, general audience magazines, and trade publications focused on the issuer's industry.

For many years, tombstones were read left to right, top to bottom, in alphabetical order by significance and by underwriting or risk commitment (bracketing), with the lead or book running manager appearing on the left of the first line of underwriters and the ad running in the typeface, style, and distinctive border associated with that particular firm. Securities lawyers have always been overly careful to make sure that a tombstone in no way is deemed a "selling" prospectus, and therefore the tombstone's look has changed little over the years. In fact, it was a major breakthrough in the late 1950s when simple logos were included in such ads, be it the issuer client's or the managing underwriter's.

Since the SEC rule governing the content of tombstone ads is legally limiting (and precludes creative, hard sell solicitation), investment banking firms have successfully adapted to the ad's confining structure. The type size of the lead and co-managers began to be larger than that of the other underwriters in the early-to-mid 1980s. In the mid-to-late 1990s, some firms began to experiment with other than traditional formats such as full-page layouts in financial publications that often encompassed multiple offerings and carried promotional messages trumpeting only the capabilities and accomplishments of the lead manager.

Students of the industry should understand that there is no legal requirement for an underwriting firm to appear in a tombstone (giving rise to the phrase "non-appearing" underwriter). Non-appearance, while rare, usually relates to a disagreement between the book running manager and the participating underwriter over the latter's role in the financing or the size of the participation offered it, either in terms of underwriting commitment (bracketing) or free retention or both.

For the most part, the names of selected dealers (the selling group) do not appear in a tombstone ad, although some lead managers have listed such firms under a separate heading. The actual positioning of individual firms in an ad has always been taken more seriously by Wall Street than Main Street because the line up inevitably becomes the most current version of Wall Street's social pecking order or power structure. In general, the tombstone ad has evolved over time to become an important vehicle for investment banks to conduct targeted advertising that brings attention to the firm's successful financing accomplishments.[2]

On occasion, firms have placed pre-effective tombstone advertisements in an effort to generate interest in a forthcoming offering. Such ads, by their nature, carry no details of final price and size, but

---

2. The editors thank John E. Eckelberry, an industry professional with over 40 years of experience, for major contributions to this chapter.

rather announce the intention of the issuer and often include names, addresses, telephone numbers, and e-mail addresses of underwriters and/or selected dealers to enable potential investors to obtain a preliminary prospectus.

Firms generally acknowledged to be in the tombstone production business as of the date of publication of this handbook are listed below. The reader should know that from time to time, certain investment banks have employed Madison Avenue advertising agencies on either an ad hoc or dedicated basis.

Citigate Albert Frank
850 Third Avenue
11th Floor
New York, NY 10022-6222
212-508-3400/3544 fax
www.citigate.com

John McNamara Advertising, Inc.
27 Whitehall Street
6th Floor
New York, NY 10004-2117
212-509-7779/797-9586 fax
no Web site

Doremus & Company
200 Varick Street
11th Floor
New York, NY 10014-4810
212-366-3000/3660 Fax
www.doremus.com

Appendix 4

RATING AGENCIES

Simply stated, a debt rating is an attempt to ". . . determine how likely it is that the issuer of the debt will be able to pay back the principal (amount) it borrows, plus interest, and make those payments at those times at which it has been legally agreed."[1] A preferred stock rating addresses the same topics with regard to sinking fund issues and dividend payments only with regard to perpetual issues.

As of January 2000, there were five organizations that carried the qualification of a Nationally Recognized Statistical Rating Organization (NRSRO), an SEC defined term that, when granted, qualifies an agency's ratings for legal and technical use—Duff & Phelps (D&P), Fitch IBCA (Fitch), Moody's Investors Service (Moody's), Standard & Poors (S&P), and Thomson Bankwatch (Thomson).[2] As of this writing, Moody's and S&P rate almost all new issues of fixed income securities (debt and preferred), while D&P and Fitch rate only upon request, and Thomson restricts its ratings to commercial bank issues.

Ironically, while rating agencies in effect work for investors who use these ratings in investment decisions, the agencies almost never

---

1. The editors thank Byron D. Klapper, a 29-year veteran of the credit market scene as a reporter (*Wall Street Journal,* "Credit Markets" column) and rating agency publisher/senior executive, for his help with this chapter. Additionally, we are grateful for the assistance James J. Jockle of Fitch gave us for the Second Edition.

2. Editors' note: Fitch IBCA and Duff & Phelps merged on June 1, 2000 to become Fitch. The new entity expects to have a consolidated Web site ready by late 2000.

see these investors; and the agencies receive most of their fee revenue from the very companies or government entities that they rate. By the very nature of its work, a rating agency often finds itself writing less than flattering or complimentary observations on the credit characteristics of its subject. In the words of one rating agency veteran, a negative credit report on its face theoretically presents ". . . a prima facie case for libel—the presence of defamation and monetary loss . . . .[3]" Thankfully, and not unlike the press, rating agencies operate under the First Amendment to the United States Constitution protective umbrella of the right of free speech ". . . fair, arm's length comment and criticism with the absence of malice; an objective opinion on the underlying credit worthiness of an issuer . . . .[4]"

Investors have long looked to rating agencies for guidance on credit evaluation. For example, many institutional investors require two rating agency reviews before purchasing a security, and the significant increase in new issue activity for companies carrying a less than investment grade ("junk" or "high yield") rating argues well for the continued need for multiple independent agencies going forward. Rating categories are relatively simplistic—usually gradations of the first four letters of the alphabet or a combination of letters and numbers that describe the various levels of risk. Each service publishes an extremely detailed monthly guide, a calendar year-end summary, and ad hoc literature to define its rating categories and announce rating changes on existing securities or coverage of newly issued ones. Contact information on each agency follows.

Duff & Phelps Credit Rating
  Company[5]
55 East Monroe Street
Suite 3500
Chicago, IL 60603
312-368-3100
312-263-1032 fax
www.dcrco.com

Fitch, Inc.[6]
1 State Street Plaza
New York, NY 10004
1-800-75-FITCH
212-908-0500
www.fitchratings.com

---

3. *Id.*
4. *Id.*
5. *See* Appendix 4 note 2.
6. *See* Appendix 4 note 2.

Merrill Corporation
225 Varick Street
New York, NY 10014
800-888-2677/212-620-5600
Fx: 212-675-2805 (Financial
   Documents Services)
Fx: 212-367-5900 (Investment
   Company Services)

Moody's Investor Services
99 Church Street
New York, NY 10007
212-553-0300/0882 fax
www.stagingmoodys.com

Standard & Poors Ratings
   Services
55 Water Street, 37th Floor
New York, NY 10041
212-438-2400
www.standardandpoors.com/
   ratings

Thomson Financial Bank
   Watch
61 Broadway, 3rd Floor
New York, NY 10006
212-845-0300/0502 fax
www.bankwatch.com

Appendix 5

SIGNIFICANT DATES IN SECURITIES INDUSTRY HISTORY

The following are significant dates in securities industry history.

1653   **Wall Street**

Operating under a proclamation issued by then Governor Kieft, on March 13, 1653, settlers of New Amsterdam on the southern tip of Manhattan, erected a wooden fence backed by a ditch to keep their livestock within the boundaries of their tiny community.[1] The fence became a wall, and today's Wall Street, in the heart of the New York financial district, roughly approximates the east-west axis of the old wooden fence. Oddly, Wall Street is one of the few streets in the world with a river (East) at one end and a grave yard at the other (part of Trinity Church).

1792   **Hamilton intervention in market**

The 1790 reorganization of Revolutionary War debt ("Stock in the Public Funds of the United States" exchange offer) and subsequent Alexander Hamilton (Secretary of the Treasury) intervention in the then nascent U.S. Government Bond Market, resulting from April 1792 stock market crash, led to signing of Button Wood Tree Agreement on May 17,

---

1. Adapted from Museum of American Financial History's invitation to its reception celebrating the 345th Birthday of Wall Street.

1792. A landmark plaque on Broad Street outside NYSE commemorates the event and its two-sentence document.

1800   **Linen merchant Alexander Brown moves to Baltimore from Belfast**
Establishing roots of what became America's oldest investment bank, Alex. Brown & Sons.

1817   **New York Stock and Exchange Board constitution adopted**

1837   **Panic of 1837**
The result of a dispute between President Andrew Jackson and banker Nicholas Biddle over the destiny of The Bank of the United States.

1844   **Invention of the Morse telegraph**
The Morse telegraph was adopted as the European standard in 1851.[2]

1850   **Henry, Emanuel, and Mayer Lehman open Lehman Brothers**
Originally operated as cotton brokers in Montgomery, AL.

1862   **Lincoln administration sells government bonds to the public to help finance the Civil War**
Philadelphia investment banker Jay Cooke convinces Treasury Department to try novel approach—first documented U.S. use of syndicate underwriting/distribution and offering price stabilization techniques used to distribute annuities to individuals.

1864   **National Banking Act of 1864**
This Act mandated that only the U.S. federal government could print paper money, thus stabilizing the flow of currency in the country.

1865   **NYSE locates at current site**

---

2. *The Economist,* January 23, 1999, pg. 71.

1866   **First trans-Atlantic cable laid**

1867   **Introduction of stock ticker**

1869   **Marcus Goldman begins dealing in commercial paper**
       Establishing roots of investment bank Goldman, Sachs.

1871   **Continuous auction market replaces call market on floor of NYSE**
       Members had assigned seats during operating hours of call market. The term "seat" endures to this day as an indication of exchange membership.

1873   **Panic of 1873**
       Precipitated by the bankruptcy of financier/speculator Jay Cooke.

1878   **First telephone installed on NYSE floor**

1886   **NYSE daily trading volume tops 1 million for first time**

1891   **Sherman Anti-Trust Act passed**
       This Act was passed to deter monopolies and combinations in restraint of trade.

1893   **Panic of 1893**
       Resulted from increased productivity in factories and on farms. This resulting over-supply of goods caused a short but severe economic recession.

1896   **Charles Henry Dow creates first industrial stock index**

1899   **The Wall Street Journal begins publication of economic news**

1907   **Panic of 1907**
       Jones Industrial Index declines 45 percent. New York banker J.P. Morgan instrumental in restoring order.

1913   **Federal Reserve Act signed December 23, 1913**
        This Act created the Federal Reserve System that is in
        place today.

1917   **U.S. Liberty bonds offered via NYSE to help finance
        World War I**

1921   **Last day of outdoor trading at New York Curb Market—
        June 25, 1921**
        This market is now the American Stock Exchange.

1924   **First Mutual Fund**
        Massachusetts Investor's Trust (MIT) formed.

1929   **Black Tuesday—October 29, 1929**
        Stock market crash . . . end of the Roaring 20s.

1930   **The Depression**
        25 percent unemployment . . . US savings rate plummets
        . . . new job formation stalls . . . breadlines . . . indelible
        impression left on an entire generation.

1930   **The New Deal**
        Securities Act of 1933—registration and full disclosure re-
        quired of issuers of securities—"truth in securities" act.
        The Banking Act of 1933 (Glass-Steagall)—mandates sep-
        aration of commercial banking (deposit taking), investment
        banking (capital formation/risk taking), and insurance
        underwriting. Sponsored by Senator Carter Glass (D-VA)
        and Congressman Henry Steagall (D-AL). Securities
        Exchange Act of 1934—market regulation, establishment
        of the SEC, and self-regulatory concept. Public Utility Hold-
        ing Company Act of 1935—registration requirement with
        SEC . . . Competitive bidding (William O. Douglas's speech
        to Bond Club of NY) for utility securities required as of
        April 8, 1941 (SEC rule U-50). Trust and Indenture Act of
        1939, Investment Company Act of 1940—mutual funds,
        Investment Advisor Act of 1940.

1939   **World War II 1939-1945**
       "The Arsenal of Democracy" . . . pegged interest rates . . .
       rationing/suppression of consumer demand sends individ-
       ual savings rate soaring. . . Bretton Woods Agreement—
       1944 . . . free world fixing of international currency
       exchange rates tied to the Gold Standard (@ US$ 35 to the
       ounce).

Post WWII
       Low inflation . . . rising stock market prices . . . release of
       pent-up consumer demand . . . GI Bill . . . an economic
       boom commences.

       Wall Street a cottage industry . . . wholesalers . . . retailers
       . . . all with little appetite for risk.

1947   **U.S. v. Henry S. Morgan et al.—October 30, 1947**
       U.S. Attorney General filed a civil anti-trust suit against 17
       investment banks accused of violating the Sherman Anti-
       Trust Act—presiding Judge Harold R. Medina's decision
       of October 14, 1953 absolved all firms so charged.

1954   **Monthly Investment Plan (MIP) introduced June 25, 1954**
       This Plan encouraged individual investor participation in
       stock market.

1956   **Ford Motor Company IPO—January 1956**
       Blyth & Co., Inc. led $657 million secondary sale of a por-
       tion of the Ford Foundation shares—offering represents
       zenith of broad underwriting syndication (722 underwrit-
       ers and over 1,000 selected dealers).

1958   **British Aluminum versus Reynolds Metals/Tube Invest-
       ment joint venture**
       S.G. Warburg representing British Aluminum successfully
       takes on London "City" establishment in hostile takeover.

1960   **The "Go-Go" years**
       Mutual fund "gunslingers" . . . individual investors flock to
       equity markets creating paper crunch/capital crisis. Wed-

nesday shut-down—industry unable to cope with increased volume of business—and failure of many firms culminates with Merrill Lynch–Goodbody combination (industry indemnification of Merrill acquisition critical aspect of transaction) and birth of Depository Trust Company (1973), Securities Industry Automation Corporation and Securities Investor Protection Corporation (1970) . . . appearance of H. Ross Perot in Wall Street . . . Francis I. duPont/Glore Forgan/Walston . . . Perot's imaginative but at the time naive "triangle of investing" concept does not take hold.

1963   **SEC Special Study of Securities Markets**
Publication causes first cracks to appear in NYSE minimum fixed rate commission schedule—beginning of negotiated rates for secondary market transactions.

1963   **Birth of Eurobond Market**
Incentive—avoidance of U.S. interest equalization tax implemented by JFK administration/access to growing offshore deposits of US$'s. S.G. Warburg lead manages US$ 15MM 15-year deal for Autostrade (Italian highway authority)—first eurobond new issue.

1960s   **Re-alignment of special/bulge bracket in underwriting business occurs in late 1960s**
was: First Boston   added: Merrill Lynch Pearce Fenner
Dillon Read   & Beane
Kuhn Loeb   Salomon Brothers & Hutzler
Morgan Stanley

1970   **Donaldson Lufkin & Jenrette IPO**
Until 1970, only First Boston, Discount Corporation, and Weeden were publicly held. Merrill Lynch follows as do CBWL-Hayden Stone, A.G. Edwards, Reynolds, E.F. Hutton, PaineWebber, Dean Witter, and others including regional firms like Piper Jaffray & Hopwood, Mitchum, Jones & Templeton, First of Michigan; local firms like First Equity Corporation of Florida; and boutiques like Oliphant.

1971   **Onset of Nasdaq trading**
Revolution in OTC market making. Trading spreads tighten but volume soars.

1971   **Birth of Securities Industry Association**
Amalgamation of Investment Bankers Association and Association of Stock Exchange Firms created industry's first united trade group.

1971   **President Nixon renounces U.S. adherence to gold standard**
Bretton Woods fixed rate currency exchange agreement scrapped.

1972   **Money Market funds introduced**

1973   **Bear Market of 1973-1974**
OPEC crisis . . . over 500 securities firms merge or go out of business . . . new issue equity business all but disappears (nine IPO's occur in all of 1974).

1974   **Employee Retirement Income Securities Act (ERISA) of 1974 enacted**
Foundation for dynamic growth of institutional equity business.

1974   **International Nickel acquisition of Electronic Storage Battery**
Morgan Stanley representation of International Nickel legitimizes hostile takeover business.

1975   **Securities Acts Amendments—May 1975**
Final abolition of NYSE minimum fixed rate commissions—"May Day"—rates for secondary equity market institutional transactions plummet, exceeding most predictions with respect to both magnitude and speed of decline.

1976   **Papilsky legal action—October 1976**
        Unsuccessful attempt by mutual fund investor to force
        institutional (investment management company) pur-
        chasers of new issues to seek recapture of portion of under-
        writing compensation of purchased new issues.

1977   **Merrill Lynch introduces CMA (cash management
        account)**
        Quantum leap forward in providing full service to retail
        investor client, particularly with regard to dividend/inter-
        est sweep into money market account and customer state-
        ment consolidation/simplification.

        Lehman Brothers acquires Kuhn Loeb
        Two grand names in investment banking become one.

1978   **A.G. Becker-Bankers Trust commercial paper lawsuit**
        Glass-Steagall Chinese wall separating commercial and
        investment banking starts to crumble as Bankers Trust pre-
        vails and enters commercial paper business as dealer.

        Merrill Lynch purchases White, Weld & Co.
        A significant step in Merrill's ascendancy in investment
        banking. White, Weld's European affiliate—Credit Suisse
        White Weld—becomes Credit Suisse First Boston.

1979   **IBM $1 Billion 2-Tranche bond offering—October 1979**
        This deal marks the beginning of the end of sole-managed
        high-grade bond issues. Morgan Stanley refuses to co-man-
        age this offering with Salomon Brothers. IBM gives Salo-
        mon the books, and adds Merrill Lynch as co-manager.
        Morgan withdraws as a manager but participates in a super
        bulge bracket by itself.

1970s   **Emergence of high yield/junk bond market—late 1970s**
        Michael Milken . . . Drexel Burnham Lambert . . . lever-
        aged buyouts . . . state pension plans legitimize business
        with significant commitments of retirement plan assets.

1981   **Salomon Brothers/Phibro amalgamation**
       Ends one of Street's oldest partnerships, but gives Salomon
       permanent public capital and its balance sheet starts to
       grow more rapidly.

1981   **Economic Recovery Tax Act of 1981**
       This Act made Individual Retirement Accounts (IRAs)
       available to all workers.

1982   **Enactment of Tax Equity and Fiscal Responsibility Act
       (TEFRA)**

1982   **SEC Shelf Registration Temporary Rule 415—made per-
       manent in 1983**
       Citibank is first filer . . . "historical" investment banking/
       issuer relationships begin to transform.

1984   **Merrill Lynch purchases A.G. Becker Paribas**
       Another significant step in Merrill's ascendancy in invest-
       ment banking.

1985   **Globalization of securities business accelerates**
       U.S. Treasury market expands . . . non-U.S. government
       equity privatization begins in earnest (initially in U.K.) . . .
       IBM and Citibank US$ 30-year bond new issues widely
       purchased in Japan.

1986   **Big Bang—October 27, 1986**
       London securities industry deregulation . . . consolidation
       of firms accelerates as competition unleashed.

1986   **Morgan Stanley—IPO March 21, 1986**
       Founded as private partnership in September 1935 by ex-
       employees of the old House of Morgan—an early result of
       Glass-Steagall mandate to separate investment banking
       from commercial banking.

1987   **Monday October 19, 1987**
        NYSE barely escapes meltdown . . . Dow Jones Industrial
        Average fell 508 points (22.6 percent) on then record vol-
        ume of 608,000,000 shares . . . CBOE . . . Merc . . . CBOT
        all close to shut down . . . Brady Commission formed to
        investigate circumstances . . . trading collars/"circuit
        breaker" concept born . . . Nasdaq market ceases to function
        as few firms reportedly answer their phones . . . seeds of
        development of Nasdaq Small Order Entry System (SOES)
        sown . . . British Petroleum global equity underwriting cre-
        ates large US$ marked-to-market underwriting loss for
        managers of U.S. tranche — Goldman, Morgan, Salomon
        and Shearson Lehman — and marks the end of conformance
        to off-shore underwriting customs and practices for U.S.
        portion of such distributions (October 30, 1987).

1988   **Insider Trading and Securities Fraud Enforcement Act en-
        acted**
        Fulfilling promise of then SEC Commissioner and long-
        time E.F. Hutton senior executive John S. R. Shad.

1980s   **Impact of public ownership of securities firms**
        Easier access to capital permits rapid expansion of balance
        sheets and more tolerance for principal risk.

1980s   **Insider trading scandals — late 1980s**
        Ivan Boesky . . . Marty Siegel-Kidder Peabody . . . Mike
        Milken — beginning of the fall of Drexel . . . industry Chi-
        nese Wall procedures rethought and strengthened.

1990   **Drexel Burnham Lambert fails May 29, 1990**
        Files for protection from creditors under Chapter 11 of the
        Federal Bankruptcy Code.

1990   **144A Market opens**
        Implementation of concept of capital markets efficiency . . .
        qualified institutional buyer (QIB) term born.

1993   **Vanderbilt University and Ohio State University profes-
        sors question Nasdaq trading procedures**
        Issue of secondary market trading spreads. Collusion? Long-
        term impact on depth of market making and capital raising
        for small companies still unknown . . . widespread trading
        in 1/16's, 1/32's commences in 1996 . . . 1997 $1B settle-
        ment/consent decree signed by almost all industry parties
        to formal complaint.

1990s   **SEC under Chairman Arthur Levitt continues tradition
        of activism**
        Capital raising hopefully made easier for issuers . . . in-
        vestor awareness heightened through mechanism of infor-
        mational "town meetings" hosted by SEC Chairman . . .
        mutual fund prospectus simplification program and plain
        language initiative implemented.

1993   **T + 3**
        Three-day settlement for corporate securities goes into
        effect replacing five-day settlement (in place since June
        1968 when it was four-day).

1996   **Glass-Steagall 60 + years later 1996**
        Federal Reserve Section 20 authorization expanded (Dec
        1996) . . . banks start to buy securities firms . . . securities
        firms would like to buy banks but cannot . . . concept of
        world class global investment bank begins to emerge and
        take shape.

1997   **The Year of Consolidation**
        ABN AMRO - Chicago Corporation
        BancAmerica - Robertson Stephens
        Bank of New York - ESI Securities
        BankersTrust - Alex Brown
        BZW—dissolution/break up of investment banking
        CIBC - Oppenheimer
        CS First Boston - Volpe Brown Whelan
        Everen - Principal Financial
        Fahnestock - First of Michigan

Fifth Third Bank - Ohio Company
First Union - Wheat First Butcher Singer
Fleet Bank - Quick & Reilly
Friedman Billings Ramsey - IPO
GKN - South East Research Partners
Gruntal - Hampshire Securities
ING - Furman Selz
Investec - Ernst
Morgan Stanley - Dean Witter Discover
Nat West—investment banking dissolution/breakup
NationsBanc - Montgomery Securities
NBD First Chicago - Roney
Smith Barney - Salomon Brothers
Southern National - Craigie
SunTrust - Equitable Securities
Swiss Bank - UBS
Swiss Bank Warburg - Dillon Read
USBancorp - Piper Jaffray
Yamaichi - bankruptcy

1998   **Japanese "Big Bang"**
        Deregulation of Japan's financial system . . . Merrill Lynch
        takeover of Yamaichi branch offices . . . Salomon Smith
        Barney investment in Nikko.

1998   **Megamerger announcements**
        Travelers - Citicorp become Citigroup . . . First Chicago
        NBD - BancOne . . . NationsBanc - BancAmerica become
        Bank of America (and sell Robertson Stephens to Bank
        Boston) . . . Deutsche Bank announces purchase of Bankers
        Trust/Alex.Brown.

1998   **Goldman, Sachs & Co. announces plan to go public**
        Files registration statement in August and withdraws it in
        September amid global financial uncertainty.

1998   **Global Financial Crisis**
      Long Term Capital Management hedge fund, tottering on
      brink of insolvency, rescued and restructured by Fed-
      brokered consortium of commercial and investment banks.

1999   **Goldman Sachs & Co. IPO**
      US$ 3.7B public offering ends 130 year old private part-
      nership.

Editors' note—for those interested in the history of finance, investment banking, the capital raising process, and the securities markets of the United States, a visit or involvement with the Museum of
American Financial History may be rewarding. Founded in 1988
by John E. Herzog, its address is 26 Broadway, New York, NY 10004.
Telephone: 212-908-4519/4601 fax. Web site: www.financialhistory.
org.

Appendix 6

SECURITIES ACT OF 1933

INDEX

SECTION 1—SHORT TITLE

This title may be cited as the "Securities Act of 1933."

SECTION 2—DEFINITIONS; PROMOTION OF EFFICIENCY, COMPETITION, AND CAPITAL FORMATION

a. **Definitions.** When used in this subchapter, unless the context otherwise requires—

   1. The term "security" means any note, stock, treasury stock, bond, debenture, evidence of indebtedness, certificate of interest or participation in any profit-sharing agreement, collateral-trust certificate, preorganization certificate or subscription, transferable share, investment contract, voting-trust certificate, certificate of deposit for a security, fractional undivided interest in oil, gas, or other mineral rights, any put, call, straddle, option, or privilege on any security, certificate of deposit, or group or index of securities (including any interest therein or based on the value thereof), or any put, call, straddle, option, or privilege entered into

on a national securities exchange relating to foreign currency, or, in general, any interest or instrument commonly known as a "security", or any certificate of interest or participation in, temporary or interim certificate for, receipt for, guarantee of, or warrant or right to subscribe to or purchase, any of the foregoing.

2. The term "person" means an individual, a corporation, a partnership, an association, a joint-stock company, a trust, any unincorporated organization, or a government or political subdivision thereof. As used in this paragraph the term "trust" shall include only a trust where the interest or interests of the beneficiary or beneficiaries are evidenced by a security.

3. The term "sale" or "sell" shall include every contract of sale or disposition of a security or interest in a security, for value. The term "offer to sell", "offer for sale", or "offer" shall include every attempt or offer to dispose of, or solicitation of an offer to buy, a security or interest in a security, for value. The terms defined in this paragraph and the term "offer to buy" as used in <u>subsection (c)</u> of section 5 of this title shall not include preliminary negotiations or agreements between an issuer (or any person directly or indirectly controlling or controlled by an issuer, or under direct or indirect common control with an issuer) and any underwriter or among underwriters who are or are to be in privity of contract with an issuer (or any person directly or indirectly controlling or controlled by an issuer, or under direct or indirect common control with an issuer). Any security given or delivered with, or as a bonus on account of, any purchase of securities or any other thing, shall be conclusively presumed to constitute a part of the subject of such purchase and to have been offered and sold for value. The issue or transfer of a right or privilege, when originally issued or transferred with a security, giving the holder of such security the right to convert such security into another security of the same issuer or of another person, or giving a right to subscribe to another security of the same issuer or of another person, which right cannot be exercised until

some future date, shall not be deemed to be an offer or sale of such other security; but the issue or transfer of such other security upon the exercise of such right of conversion or subscription shall be deemed a sale of such other security.

4. The term "issuer" means every person who issues or proposes to issue any security; except that with respect to certificates of deposit, voting-trust certificates, or collateral-trust certificates, or with respect to certificates of interest or shares in an unincorporated investment trust not having a board of directors (or persons performing similar functions) or of the fixed, restricted management, or unit type, the term "issuer" means the person or persons performing the acts and assuming the duties of depositor or manager pursuant to the provisions of the trust or other agreement or instrument under which such securities are issued; except that in the case of an unincorporated association which provides by its articles for limited liability of any or all of its members, or in the case of a trust, committee, or other legal entity, the trustees or members thereof shall not be individually liable as issuers of any security issued by the association, trust, committee, or other legal entity; except that with respect to equipment-trust certificates or like securities, the term "issuer" means the person by whom the equipment or property is or is to be used; and except that with respect to fractional undivided interests in oil, gas, or other mineral rights, the term "issuer" means the owner of any such right or of any interest in such right (whether whole or fractional) who creates fractional interests therein for the purpose of public offering.

5. The term "Commission" means the Securities and Exchange Commission.

6. The term "Territory" means Puerto Rico, the Virgin Islands, and the insular possessions of the United States.

7. The term "interstate commerce" means trade or commerce in securities or any transportation or communication relating thereto among the several States or between the District of Columbia or any Territory of the United States and any

State or other Territory, or between any foreign country and any State, Territory, or the District of Columbia, or within the District of Columbia.

8.   The term "registration statement" means the statement provided for in section 6 of this title, and includes any amendment thereto and any report, document, or memorandum filed as part of such statement or incorporated therein by reference.

9.   The term "write" or "written" shall include printed, lithographed, or any means of graphic communication.

10.   The term "prospectus" means any prospectus, notice, circular, advertisement, letter, or communication, written or by radio or television, which offers any security for sale or confirms the sale of any security; except that (a) a communication sent or given after the effective date of the registration statement (other than a prospectus permitted under subsection (b) of section 10 of this title) shall not be deemed a prospectus if it is proved that prior to or at the same time with such communication a written prospectus meeting the requirements of subsection (a) of section 10 of this title at the time of such communication was sent or given to the person to whom the communication was made, and (b) a notice, circular, advertisement, letter, or communication in respect of a security shall not be deemed to be a prospectus if it states from whom a written prospectus meeting the requirements of section 10 of this title may be obtained and, in addition, does no more than identify the security, state the price thereof, state by whom orders will be executed, and contain such other information as the Commission, by rules or regulations deemed necessary or appropriate in the public interest and for the protection of investors, and subject to such terms and conditions as may be prescribed therein, may permit.

11.   The term "underwriter" means any person who has purchased from an issuer with a view to, or offers or sells for an issuer in connection with, the distribution of any security, or participates or has a direct or indirect participation in

any such undertaking, or participates or has a participation in the direct or indirect underwriting of any such under-taking; but such term shall not include a person whose interest is limited to a commission from an underwriter or dealer not in excess of the usual and customary distributors' or sellers' commission. As used in this paragraph the term "issuer" shall include, in addition to an issuer, any person directly or indirectly controlling or controlled by the issuer, or any person under direct or indirect common control with the issuer.

12. The term "dealer" means any person who engages either for all or part of his time, directly or indirectly, as agent, broker, or principal, in the business of offering, buying, selling, or otherwise dealing or trading in securities issued by another person.

13. The term "insurance company" means a company which is organized as an insurance company, whose primary and predominant business activity is the writing of insurance or the reinsuring of risks underwritten by insurance compa-nies, and which is subject to supervision by the insurance commissioner, or a similar official or agency, of a State or territory or the District of Columbia; or any receiver or sim-ilar official or any liquidating agent for such company, in his capacity as such.

14. The term "separate account" means an account established and maintained by an insurance company pursuant to the laws of any State or territory of the United States, the Dis-trict of Columbia, or of Canada or any province thereof, under which income, gains and losses, whether or not real-ized, from assets allocated to such account, are, in accor-dance with the applicable contract, credited to or charged against such account without regard to other income, gains, or losses of the insurance company.

15. The term "accredited investor" shall mean—

    i.   a bank as defined in section 3(a)(2) whether act-ing in its individual or fiduciary capacity; an in-surance company as defined in paragraph (13); an investment company registered under the Investment Company Act of 1940 or a business development company as defined in section 2(a)(48) of that Act); a Small Business Investment Company licensed by the Small Business Administration; or an employee benefit plan, including an individual retirement account, which is subject to the provisions of the Employee Retirement Income Security Act of 1974, if the investment decision is made by a plan fiduciary, as defined in section 3(21) of such Act), which is either a bank, insurance company, or registered investment adviser; or

    ii. any person who, on the basis of such factors as financial sophistication, net worth, knowledge, and experience in financial matters, or amount of assets under management qualifies as an accredited investor under rules and regulations which the Commission shall prescribe.

b. **Consideration of Promotion of Efficiency, Competition, and Capital Formation.** Whenever pursuant to this title the Commission is engaged in rulemaking and is required to consider or determine whether an action is necessary or appropriate in the public interest, the Commission shall also consider, in addition to the protection of investors, whether the action will promote efficiency, competition, and capital formation.

SECTION 3—CLASSES OF SECURITIES UNDER THIS TITLE

a. **Exempted securities.** Except as hereinafter expressly provided, the provisions of this subchapter shall not apply to any of the following classes of securities:

    1. Reserved.

    2. Any security issued or guaranteed by the United States or any territory thereof, or by the District of Columbia, or by any State of the United States, or by any political subdivision of a State or territory, or by any public instrumentality

of one or more States or territories, or by any person controlled or supervised by and acting as an instrumentality of the Government of the United States pursuant to authority granted by the Congress of the United States; or any certificate of deposit for any of the foregoing; or any security issued or guaranteed by any bank; or any security issued by or representing an interest in or a direct obligation of a Federal Reserve bank; or any interest or participation in any common trust fund or similar fund maintained by a bank exclusively for the collective investment and reinvestment of assets contributed thereto by such bank in its capacity as trustee, executor, administrator, or guardian; or any security which is an industrial development bond (as defined in section 103(c)(2) of the Internal Revenue Code of 1954) the interest on which is excludable from gross income under section 103(a)(1) of such Code if, by reason of the application of paragraph (4) or (6) of section 103(c) of such Code (determined as if paragraphs (4)(A), (5), and (7) were not included in such section 103(c)), paragraph (1) of such section 103(c) does not apply to such security; or any interest or participation in a single trust fund, or in a collective trust fund maintained by a bank, or any security arising out of a contract issued by an insurance company, which interest, participation, or security is issued in connection with

A. a stock bonus, pension, or profit-sharing plan which meets the requirements for qualification under section 401 of the Internal Revenue Code of 1954,

B. an annuity plan which meets the requirements for the deduction of the employer's contributions under section 404(a)(2) of such Code, or

C. a governmental plan as defined in section 414(d) of such Code which has been established by an employer for the exclusive benefit of its employees or their beneficiaries for the purpose of distributing to such employees or their beneficiaries the corpus and income of the funds accumulated under such plan, if under such plan it is impossible, prior to the satisfaction of all liabilities with respect to such employees and their beneficiaries, for any part of the corpus or income to be used for, or diverted to, purposes other than the exclusive benefit of such employees or their beneficiaries, other than any plan described in clause (A), (B), or (C) of this paragraph

    i.   the contributions under which are held in a single trust fund or in a separate account maintained by an insurance company for a single employer and under which an amount in excess of the employer's contribution is allocated to the purchase of securities (other than interests or participations in the trust or separate account itself) issued by the employer or any company directly or indirectly controlling, controlled by, or under common control with the employer,

    ii. which covers employees some or all of whom are employees within the meaning of section 401(c)(1) of such Code, or

    iii. which is a plan funded by an annuity contract described in section 403(b) of such Code.

The Commission, by rules and regulations or order, shall exempt from the provisions of section 5 of this Act any interest or participation issued in connection with a stock bonus, pension, profit-sharing, or annuity plan which covers employees some or all of whom are employees within the meaning of section 401(c)(1) of the Internal Revenue Code of 1954, if and to the extent that the Commission determines this to be necessary or appropriate in the public interest and consistent with the protection of investors and the purposes fairly intended by the policy and provisions of this subchapter. For purposes of this paragraph, a security issued or guaranteed by a bank shall not include any interest or participation any collective trust fund maintained by a bank; and the term "bank" means any national bank, or any banking institution organized under the laws of any State, Territory, or the District of Columbia, the business of which is substantially confined to banking and is supervised by the State or territorial banking commission or similar official; except that in the case of a common trust fund or similar fund, or a collective trust fund, the term "bank" has the same meaning as in the Investment Company Act of 1940;

3. Any note, draft, bill of exchange, or banker's acceptance which arises out of a current transaction or the proceeds of which have been or are to be used for current transactions, and which has a maturity at the time of issuance of not exceeding nine months, exclusive of days of grace, or any renewal thereof the maturity of which is likewise limited;

4. Any security issued by a person organized and operated exclusively for religious, educational, benevolent, fraternal, charitable, or reformatory purposes and not for pecuniary profit, and no part of the net earnings of which inures to the benefit of any person, private stockholder, or individual; or any security of a fund that is excluded from the definition of an investment company under section 3(c)(10)(B) of the Investment Company Act of 1940;

5. Any security issued (a) by a savings and loan association, building and loan association, cooperative bank, homestead association, or similar institution, which is supervised and examined by State or Federal authority having supervision over any such institution; or (b) by (i) a farmer's cooperative organization exempt from tax under section 521 of the Internal Revenue Code of 1954, (ii) a corporation described in section 501(c)(16) of such Code and exempt from tax under section 501(a) of such Code, or (iii) a corporation described in section 501(c)(2) of such Code which is exempt from tax under section 501(a) of such Code and is organized for the exclusive purpose of holding title to property, collecting income therefrom, and turning over the entire

amount thereof, less expenses, to an organization or corporation described in clause (i) or (ii);

6. Any interest in a railroad equipment trust. For purposes of this paragraph "interest in a railroad equipment trust" means any interest in an equipment trust, lease, conditional sales contract, or other similar arrangement entered into, issued, assumed, guaranteed by, or for the benefit of, a common carrier to finance the acquisition of rolling stock, including motive power;

7. Certificates issued by a receiver or by a trustee or debtor in possession in a case under title 11 of the United States Code, with the approval of the court;

8. Any insurance or endowment policy or annuity contract or optional annuity contract, issued by a corporation subject to the supervision of the insurance commissioner, bank commissioner, or any agency or officer performing like functions, of any State or Territory of the United States or the District of Columbia;

9. Except with respect to a security exchanged in a case under title 11 of the United States Code, any security exchanged by the issuer with its existing security holders exclusively where no commission or other remuneration is paid or given directly or indirectly for soliciting such exchange;

10. Except with respect to a security exchanged in a case under title 11 of the United States Code, any security which is issued in exchange for one or more bona fide outstanding securities, claims or property interests, or partly in such exchange and partly for cash, where the terms and conditions of such issuance and exchange are approved, after a hearing upon the fairness of such terms and conditions at which all persons to whom it is proposed to issue securities in such exchange shall have the right to appear, by any court, or by any official or agency of the United States, or by any State or Territorial banking or insurance commission or other governmental authority expressly authorized by law to grant such approval;

11. Any security which is a part of an issue offered and sold only to persons resident within a single State or Territory, where the issuer of such security is a person resident and doing business within or, if a corporation, incorporated by and doing business within, such State or Territory.

12. Any equity security issued in connection with the acquisition by a holding company of a bank under section 3(a) of the Bank Holding Company Act of 1956 or a savings association under section 10(e) of the Home Owners' Loan Act, if—

   A. the acquisition occurs solely as part of a reorganization in which security holders exchange their shares of a bank or savings association for shares of a newly formed holding company with no significant assets other than securities of the bank or savings association and the existing subsidiaries of the bank or savings association;

   B. the security holders receive, after that reorganization, substantially the same proportional share interests in the holding company as they held in the bank or savings association, except for nominal changes in shareholders' interests resulting from lawful elimination of fractional interests and the exercise of dissenting shareholders' rights under State or Federal law;

   C. the rights and interests of security holders in the holding company are substantially the same as those in the bank or savings association prior to the transaction, other than as may be required by law; and

   D. the holding company has substantially the same assets and liabilities, on a consolidated basis, as the bank or savings association had prior to the transaction.

   For purposes of this paragraph, the term "savings association" means a savings association (as defined in <u>section 3(b)</u> of the Federal Deposit Insurance Act) the deposits of which are insured by the Federal Deposit Insurance Corporation.

13. Any security issued by or any interest or participation in any church plan, company or account that is excluded from the definition of an investment company under <u>section 3(c)(14)</u>.

b. **Additional exemptions.** The Commission may from time to time by its rules and regulations, and subject to such terms and conditions as may be prescribed therein, add any class of securities to the securities exempted as provided in this section, if it finds that the enforcement of this subchapter with respect to such securities is not necessary in the public interest and for the protection of investors by reason of the small amount involved or the limited character of the public offering; but no issue of securities shall be exempted under this subsection where the aggregate amount at which such issue is offered to the public exceeds $5,000,000.

c. **Securities issued by small investment company.** The Commission may from time to time by its rules and regulations and subject to such terms and conditions as may be prescribed therein, add to the securities exempted as provided in this section any class of securities issued by a small business investment company under the <u>Small Business Investment Act of 1958</u> if it finds, having regard to the purposes of that Act, that the enforcement of this subchapter with respect to such securities is not necessary in the public interest and for the protection of investors.

SECTION 4—EXEMPTED TRANSACTIONS

The provisions of <u>section 5</u> shall not apply to—

1. transactions by any person other than an issuer, underwriter, or dealer.

2. transactions by an issuer not involving any public offering.

3. transactions by a dealer (including an underwriter no longer acting as an underwriter in respect of the security involved in such transaction), except—

A. transactions taking place prior to the expiration of forty days after the first date upon which the security was bona fide offered to the public by the issuer or by or through an underwriter,

B. transactions in a security as to which a registration statement has been filed taking place prior to the expiration of forty days after the effective date of such registration statement or prior to the expiration of forty days after the first date upon which the security was bona fide offered to the public by the issuer or by or through an underwriter after such effective date, whichever is later (excluding in the computation of such forty days any time during which a stop order issued under section 8 of this title is in effect as to the security), or such shorter period as the Commission may specify by rules and regulations or order, and

C. transactions as to securities constituting the whole or a part of an unsold allotment to or subscription by such dealer as a participant in the distribution of such securities by the issuer or by or through an underwriter.

With respect to transactions referred to in clause (B), if securities of the issuer have not previously been sold pursuant to an earlier effective registration statement the applicable period, instead of forty days, shall be ninety days, or such shorter period as the Commission may specify by rules and regulations or order.

4. brokers' transactions executed upon customers' orders on any exchange or in the over-the-counter market but not the solicitation of such orders.

5.

A. transactions involving offers or sales of one or more promissory notes directly secured by a first lien on a single parcel of real estate upon which is located a dwelling or other residential or commercial structure, and participation interests in such notes—

    i. where such securities are originated by a savings and loan association, savings bank, commercial bank, or similar banking institution which is supervised and examined by a Federal or State authority, and are offered and sold subject to the following conditions:

        a. the minimum aggregate sales price per purchaser shall not be less than $250,000;

        b. the purchaser shall pay cash either at the time of the sale or within sixty days thereof; and

        c. each purchaser shall buy for his own account only; or

    ii. where such securities are originated by a mortgagee approved by the Secretary of Housing and Urban Development pursuant to sections 203 and 211 of the National Housing Act and are offered or sold subject to the three conditions specified in subparagraph (A)(i) to any institution described in such subparagraph or to any insurance company subject to the supervision of the insurance commissioner, or any agency or officer performing like function, of any State or territory of the United States or the District of Columbia, or the Federal Home Loan Mortgage Corporation, the Federal National Mortgage Association, or the Government National Mortgage Association.

  B. transactions between any of the entities described in subparagraph (A)(i) or (A)(ii) involving non-assignable contracts to buy or sell the foregoing securities which are to be completed within two years, where the seller of the foregoing securities pursuant to any such contract is one of the parties described in subparagraph (A)(i) or (A)(ii) who may originate such securities and the purchaser of such securities pursuant to any such contract is any institution described in subparagraph (A)(i) or any insurance company described in subparagraph (A)(ii), the Federal Home Loan Mortgage Corporation, Federal National Mortgage Association, or the Government National Mortgage Association and where the foregoing securities are subject to the three conditions for sale set forth in subparagraphs (A)(i)(a) through (c).

C.   The exemption provided by subparagraphs (A) and (B) shall not apply to resales of the securities acquired pursuant thereto, unless each of the conditions for sale contained in subparagraphs (A)(i)(a) through (c) are satisfied.

6.   transactions involving offers or sales by an issuer solely to one or more accredited investors, if the aggregate offering price of an issue of securities offered in reliance on this paragraph does not exceed the amount allowed under section 3(b), if there is no advertising or public solicitation in connection with the transaction by the issuer or anyone acting on the issuer's behalf, and if the issuer files such notice with the Commission as the Commission shall prescribe.

SECTION 5—PROHIBITIONS RELATING TO INTERSTATE COMMERCE AND THE MAILS

a.   **Sale or delivery after sale of unregistered securities.** Unless a registration statement is in effect as to a security, it shall be unlawful for any person, directly or indirectly—

1.   to make use of any means or instruments of transportation or communication in interstate commerce or of the mails to sell such security through the use or medium of any prospectus or otherwise; or

      2. to carry or cause to be carried through the mails or in interstate commerce, by any means or instruments of transportation, any such security for the purpose of sale or for delivery after sale.

b. **Necessity of prospectus meeting requirements of section 10.** It shall be unlawful for any person, directly or indirectly—

      1. to make use of any means or instruments of transportation or communication in interstate commerce or of the mails to carry or transmit any prospectus relating to any security with respect to which a registration statement has been filed under this title, unless such prospectus meets the requirements of section 10; or

      2. to carry or cause to be carried through the mails or in interstate commerce any such security for the purpose of sale or for delivery after sale, unless accompanied or preceded by a prospectus that meets the requirements of subsection (a) of section 10.

c. **Necessity of filing registration statement.** It shall be unlawful for any person, directly or indirectly, to make use of any means or instruments of transportation or communication in interstate commerce or of the mails to offer to sell or offer to buy through the use or medium of any prospectus or otherwise any security, unless a registration statement has been filed as to such security, or while the registration statement is the subject of a refusal order or stop order or (prior to the effective date of the registration statement) any public proceeding or examination under section 8.

SECTION 6—REGISTRATION OF SECURITIES

a. **Method of registration.** Any security may be registered with the Commission under the terms and conditions hereinafter provided, by filing a registration statement in triplicate, at least one of which shall be signed by each issuer, its principal executive officer or officers, its principal financial officer, its comptroller or principal accounting officer, and the majority of its board of directors or persons performing similar functions (or, if there is no board of

directors or persons performing similar functions, by the majority
of the persons or board having the power of management of the
issuer), and in case the issuer is a foreign or Territorial person by
its duly authorized representative in the United States; except that
when such registration statement relates to a security issued by
a foreign government, or political subdivision thereof, it need be
signed only by the underwriter of such security. Signatures of all
such persons when written on the said registration statements shall
be presumed to have been so written by authority of the person
whose signature is so affixed and the burden of proof, in the event
such authority shall be denied, shall be upon the party denying
the same. The affixing of any signature without the authority of the
purported signer shall constitute a violation of this title. A registration statement shall be deemed effective only as to the securities specified therein as proposed to be offered.

b. **Registration Fee.**

1. **Recovery of cost of services.** The commission shall, in
    accordance with this subsection, collect registration fees
    that are designed to recover the costs to the government of
    the securities registration process, and costs related to such
    process, including enforcement activities, policy and rule-
    making activities, administration, legal services, and inter-
    national regulatory activities.

2. **Fee payment required.** At the time of filing a registration
    statement, the applicant shall pay to the Commission a fee
    that shall be equal to the sum of the amounts (if any) deter-
    mined under the rates established by paragraphs (3) and (4).
    The commission shall publish in the Federal Register
    notices of the fee rates applicable under this section for
    each fiscal year.

3. **General revenue fees.** The rate determined under this
    paragraph is a rate equal to $200 per $1,000,000 of the
    maximum aggregate price at which such activities are pro-
    posed to be offered, except that during fiscal year 2007
    and any succeeding fiscal year such rate is equal to $67 per
    $1,000,000 of the maximum aggregate price at which such
    securities are proposed to be offered. Fees collected during

any fiscal year pursuant to this paragraph shall be deposited and credited as general revenues of the Treasury.

4. **Offsetting collection fees.**

   A. **In general.** Except as provided in subparagraphs (B) and (C), the rate determined under this paragraph is a rate equal to the following amount per $1,000,000 of the maximum aggregate price at which such securities are proposed to be offered:

      i. $95 during fiscal year 1998;

      ii. $78 during fiscal year 1999;

      iii. $64 during fiscal year 2000;

      iv. $50 during fiscal year 2001;

      v. $39 during fiscal year 2002;

      vi. $28 during fiscal year 2003;

      vii. $9 during fiscal year 2004;

      viii. $5 during fiscal year 2005;

      ix. $0 during fiscal year 2006 or any succeeding fiscal year.

   B. **Limitation; deposit.** Except as provided in subparagraph (C), no amounts shall be collected pursuant to this paragraph (4) for any fiscal year except to the extent provided in advance in appropriation Acts. Fees collected during any fiscal year pursuant to this paragraph shall be deposited and credited as offsetting collections in accordance with appropriations Acts.

   C. **Lapse of appropriations.** If on the first day of a fiscal year a regular appropriation to the Commission has not been enacted, the Commission shall continue to collect fees (as offsetting collections) under this paragraph at the rate in effect during the preceding fiscal year, until such a regular appropriation is enacted.

    5. **Pro rata application of rates.** The rates required by this subsection shall be applied pro rata to amounts and balances equal to less than $1,000,000.

c. **Time registration effective.** The filing with the Commission of a registration statement, or of an amendment to a registration statement, shall be deemed to have taken place upon the receipt thereof, but the filing of a registration statement shall not be deemed to have taken place unless it is accompanied by a United States postal money order or a certified bank check or cash for the amount of the fee required under subsection (b).

d. **Information available to public.** The information contained in or filed with any registration statement shall be made available to the public under such regulations as the Commission may prescribe, and copies thereof, photostatic or otherwise, shall be furnished to every applicant at such reasonable charge as the Commission may prescribe.

SECTION 7—INFORMATION REQUIRED IN REGISTRATION STATEMENT

a. The registration statement, when relating to a security other than a security issued by a foreign government, or political subdivision thereof, shall contain the information, and be accompanied by the documents, specified in Schedule A, and when relating to a security issued by a foreign government, or political subdivision thereof, shall contain the information, and be accompanied by the documents, specified in Schedule B; except that the Commission may by rules or regulations provide that any such information or document need not be included in respect of any class of issuers or securities if it finds that the requirement of such information or document is inapplicable to such class and that disclosure fully adequate for the protection of investors is otherwise required to be included within the registration statement. If any accountant, engineer, or appraiser, or any person whose profession gives authority to a statement made by him, is named as having prepared or certified any part of the registration statement, or is named as having prepared or certified a report or valuation for use in connection with the registration statement, the written consent of such person shall be filed with the registration statement. If any such person is named as having prepared or certified a report or valuation (other than a public official document or statement) which is used in connection with the registration statement, but is not named as having prepared or certified such report or valuation for use in connection with the registration statement, the written consent of such person shall be filed with the registration statement unless the Commission dispenses with such filing as impracticable or as involving undue hardship on the person filing the registration statement. Any such registration statement shall contain such other information, and be accompanied by such other documents, as the Commission may by rules or regulations require as being necessary or appropriate in the public interest or for the protection of investors.

b.

1. The Commission shall prescribe special rules with respect to registration statements filed by any issuer that is a blank check company. Such rules may, as the Commission determines necessary or appropriate in the public interest or for the protection of investors—

    A. require such issuers to provide timely disclosure, prior to or after such statement becomes effective under section 8, of (i) information regarding the company to be acquired and the specific application of the proceeds of the offering, or (ii) additional information necessary to prevent such statement from being misleading;

    B. place limitations on the use of such proceeds and the distribution of securities by such issuer until the disclosures required under subparagraph (A) have been made; and

    C. provide a right of rescission to shareholders of such securities.

2. The Commission may, as it determines consistent with the public interest and the protection of investors, by rule or order exempt any issuer or class of issuers from the rules prescribed under paragraph (1).

3. For purposes of paragraph (1) of this subsection, the term "blank check company" means any development stage company that is issuing a penny stock (within the meaning of section 3 (a)(51) of the Securities Exchange Act of 1934) and that—

   A. has no specific business plan or purpose; or

   B. has indicated that its business plan is to merge with an unidentified company or companies.

SECTION 8—TAKING EFFECT OF REGISTRATION STATEMENTS AND AMENDMENTS THERETO

a. **Effective date of registration statement.** Except as hereinafter provided, the effective date of a registration statement shall be the twentieth day after the filing thereof or such earlier date as the Commission may determine, having due regard to the adequacy of the information respecting the issuer theretofore available to the public, to the facility with which the nature of the securities to be registered, their relationship to the capital structure of the issuer and the rights of holders thereof can be understood, and to the public interest and the protection of investors. If any amendment to any such statement is filed prior to the effective date of such statement, the registration statement shall be deemed to have been filed when such amendment was filed; except that an amendment filed with the consent of the Commission, prior to the effective date of the registration statement, or filed pursuant to an order of the Commission, shall be treated as a part of the registration statement.

b. **Incomplete or inaccurate registration statement.** If it appears to the Commission that a registration statement is on its face incomplete or inaccurate in any material respect, the Commission may, after notice by personal service or the sending of confirmed telegraphic notice not later than ten days after the filing of the registration statement, and opportunity for hearing (at a time fixed by the Commission) within ten days after such notice by personal service or the sending of such telegraphic notice, issue an order prior to the effective date of registration refusing to permit such statement to become effective until it has been amended in accordance with such order. When such statement has been amended in accordance with such order the Commission shall so declare and the registration shall become effective at the time provided in subsection (a) of this section or upon the date of such declaration, whichever date is the later.

c. **Effective date of amendment to registration statement.** An amendment filed after the effective date of the registration statement, if such amendment, upon its face, appears to the Commission not to be incomplete or inaccurate in any material respect, shall become effective on such date as the Commission may determine, having due regard to the public interest and the protection of investors.

d. **Untrue statements or omissions in registration statement.** If it appears to the Commission at any time that the registration statement includes any untrue statement of a material fact or omits to state any material fact required to be stated therein or necessary to make the statements therein not misleading, the Commission may, after notice by personal service or the sending of confirmed telegraphic notice, and after opportunity for hearing (at a time fixed by the Commission) within fifteen days after such notice by personal service or the sending of such telegraphic notice, issue a stop order suspending the effectiveness of the registration statement. When such statement has been amended in accordance with such stop order, the Commission shall so declare and thereupon the stop order shall cease to be effective.

e. **Examination for issuance of stop order.** The Commission is empowered to make an examination in any case in order to determine whether a stop order should issue under subsection (d) of this section. In making such examination the Commission or any officer or officers designated by it shall have access to and may demand the production of any books and papers of, and may administer oaths and affirmations to and examine, the issuer, underwriter, or any other person, in respect of any matter relevant to the examination, and may, in its discretion, require the production of a balance sheet exhibiting the assets and liabilities of the issuer, or its income statement, or both, to be certified to by a public or certified accountant approved by the Commission. If the issuer or underwriter shall fail to cooperate, or shall obstruct or refuse to permit the making of an examination, such conduct shall be proper ground for the issuance of a stop order.

f. **Notice requirements.** Any notice required under this section shall be sent to or served on the issuer, or, in case of a foreign government or political subdivision thereof, to or on the underwriter, or, in the case of a foreign or Territorial person, to or on its duly authorized representative in the United States named in the registration statement, properly directed in each case of telegraphic notice to the address given in such statement.

SECTION 8A—CEASE-AND-DESIST PROCEEDINGS

a. **Authority of the Commission.** If the Commission finds, after notice and opportunity for hearing, that any person is violating, has violated, or is about to violate any provision of this title, or any rule or regulation thereunder, the Commission may publish its findings and enter an order requiring such person, and any other person that is, was, or would be a cause of the violation, due to an act or omission the person knew or should have known would contribute to such violation, to cease and desist from committing or causing such violation and any future violation of the same provision, rule, or regulation. Such order may, in addition to requiring a person to cease and desist from committing or causing a violation, require such person to comply, or to take steps to effect compliance, with such provision, rule, or regulation, upon such terms and conditions and within such time as the Commission may specify in such order. Any such order may, as the Commission deems appropriate, require future compliance or steps to effect future compliance, either permanently or for such period of time as the Commission may specify, with such provision, rule, or regulation with respect to any security, any issuer, or any other person.

b. **Hearing.** The notice instituting proceedings pursuant to subsection (a) of this section shall fix a hearing date not earlier than 30 days nor later than 60 days after service of the notice unless an earlier or a later date is set by the Commission with the consent of any respondent so served.

c. **Temporary order.**

   1. **In general.** Whenever the Commission determines that the alleged violation or threatened violation specified in the

notice instituting proceedings pursuant to <u>subsection (a)</u> of this section, or the continuation thereof, is likely to result in significant dissipation or conversion of assets, significant harm to investors, or substantial harm to the public inter- est, including, but not limited to, losses to the Securities Investor Protection Corporation, prior to the completion of the proceedings, the Commission may enter a temporary order requiring the respondent to cease and desist from the violation or threatened violation and to take such action to prevent the violation or threatened violation and to prevent dissipation or conversion of assets, significant harm to investors, or substantial harm to the public interest as the Commission deems appropriate pending completion of such proceeding. Such an order shall be entered only after notice and opportunity for a hearing, unless the Commis- sion determines that notice and hearing prior to entry would be impracticable or contrary to the public interest. A temporary order shall become effective upon service upon the respondent and, unless set aside, limited, or sus- pended by the Commission or a court of competent juris- diction, shall remain effective and enforceable pending the completion of the proceedings.

2. **Applicability.** This subsection shall apply only to a respon- dent that acts, or, at the time of the alleged misconduct acted, as a broker, dealer, investment adviser, investment company, municipal securities dealer, government securi- ties broker, government securities dealer, or transfer agent, or is, or was at the time of the alleged misconduct, an asso- ciated person of, or a person seeking to become associated with, any of the foregoing.

d. **Review of Temporary Orders.**

1. **Commission review.** At any time after the respondent has been served with a temporary cease-and-desist order pur- suant to subsection (c) of this section, the respondent may apply to the Commission to have the order set aside, lim- ited, or suspended. If the respondent has been served with a temporary cease-and-desist order entered without a prior

Commission hearing, the respondent may, within 10 days after the date on which the order was served, request a hearing on such application and the Commission shall hold a hearing and render a decision on such application at the earliest possible time.

2. **Judicial review.** Within—

   A. 10 days after the date the respondent was served with a temporary cease-and-desist order entered with a prior Commission hearing, or

   B. 10 days after the Commission renders a decision on an application and hearing under paragraph (1), with respect to any temporary cease-and-desist order entered without a prior Commission hearing, the respondent may apply to the United States district court for the district in which the respondent resides or has its principal place of business, or for the District of Columbia, for an order setting aside, limiting, or suspending the effectiveness or enforcement of the order, and the court shall have jurisdiction to enter such an order. A respondent served with a temporary cease-and-desist order entered without a prior Commission hearing may not apply to the court except after hearing and decision by the Commission on the respondent's application under paragraph (1) of this subsection.

3. **No automatic stay of temporary order.** The commencement of proceedings under paragraph (2) of this subsection shall not, unless specifically ordered by the court, operate as a stay of the Commission's order.

4. **Exclusive review.** Section 9(a) shall not apply to a temporary order entered pursuant to this section.

e. **Authority to enter order requiring accounting and disgorgement.** In any cease-and-desist proceeding under subsection (a) of this section, the Commission may enter an order requiring accounting and disgorgement, including reasonable interest. The Commission is authorized to adopt rules, regulations, and orders concerning payments to investors, rates of interest, periods of accrual, and such other matters as it deems appropriate to implement this subsection.

SECTION 9—COURT REVIEW OF ORDERS

a.   Any person aggrieved by an order of the Commission may obtain a review of such order in the court of appeals of the United States, within any circuit wherein such person resides or has his principal place of business, or in the United States Court of Appeals for the District of Columbia, by filing in such Court, within sixty days after the entry of such order, a written petition praying that the order of the Commission be modified or be set aside in whole or in part. A copy of such petition shall be forthwith transmitted by the clerk of the court to the Commission, and thereupon the Commission shall file in the court the record upon which the order complained of was entered, as provided in section 2112 of Title 28. No objection to the order of the Commission shall be considered by the court unless such objection shall have been urged before the Commission. The finding of the Commission as to the facts, if supported by evidence, shall be conclusive. If either party shall apply to the court for leave to adduce additional evidence, and shall show to the satisfaction of the court that such additional evidence is material and that there were reasonable grounds for failure to adduce such evidence in the hearing before the Commission, the court may order such additional evidence to be taken before the Commission and to be adduced upon the hearing in such manner and upon such terms and conditions as to the court may seem proper. The Commission may modify its findings as to the facts, by reason of the additional evidence so taken, and it shall file such modified or new findings, which, if supported by evidence, shall be conclusive, and its recommendation, if any, for the modification or setting aside of the original order. The jurisdiction of the court shall be exclusive and its judgment and decree, affirming, modifying, or setting aside, in whole or in part, any order of the Commission, shall be final, subject to review by the Supreme Court of the United States upon certiorari or certification as provided in section 1254 of Title 28.

b. The commencement of proceedings under subsection (a) of this section shall not, unless specifically ordered by the court, operate as a stay of the Commission's order.

SECTION 10—INFORMATION REQUIRED IN PROSPECTUS

a. **Information in registration statement; documents not required.** Except to the extent otherwise permitted or required pursuant to this subsection or subsections (c), (d), or (e) of this section—

1. a prospectus relating to a security other than a security issued by a foreign government or political subdivision thereof, shall contain the information contained in the registration statement, but it need not include the documents referred to in paragraphs (28) to (32), inclusive, of Schedule A;

2. a prospectus relating to a security issued by a foreign government or political subdivision thereof shall contain the information contained in the registration statement, but it need not include the documents referred to in paragraphs (13) and (14) of Schedule B;

3. notwithstanding the provisions of paragraphs (1) and (2) of this subsection when a prospectus is used more than nine months after the effective date of the registration statement, the information contained therein shall be as of a date not more than sixteen months prior to such use, so far as such information is known to the user of such prospectus or can be furnished by such user without unreasonable effort or expense;

4. there may be omitted from any prospectus any of the information required under this subsection which the Commission may by rules or regulations designate as not being necessary or appropriate in the public interest or for the protection of investors.

b. **Summarizations and omissions allowed by rules and regulations.** In addition to the prospectus permitted or required in subsection (a) of this section, the Commission shall by rules or regulations deemed necessary or appropriate in the public interest or for the protection of investors permit the use of a prospectus for the purposes of sub-section (b)(1) of section 5 which omits in part or summarizes information in the prospectus specified in subsection (a) of this section. A prospectus permitted under this subsection shall, except to the extent the Commission by rules or regulations deemed necessary or appropriate in the public interest or for the protection of investors otherwise provides, be filed as part of the registration statement but shall not be deemed a part of such registration statement for the purposes of section 11 of this title. The Commission may at any time issue an order preventing or suspending the use of a prospectus permitted under this subsection, if it has reason to believe that such prospectus has not been filed (if required to be filed as part of the registration statement) or includes any untrue statement of a material fact or omits to state any material fact required to be stated therein or necessary to make the statements therein, in the light of the circumstances under which such prospectus is or is to be used, not misleading. Upon issuance of an order under this subsection, the Commission shall give notice of the issuance of such order and opportunity for hearing by personal service or the sending of confirmed telegraphic notice. The Commission shall vacate or modify the order at any time for good cause or if such prospectus has been filed or amended in accordance with such order.

c. **Additional information required by rules and regulations.** Any prospectus shall contain such other information as the Commission may by rules or regulations require as being necessary or appropriate in the public interest or for the protection of investors.

d. **Classification of prospectuses.** In the exercise of its powers under subsections (a), (b), or (c) of this section, the Commission shall have authority to classify prospectuses according to the nature and circumstances of their use or the nature of the security, issue, issuer, or otherwise, and, by rules and regulations and subject to such terms and conditions as it shall specify therein, to prescribe as to each class the form and contents which it may find appropriate and consistent with the public interest and the protection of investors.

e. **Information in conspicuous part of prospectus.** The statements or information required to be included in a prospectus by or under authority of subsections (a), (b), (c), or (d) of this section, when written, shall be placed in a conspicuous part of the prospectus and, except as otherwise permitted by rules or regulations, in type as large as that used generally in the body of the prospectus.

f. **Prospectus consisting of radio or television broadcast.** In any case where a prospectus consists of a radio or television broadcast, copies thereof shall be filed with the Commission under such rules and regulations as it shall prescribe. The Commission may by rules and regulations require the filing with it of forms and prospectuses used in connection with the offer or sale of securities registered under this title.

SECTION 11—CIVIL LIABILITIES ON ACCOUNT OF FALSE REGISTRATION STATEMENT

a. **Persons possessing cause of action; persons liable.** In case any part of the registration statement, when such part became effective, contained an untrue statement of a material fact or omitted to state a material fact required to be stated therein or necessary to make the statements therein not misleading, any person acquiring such security (unless it is proved that at the time of such acquisition he knew of such untruth or omission) may, either at law or in equity, in any court of competent jurisdiction, sue—

　　1. every person who signed the registration statement;

　　2. every person who was a director of (or person performing similar functions) or partner in the issuer at the time of the filing of the part of the registration statement with respect to which his liability is asserted;

　　3. every person who, with his consent, is named in the registration statement as being or about to become a director, person performing similar functions, or partner;

　　4. every accountant, engineer, or appraiser, or any person whose profession gives authority to a statement made by him, who has with his consent been named as having prepared or certified any part of the registration statement, or

as having prepared or certified any report or valuation which is used in connection with the registration statement, with respect to the statement in such registration statement, report, or valuation, which purports to have been prepared or certified by him;

5. every underwriter with respect to such security.

If such person acquired the security after the issuer has made generally available to its security holders an earning statement covering a period of at least twelve months beginning after the effective date of the registration statement, then the right of recovery under this subsection shall be conditioned on proof that such person acquired the security relying upon such untrue statement in the registration statement or relying upon the registration statement and not knowing of such omission, but such reliance may be established without proof of the reading of the registration statement by such person.

b. **Persons exempt from liability upon proof of issues.** Notwithstanding the provisions of subsection (a) of this section no person, other than the issuer, shall be liable as provided therein who shall sustain the burden of proof—

1. that before the effective date of the part of the registration statement with respect to which his liability is asserted (A) he had resigned from or had taken such steps as are permitted by law to resign from, or ceased or refused to act in, every office, capacity, or relationship in which he was described in the registration statement as acting or agreeing to act, and (B) he had advised the Commission and the issuer in writing that he had taken such action and that he would not be responsible for such part of the registration statement; or

2. that if such part of the registration statement became effective without his knowledge, upon becoming aware of such fact he forthwith acted and advised the Commission, in accordance with paragraph (1) of this subsection, and, in addition, gave reasonable public notice that such part of the registration statement had become effective without his knowledge; or

3. that (A) as regards any part of the registration statement not purporting to be made on the authority of an expert, and not purporting to be a copy of or extract from a report or valuation of an expert, and not purporting to be made on the authority of a public official document or statement, he had, after reasonable investigation, reasonable ground to believe and did believe, at the time such part of the registration statement became effective, that the statements therein were true and that there was no omission to state a material fact required to be stated therein or necessary to make the statements therein not misleading; and (B) as regards any part of the registration statement purporting to be made upon his authority as an expert or purporting to be a copy of or extract from a report or valuation of himself as an expert, (i) he had, after reasonable investigation, reasonable ground to believe and did believe, at the time such part of the registration statement became effective, that the statements therein were true and that there was no omission to state a material fact required to be stated therein or necessary to make the statements therein not misleading, or (ii) such part of the registration statement did not fairly represent his statement as an expert or was not a fair copy of or extract from his report or valuation as an expert; and (C) as regards any part of the registration statement purporting to be made on the authority of an expert (other than himself) or purporting to be a copy of or extract from a report or valuation of an expert (other than himself), he had no reasonable ground to believe and did not believe, at the time such part of the registration statement became effective, that the statements therein were untrue or that there was an omission to state a material fact required to be stated therein or necessary to make the statements therein not misleading, or that such part of the registration statement did not fairly represent the statement of the expert or was not a fair copy of or extract from the report or valuation of the expert; and (D) as regards any part of the registration statement purporting to be a statement made by an official person or purporting to be a copy of or extract from a public official document, he had no reasonable ground to believe

and did not believe, at the time such part of the registration statement became effective, that the statements therein were untrue, or that there was an omission to state a material fact required to be stated therein or necessary to make the statements therein not misleading, or that such part of the registration statement did not fairly represent the statement made by the official person or was not a fair copy of or extract from the public official document.

c. **Standard of reasonableness.** In determining, for the purpose of paragraph (3) of subsection (b) of this section, what constitutes reasonable investigation and reasonable ground for belief, the standard of reasonableness shall be that required of a prudent man in the management of his own property.

d. **Effective date of registration statement with regard to underwriters.** If any person becomes an underwriter with respect to the security after the part of the registration statement with respect to which his liability is asserted has become effective, then for the purposes of paragraph (3) of subsection (b) of this section such part of the registration statement shall be considered as having become effective with respect to such person as of the time when he became an underwriter.

e. **Measure of damages; undertaking for payment of costs.** The suit authorized under subsection (a) of this section may be to recover such damages as shall represent the difference between the amount paid for the security (not exceeding the price at which the security was offered to the public) and (1) the value thereof as of the time such suit was brought, or (2) the price at which such security shall have been disposed of in the market before suit, or (3) the price at which such security shall have been disposed of after suit but before judgment if such damages shall be less than the damages representing the difference between the amount paid for the security (not exceeding the price at which the security was offered to the public) and the value thereof as of the time such suit was brought: Provided, That if the defendant proves that any portion or all of such damages represents other than the depreciation in value of such security resulting from such part of the registration statement, with respect to which his liability is asserted, not being true or omitting to state a material fact required to be stated therein or necessary to make the statements therein not misleading, such portion of or all such damages shall not be recoverable. In no event shall any underwriter (unless such underwriter shall have knowingly received from the issuer for acting as an underwriter some benefit, directly or indirectly, in which all other underwriters similarly situated did not share in proportion to their respective interests in the underwriting) be liable in any suit or as a consequence of suits authorized under subsection (a) of this section for damages in excess of the total price at which the securities underwritten by him and distributed to the public were offered to the public. In any suit under this or any other section of this title the court may, in its discretion, require an undertaking for the payment of the costs of such suit, including reasonable attorney's fees, and if judgment shall be rendered against a party litigant, upon the motion of the other party litigant, such costs may be assessed in favor of such party litigant (whether or not such undertaking has been required) if the court believes the suit or the defense to have been without merit, in an amount sufficient to reimburse him for the reasonable expenses incurred by him, in connection with such suit, such costs to be taxed in the manner usually provided for taxing of costs in the court in which the suit was heard.

f.   **Joint and several liability; liability of outside director.**

     1.   Except as provided in paragraph (2), all or any one or more of the persons specified in subsection (a) of this section shall be jointly and severally liable, and every person who becomes liable to make any payment under this section may recover contribution as in cases of contract from any person who, if sued separately, would have been liable to make the same payment, unless the person who has become liable was, and the other was not, guilty of fraudulent misrepresentation.

     2.

         A.   The liability of an outside director under subsection (e) shall be determined in accordance with section 21D(f) of the Securities Exchange Act of 1934.

        B. For purposes of this paragraph, the term "outside director" shall have the meaning given such term by rule or regulation of the Commission.

g. **Offering price to public as maximum amount recoverable.** In no case shall the amount recoverable under this section exceed the price at which the security was offered to the public.

SECTION 12—CIVIL LIABILITIES ARISING IN CONNECTION WITH PROSPECTUSES AND COMMUNICATIONS

a. **In General.** Any person who—

    1. offers or sells a security in violation of <u>section 5</u>, or

    2. offers or sells a security (whether or not exempted by the provisions of <u>section 3</u>, other than <u>paragraph (2)</u> of subsection (a) of said section), by the use of any means or instruments of transportation or communication in interstate commerce or of the mails, by means of a prospectus or oral communication, which includes an untrue statement of a material fact or omits to state a material fact necessary in order to make the statements, in the light of the circumstances under which they were made, not misleading (the purchaser not knowing of such untruth or omission), and who shall not sustain the burden of proof that he did not know, and in the exercise of reasonable care could not have known, of such untruth or omission, shall be liable, subject to subsection (b), to the person purchasing such security from him, who may sue either at law or in equity in any court of competent jurisdiction, to recover the consideration paid for such security with interest thereon, less the amount of any income received thereon, upon the tender of such security, or for damages if he no longer owns the security.

b. **Loss Causation.**—In an action described in subsection (a)(2), if the person who offered or sold such security proves that any portion or all of the amount recoverable under subsection (a)(2) represents other than the depreciation in value of the subject security resulting from such part of the prospectus or oral communication, with respect to which the liability of that person is asserted, not being true or omitting to state a material fact required to be stated therein or necessary to make the statement not misleading, then such portion or amount, as the case may be, shall not be recoverable.

SECTION 13—LIMITATION OF ACTIONS

No action shall be maintained to enforce any liability created under section 11 or 12(a)(2) unless brought within one year after the discovery of the untrue statement or the omission, or after such discovery should have been made by the exercise of reasonable diligence, or, if the action is to enforce a liability created under section 12(a)(1), unless brought within one year after the violation upon which it is based. In no event shall any such action be brought to enforce a liability created under section 11 or 12(a)(1) more than three years after the security was bona fide offered to the public, or under section 12(a)(2) more than three years after the sale.

SECTION 14—CONTRARY STIPULATIONS VOID

Any condition, stipulation, or provision binding any person acquiring any security to waive compliance with any provision of this title or of the rules and regulations of the Commission shall be void.

SECTION 15—LIABILITY OF CONTROLLING PERSONS

Every person who, by or through stock ownership, agency, or otherwise, or who, pursuant to or in connection with an agreement or understanding with one or more other persons by or through stock ownership, agency, or otherwise, controls any person liable under sections 11 or 12, shall also be liable jointly and severally with and to the same extent as such controlled person to any person to whom such controlled person is liable, unless the controlling person had no knowledge of or reasonable ground to believe in the existence of the facts by reason of which the liability of the controlled person is alleged to exist.

SECTION 16—ADDITIONAL REMEDIES; LIMITATION ON REMEDIES

a. **Remedies additional.** Except as provided in subsection (b), the rights and remedies provided by this subchapter shall be in addition to any and all other rights and remedies that may exist at law or in equity.

b. **Class action limitations.** No covered class action based upon the statutory or common law of any State or subdivision thereof may be maintained in any State or Federal court by any private party alleging—

    1. an untrue statement or omission of a material fact in connection with the purchase or sale of a covered security; or

    2. that the defendant used or employed any manipulative or deceptive device or contrivance in connection with the purchase or sale of a covered security.

c. **Removal of covered class actions.** Any covered class action brought in any State court involving a covered security, as set forth in subsection (b), shall be removable to the Federal district court for the district in which the action is pending, and shall be subject to subsection (b).

d. **Preservation of certain actions.**

    1. **Actions under State law of State of incorporation.**

        A. **Actions preserved.** Notwithstanding subsection (b) or (c), a covered class action described in subparagraph (B) of this paragraph that is based upon the statutory or common law of the State in which the issuer is incorporated (in the case of a corporation) or organized (in the case of any other entity) may be maintained in a State or Federal court by a private party.

        B. **Permissible actions.** A covered class action is described in this subparagraph if it involves—

            i. the purchase or sale of securities by the issuer or an affiliate of the issuer exclusively from or to holders of equity securities of the issuer; or

    ii. any recommendation, position, or other communication with respect to the sale of securities of the issuer that—

        I. is made by or on behalf of the issuer or an affiliate of the issuer to holders of equity securities of the issuer; and

        II. concerns decisions of those equity holders with respect to voting their securities, acting in response to a tender or exchange offer, or exercising dissenters' or appraisal rights.

2. **State actions.**

    A. **In general.** Notwithstanding any other provision of this section, nothing in this section may be construed to preclude a State or political subdivision thereof or a State pension plan from bringing an action involving a covered security on its own behalf, or as a member of a class comprised solely of other States, political subdivisions, or State pension plans that are named plaintiffs, and that have authorized participation, in such action.

    B. **State pension plan defined.** For purposes of this paragraph, the term "State pension plan" means a pension plan established and maintained for its employees by the government of the State or political subdivision thereof, or by any agency or instrumentality thereof.

3. **Actions under contractual agreements between issuers and indenture trustees.** Notwithstanding subsection (b) or (c), a covered class action that seeks to enforce a contractual agreement between an issuer and an indenture trustee may be maintained in a State or Federal court by a party to the agreement or a successor to such party.

4. **Remand of removed actions.** In an action that has been removed from a State court pursuant to subsection (c), if the Federal court determines that the action may be maintained in State court pursuant to this subsection, the Federal court shall remand such action to such State court.

e. **Preservation of State jurisdiction.** The securities commission (or any agency or office performing like functions) of any State shall retain jurisdiction under the laws of such State to investigate and bring enforcement actions.

f. **Definitions.** For purposes of this section, the following definitions shall apply:

1. **Affiliate of the issuer.** The term "affiliate of the issuer" means a person that directly or indirectly, through one or more intermediaries, controls or is controlled by or is under common control with, the issuer.

2. **Covered class action—**

   A. **In general.** The term "covered class action" means—

      i. any single lawsuit in which—

         I. damages are sought on behalf of more than 50 persons or prospective class members, and questions of law or fact common to those persons or members of the prospective class, without reference to issues of individualized reliance on an alleged misstatement or omission, predominate over any questions affecting only individual persons or members; or

         II. one or more named parties seek to recover damages on a representative basis on behalf of themselves and other unnamed parties similarly situated, and questions of law or fact common to those persons or members of the prospective class predominate over any questions affecting only individual persons or members; or

   ii. any group of lawsuits filed in or pending in the same court and involving common questions of law or fact, in which—

      I. damages are sought on behalf of more than 50 persons; and

      II. the lawsuits are joined, consolidated, or otherwise proceed as a single action for any purpose.

B. **Exception for derivative actions.** Notwithstanding subparagraph (A), the term "covered class action" does not include an exclusively derivative action brought by one or more shareholders on behalf of a corporation.

C. **Counting of certain class members.** For purposes of this paragraph, a corporation, investment company, pension plan, partnership, or other entity, shall be treated as one person or prospective class member, but only if the entity is not established for the purpose of participating in the action.

D. **Rule of construction.** Nothing in this paragraph shall be construed to affect the discretion of a State court in determining whether actions filed in such court should be joined, consolidated, or otherwise allowed to proceed as a single action.

3. **Covered security.** The term "covered security" means a security that satisfies the standards for a covered security specified in paragraph (1) or (2) of section 18(b) of this title at the time during which it is alleged that the misrepresentation, omission, or manipulative or deceptive conduct occurred, except that such term shall not include any debt

security that is exempt from registration under this title pursuant to rules issued by the Commission under section 4(2) of this title.

SECTION 17—FRAUDULENT INTERSTATE TRANSACTIONS

a.   **Use of interstate commerce for purpose of fraud or deceit.** It shall be unlawful for any person in the offer or sale of any securities by the use of any means or instruments of transportation or communication in interstate commerce or by the use of the mails, directly or indirectly—

1.   to employ any device, scheme, or artifice to defraud, or

2.   to obtain money or property by means of any untrue statement of a material fact or any omission to state a material fact necessary in order to make the statements made, in the light of the circumstances under which they were made, not misleading, or

3.   to engage in any transaction, practice, or course of business which operates or would operate as a fraud or deceit upon the purchaser.

b.   **Use of interstate commerce for purpose of offering for sale.** It shall be unlawful for any person, by the use of any means or instruments of transportation or communication in interstate commerce or by the use of the mails, to publish, give publicity to, or circulate any notice, circular, advertisement, newspaper, article, letter, investment service, or communication which, though not purporting to offer a security for sale, describes such security for a consideration received or to be received, directly or indirectly, from an issuer, underwriter, or dealer, without fully disclosing the receipt, whether past or prospective, of such consideration and the amount thereof.

c.   **Exemptions, of section 3 not applicable to this section.** The exemptions provided in section 3 shall not apply to the provisions of this section.

SECTION 18—EXEMPTION FROM STATE
REGULATION OF SECURITIES OFFERINGS

a. **Scope of Exemption.** Except as otherwise provided in this section, no law, rule, regulation, or order, or other administrative action of any State or any political subdivision thereof—

1. requiring, or with respect to, registration or qualification of securities, or registration or qualification of securities transactions, shall directly or indirectly apply to a security that—

   A. is a covered security; or

   B. will be a covered security upon completion of the transaction;

2. shall directly or indirectly prohibit, limit, or impose any conditions upon the use of—

   A. with respect to a covered security described in subsection (b), any offering document that is prepared by or on the behalf of the issuer; or

   B. any proxy statement, report to shareholders, or other disclosure document relating to a covered security or the issuer thereof that is required to be and is filed with the Commission or any national thereof that is required to be and is filed with the Commission or any national securities organization registered under section 15A of the Securities Exchange Act of 1934, except that this subparagraph does not apply to the laws, rules, regulations, or orders, or other administrative actions of the State of incorporation of the issuer; or

3. shall directly or indirectly prohibit, limit, or impose conditions, based on the merits of such offering or issuer, upon the offer or sale of any security described in paragraph (1).

b. **Covered Securities.** For the purposes of this section, the following are covered securities:

1. **Exclusive federal registration of nationally traded securities.** A security is a covered security if such security is—

    A. listed, or authorized for listing, on the New York Stock Exchange or the American Stack Exchange, or listed, or authorized for listing, on the National Market System of the Nasdaq Stock Market (or any successor to such entities);

    B. listed, or authorized for listing, on a national securities exchange (or tier or segment thereof) that has listing standards that the Commission determines by rule (on its own initiative or on the basis of a petition) are substantially similar to the listing standards applicable to securities describe in subparagraph (A); or

    C. is a security of the same issuer that is equal in seniority or that is a senior security to a security described in subparagraph (A) or (B).

2. **Exclusive federal registration of investment companies.** A security is a covered security if such security is a security issued by an investment company that is registered, or that has filed a registration statement, under the Investment Company Act of 1940.

3. **Sales to qualified purchasers.** A security is a covered security with respect to the offer or sale of the security to qualified purchasers, as defined by the Commission by rule. In prescribing such rule, the Commission may define the term "qualified purchaser" differently with respect to different categories of securities, consistent with the public interest and the protection of investors.

4. **Exemption in connection with certain exempt offerings.** A security is a covered security with respect to a transaction that is exempt from registration under this title pursuant to—

    A. paragraph (1) or (3) of section 4, and the issuer of such security files reports with the Commission pursuant to section 13 or 15(d) of the Securities Exchange Act of 1934;

B. section 4(4);

C. section 3(a), other than the offer or sale of a security that is exempt from such registration pursuant to paragraph (4), (10) or (11) of such section, except that a municipal security that is exempt from such a registration pursuant to paragraph (2) of such section is not a covered security with respect to the offer or sale of such security in the State in which the issuer of such security is located; or

D. Commission rules or regulations issued under section 4(2), except that this subparagraph does not prohibit a State from imposing notice filing requirements that are substantially similar to those required by rule or regulation under section 4(2) that are in effect on September 1, 1996.

c. **Preservation of Authority.**

1. **Fraud authority.** Consistent with this section, the securities commission (or agency or office performing like functions) of any State shall retain jurisdiction under the laws of such State to investigate and bring enforcement actions with respect to fraud or deceit, or unlawful conduct by a broker or dealer, in connection with securities or securities transactions.

2. **Preservation of filing requirements.**

A. **Notice filings permitted.** Nothing in this section prohibits the securities commission (or any agency or office performing like functions) of any State from requiring the filing of any document filed with the Commission pursuant to this title, together with annual or periodic reports of the value of securities sold or offered to be sold to persons located in the State (if such sales data is not included in documents filed with the Commission), solely for notice purposes and the assessment of any fee, together with a consent to service of process and any required fee.

B. **Preservation of fees.**

    i. **In general.** Until otherwise provided by law, rule, regulation, or order, or other administrative action of any State, or any political subdivision thereof, adopted after the date of enactment of the National Securities Markets Improvement Act of 1996, filing or registration fees with respect to securities or securities transactions shall continue to be collected in amounts determined pursuant to State law as in effect on the day before such date.

    ii. **Schedule.** The fees required by this subparagraph shall be paid, and all necessary supporting data on sales or offers for sales required under subparagraph (A), shall be reported on the same schedule as would have been applicable had the issuer not relied on the exemption provided in <u>subsection (a)</u>.

C. **Availability of preemption contingent on payment of fees.**

    i. **In general.** During the period beginning on the date of enactment of the National Securities Markets Improvement Act of 1996 and ending 3 years after that date of enactment, the securities commission (or any agency or office performing like functions) of any State may require the registration of securities issued by any issuer who refuses to pay the fees required by subparagraph (B).

    ii. **Delays.** For purposes of this subparagraph, delays in payment of fees or underpayments of fees that are promptly remedied shall not constitute a refusal to pay fees.

   D. **Fees not permitted on listed securities.** Notwithstanding subparagraphs (A), (B), and (C), no filing or fee may be required with respect to any security that is a covered security pursuant to <u>subsection (b)(1)</u>, or will be such a covered security upon completion of the transaction, or is a security of the same issuer that is equal in seniority or that is a senior security to a security that is a covered security pursuant to subsection (b)(1).

3. **Enforcement of requirements.** Nothing in this section shall prohibit the security commission (or any agency or office performing like functions) of any State from suspending the offer or sale of securities within such State as a result of the failure to submit any filing or fee required under law and permitted under this section.

d. **Definitions.** For purposes of this section, the following definitions shall apply:

   1. **Offering document.** The term "offering document"—

      A. has the meaning given the term "prospectus" in <u>section 2(a)(10)</u>, but without regard to the provisions of subparagraphs <u>(a)</u> and <u>(b)</u> of that section; and

      B. includes a communication that is not deemed to offer a security pursuant to a rule of the Commission.

   2. **Prepared by or on behalf of the issuer.** Not later than 6 months after the date of enactment of the National Securities Markets Improvement Act of 1996 [enacted October 11, 1996], the Commission shall, by rule, define the term "prepared by or on behalf of the issuer" for purposes of this section.

   3. **State.** The term "State" has the same meaning as on <u>section 3</u> of the Securities Exchange Act of 1934.

4. **Senior security.** The term "senior security" means any bond, debenture, note, or similar obligation or instrument constituting a security and evidencing indebtedness, and any stock of a class having priority over any other class as to distribution of assets or payments of dividends.

SECTION 18A—PREEMPTION OF STATE LAW

a. **Authority to purchase, hold, and invest in securities; securities considered as obligations of United States.**

1. Any person, trust, corporation, partnership, association, business trust, or business entity created pursuant to or existing under the laws of the United States or any State shall be authorized to purchase, hold, and invest in securities that are—

   A. offered and sold pursuant to section 4(5),

   B. mortgage related securities (as that term is defined in section 3(a)(41)),

   C. small business related securities (as defined in section 3(a)(53)), or

   D. securities issued or guaranteed by the Federal Home Loan Mortgage Corporation or the Federal National Mortgage Association, to the same extent that such person, trust, corporation, partnership, association, business trust, or business entity is authorized under any applicable law to purchase, hold or invest in obligations issued by or guaranteed as to principal and interest by the United States or any agency or instrumentality thereof.

2. Where State law limits the purchase, holding, or investment in obligations issued by the United States by such a person, trust, corporation, partnership, association, business trust, or business entity, such securities that are—

   A. offered and sold pursuant to section 4(5),

   B. mortgage related securities (as that term is defined
       in section 3(a)(41)),

   C. small business related securities (as defined in sec-
       tion 3(a)(53)), or

   D. securities issued or guaranteed by the Federal
       Home Loan Mortgage Corporation or the Federal
       National Mortgage Association, shall be consid-
       ered to be obligations issued by the United States
       for purposes of the limitation.

b. **Exception; validity of contracts under prior law.** The provisions
    of subsection (a) of this section shall not apply with respect to a par-
    ticular person, trust, corporation, partnership, association, business
    trust, or business entity or class thereof in any State that, prior to
    the expiration of seven years after October 3, 1984, enacts a statute
    that specifically refers to this section and either prohibits or pro-
    vides for a more limited authority to purchase, hold, or invest in
    such securities by any person, trust, corporation, partnership, asso-
    ciation, business trust, or business entity or class thereof than is pro-
    vided in subsection (a) of this section. The enactment by any State
    of any statute of the type described in the preceding sentence shall
    not affect the validity of any contractual commitment to purchase,
    hold, or invest that was made prior thereto and shall not require the
    sale or other disposition of any securities acquired prior thereto.

c. **Registration and qualification requirements; exemption; sub-
    sequent enactment by State.** Any securities that are offered and
    sold pursuant to section 4(5), that are mortgage related securities
    (as that term is defined in section 3(a)(41)), or that are small busi-
    ness related securities (as defined in section 3(a)(53)) shall be
    exempt from any law of any State with respect to or requiring reg-
    istration or qualification of securities or real estate to the same
    extent as any obligation issued by or guaranteed as to principal and
    interest by the United States or any agency or instrumentality
    thereof. Any State may, prior to the expiration of seven years after
    October 3, 1984, enact a statute that specifically refers to this sec-
    tion and requires registration or qualification of any such security
    on terms that differ from those applicable to any obligation issued
    by the United States.

d. **Implementation.**

    1. **Limitation.** The provisions of subsections (a) and (b) of this section concerning small business related securities shall not apply with respect to a particular person, trust, corporation, partnership, association, business trust, or business entity or class thereof in any State that, prior to the expiration of 7 years after September 23, 1994, enacts a statute that specifically refers to this section and either prohibits or provides for a more limited authority to purchase, hold, or invest in such small business related securities by any person, trust, corporation, partnership, association, business trust, or business entity or class thereof than is provided in this section. The enactment by any State of any statute of the type described in the preceding sentence shall not affect the validity of any contractual commitment to purchase, hold, or invest that was made prior to such enactment, and shall not require the sale or other disposition of any small business related securities acquired prior to the date of such enactment.

    2. **State registration or qualification requirements.** Any State may, not later than 7 years after September 23, 1994, enact a statute that specifically refers to this section and requires registration or qualification of any small business related securities on terms that differ from those applicable to any obligation issued by the United States.

SECTION 19—SPECIAL POWERS OF COMMISSION

a. The Commission shall have authority from time to time to make, amend, and rescind such rules and regulations as may be necessary to carry out the provisions of this title, including rules and regulations governing registration statements and prospectuses for various classes of securities and issuers, and defining accounting, technical, and trade terms used in this title. Among other things, the Commission shall have authority, for the purposes of this title, to prescribe the form or forms in which required information shall be set forth, the items or details to be shown in the balance sheet and earning statement, and the methods to be followed in the preparation of accounts, in the appraisal or valuation of assets and liabilities, in the determination of depreciation and depletion, in the differentiation of recurring and nonrecurring income, in the differentiation of investment and operating income, and in the preparation, where the Commission deems it necessary or desirable, of consolidated balance sheets or income accounts of any person directly or indirectly controlling or controlled by the issuer, or any person under direct or indirect common control with the issuer. The rules and regulations of the Commission shall be effective upon publication in the manner which the Commission shall prescribe. No provision of this title imposing any liability shall apply to any act done or omitted in good faith in conformity with any rule or regulation of the Commission, notwithstanding that such rule or regulation may, after such act or omission, be amended or rescinded or be determined by judicial or other authority to be invalid for any reason.

b. For the purpose of all investigations which, in the opinion of the Commission, are necessary and proper for the enforcement of this title, any member of the Commission or any officer or officers designated by it are empowered to administer oaths and affirmations, subpoena witnesses, take evidence, and require the production of any books, papers, or other documents which the Commission deems relevant or material to the inquiry. Such attendance of witnesses and the production of such documentary evidence may be required from any place in the United States or any Territory at any designated place of hearing.

c.

1. The Commission is authorized to cooperate with any association composed of duly constituted representatives of State governments whose primary assignment is the regulation of the securities business within those States, and which, in the judgment of the Commission, could assist in effectuating greater uniformity in Federal-State securities matters. The Commission shall, at its discretion, cooperate, coordinate, and share information with such an association for the purposes of carrying out the policies and projects set forth in paragraphs (2) and (3).

2. It is the declared policy of this subsection that there should be greater Federal and State cooperation in securities matters, including

    A. maximum effectiveness of regulation,

    B. maximum uniformity in Federal and State regulatory standards,

    C. minimum interference with the business of capital formation, and

    D. a substantial reduction in costs and paperwork to diminish the burdens of raising investment capital (particularly by small business) and to diminish the costs of the administration of the Government programs involved.

3. The purpose of this subsection is to engender cooperation between the Commission, any such association of State securities officials, and other duly constituted securities associations in the following areas:

    A. the sharing of information regarding the registration or exemption of securities issues applied for in the various States;

    B. the development and maintenance of uniform securities forms and procedures; and

    C. the development of a uniform exemption from registration for small issuers which can be agreed upon among several States or between the States and the Federal Government. The Commission shall have the authority to adopt such an exemption as agreed upon for Federal purposes. Nothing in this chapter shall be construed as authorizing preemption of State law.

4. In order to carry out these policies and purposes, the Commission shall conduct an annual conference as well as such other meetings as are deemed necessary, to which representatives from such securities associations, securities

self-regulatory organizations, agencies, and private organizations involved in capital formation shall be invited to
participate.

5. For fiscal year 1982, and for each of the three succeeding
   fiscal years, there are authorized to be appropriated such
   amounts as may be necessary and appropriate to carry out
   the policies, provisions, and purposes of this subsection.
   Any sums so appropriated shall remain available until expended.

6. Notwithstanding any other provision of law, neither the
   Commission nor any other person shall be required to
   establish any procedures not specifically required by the
   securities laws, as that term is defined in section 3(a)(47)
   of the Securities Exchange Act of 1934, or by chapter 5 of
   title 5 of the United States Code, in connection with cooperation, coordination, or consultation with—

   A. any association referred to in paragraph (1) or (3)
      or any conference or meeting referred to in para-
      graph (4), while such association, conference, or
      meeting is carrying out activities in furtherance of
      the provisions of this subsection; or

   B. any forum, agency, or organization, or group re-
      ferred to in section 503 of the Small Business In-
      vestment Incentive Act of 1980, while such forum,
      agency, organization, or group is carrying out activ-
      ities in furtherance of the provisions of such sec-
      tion 503.

As used in this paragraph, the terms 'association', 'conference', 'meeting', 'forum', 'agency', 'organization', and
'group' include any committee, subgroup, or representative
of such entities.

SECTION 20—INJUNCTIONS AND PROSECUTION
OF OFFENSES

a. **Investigation of violations.** Whenever it shall appear to the Commission, either upon complaint or otherwise, that the provisions of

this title, or of any rule or regulation prescribed under authority thereof, have been or are about to be violated, it may, in its discretion, either require or permit such person to file with it a statement in writing, under oath, or otherwise, as to all the facts and circumstances concerning the subject matter which it believes to be in the public interest to investigate, and may investigate such facts.

b. **Action for injunction or criminal prosecution in district court.** Whenever it shall appear to the Commission that any person is engaged or about to engage in any acts or practices which constitute or will constitute a violation of the provisions of this title, or of any rule or regulation prescribed under authority thereof, the Commission may, in its discretion, bring an action in any district court of the United States, or United States court of any Territory, to enjoin such acts or practices, and upon a proper showing, a permanent or temporary injunction or restraining order shall be granted without bond. The Commission may transmit such evidence as may be available concerning such acts or practices to the Attorney General who may, in his discretion, institute the necessary criminal proceedings under this title. Any such criminal proceeding may be brought either in the district wherein the transmittal of the prospectus or security complained of begins, or in the district wherein such prospectus or security is received.

c. **Writ of mandamus.** Upon application of the Commission, the district courts of the United States and the United States courts of any Territory shall have jurisdiction to issue writs of mandamus commanding any person to comply with the provisions of this title or any order of the Commission made in pursuance thereof.

d. **Money penalties in civil actions.**

   1. **Authority of commission.** Whenever it shall appear to the Commission that any person has violated any provision of this title, the rules or regulations thereunder, or a cease-and-desist order entered by the Commission pursuant to section 8A, other than by committing a violation subject to a penalty pursuant to section 21A of the Securities Exchange Act of 1934, the Commission may bring an action in a United States district court to seek, and the court shall have jurisdiction to impose, upon a proper showing, a civil penalty to be paid by the person who committed such violation.

2. **Amount of penalty.**

   A. **First tier.** The amount of the penalty shall be determined by the court in light of the facts and circumstances. For each violation, the amount of the penalty shall not exceed the greater of (i) $5,000 for a natural person or $50,000 for any other person, or (ii) the gross amount of pecuniary gain to such defendant as a result of the violation.

   B. **Second tier.** Notwithstanding subparagraph (A), the amount of penalty for each such violation shall not exceed the greater of (i) $50,000 for a natural person or $250,000 for any other person, or (ii) the gross amount of pecuniary gain to such defendant as a result of the violation, if the violation described in paragraph (1) involved fraud, deceit, manipulation, or deliberate or reckless disregard of a regulatory requirement.

   C. **Third tier.** Notwithstanding subparagraphs (A) and (B), the amount of penalty for each such violation shall not exceed the greater of (i) $100,000 for a natural person or $500,000 for any other person, or (ii) the gross amount of pecuniary gain to such defendant as a result of the violation, if—

      I. the violation described in paragraph (1) involved fraud, deceit, manipulation, or deliberate or reckless disregard of a regulatory requirement; and

      II. such violation directly or indirectly resulted in substantial losses or created a significant risk of substantial losses to other persons.

3. **Procedures for collections.**

   A. **Payment of penalty to treasury.** A penalty imposed under this section shall be payable into the Treasury of the United States.

B. **Collection of penalty.** If a person upon whom such a penalty is imposed shall fail to pay such penalty within the time prescribed in the court's order, the Commission may refer the matter to the Attorney General who shall recover such penalty by action in the appropriate United States district court.

C. **Remedy not exclusive.** The actions authorized by this subsection may be brought in addition to any other action that the Commission or the Attorney General is entitled to bring.

D. **Jurisdiction and venue.** For purposes of section 22, actions under this section shall be actions to enforce a liability or a duty created by this title.

4. **Special provisions relating to a violation of a cease-and-desist order.** In an action to enforce a cease-and-desist order entered by the Commission pursuant to section 8A, each separate violation of such order shall be a separate offense, except that in the case of a violation through a continuing failure to comply with such an order, each day of the failure to comply with the order shall be deemed a separate offense.

e. **Authority of a court to prohibit persons from serving as officers or directors.** In any proceeding under subsection (b), the court may prohibit, conditionally or unconditionally, and permanently or for such period of time as it shall determine, any person who violated section 17(a)(1) from acting as an officer or director of any issuer that has a class of securities registered pursuant to section 12 of the Securities Exchange Act of 1934 or that is required to file reports pursuant to section 15(d) of such Act if the person's conduct demonstrates substantial unfitness to serve as an officer or director of any such issuer.

f. **Prohibition of attorneys' fees paid from commission disgorgement.** Except as otherwise ordered by the court upon motion by the Commission, or, in the case of an administrative action, as otherwise ordered by the Commission, funds disgorged as the result of an action brought by the Commission in Federal court, or as a result of any Commission administrative action, shall not be distributed as payment for attorneys' fees or expenses incurred by private parties seeking distribution of the disgorged funds.

SECTION 21—HEARINGS BY COMMISSION

All hearings shall be public and may be held before the Commission or an officer or officers of the Commission designated by it, and appropriate records thereof shall be kept.

SECTION 22—JURISDICTION OF OFFENSES AND SUITS

a. **Federal and State courts; venue; service of process; review; removal; costs.** The district courts of the United States and the United States courts of any Territory shall have jurisdiction of offenses and violations under this title and under the rules and regulations promulgated by the Commission in respect thereto, and, concurrent with State and Territorial courts, except as provided in section 16 with respect to covered class actions, of all suits in equity and actions at law brought to enforce any liability or duty created by this title. Any such suit or action may be brought in the district wherein the defendant is found or is an inhabitant or transacts business, or in the district where the offer or sale took place, if the defendant participated therein, and process in such cases may be served in any other district of which the defendant is an inhabitant or wherever the defendant may be found. Judgments and decrees so rendered shall be subject to review as provided in sections 1254, 1291, 1292, and 1294 of title 28, United States Code. Except as provided in section 16(c), no case arising under this title and brought in any State court of competent jurisdiction shall be removed to any court of the United States. No costs shall be assessed for or against the Commission in any proceeding under this title brought by or against it in the Supreme Court or such other courts.

b. **Contumacy or refusal to obey subpoena; contempt.** In case of contumacy or refusal to obey a subpoena issued to any person, any of the said United States courts, within the jurisdiction of which said person guilty of contumacy or refusal to obey is found or resides, upon application by the Commission may issue to such person an order requiring such person to appear before the Commission, or one of its examiners designated by it, there to produce documentary evidence if so ordered, or there to give evidence touching the matter in question; and any failure to obey such order of the court may be punished by said court as a contempt thereof.

SECTION 23 — UNLAWFUL REPRESENTATIONS

Neither the fact that the registration statement for a security has been filed or is in effect nor the fact that a stop order is not in effect with respect thereto shall be deemed a finding by the Commission that the registration statement is true and accurate on its face or that it does not contain an untrue statement of fact or omit to state a material fact, or be held to mean that the Commission has in any way passed upon the merits of, or given approval to, such security. It shall be unlawful to make, or cause to be made to any prospective purchaser any representation contrary to the foregoing provisions of this section.

SECTION 24—PENALTIES

Any person who willfully violates any of the provisions of this title, or the rules and regulations promulgated by the Commission under authority thereof, or any person who willfully, in a registration statement filed under this title, makes any untrue statement of a material fact or omits to state any material fact required to be stated therein or necessary to make the statements therein not misleading, shall upon conviction be fined not more than $10,000 or imprisoned not more than five years, or both.

SECTION 25—JURISDICTION OF OTHER GOVERNMENT AGENCIES OVER SECURITIES

Nothing in this title shall relieve any person from submitting to the respective supervisory units of the Government of the United States information, reports, or other documents that may be required by any provision of law.

SECTION 26—SEPARABILITY OF PROVISIONS

If any provision of this Act, or the application of such provision to any person or circumstance, shall be held invalid, the remainder of this Act, or the application of such provision to persons or circumstances other than those as to which it is held invalid, shall not be affected thereby.

SECTION 27—PRIVATE SECURITIES LITIGATION

a. **Private class actions.**

    1. **In general.** The provisions of this subsection shall apply to each private action arising under this title that is brought as a plaintiff class action pursuant to the <u>Federal Rules of Civil Procedure</u>.

    2. **Certification filed with complaint.**

        A. **In general.** Each plaintiff seeking to serve as a representative party on behalf of a class shall provide a sworn certification, which shall be personally signed by such plaintiff and filed with the complaint, that—

            i. states that the plaintiff has reviewed the complaint and authorized its filing;

            ii. states that the plaintiff did not purchase the security that is the subject of the complaint at the direction of plaintiff's counsel or in order to participate in any private action arising under this title;

            iii. states that the plaintiff is willing to serve as a representative party on behalf of a class, including providing testimony at deposition and trial, if necessary;

            iv. sets forth all of the transactions of the plaintiff in the security that is the subject of the complaint during the class period specified in the complaint;

v. identifies any other action under this title, filed during the 3-year period preceding the date on which the certification is signed by the plaintiff, in which the plaintiff has sought to serve, or served, as a representative party on behalf of a class; and

vi. states that the plaintiff will not accept any payment for serving as a representative party on behalf of a class beyond the plaintiff's pro rata share of any recovery, except as ordered or approved by the court in accordance with paragraph (4).

B. **Nonwaiver of attorney-client privilege.** The certification filed pursuant to subparagraph (A) shall not be construed to be a waiver of the attorney-client privilege.

3. **Appointment of lead plaintiff.**

A. **Early notice to class members.**

i. **In general.** Not later than 20 days after the date on which the complaint is filed, the plaintiff or plaintiffs shall cause to be published, in a widely circulated national business-oriented publication or wire service, a notice advising members of the purported plaintiff class—

I. of the pendency of the action, the claims asserted therein, and the purported class period; and

II. that, not later than 60 days after the date on which the notice is published, any member of the purported class may move the court to serve as lead plaintiff of the purported class.

ii. **Multiple actions.** If more than one action on behalf of a class asserting substantially the same claim or claims arising under this title is filed, only the plaintiff or plaintiffs in the first filed action shall be required to cause notice to be published in accordance with clause (i).

iii. **Additional notices may be required under Federal Rules.** Notice required under clause (i) shall be in addition to any notice required pursuant to the Federal Rules of Civil Procedure.

B. **Appointment of lead plaintiff.**

i. **In general.** Not later than 90 days after the date on which a notice is published under subparagraph (A)(i), the court shall consider any motion made by a purported class member in response to the notice, including any motion by a class member who is not individually named as a plaintiff in the complaint or complaints, and shall appoint as lead plaintiff the member or members of the purported plaintiff class that the court determines to be most capable of adequately representing the interests of class members (hereafter in this paragraph referred to as the "most adequate plaintiff") in accordance with this subparagraph.

ii. **Consolidated actions.** If more than one action on behalf of a class asserting substantially the same claim or claims arising under this title has been filed, and any party has sought to consolidate those actions for pretrial purposes or for trial, the court shall not make the determination required by clause (i) until after the decision on the motion to consolidate is rendered. As soon as practicable after such decision is rendered, the court shall appoint the most adequate plaintiff as lead plaintiff for the consolidated actions in accordance with this subparagraph.

iii. **Rebuttable presumption.**

I. **In general.** Subject to subclause (II), for purposes of clause (i), the court shall adopt a presumption that the most adequate plaintiff in any private action arising under this title is the person or group of persons that—

(aa) has either filed the complaint or made a motion in response to a notice under Subparagraph (A)(i);

(bb) in the determination of the court, has the largest financial interest in the relief sought by the class; and

(cc) otherwise satisfies the requirements of Rule 23 of the Federal Rules of Civil Procedure.

II. **Rebuttable evidence.** The presumption described in subclause (I) may be rebutted only upon proof by a member of the purported plaintiff class that the presumptively most adequate plaintiff—

(aa) will not fairly and adequately protect the interests of the class; or

(bb) is subject to unique defenses that render such plaintiff incapable of adequately representing the class.

iv. **Discovery.** For purposes of this subparagraph, discovery relating to whether a member or members of the purported plaintiff class is the most adequate plaintiff may be conducted by a plaintiff only if the plaintiff first demonstrates a reasonable basis for a finding that the presumptively most adequate plaintiff is incapable of adequately representing the class.

v.   **Selection of lead counsel.** The most adequate plaintiff shall, subject to the approval of the court, select and retain counsel to represent the class.

vi. **Restrictions on professional plaintiffs.** Except as the court may otherwise permit, consistent with the purposes of this section, a person may be a lead plaintiff, or an officer, director, or fiduciary of a lead plaintiff, in no more than 5 securities class actions brought as plaintiff class actions pursuant to the Federal Rules of Civil Procedure during any 3-year period.

4. **Recovery by plaintiffs.** The share of any final judgment or of any settlement that is awarded to a representative party serving on behalf of a class shall be equal, on a per share basis, to the portion of the final judgment or settlement awarded to all other members of the class. Nothing in this paragraph shall be construed to limit the award of reasonable costs and expenses (including lost wages) directly relating to the representation of the class to any representative party serving on behalf of the class.

5. **Restrictions on settlements under seal.** The terms and provisions of any settlement agreement of a class action shall not be filed under seal, except that on motion of any party to the settlement, the court may order filing under seal for those portions of a settlement agreement as to which good cause is shown for such filing under seal. For purposes of this paragraph, good cause shall exist only if publication of a term or provision of a settlement agreement would cause direct and substantial harm to any party.

6. **Restrictions on payment of attorneys' fees and expenses.** Total attorneys' fees and expenses awarded by the court to counsel for the plaintiff class shall not exceed a reasonable percentage of the amount of any damages and prejudgment interest actually paid to the class.

7. **Disclosure of settlement terms to class members.** Any proposed or final settlement agreement that is published or otherwise disseminated to the class shall include each of the following statements, along with a cover page summarizing the information contained in such statements:

    A. **Statement of plaintiff recovery.** The amount of the settlement proposed to be distributed to the parties to the action, determined in the aggregate and on an average per share basis.

    B. **Statement of potential outcome of case.**

        i.   **Agreement on the amount of damages.** If the settling parties agree on the average amount of damages per share that would be recoverable if the plaintiff prevailed on each claim alleged under this title, a statement concerning the average amount of such potential damages per share.

        ii. **Disagreement on the amount of damages.** If the parties do not agree on the average amount of damages per share that would be recoverable if the plaintiff prevailed on each claim alleged under this title, a statement from each settling party concerning the issue or issues on which the parties disagree.

        iii. **Inadmissibility for certain purposes.** A statement made in accordance with clause (i) or (ii) concerning the amount of damages shall not be admissible in any Federal or State judicial action or administrative proceeding, other than an action or proceeding arising out of such statement.

C. **Statement of attorneys' fees or costs sought.** If any of the settling parties or their counsel intend to apply to the court for an award of attorneys' fees or costs from any fund established as part of the settlement, a statement indicating which parties or counsel intend to make such an application, the amount of fees and costs that will be sought (including the amount of such fees and costs determined on an average per share basis), and a brief explanation supporting the fees and costs sought.

D. **Identification of lawyers' representatives.** The name, telephone number, and address of one or more representatives of counsel for the plaintiff class who will be reasonably available to answer questions from class members concerning any matter contained in any notice of settlement published or otherwise disseminated to the class.

E. **Reasons for settlement.** A brief statement explaining the reasons why the parties are proposing the settlement.

F. **Other information.** Such other information as may be required by the court.

8. **Attorney conflict of interest.** If a plaintiff class is represented by an attorney who directly owns or otherwise has a beneficial interest in the securities that are the subject of the litigation, the court shall make a determination of whether such ownership or other interest constitutes a conflict of interest sufficient to disqualify the attorney from representing the plaintiff class.

b. **Stay of discovery; preservation of evidence.**

1. **In general.** In any private action arising under this title, all discovery and other proceedings shall be stayed during the pendency of any motion to dismiss, unless the court finds, upon the motion of any party, that particularized discovery is necessary to preserve evidence or to prevent undue prejudice to that party.

2. **Preservation of evidence.** During the pendency of any stay of discovery pursuant to this subsection, unless otherwise ordered by the court, any party to the action with actual notice of the allegations contained in the complaint shall treat all documents, data compilations (including electronically recorded or stored data), and tangible objects that are in the custody or control of such person and that are relevant to the allegations, as if they were the subject of a continuing request for production of documents from an opposing party under the Federal Rules of Civil Procedure.

3. **Sanction for willful violation.** A party aggrieved by the willful failure of an opposing party to comply with paragraph (2) may apply to the court for an order awarding appropriate sanctions.

4. **Circumvention of stay of discovery.** Upon a proper showing, a court may stay discovery proceedings in any private action in a State court as necessary in aid of its jurisdiction, or to protect or effectuate its judgments, in an action subject to a stay of discovery pursuant to this subsection.

c. **Sanctions for abusive litigation.**

1. **Mandatory review by court.** In any private action arising under this title, upon final adjudication of the action, the court shall include in the record specific findings regarding compliance by each party and each attorney representing any party with each requirement of Rule 11(b) of the Federal Rules of Civil Procedure as to any complaint, responsive pleading, or dispositive motion.

2. **Mandatory sanctions.** If the court makes a finding under paragraph (1) that a party or attorney violated any requirement of Rule 11(b) of the Federal Rules of Civil Procedure as to any complaint, responsive pleading, or dispositive motion, the court shall impose sanctions on such party or attorney in accordance with Rule 11 of the Federal Rules of Civil Procedure. Prior to making a finding that any party or attorney has violated Rule 11 of the Federal Rules of Civil Procedure, the court shall give such party or attorney notice and an opportunity to respond.

3. Presumptions in favor of attorneys' fees and costs.

A. **In general.** Subject to subparagraphs (B) and (C), for purposes of paragraph (2), the court shall adopt a presumption that the appropriate sanction—

   i. for failure of any responsive pleading or dispositive motion to comply with any requirement of Rule 11(b) of the Federal Rules of Civil Procedure is an award to the opposing party of the reasonable attorneys' fees and other expenses incurred as a direct result of the violation; and

   ii. for substantial failure of any complaint to comply with any requirement of <u>Rule 11(b) of the Federal Rules of Civil Procedure</u> is an award to the opposing party of the reasonable attorneys' fees and other expenses incurred in the action.

B. **Rebuttal evidence.** The presumption described in subparagraph (A) may be rebutted only upon proof by the party or attorney against whom sanctions are to be imposed that—

   i. the award of attorneys' fees and other expenses will impose an unreasonable burden on that party or attorney and would be unjust, and the failure to make such an award would not impose a greater burden on the party in whose favor sanctions are to be imposed; or

   ii. the violation of Rule 11(b) of the Federal Rules of Civil Procedure was de minimis.

C. **Sanctions.** If the party or attorney against whom sanctions are to be imposed meets its burden under subparagraph (B), the court shall award the sanctions that the court deems appropriate pursuant to Rule 11 of the Federal Rules of Civil Procedure.

d. **Defendant's right to written interrogatories.** In any private action arising under this title in which the plaintiff may recover money damages only on proof that a defendant acted with a particular state of mind, the court shall, when requested by a defendant, submit to the jury a written interrogatory on the issue of each such defendant's state of mind at the time the alleged violation occurred.

SECTION 27A—APPLICATION OF SAFE HARBOR FOR FORWARD-LOOKING STATEMENTS

a. **Applicability.** This section shall apply only to a forward-looking statement made by—

> 1. an issuer that, at the time that the statement is made, is subject to the reporting requirements of section 13(a) or section 15(d) of the Securities Exchange Act of 1934;
>
> 2. a person acting on behalf of such issuer;
>
> 3. an outside reviewer retained by such issuer making a statement on behalf of such issuer; or
>
> 4. an underwriter, with respect to information provided by such issuer or information derived from information provided by the issuer.

b. **Exclusions.** Except to the extent otherwise specifically provided by rule, regulation, or order of the Commission, this section shall not apply to a forward-looking statement—

> 1. that is made with respect to the business or operations of the issuer, if the issuer—
>
>> A. during the 3-year period preceding the date on which the statement was first made—
>>
>>> i. was convicted of any felony or misdemeanor described in clauses (i) through (iv) of section 15 (b)(4)(B) of the Securities Exchange Act of 1934; or
>>>
>>> ii. has been made the subject of a judicial or administrative decree or order arising out of a governmental action that—

    I.   prohibits future violations of the antifraud provisions of the securities laws;

    II.   requires that the issuer cease and desist from violating the antifraud provisions of the securities laws; or

    III.   determines that the issuer violated the antifraud provisions of the securities laws;

B.   makes the forward-looking statement in connection with an offering of securities by a blank check company;

C.   issues penny stock;

D.   makes the forward-looking statement in connection with a rollup transaction; or

E.   makes the forward-looking statement in connection with a going private transaction; or

2.   that is—

A.   included in a financial statement prepared in accordance with generally accepted accounting principles;

B.   contained in a registration statement of, or otherwise issued by, an investment company;

C.   made in connection with a tender offer;

D.   made in connection with an initial public offering;

E.   made in connection with an offering by, or relating to the operations of, a partnership, limited liability company, or a direct participation investment program; or

F.   made in a disclosure of beneficial ownership in a report required to be filed with the Commission pursuant to section 13(d) of the Securities Exchange Act of 1934.

c. **Safe harbor.**

    1. **In general.** Except as provided in subsection (b), in any private action arising under this title that is based on an untrue statement of a material fact or omission of a material fact necessary to make the statement not misleading, a person referred to in subsection (a) shall not be liable with respect to any forward-looking statement, whether written or oral, if and to the extent that—

        A. the forward-looking statement is—

            i. identified as a forward-looking statement, and is accompanied by meaningful cautionary statements identifying important factors that could cause actual results to differ materially from those in the forward-looking statement; or

            ii. immaterial; or

        B. the plaintiff fails to prove that the forward-looking statement—

            i. if made by a natural person, was made with actual knowledge by that person that the statement was false or misleading; or

            ii. if made by a business entity, was—

                I. made by or with the approval of an executive officer of that entity, and

                II. made or approved by such officer with actual knowledge by that officer that the statement was false or misleading.

    2. **Oral forward-looking statements.** In the case of an oral forward-looking statement made by an issuer that is subject to the reporting requirements of section 13(a) or section 15(d) of the Securities Exchange Act of 1934, or by a person acting on behalf of such issuer, the requirement set forth in paragraph (1)(A) shall be deemed to be satisfied—

    A. if the oral forward-looking statement is accompanied by a cautionary statement—

        i. that the particular oral statement is a forward-looking statement; and

        ii. that the actual results could differ materially from those projected in the forward-looking statement; and

    B. if—

        i. the oral forward-looking statement is accompanied by an oral statement that additional information concerning factors that could cause actual results to differ materially from those in the forward-looking statement is contained in a readily available written document, or portion thereof;

        ii. the accompanying oral statement referred to in clause (i) identifies the document, or portion thereof, that contains the additional information about those factors relating to the forward-looking statement; and

        iii. the information contained in that written document is a cautionary statement that satisfies the standard established in paragraph (1)(A).

3. **Availability.** Any document filed with the Commission or generally disseminated shall be deemed to be readily available for purposes of paragraph (2).

4. **Effect on other safe harbors.** The exemption provided for in paragraph (1) shall be in addition to any exemption that the Commission may establish by rule or regulation under subsection (g).

d. **Duty to update.** Nothing in this section shall impose upon any person a duty to update a forward-looking statement.

e. **Dispositive motion.** On any motion to dismiss based upon subsection (c)(1), the court shall consider any statement cited in the complaint and cautionary statement accompanying the forward-looking statement, which are not subject to material dispute, cited by the defendant.

f. **Stay pending decision on motion.** In any private action arising under this title, the court shall stay discovery (other than discovery that is specifically directed to the applicability of the exemption provided for in this section) during the pendency of any motion by a defendant for summary judgment that is based on the grounds that—

1. the statement or omission upon which the complaint is based is a forward-looking statement within the meaning of this section; and

2. the exemption provided for in this section precludes a claim for relief.

g. **Exemption authority.** In addition to the exemptions provided for in this section, the Commission may, by rule or regulation, provide exemptions from or under any provision of this title, including with respect to liability that is based on a statement or that is based on projections or other forward-looking information, if and to the extent that any such exemption is consistent with the public interest and the protection of investors, as determined by the Commission.

h. **Effect on other authority of commission.** Nothing in this section limits, either expressly or by implication, the authority of the Commission to exercise similar authority or to adopt similar rules and regulations with respect to forward-looking statements under any other statute under which the Commission exercises rulemaking authority.

i. **Definitions.** For purposes of this section, the following definitions shall apply:

1. **Forward-looking statement.** The term "forward-looking statement" means—

A. a statement containing a projection of revenues, income (including income loss), earnings (including earnings loss) per share, capital expenditures, dividends, capital structure, or other financial items;

B.   a statement of the plans and objectives of management for future operations, including plans or objectives relating to the products or services of the issuer;

C.   a statement of future economic performance, including any such statement contained in a discussion and analysis of financial condition by the management or in the results of operations included pursuant to the rules and regulations of the Commission;

D.   any statement of the assumptions underlying or relating to any statement described in subparagraph (A), (B), or (C);

E.   any report issued by an outside reviewer retained by an issuer, to the extent that the report assesses a forward-looking statement made by the issuer; or

F.   a statement containing a projection or estimate of such other items as may be specified by rule or regulation of the Commission.

2.   **Investment company.** The term "investment company" has the same meaning as in <u>section 3(a)</u> of the Investment Company Act of 1940.

3.   **Penny stock.** The term "penny stock" has the same meaning as in <u>section 3(a)(51)</u> of the Securities Exchange Act of 1934, and the rules and regulations, or orders issued pursuant to that section.

4.   **Going private transaction.** The term "going private transaction" has the meaning given that term under the rules or regulations of the Commission issued pursuant to <u>section 13(e)</u> of the Securities Exchange Act of 1934.

5.   **Security laws.** The term "securities laws" has the same meaning as in <u>section 3</u> of the Securities Exchange Act of 1934.

6.   **Person acting on behalf of an issuer.** The term "person acting on behalf of an issuer" means an officer, director, or employee of the issuer.

7. **Other terms.** The terms "blank check company", "rollup transaction", "partnership", "limited liability company", "executive officer of an entity" and "direct participation investment program", have the meanings given those terms by rule or regulation of the Commission.

SECTION 28—GENERAL EXEMPTIVE AUTHORITY

The Commission, by rule or regulation, may conditionally or unconditionally exempt any person, security, or transaction, or any class of persons, securities, or transactions, from any provision or provisions of this title or of any rule or regulation issued under this title, to the extent that such exemption is necessary or appropriate in the public interest, and is consistent with the protection of investors.

SCHEDULE A

1. The name under which the issuer is doing or intends to do business;

2. the name of the State or other sovereign power under which the issuer is organized;

3. the location of the issuer's principal business office, and if the issuer is a foreign or territorial person, the name and address of its agent in the United States authorized to receive notice;

4. the names and addresses of the directors or persons performing similar functions, and the chief executive, financial and accounting officers, chosen or to be chosen if the issuer be a corporation, association, trust, or other entity; of all partners, if the issuer be a partnership; and of the issuer, if the issuer be an individual; and of the promoters in the case of a business to be formed, or formed within two years prior to the filing of the registration statement;

5. the names and addresses of the underwriters;

6. the names and addresses of all persons, if any, owning of record or beneficially, if known, more than 10 per centum of any class of stock of the issuer, or more than 10 per centum in the aggregate of the outstanding stock of the issuer as of a date within twenty days prior to the filing of the registration statement;

7. the amount of securities of the issuer held by any person specified in paragraphs (4), (5), and (6) of this schedule, as of a date within twenty days prior to the filing of the registration statement, and, if possible, as of one year prior thereto, and the amount of the securities, for which the registration statement is filed, to which such persons have indicated their intention to subscribe;

8. the general character of the business actually transacted or to be transacted by the issuer;

9. a statement of the capitalization of the issuer, including the authorized and outstanding amounts of its capital stock and the proportion thereof paid up, the number and classes of shares in which such capital stock is divided, par value thereof, or if it has no par value, the stated or assigned value thereof, a description of the respective voting rights, preferences, conversion and exchange rights, rights to dividends, profits, or capital of each class, with respect to each other class, including the retirement and liquidation rights or values thereof;

10. a statement of the securities, if any, covered by options outstanding or to be created in connection with the security to be offered, together with the names and addresses of all persons, if any, to be allotted more than 10 per centum in the aggregate of such options;

11. the amount of capital stock of each class issued or included in the shares of stock to be offered;

12. the amount of the funded debt outstanding and to be created by the security to be offered, with a brief description of the date, maturity, and character of such debt, rate of interest, character of amortization provisions, and the security, if any, therefor. If substitution of any security is permissible, a summarized statement of the conditions under which such substitution is permitted. If substitution is permissible without notice, a specific statement to that effect;

13. the specific purposes in detail and the approximate amounts to be devoted to such purposes, so far as determinable, for which the security to be offered is to supply funds, and if the funds are to be raised in part from other sources, the amounts thereof and the sources thereof, shall be stated;

14. the remuneration, paid or estimated to be paid, by the issuer or its predecessor, directly or indirectly, during the past year and

ensuing year to (a) the directors or persons performing similar functions, and (b) its officers and other persons, naming them wherever such remuneration exceeded $25,000 during any such year;

15. the estimated net proceeds to be derived from the security to be offered;

16. the price at which it is proposed that the security shall be offered to the public or the method by which such price is computed and any variation therefrom at which any portion of such security is proposed to be offered to any persons or classes of persons, other than the underwriters, naming them or specifying the class. A variation in price may be proposed prior to the date of the public offering of the security, but the Commission shall immediately be notified of such variation;

17. all commissions or discounts paid or to be paid, directly or indirectly, by the issuer to the underwriters in respect of the sale of the security to be offered. Commissions shall include all cash, securities, contracts, or anything else of value, paid, to be set aside, disposed of, or understandings with or for the benefit of any other persons in which any underwriter is interested, made, in connection with the sale of such security. A commission paid or to be paid in connection with the sale of such security by a person in which the issuer has an interest or which is controlled or directed by, or under common control with, the issuer shall be deemed to have been paid by the issuer. Where any such commission is paid the amount of such commission paid to each underwriter shall be stated;

18. the amount or estimated amounts, itemized in reasonable detail, of expenses, other than commissions specified in paragraph (17) of this schedule, incurred or borne by or for the account of the issuer in connection with the sale of the security to be offered or properly chargeable thereto, including legal, engineering, certification, authentication, and other charges;

19. the net proceeds derived from any security sold by the issuer during the two years preceding the filing of the registration statement, the price at which such security was offered to the public, and the names of the principal underwriters of such security;

20. any amount paid within two years preceding the filing of the registration statement or intended to be paid to any promoter and the consideration for any such payment;

21. the names and addresses of the vendors and the purchase price of any property, or good will, acquired or to be acquired, not in the ordinary course of business, which is to be defrayed in whole or in part from the proceeds of the security to be offered, the amount of any commission payable to any person in connection with such acquisition, and the name or names of such person or persons, together with any expense incurred or to be incurred in connection with such acquisition, including the cost of borrowing money to finance such acquisition;

22. full particulars of the nature and extent of the interest, if any, of every director, principal executive officer, and of every stockholder holding more than 10 per centum of any class of stock or more than 10 per centum in the aggregate of the stock of the issuer, in any property acquired, not in the ordinary course of business of the issuer, within two years preceding the filing of the registration statement or proposed to be acquired at such date;

23. the names and addresses of counsel who have passed on the legality of the issue;

24. dates of and parties to, and the general effect concisely stated of every material contract made, not in the ordinary course of business, which contract is to be executed in whole or in part at or after the filing of the registration statement or which contract has been made not more than two years before such filing. Any management contract or contract providing for special bonuses or profit-sharing arrangements, and every material patent or contract for a material patent right, and every contract by or with a public utility company or an affiliate thereof, providing for the giving or receiving of technical or financial advice or service (if such contract may involve a charge to any party thereto at a rate in excess of $2,500 per year in cash or securities or anything else of value), shall be deemed a material contract;

25. a balance sheet as of a date not more than ninety days prior to the date of the filing of the registration statement showing all of the assets of the issuer, the nature and cost thereof, whenever

determinable, in such detail and in such form as the Commission shall prescribe (with intangible items segregated), including any loan in excess of $20,000 to any officer, director, stockholder or person directly or indirectly controlling or controlled by the issuer, or person under direct or indirect common control with the issuer. All the liabilities of the issuer in such detail and such form as the Commission shall prescribe, including surplus of the issuer showing how and from what sources such surplus was created, all as of a date not more than ninety days prior to the filing of the registration statement. If such statement be not certified by an independent public or certified accountant, in addition to the balance sheet required to be submitted under this schedule, a similar detailed balance sheet of the assets and liabilities of the issuer, certified by an independent public or certified accountant, of a date not more than one year prior to the filing of the registration statement, shall be submitted;

26. a profit and loss statement of the issuer showing earnings and income, the nature and source thereof, and the expenses and fixed charges in such detail and such form as the Commission shall prescribe for the latest fiscal year for which such statement is available and for the two preceding fiscal years, year by year, or, if such issuer has been in actual business for less than three years, then for such time as the issuer has been in actual business, year by year. If the date of the filing of the registration statement is more than six months after the close of the last fiscal year, a statement from such closing date to the latest practicable date. Such statement shall show what the practice of the issuer has been during the three years or lesser period as to the character of the charges, dividends or other distributions made against its various surplus accounts, and as to depreciation, depletion, and maintenance charges, in such detail and form as the Commission shall prescribe, and if stock dividends or avails from the sale of rights have been credited to income, they shall be shown separately with a statement of the basis upon which the credit is computed. Such statement shall also differentiate between any recurring and non-recurring income and between any investment and operating income. Such statement shall be certified by an independent public or certified accountant;

27. if the proceeds, or any part of the proceeds, of the security to be issued is to be applied directly or indirectly to the purchase of any business, a profit and loss statement of such business certified by an independent public or certified accountant, meeting the requirements of paragraph (26) of this schedule, for the three preceding fiscal years, together with a balance sheet, similarly certified, of such business, meeting the requirements of paragraph (25) of this schedule of a date not more than ninety days prior to the filing of the registration statement or at the date such business was acquired by the issuer if the business was acquired by the issuer more than ninety days prior to the filing of the registration statement;

28. a copy of any agreement or agreements (or, if identical agreements are used, the forms thereof) made with any underwriter, including all contracts and agreements referred to in paragraph (17) of this schedule;

29. a copy of the opinion or opinions of counsel in respect to the legality of the issue, with a translation of such opinion, when necessary, into the English language;

30. a copy of all material contracts referred to in paragraph (24) of this schedule, but no disclosure shall be required of any portion of any such contract if the Commission determines that disclosure of such portion would impair the value of the contract and would not be necessary for the protection of the investors;

31. unless previously filed and registered under the provisions of this title, and brought up to date, (a) a copy of its articles of incorporation, with all amendments thereof and of its existing bylaws or instruments corresponding thereto, whatever the name, if the issuer be a corporation; (b) copy of all instruments by which the trust is created or declared, if the issuer is a trust; (c) a copy of its articles of partnership or association and all other papers pertaining to its organization, if the issuer is a partnership, unincorporated association, joint-stock company, or any other form of organization; and

32. a copy of the underlying agreements or indentures affecting any stock, bonds, or debentures offered or to be offered.

In case of certificates of deposit, voting trust certificates, collateral trust certificates, certificates of interest or shares in unincorporated investment trusts, equipment trust certificates, interim or other receipts for certificates, and like securities, the Commission shall establish rules and regulations requiring the submission of information of a like character applicable to such cases, together with such other information as it may deem appropriate and necessary regarding the character, financial or otherwise, of the actual issuer of the securities and/or the person performing the acts and assuming the duties of depositor or manager.

SCHEDULE B

1. Name of borrowing government or subdivision thereof;

2. specific purposes in detail and the approximate amounts to be devoted to such purposes, so far as determinable, for which the security to be offered is to supply funds, and if the funds are to be raised in part from other sources, the amounts thereof and the sources thereof, shall be stated;

3. the amount of the funded debt and the estimated amount of the floating debt outstanding and to be created by the security to be offered, excluding intergovernmental debt, and a brief description of the date, maturity, character of such debt, rate of interest, character of amortization provisions, and the security, if any, therefor. If substitution of any security is permissible, a statement of the conditions under which such substitution is permitted. If substitution is permissible without notice, a specific statement to that effect;

4. whether or not the issuer or its predecessor has, within a period of twenty years prior to the filing of the registration statement, defaulted on the principal or interest of any external security, excluding intergovernmental debt, and, if so, the date, amount, and circumstances of such default, and the terms of the succeeding arrangement, if any;

5. the receipts, classified by source, and the expenditures, classified by purpose, in such detail and form as the Commission shall prescribe for the latest fiscal year for which such information is available and the two preceding fiscal years, year by year;

6. the names and addresses of the underwriters;

7. the name and address of its authorized agent, if any, in the United States;

8. the estimated net proceeds to be derived from the sale in the United States of the security to be offered;

9. the price at which it is proposed that the security shall be offered in the United States to the public or the method by which such price is computed. A variation in price may be proposed prior to the date of the public offering of the security, but the Commission shall immediately be notified of such variation;

10. all commissions paid or to be paid, directly or indirectly, by the issuer to the underwriters in respect of the sale of the security to be offered. Commissions shall include all cash, securities, contracts, or anything else of value, paid, to be set aside, disposed of, or understandings with or for the benefit of any other persons in which the underwriter is interested, made, in connection with the sale of such security. Where any such commission is paid, the amount of such commission paid to each underwriter shall be stated;

11. the amount or estimated amounts, itemized in reasonable detail, of expenses, other than the commissions specified in paragraph (10) of this schedule, incurred or borne by or for the account of the issuer in connection with the sale of the security to be offered or properly chargeable thereto, including legal, engineering, certification, and other charges;

12. the names and addresses of counsel who have passed upon the legality of the issue;

13. a copy of any agreement or agreements made with any underwriter governing the sale of the security within the United States; and

14. an agreement of the issuer to furnish a copy of the opinion or opinions of counsel in respect to the legality of the issue, with a translation, where necessary, into the English language. Such opinion shall set out in full all laws, decrees, ordinances, or other acts of Government under which the issue of such security has been authorized.

Appendix 7

SECURITIES EXCHANGE ACT OF 1934

INDEX

SECTION 1—SHORT TITLE

This Act may be cited as the "Securities Exchange Act of 1934."

SECTION 2—NECESSITY FOR REGULATION AS PROVIDED IN THIS TITLE

For the reasons hereinafter enumerated, transactions in securities as commonly conducted upon securities exchanges and over-the-counter markets are affected with a national public interest which makes it necessary to provide for regulation and control of such transactions and of practices and matters related thereto, including transactions by officers, directors, and principal security holders, to require appropriate reports, to remove impediments to and perfect the mechanisms of a national market system for securities and a national system for the clearance and settlement of securities transactions and the safeguarding of securities and funds related thereto, and to impose requirements necessary to make such regulation and control reasonably complete and effective, in order to protect interstate commerce, the national credit, the Federal taxing power, to protect and make more effective the national banking system and Federal Reserve System, and to insure the maintenance of fair and honest markets in such transactions:

1. Such transactions

    a. are carried on in large volume by the public generally and in large part originate outside the States in which the exchanges and over-the-counter markets are located and/or are effected by means of the mails and instrumentalities of interstate commerce;

    b. constitute an important part of the current of interstate commerce;

    c. involve in large part the securities of issuers engaged in interstate commerce;

     d. involve the use of credit, directly affect the financing of trade, industry, and transportation in interstate commerce, and directly affect and influence the volume of interstate commerce; and affect the national credit.

2. The prices established and offered in such transactions are generally disseminated and quoted throughout the United States and foreign countries and constitute a basis for determining and establishing the prices at which securities are bought and sold, the amount of certain taxes owing to the United States and to the several States by owners, buyers, and sellers of securities, and the value of collateral for bank loans.

3. Frequently the prices of securities on such exchanges and markets are susceptible to manipulation and control, and the dissemination of such prices gives rise to excessive speculation, resulting in sudden and unreasonable fluctuations in the prices of securities which

     a. cause alternately unreasonable expansion and unreasonable contraction of the volume of credit available for trade, transportation, and industry in interstate commerce,

     b. hinder the proper appraisal of the value of securities and thus prevent a fair calculation of taxes owing to the United States and to the several States by owners, buyers, and sellers of securities, and

     c. prevent the fair valuation of collateral for bank loans and/or obstruct the effective operation of the national banking system and Federal Reserve System.

4. National emergencies, which produce widespread unemployment and the dislocation of trade, transportation, and industry, and which burden interstate commerce and adversely affect the general welfare, are precipitated, intensified, and prolonged by manipulation and sudden and unreasonable fluctuations of security prices and by excessive speculation on such exchanges and markets, and to meet such emergencies the Federal Government is put to such great expense as to burden the national credit.

SECTION 3—DEFINITIONS AND APPLICATION OF TITLE

a. When used in this title, unless the context otherwise requires—

  1. The term "exchange" means any organization, association, or group of persons, whether incorporated or unincorporated, which constitutes, maintains, or provides a market place or facilities for bringing together purchasers and sellers of securities or for otherwise performing with respect to securities the functions commonly performed by a stock exchange as that term is generally understood, and includes the market place and the market facilities maintained by such exchange.

  2. The term "facility" when used with respect to an exchange includes its premises, tangible or intangible property whether on the premises or not, any right to the use of such premises or property or any service thereof for the purpose of effecting or reporting a transaction on an exchange (including, among other things, any system of communication to or from the exchange, by ticker or otherwise, maintained by or with the consent of the exchange), and any right of the exchange to the use of any property or service.

  3.

  A. The term "member" when used with respect to a national securities exchange means

  i. any natural person permitted to effect transactions on the floor of the exchange without the services of another person acting as broker,

  ii. any registered broker or dealer with which such a natural person is associated,

  iii. any registered broker or dealer permitted to designate as a representative such a natural person, and

  iv. any other registered broker or dealer which agrees to be regulated by such exchange and with respect to which the exchange undertakes to enforce compliance with the provisions of this title, the rules and regulations thereunder, and its own rules.

For purposes of sections [6](b)(1), 6(b)(4), 6(b)(6), 6(b)(7), 6(d), 17(d), 19(d), 19(e), 19(g), 19(h), and 21 of this title, the term "member" when used with respect to a national securities exchange also means, to the extent of the rules of the exchange specified by the Commission, any person required by the Commission to comply with such rules pursuant to section 6(f) of this title.

B. The term "member" when used with respect to a registered securities association means any broker or dealer who agrees to be regulated by such association and with respect to whom the association undertakes to enforce compliance with the provisions of this title, the rules and regulations thereunder, and its own rules.

4. The term "broker" means any person engaged in the business of effecting transactions in securities for the account of others, but does not include a bank.

5. The term "dealer" means any person engaged in the business of buying and selling securities for his own account, through a broker or otherwise, but does not include a bank, or any person insofar as he buys or sells securities for his own account, either individually or in some fiduciary capacity, but not as a part of a regular business.

6. The term "bank" means

A. a banking institution organized under the laws of the United States,

B. a member bank of the Federal Reserve System,

C. any other banking institution, whether incorporated or not, doing business under the laws of any State or of the United States, a substantial portion of the business of which consists of receiving deposits or exercising fiduciary powers similar to those permitted to national banks under the authority of the Comptroller of the Currency pursuant to the first section of Public Law 87-722, and which is supervised and examined by State or Federal authority having supervision over banks, and which is not operated for the purpose of evading the provisions of this title, and

D. a receiver, conservator, or other liquidating agent of any institution or firm included in clauses (A), (B), or (C) of this paragraph.

7. The term "director" means any director of a corporation or any person performing similar functions with respect to any organization, whether incorporated or unincorporated.

8. The term "issuer" means any person who issues or proposes to issue any security; except that with respect to certificates of deposit for securities, voting-trust certificates, or collateral-trust certificates, or with respect to certificates of interest or shares in an unincorporated investment trust not having a board of directors or of the fixed, restricted management, or unit type, the term "issuer" means the person or persons performing the acts and assuming the duties of depositor or manager pursuant to the provisions of the trust or other agreement or instrument under which such securities are issued; and except that with respect to equipment-trust certificates or like securities, the term "issuer" means the person by whom the equipment or property is, or is to be, used.

9. The term "person" means a natural person, company, government, or political subdivision, agency, or instrumentality of a government.

10. The term "security" means any note, stock, treasury stock, bond, debenture, certificate of interest or participation in any profit-sharing agreement or in any oil, gas, or other mineral royalty or lease, any collateral-trust certificate, pre-organization certificate or subscription, transferable share, investment contract, voting-trust certificate, certificate of

deposit for a security, any put, call, straddle, option, or privilege on any security, certificate of deposit, or group or index of securities (including any interest therein or based on the value thereof), or any put, call, straddle, option, or privilege entered into on a national securities exchange relating to foreign currency, or in general, any instrument commonly known as a "security"; or any certificate of interest or participation in, temporary or interim certificate for, receipt for, or warrant or right to subscribe to or purchase, any of the foregoing; but shall not include currency or any note, draft, bill of exchange, or banker's acceptance which has a maturity at the time of issuance of not exceeding nine months, exclusive of days of grace, or any renewal thereof the maturity of which is likewise limited.

11. The term "equity security" means any stock or similar security; or any security convertible, with or without consideration, into such a security, or carrying any warrant or right to subscribe to or purchase such a security; or any such warrant or right; or any other security which the Commission shall deem to be of similar nature and consider necessary or appropriate, by such rules and regulations as it may prescribe in the public interest or for the protection of investors, to treat as an equity security.

12.

   A. The term "exempted security" or "exempted securities" includes—

      i.   government securities, as defined in paragraph (42) of this subsection;

      ii. municipal securities, as defined in paragraph (29) of this subsection;

      iii. any interest or participation in any common trust fund or similar fund maintained by a bank exclusively for the collective investment and reinvestment of assets contributed thereto by such bank in its capacity as trustee, executor, administrator, or guardian;

iv. any interest or participation in a single trust fund, or a collective trust fund maintained by a bank, or any security arising out of a contract issued by an insurance company, which interest, participation, or security is issued in connection with a qualified plan as defined in subparagraph (C) of this paragraph;

v. any security issued by or any interest or participation in any pooled income fund, collective trust fund, collective investment fund, or similar fund that is excluded from the definition of an investment company under section 3(c)(10)(B) of the Investment Company Act of 1940;

vi. solely for purpose of sections 12, 13, 14, and 16 of this title, any security issued by or any interest or participation in any church plan, company, or account that is excluded from the definition of an investment company under section 3(c)(14) of the Investment Company Act of 1940; and

vii. such other securities (which may include, among others, unregistered securities, the market in which is predominantly intrastate) as the Commission may, by such rules and regulations as it deems consistent with the public interest and the protection of investors, either unconditionally or upon specified terms and conditions or for stated periods, exempt from the operation of any one or more provisions of this title which by their terms do not apply to an "exempted security" or to "exempted securities".

B.

i. Notwithstanding subparagraph (A)(i) of this paragraph, government securities shall not be deemed to be "exempted securities" for the purposes of section 17A of this title.

ii. Notwithstanding subparagraph (A)(ii) of this paragraph, municipal securities shall not be deemed to be "exempted securities" for the purposes of sections 15 and 17A of this title.

C. For purposes of subparagraph (A)(iv) of this paragraph, the term "qualified plan" means

i. a stock bonus, pension, or profit-sharing plan which meets the requirements for qualification under section 401 of the Internal Revenue Code of 1954,

ii. an annuity plan which meets the requirements for the deduction of the employer's contribution under section 404(a)(2) of such Code, or

iii. a governmental plan as defined in section 414(d) of such Code which has been established by an employer for the exclusive benefit of its employees or their beneficiaries for the purpose of distributing to such employees or their beneficiaries the corpus and income of the funds accumulated under such plan, if under such plan it is impossible, prior to the satisfaction of all liabilities with respect to such employees and their beneficiaries, for any part of the corpus or income to he used for, or diverted to, purposes other than the exclusive benefit of such employees or their beneficiaries, other than any plan described in clause (i), (ii), or (iii) of this subparagraph which

I. covers employees some or all of whom are employees within the meaning of section 401(c) of such Code, or

      II. is a plan funded by an annuity contract described in section 403(b) of such Code.

13. The terms "buy" and "purchase" each include any contract to buy, purchase, or otherwise acquire.

14. The terms "sale" and "sell" each include any contract to sell or otherwise dispose of.

15. The term "Commission" means the Securities and Exchange Commission established by section 4 of this title.

16. The term "State" means any State of the United States, the District of Columbia, Puerto Rico, the Virgin Islands, or any other possession of the United States.

17. The term "interstate commerce" means trade, commerce, transportation, or communication among the several States, or between any foreign country and any State, or between any State and any place or ship outside thereof. The term includes intrastate use of

    A. any facility of a national securities exchange or of a telephone or other interstate means of communication, or

    B. any other interstate instrumentality.

18. The term "person associated with a broker or dealer" or "associated person of a broker or dealer" means any partner, officer, director, or branch manager of such broker or dealer (or any person occupying a similar status or performing similar functions), any person directly or indirectly controlling, controlled by, or under common control with such broker or dealer, or any employee of such broker or dealer, except that any person associated with a broker or dealer whose functions are solely clerical or ministerial shall not be included in the meaning of such term for purposes of section 15(b) of this title (other than paragraph (6) thereof).

19. The terms "investment company", "affiliated person", "insurance company", "separate account", and "company" have the same meanings as in the Investment Company Act of 1940.

20. The terms "investment adviser" and "underwriter" have the same meaning as in the Investment Advisers Act of 1940.

21. The term "person associated with a member" or "associated person of a member" when used with respect to a member of a national securities exchange or registered securities association means any partner, officer, director, or branch manager of such member (or any person occupying a similar status or performing similar functions), any person directly or indirectly controlling, controlled by, or under common control with such member, or any employee of such member.

22.

    A. The term "securities information processor" means any person engaged in the business of

        i. collecting, processing, or preparing for distribution or publication, or assisting, participating in, or coordinating the distribution or publication of, information with respect to transactions in or quotations for any security (other than an exempted security) or

        ii. distributing or publishing (whether by means of a ticker tape, a communications network, a terminal display device, or otherwise) on a current and continuing basis, information with respect to such transactions or quotations. The term "securities information processor" does not include any bona fide newspaper, news magazine, or business or financial publication of general and regular circulation, any self-regulatory organization, any bank, broker, dealer, building and loan, savings and loan, or homestead association, or cooperative bank, if such bank, broker, dealer, association, or cooperative bank would be deemed to be a securities information processor solely by reason of functions performed by such institutions as part of customary banking, brokerage, dealing, association, or cooperative bank activities, or any common carrier, as defined in section 3 of the Communications Act of 1934, subject to the jurisdiction of the Federal Communications Commission or a State commission, as defined in section 3 of that Act, unless the Commission determines that such carrier is engaged in the business of collecting, processing, or preparing for distribution or publication, information with respect to transactions in or quotations for any security.

B. The term "exclusive processor" means any securities information processor or self-regulatory organization which, directly or indirectly, engages on an exclusive basis on behalf of any national securities exchange or registered securities association, or any national securities exchange or registered securities association which engages on an exclusive basis on its own behalf, in collecting, processing, or preparing for distribution or publication any information with respect to

   i. transactions or quotations on or effected or made by means of any facility of such exchange or

   ii. quotations distributed or published by means of any electronic system operated or controlled by such association.

23.

A. The term "clearing agency" means any person who acts as an intermediary in making payments or deliveries or both in connection with transactions in securities or who provides facilities for comparison of data respecting the terms of settlement of securities transactions, to reduce the number of settlements of securities transactions, or for the allocation of securities settlement responsibilities. Such term also means any person, such as a securities depository, who

    i.   acts as a custodian of securities in connection with a system for the central handling of securities whereby all securities of a particular class or series of any issuer deposited within the system are treated as fungible and may be transferred, loaned, or pledged by bookkeeping entry without physical delivery of securities certificates, or

    ii. otherwise permits or facilitates the settlement of securities transactions or the hypothecation or lending of securities without physical delivery of securities certificates.

B. The term "clearing agency" does not include

    i.   any Federal Reserve bank, Federal home loan bank, or Federal land bank;

    ii. any national securities exchange or registered securities association solely by reason of its providing facilities for comparison of data respecting the terms of settlement of securities transactions effected on such exchange or by means of any electronic system operated or controlled by such association;

    iii. any bank, broker, dealer, building and loan, savings and loan, or homestead association, or cooperative bank if such bank, broker, dealer, association, or cooperative bank would be deemed to be a clearing agency solely by reason of functions performed by such institution as part of customary banking, brokerage, dealing, association, or cooperative banking activities, or solely by reason of acting on behalf of a clearing agency or a participant therein in connection with the furnishing by the clearing agency of services to its participants or the use of services of the clearing agency by its participants, unless the Commission, by rule, otherwise provides as necessary or appropriate to assure the prompt and accurate clearance and settlement of securities transactions or to prevent evasion of this title;

iv. any life insurance company, its registered separate accounts, or a subsidiary of such insurance company solely by reason of functions commonly performed by such entities in connection with variable annuity contracts or variable life policies issued by such insurance company or its separate accounts;

v. any registered open-end investment company or unit investment trust solely by reason of functions commonly performed by it in connection with shares in such registered open-end investment company or unit investment trust,[;] or

vi. any person solely by reason of its performing functions described in paragraph 25(E) of this subsection.

24. The term "participant" when used with respect to a clearing agency means any person who uses a clearing agency to clear or settle securities transactions or to transfer, pledge, lend, or hypothecate securities. Such term does not include a person whose only use of a clearing agency is

A. through another person who is a participant or

B. as a pledgee of securities.

25. The term "transfer agent" means any person who engages on behalf of an issuer of securities or on behalf of itself as an issuer of securities in

   A. countersigning such securities upon issuance;

   B. monitoring the issuance of such securities with a view to preventing unauthorized issuance, a function commonly performed by a person called a registrar;

   C. registering the transfer of such securities;

   D. exchanging or converting such securities; or

   E. transferring record ownership of securities by bookkeeping entry without physical issuance of securities certificates. The term "transfer agent" does not include any insurance company or separate account which performs such functions solely with respect to variable annuity contracts or variable life policies which it issues or any registered clearing agency which performs such functions solely with respect to options contracts which it issues.

26. The term "self-regulatory organization" means any national securities exchange, registered securities association, or registered clearing agency, or (solely for purposes of sections 19(b), 19(c), and 23(b) of this title) the Municipal Securities Rulemaking Board established by section 15B of this title.

27. The term "rules of an exchange", "rules of an association", or "rules of a clearing agency" means the constitution, articles of incorporation, bylaws, and rules, or instruments corresponding to the foregoing, of an exchange, association of brokers and dealers, or clearing agency, respectively, and such of the stated policies, practices, and interpretations of such exchange, association, or clearing agency as the Commission, by rule, may determine to be necessary or appropriate in the public interest or for the protection of investors

to be deemed to be rules of such exchange, association or clearing agency.

28. The term "rules of a self-regulatory organization" means the rules of an exchange which is a national securities exchange, the rules of an association of brokers and dealers which is a registered securities association, the rules of a clearing agency which is a registered clearing agency, or the rules of the Municipal Securities Rulemaking Board.

29. The term "municipal securities" means securities which are direct obligations of, or obligations guaranteed as to principal or interest by, a State or any political subdivision thereof, or any agency or instrumentality of a State or any political subdivision thereof, or any municipal corporate instrumentality of one or more States, or any security which is an industrial development bond (as defined in section 103(c)(2) of the Internal Revenue Code of 1954) the interest on which is excludable from gross income under section 103(a)(1) of such Code if, by reason of the application of paragraph (4) or (6) of section 103(c) of such Code (determined as if paragraphs 4(A), (5), and (7) were not included in such section 103(c)), paragraph (1) of such section 103(c) does not apply to such security.

30. The term "municipal securities dealer" means any person (including a separately identifiable department or division of a bank) engaged in the business of buying and selling municipal securities for his own account, through a broker or otherwise, but does not include—

    A. any person insofar as he buys or sells such securities for his own account, either individually or in some fiduciary capacity, but not as a part of a regular business; or

    B. a bank, unless the bank is engaged in the business of buying and selling municipal securities for its own account other than in a fiduciary capacity, through a broker or otherwise: Provided, however, That if the bank is engaged in such business through a separately identifiable department or division (as defined by the Municipal Securities Rulemaking Board in accordance with Section 15B(b)(2)(H) of this title), the department or division and not the bank itself shall be deemed to be the municipal securities dealer.

31. The term "municipal securities broker" means a broker engaged in the business of effecting transactions in municipal securities for the account of others.

32. The term "person associated with a municipal securities dealer" when used with respect to a municipal securities dealer which is a bank or a division or department of a bank means any person directly engaged in the management, direction, supervision, or performance of any of the municipal securities dealer's activities with respect to municipal securities, and any person directly or indirectly controlling such activities or controlled by the municipal securities dealer in connection with such activities.

33. The term "municipal securities investment portfolio" means all municipal securities held for investment and not for sale as part of a regular business by a municipal securities dealer or by a person, directly or indirectly, controlling, controlled by, or under common control with a municipal securities dealer.

34. The term "appropriate regulatory agency" means—

   A. When used with respect to a municipal securities dealer:

      i. the Comptroller of the Currency, in the case of a national bank or a bank operating under the Code of Law for the District of Columbia, or a subsidiary or a department or division of any such bank;

      ii. the Board of Governors of the Federal Reserve System, in the case of a State member bank of the Federal Reserve System, a subsidiary or a department or division thereof, a bank holding company, a subsidiary of a bank holding company which is a bank other than a bank specified in clause (i) or (iii) of this subparagraph, or a subsidiary or a department or division of such subsidiary;

iii. the Federal Deposit Insurance Corporation, in the case of a bank insured by the Federal Deposit Insurance Corporation (other than a member of the Federal Reserve System), or a subsidiary or a department or division thereof; and

iv. the Commission in the case of all other municipal securities dealers;

B. When used with respect to a clearing agency or transfer agent:

i. the Comptroller of the Currency, in the case of a national bank or a bank operating under the Code of Law for the District of Columbia, or a subsidiary of any such bank;

ii. the Board of Governors of the Federal Reserve System, in the case of a State member bank of the Federal Reserve System, a bank holding company, [or a subsidiary of a bank holding company,] or a subsidiary of a bank holding company which is a bank other than a bank specified in clause (i) or (iii) of this subparagraph when the appropriate regulatory agency for such clearing agency is not the Commission;

iii. the Federal Deposit Insurance Corporation, in the case of a bank insured by the Federal Deposit Insurance Corporation (other than a member of the Federal Reserve System) when the appropriate regulatory agency for such clearing agency is not the Commission; and

iv. the Commission in the case of all other clearing agencies and transfer agents.

C. When used with respect to a participant or applicant to become a participant in a clearing agency or a person requesting or having access to services offered by a clearing agency:

    i. the Comptroller of the Currency, in the case of a national bank or a bank operating under the Code of Law for the District of Columbia when the appropriate regulatory agency for such clearing agency is not the Commission;

    ii. the Board of Governors of the Federal Reserve System in the case of a State member bank of the Federal Reserve System, a bank holding company, or a subsidiary of a bank holding company, or a subsidiary of a bank holding company which is a bank other than a bank specified in clause (i) or (iii) of this subparagraph when the appropriate regulatory agency for such clearing agency is not the Commission;

    iii. the Federal Deposit Insurance Corporation, in the case of a bank insured by the Federal Deposit Insurance Corporation (other than a member of the Federal Reserve System) when the appropriate regulatory agency for such clearing agency is not the Commission; and

    iv. the Commission in all other cases.

D. When used with respect to an institutional investment manager which is a bank the deposits of which are insured in accordance with the Federal Deposit Insurance Act:

    i. the Comptroller of the Currency, in the case of a national bank or a bank operating under the Code of Law for the District of Columbia;

ii. the Board of Governors of the Federal Reserve System, in the case of any other member bank of the Federal Reserve System; and

iii. the Federal Deposit Insurance Corporation, in the case of any other insured bank.

E. When used with respect to a national securities exchange or registered securities association, member thereof, person associated with a member thereof, applicant to become a member thereof or to become associated with a member thereof, or person requesting or having access to services offered by such exchange or association or member thereof, or the Municipal Securities Rulemaking Board, the Commission.

F. When used with respect to a person exercising investment discretion with respect to an account;[:]

i. the Comptroller of the Currency, in the case of a national bank or a bank operating under the Code of Law for the District of Columbia;

ii. the Board of Governors of the Federal Reserve System in the case of any other member bank of the Federal Reserve System;

iii. the Federal Deposit Insurance Corporation, in the case of any other bank the deposits of which are insured in accordance with the Federal Deposit Insurance Act; and

iv. the Commission in the case of all other such persons.

G. When used with respect to a government securities broker or government securities dealer, or person associated with a government securities broker or government securities dealer:

i.   the Comptroller of the Currency, in the case of a national bank, a bank in the District of Columbia examined by the Comptroller of the Currency, or a Federal branch or Federal agency of a foreign bank (as such terms are used in the International Banking Act of 1978);

ii. the Board of Governors of the Federal Reserve System, in the case of a State member bank of the Federal Reserve System, a foreign bank, an uninsured State branch or State agency of a foreign bank, a commercial lending company owned or controlled by a foreign bank (as such terms are used in the International Banking Act of 1978), or a corporation organized or having an agreement with the Board of Governors of the Federal Reserve System pursuant to section 25 or section 25A of the Federal Reserve Act;

iii. the Federal Deposit Insurance Corporation, in the case of a bank insured by the Federal Deposit Insurance Corporation (other than a member of the Federal Reserve System or a Federal savings bank) or an insured State. branch of a foreign bank (as such terms are used in the International Banking Act of 1978);

iv. the Director of the Office of Thrift Supervision, in the case of a savings association (as defined in section 3(b) of the Federal Deposit Insurance Act) the deposits of which are insured by the Federal Deposit Insurance Corporation; [and]

        v. the Commission, in the case of all other government securities brokers and government securities dealers.

As used in this paragraph, the terms "bank holding company" and "subsidiary of a bank holding company" have the meanings given them in section 2 of the Bank Holding Company Act of 1956, and the term "District of Columbia savings and loan association" means any association subject to examination and supervision by the Office of Thrift Supervision under section 8 of the Home Owners' Loan Act of 1933.

35. A person exercises "investment discretion" with respect to an account if, directly or indirectly, such person

    A. is authorized to determine what securities or other property shall he purchased or sold by or for the account,

    B. makes decisions as to what securities or other property shall be purchased or sold by or for the account even though some other person may have responsibility for such investment decisions, or

    C. otherwise exercises such influence with respect to the purchase and sale of securities or other property by or for the account as the Commission, by rule, determines, in the public interest or for the protection of investors, should be subject to the operation of the provisions of this title and the rules and regulations thereunder.

36. A class of persons or markets is subject to "equal regulation" if no member of the class has a competitive advantage over any other member thereof resulting from a disparity in their regulation under this title which the Commission determines is unfair and not necessary or appropriate in furtherance of the purposes of this title.

37. The term "records" means accounts, correspondence, memorandums, tapes, discs, papers, books, and other documents

or transcribed information of any type, whether ex-pressed in ordinary or machine language.

38. The term "market maker" means any specialist permitted to act as a dealer, any dealer acting in the capacity of block positioner, and any dealer who, with respect to a security, holds himself out (by entering quotations in an inter-dealer communications system or otherwise) as being willing to buy and sell such security for his own account on a regular or continuous basis.

39. A person is subject to a "statutory disqualification" with respect to membership or participation in, or association with a member of, a self-regulatory organization, if such person—

    A. has been and is expelled or suspended from membership or participation in, or barred or suspended from being associated with a member of, any self-regulatory organization, foreign equivalent of a self-regulatory organization, foreign or international securities exchange, contract market designated pursuant to section 5 of the Commodity Exchange Act, or any substantially equivalent foreign statute or regulation or futures associates registered under section 17 of such Act, or any substantially foreign statute or regulation or has been and is denied trading privileges on any such contract market or foreign equivalent;

    B. is subject to—

        i. an order of the Commission, other appropriate regulatory agency, or foreign financial regulatory authority—

            I. denying, suspending for a period not exceeding 12 months, or revoking his registration as a broker, dealer, municipal securities dealer, government securities broker, or government securities dealer or limiting his activities as a foreign person performing a function substantially equivalent to any of the above; or

II. barring or suspending for a period not exceeding 12 months his being associated with a broker, dealer, municipal securities dealer, government securities broker, government securities dealer, or foreign person performing a function substantially equivalent to any of the above;

ii. an order of the Commodity Futures Trading Commission denying, suspending, or revoking his registration under the Commodity Exchange Act; or

iii. an order by a foreign financial regulatory authority denying, suspending, or revoking the person's authority to engage in transactions in contracts of sale of a commodity for future delivery or other instruments traded on or subject to the rules of a contract market, board of trade, or foreign equivalent thereof;

C. by his conduct while associated with a broker, dealer, municipal securities dealer, government securities broker, or government securities dealer, or while associated with an entity or person required to be registered under the Commodity Exchange Act, has been found to be a cause of any effective suspension, expulsion, or order of the character described in subparagraph (A) or (B) of this paragraph, and in entering such a suspension, expulsion, or order, the Commission, an appropriate regulatory agency, or any such self-regulatory organization shall have jurisdiction to find whether or not any person was a cause thereof;

D. by his conduct while associated with any broker, dealer, municipal securities dealer, government securities broker, government securities dealer, or any other entity engaged in transactions in securities, or while associated with an entity engaged in transactions in contracts of sale of a commodity for future delivery or other instruments traded on or subject to the rules of a contract market, board of trade, or foreign equivalent thereof, has been found to be a cause of any effective suspension, expulsion, or order by a foreign or international securities exchange or foreign financial regulatory authority empowered by a foreign government to administer or enforce its laws relating to financial transactions as described in subparagraph (A) or (B) of this paragraph;

E. has associated with him any person who is known, or in the exercise of reasonable care should be known, to him to be a person described by subparagraph (A), (B), (C), or (D) of this paragraph; or

F. has committed or omitted any act enumerated in subparagraph (D), (E), or (G) of paragraph (4) of section 15(b) of this title, has been convicted of any offense specified in subparagraph (B) of such paragraph (4) or any other felony within ten years of the date of the filing of an application for membership or participation in, or to become associated with a member of, such self-regulatory organization, is enjoined from any action, conduct, or practice specified in subparagraph (C) of such paragraph (4), has willfully made or caused to be made in any application for membership or participation in, or to become associated with a member of, a self-regulatory organization, report required to be filed with a self-regulatory organization, or proceeding before a self-regulatory organization, any statement which was at the time, and in the light of the circumstances under which it was made, false or misleading with respect to any material fact, or has omitted to state in any such application, report, or proceeding any material fact which is required to be stated therein.

40. The term "financial responsibility rules" means the rules and regulations of the Commission or the rules and regulations prescribed by any self-regulatory organization relating to financial responsibility and related practices which are designated by the Commission, by rule or regulation, to be financial responsibility rules.

41. The term "mortgage related security" means a security that is rated in one of the two highest rating categories by at least one nationally recognized statistical rating organization, and either:

   A. represents ownership of one or more promissory notes or certificates of interest or participation in such notes (including any rights designed to assure servicing of, or the receipt or timeliness of receipt by the holders of such notes, certificates, or participations of amounts payable under, such notes, certificates, or participations), which notes:

      i. are directly secured by a first lien on a single parcel of real estate, including stock allocated to a dwelling unit in a residential cooperative housing corporation, upon which is located a dwelling or mixed residential and commercial structure, on a residential manufactured home as defined in section 603(6) of the National Manufactured Housing Construction and Safety Standards Act of 1974, whether such manufactured home is considered real or personal property under the laws of the State in which it is to be located, or on one or more parcels of real estate upon which is located one or more commercial structures; and

      ii. were originated by a savings and loan association, savings bank, commercial bank, credit union, insurance company, or similar institution which is supervised and examined by a Federal or State authority, or by a mortgagee approved by the Secretary of Housing and Urban Development pursuant to sections <u>203</u> and <u>211</u> of the National Housing Act, or, where such notes involve a lien on the manufactured home, by any such institution or by any financial institution approved for insurance by the Secretary of Housing and Urban Development pursuant to <u>section 2 of the National Housing Act</u>; or

  B. is secured by one or more promissory notes or certificates of interest or participations in such notes (with or without recourse to the issuer thereof) and, by its terms, provides for payments of principal in relation to payments, or reasonable projections of payments, on notes meeting the requirements of subparagraphs (A)<u>(i)</u> and <u>(ii)</u> or certificates of interest or participations in promissory notes meeting such requirements.

For the purpose of this paragraph, the term "promissory note", when used in connection with a manufactured home, shall also include a loan, advance, or credit sale as evidence [evidenced] by a retail installment sales contract or other instrument.

42. The term "government securities" means—

  A. securities which are direct obligations of, or obligations guaranteed as to principal or interest by, the United States;

  B. securities which are issued or guaranteed by corporations in which the United States has a direct or indirect interest and which are designated by the Secretary of the Treasury for exemption as necessary or appropriate in the public interest or for the protection of investors;

C. securities issued or guaranteed as to principal or interest by any corporation the securities of which are designated, by statute specifically naming such corporation, to constitute exempt securities within the meaning of the laws administered by the Commission; or

D. for purposes of sections 15C and 17A, any put, call, straddle, option, or privilege on a security described in subparagraph (A), (B), or (C) other than a put, call, straddle, option, or privilege—

   i.   that is traded on one or more national securities exchanges; or

   ii. for which quotations are disseminated through an automated quotation system operated by a registered securities association.

43. The term "government securities broker" means any person regularly engaged in the business of effecting transactions in government securities for the account of others, but does not include—

A. any corporation the securities of which are government securities under subparagraph (B) or (C) of paragraph (42) of this subsection; or

B. any person registered with the Commodity Futures Trading Commission, any contract market designated by the Commodity Futures Trading Commission, such contract market's affiliated clearing organization, or any floor trader on such contract market, solely because such person effects transactions in government securities that the Commission, after consultation with the Commodity Futures Trading Commission, has determined by rule or order to be incidental to such person's futures-related business.

44. The term "government securities dealer" means any person engaged in the business of buying and selling government securities for his own account, through a broker or otherwise, but does not include—

   1. any person insofar as he buys or sells such securities for his own account, either individually or in some fiduciary capacity, but not as a part of a regular business;

   2. any corporation the securities of which are government securities under subparagraph (B) or (C) of paragraph (42) of this subsection;

   3. any bank, unless the bank is engaged in the business of buying and selling government securities for its own account other than in a fiduciary capacity, through a broker or otherwise; or

   4. any person registered with the Commodity Futures Trading Commission, any contract market designated by the Commodity Futures Trading Commission, such contract market's affiliated clearing organization, or any floor trader on such contract market, solely because such person effects transactions in government securities that the Commission, after consultation with the Commodity Futures Trading Commission, has determined by rule or order to be incidental to such person's futures-related business.

45. The term "person associated with a government securities broker or government securities dealer" means any partner, officer, director, or branch manager of such government securities broker or government securities dealer (or any person occupying a similar status or performing similar functions), and any other employee of such government securities broker or government securities dealer who is engaged in the management, direction, supervision, or performance of any activities relating to government securities, and any person directly or indirectly controlling, controlled

by, or under common control with such government securities broker or government securities dealer.

46. The term "financial institution" means—

    A. a bank (as defined in paragraph (6) of this subsection);

    B. a foreign bank (as such term is used in the International Banking Act of 1978); and

    C. a savings association (as defined in section 3(b) of the Federal Deposit Insurance Act) the deposits of which are insured by the Federal Deposit Insurance Corporation.

47. The term "securities laws" means the Securities Act of 1933, the Securities Exchange Act of 1934, the Public Utility Holding Company Act of 1935, the Trust Indenture Act of 1939, the Investment Company Act of 1940, the Investment Advisers Act of 1940, and the Securities Investor Protection Act of 1970.

48. The term "registered broker or dealer" means a broker or dealer registered or required to register pursuant to section 15 or 15B of this title, except that in paragraph (3) of this subsection and sections 6 and 15A the term means such a broker or dealer and a government securities broker or government securities dealer registered or required to register pursuant to section 15C(a)(1)(A) of this title.

49. The term "person associated with a transfer agent" and "associated person of a transfer agent" mean any person (except an employee, whose functions are solely clerical or ministerial) directly engaged in the management, direction, supervision, or performance of any of the transfer agent's activities with respect to transfer agent functions, and any person directly or indirectly controlling such activities or controlled by the transfer agent in connection with such activities.

50. The term "foreign securities authority" means any foreign government, or any governmental body or regulatory organization empowered by a foreign government to administer or enforce its laws as they relate to securities matters.

51.

    A. The term "penny stock" means any equity security other than a security that is—

        i. registered or approved for registration and traded on a national securities exchange that meets such criteria as the Commission shall prescribe by rule or regulation for purposes of this paragraph;

        ii. authorized for quotation on an automated quotation system sponsored by a registered securities association, if such system

            I. was established and in operation before January 1, 1990, and

            II. meets such criteria as the Commission shall prescribe by rule or regulation for purposes of this paragraph;

        iii. issued by an investment company registered under the <u>Investment Company Act of 1940</u>;

        iv. excluded, on the basis of exceeding a minimum price, net tangible assets of the issuer, or other relevant criteria, from the definition of such term by rule or regulation which the Commission shall prescribe for purposes of this paragraph; or

        v. exempted, in whole or in part, conditionally or unconditionally, from the definition of such term by rule, regulation, or order prescribed by the Commission.

    B. The Commission may, by rule, regulation, or order, designate any equity security or class of equity securities described in clause <u>(i)</u> or <u>(ii)</u> of subparagraph (A) as within the meaning of the term 'penny stock' if such security or class of securities is traded other than on a national securities exchange or through an automated quotation system described in clause (ii) of subparagraph (A).

C. In exercising its authority under this paragraph to prescribe rules, regulations, and orders, the Commission shall determine that such rule, regulation, or order is consistent with the public interest and the protection of investors.

52. The term "foreign financial regulatory authority" means any

A. foreign securities authority,

B. other governmental body or foreign equivalent of a self-regulatory organization empowered by a foreign government to administer or enforce its laws relating to the regulation of fiduciaries, trusts, commercial lending, insurance, trading in contracts of sale of a commodity for future delivery, or other instruments traded on or subject to the rules of a contract market, board of trade, or foreign equivalent, or other financial activities, or

C. membership organization a function of which is to regulate participation of its members in activities listed above.

53.

A. The term "small business related security" means a security that is rated in 1 of the 4 highest rating categories by at least 1 nationally recognized statistical rating organization, and either—

i. represents an interest in 1 or more promissory notes or leases of personal property evidencing the obligation of a small business concern and originated by an insured depository institution, insured credit union, insurance company, or similar institution which is supervised and examined by a

Federal or State authority, or a finance company or leasing company; or

  ii. is secured by an interest in 1 or more promissory notes or leases of personal property (with or without recourse to the issuer or lessee) and provides for payments of principal in relation to payments, or reasonable projections of payments, on notes or leases described in clause (i).

B. For purposes of this paragraph—

  i. an "interest in a promissory note or a lease of personal property" includes ownership rights, certificates of interest or participation in such notes or leases, and rights designed to assure servicing of such notes or leases, or the receipt or timely receipt of amounts payable under such notes or leases;

  ii. the term "small business concern" means a business that meets the criteria for a small business concern established by the Small Business Administration under section 3(a) of the Small Business Act;

  iii. the term "insured depository institution" has the same meaning as in section 3 of the Federal Deposit Insurance Act; and

  iv. the term "insured credit union" has the same meaning as in section 101 of the Federal Credit Union Act.

b. The Commission and the Board of Governors of the Federal Reserve System, as to matters within their respective jurisdictions, shall have power by rules and regulations to define technical, trade, accounting, and other terms used in this title, consistently with the provisions and purposes of this title.

c. No provision of this title shall apply to, or be deemed to include, any executive department or independent establishment of the

United States, or any lending agency which is wholly owned, directly or indirectly, by the United States, or any officer, agent, or employee of any such department, establishment, or agency, acting in the course of his official duty as such, unless such provision makes specific reference to such department, establishment, or agency.

d. No issuer of municipal securities or officer or employee thereof acting in the course of his official duties as such shall be deemed to be a "broker", "dealer", or "municipal securities dealer" solely by reason of buying, selling, or effecting transactions in the issuer's securities.

e. Charitable Organizations.

1. Exemption. Notwithstanding any other provision of this title, but subject to paragraph (2) of this subsection, a charitable organization, as defined in section 3(c)(10)(D) of the Investment Company Act of 1940, or any trustee, director, officer, employee, or volunteer of such a charitable organization acting within the scope of such person's employment or duties with such organization, shall not be deemed to be a "broker", "dealer", "municipal securities broker", "municipal securities dealer", "government securities broker", or " government securities dealer" for purposes of this title solely because such organization or person buys, holds, sells, or trades in securities for its own account in its capacity as trustee or administrator of, or otherwise on behalf of or for the account of—

    A. such a charitable organization;

    B. a fund that is excluded from the definition of an investment company under section 3(c)(10)(B) of the Investment Company Act of 1940; or

    C. a trust or other donative instrument described in section 3(c)(10)(B) of the Investment Company Act of 1940, or the settlors (or potential settlors) or beneficiaries of any such trust or other instrument.

2. Limitation on Compensation. The exemption provided under paragraph (1) shall not be available to any charitable

organization, or any trustee, director, officer, employee, or volunteer of such a charitable organization, unless each person who, on or after 90 days after the date of enactment of this subsection, solicits donations on behalf of such charitable organization from any donor to a fund that is excluded from the definition of an investment company under section 3(c)(10)(B) of the Investment Company Act of 1940, is either a volunteer or is engaged in the overall fund raising activities of a charitable organization and receives no commission or other special compensation based on the number or the value of donations collected for the fund.

f. Consideration of Promotion of Efficiency, Competition, and Capital Formation.

Whenever pursuant to this title the Commission is engaged in rulemaking, or the review of a rule of a self-regulatory organization, and is required to consider or determine whether an action is necessary or appropriate in the public interest, the Commission shall also consider, in addition to the protection of investors, whether the action will promote efficiency, competition, and capital formation.

g. Church Plans. No church plan described in section 414(e) of the Internal Revenue Code of 1986, no person or entity eligible to establish and maintain such a plan under the Internal Revenue code of 1986, no company or account that is excluded from the definition of an investment company under section 3(c)(14) of the Investment Company Act of 1940, and no trustee, director, officer or employee of or volunteer for such plan, company, account person, or entity, acting within the scope of that persons' employment or activities with respect to such plan, shall be deemed to be a "broker", "dealer", "municipal securities broker", "municipal securities dealer", "government securities broker", "government securities dealer," "clearing agency", or "transfer agent" for purposes of this title—

1. solely because such plan, company, person, or entity buys, holds, sells, trades in, or transfers securities or acts as an intermediary in making payments in connection with transactions in securities for its own account in its capacity as trustee or administrator of, or otherwise on behalf of, or for

the account of, any church plan, company, or account that is excluded from the definition of an investment company under section 3(c)(14) of the Investment Company Act of 1940; and

2. if no such person or entity receives a commission or other transaction-related sales compensation in connection with any activities conduced in reliance on the exemption provided by this subsection.

SECTION 4—SECURITIES AND EXCHANGE COMMISSION

a. There is hereby established a Securities and Exchange Commission (hereinafter referred to as the "Commission") to be composed of five commissioners to be appointed by the President by and with the advice and consent of the Senate. Not more than three of such commissioners shall be members of the same political party, and in making appointments members of different political parties shall be appointed alternately as nearly as may be practicable. No commissioner shall engage in any other business, vocation, or employment than that of serving as commissioner, nor shall any commissioner participate, directly or indirectly, in any stock-market operations or transactions of a character subject to regulation by the Commission pursuant to this title. Each commissioner shall hold office for a term of five years and until his successor is appointed and has qualified, except that he shall not so continue to serve beyond the expiration of the next session of Congress subsequent to the expiration of said fixed term of office, and except

1. any Commissioner appointed to fill a vacancy occurring prior to the expiration of the term for which his predecessor was appointed shall be appointed for the remainder of such term, and

2. the terms of office of the Commissioners first taking office after the enactment of this title shall expire as designated by the President at the time of nomination, one at the end of one year, one at the end of two years, one at the end of three years, one at the end of four years, and one at the end of five years, after the date of the enactment of this title.

b. **Appointment and Compensation of Staff and Leasing Authority—**

1. **Appointment and Compensation.**—The Commission is authorized to appoint and fix the compensation of such officers, attorneys, examiners, and other experts as may be necessary for carrying out its functions under this Act, without regard to the provisions of other laws applicable to the employment and compensation of officers and employees of the United States, and the Commission may, subject to the civil-service laws, appoint such other officers and employees as are necessary in the execution of its functions and fix their salaries in accordance with the Classification Act of 1923, as amended.

2. **Leasing Authority.**—Notwithstanding any other provision of law, the Commission is authorized to enter directly into leases for real property for office, meeting, storage, and such other space as is necessary to carry out its functions, and shall be exempt from any General Services Administration space management regulations or directives.

c. Notwithstanding any other provision of law, in accordance with regulations which the Commission shall prescribe to prevent conflicts of interest, the Commission may accept payment and reimbursement, in cash or in kind, from non-Federal agencies, organizations, and individuals for travel, subsistence, and other necessary expenses incurred by Commission members and employees in attending meetings and conferences concerning the functions or activities of the Commission. Any payment or reimbursement accepted shall be credited to the appropriated funds of the Commission. The amount of travel, subsistence, and other necessary expenses for members and employees paid or reimbursed under this subsection may exceed per diem amounts established in official travel regulations, but the Commission may include in its regulations under this subsection a limitation on such amounts.

d. Notwithstanding any other provision of law, former employers of participants in the Commission's professional fellows programs may pay such participants their actual expenses for relocation to Washington, District of Columbia, to facilitate their participation in such programs, and program participants may accept such payments.

e. Notwithstanding any other provision of law, whenever any fee is required to be paid to the Commission pursuant to any provision of the securities laws or any other law, the Commission may provide by rule that such fee shall be paid in a manner other than in cash and the Commission may also specify the time that such fee shall be determined and paid relative to the filing of any statement or document with the Commission.

f. **Reimbursement of Expenses for Assisting Foreign Securities Authorities.**—Notwithstanding any other provision of law, the Commission may accept payment and reimbursement, in cash or in kind, from a foreign securities authority, or made on behalf of such authority, for necessary expenses incurred by the Commission, its members, and employees in carrying out any investigation pursuant to Section 21(a)(2) of this title or in providing any other assistance to a foreign securities authority. Any payment or reimbursement accepted shall be considered a reimbursement to the appropriated funds of the Commission.

SECTION 4A—DELEGATION OF FUNCTIONS BY COMMISSION

a. In addition to its existing authority, the Securities and Exchange Commission shall have the authority to delegate, by published order or rule, any of its functions to a division of the Commission, an individual Commissioner, an administrative law judge, or an employee or employee board, including functions with respect to hearing, determining, ordering, certifying, reporting, or otherwise acting as to any work, business or matter. Nothing in this section shall be deemed to supersede the provisions of Section 556(b) of Title 5, or to authorize the delegation of the function of rule-making as defined in subchapter II of chapter 5 of title 5, United States Code, with reference to general rules as distinguished from rules of particular applicability, or of the making of any rule pursuant to Section 19(c) of this title.

b. With respect to the delegation of any of its functions, as provided in subsection (a) of this section, the Commission shall retain a discretionary right to review the action of any such division of the Commission, individual Commissioner, administrative law judge, employee, or employee board, upon its own initiative or upon petition of a party to or intervenor in such action, within such time and in such manner as the Commission by rule shall prescribe. The vote of one member of the Commission shall be sufficient to bring any such action before the Commission for review. A person or party shall be entitled to review by the Commission if he or it is adversely affected by action at a delegated level which

1. denies any request for action pursuant to Section 8(a) or Section 8(c) of the Securities Act of 1933 or the first sentence of Section 12(d) of this title;

2. suspends trading in a security pursuant to Section 12(k) of this title; or

3. is pursuant to any provision of this title in a case of adjudication, as defined in Section 551 of Title 5, United States Code, not required by this title to be determined on the record after notice and opportunity for hearing (except to the extent there is involved a matter described in Section 554(a)(1) through (6) of such Title 5).

c. If the right to exercise such review is declined, or if no such review is sought within the time stated in the rules promulgated by the Commission, then the action of any such division of the Commission, individual Commissioner, administrative law judge, employee, or employee board, shall, for all purposes, including appeal or review thereof, be deemed the action of the Commission.

SECTION 4B—TRANSFER OF FUNCTIONS WITH RESPECT TO ASSIGNMENT OF PERSONNEL TO CHAIRMAN

In addition to the functions transferred by the provisions of Reorganization Plan Numbered 10 of 1950, there are hereby transferred from the Commission to the Chairman of the Commission the functions of the Commission with respect to the assignment of Commission personnel, including Commissioners, to perform such functions as may have been delegated by the Commission to the Commission personnel, including Commissioners, pursuant to Section 4A of this title.

SECTION 5—TRANSACTIONS ON UNREGISTERED EXCHANGES

It shall be unlawful for any broker, dealer, or exchange, directly or indirectly, to make use of the mails or any means or instrumentality of interstate commerce for the purpose of using any facility of an exchange within or subject to the jurisdiction of the United States to effect any transaction in a security, or to report any such transaction, unless such exchange

1. is registered as a national securities exchange under Section 6 of this title, or

2. is exempted from such registration upon application by the exchange because, in the opinion of the Commission, by reason of the limited volume of transactions effected on such exchange, it is not practicable and not necessary or appropriate in the public interest or for the protection of investors to require such registration.

SECTION 6—NATIONAL SECURITIES EXCHANGES

a. An exchange may be registered as a national securities exchange under the terms and conditions hereinafter provided in this section and in accordance with the provisions of Section 19(a) of this title, by filing with the Commission an application for registration in such form as the Commission, by rule, may prescribe containing the rules of the exchange and such other information and documents as the Commission, by rule, may prescribe as necessary or appropriate in the public interest or for the protection of investors.

b. An exchange shall not be registered as a national securities exchange unless the Commission determines that—

1. Such exchange is so organized and has the capacity to be able to carry out the purposes of this title and to comply, and (subject to any rule or order of the Commission pursuant to Section 17(d) or 19(g)(2) of this title) to enforce

compliance by its members and persons associated with its members, with the provisions of this title, the rules and regulations thereunder, and the rules of the exchange.

2. Subject to the provisions of <u>subsection (c)</u> of this section, the rules of the exchange provide that any registered broker or dealer or natural person associated with a registered broker or dealer may become a member of such exchange and any person may become associated with a member thereof.

3. The rules of the exchange assure a fair representation of its members in the selection of its directors and administration of its affairs and provide that one or more directors shall be representative of issuers and investors and not be associated with a member of the exchange, broker, or dealer.

4. The rules of the exchange provide for the equitable allocation of reasonable dues, fees, and other charges among its members and issuers and other persons using its facilities.

5. The rules of the exchange are designed to prevent fraudulent and manipulative acts and practices, to promote just and equitable principles of trade, to foster cooperation and coordination with persons engaged in regulating, clearing, settling, processing information with respect to, and facilitating transactions in securities, to remove impediments to and perfect the mechanism of a free and open market and a national market system, and, in general, to protect investors and the public interest; and are not designed to permit unfair discrimination between customers, issuers, brokers, or dealers, or to regulate by virtue of any authority conferred by this title matters not related to the purposes of this title or the administration of the exchange.

6. The rules of the exchange provide that (subject to any rule or order of the Commission pursuant to section <u>17(d)</u> or <u>19(g)(2)</u> of this title) its members and persons associated with its members shall be appropriately disciplined for violation of the provisions of this title, the rules or regulations thereunder, or the rules of the exchange, by expulsion, suspension, limitation of activities, functions, and operations,

fine, censure, being suspended or barred from being associated with a member, or any other fitting sanction.

7. The rules of the exchange are in accordance with the provisions of subsection (d) of this section, and, in general,
provide a fair procedure for the disciplining of members
and persons associated with members, the denial of membership to any person seeking membership therein, the barring of any person from becoming associated with a
member thereof, and the prohibition or limitation by the
exchange of any person with respect to access to services
offered by the exchange or a member thereof.

8. The rules of the exchange do not impose any burden on
competition not necessary or appropriate in furtherance of
the purposes of this title.

9. The rules of the exchange prohibit the listing of any security issued in a limited partnership rollup transaction (as
such term is defined in paragraphs (4) and (5) of section
14(h)), unless such transaction was conducted in accordance with procedures designed to protect the rights of limited partners, including—

   A. the right of dissenting limited partners to one of the
   following:

      i.   an appraisal and compensation;

      ii. retention of a security under substantially
           the same terms and conditions as the orig-
           inal issue;

      iii. approval of the limited partnership rollup
           transaction by not less than 75 percent of
           the outstanding securities of each of the
           participating limited partnerships;

      iv. the use of a committee of limited partners
           that is independent, as determined in accor-
           dance with rules prescribed by the exchange,
           of the general partner or sponsor, that has
           been approved by a majority of the out-
           standing units of each of the participating

limited partnerships, and that has such authority as is necessary to protect the interest of limited partners, including the authority to hire independent advisors, to negotiate with the general partner or sponsor on behalf the limited partners, and to make a recommendation to the limited partners with respect to the proposed transaction; or

    v. other comparable rights that are prescribed by rule by the exchange and that are designed to protect dissenting limited partners;

B. the right not to have their voting power unfairly reduced or abridged;

C. the right not to bear an unfair portion of the costs of a proposed limited partnership rollup transaction that is rejected; and

D. restrictions on the conversion of contingent interests or fees into non-contingent interests or fees and restrictions on the receipt of a non-contingent equity interest in exchange for fees for services which have not yet been provided.

As used in this paragraph, the term "dissenting limited partner" means a person who, on the date on which soliciting material is mailed to investors, is a holder of a beneficial interest in a limited partnership that is the subject of a limited partnership rollup transaction, and who casts a vote against the transaction and complies with procedures established by the exchange, except that for purposes of an exchange or tender offer, such person shall file an objection in writing under the rules of the exchange during the period during which the offer is outstanding.

c.

1. A national securities exchange shall deny membership to

A. any person, other than a natural person, which is not a registered broker or dealer or

  B. any natural person who is not, or is not associated
  with, a registered broker or dealer.

2. A national securities exchange may, and in cases in which
the Commission, by order, directs as necessary or appropriate in the public interest or for the protection of the
investors shall, deny membership to any registered broker
or dealer or natural person associated with a registered broker or dealer, and bar from becoming associated with a
member any person, who is subject to a statutory disqualification. A national securities exchange shall file notice
with the Commission not less than thirty days prior to admitting any person to membership or permitting any person to become associated with a member, if the exchange
knew, or in the exercise of reasonable care should have
known, that such person was subject to a statutory disqualification. The notice shall be in such form and contain
such information as the Commission, by rule, may prescribe as necessary or appropriate in the public interest or
for the protection of investors.

3.

  A. A national securities exchange may deny membership to, or condition the membership of, a registered broker or dealer if

    i. such broker or dealer does not meet such
    standards of financial responsibility or oper-
    ational capability or such broker or dealer
    or any natural person associated with such
    broker or dealer does not meet such stan-
    dards of training, experience, and compe-
    tence as are prescribed by the rules of the
    exchange or

    ii. such broker or dealer or person associated
    with such broker or dealer has engaged
    and there is a reasonable likelihood he will
    again engage in acts or practices inconsis-
    tent with just and equitable principles of
    trade. A national securities exchange may

examine and verify the qualifications of an applicant to become a member and the natural persons associated with such an applicant in accordance with procedures established by the rules of the exchange.

B. A national securities exchange may bar a natural person from becoming a member or associated with a member, or condition the membership of a natural person or association of a natural person with a member, if such natural person

   i.   does not meet such standards of training, experience, and competence as are prescribed by the rules of the exchange or

   ii. has engaged and there is a reasonable likelihood he will again engage in acts or practices inconsistent with just and equitable principles of trade. A national securities exchange may examine and verify the qualifications of an applicant to become a person associated with a member in accordance with procedures established by the rules of the exchange and require any person associated with a member, or any class of such persons, to be registered with the exchange in accordance with procedures so established.

C. A national securities exchange may bar any person from becoming associated with a member if such person does not agree

   i.   to supply the exchange with such information with respect to its relationship and dealings with the member as may be specified in the rules of the exchange and

   ii. to permit the examination of its books and records to verify the accuracy of any information so supplied.

4. A national securities exchange may limit

   A. the number of members of the exchange and

   B. the number of members and designated represen-
       tatives of members permitted to effect transactions
       on the floor of the exchange without the services
       of another person acting as broker: Provided, how-
       ever, That no national securities exchange shall have
       the authority to decrease the number of member-
       ships in such exchange, or the number of members
       and designated representatives of members permit-
       ted to effect transactions on the floor of such ex-
       change without the services of another person acting
       as broker, below such number in effect on May 1,
       1975, or the date such exchange was registered with
       the Commission, whichever is later: And provided
       further, That the Commission, in accordance with
       the provisions of Section 19(c) of this title, may
       amend the rules of any national securities exchange
       to increase (but not to decrease) or to remove any
       limitation on the number of memberships in such
       exchange or the number of members or designated
       representatives of members permitted to effect
       transactions on the floor of the exchange without
       the services of another person acting as broker, if
       the Commission finds that such limitation imposes
       a burden on competition not necessary or appro-
       priate in furtherance of the purposes of this title.

d.

1. In any proceeding by a national securities exchange to
    determine whether a member or person associated with a
    member should be disciplined (other than a summary pro-
    ceeding pursuant to paragraph (3) of this subsection), the
    exchange shall bring specific charges, notify such member
    or person of, and give him an opportunity to defend against,
    such charges, and keep a record. A determination by the
    exchange to impose a disciplinary sanction shall be sup-
    ported by a statement setting forth—

A. any act or practice in which such member or person associated with a member has been found to have engaged, or which such member or person has been found to have omitted;

B. the specific provision of this title, the rules or regulations thereunder, or the rules of the exchange which any such act or practice, or omission to act, is deemed to violate; and

C. the sanction imposed and the reasons therefor.

2. In any proceeding by a national securities exchange to determine whether a person shall be denied membership, barred from becoming associated with a member, or prohibited or limited with respect to access to services offered by the exchange or a member thereof (other than a summary proceeding pursuant to paragraph (3) of this subsection), the exchange shall notify such person of, and give him an opportunity to be heard upon, the specific grounds for denial, bar, or prohibition or limitation under consideration and keep a record. A determination by the exchange to deny membership, bar a person from becoming associated with a member, or prohibit or limit a person with respect to access to services offered by the exchange or a member thereof shall be supported by a statement setting forth the specific grounds on which the denial, bar, or prohibition or limitation is based.

3. A national securities exchange may summarily

A. suspend a member or person associated with a member who has been and is expelled or suspended from any self-regulatory organization or barred or suspended from being associated with a member of any self-regulatory organization,

B. suspend a member who is in such financial or operating difficulty that the exchange determines and so notifies the Commission that the member cannot be permitted to continue to do business as a member with safety to investors, creditors, other members, or the exchange, or

C. limit or prohibit any person with respect to access to services offered by the exchange if subparagraph (A) or (B) of this paragraph is applicable to such person or, in the case of a person who is not a member, if the exchange determines that such person does not meet the qualification requirements or other prerequisites for such access and such person cannot be permitted to continue to have such access with safety to investors, creditors, members, or the exchange. Any person aggrieved by any such summary action shall be promptly afforded an opportunity for a hearing by the exchange in accordance with the provisions of paragraph (1) or (2) of this subsection. The Commission, by order, may stay any such summary action on its own motion or upon application by any person aggrieved thereby, if the Commission determines summarily or after notice and opportunity for hearing (which hearing may consist solely of the submission of affidavits or presentation of oral arguments) that such stay is consistent with the public interest and the protection of investors.

e.

1. On and after the date of enactment of the Securities Acts Amendments of 1975, no national securities exchange may impose any schedule or fix rates of commissions, allowances, discounts, or other fees to be charged by its members: Provided, however, That until May 1, 1976, the preceding provisions of this paragraph shall not prohibit any such exchange from imposing or fixing any schedule of commissions, allowances, discounts, or other fees to be charged by its members for acting as broker on the floor of the exchange or as odd-lot dealer: And provided further, That the Commission, in accordance with the provisions of Section 19(b) of this title as modified by the provisions of paragraph (3) of this subsection, may—

    A. permit a national securities exchange, by rule, to impose a reasonable schedule or fix reasonable rates of commissions, allowances, discounts, or other fees to be charged by its members for effecting transactions on such exchange prior to November 1, 1976, if the Commission finds that such schedule or fixed rates of commissions, allowances, discounts, or other fees are in the public interest; and

B. permit a national securities exchange, by rule, to impose a schedule or fix rates of commissions, allowances, discounts, or other fees to be charged by its members for effecting transactions on such exchange after November 1, 1976, if the Commission finds that such schedule or fixed rates of commissions, allowances, discounts, or other fees

    i. are reasonable in relation to the costs of providing the service for which such fees are charged (and the Commission publishes the standards employed in adjudging reasonableness) and

    ii. do not impose any burden on competition not necessary or appropriate in furtherance of the purposes of this title, taking into consideration the competitive effects of permitting such schedule or fixed rates weighed against the competitive effects of other lawful actions which the Commission is authorized to take under this title.

2. Notwithstanding the provisions of Section 19(c) of this title, the Commission, by rule, may abrogate any exchange rule which imposes a schedule or fixes rates of commissions, allowances, discounts, or other fees, if the Commission determines that such schedule or fixed rates are no longer reasonable, in the public interest, or necessary to accomplish the purposes of this title.

3.

A. Before approving or disapproving any proposed rule change submitted by a national securities exchange which would impose a schedule or fix rates of commissions, allowances, discounts, or other fees to be charged by its members for effecting transactions on such exchange, the Commission shall afford interested persons

    i.   an opportunity for oral presentation of data, views, and arguments and

    ii. with respect to any such rule concerning transactions effected after November 1, 1976, if the Commission determines there are disputed issues of material fact, to present such rebuttal submissions and to conduct (or have conducted under subparagraph (B) of this paragraph) such cross-examination as the Commission determines to be appropriate and required for full disclosure and proper resolution of such disputed issues of material fact.

B. The Commission shall prescribe rules and make rulings concerning any proceeding in accordance with subparagraph (A) of this paragraph designed to avoid unnecessary costs or delay. Such rules or rulings may

    i.   impose reasonable time limits on each interested person's oral presentations, and

    ii. require any cross-examination to which a person may be entitled under subparagraph (A) of this paragraph to be conducted by the Commission on behalf of that person in such manner as the Commission determines to be appropriate and required for full disclosure and proper resolution of disputed issues of material fact.

C.

    i.   If any class of persons, the members of which are entitled to conduct (or have conducted) cross-examination under sub-paragraphs (A) and (B) of this paragraph and which have, in the view of the Commission, the same or similar interests in the proceeding, cannot agree upon a single representative of such interests for purposes of cross-examination, the Commission may make rules and rulings specifying the manner in which such interests shall be represented and such cross-examination conducted.

    ii. No member of any class of persons with respect to which the Commission has specified the manner in which its interests shall be represented pursuant to clause (i) of this subparagraph shall be denied, pursuant to such clause (i), the opportunity to conduct (or have conducted) cross-examination as to issues affecting his particular interests if he satisfies the Commission that he has made a reasonable and good faith effort to reach agreement upon group representation and there are substantial and relevant issues which would not be presented adequately by group representation.

D. A transcript shall be kept of any oral presentation and cross-examination.

E. In addition to the bases specified in subsection 25(a), a reviewing Court may set aside an order of the Commission under Section 19(b) approving an exchange rule imposing a schedule or fixing rates of commissions, allowances, discounts, or other fees, if the Court finds—

    1. a Commission determination under subparagraph (A) of this paragraph that an interested person is not entitled to conduct cross-examination or make rebuttal submissions, or

2. a Commission rule or ruling under sub-paragraph (B) of this paragraph limiting the petitioner's cross-examination or rebuttal submissions,

F. has precluded full disclosure and proper resolution of disputed issues of material fact which were necessary for fair determination by the Commission.

f. The Commission, by rule or order, as it deems necessary or appropriate in the public interest and for the protection of investors, to maintain fair and orderly markets, or to assure equal regulation, may require—

1. any person not a member or a designated representative of a member of a national securities exchange effecting transactions on such exchange without the services of another person acting as a broker, or

2. any broker or dealer not a member of a national securities exchange effecting transactions on such exchange on a regular basis, to comply with such rules of such exchange as the Commission may specify.

SECTION 7—MARGIN REQUIREMENTS

a. For the purpose of preventing the excessive use of credit for the purchase or carrying of securities, the Board of Governors of the Federal Reserve System shall, prior to the effective date of this section and from time to time thereafter, prescribe rules and regulations with respect to the amount of credit that may be initially extended and subsequently maintained on any security (other than an exempted security). For the initial extension of credit, such rules and regulations shall be based upon the following standard: An amount not greater than whichever is the higher of—

1. 55 per centum of the current market price of the security, or

2. 100 per centum of the lowest market price of the security during the preceding thirty-six calendar months, but not more than 75 per centum of the current market price.

Such rules and regulations may make appropriate provision with respect to the carrying of undermargined accounts for limited periods and under specified conditions; the withdrawal of funds or securities; the substitution or additional purchases of securities; the transfer of accounts from one lender to another; special or different margin requirements for delayed deliveries, short sales, arbitrage transactions, and securities to which paragraph (2) of this subsection does not apply; the bases and the methods to be used in calculating loans, and margins and market prices; and similar administrative adjustments and details. For the purposes of paragraph (2) of this subsection, until July 1, 1936, the lowest price at which a security has sold on or after July 1, 1933, shall be considered as the lowest price at which such security has sold during the preceding thirty-six calendar months.

b. Notwithstanding the provisions of <u>subsection (a)</u> of this section, the Board of Governors of the Federal Reserve System, may, from time to time, with respect to all or specified securities or transactions, or classes of securities, or classes of transactions, by such rules and regulations

1. prescribe such lower margin requirements for the initial extension or maintenance of credit as it deems necessary or appropriate for the accommodation of commerce and industry, having due regard to the general credit situation of the country, and

2. prescribe such higher margin requirements for the initial extension or maintenance of credit as it may deem necessary or appropriate to prevent the excessive use of credit to finance transactions in securities.

c. Unlawful Credit Extension to Customers.—

1. Prohibition.—It shall be unlawful for any member of a national securities exchange or any broker or dealer, directly or indirectly, to extend or maintain credit or arrange for the extension or maintenance of credit to or for any customer—

   A. On any security (other than an exempted security), in contravention of the rules and regulations which the Board of Governors of the Federal Reserve

System (hereafter in this section referred to as the 'Board') shall prescribe under subsections (a) and (b) of this section;

B. Without collateral or on any collateral other than securities, except in accordance with such rules and regulations as the Board may prescribe—

    i. to permit under specified conditions and for a limited period any such member, broker, or dealer to maintain a credit initially extended in conformity with the rules and regulations of the Board; and

    ii. to permit the extension or maintenance of credit in cases where the extension or maintenance of credit is not for the purpose of purchasing or carrying securities or of evading or circumventing the provisions of subparagraph (A).

2. Exception.—This subsection and the rules and regulations issued under this subsection shall not apply to any credit extended, maintained, or arranged by a member of a national securities exchange or a broker or dealer to or for a member of a national securities exchange or a registered broker or dealer—

A. a substantial portion of whose business consists of transactions with persons other than brokers or dealers; or

B. to finance its activities as a market maker or an underwriter;

except that the Board may impose such rules and regulations, in whole or in part, on any credit otherwise exempted by this paragraph if the Board determines that such action is necessary or appropriate in the public interest or for the protection of investors.

d. Unlawful Credit Extension in Violation of Rules and Regulations; Exception to Application of Rules, Etc.—

1. Prohibition.—It shall be unlawful for any person not subject to subsection (c) to extend or maintain credit or to arrange for the extension or maintenance of credit for the purpose of purchasing or carrying any security, in contravention of such rules and regulations as the Board of Governors of the Federal Reserve System shall prescribe to prevent the excessive use of credit for the purchasing or carrying of or trading in securities in circumvention of the other provisions of this section. Such rules and regulations may impose upon all loans made for the purpose of purchasing or carrying securities limitations similar to those imposed upon members, brokers, or dealers by subsection (c) of this section and the rules and regulations thereunder.

2. Exceptions.—This subsection and the rules and regulations thereunder shall not apply to any credit extended, maintained, or arranged—

   A. by a person not in the ordinary course of his business,

   B. on an exempted security,

   C. to or for a member of a national securities exchange or a registered broker or dealer—

      i. a substantial portion of whose business consists of transactions with persons other than brokers or dealers; or

      ii. to finance its activities as a market maker or an underwriter;

   D. by a bank on a security other than an equity security, or

   E. as the Board shall, by such rules, regulations, or orders as it may deem necessary or appropriate in the public interest or for the protection of investors, exempt, either unconditionally or upon specified terms and conditions or for stated periods, from the operation of this subsection and the rules and regulations thereunder.

3. Board authority.—The Board may impose such rules and regulations, in whole or in part, on any credit otherwise exempted by subparagraph (c) if it determines that such action is necessary or appropriate in the public interest or for the protection of investors.

e. The provisions of this section or the rules and regulations thereunder shall not apply on or before July 1, 1937, to any loan or extension of credit made prior to the enactment of this title or to the maintenance, renewal, or extension of any such loan or credit, except to the extent that the Board of Governors of the Federal Reserve System may by rules and regulations prescribe as necessary to prevent the circumvention of the provisions of this section or the rules and regulations thereunder by means of withdrawals of funds or securities, substitutions of securities, or additional purchases or by any other device.

f.

1. It is unlawful for any United States person, or any foreign person controlled by a United States person or acting on behalf of or in conjunction with such person, to obtain, receive, or enjoy the beneficial use of a loan or other extension of credit from any lender (without regard to whether the lender's office or place of business is in a State or the transaction occurred in whole or in part within a State) for the purpose of

 A. purchasing or carrying United States securities, or

 B. purchasing or carrying within the United States of any other securities, if, under this section or rules and regulations prescribed thereunder, the loan or other credit transaction is prohibited or would be prohibited if it had been made or the transaction had otherwise occurred in a lender's office or other place of business in a State.

2. For the purposes of this subsection—

 A. The term "United States person" includes a person which is organized or exists under the laws of any State or, in the case of a natural person, a citizen or resident of the United States; a domestic estate; or a trust in which one or more of the foregoing persons has a cumulative direct or indirect beneficial interest in excess of 50 per centum of the value of the trust.

   B. The term "United States security" means a security (other than an exempted security) issued by a person incorporated under the laws of any State, or whose principal place of business is within a State.

   C. The term "foreign person controlled by a United States person" includes any noncorporate entity in which United States persons directly or indirectly have more than a 50 per centum beneficial interest, and any corporation in which one or more United States persons, directly or indirectly, own stock possessing more than 50 per centum of the total combined voting power of all classes of stock entitled to vote, or more than 50 per centum of the total value of shares of all classes of stock.

  3. The Board of Governors of the Federal Reserve System may, in its discretion and with due regard for the purposes of this section, by rule or regulation exempt any class of United States persons or foreign persons controlled by a United States person from the application of this subsection.

 g. Subject to such rules and regulations as the Board of Governors of the Federal Reserve System may adopt in the public interest and for the protection of investors, no member of a national securities exchange or broker or dealer shall be deemed to have extended or maintained credit or arranged for the extension or maintenance of credit for the purpose of purchasing a security, within the meaning of this section, by reason of a bona fide agreement for delayed delivery of a mortgage related security or a small business related security against full payment of the purchase price thereof upon such delivery within one hundred and eighty days after the purchase, or within such shorter period as the Board of Governors of the Federal Reserve System may prescribe by rule or regulation.

SECTION 8—RESTRICTIONS ON BORROWING BY MEMBERS, BROKERS, AND DEALERS

It shall be unlawful for any registered broker or dealer, member of a national securities exchange, or broker or dealer who transacts a business in securities through the medium of any member of a national securities exchange, directly or indirectly—

a. To borrow in the ordinary course of business as a broker or dealer on any security (other than an exempted security) registered on a national securities exchange except

　　1. from or through a member bank of the Federal Reserve System,

　　2. from any nonmember bank which shall have filed with the Board of Governors of the Federal Reserve System an agreement, which is still in force and which is in the form prescribed by the Board, undertaking to comply with all provisions of this chapter, the Federal Reserve Act as amended, and the Banking Act of 1933, which are applicable to member banks and which relate to the use of credit to finance transactions in securities, and with such rules and regulations as may be prescribed pursuant to such provisions of law or for the purpose of preventing evasions thereof, or

　　3. in accordance with such rules and regulations as the Board of Governors of the Federal Reserve System may prescribe to permit loans between such members and/or brokers and/or dealers, or to permit loans to meet emergency needs. Any such agreement filed with the Board of Governors of the Federal Reserve System shall be subject to termination at any time by order of the Board, after appropriate notice and opportunity for hearing, because of any failure by such bank to comply with the provisions thereof or with such provisions of law or rules or regulations; and, for any willful violation of such agreement, such bank shall be subject to the penalties provided for violations of rules and regulations prescribed under this Act. The provisions of Sections 21 and 25 of this Act shall apply in the case of any

such proceeding or order of the Board of Governors of the Federal Reserve System in the same manner as such provisions apply in the case of proceedings and orders of the Commission. Subject to such rules and regulations as the Board of Governors of the Federal Reserve System may adopt in the public interest and for the protection of investors, no person shall be deemed to have borrowed within the ordinary course of business, within the meaning of this section, by reason of a bona fide agreement for delayed delivery of a mortgage related security or a small business related security against full payment of the purchase price thereof upon such delivery within one hundred and eighty days after the purchase, or within such shorter period as the Board of Governors of the Federal Reserve System may prescribe by rule or regulation.

b. In contravention of such rules and regulations as the Commission shall prescribe for the protection of investors to hypothecate or arrange for the hypothecation of any securities carried for the account of any customer under circumstances

   1. that will permit the commingling of his securities without his written consent with the securities of any other customer,

   2. that will permit such securities to be commingled with the securities of any person other than a bona fide customer, or

   3. that will permit such securities to be hypothecated, or subjected to any lien or claim of the pledgee, for a sum in excess of the aggregate indebtedness of such customers in respect of such securities.

c. To lend or arrange for the lending of any securities carried for the account of any customer without the written consent of such customer or in contravention of such rules and regulations as the Commission shall prescribe for the protection of investors. It shall be unlawful for any registered broker or dealer, member of a national securities exchange, or broker or dealer who transacts a business in securities through the medium of any member of a national securities exchange, directly or indirectly—

SECTION 9—PROHIBITION AGAINST MANIPULATION OF SECURITY PRICES

a. It shall be unlawful for any person, directly or indirectly, by the use of the mails or any means or instrumentality of interstate commerce, or of any facility of any national securities exchange, or for any member of a national securities exchange—

1. For the purpose of creating a false or misleading appearance of active trading in any security registered on a national securities exchange, or a false or misleading appearance with respect to the market for any such security,

    A. to effect any transaction in such security which involves no change in the beneficial ownership thereof, or

    B. to enter an order or orders for the purchase of such security with the knowledge that an order or orders of substantially the same size, at substantially the same time, and at substantially the same price, for the sale of any such security, has been or will be entered by or for the same or different parties, or

    C. to enter any order or orders for the sale of any such security with the knowledge that an order or orders of substantially the same size, at substantially the same time, and at substantially the same price, for the purchase of such security, has been or will be entered by or for the same or different parties.

2. To effect, alone or with one or more other persons, a series of transactions in any security registered on a national securities exchange creating actual or apparent active trading in such security, or raising or depressing the price of such security, for the purpose of inducing the purchase or sale of such security by others.

3. If a dealer or broker, or other person selling or offering for sale or purchasing or offering to purchase the security, to induce the purchase or sale of any security registered on a national securities exchange by the circulation or dissemination in the ordinary course of business of information to

the effect that the price of any such security will or is likely to rise or fall because of market operations of any one or more persons conducted for the purpose of raising or depressing the price of such security.

4. If a dealer or broker, or other person selling or offering for sale or purchasing or offering to purchase the security, to make, regarding any security registered on a national securities exchange, for the purpose of inducing the purchase or sale of such security, any statement which was at the time and in the light of the circumstances under which it was made, false or misleading with respect to any material fact, and which he knew or had reasonable ground to believe was so false or misleading.

5. For a consideration, received directly or indirectly from a dealer or broker, or other person selling or offering for sale or purchasing or offering to purchase the security, to induce the purchase of any security registered on a national securities exchange by the circulation or dissemination of information to the effect that the price of any such security will or is likely to rise or fall because of the market operations of any one or more persons conducted for the purpose of raising or depressing the price of such security.

6. To effect either alone or with one or more other persons any series of transactions for the purchase and/or sale of any security registered on a national securities exchange for the purpose of pegging, fixing, or stabilizing the price of such security in contravention of such rules and regulations as the Commission may prescribe as necessary or appropriate in the public interest or for the protection of investors.

b. It shall be unlawful for any person to effect, by use of any facility of a national securities exchange, in contravention of such rules and regulations as the Commission may prescribe as necessary or appropriate in the public interest or for the protection of investors—

1. any transaction in connection with any security whereby any party to such transaction acquires any put, call, straddle,

or other option or privilege of buying the security from or selling the security to another without being bound to do so; or

2. any transaction in connection with any security with relation to which he has, directly or indirectly, any interest in any such put, call, straddle, option, or privilege; or

3. any transaction in any security for the account of any person who he has reason to believe has, and who actually has, directly or indirectly, any interest in any such put, call, straddle, option, or privilege with relation to such security.

c. It shall be unlawful for any member of a national securities exchange directly or indirectly to endorse or guarantee the performance of any put, call, straddle, option, or privilege in relation to any security registered on a national securities exchange, in contravention of such rules and regulations as the Commission may prescribe as necessary or appropriate in the public interest or for the protection of investors.

d. The terms "put," "call," "straddle," "option," or "privilege" as used in this section shall not include any registered warrant, right, or convertible security.

e. Any person who willfully participates in any act or transaction in violation of subsections (a), (b), or (c) of this section, shall be liable to any person who shall purchase or sell any security at a price which was affected by such act or transaction, and the person so injured may sue in law or in equity in any court of competent jurisdiction to recover the damages sustained as a result of any such act or transaction. In any such suit the court may, in its discretion, require an undertaking for the payment of the costs of such suit, and assess reasonable costs, including reasonable attorneys' fees, against either party litigant. Every person who becomes liable to make any payment under this subsection may recover contribution as in cases of contract from any person who, if joined in the original suit, would have been liable to make the same payment. No action shall be maintained to enforce any liability created under this section, unless brought within one year after the discovery of the facts constituting the violation and within three years after such violation.

f. The provisions of <u>subsection (a)</u> shall not apply to an exempted security.

g. Notwithstanding any other provision of law, the Commission shall have the authority to regulate the trading of any put, call, straddle, option, or privilege on any security, certificate of deposit, or group or index of securities (including any interest therein or based on the value thereof), or any put, call, straddle, option, or privilege entered into on a national securities exchange relating to foreign currency (but not, with respect to any of the foregoing, an option on a contract for future delivery).

h. **Limitations on Practices That Affect Market Volatility.**—It shall be unlawful for any person, by the use of the mails or any means or instrumentality of interstate commerce or of any facility of any national securities exchange, to use or employ any act or practice in connection with the purchase or sale of any equity security in contravention of such rules or regulations as the Commission may adopt, consistent with the public interest, the protection of investors, and the maintenance of fair and orderly markets—

   1. to prescribe means reasonably designed to prevent manipulation of price levels of the equity securities market or a substantial segment thereof; and

   2. to prohibit or constrain, during periods of extraordinary market volatility, any trading practice in connection with the purchase or sale of equity securities that the Commission determines

      A. has previously contributed significantly to extraordinary levels of volatility that have threatened the maintenance of fair and orderly markets; and

      B. is reasonably certain to engender such levels of volatility if not prohibited or constrained.

   3. In adopting rules under paragraph (2), the Commission shall, consistent with the purposes of this subsection, minimize the impact on the normal operations of the market and a natural person's freedom to buy or sell any equity security.

SECTION 10—REGULATION OF THE USE OF MANIPULATIVE AND DECEPTIVE DEVICES

It shall be unlawful for any person, directly or indirectly, by the use of any means or instrumentality of interstate commerce or of the mails, or of any facility of any national securities exchange—

a. To effect a short sale, or to use or employ any stop-loss order in connection with the purchase or sale, of any security registered on a national securities exchange, in contravention of such rules and regulations as the Commission may prescribe as necessary or appropriate in the public interest or for the protection of investors.

b. To use or employ, in connection with the purchase or sale of any security registered on a national securities exchange or any security not so registered, any manipulative or deceptive device or contrivance in contravention of such rules and regulations as the Commission may prescribe as necessary or appropriate in the public interest or for the protection of investors.

SECTION 10A—AUDIT REQUIREMENTS

a. **In General.**—Each audit required pursuant to this title of the financial statements of an issuer by an independent public accountant shall include, in accordance with generally accepted auditing standards, as may be modified or supplemented from time to time by the Commission—

   1. procedures designed to provide reasonable assurance of detecting illegal acts that would have a direct and material effect on the determination of financial statement amounts;

   2. procedures designed to identify related party transactions that are material to the financial statements or otherwise require disclosure therein; and

   3. an evaluation of whether there is substantial doubt about the ability of the issuer to continue as a going concern during the ensuing fiscal year.

b. **Required response to audit discoveries.**—

1. **Investigation and report to management.**—If, in the course of conducting an audit pursuant to this title to which subsection (a) applies, the independent public accountant detects or otherwise becomes aware of information indicating that an illegal act (whether or not perceived to have a material effect on the financial statements of the issuer) has or may have occurred, the accountant shall, in accordance with generally accepted auditing standards, as may be modified or supplemented from time to time by the Commission—

     A.

          i.   determine whether it is likely that an illegal act has occurred; and

          ii. if so, determine and consider the possible effect of the illegal act on the financial statements of the issuer, including any contingent monetary effects, such as fines, penalties, and damages; and

     B.   as soon as practicable, inform the appropriate level of the management of the issuer and assure that the audit committee of the issuer, or the board of directors of the issuer in the absence of such a committee, is adequately informed with respect to illegal acts that have been detected or have otherwise come to the attention of such accountant in the course of the audit, unless the illegal act is clearly inconsequential.

2. **Response to failure to take remedial action.**—If, after determining that the audit committee of the board of directors of the issuer, or the board of directors of the issuer in the absence of an audit committee, is adequately informed with respect to illegal acts that have been detected or have otherwise come to the attention of the accountant in the course of the audit of such accountant, the independent public accountant concludes that—

     A.   the illegal act has a material effect on the financial statements of the issuer;

    B. the senior management has not taken, and the board of directors has not caused senior management to take, timely and appropriate remedial actions with respect to the illegal act; and

    C. the failure to take remedial action is reasonably expected to warrant departure from a standard report of the auditor, when made, or warrant resignation from the audit engagement; the independent public accountant shall, as soon as practicable, directly report its conclusions to the board of directors.

3. **Notice to commission; response to failure to notify.**—An issuer whose board of directors receives a report under paragraph (2) shall inform the Commission by notice not later than 1 business day after the receipt of such report and shall furnish the independent public accountant making such report with a copy of the notice furnished to the Commission. If the independent public accountant fails to receive a copy of the notice before the expiration of the required 1 business day period, the independent public accountant shall—

    A. resign from the engagement; or

    B. furnish to the Commission a copy of its report (or the documentation of any oral report given) not later than 1 business day following such failure to receive notice.

4. **Report after resignation.**—If an independent public accountant resigns from an engagement under paragraph (3)(A), the accountant shall, not later than 1 business day following the failure by the issuer to notify the Commission under paragraph (3), furnish to the Commission a copy of the accountant's report (or the documentation of any oral report given).

c. **Auditor liability limitation.**—No independent public accountant shall be liable in a private action for any finding, conclusion, or statement expressed in a report made pursuant to paragraph (3) or (4) of subsection (b), including any rule promulgated pursuant thereto.

d. **Civil penalties in cease-and-desist proceedings.**—If the Commission finds, after notice and opportunity for hearing in a proceeding instituted pursuant to section 21C, that an independent public accountant has willfully violated paragraph (3) or (4) of subsection (b), the Commission may, in addition to entering an order under section 21C, impose a civil penalty against the independent public accountant and any other person that the Commission finds was a cause of such violation. The determination to impose a civil penalty and the amount of the penalty shall be governed by the standards set forth in section 21B.

e. **Preservation of existing authority.**—Except as provided in subsection (d), nothing in this section shall be held to limit or otherwise affect the authority of the Commission under this title.

f. **Definition.**—As used in this section, the term "illegal act" means an act or omission that violates any law, or any rule or regulation having the force of law.

SECTION 11—TRADING BY MEMBERS OF EXCHANGES, BROKERS, AND DEALERS

a.

1. It shall be unlawful for any member of a national securities exchange to effect any transaction on such exchange for its own account, the account of an associated'person, or an account with respect to which it or an associated person thereof exercises investment discretion:

   Provided, however,

   That this paragraph shall not make unlawful—

   A. any transaction by a dealer acting in the capacity of market maker;

   B. any transaction for the account of an odd-lot dealer in a security in which he is so registered;

   C. any stabilizing transaction effected in compliance with rules under section 10(b) of this title to facilitate a distribution of a security in which the member effecting such transaction is participating;

D. any bona fide arbitrage transaction, any bona fide hedge transaction involving a long or short position in an equity security and a long or short position in a security entitling the holder to acquire or sell such equity security, or any risk arbitrage transaction in connection with a merger, acquisition tender offer, or similar transaction involving a recapitalization;

E. any transaction for the account of a natural person, the estate of a natural person, or a trust (other than an investment company) created by a natural person for himself or another natural person;

F. any transaction to offset a transaction made in error;

G. any other transaction for a member's own account provided that

  i. such member is primarily engaged in the business of underwriting and distributing securities issued by other persons, selling securities to customers, and acting as broker, or any one or more of such activities, and whose gross income normally is derived principally from such business and related activities and

  ii. such transaction is effected in compliance with rules of the Commission which, as a minimum, assure that the transaction is not inconsistent with the maintenance of fair and orderly markets and yields priority, parity, and precedence in execution to orders for the account of persons who are not members or associated with members of the exchange; and

H. any transaction for an account with respect to which such member or an associated person thereof exercises investment discretion if such member—

    i. has obtained, from the person or persons authorized to transact business for the account, express authorization for such member or associated person to effect such transactions prior to engaging in the practice of effecting such transactions;

   ii. furnishes the person or persons authorized to transact business for the account with a statement at least annually disclosing the aggregate compensation received by the exchange member in effecting such transactions; and

  iii. complies with any rules the Commission has prescribed with respect to the requirements of clauses (i) and (ii); and

          I. any other transaction of a kind which the Commission, by rule, determines is consistent with the purposes of this paragraph, the protection of investors, and the maintenance of fair and orderly markets.

        II. The Commission, by rule, as it deems necessary or appropriate in the public interest and for the protection of investors, to maintain fair and orderly markets, or to assure equal regulation of exchange markets and markets occurring otherwise than on an exchange, may regulate or prohibit:

            A. transactions on a national securities exchange not unlawful under paragraph (1) of this subsection effected by any member thereof for its own account (unless such member is acting in the capacity of market maker or odd-lot dealer), the account of an associated person, or an account with respect to which such member or an associated person thereof exercises investment discretion;

B. transactions otherwise than on a national securities exchange effected by use of the mails or any means or instrumentality of interstate commerce by any member of a national securities exchange, broker, or dealer for the account of such member, broker, or dealer (unless such member, broker, or dealer is acting in the capacity of a market maker) the account of an associated person, or an account with respect to which such member, broker, or dealer or associated person thereof exercises investment discretion; and

C. transactions on a national securities exchange effected by any broker or dealer not a member thereof for the account of such broker or dealer (unless such broker or dealer is acting in the capacity of market maker), the account of an associated person, or an account with respect to which such broker or dealer or associated person thereof exercises investment discretion.

3. The provisions of <u>paragraph (1)</u> of this subsection insofar as they apply to transactions on a national securities exchange effected by a member thereof who was a member on February 1, 1978 shall not become effective until February 1, 1979. Nothing in this paragraph shall be construed to impair or limit the authority of the Commission to regulate or prohibit such transactions prior to February 1, 1979, pursuant to <u>paragraph (2)</u> of this subsection.

b. When not in contravention of such rules and regulations as the Commission may prescribe as necessary or appropriate in the public interest and for the protection of investors, to maintain fair and orderly markets, or to remove impediments to and perfect the mechanism of a national market system, the rules of a national securities exchange may permit (1) a member to be registered as an odd-lot dealer and as such to buy and sell for his own account so far as may be reasonably necessary to carry on such odd-lot transactions, and (2) a member to be registered as a specialist. Under the rules and regulations of the Commission a specialist may be permitted to act as a broker and dealer or limited to acting as a broker or dealer. It shall be unlawful for a specialist or an official of the exchange to disclose information in regard to orders placed with such specialist which is not available to all members of the exchange, to any person other than an official of the exchange, a representative of the Commission, or a specialist who may be acting for such specialist: Provided, however, That the Commission, by rule, may require disclosure to all members of the exchange of all orders placed with specialists, under such rules and regulations as the Commission may prescribe as necessary or appropriate in the public interest or for the protection of investors. It shall also be unlawful for a specialist permitted to act as a broker and dealer to effect on the exchange as broker any transaction except upon a market or limited price order.

c. If because of the limited volume of transactions effected on an exchange, it is in the opinion of the Commission impracticable and not necessary or appropriate in the public interest or for the protection of investors to apply any of the foregoing provisions of this section or the rules and regulations thereunder, the Commission shall have power, upon application of the exchange and on a showing that the rules of such exchange are otherwise adequate for the protection of investors, to exempt such exchange and its members from any such provision or rules and regulations.

d.   It shall be unlawful for a member of a national securities exchange who is both a dealer and a broker, or for any person who both as a broker and a dealer transacts a business in securities through the medium of a member or otherwise, to effect through the use of any facility of a national securities exchange or of the mails or of any means or instrumentality of interstate commerce, or otherwise in the case of a member,

1.   any transaction in connection with which, directly or indirectly, he extends or maintains or arranges for the extension or maintenance of credit to or for a customer on any security (other than an exempted security) which was a part of a new issue in the distribution of which he participated as a member of a selling syndicate or group within thirty days prior to such transaction: Provided, That credit shall not be deemed extended by reason of a bona fide delayed delivery of

i.   any such security against full payment of the entire purchase price thereof upon such delivery within thirty-five days after such purchase or

ii.   any mortgage related security or any small business related security against full payment of the entire purchase price thereof upon such delivery within one hundred and eighty days after such purchase, or within such shorter period as the Commission may prescribe by rule or regulation, or

2.   any transaction with respect to any security (other than an exempted security) unless, if the transaction is with a customer, he discloses to such customer in writing at or before the completion of the transaction whether he is acting as a dealer for his own account, as a broker for such customer, or as a broker for some other person.

SECTION 11A—NATIONAL MARKET SYSTEM FOR SECURITIES; SECURITIES INFORMATION PROCESSORS

a.

1. The Congress finds that—

    A. The securities markets are an important national asset which must be preserved and strengthened.

    B. New data processing and communications techniques create the opportunity for more efficient and effective market operations.

    C. It is in the public interest and appropriate for the protection of investors and the maintenance of fair and orderly markets to assure—

        i.   economically efficient execution of securities transactions;

        ii. fair competition among brokers and dealers, among exchange markets, and between exchange markets and markets other than exchange markets;

        iii. the availability to brokers, dealers, and investors of information with respect to quotations for and transactions in securities;

        iv. the practicability of brokers executing investors' orders in the best market; and

        v.   an opportunity, consistent with the provisions of clauses (i) and (iv) of this subparagraph, for investors' orders to be executed without the participation of a dealer.

    D. The linking of all markets for qualified securities through communication and data processing facilities will foster efficiency, enhance competition, increase the information available to brokers, dealers, and investors, facilitate the offsetting of investors' orders, and contribute to best execution of such orders.

2. The Commission is directed, therefore, having due regard for the public interest, the protection of investors, and the maintenance of fair and orderly markets, to use its authority under this title to facilitate the establishment of a national market system for securities (which may include subsystems for particular types of securities with unique trading characteristics) in accordance with the findings and to carry out the objectives set forth in paragraph (1) of this subsection. The Commission, by rule, shall designate the securities or classes of securities qualified for trading in the national market system from among securities other than exempted securities. (Securities or classes of securities so designated hereinafter in this section referred to as "qualified securities".)

3. The Commission is authorized in furtherance of the directive in paragraph (2) of this subsection—

    A. to create one or more advisory committees pursuant to the Federal Advisory Committee Act (which shall be in addition to the National Market Advisory Board established pursuant to subsection (d) of this section) and to employ one or more outside experts;

    B. by rule or order, to authorize or require self-regulatory organizations to act jointly with respect to matters as to which they share authority under this title in planning, developing, operating, or regulating a national market system (or a subsystem thereof) or one or more facilities thereof; and

    C. to conduct studies and make recommendations to the Congress from time to time as to the possible need for modifications of the scheme of self-regulation provided for in this title so as to adapt it to a national market system.

b.

1. Except as otherwise provided in this section, it shall be unlawful for any securities information processor unless registered in accordance with this subsection, directly or indirectly, to make use of the mails or any means or instrumentality of interstate commerce to perform the functions of a securities information processor. The Commission, by rule or order, upon its own motion or upon application, may conditionally or unconditionally exempt any securities information processor or class of securities information processors or security or class of securities from any provision of this section or the rules or regulations thereunder, if the Commission finds that such exemption is consistent with the public interest, the protection of investors, and the purposes of this section, including the maintenance of fair and orderly markets in securities and the removal of impediments to and perfection of the mechanism of a national market system:

   Provided, however,

   That a securities information processor not acting as the exclusive processor of any information with respect to quotations for or transactions in securities is exempt from the requirement to register in accordance with this subsection unless the Commission, by rule or order, finds that the registration of such securities information processor is necessary or appropriate in the public interest, for the protection of investors, or for the achievement of the purposes of this section.

2. A securities information processor may be registered by filing with the Commission an application for registration in such form as the Commission, by rule, may prescribe containing the address of its principal office, or offices, the names of the securities and markets for which it is then acting and for which it proposes to act as a securities information processor, and such other information and documents as the Commission, by rule, may prescribe with regard to performance capability, standards and procedures

for the collection, processing, distribution, and publication of information with respect to quotations for and transactions in securities, personnel qualifications, financial condition, and such other matters as the Commission determines to be germane to the provisions of this title and the rules and regulations thereunder, or necessary or appropriate in furtherance of the purposes of this section.

3. The Commission shall, upon the filing of an application for registration pursuant to paragraph (2) of this subsection, publish notice of the filing and afford interested persons an opportunity to submit written data, views, and arguments concerning such application. Within ninety days of the date of the publication of such notice (or within such longer period as to which the applicant consents) the Commission shall—

   A. by order grant such registration, or

   B. institute proceedings to determine whether registration should be denied. Such proceedings shall include notice of the grounds for denial under consideration and opportunity for hearing and shall be concluded within one hundred eighty days of the date of publication of notice of the filing of the application for registration. At the conclusion of such proceedings the Commission, by order, shall grant or deny such registration. The Commission may extend the time for the conclusion of such proceedings for up to sixty days if it finds good cause for such extension and publishes its reasons for so finding or for such longer periods as to which the applicant consents.

   The Commission shall grant the registration of a securities information processor if the Commission finds that such securities information processor is so organized, and has the capacity, to be able to assure the prompt, accurate, and reliable performance of its functions as a securities information processor, comply with the provisions of this title and the rules and regulations thereunder, carry out its functions in a manner consistent with the purposes of this section, and, insofar as it is acting as an exclusive processor, operate fairly and efficiently. The Commission shall deny the registration of a securities information processor if the Commission does not make any such finding.

4. A registered securities information processor may, upon such terms and conditions as the Commission deems necessary or appropriate in the public interest or for the protection of investors, withdraw from registration by filing a written notice of withdrawal with the Commission. If the Commission finds that any registered securities information processor is no longer in existence or has ceased to do business in the capacity specified in its application for registration, the Commission, by order, shall cancel the registration.

5.

   A. If any registered securities information processor prohibits or limits any person in respect of access to services offered, directly or indirectly, by such securities information processor, the registered securities information processor shall promptly file notice thereof with the Commission. The notice shall be in such form and contain such information as the Commission, by rule, may prescribe as necessary or appropriate in the public interest or for the protection of investors. Any prohibition or limitation on access to services with respect to which a registered securities information processor is required by this paragraph to file notice shall be subject to review by the Commission on its own motion, or upon application by any person aggrieved thereby filed within thirty days after such notice has been filed with the Commission and received by such aggrieved person, or within such longer period as the Commission may determine. Application to the Commission for review, or the institution of review by the Commission on its own motion, shall not operate as a stay of such prohibition or limitation, unless the Commission otherwise orders, summarily or after notice and opportunity for hearing on the question of a stay (which hearing may consist solely of the submission of affidavits or presentation of oral arguments). The Commission shall establish for appropriate cases an expedited procedure for consideration and determination of the question of a stay.

B.   In any proceeding to review the prohibition or limitation of any person in respect of access to services offered by a registered securities information processor, if the Commission finds, after notice and opportunity for hearing, that such prohibition or limitation is consistent with the provisions of this title and the rules and regulations thereunder and that such person has not been discriminated against unfairly, the Commission, by order, shall dismiss the proceeding. If the Commission does not make any such finding or if it finds that such prohibition or limitation imposes any burden on competition not necessary or appropriate in furtherance of the purposes of this title, the Commission, by order, shall set aside the prohibition or limitation and require the registered securities information processor to permit such person access to services offered by the registered securities information processor.

6.   The Commission, by order, may censure or place limitations upon the activities, functions, or operations of any registered securities information processor or suspend for a period not exceeding twelve months or revoke the registration of any such processor, if the Commission finds, on the record after notice and opportunity for hearing, that such censure, placing of limitations, suspension, or revocation is in the public interest and necessary or appropriate for the protection of investors or to assure the prompt,

accurate, or reliable performance of the functions of such securities information processor and that such securities information processor has violated or is unable to comply with any provision of this title or the rules or regulations thereunder.

c.

1. No self-regulatory organization, member thereof, securities information processor, broker, or dealer shall make use of the mails or any means or instrumentality of interstate commerce to collect, process, distribute, publish, or prepare for distribution or publication any information with respect to quotations for or transactions in any security other than an exempted security, to assist, participate in, or coordinate the distribution or publication of such information, or to effect any transaction in, or to induce or attempt to induce the purchase or sale of, any such security in contravention of such rules and regulations as the Commission shall prescribe as necessary or appropriate in the public interest, for the protection of investors, or otherwise in furtherance of the purposes of this title to—

   A. prevent the use, distribution, or publication of fraudulent, deceptive, or manipulative information with respect to quotations for and transactions in such securities;

   B. assure the prompt, accurate, reliable, and fair collection, processing, distribution, and publication of information with respect to quotations for and transactions in such securities and the fairness and usefulness of the form and content of such information;

   C. assure that all securities information processors may, for purposes of distribution and publication, obtain on fair and reasonable terms such information with respect to quotations for and transactions in such securities as is collected, processed, or prepared for distribution or publication by any exclusive processor of such information acting in such capacity;

    D. assure that all exchange members, brokers, dealers, securities information processors, and, subject to such limitations as the Commission, by rule, may impose as necessary or appropriate for the protection of investors or maintenance of fair and orderly markets, all other persons may obtain on terms which are not unreasonably discriminatory such information with respect to quotations for and transactions in such securities as is published or distributed by any self-regulatory organization or securities information processor;

    E. assure that all exchange members, brokers, and dealers transmit and direct orders for the purchase or sale of qualified securities in a manner consistent with the establishment and operation of a national market system; and

    F. assure equal regulation of all markets for qualified securities and all exchange members, brokers, and dealers effecting transactions in such securities.

2. The Commission, by rule, as it deems necessary or appropriate in the public interest or for the protection of investors, may require any person who has effected the purchase or sale of any qualified security by use of the mails or any means or instrumentality of interstate commerce to report such purchase or sale to a registered securities information processor, national securities exchange, or registered securities association and require such processor, exchange, or association to make appropriate distribution and publication of information with respect to such purchase or sale.

3.

    A. The Commission, by rule, is authorized to prohibit brokers and dealers from effecting transactions in securities registered pursuant to section 12(b) otherwise than on a national securities exchange, if the Commission finds, on the record after notice and opportunity for hearing, that—

    i.   as a result of transactions in such securities effected otherwise than on a national securities exchange the fairness or orderliness of the markets for such securities has been affected in a manner contrary to the public interest or the protection of investors;

    ii. no rule of any national securities exchange unreasonably impairs the ability of any dealer to solicit or effect transactions in such securities for his own account or unreasonably restricts competition among dealers in such securities or between dealers acting in the capacity of market makers who are specialists in such securities and such dealers who are not specialists in such securities; and

    iii. the maintenance or restoration of fair and orderly markets in such securities may not be assured through other lawful means under this title.

The Commission may conditionally or unconditionally exempt any security or transaction or any class of securities or transactions from any such prohibition if the Commission deems such exemption consistent with the public interest, the protection of investors, and the maintenance of fair and orderly markets.

B. For the purposes of subparagraph (A) of this paragraph, the ability of a dealer to solicit or effect transactions in securities for his own account shall not be deemed to be unreasonably impaired by any rule of an exchange fairly and reasonably prescribing the sequence in which orders brought to the exchange must be executed or which has been adopted to effect compliance with a rule of the Commission promulgated under this title.

4. The Commission is directed to review any and all rules of national securities exchanges which limit or condition the ability of members to effect transactions in securities otherwise than on such exchanges.

5. No national securities exchange or registered securities association may limit or condition the participation of any member in any registered clearing agency.

d.

1. Not later than one hundred eighty days after the date of enactment of the Securities Acts Amendments of 1975, the Commission shall establish a National Market Advisory Board (hereinafter in this section referred to as the "Advisory Board") to be composed of fifteen members, not all of whom shall be from the same geographical area of the United States, appointed by the Commission for a term specified by the Commission of not less than two years or more than five years. The Advisory Board shall consist of persons associated with brokers and dealers (who shall be a majority) and persons not so associated who are representative of the public and, to the extent feasible, have knowledge of the securities markets of the United States.

2. It shall be the responsibility of the Advisory Board to formulate and furnish to the Commission its views on significant regulatory proposals made by the Commission or any self-regulatory organization concerning the establishment, operation, and regulation of the markets for securities in the United States.

3.

A. The Advisory Board shall study and make recommendations to the Commission as to the steps it finds appropriate to facilitate the establishment of a national market system. In so doing, the Advisory Board shall assume the responsibilities of any advisory committee appointed to advise the Commission with respect to the national market system which is in existence at the time of the establishment of the Advisory Board.

B. The Advisory Board shall study the possible need for modifications of the scheme of self-regulation provided for in this title so as to adapt it to a national market system, including the need for the establishment of a new self-regulatory organization (hereinafter in this section referred to as a "National Market Regulatory Board" or "Regulatory Board") to administer the national market system. In the event the Advisory Board determines a National Market Regulatory Board should be established, it shall make recommendations as to:

    i.   the point in time at which a Regulatory Board should be established;

    ii. the composition of a Regulatory Board;

    iii. the scope of the authority of a Regulatory Board;

    iv. the relationship of a Regulatory Board to the Commission and to existing self-regulatory organizations; and

    v. the manner in which a Regulatory Board should be funded.

The Advisory Board shall report to the Congress, on or before December 31, 1976, the results of such study and its recommendations, including such recommendations for legislation as it deems appropriate.

C. In carrying out its responsibilities under this paragraph, the Advisory Board shall consult with self-regulatory organizations, brokers, dealers, securities information processors, issuers, investors, representatives of Government agencies, and other persons interested or likely to participate in the establishment, operation, or regulation of the national market system.

SECTION 12—REGISTRATION REQUIREMENTS FOR SECURITIES

a. It shall be unlawful for any member, broker, or dealer to effect any transaction in any security (other than an exempted security) on a national securities exchange unless a registration is effective as to such security for such exchange in accordance with the provisions of this title and the rules and regulations thereunder.

b. A security may be registered on a national securities exchange by the issuer filing an application with the exchange (and filing with the Commission such duplicate originals thereof as the Commission may require), which application shall contain—

1. Such information, in such detail, as to the issuer and any person directly or indirectly controlling or controlled by, or under direct or indirect common control with, the issuer, and any guarantor of the security as to principal or interest or both, as the Commission may by rules and regulations require, as necessary or appropriate in the public interest or for the protection of investors, in respect of the following:

    A. the organization, financial structure and nature of the business;

    B. the terms, position, rights, and privileges of the different classes of securities outstanding;

    C. the terms on which their securities are to be, and during the preceding three years have been, offered to the public or otherwise;

    D. the directors, officers, and underwriters, and each security holder of record holding more than 10 per centum of any class of any equity security of the issuer (other than an exempted security), their remuneration and their interests in the securities of, and their material contracts with, the issuer and any person directly or indirectly controlling or controlled by, or under direct or indirect common control with, the issuer;

E.   remuneration to others than directors and officers exceeding $20,000 per annum;

F.   bonus and profit-sharing arrangements;

G.   management and service contracts;

H.   options existing or to be created in respect of their securities;

I.   material contracts, not made in the ordinary course of business, which are to be executed in whole or in part at or after the filing of the application or which were made not more than two years before such filing, and every material patent or contract for a material patent right shall be deemed a material contract;

J.   balance sheets for not more than the three preceding fiscal years, certified if required by the rules and regulations of the Commission by independent public accountants;

K.   profit and loss statements for not more than the three preceding fiscal years, certified if required by the rules and regulations of the Commission by independent public accountants; and

L.   any further financial statements which the Commission may deem necessary or appropriate for the protection of investors.

2.   Such copies of articles of incorporation, by-laws, trust indentures, or corresponding documents by whatever name known, underwriting arrangements, and other similar documents of, and voting trust agreements with respect to, the issuer and any person directly or indirectly controlling or controlled by, or under direct or indirect common control with, the issuer as the Commission may require as necessary or appropriate for the proper protection of investors and to insure fair dealing in the security.

3.   Such copies of material contracts, referred to in paragraph (1)(I) above, as the Commission may require as necessary

or appropriate for the proper protection of investors and to insure fair dealing in the security.

c. If in the judgment of the Commission any information required under subsection (b) is inapplicable to any specified class or classes of issuers, the Commission shall require in lieu thereof the submission of such other information of comparable character as it may deem applicable to such class of issuers.

d. If the exchange authorities certify to the Commission that the security has been approved by the exchange for listing and registration, the registration shall become effective thirty days after the receipt of such certification by the Commission or within such shorter period of time as the Commission may determine. A security registered with a national securities exchange may be withdrawn or stricken from listing and registration in accordance with the rules of the exchange and, upon such terms as the Commission may deem necessary to impose for the protection of investors, upon application by the issuer or the exchange to the Commission; whereupon the issuer shall be relieved from further compliance with the provisions of this section and section 13 of this title and any rules or regulations under such sections as to the securities so withdrawn or stricken.

An unissued security may be registered only in accordance with such rules and regulations as the Commission may prescribe as necessary or appropriate in the public interest or for the protection of investors.

e. Notwithstanding the foregoing provisions of this section, the Commission may by such rules and regulations as it deems necessary or appropriate in the public interest or for the protection of investors permit securities listed on any exchange at the time the registration of such exchange as a national securities exchange becomes effective, to be registered for a period ending not later than July 1, 1935, without complying with the provisions of this section.

f.

    1.

        A. Notwithstanding the preceding subsections of this section, any national securities exchange, in accordance with the requirements of this subsection and the rules hereunder, may extend unlisted trading privileges to—

    i.   any security that is listed and registered on a national securities exchange, subject to subparagraph (B); and

    ii.   any security that is otherwise registered pursuant to this section, or that would be required to be so registered except for the exemption from registration provided in subparagraph (B) or (G) of subsection (g)(2), subject to subparagraph (E) of this paragraph.

B.   A national securities exchange may not extend unlisted trading privileges to a security described in subparagraph (A)(i) during such interval, if any, after the commencement of an initial public offering of such security, as is or may be required pursuant to subparagraph (C).

C.   Not later than 180 days after the date of enactment of the Unlisted Trading Privileges Act of 1994, the Commission shall prescribe, by rule or regulation, the duration of the interval referred to in subparagraph (B), if any, as the Commission determines to be necessary or appropriate for the maintenance of fair and orderly markets, the protection of investors and the public interest, or otherwise in furtherance of the purposes of this title. Until the earlier of the effective date of such rule or regulation or 240 days, after such date of enactment, such interval shall begin at the opening of trading on the day on which such security commences trading on the national securities exchange with which such security is registered and end at the conclusion of the next day of trading.

D.   The Commission may prescribe, by rule or regulation such additional procedures or requirements for extending unlisted trading privileges to any security as the Commission deems necessary or appropriate for the maintenance of fair and orderly markets, the protection of investors and the public interest, or otherwise in furtherance of the purposes of this title.

E. No extension of unlisted trading privileges to securities described in subparagraph (A)(ii) may occur except pursuant to a rule, regulation, or order of the Commission approving such extension or extensions. In promulgating such rule or regulation or in issuing such order, the Commission—

    i. shall find that such extension or extensions of unlisted trading privileges is consistent with the maintenance of fair and orderly markets, the protection of investors and the public interest, and otherwise in furtherance of the purposes of this title;

    ii. shall take account of the public trading activity in such securities, the character of such trading, the impact of such extension on the existing markets for such securities, and the desirability of removing impediments to and the progress that has been made toward the development of a national market system; and

    iii. shall not permit a national securities exchange to extend unlisted trading privileges to such securities if any rule of such national securities exchange would unreasonably impair the ability of a dealer to solicit or effect transactions in such securities for its own account, or would unreasonably restrict competition among dealers in such securities or between such dealers acting in the capacity of market makers who are specialists and such dealers who are not specialists.

F. An exchange may continue to extend unlisted trading privileges in accordance with this paragraph only if the exchange and the subject security continue to satisfy the requirements for eligibility under this paragraph, including any rules and regulations issued by the Commission pursuant to this paragraph, except that unlisted trading privileges may continue with regard to securities which had been admitted on such exchange prior to July 1, 1964, notwithstanding the failure to satisfy such requirements. If unlisted trading privileges in a security are discontinued pursuant to this subparagraph, the exchange shall cease trading in that security, unless the exchange and the subject security thereafter satisfy the requirements of this paragraph and the rules issued hereunder.

G. For purposes of this paragraph—

    i. a security is the subject of an initial public offering if—

        I. the offering of the subject security is registered under the Securities Act of 1933; and

        II. the issuer of the security, immediately prior to filing the registration statement with respect to the offering, was not subject to the reporting requirements of section 13 or 15(d) of this title; and

    ii. an initial public offering of such security commences at the opening of trading on the day on which such security commences trading on the national securities exchange with which such security is registered.

2.

A. At any time within 60 days of commencement of trading on an exchange of a security pursuant to unlisted trading privileges, the Commission may summarily suspend such unlisted trading privileges on the exchange. Such suspension shall not be reviewable under section 25 of this title and shall not be deemed to be a final agency action for purposes of section 704 of title 5, United States Code. Upon such suspension—

    i.   the exchange shall cease trading in the security by the close of business on the date of such suspension, or at such time as the Commission may prescribe by rule or order for the maintenance of fair and orderly markets, the protection of investors and the public interest, or otherwise in furtherance of the purposes of this title; and

    ii. if the exchange seeks to extend unlisted trading privileges to the security, the exchange shall file an application to reinstate its ability to do so with the Commission pursuant to such procedures as the Commission may prescribe by rule or order for the maintenance of fair and orderly markets, the protection of investors and the public interest, or otherwise in furtherance of the purposes of this title.

B. A suspension under subparagraph (A) shall remain in effect until the Commission, by order, grants approval of an application to reinstate, as described in subparagraph (A)(ii).

C. A suspension under subparagraph (A) shall not affect the validity or force of an extension of unlisted trading privileges in effect prior to such suspension.

D. The Commission shall not approve an application by a national securities exchange to reinstate its ability to extend unlisted trading privileges to a security unless the Commission finds, after notice and opportunity for hearing, that the extension of unlisted trading privileges pursuant to such application is consistent with the maintenance of fair and orderly markets, the protection of investors and the public interest, and otherwise in furtherance of the purposes of this title. If the application is made to reinstate unlisted trading privileges to a security described in paragraph (1)(A)(ii), the Commission—

    i.   shall take account of the public trading activity in such security, the character of such trading, the impact of such extension on the existing markets for such a security, and the desirability of removing impediments to and the progress that has been made toward the development of a national market system; and

    ii.   shall not grant any such application if any rule of the national securities exchange making application under this subsection would unreasonably impair the ability of a dealer to solicit or effect transactions in such security for its own account, or would unreasonably restrict competition among dealers in such security or between such dealers acting in the capacity of market makers who are specialists and such dealers who are not specialists.

3.   Notwithstanding paragraph (2), the Commission shall by rules and regulations suspend unlisted trading privileges in whole or in part for any or all classes of securities for a period not exceeding twelve months, if it deems such suspension necessary or appropriate in the public interest or for the protection of investors or to prevent evasion of the purposes of this title.

4.   On the application of the issuer of any security for which unlisted trading privileges on any exchange have been continued or extended pursuant to this subsection, or of any

broker or dealer who makes or creates a market for such security, or of any other person having a bona fide interest in the question of termination or suspension of such unlisted trading privileges, or on its own motion, the Commission shall by order terminate, or suspend for a period not exceeding twelve months, such unlisted trading privileges for such security if the Commission finds, after appropriate notice and opportunity for hearing, that such termination or suspension is necessary or appropriate in the public interest or for the protection of investors.

5. In any proceeding under this subsection in which appropriate notice and opportunity for hearing are required, notice of not less than ten days to the applicant in such proceeding, to the issuer of the security involved, to the exchange which is seeking to continue or extend or has continued or extended unlisted trading privileges for such security, and to the exchange, if any, on which such security is listed and registered, shall be deemed adequate notice, and any broker or dealer who makes or creates a market for such security, and any other person having a bona fide interest in such proceeding, shall upon application be entitled to be heard.

6. Any security for which unlisted trading privileges are continued or extended pursuant to this subsection shall be deemed to be registered on a national securities exchange within the meaning of this title. The powers and duties of the Commission under this title shall be applicable to the rules of an exchange in respect of any such security. The Commission may, by such rules and regulations as it deems necessary or appropriate in the public interest or for the protection of investors, either unconditionally or upon specified terms and conditions, or for stated periods, exempt such securities from the operation of any provision of section 13, 14, or 16 of this title.

g.

1. Every issuer which is engaged in interstate commerce, or in a business affecting interstate commerce, or whose

securities are traded by use of the mails or any means or instrumentality of interstate commerce shall—

A.　within one hundred and twenty days after the last day of its first fiscal year ended after the effective date of this subsection on which the issuer has total assets exceeding $1,000,000 and a class of equity security (other than an exempted security) held of record by seven hundred and fifty or more persons; and

B.　within one hundred and twenty days after the last day of its first fiscal year ended after two years from the effective date of this subsection on which the issuer has total assets exceeding $1,000,000 and a class of equity security (other than an exempted security) held of record by five hundred or more but less than seven hundred and fifty persons,

register such security by filing with the Commission a registration statement (and such copies thereof as the Commission may require) with respect to such security containing such information and documents as the Commission may specify comparable to that which is required in an application to register a security pursuant to subsection (b) of this section. Each such registration statement shall become effective sixty days after filing with the Commission or within such shorter period as the Commission may direct. Until such registration statement becomes effective it shall not be deemed filed for the purposes of section 18 of this title. Any issuer may register any class of equity security not required to be registered by filing a registration statement pursuant to the provisions of this paragraph. The Commission is authorized to extend the date upon which any issuer or class of issuers is required to register a security pursuant to the provisions of this paragraph.

2. The provisions of this subsection shall not apply in respect of—

    A. any security listed and registered on a national securities exchange.

    B. any security issued by an investment company registered pursuant to section 8 of the Investment Company Act of 1940.

    C. any security, other than permanent stock, guaranty stock, permanent reserve stock, or any similar certificate evidencing nonwithdrawable capital, issued by a savings and loan association, building and loan association, cooperative bank, homestead association, or similar institution, which is supervised and examined by State or Federal authority having supervision over any such institution.

    D. any security of an issuer organized and operated exclusively for religious, educational, benevolent, fraternal, charitable, or reformatory purposes and not for pecuniary profit, and no part of the net earnings of which inures to the benefit of any private shareholder or individual; or any security of a fund that is excluded from the definition of an investment company under section 3(c)(10)(B) of the Investment Company Act of 1940.

    E. any security of an issuer which is a "cooperative association" as defined in the Agricultural Marketing Act, approved June 15, 1929, as amended, or a federation of such cooperative associations, if such federation possesses no greater powers or purposes than cooperative associations so defined.

    F. any security issued by a mutual or cooperative organization which supplies a commodity or service primarily for the benefit of its members and operates not for pecuniary profit, but only if the security is part of a class issuable only to persons who purchase commodities or services from the issuer, the security is transferable only to a successor in interest or occupancy of premises serviced or to be served by the issuer, and no dividends are payable to the holder of the security.

G. any security issued by an insurance company if all of the following conditions are met:

  i. Such insurance company is required to and does file an annual statement with the Commissioner of Insurance (or other officer or agency performing a similar function) of its domiciliary State, and such annual statement conforms to that prescribed by the National Association of Insurance Commissioners or in the determination of such State commissioner, officer or agency substantially conforms to that so prescribed.

  ii. Such insurance company is subject to regulation by its domiciliary State of proxies, consents, or authorizations in respect of securities issued by such company and such regulation conforms to that prescribed by the National Association of Insurance Commissioners.

  iii. After July 1, 1966, the purchase and sales of securities issued by such insurance company by beneficial owners, directors, or officers of such company are subject to regulation (including reporting) by its domiciliary State substantially in the manner provided in section 16 of this title.

H. any interest or participation in any collective trust funds maintained by a bank or in a separate account maintained by an insurance company which interest or participation is issued in connection with

  i. a stock-bonus, pension, or profit-sharing plan which meets the requirements for qualification under section 401 of the Internal Revenue Code of 1954, or

    ii.   an annuity plan which meets the requirements for deduction of the employer's contribution under section 404(a)(2) of such Code.

3. The Commission may by rules or regulations or, on its own motion, after notice and opportunity for hearing, by order, exempt from this subsection any security of a foreign issuer, including any certificate of deposit for such a security, if the Commission finds that such exemption is in the public interest and is consistent with the protection of investors.

4. Registration of any class of security pursuant to this subsection shall be terminated ninety days, or such shorter period as the Commission may determine, after the issuer files a certification with the Commission that the number of holders of record of such class of security is reduced to less than three hundred persons. The Commission shall after notice and opportunity for hearing deny termination of registration if it finds that the certification is untrue. Termination of registration shall be deferred pending final determination on the question of denial.

5. For the purposes of this subsection the term "class" shall include all securities of an issuer which are of substantially similar character and the holders of which enjoy substantially similar rights and privileges. The Commission may for the purpose of this subsection define by rules and regulations the terms "total assets" and "held of record" as it deems necessary or appropriate in the public interest or for the protection of investors in order to prevent circumvention of the provisions of this subsection.

h. The Commission may by rules and regulations, or upon application of an interested person, by order, after notice and opportunity for hearing, exempt in whole or in part any issuer or class of issuers from the provisions of subsection (g) of this section or from section 13, 14, or 15(d) or may exempt from section 16 any officer, director, or beneficial owner of securities of any issuer, any security of which is required to be registered pursuant to subsection (g) hereof, upon such terms and conditions and for such period as it deems necessary or appropriate, if the Commission finds, by reason of the number of public investors, amount of trading interest in the securities, the nature and extent of the activities of the issuer, income or assets of the issuer, or otherwise, that such action is not inconsistent with the public interest or the protection of investors. The Commission may, for the purposes of any of the above-mentioned sections or subsections of this title, classify issuers and prescribe requirements appropriate for each such class.

i.   In respect of any securities issued by banks and savings associations the deposits of which are insured in accordance with the Federal Deposit Insurance Act, the powers, functions, and duties vested in the Commission to administer and enforce sections 12, 13, 14(a), 14(c), 14(d), 14(f), and 16, (1) with respect to national banks and banks operating under the Code of Law for the District of Columbia are vested in the Comptroller of the Currency, (2) with respect to all other member banks of the Federal Reserve System are vested in the Board of Governors of the Federal Reserve System, (3) with respect to all other insured banks are vested in the Federal Deposit Insurance Corporation, and (4) with respect to savings associations the accounts of which are insured by the Federal Deposit Insurance Corporation are vested in the Office of Thrift Supervision. The Comptroller of the Currency, the Board of Governors of the Federal Reserve System, the Federal Deposit Insurance Corporation, and the Office of Thrift Supervision shall have the power to make such rules and regulations as may be necessary for the execution of the functions vested in them as provided in this subsection. In carrying out their responsibilities under this subsection, the agencies named in the first sentence of this subsection shall issue substantially similar regulations to regulations and rules issued by the Commission under sections 12, 13, 14(a), 14(c), 14(d), 14(f), and 16, unless they find that implementation of substantially similar regulations with respect to insured banks and insured institutions are not necessary or appropriate in the public interest or for protection of investors, and publish such findings, and the detailed reasons therefor, in the Federal Register. Such regulations of the above-named agencies, or the reasons for failure to publish such substantially similar regulations to those of the Commission, shall be published in the Federal Register within 120 days of the date of enactment of this subsection, and, thereafter, within 60 days of any changes made by the Commission in its relevant regulations and rules.

j. The Commission is authorized, by order, as it deems necessary or appropriate for the protection of investors to deny, to suspend the effective date of, to suspend for a period not exceeding twelve months, or to revoke the registration of a security, if the Commission finds, on the record after notice and opportunity for hearing, that the issuer of such security has failed to comply with any provision of this title or the rules and regulations thereunder. No member of a national securities exchange, broker, or dealer shall make use of the mails or any means or instrumentality of interstate commerce to effect any transaction in, or to induce the purchase or sale of, any security the registration of which has been and is suspended or revoked pursuant to the preceding sentence.

k. Trading Suspensions: Emergency Authority.—

    1. Trading suspensions.—If in its opinion the public interest and the protection of investors so require, the Commission is authorized by order—

        A. summarily to suspend trading in any security (other than an exempted security) for a period not exceeding 10 business days, and

        B. summarily to suspend all trading on any national securities exchange or otherwise, in securities other than exempted securities, for a period not exceeding 90 calendar days.

    The action described in subparagraph (B) shall not take effect unless the Commission notifies the President of its decision and the President notifies the Commission that the President does not disapprove of such decision.

    2. Emergency orders.—

        A. The Commission, in an emergency, may by order summarily take such action to alter, supplement, suspend, or impose requirements or restrictions with respect to any matter or action subject to regulation by the Commission or a self-regulatory organization under this title, as the Commission determines is necessary in the public interest and for the protection of investors—

    i.   to maintain or restore fair and orderly securities markets (other than markets in exempted securities); or

    ii. to ensure prompt, accurate, and safe clearance and settlement of transactions in securities (other than exempted securities).

B. An order of the Commission under this paragraph (2) shall continue in effect for the period specified by the Commission, and may be extended, except that in no event shall the Commission's action continue in effect for more than 10 business days, including extensions. In exercising its authority under this paragraph, the Commission shall not be required to comply with the provisions of section 553 of title 5, United States Code, or with the provisions of section 19(c) of this title.

3. Termination of emergency actions by President.—The President may direct that action taken by the Commission under paragraph (1)(B) or paragraph (2) of this subsection shall not continue in effect.

4. Compliance with orders.—No member of a national securities exchange, broker, or dealer shall make use of the mails or any means or instrumentality of interstate commerce to effect any transaction in, or to induce the purchase or sale of, any security in contravention of an order of the Commission under this subsection unless such order has been stayed, modified, or set aside as provided in paragraph (5) of this subsection or has ceased to be effective upon direction of the President as provided in paragraph (3).

5. Limitations on review of orders.—An order of the Commission pursuant to this subsection shall be subject to review only as provided in section 25(a) of this title. Review

shall be based on an examination of all the information before the Commission at the time such order was issued. The reviewing court shall not enter a stay, writ of mandamus, or similar relief unless the court finds, after notice and hearing before a panel of the court, that the Commission's action is arbitrary, capricious, an abuse of discretion, or otherwise not in accordance with law.

6. Definition of emergency.—For purposes of this subsection, the term "emergency" means a major market disturbance characterized by or constituting—

   A. sudden and excessive fluctuations of securities prices generally, or a substantial threat thereof, that threaten fair and orderly markets, or

   B. a substantial disruption of the safe or efficient operation of the national system for clearance and settlement of securities, or a substantial threat thereof.

l. It shall be unlawful for an issuer, any class of whose securities is registered pursuant to this section or would be required to be so registered except for the exemption from registration provided by subsection (g)(2)(B) or (g)(2)(G) of this section, by the use of any means or instrumentality of interstate commerce, or of the mails, to issue, either originally or upon transfer, any of such securities in a form or with a format which contravenes such rules and regulations as the Commission may prescribe as necessary or appropriate for the prompt and accurate clearance and settlement of transactions in securities. The provisions of this subsection shall not apply to variable annuity contracts or variable life policies issued by an insurance company or its separate accounts.

SECTION 13—PERIODICAL AND OTHER REPORTS

a. Every issuer of a security registered pursuant to Section 12 of this title shall file with the Commission, in accordance with such rules and regulations as the Commission may prescribe as necessary or appropriate for the proper protection of investors and to insure fair dealing in the security—

1. Such information and documents (and such copies thereof) as the Commission shall require to keep reasonably current the information and documents required to be included in or filed with an application or registration statement filed pursuant to <u>Section 12</u>, except that the Commission may not require the filing of any material contract wholly executed before July 1, 1962.

2. Such annual reports (and such copies thereof), certified if required by the rules and regulations of the Commission by independent public accountants, and such quarterly reports (and such copies thereof), as the Commission may prescribe.

Every issuer of a security registered on a national securities exchange shall also file a duplicate original of such information, documents, and reports with the exchange.

b.

1. The Commission may prescribe, in regard to reports made pursuant to this title, the form or forms in which the required information shall be set forth, the items or details to be shown in the balance sheet and the earnings statement, and the methods to be followed in the preparation of reports, in the appraisal or valuation of assets and liabilities, in the determination of depreciation and depletion, in the differentiation of recurring and nonrecurring income, in the differentiation of investment and operating income, and in the preparation, where the Commission deems it necessary or desirable, of separate and/or consolidated balance sheets or income accounts of any person directly or indirectly controlling or controlled by the issuer, or any person under direct or indirect common control with the issuer; but in the case of the reports of any person whose methods of accounting are prescribed under the provisions of any law of the United States, or any rule or regulation thereunder, the rules and regulations of the Commission with respect to reports shall not be inconsistent with the requirements imposed by such law or rule or regulation in respect of the same subject matter (except that such rules and regulations

of the Commission may be inconsistent with such requirements to the extent that the Commission determines that the public interest or the protection of investors so requires).

2.   Every issuer which has a class of securities registered pursuant to Section 12 of this title and every issuer which is required to file reports pursuant to Section 15(d) of this title shall—

   A.   make and keep books, records, and accounts, which, in reasonable detail, accurately and fairly reflect the transactions and dispositions of the assets of the issuer; and

   B.   devise and maintain a system of internal accounting controls sufficient to provide reasonable assurances that—

      i.   transactions are executed in accordance with management's general or specific authorization;

      ii.   transactions are recorded as necessary (I) to permit preparation of financial statements in conformity with generally accepted accounting principles or any other criteria applicable to such statements, and (II) to maintain accountability for assets;

      iii.   access to assets is permitted only in accordance with management's general or specific authorization; and

      iv.   the recorded accountability for assets is compared with the existing assets at reasonable intervals and appropriate action is taken with respect to any differences.

3.

   A.   With respect to matters concerning the national security of the United States, no duty or liability under paragraph (2) of this subsection shall be imposed upon any person acting in cooperation with the head of any Federal department or agency responsible for such matters if such act in cooperation with such head of a department or agency was done upon the specific, written directive of the head of such department or agency pursuant to Presidential authority to issue such directives. Each directive issued under this paragraph shall set forth the specific facts and circumstances with respect to which the provisions of this paragraph are to be invoked. Each such directive shall, unless renewed in writing, expire one year after the date of issuance.

B. Each head of a Federal department or agency of the United States who issues a directive pursuant to this paragraph shall maintain a complete file of all such directives and shall, on October 1 of each year, transmit a summary of matters covered by such directives in force at any time during the previous year to the Permanent Select Committee on Intelligence of the House of Representatives and the Select Committee on Intelligence of the Senate.

4. No criminal liability shall be imposed for failing to comply with the requirements of paragraph (2) of this subsection except as provided in paragraph (5) of this subsection.

5. No person shall knowingly circumvent or knowingly fail to implement a system of internal accounting controls or knowingly falsify any book, record, or account described in paragraph (2).

6. Where an issuer which has a class of securities registered pursuant to Section 12 of this title or an issuer which is required to file reports pursuant to Section 15(d) of this title holds 50 per centum or less of the voting power with respect to a domestic or foreign firm, the provisions of paragraph (2) require only that the issuer proceed in good faith to use its influence, to the extent reasonable under the issuer's circumstances, to cause such domestic or foreign firm to devise and maintain a system of internal accounting controls consistent with paragraph (2). Such circumstances

include the relative degree of the issuer's ownership of the domestic or foreign firm and the laws and practices governing the business operations of the country in which such firm is located. An issuer which demonstrates good faith efforts to use such influence shall be conclusively presumed to have complied with the requirements of paragraph (2).

7. For the purpose of paragraph (2) of this subsection, the terms 'reasonable assurances' and 'reasonable detail' mean such level of detail and degree of assurance as would satisfy prudent officials in the conduct of their own affairs.

c. If in the judgment of the Commission any report required under subsection (a) is inapplicable to any specified class or classes of issuers, the Commission shall require in lieu thereof the submission of such reports of comparable character as it may deem applicable to such class or classes of issuers.

d.

1. Any person who, after acquiring directly or indirectly the beneficial ownership of any equity security of a class which is registered pursuant to Section 12 of this title, or any equity security of an insurance company which would have been required to be so registered except for the exemption contained in Section 12(g)(2)(G) of this title, or any equity security issued by a closed-end investment company registered under the Investment Company Act of 1940 or any equity security issued by a Native Corporation pursuant to Section 37(d)(6) of the Alaska Native Claims Settlement Act, is directly or indirectly the beneficial owner of more than 5 per centum of such class shall, within ten days after such acquisition, send to the issuer of the security at its principal executive office, by registered or certified mail, send to each exchange where the security is traded, and file with the Commission, a statement containing such of the following information, and such additional information, as the Commission may by rules and regulations prescribe as necessary or appropriate in the public interest or for the protection of investors—

A. The background, and identity, residence, and citizenship of, and the nature of such beneficial ownership by, such person and all other persons by whom or on whose behalf the purchases have been or are to be effected;

B. the source and amount of the funds or other consideration used or to be used in making the purchases, and if any part of the purchase price or proposed purchase price is represented or is to be represented by funds or other consideration borrowed or otherwise obtained for the purpose of acquiring, holding, or trading such security, a description of the transaction and the names of the parties thereto, except that where a source of funds is a loan made in the ordinary course of business by a bank, as defined in Section 3(a)(6) of this title, if the person filing such statement so requests, the name of the bank shall not be made available to the public;

C. if the purpose of the purchases or prospective purchases is to acquire control of the business of the issuer of the securities, any plans or proposals which such persons may have to liquidate such issuer, to sell its assets to or merge it with any other persons, or to make any other major change in its business or corporate structure;

D. the number of shares of such security which are beneficially owned, and the number of shares concerning which there is a right to acquire, directly or indirectly, by

    i.   (i) such person, and

    ii. (ii) by each associate of such person, giving the background, identity, residence and citizenship of each such associate; and

E. (E) information as to any contracts, arrangements, or understandings with any person with respect to any securities of the issuer, including but not limited to transfer of any of the securities, joint ventures, loan or option arrangements, puts or calls, guaranties of loans, guaranties against loss or guaranties of profits, division of losses or profits, or the giving or withholding of proxies, naming the persons with whom such contracts, arrangements, or understandings have been entered into, and giving the details thereof.

2. If any material change occurs in the facts set forth in the statements to the issuer and the exchange, and in the statement filed with the Commission, an amendment shall be transmitted to the issuer and the exchange and shall be filed with the Commission, in accordance with such rules and regulations as the Commission may prescribe as necessary or appropriate in the public interest or for the protection of investors.

3. When two or more persons act as a partnership, limited partnership, syndicate, or other group for the purpose of acquiring, holding, or disposing of securities of an issuer, such syndicate or group shall be deemed a "person" for the purposes of this subsection.

4. In determining, for purposes of this subsection, any percentage of a class of any security, such class shall be deemed to consist of the amount of the outstanding securities of such class, exclusive of any securities of such class held by or for the account of the issuer or a subsidiary of the issuer.

5. The Commission, by rule or regulation or by order, may permit any person to file in lieu of the statement required by paragraph (1) of this subsection or the rules and regulations thereunder, a notice stating the name of such person, the number of shares of any equity securities subject to paragraph (1) which are owned by him, the date of their acquisition and such other information as the Commission may specify, if it appears to the Commission that such securities were acquired by such person in the ordinary course of his business and were not acquired for the purpose of and do not have the effect of changing or influencing the control of the issuer nor in connection with or as a participant in any transaction having such purpose or effect.

6. The provisions of this subsection shall not apply to—

    A. any acquisition or offer to acquire securities made or proposed to be made by means of a registration statement under the Securities Act of 1933;

    B. any acquisition of the beneficial ownership of a security which, together with all other acquisitions by the same person of securities of the same class during the preceding twelve months, does not exceed 2 per centum of that class;

    C. any acquisition of an equity security by the issuer of such security;

    D. any acquisition or proposed acquisition of a security which the Commission, by rules or regulations or by order, shall exempt from the provisions of this subsection as not entered into for the purpose of, and not having the effect of, changing or influencing the control of the issuer or otherwise as not comprehended within the purposes of this subsection.

e.

1. It shall be unlawful for an issuer which has a class of equity securities registered pursuant to Section 12 of this title, or which is a closed-end investment company registered under the Investment Company Act of 1940, to purchase any equity security issued by it if such purchase is in contravention of such rules and regulations as the Commission, in the public interest or for the protection of investors, may adopt

    A. to define acts and practices which are fraudulent, deceptive, or manipulative, and

    B. to prescribe means reasonably designed to prevent such acts and practices.

Such rules and regulations may require such issuer to provide holders of equity securities of such class with such information relating to the reasons for such purchase, the source of funds, the number of shares to be purchased, the price to be paid for such securities, the method of purchase, and such additional information, as the Commission deems necessary or appropriate in the public interest or for the protection of investors, or which the Commission deems to be material to a determination whether such security should be sold.

2. For the purpose of this subsection, a purchase by or for the issuer or any person controlling, controlled by, or under common control with the issuer, or a purchase subject to control of the issuer or any such person, shall be deemed to be a purchase by the issuer. The Commission shall have power to make rules and regulations implementing this paragraph in the public interest and for the protection of investors, including exemptive rules and regulations covering situations in which the Commission deems it unnecessary or inappropriate that a purchase of the type described in this paragraph shall be deemed to be a purchase by the issuer for purposes of some or all of the provisions of paragraph (1) of this subsection.

3. At the time of filing such statement as the Commission may require by rule pursuant to paragraph (1) of this subsection, the person making the filing shall pay to the Commission a fee of 1/50 of 1 per centum of the value of securities proposed to be purchased. The fee shall be reduced with respect to securities in an amount equal to any fee paid with respect to any securities issued in connection with the proposed transaction under Section 6(b) of the Securities Act of 1933, or the fee paid under that section shall be reduced in an amount equal to the fee paid to the Commission in connection with such transaction under this paragraph.

f.

1. Every institutional investment manager which uses the mails, or any means or instrumentality of interstate commerce in the course of its business as an institutional investment manager and which exercises investment discretion with respect to accounts holding equity securities of a class

described in Section 13(d)(1) of this title having an aggregate fair market value on the last trading day in any of the preceding twelve months of at least $100,000,000 or such lesser amount (but in no case less than $10,000,000) as the Commission, by rule, may determine, shall file reports with the Commission in such form, for such periods, and at such times after the end of such periods as the Commission, by rule, may prescribe, but in no event shall such reports be filed for periods longer than one year or shorter than one quarter. Such reports shall include for each such equity security held on the last day of the reporting period by accounts (in aggregate or by type as the Commission, by rule, may prescribe) with respect to which the institutional investment manager exercises investment discretion (other than securities held in amounts which the Commission, by rule, determines to be insignificant for purposes of this subsection), the name of the issuer and the title, class, CUSIP number, number of shares or principal amount, and aggregate fair market value of each such security. Such reports may also include for accounts (in aggregate or by type) with respect to which the institutional investment manager exercises investment discretion such of the following information as the Commission, by rule, prescribes—

A. the name of the issuer and the title, class, CUSIP number, number of shares or principal amount, and aggregate fair market value or cost or amortized cost of each other security (other than an exempted security) held on the last day of the reporting period by such accounts;

B. the aggregate fair market value or cost or amortized cost of exempted securities (in aggregate or by class) held on the last day of the reporting period by such accounts;

C. the number of shares of each equity security of a class described in Section 13(d)(1) of this title held on the last day of the reporting period by such accounts with respect to which the institutional investment manager possesses sole or shared authority to exercise the voting rights evidenced by such securities;

D. the aggregate purchases and aggregate sales during the reporting period of each security (other than an exempted security) effected by or for such accounts; and

E. with respect to any transaction or series of transactions having a market value of at least $500,000 or such other amount as the Commission, by rule, may determine effected during the reporting period by or for such accounts in any equity security of a class described in Section 13(d)(1) of this title—

   i.   the name of the issuer and the title, class, and CUSIP number of the security;

   ii.   the number of shares or principal amount of the security involved in the transaction;

   iii. whether the transaction was a purchase or sale;

   iv.   the per share price or prices at which the transaction was effected;

   v.   the date or dates of the transaction;

   vi.   the date or dates of the settlement of the transaction;

   vii. the broker or dealer through whom the transaction was effected;

   viii. the market or markets in which the transaction was effected; and

   ix.   such other related information as the Commission, by rule, may prescribe.

2. The Commission, by rule or order, may exempt, conditionally or unconditionally, any institutional investment manager or security or any class of institutional investment managers or securities from any or all of the provisions of this subsection or the rules thereunder.

3. The Commission shall make available to the public for a reasonable fee a list of all equity securities of a class described in Section 13(d)(1) of this title, updated no less frequently than reports are required to be filed pursuant to paragraph(1) of this subsection. The Commission shall tabulate the information contained in any report filed pursuant to this subsection in a manner which will, in the view of the Commission, maximize the usefulness of the information to other Federal and State authorities and the public. Promptly after the filing of any such report, the Commission shall make the information contained therein conveniently available to the public for a reasonable fee in such form as the Commission, by rule, may prescribe, except that the Commission, as it determines to be necessary or appropriate in the public interest or for the protection of investors, may delay or prevent public disclosure of any such information in accordance with Section 552 of title 5, United States Code. Notwithstanding the preceding sentence, any such information identifying the securities held by the account of a natural person or an estate or trust (other than a business trust or investment company) shall not be disclosed to the public.

4. In exercising its authority under this subsection, the Commission shall determine (and so state) that its action is necessary or appropriate in the public interest and for the protection of investors or to maintain fair and orderly markets or, in granting an exemption, that its action is consistent with the protection of investors and the purposes of this subsection. In exercising such authority the Commission shall take such steps as are within its power, including consulting with the Comptroller General of the United States, the Director of the Office of Management and Budget, the appropriate regulatory agencies, Federal and State authorities which, directly or indirectly, require reports from institutional investment managers of information substantially similar to that called for by this subsection, national securities exchanges, and registered securities associations,

    A. to achieve uniform, centralized reporting of information concerning the securities holdings of and transactions by or for accounts with respect to which institutional investment managers exercise investment discretion, and

B. consistently with the objective set forth in the preceding subparagraph, to avoid unnecessarily duplicative reporting by, and minimize the compliance burden on, institutional investment managers.

Federal authorities which, directly or indirectly, require reports from institutional investment managers of information substantially similar to that called for by this subsection shall cooperate with the Commission in the performance of its responsibilities under the preceding sentence. An institutional investment manager which is a bank, the deposits of which are insured in accordance with the Federal Deposit Insurance Act, shall file with the appropriate regulatory agency a copy of every report filed with the Commission pursuant to this subsection.

5.

A. For purposes of this subsection the term "institutional investment manager" includes any person, other than a natural person, investing in or buying and selling securities for its own account, and any person exercising investment discretion with respect to the account of any other person.

B. The Commission shall adopt such rules as it deems necessary or appropriate to prevent duplicative reporting pursuant to this subsection by two or more institutional investment managers exercising investment discretion with respect to the same amount.

g.

1. Any person who is directly or indirectly the beneficial owner of more than 5 per centum of any security of a class described in subsection (d)(1) of this section shall send to the issuer of the security and shall file with the Commission a statement setting forth, in such form and at such time as the Commission may, by rule, prescribe—

    A. such person's identity, residence, and citizenship; and

    B. the number and description of the shares in which such person has an interest and the nature of such interest.

2. If any material change occurs in the facts set forth in the statement sent to the issuer and filed with the Commission, an amendment shall be transmitted to the issuer and shall be filed with the Commission, in accordance with such rules and regulations as the Commission may prescribe as necessary or appropriate in the public interest or for the protection of investors.

3. When two or more persons act as a partnership, limited partnership, syndicate, or other group for the purpose of acquiring, holding, or disposing of securities of an issuer, such syndicate or group shall be deemed a "person" for the purposes of this subsection.

4. In determining, for purposes of this subsection, any percentage of a class of any security, such class shall be deemed to consist of the amount of the outstanding securities of such class, exclusive of any securities of such class held by or for the account of the issuer or a subsidiary of the issuer.

5. In exercising its authority under this subsection, the Commission shall take such steps as it deems necessary or appropriate in the public interest or for the protection of investors

    A. to achieve centralized reporting of information regarding ownership,

    B. to avoid unnecessarily duplicative reporting by and minimize the compliance burden on persons required to report, and

    C. to tabulate and promptly make available the information contained in any report filed pursuant to this subsection in a manner which will, in the view of the Commission, maximize the usefulness of the information to other Federal and State agencies and the public.

6. The Commission may, by rule or order, exempt, in whole or in part, any person or class of persons from any or all of the reporting requirements of this subsection as it deems necessary or appropriate in the public interest or for the protection of investors.

h. **Large Trader Reporting.**—

1. **Identification Requirements For Large Traders.**—For the purpose of monitoring the impact on the securities markets of securities transactions involving a substantial volume or a large fair market value or exercise value and for the purpose of otherwise assisting the Commission in the enforcement of this title, each large trader shall—

   A. provide such information to the Commission as the Commission may by rule or regulation prescribe as necessary or appropriate, identifying such large trader and all accounts in or through which such large trader effects such transactions; and

   B. identify, in accordance with such rules or regulations as the Commission may prescribe as necessary or appropriate, to any registered broker or dealer by or through whom such large trader directly or indirectly effects securities transactions, such large trader and all accounts directly or indirectly maintained with such broker or dealer by such large trader in or through which such transactions are effected.

2. Recordkeeping and reporting requirements for brokers and dealers.—Every registered broker or dealer shall make and keep for prescribed periods such records as the Commission by rule or regulation prescribes as necessary or appropriate in the public interest, for the protection of investors, or otherwise in furtherance of the purposes of this title, with respect to securities transactions that equal or exceed the reporting activity level effected directly or indirectly by or

through such registered broker or dealer of or for any person that such broker or dealer knows is a large trader, or any person that such broker or dealer has reason to know is a large trader on the basis of transactions in securities effected by or through such broker or dealer. Such records shall be available for reporting to the Commission, or any self-regulatory organization that the Commission shall designate to receive such reports, on the morning of the day following the day the transactions were effected, and shall be reported to the Commission or a self-regulatory organization designated by the Commission immediately upon request by the Commission or such a self-regulatory organization. Such records and reports shall be in a format and transmitted in a manner prescribed by the Commission (including, but not limited to, machine readable form).

3. Aggregation rules.—The Commission may prescribe rules or regulations governing the manner in which transactions and accounts shall be aggregated for the purpose of this subsection, including aggregation on the basis of common ownership or control.

4. Examination of broker and dealer records.—All records required to be made and kept by registered brokers and dealers pursuant to this subsection with respect to transactions effected by large traders are subject at any time, or from time to time, to such reasonable periodic, special, or other examinations by representatives of the Commission as the Commission deems necessary or appropriate in the public interest, for the protection of investors, or otherwise in furtherance of the purposes of this title.

5. Factors to be considered in Commission actions.—In exercising its authority under this subsection, the Commission shall take into account—

   A. existing reporting systems;

   B. the costs associated with maintaining information with respect to transactions effected by large traders and reporting such information to the Commission or self regulatory organizations; and

      C. the relationship between the United States and international securities markets.

6. Exemptions.—The Commission, by rule, regulation, or order, consistent with the purposes of this title, may exempt any person or class of persons or any transaction or class of transactions, either conditionally or upon specified terms and conditions or for stated periods, from the operation of this subsection, and the rules and regulations thereunder.

7. Authority of Commission to limit disclosure of information.—Notwithstanding any other provision of law, the Commission shall not be compelled to disclose any information required to be kept or reported under this subsection. Nothing in this subsection shall authorize the Commission to withhold information from Congress, or prevent the Commission from complying with a request for information from any other Federal department or agency requesting information for purposes within the scope of its jurisdiction, or complying with an order of a court of the United States in an action brought by the United States or the Commission. For purposes of <u>Section 552 of Title 5, United States Code</u>, this subsection shall be considered a statute described in subsection (b)(3)(B) of such section 552.

8. Definitions.—For purposes of this subsection—

    1. the term "large trader" means every person who, for his own account or an account for which he exercises investment discretion, effects transactions for the purchase or sale of any publicly traded security or securities by use of any means or instrumentality of interstate commerce or of the mails, or of any facility of a national securities exchange, directly or indirectly by or through a registered broker or dealer in an aggregate amount equal to or in excess of the identifying activity level;

    2. the term "publicly traded security" means any equity security (including an option on individual equity securities, and an option on a group or index of such securities) listed, or admitted to unlisted

trading privileges, on a national securities exchange, or quoted in an automated interdealer quotation system;

3. the term "identifying activity level" means transactions in publicly traded securities at or above a level of volume, fair market value, or exercise value as shall be fixed from time to time by the Commission by rule or regulation, specifying the time interval during which such transactions shall be aggregated;

4. the term "reporting activity level" means transactions in publicly traded securities at or above a level of volume, fair market value, or exercise value as shall be fixed from time to time by the Commission by rule, regulation, or order, specifying the time interval during which such transactions shall be aggregated; and

5. the term "person" has the meaning given in Section 3(a)(9) of this title and also includes two or more persons acting as a partnership, limited partnership, syndicate, or other group, but does not include a foreign central bank.

SECTION 14—PROXIES

a. It shall be unlawful for any person, by the use of the mails or by any means or instrumentality of interstate commerce or of any facility of a national securities exchange or otherwise, in contravention of such rules and regulations as the Commission may prescribe as necessary or appropriate in the public interest or for the protection of investors, to solicit or to permit the use of his name to solicit any proxy or consent or authorization in respect of any security (other than an exempted security) registered pursuant to Section 12 of this title.

b.

1. It shall be unlawful for any member of a national securities exchange, or any broker or dealer registered under this title,

or any bank, association, or other entity that exercises fiduciary powers, in contravention of such rules and regulations as the Commission may prescribe as necessary or appropriate in the public interest or for the protection of investors, to give, or to refrain from giving a proxy, consent, or authorization in respect of any security registered pursuant to Section 12 of this title, or any security issued by an investment company registered under the Investment Company Act of 1940, and carried for the account of a customer.

2. With respect to banks, the rules and regulations prescribed by the Commission under paragraph (1) shall not require the disclosure of the names of beneficial owners of securities in an account held by the bank on the date of enactment of this paragraph unless the beneficial owner consents to the disclosure. The provisions of this paragraph shall not apply in the case of a bank which the Commission finds has not made a good faith effort to obtain such consent from such beneficial owners.

c. Unless proxies, consents, or authorizations in respect of a security registered pursuant to Section 12 of this title, or a security issued by an investment company registered under the Investment Company Act of 1940, are solicited by or on behalf of the management of the issuer from the holders of record of such security in accordance with the rules and regulations prescribed under subsection (a) of this section, prior to any annual or other meeting of the holders of such security, such issuer shall, in accordance with rules and regulations prescribed by the Commission, file with the Commission and transmit to all holders of record of such security information substantially equivalent to the information which would be required to be transmitted if a solicitation were made, but no information shall be required to be filed or transmitted pursuant to this subsection before July 1, 1964.

d.

1. It shall be unlawful for any person, directly or indirectly, by use of the mails or by any means or instrumentality of interstate commerce or of any facility of a national securities exchange or otherwise, to make a tender offer for, or a

request or invitation for tenders of, any class of any equity security which is registered pursuant to Section 12 of this title, or any equity security of an insurance company which would have been required to be so registered except for the exemption contained in Section 12(g)(2)(G) of this title, or any equity security issued by a closed-end investment company registered under the Investment Company Act of 1940, if, after consummation thereof, such person would, directly or indirectly, be the beneficial owner of more than 5 per centum of such class, unless at the time copies of the offer or request or invitation are first published or sent or given to security holders such person has filed with the Commission a statement containing such of the information specified in Section 13(d) of this title, and such additional information as the Commission may by rules and regulations prescribe as necessary or appropriate in the public interest or for the protection of investors. All requests or invitations for tenders or advertisements making a tender offer or requesting or inviting tenders of such a security shall be filed as a part of such statement and shall contain such of the information contained in such statement as the Commission may by rules and regulations prescribe. Copies of any additional material soliciting or requesting such tender offers subsequent to the initial solicitation or request shall contain such information as the Commission may by rules and regulations prescribe as necessary or appropriate in the public interest or for the protection of investors, and shall be filed with the Commission not later than the time copies of such material are first published or sent or given to security holders. Copies of all statements, in the form in which such material is furnished to security holders and the Commission, shall be sent to the issuer not later than the date such material is first published or sent or given to any security holders.

2. When two or more persons act as a partnership, limited partnership, syndicate, or other group for the purpose of acquiring, holding, or disposing of securities of an issuer, such syndicate or group shall be deemed a "person" for purposes of this subsection.

3. In determining, for purposes of this subsection, any percentage of a class of any security, such class shall be deemed to consist of the amount of the outstanding securities of such class, exclusive of any securities of such class held by or for the account of the issuer or a subsidiary of the issuer.

4. Any solicitation or recommendation to the holders of such a security to accept or reject a tender offer or request or invitation for tenders shall be made in accordance with such rules and regulations as the Commission may prescribe as necessary or appropriate in the public interest or for the protection of investors.

5. Securities deposited pursuant to a tender offer or request or invitation for tenders may be withdrawn by or on behalf of the depositor at any time until the expiration of seven days after the time definitive copies of the offer or request or invitation are first published or sent or given to security holders, and at any time after sixty days from the date of the original tender offer or request or invitation, except as the Commission may otherwise prescribe by rules, regulations, or order as necessary or appropriate in the public interest or for the protection of investors.

6. Where any person makes a tender offer, or request or invitation for tenders, for less than all the outstanding equity securities of a class, and where a greater number of securities is deposited pursuant thereto within ten days after copies of the offer or request or invitation are first published or sent or given to security holders than such person is bound or willing to take up and pay for, the securities taken up shall be taken up as nearly as may be pro rata, disregarding fractions, according to the number of securities deposited by each depositor. The provisions of this subsection shall also apply to securities deposited within ten days after notice of an increase in the consideration offered to security holders, as described in paragraph (7), is first published or sent or given to security holders.

7. Where any person varies the terms of a tender offer or request or invitation for tenders before the expiration thereof by increasing the consideration offered to holders of such

securities, such person shall pay the increased consideration to each security holder whose securities are taken up and paid for pursuant to the tender offer or request or invitation for tenders whether or not such securities have been taken up by such person before the variation of the tender offer or request or invitation.

8. The provisions of this subsection shall not apply to any offer for, or request or invitation for tenders of, any security—

A. if the acquisition of such security, together with all other acquisitions by the same person of securities of the same class during the preceding twelve months, would not exceed 2 per centum of that class;

B. by the issuer of such security; or

C. which the Commission, by rules or regulations or by order, shall exempt from the provisions of this subsection as not entered into for the purpose of, and not having the effect of, changing or influencing the control of the issuer or otherwise as not comprehended within the purposes of this subsection.

e. It shall be unlawful for any person to make any untrue statement of a material fact or omit to state any material fact necessary in order to make the statements made, in the light of the circumstances under which they are made, not misleading, or to engage in any fraudulent, deceptive, or manipulative acts or practices, in connection with any tender offer or request or invitation for tenders, or any solicitation of security holders in opposition to or in favor of any such offer, request, or invitation. The Commission shall, for the purposes of this subsection, by rules and regulations define, and prescribe means reasonably designed to prevent, such acts and practices as are fraudulent, deceptive, or manipulative.

f. If, pursuant to any arrangement or understanding with the person or persons acquiring securities in a transaction subject to subsection (d) of this section or subsection (d) of Section 13 of this title, any persons are to be elected or designated as directors of the issuer, otherwise than at a meeting of security holders, and the persons so elected or designated will constitute a majority of the directors of the issuer, then, prior to the time any such person takes office as a director, and in accordance with rules and regulations prescribed by the Commission, the issuer shall file with the Commission, and transmit to all holders of record of securities of the issuer who would be entitled to vote at a meeting for election of directors, information substantially equivalent to the information which would be required by subsection (a) or (c) of this section to be transmitted if such person or persons were nominees for election as directors at a meeting of such security holders.

g.

1.

  A. At the time of filing such preliminary proxy solicitation material as the Commission may require by rule pursuant to subsection (a) of this section that concerns an acquisition, merger, consolidation, or proposed sale or other disposition of substantially all the assets of a company, the person making such filing, other than a company registered under the Investment Company Act of 1940, shall pay to the Commission the following fees:

     i. for preliminary proxy solicitation material involving an acquisition, merger, or consolidation, if there is a proposed payment of cash or transfer of securities or property to shareholders, a fee of 1/50 of 1 per centum of such proposed payment, or of the value of such securities or other property proposed to be transferred; and

     ii. for preliminary proxy solicitation material involving a proposed sale or other disposition of substantially all of the assets of a company, a fee of 1/50 of 1 per centum of the cash or of the value of any securities or other property proposed to be received upon such sale or disposition.

B. The fee imposed under subparagraph (A) shall be reduced with respect to securities in an amount equal to any fee paid to the Commission with respect to such securities in connection with the proposed transaction under Section 6(b) of the Securities Act of 1933, or the fee paid under that section shall be reduced in an amount equal to the fee paid to the Commission in connection with such transaction under this subsection. Where two or more companies involved in an acquisition, merger, consolidation, sale or other disposition of substantially all the assets of a company must file such proxy material with the Commission, each shall pay a proportionate share of such fee.

2. At the time of filing such preliminary information statement as the Commission may require by rule pursuant to subsection (c) of this section, the issuer shall pay to the Commission the same fee as required for preliminary proxy solicitation material under paragraph (1) of this subsection.

3. At the time of filing such statement as the Commission may require by rule pursuant to subsection (d)(1) of this section, the person making the filing shall pay to the Commission a fee of 1/50 of 1 per centum of the aggregate amount of cash or of the value of securities or other property proposed to be offered. The fee shall be reduced with respect to securities in an amount equal to any fee paid with respect to such securities in connection with the proposed transaction under Section 6(b) of the Securities Act of 1933, or the fee paid under that section shall be reduced in an amount equal to the fee paid to the Commission in connection with such transaction under this subsection.

4. Notwithstanding any other provision of law, the Commission may impose fees, charges, or prices for matters not involving any acquisition, merger, consolidation, sale, or other disposition of assets described in this subsection, as authorized by Section 9701 of Title 31, United States Code, or otherwise.

h. **Proxy Solicitations And Tender Offers In Connection With Limited Partnership Rollup Transactions.**—

   1. **Proxy Rules To Contain Special Provisions.**—It shall be unlawful for any person to solicit any proxy, consent, or authorization concerning a limited partnership rollup transaction, or to make any tender offer in furtherance of a limited partnership rollup transaction, unless such transaction is conducted in accordance with rules prescribed by the Commission under subsections (a) and (d) as required by this subsection. Such rules shall—

      A. permit any holder of a security that is the subject of the proposed limited partnership rollup transaction to engage in preliminary communications for the purpose of determining whether to solicit proxies, consents, or authorizations in opposition to the proposed limited partnership rollup transaction, without regard to whether any such communication would otherwise be considered a solicitation of proxies, and without being required to file soliciting material with the Commission prior to making that determination, except that—

         i. nothing in this subparagraph shall be construed to limit the application of any provision of this title prohibiting, or reasonably designed to prevent, fraudulent, deceptive, or manipulative acts or practices under this title; and

         ii. any holder of not less than 5 percent of the outstanding securities that are the subject of the proposed limited partnership rollup transaction who engages in the business of buying and selling limited partnership interests in the secondary market shall be required to disclose such ownership interests and any potential conflicts of interests in such preliminary communications;

B. require the issuer to provide to holders of the secu-
    rities that are the subject of the limited partnership
    rollup transaction such list of the holders of the
    issuer's securities as the Commission may deter-
    mine in such form and subject to such terms and
    conditions as the Commission may specify;

C. prohibit compensating any person soliciting prox-
    ies, consents, or authorizations directly from secu-
    rity holders concerning such a limited partnership
    rollup transaction—

    i.   on the basis of whether the solicited proxy,
         consent, or authorization either approves or
         disapproves the proposed limited partner-
         ship rollup transaction; or

    ii. contingent on the approval, disapproval, or
         completion of the limited partnership roll-
         up transaction;

D. set forth disclosure requirements for soliciting ma-
    terial distributed in connection with a limited part-
    nership rollup transaction, including requirements
    for clear, concise, and comprehensible disclosure
    with respect to—

    i.   any changes in the business plan, voting
         rights, form of ownership interest, or the
         compensation of the general partner in the
         proposed limited partnership rollup trans-
         action from each of the original limited
         partnerships;

    ii. the conflicts of interest, if any, of the gen-
         eral partner;

    iii. whether it is expected that there will be
         a significant difference between the ex-
         change values of the limited partnerships
         and the trading price of the securities to
         be issued in the limited partnership rollup
         transaction;

      iv. the valuation of the limited partnerships and the method used to determine the value of the interests of the limited partners to be exchanged for the securities in the limited partnership rollup transaction;

      v. the differing risks and effects of the limited partnership rollup transaction for investors in different limited partnership proposed to be included, and the risks and effects of completing the limited partnership rollup transaction with less than all limited partnerships;

      vi. the statement by the general partner required under subparagraph (E);

      vii. such other matters deemed necessary or appropriate by the Commission;

E. require a statement by the general partner as to whether the proposed limited partnership rollup transaction is fair or unfair to investors in each limited partnership, a discussion of the basis for that conclusion, and an evaluation and a description by the general partner of alternatives to the limited partnership rollup transaction, such as liquidation;

F. provide that, if the general partner or sponsor has obtained any opinion (other than an opinion of counsel), appraisal, or report that is prepared by an outside party and that is materially related to the limited partnership rollup transaction, such soliciting materials shall contain or be accompanied by clear, concise, and comprehensible disclosure with respect to—

      i. the analysis of the transaction, scope of review, preparation of the opinion, and basis for and methods of arriving at conclusions, and any representations and undertakings with respect thereto;

      ii. the identity and qualifications of the person who prepared the opinion, the method of selection of such person, and any material past, existing, or contemplated relationships between the person or any of its affiliates and the general partner, sponsor, successor, or any other affiliate;

      iii. any compensation of the preparer of such opinion, appraisal, or report that is contingent on the transaction's approval or completion; and

      iv. any limitations imposed by the issuer on the access afforded to such preparer to the issuer's personnel, premises, and relevant books and records;

G. provide that, if the general partner or sponsor has obtained any opinion, appraisal, or report as described in subparagraph (F) from any person whose compensation is contingent on the transaction's approval or completion or who has not been given access by the issuer to its personnel and premises and relevant books and records, the general partner or sponsor shall state the reasons therefor;

H. provide that, if the general partner or sponsor has not obtained any opinion on the fairness of the proposed limited partnership rollup transaction to investors in each of the affected partnerships, such soliciting materials shall contain or be accompanied by a statement of such partner's or sponsor's reasons for concluding that such an opinion is not necessary in order to permit the limited partners to make an informed decision on the proposed transaction;

I. require that the soliciting material include a clear, concise, and comprehensible summary of the limited partnership rollup transaction (including a summary of the matters referred to in clauses (i) through (vii) of <u>subparagraph (D)</u> and a summary of the matter referred to in <u>subparagraphs (F)</u>, <u>(G)</u>, and <u>(H)</u>), with the risks of the limited partnership rollup transaction set forth prominently in the fore part thereof;

J. provide that any solicitation or offering period with respect to any proxy solicitation, tender offer, or information statement in a limited partnership rollup transaction shall be for not less than the lesser of 60 calendar days or the maximum number of days permitted under applicable State law; and

K. contain such other provisions as the Commission determines to be necessary or appropriate for the protection of investors in limited partnership rollup transactions.

2. **Exemptions.**—The Commission may, consistent with the public interest, the protection of investors, and the purposes of this title, exempt by rule or order any security or class of securities, any transaction or class of transactions, or any person or class of persons, in whole or in part, conditionally or unconditionally, from the requirements imposed pursuant to <u>paragraph (1)</u> or from the definition contained in <u>paragraph (4)</u>.

3. **Effect On Commission Authority.**—Nothing in this subsection limits the authority of the Commission under <u>subsection (a)</u> or <u>(d)</u> or any other provision of this title or precludes the Commission from imposing, under <u>subsection (a)</u> or <u>(d)</u> or any other provision of this title, a remedy or procedure required to be imposed under this subsection.

4. **Definition Of Limited Partnership Rollup Transaction.**—Except as provided in <u>paragraph (5)</u>, as used in this subsection, the term "limited partnership rollup transaction" means a transaction involving the combination or reorganization of one or more limited partnerships, directly or indirectly, in which—

A. some or all of the investors in any of such limited partnerships will receive new securities, or securities in another entity, that will be reported under a transaction reporting plan declared effective before the date of enactment of this subsection by the Commission under Section 11A;

B. any of the investors' limited partnership securities are not, as of the date of filing, reported under a transaction reporting plan declared effective before the date of enactment of this subsection by the Commission under Section 11A;

C. investors in any of the limited partnerships involved in the transaction are subject to a significant adverse change with respect to voting rights, the term of existence of the entity, management compensation, or investment objectives; and

D. any of such investors are not provided an option to receive or retain a security under substantially the same terms and conditions as the original issue.

5. **Exclusions From Definition.**—Notwithstanding paragraph (4), the term "limited partnership rollup transaction" does not include—

A. a transaction that involves only a limited partnership or partnerships having an operating policy or practice of retaining cash available for distribution and reinvesting proceeds from the sale, financing, or refinancing of assets in accordance with such criteria as the Commission determines appropriate;

B. a transaction involving only limited partnerships wherein the interests of the limited partners are repurchased, recalled, or exchanged in accordance with the terms of the preexisting limited partnership agreements for securities in an operating company specifically identified at the time of the formation of the original limited partnership;

C. a transaction in which the securities to be issued or exchanged are not required to be and are not registered under the Securities Act of 1933;

D. a transaction that involves only issuers that are not required to register or report under Section 12, both before and after the transaction;

E. a transaction, except as the Commission may otherwise provide by rule for the protection of investors, involving the combination or reorganization of one or more limited partnerships in which a non-affiliated party succeeds to the interests of a general partner or sponsor, if—

    i. such action is approved by not less than 66 percent of the outstanding units of each of the participating limited partnerships; and

    ii. as a result of the transaction, the existing general partners will receive only compensation to which they are entitled as expressly provided for in the preexisting limited partnership agreements; or

F. a transaction, except as the Commission may otherwise provide by rule for the protection of investors, in which the securities offered to investors are securities of another entity that are reported under a transaction reporting plan declared effective before the date of enactment of this subsection by the Commission under Section 11A, if—

    i. such other entity was formed, and such class of securities was reported and regularly traded, not less than 12 months before the date on which soliciting material is mailed to investors; and

    ii. the securities of that entity issued to investors in the transaction do not exceed 20 percent of the total outstanding securities of the entity, exclusive of any securities of such class held by or for the account of the entity or a subsidiary of the entity.

SECTION 15—REGISTRATION AND REGULATION OF BROKERS AND DEALERS

a.

1. It shall be unlawful for any broker or dealer which is either a person other than a natural person or a natural person not associated with a broker or dealer which is a person other than a natural person (other than such a broker or dealer whose business is exclusively intrastate and who does not make use of any facility of a national securities exchange) to make use of the mails or any means or instrumentality of interstate commerce to effect any transactions in, or to induce or attempt to induce the purchase or sale of, any security (other than an exempted security or commercial paper, bankers' acceptances, or commercial bills) unless such broker or dealer is registered in accordance with sub-section (b) of this section.

2. The Commission, by rule or order, as it deems consistent with the public interest and the protection of investors, may conditionally or unconditionally exempt from paragraph (1) of this subsection any broker or dealer or class of brokers or dealers specified in such rule or order.

b.

1. A broker or dealer may be registered by filing with the Commission an application for registration in such form and containing such information and documents concerning such broker or dealer and any persons associated with such broker or dealer as the Commission, by rule, may prescribe as necessary or appropriate in the public interest or for the protection of investors. Within forty-five days of the date of the filing of such application (or within such longer period as to which the applicant consents), the Commission shall—

   A. by order grant registration, or

   B. institute proceedings to determine whether registration should be denied. Such proceedings shall include notice of the grounds for denial under consideration and opportunity for hearing and shall be concluded within one hundred twenty days of the date of the filing of the application for registration. At the conclusion of such proceedings, the Commission, by order, shall grant or deny such registration. The order granting registration shall not be effective until such broker or dealer has become a member of a registered securities association, or until such broker or dealer has become a member of a national securities exchange if such broker or dealer effects transactions solely on that exchange, unless the Commission has exempted such broker or dealer, by rule or order, from such membership. The Commission may extend the time for conclusion of such proceedings for up to ninety days if it finds good cause for such extension and publishes its reasons for so finding or for such longer period as to which the applicant consents.

The Commission shall grant such registration if the Commission finds that the requirements of this section are satisfied. The Commission shall deny such registration if it does not make such a finding or if it finds that if the applicant were so registered, its registration would be subject to suspension or revocation under paragraph (4) of this subsection.

2.

    A. An application for registration of a broker or dealer to be formed or organized may be made by a broker or dealer to which the broker or dealer to be formed or organized is to be the successor. Such application, in such form as the Commission, by rule, may prescribe, shall contain such information and documents concerning the applicant, the successor, and any persons associated with the applicant or the successor, as the Commission, by rule, may prescribe as necessary or appropriate in the public interest or for the protection of investors.

The grant or denial of registration to such an applicant shall be in accordance with the procedures set forth in paragraph (1) of this subsection. If the Commission grants such registration, the registration shall terminate on the forty-fifth day after the effective date thereof, unless prior thereto the successor shall, in accordance with such rules and regulations as the Commission may prescribe, adopt the application for registration as its own.

B. Any person who is a broker or dealer solely by reason of acting as a municipal securities dealer or municipal securities broker, who so acts through a separately identifiable department or division, and who so acted in such a manner on the date of enactment of the Securities Acts Amendments of 1975, may, in accordance with such terms and conditions as the Commission, by rule, prescribes as necessary and appropriate in the public interest and for the protection of investors, register such separately identifiable department or division in accordance with this subsection. If any such department or division is so registered, the department or division and not such person himself shall be the broker or dealer for purposes of this title.

C. Within six months of the date of the granting of registration to a broker or dealer, the Commission, or upon the authorization and direction of the Commission, a registered securities association or national securities exchange of which such broker or dealer is a member, shall conduct an inspection of the broker or dealer to determine whether it is operating in conformity with the provisions of this title and the rules and regulations thereunder:

Provided, however,

That the Commission may delay such inspection of any class of brokers or dealers for a period not to exceed six months.

3. Any provision of this title (other than <u>section 5</u> and <u>subsection (a)</u> of this section) which prohibits any act, practice, or course of business if the mails or any means or instrumentality of interstate commerce is used in connection therewith shall also prohibit any such act, practice, or course of business by any registered broker or dealer or any person acting on behalf of such a broker or dealer, irrespective of any use of the mails or any means or instrumentality of interstate commerce in connection therewith.

4. The Commission, by order, shall censure, place limitations on the activities, functions, or operations of, suspend for a period not exceeding twelve months, or revoke the registration of any broker or dealer if it finds, on the record after notice and opportunity for hearing, that such censure, placing of limitations, suspension, or revocation is in the public interest and that such broker or dealer, whether prior or subsequent to becoming such, or any person associated with such broker or dealer, whether prior or subsequent to becoming so associated—

   A. has willfully made or caused to be made in any application for registration or report required to be filed with the Commission or with any other appropriate regulatory agency under this title, or in any proceeding before the Commission with respect to registration, any statement which was at the time and in the light of the circumstances under which it was made false or misleading with respect to any material fact, or has omitted to state in any such application or report any material fact which is required to be stated therein.

   B. has been convicted within ten years preceding the filing of any application for registration or at any time thereafter of any felony or misdemeanor or of a substantially equivalent crime by a foreign court of competent jurisdiction which the Commission finds—

      i. involves the purchase or sale of any security, the taking of a false oath, the making of a false report, bribery, perjury, burglary, any substantially equivalent activity however denominated by the laws of the relevant foreign government or conspiracy to commit any such offense;

ii. arises out of the conduct of the business of a broker, dealer, municipal securities dealer, government securities broker, government securities dealer, investment adviser, bank, insurance company, fiduciary, transfer agent, foreign person performing a function substantially equivalent to any of the above or entity or person required to be registered under the Commodity Exchange Act or any substantially equivalent foreign statute or regulation;

iii. involves the larceny, theft, robbery, extortion, forgery, counterfeiting, fraudulent concealment, embezzlement, fraudulent conversion, or misappropriation of funds or securities, or substantially equivalent activity however denominated by the laws of the relevant foreign government; or

iv. involves the violation of section 152, 1341, 1342, or 1343 or chapter 25 or 47 of title 18, United States Code, or a violation of a substantially equivalent foreign statute.

C. is permanently or temporarily enjoined by order, judgment, or decree of any court of competent jurisdiction from acting as an investment adviser, underwriter, broker, dealer, municipal securities dealer, government securities broker, government securities dealer, transfer agent, foreign person performing a function substantially equivalent to any of the above or entity or person required to be registered under the Commodity Exchange Act or any substantially equivalent foreign statute or regulation, or as an affiliated person or employee of any investment company, bank, insurance company, foreign entity substantially equivalent to any of the above, or entity or person required to be registered under the Commodity Exchange Act or any substantially equivalent foreign statute or regulation, or from engaging in or continuing any conduct or practice in connection with any such activity, or in connection with the purchase or sale of any security.

D. has willfully violated any provision of the Securities Act of 1933, the Investment Advisers Act of 1940, the Investment Company Act of 1940, the Commodity Exchange Act, this title, the rules or regulations under any of such statutes, or the rules of the Municipal Securities Rulemaking Board, or is unable to comply with any such provision.

E. has willfully aided, abetted, counseled, commanded, induced, or procured the violation by any person of any provision of the Securities Act of 1933, the Investment Advisers Act of 1940, the Investment Company Act of 1940, the Commodity Exchange Act, this title, the rules or regulations under any of such statutes, or the rules of the Municipal Securities Rulemaking Board, or has failed reasonably to supervise, with a view to preventing violations of the provisions of such statutes, rules, and regulations, another person who commits such a violation, if such other person is subject to his supervision. For the purposes of this subparagraph (E) no person shall be deemed to have failed reasonably to supervise any other person, if—

i. there have been established procedures, and a system for applying such procedures, which would reasonably be expected to prevent and detect, insofar as practicable, any such violation by such other person, and

      ii.   such person has reasonably discharged the duties and obligations incumbent upon him by reason of such procedures and system without reasonable cause to believe that such procedures and system were not being complied with.

F.   is subject to an order of the Commission entered pursuant to paragraph (6) of this subsection (b) barring or suspending the right of such person to be associated with a broker or dealer.

G.   has been found by a foreign financial regulatory authority to have —

      i.   made or caused to make in any application for registration or report required to be filed with a foreign financial regulatory authority, or in any proceeding before a foreign financial regulatory authority with respect to registration, any statement that was at the time and in the light of the circumstances under which it was made false or misleading with respect to any material fact, or has omitted to state in any application or report to the foreign financial regulatory authority any material fact that is required to be stated therein;

      ii.   violated any foreign statute or regulation regarding transactions in securities, or contracts of sale of a commodity for future delivery, traded on or subject to the rules of a contract market or any board of trade;

      iii.   aided, abetted, counseled, commanded, induced, or procured the violation by any person of any provision of any statutory provisions enacted by a foreign government, or rules or regulations thereunder, empowering a foreign financial regulatory authority regarding transactions in

securities, or contracts of sale of a commodity for future delivery, traded on or subject to the rules of a contract market or any
board of trade, or has been found, by a foreign financial regulatory authority, to have
failed reasonably to supervise, with a view
to preventing violations of such statutory
provisions, rules, and regulations, another
person who commits such a violation, if
such other person is subject to his supervision.

5. Pending final determination whether any registration under
this subsection shall be revoked, the Commission, by order,
may suspend such registration, if such suspension appears
to the Commission, after notice and opportunity for hearing, to be necessary or appropriate in the public interest
or for the protection of investors. Any registered broker or
dealer may, upon such terms and conditions as the Commission deems necessary or appropriate in the public interest or for the protection of investors, withdraw from
registration by filing a written notice of withdrawal with the
Commission. If the Commission finds that any registered
broker or dealer is no longer in existence or has ceased to
do business as a broker or dealer, the Commission, by order, shall cancel the registration of such broker or dealer.

6.

    A. With respect to any person who is associated, who
is seeking to become associated, or, at the time of
the alleged misconduct, who was associated or was
seeking to become associated with a broker or
dealer, or any person participating, or, at the time
of the alleged misconduct, who was participating,
in an offering of any penny stock, the Commission,
by order, shall censure, place limitations on the
activities or functions of such person, or suspend for
a period not exceeding 12 months, or bar such person from being associated with a broker or dealer,
or from participating in an offering of penny stock,

if the Commission finds, on the record after notice and opportunity for a hearing, that such censure, placing of limitations, suspension, or bar is in the public interest and that such person—

    i.   has committed or omitted any act or omission enumerated in subparagraph (A), (D), (E), or (G) of paragraph (4) of this subsection;

    ii. has been convicted of any offense specified in subparagraph (B) of such paragraph (4) within 10 years of the commencement of the proceedings under this paragraph; or

    iii. is enjoined from any action, conduct, or practice specified in subparagraph (C) of such paragraph (4).

B. It shall be unlawful—

    i.   for any person as to whom an order under subparagraph (A) is in effect, without the consent of the Commission, willfully to become, or to be, associated with a broker or dealer in contravention of such order, or to participate in an offering of penny stock in contravention of such order;

    ii. for any broker or dealer to permit such a person, without the consent of the Commission, to become or remain, a person associated with the broker or dealer in contravention of such order, if such broker or dealer knew, or in the exercise of reasonable care should have known, of such order; or

    iii. for any broker or dealer to permit such a person, without the consent of the Commission, to participate in an offering of penny stock in contravention of such order, if such broker or dealer knew, or in the exercise of reasonable care should have known, of such order and of such participation.

C. For purposes of this paragraph, the term "person participating in an offering of penny stock" includes any person acting as any promoter, finder, consultant, agent, or other person who engages in activities with a broker, dealer, or issuer for purposes of the issuance or trading in any penny stock, or inducing or attempting to induce the purchase or sale of any penny stock. The Commission may, by rule or regulation, define such term to include other activities, and may, by rule, regulation, or order, exempt any person or class of persons, in whole or in part, conditionally or unconditionally, from such term.

7. No registered broker or dealer or government securities broker or government securities dealer registered (or required to register) under section 15C(a)(1)(A) shall effect any transaction in, or induce the purchase or sale of, any security unless such broker or dealer meets such standards of operational capability and such broker or dealer and all natural persons associated with such broker or dealer meet such standards of training, experience, competence, and such other qualifications as the Commission finds necessary or appropriate in the public interest or for the protection of investors. The Commission shall establish such standards by rules and regulations, which may—

A. specify that all or any portion of such standards shall be applicable to any class of brokers and dealers and persons associated with brokers and dealers;

B. require persons in any such class to pass tests prescribed in accordance with such rules and regulations, which tests shall, with respect to any class of partners, officers, or supervisory employees (which latter term may be defined by the Commission's rules and regulations and as so defined shall include branch managers of brokers or dealers) engaged in the management of the broker or dealer, include questions relating to bookkeeping, accounting, internal control over cash and securities, supervision of employees, maintenance of records, and other appropriate matters; and

C. provide that persons in any such class other than brokers and dealers and partners, officers, and supervisory employees of brokers or dealers, may be qualified solely on the basis of compliance with such standards of training and such other qualifications as the Commission finds appropriate.

The Commission, by rule, may prescribe reasonable fees and charges to defray its costs in carrying out this paragraph, including, but not limited to, fees for any test administered by it or under its direction. The Commission may cooperate with registered securities associations and national securities exchanges in devising and administering tests and may require registered brokers and dealers and persons associated with such brokers and dealers to pass tests administered by or on behalf of any such association or exchange and to pay such association or exchange reasonable fees or charges to defray the costs incurred by such association or exchange in administering such tests.

8. It shall be unlawful for any registered broker or dealer to effect any transactions in, or induce or attempt to induce the purchase or sale of, any security (other than commercial paper, bankers' acceptances, or commercial bills), unless such broker or dealer is a member of a securities association registered pursuant to section 15A of this title or effects transactions in securities solely on a national securities exchange of which it is a member.

9. The Commission by rule or order, as it deems consistent with the public interest and the protection of investors, may conditionally or unconditionally exempt from paragraph (8) of this subsection any broker or dealer or class of brokers or dealers specified in such rule or order.

10. For purposes of determining whether a person is subject to a statutory disqualification under section 6(c)(2), 15A(g)(2), or 17A(b)(4)(A) of this title, the term "Commission" in paragraph (4)(B) of this subsection shall mean "exchange", "association", or "clearing agency", respectively.

c.

  1.

  A. No broker or dealer shall make use of the mails or any means or instrumentality of interstate commerce to effect any transaction in, or to induce or attempt to induce the purchase or sale of, any security (other than commercial paper, bankers' acceptances, or commercial bills) otherwise than on a national securities exchange of which it is a member by means of any manipulative, deceptive, or other fraudulent device or contrivance.

  B. No municipal securities dealer shall make use of the mails or any means or instrumentality of interstate commerce to effect any transaction in, or to induce or attempt to induce the purchase or sale of, any municipal security by means of any manipulative, deceptive, or other fraudulent device or contrivance.

  C. No government securities broker or government securities dealer shall make use of the mails or any means or instrumentality of interstate commerce to effect any transaction in, or to induce or attempt to induce the purchase or sale of, any government security by means of any manipulative, deceptive, or other fraudulent device or contrivance.

  D. The Commission shall, for the purposes of this paragraph, by rules and regulations define such devices or contrivances as are manipulative, deceptive, or otherwise fraudulent.

  E. The Commission shall, prior to adopting any rule or regulation under subparagraph (C), consult with and consider the views of the Secretary of the Treasury and each appropriate regulatory agency. If the Secretary of the Treasury or any appropriate regulatory agency comments in writing on a proposed rule or regulation of the Commission under such subparagraph (C) that has been published for comment, the Commission shall respond in writing to such written comment before adopting the proposed rule. If the Secretary of the Treasury determines, and notifies the Commission, that such rule or regulation, if implemented, would, or as applied does

    i.   adversely affect the liquidity or efficiency of the market for government securities; or

    ii.   impose any burden on competition not necessary or appropriate in furtherance of the purposes of this section,

the Commission shall, prior to adopting the proposed rule or regulation, find that such rule or regulation is necessary and appropriate in furtherance of the purposes of this section notwithstanding the Secretary's determination.

2.

A. No broker or dealer shall make use of the mails or any means or instrumentality of interstate commerce to effect any transaction in, or to induce or attempt to induce the purchase or sale of, any security (other than an exempted security or commercial paper, bankers' acceptances, or commercial bills) otherwise than on a national securities exchange of which it is a member, in connection with which such broker or dealer engages in any fraudulent, deceptive, or manipulative act or practice, or makes any fictitious quotation.

B. No municipal securities dealer shall make use of the mails or any means or instrumentality of interstate commerce to effect any transaction in, or to induce or attempt to induce the purchase or sale of, any municipal security in connection with which such municipal securities dealer engages in any fraudulent, deceptive, or manipulative act or practice, or makes any fictitious quotation.

C. No government securities broker or government securities dealer shall make use of the mails or any means or instrumentality of interstate commerce to effect any transaction in, or induce or attempt to induce the purchase or sale of, any government security in connection with which such government securities broker or government securities dealer engages in any fraudulent, deceptive, or manipulative act or practice, or makes any fictitious quotation.

D. The Commission shall, for the purposes of this paragraph, by rules and regulations define. and prescribe means reasonably designed to prevent, such acts and practices as are fraudulent, deceptive, or manipulative and such quotations as are fictitious.

E. The Commission shall, prior to adopting any rule or regulation under subparagraph (C), consult with and consider the views of the Secretary of the Treasury and each appropriate regulatory agency. If the Secretary of the Treasury or any appropriate regulatory agency comments in writing on a proposed rule or regulation of the Commission under such subparagraph (C) that has been published for comment, the Commission shall respond in writing to such written comment before adopting the proposed rule. If the Secretary of the Treasury determines, and notifies the Commission, that such rule or regulation, if implemented, would, or as applied does

  i. adversely affect the liquidity or efficiency of the market for government securities; or

    ii. impose any burden on competition not necessary or appropriate in furtherance of the purposes of this section,

    the Commission shall, prior to adopting the proposed rule or regulation, find that such rule or regulation is necessary and appropriate in furtherance of the purposes of this section notwithstanding the Secretary's determination.

3. No broker or dealer (other than a government securities broker or government securities dealer, except a registered broker or dealer) shall make use of the mails or any means or instrumentality of interstate commerce to effect any transaction in, or to induce or attempt to induce the purchase or sale of, any security (other than an exempted security (except a government security) or commercial paper, bankers' acceptances, or commercial bills) in contravention of such rules and regulations as the Commission shall prescribe as necessary or appropriate in the public interest or for the protection of investors to provide safeguards with respect to the financial responsibility and related practices of brokers and dealers including, but not limited to, the acceptance of custody and use of customers' securities and the carrying and use of customers' deposits or credit balances. Such rules and regulations shall

    A. require the maintenance of reserves with respect to customers' deposits or credit balances, and

    B. no later than September 1, 1975, establish minimum financial responsibility requirements for all brokers and dealers.

4. If the Commission finds, after notice and opportunity for a hearing, that any person subject to the provisions of section 12, 13, 14, or subsection (d) of section 15 of this title or any rule or regulation thereunder has failed to comply with any such provision, rule, or regulation in any material respect, the Commission may publish its findings and issue an order requiring such person, and any person who was a cause of

the failure to comply due to an act or omission the person knew or should have known would contribute to the failure to comply, to comply, or to take steps to effect compliance, with such provision or such rule or regulation thereunder upon such terms and conditions and within such time as the Commission may specify in such order.

5. No dealer (other than a specialist registered on a national securities exchange) acting in the capacity of market maker or otherwise shall make use of the mails or any means or instrumentality of interstate commerce to effect any transaction in, or to induce or attempt to induce the purchase or sale of, any security (other than an exempted security or a municipal security) in contravention of such specified and appropriate standards with respect to dealing as the Commission, by rule, shall prescribe as necessary or appropriate in the public interest and for the protection of investors, to maintain fair and orderly markets, or to remove impediments to and perfect the mechanism of a national market system. Under the rules of the Commission a dealer in a security may be prohibited from acting as a broker in that security.

6. No broker or dealer shall make use of the mails or any means or instrumentality of interstate commerce to effect any transaction in, or to induce or attempt to induce the purchase or sale of, any security (other than an exempted security, municipal security, commercial paper, bankers' acceptances, or commercial bills) in contravention of such rules and regulations as the Commission shall prescribe as necessary or appropriate in the public interest and for the protection of investors or to perfect or remove impediments to a national system for the prompt and accurate clearance and settlement of securities transactions, with respect to the time and method of, and the form and format of documents used in connection with, making settlements of and payments for transactions in securities, making transfers and deliveries of securities, and closing accounts. Nothing in this paragraph shall be construed

A. to affect the authority of the Board of Governors of the Federal Reserve System, pursuant to section 7 of this title, to prescribe rules and regulations for the purpose of preventing the excessive use of credit for the purchase or carrying of securities, or

B. to authorize the Commission to prescribe rules or regulations for such purpose.

7. In connection with any bid for or purchase of a government security related to an offering of government securities by or on behalf of an issuer, no government securities broker, government securities dealer, or bidder for or purchaser of securities in such offering shall knowingly or willfully make any false or misleading written statement or omit any fact necessary to make any written statement made not misleading.

8. **Prohibition of referral fees.**—No broker or dealer, or person associated with a broker or dealer, may solicit or accept, directly or indirectly, remuneration for assisting an attorney in obtaining the representation of any person in any private action arising under this title or under the Securities Act of 1933.

d. Each issuer which has filed a registration statement containing an undertaking which is or becomes operative under this subsection as in effect prior to the date of enactment of the Securities Acts Amendments of 1964, and each issuer which shall after such date file a registration statement which has become effective pursuant to the Securities Act of 1933, as amended, shall file with the Commission, in accordance with such rules and regulations as the Commission may prescribe as necessary or appropriate in the public interest or for the protection of investors, such supplementary and periodic information, documents, and reports as may be required pursuant to section 13 of this title in respect of a security registered pursuant to section 12 of this title. The duty to file under this subsection shall be automatically suspended if and so long as any issue of securities of such issuer is registered pursuant to section 12 of this title. The duty to file under this subsection shall also be automatically suspended as to any fiscal year, other than the fiscal year within which such registration statement became effective, if, at the beginning of such fiscal year, the securities of each class to which the registration statement relates are held of record by less than three hundred persons. For the purposes of this subsection, the term "class" shall be construed to include all securities of an issuer which are of substantially similar character and the holders of which enjoy substantially similar rights and privileges. The Commission may, for the purpose of this subsection, define by rules and regulations the term "held of record" as it deems necessary or appropriate in the public interest or for the protection of investors in order to prevent circumvention of the provisions of this subsection. Nothing in this subsection shall apply to securities issued by a foreign government or political subdivision thereof.

e. The Commission, by rule, as it deems necessary or appropriate in the public interest and for the protection of investors or to assure equal regulation, may require any member of a national securities exchange not required to register under section 15 of this title and any person associated with any such member to comply with any provision of this title (other than section 15(a)) or the rules or regulations thereunder which by its terms regulates or prohibits any act, practice, or course of business by a "broker or dealer" or "registered broker or dealer" or a "person associated with a broker or dealer," respectively.

f. Every registered broker or dealer shall establish, maintain, and enforce written policies and procedures reasonably designed, taking into consideration the nature of such broker's or dealer's business, to prevent the misuse in violation of this title, or the rules or regulations thereunder, of material, nonpublic information by such broker or dealer or any person associated with such broker or dealer. The Commission, as it deems necessary or appropriate in the public interest or for the protection of investors, shall adopt rules or regulations to require specific policies or procedures reasonably designed to prevent misuse in violation of this title (or the rules or regulations thereunder) of material, nonpublic information.

g. **Requirements for Transactions in Penny Stocks.**—

   1. **In General.**—No broker or dealer shall make use of the mails or any means or instrumentality of interstate commerce to effect any transaction in, or to induce or attempt to induce the purchase or sale of, any penny stock by any

customer except in accordance with the requirements of
this subsection and the rules and regulations prescribed under this subsection.

2. **Risk disclosure with respect to penny stocks.**—Prior to
effecting any transaction in any penny stock, a broker or
dealer shall give the customer a risk disclosure document
that—

   A. contains a description of the nature and level of
   risk in the market for penny stocks in both public
   offerings and secondary trading;

   B. contains a description of the broker's or dealer's
   duties to the customer and of the rights and remedies available to the customer with respect to
   violations of such duties or other requirements of
   Federal securities laws;

   C. contains a brief, clear, narrative description of a
   dealer market, including "bid" and "ask" prices for
   penny stocks and the significance of the spread
   between the bid and ask prices;

   D. contains the toll free telephone number for inquiries on disciplinary actions established pursuant to
   section 15A(i) of this title;

   E. defines significant terms used in the disclosure
   document or in the conduct of trading in penny
   stocks; and

   F. contains such other information, and is in such form
   (including language, type size, and format), as the
   Commission shall require by rule or regulation.

3. **Commission rules relating to disclosure.**—The Commission shall adopt rules setting forth additional standards
for the disclosure by brokers and dealers to customers of
information concerning transactions in penny stocks. Such
rules—

   A. shall require brokers and dealers to disclose to each
   customer, prior to effecting any transaction in, and

at the time of confirming any transaction with respect to any penny stock, in accordance with such
procedures and methods as the Commission may
requires consistent with the public interest and the
protection of investors—

    i.   the bid and ask prices for penny stock, or
         such other information as the Commission
         may, by rule, require to provide customers
         with more useful and reliable information
         relating to the price of such stock.

    ii. the number of shares to which such bid and
         ask prices apply, or other comparable infor-
         mation relating to the depth and liquidity
         of the market for such stock; and

    iii. the amount and a description of any com-
         pensation that the broker or dealer and the
         associated person thereof will receive or
         has received in connection with such trans-
         action;

B. shall require brokers and dealers to provide, to each
customer whose account with the broker or dealer
contains penny stocks, a monthly statement indicating the market value of the penny stocks in that
account or indicating that the market value of such
stock cannot be determined because of the unavailability of firm quotes; and

C. may, as the Commission finds necessary or appropriate in the public interest or for the protection of
investors, require brokers and dealers to disclose to
customers additional information concerning transactions in penny stocks.

4. **Exemptions.**—The Commission, as it determines consistent with the public interest and the protection of investors,
may by rule, regulation, or order exempt in whole or in
part, conditionally or unconditionally, any person or class
of persons, or any transaction or class of transactions, from
the requirements of this subsection. Such exemptions shall

include an exemption for brokers and dealers based on the minimal percentage of the broker's or dealer's commissions, commission-equivalents, and markups received from transactions in penny stocks.

5. **Regulations.**—It shall be unlawful for any person to violate such rules and regulations as the Commission shall prescribe in the public interest or for the protection of investors or to maintain fair and orderly markets—

   A. as necessary or appropriate to carry out this subsection; or

   B. as reasonably designed to prevent fraudulent, deceptive, or manipulative acts and practices with respect to penny stocks.

h. **Limitations on State Law.**—

1. **Capital, margin, books and records, bonding, and reports.**—No law, rule, regulation, or order, or other administrative action of any State or political subdivision thereof shall establish capital, custody, margin, financial responsibility, making and keeping records, bonding, or financial or operational reporting requirements for brokers, dealers, municipal securities dealers, government securities brokers, or government securities dealers that differ from, or are in addition to, the requirements in those areas established under this title. The Commission shall consult periodically the securities commissions (or any agency or office performing like functions) of the States concerning the adequacy of such requirements as established under this title.

2. **De minimis transactions by associated persons.**—No law, rule, regulation, or order, or other administrative action of any State or political subdivision thereof may prohibit an associated person of a broker or dealer from affecting a transaction described in paragraph (3) for a customer in such State if—

   A. such associated person is not ineligible to register with such State for any reason other than such a transaction;

  B. such associated person is registered with a registered securities association and at least one State; and

  C. the broker or dealer with which such person is associated is registered with such State.

 3. **Described transactions.**—

  A. **In general.**—A transaction is described in this paragraph if—

   i. such transaction is effected—

    I. on behalf of a customer that, for 30 days prior to the day of the transaction, maintained an account with the broker or dealer; and

    II. by an associated person of the broker or dealer—

     (aa) to which the customer was assigned for 14 days prior to the day of the transaction; and

     (bb) who is registered with a State in which the customer was a resident or was present for at least 30 consecutive days during the 1-year period prior to the day of the transaction;

   ii. the transaction is effected—

    I. on behalf of a customer that, for 30 days prior to the day of the transaction, maintains an account with the broker or dealer; and

    II. during the period beginning on the date on which such associated person files an application for registration with the State in which the transaction is effected and ending on the earlier of—

(aa) 60 days after the date on which the application is filed; or

(bb) the date on which such State notifies the associated person that has denied the application for registration or has stayed the pendency of the application for cause.

B. **Rules of construction.**—For purposes of subparagraph (A)(i)(II)—

    i.   each of up to 3 associated persons of a broker or dealer who are designated to effect transactions during the absence or unavailability of the principal associated person for a customer may be treated as an associated person to which such customer is assigned; and

    ii.   if the customer is present in another State for 30 or more consecutive days or has permanently changed his or her residence to another State, a transaction is not described in this paragraph, unless the association person of the broker or dealer files an application for registration with such State not later than 10 business days after the later of the date of the transaction, or the date of discovery of the presence of the customer in the other State for 30 or more consecutive days or the change in the customer's residence.

SECTION 15A—REGISTERED SECURITIES ASSOCIATIONS

a. An association of brokers and dealers may be registered as a national securities association pursuant to subsection (b), or as an affiliated securities association pursuant to subsection (d), under the terms and conditions hereinafter provided in this section and in accordance with the provisions of section 19(a) of this title, by filing with the Commission an application for registration in such form as the Commission, by rule, may prescribe containing the rules of the association and such other information and documents as the Commission, by rule, may prescribe as necessary or appropriate in the public interest or for the protection of investors.

b.   An association of brokers and dealers shall not be registered as a national securities association unless the Commission determines that—

   1.   By reason of the number and geographical distribution of its members and the scope of their transactions, such association will be able to carry out the purposes of this section.

   2.   Such association is so organized and has the capacity to be able to carry out the purposes of this title and to comply, and (subject to any rule or order of the Commission pursuant to section 17(d) or 19(g)(2) of this title) to enforce compliance by its members and persons associated with its members, with the provisions of this title, the rules and regulations thereunder, the rules of the Municipal Securities Rulemaking Board, and the rules of the association.

   3.   Subject to the provisions of subsection (g) of this section, the rules of the association provide that any registered broker or dealer may become a member of such association and any person may become associated with a member thereof.

   4.   The rules of the association assure a fair representation of its members in the selection of its directors and administration of its affairs and provide that one or more directors shall be representative of issuers and investors and not be associated with a member of the association, broker, or dealer.

   5.   The rules of the association provide for the equitable allocation of reasonable dues, fees, and other charges among members and issuers and other persons using any facility or system which the association operates or controls.

6. The rules of the association are designed to prevent fraudulent and manipulative acts and practices, to promote just and equitable principles of trade, to foster cooperation and coordination with persons engaged in regulating, clearing, settling, processing information with respect to, and facilitating transactions in securities, to remove impediments to and perfect the mechanism of a free and open market and a national market system, and, in general, to protect investors and the public interest; and are not designed to permit unfair discrimination between customers, issuers, brokers, or dealers, to fix minimum profits, to impose any schedule or fix rates of commissions, allowances, discounts, or other fees to be charged by its members, or to regulate by virtue of any authority conferred by this title matters not related to the purposes of this title or the administration of the association.

7. The rules of the association provide that (subject to any rule or order of the Commission pursuant to section 17(d) or 19(g)(2) of this title) its members and persons associated with its members shall be appropriately disciplined for violation of any provision of this title, the rules or regulations thereunder, the rules of the Municipal Securities Rulemaking Board, or the rules of the association, by expulsion, suspension, limitation of activities, functions, and operations, fine, censure, being suspended or barred from being associated with a member, or any other fitting sanction.

8. The rules of the association are in accordance with the provisions of subsection (h) of this section, and, in general, provide a fair procedure for the disciplining of members and persons associated with members, the denial of membership to any person seeking membership therein, the barring of any person from becoming associated with a member thereof, and the prohibition or limitation by the association of any person with respect to access to services offered by the association or a member thereof.

9. The rules of the association do not impose any burden on competition not necessary or appropriate in furtherance of the purposes of this title.

10. The requirements of subsection (c), insofar as these may be applicable, are satisfied.

11. The rules of the association include provisions governing the form and content of quotations relating to securities sold otherwise than on a national securities exchange which may be distributed or published by any member or person associated with a member, and the persons to whom such quotations may be supplied. Such rules relating to quotations shall be designed to produce fair and informative quotations, to prevent fictitious or misleading quotations, and to promote orderly procedures for collecting, distributing, and publishing quotations.

12. The rules of the association to promote just and equitable principles of trade, as required by paragraph (6), include rules to prevent members of the association from participating in any limited partnership rollup transaction (as such term is defined in paragraphs (4) and (5) of section 14(h)) unless such transaction was conducted in accordance with procedures designed to protect the rights of limited partners, including—

    A. the right of dissenting limited partners to one of the following:

        i.   an appraisal and compensation;

        ii. retention of a security under substantially the same terms and conditions as the original issue;

        iii. approval of the limited partnership rollup transaction by not less than 75 percent of the outstanding securities of each of the participating limited partnerships;

        iv. the use of a committee that is independent, as determined in accordance with rules prescribed by the association, of the general partner or sponsor, that has been approved by a majority of the outstanding securities of each of the participating partnerships, and that has such authority as is necessary to protect the interest of limited partners, including the authority to hire independent advisors, to negotiate with the general partner or sponsor on behalf of the limited partners, and to make a recommendation to the limited partners with respect to the proposed transaction; or

v. other comparable rights that are prescribed by rule by the association and that are designed to protect dissenting limited partners;

B. the right not to have their voting power unfairly reduced or abridged;

C. the right not to bear an unfair portion of the costs of a proposed limited partnership rollup transaction that is rejected; and

D. restrictions on the conversion of contingent interests or fees into non-contingent interests or fees and restrictions on the receipt of a non-contingent equity interest in exchange for fees for services which have not yet been provided.

As used in this paragraph, the term "dissenting limited partner" means a person who, on the date on which soliciting material is mailed to investors, is a holder of a beneficial interest in a limited partnership that is the subject of a limited partnership rollup transaction, and who casts a vote against the transaction and complies with procedures established by the association, except that for purposes of an exchange or tender offer, such person shall file an objection in writing under the rules of the association during the period in which the offer is outstanding.

13. The rules of the association prohibit the authorization for quotation on an auto-mated interdealer quotation system sponsored by the association of any security designated by the Commission as a national market system security resulting from a limited partnership rollup transaction (as such term is defined in paragraphs (4) and (5) of section

14(h)), unless such transaction was conducted in accordance with procedures designed to protect the rights of limited partners including—

   A. the right of dissenting limited partners to one of the following:

      i. an appraisal and compensation;

      ii. retention of a security under substantially the same terms and conditions as the original issue;

      iii. approval of the limited partnership rollup transaction by not less than 75 percent of the outstanding securities of each of the participating limited partnerships;

      iv. the use of a committee that is independent, as determined in accordance with rules prescribed by the association, of the general partner or sponsor, that has been approved by a majority of the outstanding securities of each of the participating partnerships, and that has such authority as is necessary to protect the interest of limited partners, including the authority to hire independent advisors, to negotiate with the general partner or sponsor on behalf of the limited partners, and to make a recommendation to the limited partners with respect to the proposed transaction; or

      v. other comparable rights that are prescribed by rule by the association and that are designed to protect dissenting limited partners;

   B. the right not to have their voting power unfairly reduced or abridged;

   C. the right not to bear an unfair portion of the costs of a proposed limited partnership rollup transaction that is rejected; and

D.	restrictions on the conversion of contingent interests or fees into non-contingent interests or fees and restrictions on the receipt of a non-contingent equity interest in exchange for fees for services which have not yet been provided.

As used in this paragraph, the term "dissenting limited partner" means a person who, on the date on which soliciting material is mailed to investors, is a holder of a beneficial interest in a limited partnership that is the subject of a limited partnership rollup transaction, and who casts a vote against the transaction and complies with procedures established by the association, except that for purposes of an exchange or tender offer, such person shall file an objection in writing under the rules of the association during the period during which the offer is outstanding.

c.	The Commission may permit or require the rules of an association applying for registration pursuant to subsection (b), to provide for the admission of an association registered as an affiliated securities association, pursuant to subsection (d), to participation in said applicant association as an affiliate thereof, under terms permitting such powers and responsibilities to such affiliate, and under such other appropriate terms and conditions, as may be provided by the rules of said applicant association, if such rules appear to the Commission to be necessary or appropriate in the public interest or for the protection of investors and to carry out the purposes of this section. The duties and powers of the Commission with respect to any national securities association or any affiliated association shall in no way be limited by reason of any such affiliation.

d.	An applicant association shall not be registered as an affiliated securities association unless it appears to the Commission that—

1.	such association, notwithstanding that it does not satisfy the requirements set forth in paragraph (1) of subsection (b), will, forthwith upon the registration thereof, be admitted to affiliation with an association registered as a national securities association pursuant to said subsection (b), in the manner and under the terms and conditions provided by the rules of said national securities association in accordance with <u>subsection (c)</u>; and

2. such association and its rules satisfy the requirements set forth in paragraphs <u>(2)</u> to <u>(10)</u> inclusive and paragraph <u>(12)</u>, of subsection <u>(b)</u>; except that in the case of any such association any restrictions upon membership therein of the type authorized by <u>paragraph (3)</u> of subsection (b) shall not be less stringent than in the case of the national securities association with which such association is to be affiliated.

e.

1. The rules of a registered securities association may provide that no member thereof shall deal with any nonmember professional (as defined in <u>paragraph (2)</u> of this subsection) except at the same prices, for the same commissions or fees, and on the same terms and conditions as are by such member accorded to the general public.

2. For the purposes of this subsection, the term "nonmember professional" shall include

    A. with respect to transactions in securities other than municipal securities, any registered broker or dealer who is not a member of any registered securities association, except such a broker or dealer who deals exclusively in commercial paper, bankers' acceptances, and commercial bills, and

    B. with respect to transactions in municipal securities, any municipal securities dealer (other than a bank or division or department of a bank) who is not a member of any registered securities association and any municipal securities broker who is not a member of any such association.

3. Nothing in this subsection shall be so construed or applied as to prevent

    A. any member of a registered securities association from granting to any other member of any registered securities association any dealer's discount, allowance, commission, or special terms, in connection with the purchase or sale of securities, or

B. any member of a registered securities association or any municipal securities dealer which is a bank or a division or department of a bank from granting to any member of any registered securities association or any such municipal securities dealer any dealer's discount, allowance, commission, or special terms in connection with the purchase or sale of municipal securities:

Provided, however,

That the granting of any such discount, allowance, commission, or special terms in connection with the purchase or sale of municipal securities shall be subject to rules of the Municipal Securities Rulemaking Board adopted pursuant to section 15B(b)(2)(K) of this title.

f. Nothing in subsection (b)(6) or (b)(11) of this section shall be construed to permit a registered securities association to make rules concerning any transaction by a registered broker or dealer in a municipal security.

g.

1. A registered securities association shall deny membership to any person who is not a registered broker or dealer.

2. A registered securities association may, and in cases in which the Commission, by order, directs as necessary or appropriate in the public interest or for the protection of investors shall, deny membership to any registered broker or dealer, and bar from becoming associated with a member any person, who is subject to a statutory disqualification. A registered securities association shall file notice with the Commission not less than thirty days prior to admitting any registered broker or dealer to membership or permitting any person to become associated with a member, if the association knew, or in the exercise of reasonable

care should have known, that such broker or dealer or person was subject to a statutory disqualification. The notice shall be in such form and contain such information as the Commission, by rule, may prescribe as necessary or appropriate in the public interest or for the protection of investors.

3.

    A. A registered securities association may deny membership to, or condition the membership of, a registered broker or dealer if

        i. such broker or dealer does not meet such standards of financial responsibility or operational capability or such broker or dealer or any natural person associated with such broker or dealer does not meet such standards of training, experience, and competence as are prescribed by the rules of the association or

        ii. such broker or dealer or person associated with such broker or dealer has engaged and there is a reasonable likelihood he will again engage in acts or practices inconsistent with just and equitable principles of trade.

        A registered securities association may examine and verify the qualifications of an applicant to become a member and the natural persons associated with such an applicant in accordance with procedures established by the rules of the association.

    B. A registered securities association may bar a natural person from becoming associated with a member or condition the association of a natural person with a member if such natural person

        i. does not meet such standards of training, experience, and competence as are prescribed by the rules of the association or

    ii. has engaged and there is a reasonable likelihood he will again engage in acts or practices inconsistent with just and equitable principles of trade.

A registered securities association may examine and verify the qualifications of an applicant to become a person associated with a member in accordance with procedures established by the rules of the association and require a natural person associated with a member, or any class of such natural persons, to be registered with the association in accordance with procedures so established.

C. A registered securities association may bar any person from becoming associated with a member if such person does not agree

    i. to supply the association with such information with respect to its relationship and dealings with the member as may be specified in the rules of the association and

    ii. to permit examination of its books and records to verify the accuracy of any information so supplied.

D. Nothing in subparagraph (A), (B), or (C) of this paragraph shall be construed to permit a registered securities association to deny membership to or condition the membership of, or bar any person from becoming associated with or condition the association of any person with, a broker or dealer that engages exclusively in transactions in municipal securities.

4. A registered securities association may deny membership to a registered broker or dealer not engaged in a type of business in which the rules of the association require members to be engaged:

Provided, however,

That no registered securities association may deny membership to a registered broker or dealer by reason of the amount of such type of business done by such broker or dealer or the other types of business in which he is engaged.

h.

1. In any proceeding by a registered securities association to determine whether a member or person associated with a member should be disciplined (other than a summary proceeding pursuant to paragraph (3) of this subsection) the association shall bring specific charges, notify such member or person of, and give him an opportunity to defend against, such charges, and keep a record. A determination by the association to impose a disciplinary sanction shall be supported by a statement setting forth—

    A. any act or practice in which such member or person associated with a member has been found to have engaged, or which such member or person has been found to have omitted;

    B. the specific provision of this title, the rules or regulations thereunder, the rules of the Municipal Securities Rulemaking Board, or the rules of the association which any such act or practice, or omission to act, is deemed to violate; and

    C. the sanction imposed and the reason therefor.

2. In any proceeding by a registered securities association to determine whether a person shall be denied membership, barred from becoming associated with a member, or prohibited or limited with respect to access to services offered by the association or a member thereof (other than a summary proceeding pursuant to paragraph (3) of this subsection), the association shall notify such person of and give him an opportunity to be heard upon, the specific grounds for denial, bar, or prohibition or limitation under consideration and keep a record. A determination by the association to deny membership, bar a person from becoming associated

with a member, or prohibit or limit a person with respect to access to services offered by the association or a member thereof shall be supported by a statement setting forth the specific grounds on which the denial, bar, or prohibition or limitation is based.

3. A registered securities association may summarily

    A. suspend a member or person associated with a member who has been and is expelled or suspended from any self-regulatory organization or barred or suspended from being associated with a member of any self-regulatory organization,

    B. suspend a member who is in such financial or operating difficulty that the association determines and so notifies the Commission that the member cannot be permitted to continue to do business as a member with safety to investors, creditors, other members, or the association, or

    C. limit or prohibit any person with respect to access to services offered by the association if subparagraph (A) or (B) of this paragraph is applicable to such person or, in the case of a person who is not a member, if the association determines that such person does not meet the qualification requirements or other prerequisites for such access and such person cannot be permitted to continue to have such access with safety to investors, creditors, members, or the association.

Any person aggrieved by any such summary action shall be promptly afforded an opportunity for a hearing by the association in accordance with the provisions of paragraph (1) or (2) of this subsection. The Commission, by order, may stay any such summary action on its own motion or upon application by any person aggrieved thereby, if the Commission determines summarily or after notice and opportunity for hearing (which hearing may consist solely of the submission of affidavits or presentation of oral arguments) that such stay is consistent with the public interest and the protection of investors.

i. A registered securities association shall, within one year from the date of enactment of this section,

    1. establish and maintain a toll-free telephone listing to receive inquiries regarding disciplinary actions involving its members and their associated persons, and

    2. promptly respond to such inquiries in writing. Such association may charge persons, other than individual investors, reasonable fees for written responses to such inquiries. Such an association shall not have any liability to any person for any actions taken or omitted in good faith under this paragraph.

SECTION 15B—MUNICIPAL SECURITIES

a.

    1. It shall be unlawful for any municipal securities dealer (other than one registered as a broker or dealer under section 15 of this title) to make use of the mails or any means or instrumentality of interstate commerce to effect any transaction in, or to induce or attempt to induce the purchase or sale of, any municipal security unless such municipal securities dealer is registered in accordance with this subsection.

    2. A municipal securities dealer may be registered by filing with the Commission an application for registration in such form and containing such information and documents concerning such municipal securities dealer and any persons associated with such municipal securities dealer as the Commission, by rule, may prescribe as necessary or appropriate in the public interest or for the protection of investors. Within forty-five days of the date of the filing of such application (or within such longer period as to which the applicant consents), the Commission shall—

        A. by order grant registration, or

B. institute proceedings to determine whether registration should be denied. Such proceedings shall include notice of the grounds for denial under consideration and opportunity for hearing and shall be concluded within one hundred twenty days of the date of the filing of the application for registration. At the conclusion of such proceedings the Commission, by order, shall grant or deny such registration. The Commission may extend the time for the conclusion of such proceedings for up to ninety days if it finds good cause for such extension and publishes its reasons for so finding or for such longer period as to which the applicant consents.

The Commission shall grant the registration of a municipal securities dealer if the Commission finds that the requirements of this section are satisfied. The Commission shall deny such registration if it does not make such a finding or if it finds that if the applicant were so registered, its registration would be subject to suspension or revocation under subsection (c) of this section.

3. Any provision of this title (other than section 5 or paragraph (1) of this subsection) which prohibits any act, practice, or course of business if the mails or any means or instrumentality of interstate commerce is used in connection therewith shall also prohibit any such act, practice, or course of business by any registered municipal securities dealer or any person acting on behalf of such municipal securities dealer, irrespective of any use of the mails or any means or instrumentality of interstate commerce in connection therewith.

4. The Commission, by rule or order, upon its own motion or upon application, may conditionally or unconditionally exempt any broker, dealer, or municipal securities dealer or class of brokers, dealers, or municipal securities dealers from any provision of this section or the rules or regulations thereunder, if the Commission finds that such exemption is consistent with the public interest, the protection of investors, and the purposes of this section.

b.

1. Not later than one hundred twenty days after the date of enactment of the Securities Acts Amendments of 1975, the Commission shall establish a Municipal Securities Rulemaking Board (hereinafter in this section referred to as the "Board") to be composed initially of fifteen members appointed by the Commission, which shall perform the duties set forth in this section. The initial members of the Board shall serve as members for a term of two years, and shall consist of

   A. five individuals who are not associated with any broker, dealer, or municipal securities dealer (other than by reason of being under common control with, or indirectly controlling, any broker or dealer which is not a municipal securities broker or municipal securities dealer), at least one of whom shall be representative of investors in municipal securities, and at least one of whom shall be representative of issuers of municipal securities (which members are hereinafter referred to as "public representatives");

   B. five individuals who are associated with and representative of municipal securities brokers and municipal securities dealers which are not banks or subsidiaries or departments or divisions of banks (which members are hereinafter referred to as "broker-dealer representatives"); and

   C. five individuals who are associated with and representative of municipal securities dealers which are banks or subsidiaries or departments or divisions of banks (which members are hereinafter referred to as "bank representatives").

   Prior to the expiration of the terms of office of the initial members of the Board, an election shall be held under rules adopted by the Board (pursuant to subsection (b)(2)(B) of this section) of the members to succeed such initial members.

2. The Board shall propose and adopt rules to effect the purposes of this title with respect to transactions in municipal securities effected by brokers, dealers and municipal securities dealers. (Such rules are hereinafter collectively referred to in this title as "rules of the Board".) The rules of the Board, as a minimum, shall:

    A. provide that no municipal securities broker or municipal securities dealer shall effect any transaction in, or induce or attempt to induce the purchase or sale of, any municipal security unless such municipal securities broker or municipal securities dealer meets such standards of operational capability and such municipal securities broker or municipal securities dealer and every natural person associated with such municipal securities broker or municipal securities dealer meets such standards of training, experience, competence, and such other qualifications as the Board finds necessary or appropriate in the public interest or for the protection of investors. In connection with the definition and application of such standards the Board may—

        i.   appropriately classify municipal securities brokers and municipal securities dealers (taking into account relevant matters, including types of business done, nature of securities other than municipal securities sold, and character of business organization), and persons associated with municipal securities brokers and municipal securities dealers;

        ii. specify that all or any portion of such standards shall be applicable to any such class;

        iii. require persons in any such class to pass tests administered in accordance with subsection (c)(7) of this section; and

iv. provide that persons in any such class other than municipal securities brokers and municipal securities dealers and partners, officers, and supervisory employees of municipal securities brokers or municipal securities dealers, may be qualified solely on the basis of compliance with such standards of training and such other qualifications as the Board finds appropriate.

B. establish fair procedures for the nomination and election of members of the Board and assure fair representation in such nominations and elections of municipal securities brokers and municipal securities dealers. Such rules shall provide that the membership of the Board shall at all times be equally divided among public representatives, broker-dealer representatives, and bank representatives, and that the public representatives shall be subject to approval by the Commission to assure that no one of them is associated with any broker, dealer, or municipal securities dealer (other than by reason of being under common control with, or indirectly controlling, any broker or dealer which is not a municipal securities broker or municipal securities dealer) and that at least one is representative of investors in municipal securities and at least one is representative of issuers of municipal securities. Such rules shall also specify the term members shall serve and may increase the number of members which shall constitute the whole Board provided that such number is an odd number.

C. be designed to prevent fraudulent and manipulative acts and practices, to promote just and equitable principles of trade, to foster cooperation and coordination with persons engaged in regulating, clearing, settling, processing information with respect to, and facilitating transactions in municipal securities, to remove impediments to and perfect the mechanism of a free and open market in municipal securities, and, in general, to protect investors and the public interest; and not be designed to permit unfair discrimination between customers, issuers, municipal securities brokers, or municipal securities dealers, to fix minimum profits, to impose any schedule or fix rates of commissions, allowances, discounts, or other fees to be charged by municipal securities brokers or municipal securities dealers, to regulate by virtue of any authority conferred by this title matters not related to the purposes of this title or the administration of the Board, or to impose any burden on competition not necessary or appropriate in furtherance of the purpose of this title.

D.   if the Board deems appropriate, provide for the arbitration of claims, disputes, and controversies relating to transactions in municipal securities:

Provided, however,

That no person other than a municipal securities broker, municipal securities dealer, or person associated with such a municipal securities broker or municipal securities dealer may be compelled to submit to such arbitration except at his instance and in accordance with section 29 of this title.

E.   provide for the periodic examination in accordance with subsection (c)(7) of this section of municipal securities brokers and municipal securities dealers to determine compliance with applicable provisions of this title, the rules and regulations thereunder, and the rules of the Board. Such rules shall specify the minimum scope and frequency of such examinations and shall be designed to avoid unnecessary regulatory duplication or undue regulatory burdens for any such municipal securities broker or municipal securities dealer.

F.   include provisions governing the form and content of quotations relating to municipal securities which may be distributed or published by any municipal securities broker, municipal securities dealer, or person associated with such a municipal securities broker or municipal securities dealer, and the persons to whom such quotations may be supplied. Such rules relating to quotations shall be designed to produce fair and informative quotations, to prevent fictitious or misleading quotations, and to promote orderly procedures for collecting, distributing, and publishing quotations.

G. prescribe records to be made and kept by municipal securities brokers and municipal securities dealers and the periods for which such records shall be preserved.

H. define the term "separately identifiable department or division", as that term is used in section 3(a)(30) of this title, in accordance with specified and appropriate standards to assure that a bank is not deemed to be engaged in the business of buying and selling municipal securities through a separately identifiable department or division unless such department or division is organized and administered so as to permit independent examination and enforcement of applicable provisions of this title, the rules and regulations thereunder and the rules of the Board. A separately identifiable department or division of a bank may be engaged in activities other than those relating to municipal securities.

I. provide for the operation and administration of the Board, including the selection of a Chairman from among the members of the Board, the compensation of the members of the Board, and the appointment and compensation of such employees, attorneys, and consultants as may be necessary or appropriate to carry out the Board's functions under this section.

J. provide that each municipal securities broker and each municipal securities dealer shall pay to the

Board such reasonable fees and charges as may be necessary or appropriate to defray the costs and expenses of operating and administering the Board. Such rules shall specify the amount of such fees and charges.

K. establish the terms and conditions under which any municipal securities dealer may sell, or prohibit any municipal securities dealer from selling, any part of a new issue of municipal securities to a municipal securities investment portfolio during the underwriting period.

3. Nothing in this section shall be construed to impair or limit the power of the Commission under this title.

c.

1. No broker, dealer, or municipal securities dealer shall make use of the mails or any means or instrumentality of interstate commerce to effect any transaction in, or to induce or attempt to induce the purchase or sale of, any municipal security in contravention of any rule of the Board.

2. The Commission, by order, shall censure, place limitations on the activities, functions, or operations, suspend for a period not exceeding twelve months, or revoke the registration of any municipal securities dealer, if it finds, on the record after notice and opportunity for hearing, that such censure, placing of limitations, denial, suspension, or revocation, is in the public interest and that such municipal securities dealer has committed or omitted any act or omission enumerated in subparagraph (A), (D), (E), or (G) of paragraph (4) of section 15(b) of this title, has been convicted of any offense specified in subparagraph (B) of such paragraph (4) within ten years of the commencement of the proceedings under this paragraph, or is enjoined from any action, conduct, or practice specified in subparagraph (C) of such paragraph (4).

3. Pending final determination whether any registration under this section shall be revoked, the Commission, by order, may suspend such registration, if such suspension appears

to the Commission, after notice and opportunity for hearing, to be necessary or appropriate in the public interest or for the protection of investors. Any registered municipal securities dealer may, upon such terms and conditions as the Commission may deem necessary in the public interest or for the protection of investors, withdraw from registration by filing a written notice of withdrawal with the Commission. If the Commission finds that any registered municipal securities dealer is no longer in existence or has ceased to do business as a municipal securities dealer, the Commission, by order, shall cancel the registration of such municipal securities dealer.

4.   The Commission, by order, shall censure or place limitations on the activities or functions of any person associated, seeking to become associated or, at the time of the alleged misconduct, associated or seeking to become associated with a municipal securities dealer, or suspend for a period not exceeding twelve months or bar any such person from being associated with a municipal securities dealer, if the Commission finds, on the record after notice and opportunity for hearing, that such censure, placing of limitations, suspension, or bar is in the public interest and that such person has committed or omitted any act or omission enumerated in subparagraph (A), (D), (E), or (G) of paragraph (4) of section 15(b) of this title, has been convicted of any offense specified in subparagraph (B) of such paragraph (4) within ten years of the commencement of the proceedings under this paragraph, or is enjoined from any action, conduct, or practice specified in subparagraph (C) of such paragraph (4). It shall be unlawful for any person as to whom an order entered pursuant to this paragraph or paragraph (5) of this subsection suspending or barring him from being associated with a municipal securities dealer is in effect willfully to become, or to be, associated with a municipal securities dealer without the consent of the Commission, and it shall be unlawful for any municipal securities dealer to permit such a person to become, or remain, a person associated with him without the consent of the Commission, if such municipal securities dealer knew,

or, in the exercise of reasonable care should have known, of such order.

5. With respect to any municipal securities dealer for which the Commission is not the appropriate regulatory agency, the appropriate regulatory agency for such municipal securities dealer may sanction any such municipal securities dealer in the manner and for the reasons specified in paragraph (2) of this subsection and any person associated with such municipal securities dealer in the manner and for the reasons specified in paragraph (4) of this subsection. In addition, such appropriate regulatory agency may, in accordance with section 8 of the Federal Deposit Insurance Act (12 U.S.C. 1818), enforce compliance by such municipal securities dealer or any person associated with such municipal securities dealer with the provisions of this section, section 17 of this title, the rules of the Board, and the rules of the Commission pertaining to municipal securities dealers, persons associated with municipal securities dealers, and transactions in municipal securities. For purposes of the preceding sentence, any violation of any such provision shall constitute adequate basis for the issuance of any order under section 8(b) or 8(c) of the Federal Deposit Insurance Act, and the customers of any such municipal securities dealer shall be deemed to be "depositors" as that term is used in section 8(c) of that Act. Nothing in this paragraph shall be construed to affect in any way the powers of such appropriate regulatory agency to proceed against such municipal securities dealer under any other provision of law.

6.

   A. The Commission, prior to the entry of an order of investigation, or commencement of any proceedings, against any municipal securities dealer, or person associated with any municipal securities dealer, for which the Commission is not the appropriate regulatory agency, for violation of any provision of this section, section 15(c)(1) or 15(c)(2) of this title, any rule or regulation under any such section, or any rule of the Board, shall

      i.   give notice to the appropriate regulatory agency for such municipal securities dealer of the identity of such municipal securities dealer or person associated with such municipal securities dealer, the nature of and basis for such proposed action and whether the Commission is seeking a monetary penalty against such municipal securities dealer or other associated person pursuant to section 21B of this title; and

     ii.   consult with such appropriate regulatory agency concerning the effect of such proposed action on sound banking practices and the feasibility and desirability of coordinating such action with any proceeding or proposed proceeding by such appropriate regulatory agency against such municipal securities dealer or associated person.

B. The appropriate regulatory agency for a municipal securities dealer (if other than the Commission), prior to the entry of an order of investigation, or commencement of any proceedings, against such municipal securities dealer or person associated with such municipal securities dealer, for violation of any provision of this section, the rules of the Board, or the rules or regulations of the Commission pertaining to municipal securities dealers, persons associated with municipal securities dealers, or transactions in municipal securities shall

      i.   give notice to the Commission of the identity of such municipal securities dealer or person associated with such municipal securities dealer and the nature of and basis for such proposed action and

     ii.   consult with the Commission concerning the effect of such proposed action on the protection of investors and the feasibility and desirability of coordinating such action with any proceeding or proposed proceeding by the Commission against such municipal securities dealer or associated person.

C. Nothing in this paragraph shall be construed to impair or limit (other than by the requirement of prior consultation) the power of the Commission or the appropriate regulatory agency for a municipal securities dealer to initiate any action of a class described in this paragraph or to affect in any way the power of the Commission or such appropriate regulatory agency to initiate any other action pursuant to this title or any other provision of law.

7.

A. Tests required pursuant to subsection (b)(2)(A)(iii) of this section shall be administered by or on behalf of and periodic examinations pursuant to subsection (b)(2)(E) of this section shall be conducted by—

    i.   a registered securities association, in the case of municipal securities brokers and municipal securities dealers who are members of such association; and

    ii. the appropriate regulatory agency for any municipal securities broker or municipal securities dealer, in the case of all other municipal securities brokers and municipal securities dealers.

B. A registered securities association shall make a report of any examination conducted pursuant to subsection (b)(2)(E) of this section and promptly furnish the Commission a copy thereof and any data supplied to it in connection with such examination. Subject to such limitations as the Commission, by rule, determines to be necessary or appropriate in the public interest or for the protection of investors, the Commission shall, on request, make available to the Board a copy of any report of an examination of a municipal securities broker or municipal securities dealer made by or furnished to the Commission pursuant to this paragraph or section 17(c)(3) of this title.

8.   The Commission is authorized, by order, if in its opinion such action is necessary or appropriate in the public interest, for the protection of investors, or otherwise, in furtherance of the purposes of this title, to remove from office or censure any member or employee of the Board, who, the Commission finds, on the record after notice and opportunity for hearing, has willfully (A) violated any provision of this title, the rules and regulations thereunder, or the rules of the Board or (B) abused his authority.

d.

1.   Neither the Commission nor the Board is authorized under this title, by rule or regulation, to require any issuer of municipal securities, directly or indirectly through a purchaser or prospective purchaser of securities from the issuer, to file with the Commission or the Board prior to the sale of such securities by the issuer any application, report, or document in connection with the issuance, sale, or distribution of such securities.

2.   The Board is not authorized under this title to require any issuer of municipal securities, directly or indirectly through a municipal securities broker or municipal securities dealer or otherwise, to furnish to the Board or to a purchaser or prospective purchaser of such securities any application, report, document or information with respect to such issuer:

Provided, however,

That the Board may require municipal securities brokers and municipal securities dealers to furnish to the Board or purchasers or prospective purchasers of municipal securities applications, reports, documents, and information with respect to the issuer thereof which are generally available from a source other than such issuer. Nothing in this paragraph shall be construed to impair or limit the power of the Commission under any provision of this title.

SECTION 15C—GOVERNMENT SECURITIES BROKERS AND DEALERS

a.

   1.

      A. It shall be unlawful for any government securities broker or government securities dealer (other than a registered broker or dealer or a financial institution) to make use of the mails or any means or instrumentality of interstate commerce to effect any transaction in, or to induce or attempt to induce the purchase or sale of, any government security unless such government securities broker or government securities dealer is registered in accordance with paragraph (2) of this subsection.

      B.

         i. It shall be unlawful for any government securities broker or government securities dealer that is a registered broker or dealer or a financial institution to make use of the mails or any means or instrumentality of interstate commerce to effect any transaction in, or to induce or attempt to induce the purchase or sale of, any government security unless such government securities broker or government securities dealer has filed with the appropriate regulatory agency written notice that it is a government securities broker or government securities dealer. When such a government securities broker or government securities dealer ceases to act as such it shall file with the appropriate regulatory agency a written notice that it is no longer acting as a government securities broker or government securities dealer.

ii. Such notices shall be in such form and contain such information concerning a government securities broker or government securities dealer that is a financial institution and any persons associated with such government securities broker or government securities dealer as the Board of Governors of the Federal Reserve System shall, by rule, after consultation with each appropriate regulatory agency (including the Commission), prescribe as necessary or appropriate in the public interest or for the protection of investors. Such notices shall be in such form and contain such information concerning a government securities broker or government securities dealer that is a registered broker or dealer and any persons associated with such government securities broker or government securities dealer as the Commission shall, by rule, prescribe as necessary or appropriate in the public interest or for the protection of investors.

iii. Each appropriate regulatory agency (other than the Commission) shall make available to the Commission the notices which have been filed with it under this subparagraph, and the Commission shall maintain and make available to the public such notices and the notices it receives under this subparagraph.

2. A government securities broker or a government securities dealer subject to the registration requirement of paragraph (1)(A) of this subsection may be registered by filing with the Commission an application for registration in such form

and containing such information and documents concerning such government securities broker or government securities dealer and any persons associated with such government securities broker or government securities dealer as the Commission, by rule, may prescribe as necessary or appropriate in the public interest or for the protection of investors. Within 45 days of the date of filing of such application (or within such longer period as to which the applicant consents), the Commission shall—

    i.   by order grant registration, or

    ii. institute proceedings to determine whether registration should be denied. Such proceedings shall include notice of the grounds for denial under consideration and opportunity for hearing and shall be concluded within 120 days of the date of the filing of the application for registration. At the conclusion of such proceedings, the Commission, by order, shall grant or deny such registration. The order granting registration shall not be effective until such government securities broker or government securities dealer has become a member of a national securities exchange registered under section 6 of this title, or a securities association registered under section 15A of this title, unless the Commission has exempted such government securities broker or government securities dealer, by rule or order, from such membership. The Commission may extend the time for the conclusion of such proceedings for up to 90 days if it finds good cause for such extension and publishes its reasons for so finding or for such longer period as to which the applicant consents.

The Commission shall grant the registration of a government securities broker or a government securities dealer if the Commission finds that the requirements of this section are satisfied. The Commission shall deny such registration if it does not make such a finding or if it finds that if the applicant were so registered, its registration would be subject to suspension or revocation under subsection (c) of this section.

3. Any provision of this title (other than section 5 or paragraph (1) of this subsection) which prohibits any act, practice, or course of business if the mails or any means or instrumentality of interstate commerce is used in connection therewith shall also prohibit any such act, practice, or course of business by any government securities broker or government securities dealer registered or having filed notice under paragraph (1) of this subsection or any person acting on behalf of such government securities broker or government securities dealer, irrespective of any use of the mails or any means or instrumentality of interstate commerce in connection therewith.

4. No government securities broker or government securities dealer that is required to register under paragraph (1)(A) and that is not a member of the Securities Investor Protection Corporation shall effect any transaction in any security in contravention of such rules as the Commission shall prescribe pursuant to this subsection to assure that its customers receive complete, accurate, and timely disclosure of the inapplicability of Securities Investor Protection Corporation coverage to their accounts

5. The Secretary of the Treasury (hereinafter in this section referred to as the "Secretary"), by rule or order, upon the Secretary's own motion or upon application, may conditionally or unconditionally exempt any government securities broker or government securities dealer, or class of government securities brokers or government securities dealers, from any provision of subsection (a), (b), or (d) of this section, other than subsection (d)(3), or the rules thereunder, if the Secretary finds that such exemption is consistent with the public interest, the protection of investors, and the purposes of this title.

b.

1. The Secretary shall propose and adopt rules to effect the purposes of this title with respect to transactions in

government securities effected by government securities brokers and government securities dealers as follows:

A. Such rules shall provide safeguards with respect to the financial responsibility and related practices of government securities brokers and government securities dealers including, but not limited to, capital adequacy standards, the acceptance of custody and use of customers' securities, the carrying and use of customers' deposits or credit balances, and the transfer and control of government securities subject to repurchase agreements and in similar transactions.

B. Such rules shall require every government securities broker and government securities dealer to make reports to and furnish copies of records to the appropriate regulatory agency, and to file with the appropriate regulatory agency, annually or more frequently, a balance sheet and income statement certified by an independent public accountant, prepared on a calendar or fiscal year basis, and such other financial statements (which shall, as the Secretary specifies, be certified) and information concerning its financial condition as required by such rules.

C. Such rules shall require records to be made and kept by government securities brokers and government securities dealers and shall specify the periods for which such records shall be preserved.

2. **Risk Assessment for Holding Company Systems.**—

A. **Obligations to obtain, maintain, and report information.**—Every person who is registered as a government securities broker or government securities dealer under this section shall obtain such information and make and keep such records as the Secretary by rule prescribes concerning the registered person's policies, procedures, or systems for monitoring and controlling financial and operational risk to it resulting from the activities of any of its associated persons, other than a natural person. Such records shall describe, in the aggregate, each of the financial and securities activities conducted by, and customary sources of capital and funding of, those of its associated persons whose business activities are reasonably likely to have a material impact on the financial or operational condition of such registered person, including its capital, its liquidity, or its ability to conduct or finance its operations. The Secretary, by rule, may require summary reports of such information to be filed with the registered person's appropriate regulatory agency no more frequently than quarterly.

B. **Authority to require additional information.**— If, as a result of adverse market conditions or based on reports provided pursuant to subparagraph (A) of this paragraph or other available information, the appropriate regulatory agency reasonably concludes it has concerns regarding the financial or operational condition of any government securities broker or government securities dealer registered under this section, such agency may require the registered person to make reports concerning the financial and securities activities of any of such person's associated persons, other than a natural person, whose business activities are reasonably likely to have a material impact on the financial or operational condition of such registered person. The appropriate regulatory agency, in requiring reports pursuant to this subparagraph, shall specify the information required, the period for which it is required, the time and date on which the information must be furnished, and whether the information is to be furnished directly to the appropriate regulatory agency or to a self-regulatory organization with primary responsibility for examining the registered person's financial and operational condition.

C. **Special provisions with respect to associated persons subject to Federal banking agency regulation.**—

    i. **Cooperation in implementation.**—In developing and implementing reporting requirements pursuant to subparagraph (A) of this paragraph with respect to associated persons subject to examination by or reporting requirements of a Federal banking agency, the Secretary shall consult with and consider the views of each such Federal banking agency. If a Federal banking agency comments in writing on a proposed rule of the Secretary under this paragraph that has been published for comment, the Secretary shall respond in writing to such written comment before adopting the proposed rule. The Secretary shall, at the request of a Federal banking agency, publish such comment and response in the Federal Register at the time of publishing the adopted rule.

    ii. **Use of banking agency reports.**—A registered government securities broker or government securities dealer shall be in compliance with any recordkeeping or reporting requirement adopted pursuant to subparagraph (A) of this paragraph concerning an associated person that is subject to examination by or reporting requirements of a Federal banking agency if such government securities broker or government securities dealer utilizes for such recordkeeping or reporting requirement copies of reports filed by the associated person with the Federal banking agency pursuant to section 5211 of the Revised Statutes, section 9 of the Federal Reserve

Act, section 7(a) of the Federal Deposit Insurance Act, section 10(b) of the Home Owners' Loan Act, or section 8 of the Bank Holding Company Act of 1956. The Secretary may, however, by rule adopted pursuant to subparagraph (A), require any registered government securities broker or government securities dealer filing such reports with the appropriate regulatory agency to obtain, maintain, or report supplemental information if the Secretary makes an explicit finding, based on information provided by the appropriate regulatory agency, that such supplemental information is necessary to inform the appropriate regulatory agency regarding potential risks to such government securities broker or government securities dealer. Prior to requiring any such supplemental information, the Secretary shall first request the Federal banking agency to expand its reporting requirements to include such information.

iii. **Procedure for requiring additional information.**—Prior to making a request pursuant to subparagraph (B) of this paragraph for information with respect to an associated person that is subject to examination by or reporting requirements of a Federal banking agency, the appropriate regulatory agency shall—

　　I.　notify such banking agency of the information required with respect to such associated person; and

　　II.　consult with such agency to determine whether the information required is available from such agency and for other purposes, unless the appropriate regulatory agency determines that any delay resulting from such consultation would be inconsistent with ensuring the financial and operational condition of the government securities broker or government securities dealer or the stability or integrity of the securities markets.

iv. **Exclusion for examination reports.**— Nothing in this subparagraph shall be construed to permit the Secretary or an appropriate regulatory agency to require any registered government securities broker or government securities dealer to obtain, maintain, or furnish any examination report of any Federal banking agency or any supervisory recommendations or analysis contained herein.

v. **Confidentiality of information provided.**—No information provided to or obtained by an appropriate regulatory agency from any Federal banking agency pursuant to a request under <u>clause (iii)</u> of this subparagraph regarding any associated person which is subject to examination by or reporting requirements of a Federal banking agency may be disclosed to any other person (other than a self-regulatory organization), without the prior written approval of the Federal banking agency. Nothing in this clause shall authorize the Secretary or any appropriate regulatory agency to withhold information from Congress, or prevent the Secretary or any appropriate regulatory agency from complying with a request for information from any other Federal department or agency requesting the information for purposes within the scope of its jurisdiction, or complying with an order of a court of the United States in an action brought by the United States or the Commission.

vi. **Notice to banking agencies concerning financial and operational condition concerns.**—The Secretary or the appropriate regulatory agency shall notify the Federal banking agency of any concerns of the Secretary or the appropriate regulatory agency regarding significant financial or operational risks resulting from the activities of any government securities broker or government securities dealer to any associated person thereof which is subject to examination by or reporting requirements of the Federal banking agency.

vii. **Definition.**—For purposes of this subparagraph, the term "Federal banking agency" shall have the same meaning as the term "appropriate Federal banking agency" in section 3(q) of the Federal Deposit Insurance Act.

D. **Exemptions.**—The Secretary by rule or order may exempt any person or class of persons, under such terms and conditions and for such periods as the Secretary shall provide in such rule or order, from the provisions of this paragraph, and the rules thereunder. In granting such exemptions, the Secretary shall consider, among other factors—

i. whether information of the type required under this paragraph is available from a supervisory agency (as defined in section 1101(6) of the Right to Financial Privacy Act of 1978), a State insurance commission or similar State agency, the Commodity

Futures Trading Commission, or a similar foreign regulator;

    ii. the primary business of any associated person;

   iii. the nature and extent of domestic or foreign regulation of the associated person's activities;

   iv. the nature and extent of the registered person's securities transactions; and

    v. with respect to the registered person and its associated persons, on a consolidated basis, the amount and proportion of assets devoted to, and revenues derived from, activities in the United States securities markets.

E. **Conformity with requirements under section 17(h).**—In exercising authority pursuant to subparagraph (A) of this paragraph concerning information with respect to associated persons of government securities brokers and government securities dealers who are also associated persons of registered brokers or dealers reporting to the Commission pursuant to section 17(h) of this title, the requirements relating to such associated person shall conform, to the greatest extent practicable, to the requirements under section 17(h).

F. **Authority to limit disclosure of information.**— Notwithstanding any other provision of law, the Secretary and any appropriate regulatory agency shall not be compelled to disclose any information required to be reported under this paragraph, or any information supplied to the Secretary or any appropriate regulatory agency by any domestic or foreign regulatory agency that relates to the financial or operational condition of any associated person of a registered government securities broker or a government securities dealer. Nothing in this paragraph shall authorize the Secretary or any appropriate regulatory agency to withhold information from Congress, or prevent the Secretary or any appropriate regulatory agency from complying with a request for information from any other Federal department or agency requesting the information for purposes within the scope of its jurisdiction, or complying with an order of a court of the United States in an action brought by the United States or the Commission. For purposes of section 552 of title 5, United States Code, this paragraph shall be considered a statute described in subsection (b)(3)(B) of such section 552.

3.

A. With respect to any financial institution that has filed notice as a government securities broker or government securities dealer or that is required to file notice under subsection (a)(1)(B), the appropriate regulatory agency for such government securities broker or government securities dealer may issue such rules and regulations with respect to transactions in government securities as may be necessary to prevent fraudulent and manipulative acts and practices and to promote just and equitable principles of trade. If the Secretary of the Treasury determines, and notifies the appropriate regulatory agency, that such rule or regulation, if implemented, would, or as applied does

   i.   adversely affect the liquidity or efficiency of the market for government securities; or

   ii. impose any burden on competition not necessary or appropriate in furtherance of the purposes of this section, the appropriate regulatory agency shall, prior to adopting the proposed rule or regulation, find that such rule or regulation is necessary and appropriate in furtherance of the purposes of this section notwithstanding the Secretary's determination.

B. The appropriate regulatory agency shall consult with and consider the views of the Secretary prior to approving or amending a rule or regulation under this paragraph, except where the appropriate regulatory agency determines that an emergency exists requiring expeditious and summary action and publishes its reasons therefor. If the Secretary comments in writing to the appropriate regulatory agency on a proposed rule or regulation that has been published for comment, the appropriate regulatory agency shall respond in writing to such written comment before approving the proposed rule or regulation.

C. In promulgating rules under this section, the appropriate regulatory agency shall consider the sufficiency and appropriateness of then existing laws and rules applicable to government securities brokers, government securities dealers, and persons associated with government securities brokers and government securities dealers.

4. Rules promulgated and orders issued under this section shall—

A. be designed to prevent fraudulent and manipulative acts and practices and to protect the integrity, liquidity, and efficiency of the market for government securities, investors, and the public interest; and

B. not be designed to permit unfair discrimination between customers, issuers, government securities brokers, or government securities dealers, or to impose any burden on competition not necessary or appropriate in furtherance of the purposes of this title.

5. In promulgating rules and issuing orders under this section, the Secretary—

A. may appropriately classify government securities brokers and government securities dealers (taking into account relevant matters, including types of business done, nature of securities other than government securities purchased or sold, and character of business organization) and persons associated with government securities brokers and government securities dealers;

B. may determine, to the extent consistent with paragraph (2) of this subsection and with the public interest, the protection of investors, and the purposes of this title, not to apply, in whole or in part, certain rules under this section, or to apply greater, lesser, or different standards, to certain classes of government securities brokers, government securities dealers, or persons associated with government securities brokers or government securities dealers;

C. shall consider the sufficiency and appropriateness of then existing laws and rules applicable to government securities brokers, government securities dealers, and persons associated with government securities brokers and government securities dealers; and

D. shall consult with and consider the views of the Commission and the Board of Governors of the Federal Reserve System, except where the Secretary determines that an emergency exists requiring expeditious or summary action and publishes its reasons for such determination.

6. If the Commission or the Board of Governors of the Federal Reserve System comments in writing on a proposed rule of the Secretary that has been published for comment, the Secretary shall respond in writing to such written comment before approving the proposed rule.

7. No government securities broker or government securities dealer shall make use of the mails or any means or instrumentality of interstate commerce to effect any transaction

in, or to induce or attempt to induce the purchase or sale of, any government security in contravention of any rule under this section.

c.

1. With respect to any government securities broker or government securities dealer registered or required to register under subsection (a)(1)(A) of this section—

   A. The Commission, by order, shall censure, place limitations on the activities, functions, or operations of, suspend for a period not exceeding 12 months, or revoke the registration of such government securities broker or government securities dealer, if it finds, on the record after notice and opportunity for hearing, that such censure, placing of limitations, suspension, or revocation is in the public interest and that such government securities broker or government securities dealer, or any person associated with such government securities broker or government securities dealer (whether prior or subsequent to becoming so associated), has committed or omitted any act or omission enumerated in subparagraph (A), (D), (E), or (G) of paragraph (4) of section 15(b) of this title, has been convicted of any offense specified in subparagraph (B) of such paragraph (4) within 10 years of the commencement of the proceedings under this paragraph, or is enjoined from any action, conduct, or practice specified in subparagraph (C) of such paragraph (4).

   B. Pending final determination whether registration of any government securities broker or government securities dealer shall be revoked, the Commission, by order, may suspend such registration, if such suspension appears to the Commission, after notice and opportunity for hearing, to be necessary or appropriate in the public interest or for the protection of investors. Any registered government securities broker or registered government securities dealer may, upon such terms and conditions as the Commission may deem necessary in the public interest or for the protection of investors, withdraw from registration by filing a written notice of withdrawal with the Commission. If the Commission finds that any registered government securities broker or registered government securities dealer is no longer in existence or has ceased to do business as a government securities broker or government securities dealer, the Commission, by order, shall cancel the registration of such government securities broker or government securities dealer.

C. The Commission, by order, shall censure or place limitations on the activities or functions of any person associated, or seeking to become associated, with a government securities broker or government securities dealer registered or required to register under subsection (a)(1)(A) of this section or suspend for a period not exceeding 12 months or bar any such person from being associated with such a government securities broker or government securities dealer, if the Commission finds, on the record after notice and opportunity for hearing, that such censure, placing of limitations, suspension, or bar is in the public interest and that such person has committed or omitted any act or omission enumerated in subparagraph (A), (D), (E), or (G) of paragraph (4) of section 15(b) of this title, has been convicted of any offense specified in subparagraph (B) of such paragraph (4) within 10 years of the commencement of the proceedings under this paragraph, or is enjoined from any action, conduct, or practice specified in subparagraph (C) of such paragraph (4).

2.

A. With respect to any government securities broker or government securities dealer which is not registered or required to register under subsection (a)(1)(A) of this section, the appropriate regulatory agency for such government securities broker or government securities dealer may, in the manner and for the reasons specified in paragraph (1)(A) of this subsection, censure, place limitations on the activities, functions, or operations of, suspend for a period not exceeding 12 months, or bar from acting as a government securities broker or government securities dealer any such government securities broker or government securities dealer, and may sanction any person associated with such government securities broker or government securities dealer in the manner and for the reasons specified in paragraph (1)(C) of this subsection.

B. In addition, where applicable, such appropriate regulatory agency may, in accordance with section 8 of the Federal Deposit Insurance Act, section 5 of the Home Owners' Loan Act of 1933, or section 407 of the National Housing Act, enforce compliance by such government securities broker or government securities dealer or any person associated with such government securities broker or government securities dealer with the provisions of this section and the rules thereunder.

C. For purposes of subparagraph (B) of this paragraph, any violation of any such provision shall constitute adequate basis for the issuance of any order under section 8(b) or 8(c) of the Federal Deposit Insurance Act, section 5(d)(2) or 5(d)(3) of the Home Owners' Loan Act of 1933, or section 407(e) or 407(f) of the National Housing Act, and the customers of any such government securities broker or government securities dealer shall be deemed, respectively, "depositors" as that term is used in section 8(c) of the Federal Deposit Insurance Act, "savings account holders" as that term is used in section 5(d)(3) of the Home Owners' Loan Act of

1933, or "insured members" as that term is used in section 407(f) of the National Housing Act.

D. Nothing in this paragraph shall be construed to affect in any way the powers of such appropriate regulatory agency to proceed against such government securities broker or government securities dealer under any other provision of law.

E. Each appropriate regulatory agency (other than the Commission) shall promptly notify the Commission after it has imposed any sanction under this paragraph on a government securities broker or government securities dealer, or a person associated with a government securities broker or government securities dealer, and the Commission shall maintain, and make available to the public, a record of such sanctions and any sanctions imposed by it under this subsection.

3. It shall be unlawful for any person as to whom an order entered pursuant to paragraph (1) or (2) of this subsection suspending or barring him from being associated with a government securities broker or government securities dealer is in effect willfully to become, or to be, associated with a government securities broker or government securities dealer without the consent of the appropriate regulatory agency, and it shall be unlawful for any government securities broker or government securities dealer to permit such a person to become, or remain, a person associated with it without the consent of the appropriate regulatory agency, if such government securities broker or government securities dealer knew, or, in the exercise of reasonable care should have known, of such order.

d.

1. All records of a government securities broker or government securities dealer are subject at any time, or from time to time, to such reasonable periodic, special, or other examinations by representatives of the appropriate regulatory agency for such government securities broker or government

securities dealer as such appropriate regulatory agency deems necessary or appropriate in the public interest, for the protection of investors, or otherwise in furtherance of the purposes of this title.

2. Information received by an appropriate regulatory agency, the Secretary, or the Commission from or with respect to any government securities broker, government securities dealer, any person associated with a government securities broker or government securities dealer, or any other person subject to this section or rules promulgated thereunder, may be made available by the Secretary or the recipient agency to the Commission, the Secretary, the Department of Just ice, the Commodity Futures Trading Commission, any appropriate regulatory agency, any self-regulatory organization, or any Federal Reserve Bank.

3. **Government securities trade reconstruction,—**

   A. **Furnishing records.**—Every government securities broker and government securities dealer shall furnish to the Commission on request such records of government securities transactions, including records of the date and time of execution of trades, as the Commission may require to reconstruct trading in the course of a particular inquiry or investigation being conducted by the Commission for enforcement or surveillance purposes. In requiring information pursuant to this paragraph, the Commission shall specify the information required, the period for which it is required, the time and date on which the information must be furnished, and whether the information is to be furnished directly to the Commission, to the Federal Reserve Bank of New York, or to an appropriate regulatory agency or self-regulatory organization with responsibility for examining the government securities broker or government securities dealer. The Commission may require that such information be furnished in machine readable form notwithstanding any limitation in subparagraph (B). In utilizing its authority to require information in machine readable form, the Commission shall minimize the burden such requirement may place on small government securities brokers and dealers.

B. **Limitation; Construction.**—The Commission shall not utilize its authority under this paragraph to develop regular reporting requirements, except that the Commission may require information to be furnished under this paragraph as frequently as necessary for particular inquiries or investigations for enforcement or surveillance purposes. This paragraph shall not be construed as requiring, or as authorizing the Commission to require, any government securities broker or government securities dealer to obtain or maintain any information for purposes of this paragraph which is not otherwise maintained by such broker or dealer in accordance with any other provision of law or usual and customary business practice. The Commission shall, where feasible, avoid requiring any information to be furnished under this paragraph that the Commission may obtain from the Federal Reserve Bank of New York.

C. **Procedures for requiring information.**—At the time the Commission requests any information pursuant to subparagraph (A) with respect to any government securities broker or government securities dealer for which the Commission is not the appropriate regulatory agency, the Commission shall notify the appropriate regulatory agency for such government securities broker or government securities dealer and, upon request, furnish to the appropriate regulatory agency any information supplied to the Commission.

D. **Consultation.**—Within 90 days after the date of enactment of this paragraph, and annually thereafter, or upon the request of any other appropriate regulatory agency, the Commission shall consult with the other appropriate regulatory agencies to determine the availability of records that may be required to be furnished under this paragraph and, for those records available directly from the other appropriate regulatory agencies, to develop a procedure for furnishing such records expeditiously upon the Commission's request.

E.   **Exclusion for examination reports.**—Nothing in this paragraph shall be construed so as to permit the Commission to require any government securities broker or government securities dealer to obtain, maintain, or furnish any examination report of any appropriate regulatory agency other than the Commission or any supervisory recommendations or analysis contained in any such examination report.

F.   **Authority to limit disclosure of information.**— Notwithstanding any other provision of law, the Commission and the appropriate regulatory agencies shall not be compelled to disclose any information required or obtained under this paragraph. Nothing in this paragraph shall authorize the Commission or any appropriate regulatory agency to withhold information from Congress, or prevent the Commission or any appropriate regulatory agency from complying with a request for information from any other Federal department or agency requesting information for purposes within the scope of its jurisdiction, or from complying with an order of a court of the United States in an action brought by the United States, the Commission, or the appropriate regulatory agency. For purposes of section 552 of title 5, United States Code, this subparagraph shall be considered a statute described in subsection (b)(3)(B) of such section 552.

e.

1.   It shall be unlawful for any government securities broker or government securities dealer registered or required to

register with the Commission under subsection (a)(1)(A) to effect any transaction in, or induce or attempt to induce the purchase or sale of, any government security, unless such government securities broker or government securities dealer is a member of a national securities exchange registered under section 6 of this title or a securities association registered under section 15A of this title.

2. The Commission, after consultation with the Secretary, by rule or order, as it deems consistent with the public interest and the protection of investors, may conditionally or unconditionally exempt from paragraph (1) of this subsection any government securities broker or government securities dealer or class of government securities brokers or government securities dealers specified in such rule or order.

f.   **Large Position Reporting.—**

1. **Reporting requirements.—**The Secretary may adopt rules to require specified persons holding, maintaining, or controlling large positions in to-be-issued or recently issued Treasury securities to file such reports regarding such positions as the Secretary determines to be necessary and appropriate for the purpose of monitoring the impact in the Treasury securities market of concentrations of positions in Treastiry securities and for the purpose of otherwise assisting the Commission in the enforcement of this title, taking into account any impact of such rules on the efficiency and liquidity of the Treasury securities market and the Cost to taxpayers of funding the Federal debt, Unless otherwise specified by the Secretary, reports required under this subsection shall be filed with the Federal Reserve Bank of New York, acting as agent for the Secretary. Such reports shall, on a timely basis, be provided directly to the Commission by the person with whom they are filed.

2. **Recordkeeping requirements—**Rules under this subsection may require persons holding, maintaining, or controlling large positions in Treasury securities to make and keep for prescribed periods such records as the Secretary determines are necessary or appropriate to ensure that such

persons can comply with reporting requirements under this subsection.

3. **Aggregation rules.**—Rules under this subsection—

   A. may prescribe the manner in which positions and accounts shall be aggregated for the purpose of this subsection, including aggregation on the basis of common ownership or control; and

   B. may define which persons (individually or as a group) hold, maintain, or control large positions.

4. **Definitional authority; determination of reporting threshold.**—

   A. In prescribing rules under this subsection, the Secretary may, consistent with the purpose of this subsection, define terms used in this subsection that are not otherwise defined in section 3 of this title

   B. Rules under this subsection shall specify—

      i.   the minimum size of positions subject to reporting under this subsection, which shall be no less than the size that provides the potential for manipulation or control of the supply or price, or the cost of financing arrangements, of an issue or the portion thereof that is available for trading;

      ii. the types of positions (which may include financing arrangements) to be reported;

      iii. the securities to be covered; and

      iv. the form and manner in which reports shall be transmitted, which may include transmission in machine readable form.

5. **Exemptions.**—Consistent with the public interest and the protection of investors, the Secretary by rule or order may exempt in whole or in part, conditionally or unconditionally, any person or class or persons, or any transaction or class of transactions, from the requirements of this subsection.

6. **Limitation on disclosure of information.**—Notwithstanding any other provision of law, the Secretary and the Commission shall not be compelled to disclose any information required to be kept or reported under this subsection. Nothing in this subsection shall authorize the Secretary or the Commission to withhold information from Congress, or prevent the Secretary or the Commission from complying with a request for information from any other Federal department or agency requesting information for purposes within the scope of its jurisdiction, or from complying with an order of a court of the United States in an action brought by the United States, the Secretary, or the Commission. For purposes of section 552 of title 5, United States Code, this paragraph shall be considered a statute described in subsection (b)(3)(B) of such section 552.

g.

1. Nothing in this section except paragraph (2) of this subsection shall be construed to impair or limit the authority under any other provision of law of the Commission, the Secretary of the Treasury, the Board of Governors of the Federal Reserve System, the Comptroller of the Currency, the Federal Deposit Insurance Corporation, the Director of the Office of Thrift Supervision, the Federal Savings and Loan Insurance Corporation, the Secretary of Housing and Urban Development, and the Government National Mortgage Association.

2. Notwithstanding any other provision of this title, the Commission shall not have any authority to make investigations of, require the filing of a statement by, or take any other action under this title against a government securities broker or government securities dealer, or any person associated with a government securities broker or government securities dealer, for any violation or threatened violation of the provisions of this section, other than subsection (d)(3), or the rules or regulations thereunder, unless the Commission is the appropriate regulatory agency for such government securities broker or government securities dealer. Nothing in the preceding sentence shall be construed to limit the

authority of the Commission with respect to violations or
threatened violations of any provision of this title other than
this section (except subsection (d)(3)), the rules or regulations under any such other provision, or investigations pursuant to section 21(a)(2) of this title to assist a foreign
securities authority.

SECTION 16—DIRECTORS, OFFICERS, AND PRINCIPAL STOCKHOLDERS

a. Every person who is directly or indirectly the beneficial owner of
more than 10 per centum of any class of any equity security (other
than an exempted security) which is registered pursuant to Section
12 of this title, or who is a director or an officer of the issuer of
such security, shall file, at the time of the registration of such security on a national securities exchange or by the effective date of a
registration statement filed pursuant to Section 12(g) of this title,
or within ten days after he becomes such beneficial owner, director, or officer, a statement with the Commission (and, if such security is registered on a national securities exchange, also with the
exchange) of the amount of all equity securities of such issuer of
which he is the beneficial owner, and within ten days after the close
of each calendar month thereafter, if there has been a change in
such ownership during such month, shall file with the Commission
(and if such security is registered on a national securities exchange,
shall also file with the exchange), a statement indicating his ownership at the close of the calendar month and such changes in his
ownership as have occurred during such calendar month.

b. For the purpose of preventing the unfair use of information which
may have been obtained by such beneficial owner, director, or officer by reason of his relationship to the issuer, any profit realized
by him from any purchase and sale, or any sale and purchase, of
any equity security of such issuer (other than an exempted security) within any period of less than six months, unless such security was acquired in good faith in connection with a debt previously
contracted, shall inure to and be recoverable by the issuer, irrespective of any intention on the part of such beneficial owner,
director, or officer in entering into such transaction of holding the
security purchased or of not repurchasing the security sold for a

period exceeding six months. Suit to recover such profit may be instituted at law or in equity in any court of competent jurisdiction by the issuer, or by the owner of any security of the issuer in the name and in behalf of the issuer if the issuer shall fail or refuse to bring such suit within sixty days after request or shall fail diligently to prosecute the same thereafter; but no such suit shall be brought more than two years after the date such profit was realized. This subsection shall not be construed to cover any transaction where such beneficial owner was not such both at the time of the purchase and sale, or the sale and purchase, of the security involved, or any transaction or transactions which the Commission by rules and regulations may exempt as not comprehended within the purpose of this subsection.

c.   It shall be unlawful for any such beneficial owner, director, or officer, directly or indirectly, to sell any equity security of such issuer (other than an exempted security), if the person selling the security or his principal

1.   does not own the security sold, or

2.   if owning the security, does not deliver it against such sale within twenty days thereafter, or does not within five days after such sale deposit it in the mails or other usual channels of transportation; but no person shall be deemed to have violated this subsection if he proves that notwithstanding the exercise of good faith he was unable to make such delivery or deposit within such time, or that to do so would cause undue inconvenience or expense.

d.   The provisions of subsection (b) of this section shall not apply to any purchase and sale, or sale and purchase, and the provisions of subsection (c) of this section shall not apply to any sale, of an equity security not then or theretofore held by him in an investment account, by a dealer in the ordinary course of his business and incident to the establishment or maintenance by him of a primary or secondary market (otherwise than on a national securities exchange or an exchange exempted from registration under Section 5 of this title) for such security. The Commission may, by such rules and regulations as it deems necessary or appropriate in the public interest, define and prescribe terms and conditions with respect to securities held in an investment account and transactions made in the ordinary course of business and incident to the establishment or maintenance of a primary or secondary market.

e. The provisions of this section shall not apply to foreign or domestic arbitrage transactions unless made in contravention of such rules and regulations as the Commission may adopt in order to carry out the purposes of this section.

SECTION 17B—AUTOMATED QUOTATION SYSTEMS FOR PENNY STOCKS

a. **Findings.**—The Congress finds that—

  1. the market for penny stocks suffers from a lack of reliable and accurate quotation and last sale information available to investors and regulators;

  2. it is in the public interest and appropriate for the protection of investors and the maintenance of fair and orderly markets to improve significantly the information available to brokers, dealers, investors, and regulators with respect to quotations for and transactions in penny stocks; and

  3. a fully implemented automated quotation system for penny stocks would meet the information needs of investors and market participants and would add visibility and regulatory and surveillance data to that market.

b. **Mandate To Facilitate The Establishment Of Automated Quotation Systems.—**

  1. **In General.**—The Commission shall facilitate the widespread dissemination of reliable and accurate last sale and quotation information with respect to penny stocks in accordance with the findings set forth in subsection (a), with a view toward establishing, at the earliest feasible time, one or more automated quotation systems that will collect and disseminate information regarding all penny stocks.

  2. **Characteristics Of Systems.**—Each such automated quotation system shall—

    A. be operated by a registered securities association or a national securities exchange in accordance with such rules as the Commission and these entities shall prescribe;

    B. collect and disseminate quotation and transaction information;

    C. except as provided in subsection (c), provide bid and ask quotations of participating brokers or dealers, or comparably accurate and reliable pricing information, which shall constitute firm bids or offers for at least such minimum numbers of shares or minimum dollar amounts as the Commission and the registered securities association or national securities exchange shall require; and

    D. provide for the reporting of the volume of penny stock transactions, including last sale reporting, when the volume reaches appropriate levels that the Commission shall specify by rule or order.

c. **Exemptive Authority.**—The Commission may, by rule or order, grant such exemptions, in whole or in part, conditionally or unconditionally, to any penny stock or class of penny stocks from the requirements of subsection (b) as the Commission determines to be consistent with the public interest, the protection of investors, and the maintenance of fair and orderly markets.

d. **Commission Reporting Requirements.**—The Commission shall, in each of the first 5 annual reports (under Section 23(b)(1) of this title) submitted more than 12 months after the date of enactment of this section, include a description of the status of the penny stock automated quotation system or systems required by subsection (b). Such description shall include—

    1. a review of the development, implementation, and progress of the project, including achievement of significant milestones and current project schedule; and

    2. a review of the activities of registered securities associations and national securities exchanges in the development of the system.

SECTION 18—LIABILITY FOR MISLEADING STATEMENTS

a. Any person who shall make or cause to be made any statement in any application, report, or document filed pursuant to this title or any rule or regulation thereunder or any undertaking contained in a registration statement as provided in subsection (d) of section 15 of this title, which statement was at the time and in the light of the circumstances under which it was made false or misleading with respect to any material fact, shall be liable to any person (not knowing that such statement was false or misleading) who, in reliance upon such statement, shall have purchased or sold a security at a price which was affected by such statement, for damages caused by such reliance, unless the person sued shall prove that he acted in good faith and had no knowledge that such statement was false or misleading. A person seeking to enforce such liability may sue at law or in equity in any court of competent jurisdiction. In any such suit the court may, in its discretion, require an undertaking for the payment of the costs of such suit, and assess reasonable costs, including reasonable attorneys' fees, against either party litigant.

b. Every person who becomes liable to make payment under this section may recover contribution as in cases of contract from any person who, if joined in the original suit, would have been liable to make the same payment.

c. No action shall be maintained to enforce any liability created under this section unless brought within one year after the discovery of the facts constituting the cause of action and within three years after such cause of action accrued.

SECTION 19—REGISTRATION, RESPONSIBILITIES, AND OVERSIGHT OF SELF-REGULATORY ORGANIZATIONS

a.

1. The Commission shall, upon the filing of an application for registration as a national securities exchange, registered securities association, or registered clearing agency, pursuant to Section 6, 15A or 17A of this title, respectively,

publish notice of the filing and afford interested persons an opportunity to submit written data, views, and arguments concerning such application. Within ninety days of the date of publication of such notice (or within such longer period as to which the applicant consents), the Commission shall—

A. by order grant such registration, or

B. institute proceedings to determine whether registration should be denied. Such proceedings shall include notice of the grounds for denial under consideration and opportunity for hearing and shall be concluded within one hundred eighty days of the date of publication of notice of the filing of the application for registration. At the conclusion of such proceedings the Commission, by order, shall grant or deny such registration. The Commission may extend the time for conclusion of such proceedings for up to ninety days if it finds good cause for such extension and publishes its reasons for so finding or for such longer period as to which the applicant consents.

The Commission shall grant such registration if it finds that the requirements of this title and the rules and regulations thereunder with respect to the applicant are satisfied. The Commission shall deny such registration if it does not make such finding.

2. With respect to an application for registration filed by a clearing agency for which the Commission is not the appropriate regulatory agency—

A. The Commission shall not grant registration prior to the sixtieth day after the date of publication of notice of the filing of such application unless the appropriate regulatory agency for such clearing agency has notified the Commission of such appropriate regulatory agency's determination that such clearing agency is so organized and has the capacity to be able to safeguard securities and funds in its custody or control or for which it is responsible and that the rules of such clearing agency are designed to assure the safeguarding of such securities and funds.

B. The Commission shall institute proceedings in accordance with paragraph (1)(B) of this subsection to determine whether registration should be denied if the appropriate regulatory agency for such clearing agency notifies the Commission within sixty days of the date of publication of notice of the filing of such application of such appropriate regulatory agency's

    i. determination that such clearing agency may not be so organized or have the capacity to be able to safeguard securities or funds in its custody or control or for which it is responsible or that the rules of such clearing agency may not be designed to assure the safeguarding of such securities and funds and

    ii. reasons for such determination.

C. The Commission shall deny registration if the appropriate regulatory agency for such clearing agency notifies the Commission prior to the conclusion of proceedings instituted in accordance with paragraph (1)(B) of this subsection of such appropriate regulatory agency's

    i. determination that such clearing agency is not so organized or does not have the capacity to be able to safeguard securities or funds in its custody or control or for which it is responsible or that the rules of such clearing agency are not designed to assure the safeguarding of such securities or funds and

    ii. reasons for such determination.

3. A self-regulatory organization may, upon such terms and conditions as the Commission, by rule, deems necessary or appropriate in the public interest or for the protection of investors, withdraw from registration by filing a written notice of withdrawal with the Commission. If the Commission finds that any self-regulatory organization is no longer in existence or has ceased to do business in the capacity specified in its application for registration, the Commission, by order, shall cancel its registration. Upon the withdrawal of a national securities association from registration or the cancellation, suspension, or revocation of the registration of a national securities association, the registration of any association affiliated therewith shall automatically terminate.

b.

1. Each self-regulatory organization shall file with the Commission, in accordance with such rules as the Commission may prescribe, copies of any proposed rule or any proposed change in, addition to, or deletion from the rules of such self-regulatory organization (hereinafter in this subsection collectively referred to as a "proposed rule change") accompanied by a concise general statement of the basis and purpose of such proposed rule change. The Commission shall, upon the filing of any proposed rule change, publish notice thereof together with the terms of substance of the proposed rule change or a description of the subjects and issues involved. The Commission shall give interested persons an opportunity to submit written data, views, and arguments concerning such proposed rule change. No proposed rule change shall take effect unless approved by the Commission or otherwise permitted in accordance with the provisions of this subsection.

2. Within thirty-five days of the date of publication of notice of the filing of a proposed rule change in accordance with paragraph (1) of this subsection, or within such longer period as the Commission may designate up to ninety days of such date if it finds such longer period to be appropriate and publishes its reasons for so finding or as to which the

self-regulatory organization consents, the Commission shall—

A. by order approve such proposed rule change, or

B. institute proceedings to determine whether the proposed rule change should be disapproved. Such proceedings shall include notice of the grounds for disapproval under consideration and opportunity for hearing and be concluded within one hundred eighty days of the date of publication of notice of the filing of the proposed rule change. At the conclusion of such proceedings the Commission, by order, shall approve or disapprove such proposed rule change. The Commission may extend the time for conclusion of such proceedings for up to sixty days if it finds good cause for such extension and publishes its reasons for so finding or for such longer period as to which the self-regulatory organization consents.

The Commission shall approve a proposed rule change of a self-regulatory organization if it finds that such proposed rule change is consistent with the requirements of this title and the rules and regulations thereunder applicable to such organization. The Commission shall disapprove a proposed rule change of a self-regulatory organization if it does not make such finding. The Commission shall not approve any proposed rule change prior to the thirtieth day after the date of publication of notice of the filing thereof, unless the Commission finds good cause for so doing and publishes its reasons for so finding.

3.

A. Notwithstanding the provisions of paragraph (2) of this subsection, a proposed rule change may take effect upon filing with the Commission if designated by the self-regulatory organization as

i. constituting a stated policy, practice, or interpretation with respect to the meaning, administration, or enforcement of an existing rule of the self-regulatory organization,

    ii. establishing or changing a due, fee, or other charge imposed by the self-regulatory organization, or

   iii. concerned solely with the administration of the self-regulatory organization or other matters which the Commission, by rule, consistent with the public interest and the purposes of this subsection, may specify as without the provisions of such paragraph (2).

B. Notwithstanding any other provision of this subsection, a proposed rule change may be put into effect summarily if it appears to the Commission that such action is necessary for the protection of investors, the maintenance of fair and orderly markets, or the safeguarding of securities or funds. Any proposed rule change so put into effect shall be filed promptly thereafter in accordance with the provisions of paragraph (1) of this subsection.

C. Any proposed rule change of a self-regulatory organization which has taken effect pursuant to subparagraph (A) or (B) of this paragraph may be enforced by such organization to the extent it is not inconsistent with the provisions of this title, the rules and regulations thereunder, and applicable Federal and State law. At any time within sixty days of the date of filing of such a proposed rule change in accordance with the provisions of paragraph (1) of this subsection, the Commission summarily may abrogate the change in the rules of the self-regulatory organization made thereby and require that the proposed rule change be refiled in accordance with the provisions of paragraph (1) of this subsection and reviewed in accordance with the provisions of paragraph (2) of this subsection, if it appears to the Commission that such action is necessary or appropriate in the public interest, for the protection of investors, or otherwise in furtherance of the purposes of this title. Commission action pursuant to the preceding sentence shall not affect the validity or force of the rule change during the period it was in effect and shall not be reviewable under Section 25 of this title nor deemed to be "final agency action" for purposes of Section 704 of title 5, United States Code.

4. With respect to a proposed rule change filed by a registered clearing agency for which the Commission is not the appropriate regulatory agency—

    A. The Commission shall not approve any such proposed rule change prior to the thirtieth day after the date of publication of notice of the filing thereof unless the appropriate regulatory agency for such clearing agency has notified the Commission of such appropriate regulatory agency's determination that the proposed rule change is consistent with the safeguarding of securities and funds in the custody or control of such clearing agency or for which it is responsible.

    B. The Commission shall institute proceedings in accordance with paragraph (2)(B) of this subsection to determine whether any such proposed rule change should be disapproved, if the appropriate regulatory agency for such clearing agency notifies the Commission within thirty days of the date of publication of notice of the filing of the proposed rule change of such appropriate regulatory agency's

        i. determination that the proposed rule change may be inconsistent with the safeguarding of securities or funds in the custody or control of such clearing agency or for which it is responsible and

        ii. reasons for such determination.

C. The Commission shall disapprove any such proposed rule change if the appropriate regulatory agency for such clearing agency notifies the Commission prior to the conclusion of proceedings instituted in accordance with paragraph (2)(B) of this subsection of such appropriate regulatory agency's

        i. determination that the proposed rule change is inconsistent with the safeguarding of securities or funds in the custody or control of such clearing agency or for which it is responsible and

        ii. reasons for such determination.

D. The Commission shall abrogate any change in the rules of such a clearing agency made by a proposed rule change which has taken effect pursuant to paragraph (3) of this subsection, require that the proposed rule change be refiled in accordance with the provisions of paragraph (1) of this subsection, and reviewed in accordance with the provisions of paragraph (2) of this subsection, if the appropriate regulatory agency for such clearing agency notifies the Commission within thirty days of the date of filing of such proposed rule change of such appropriate regulatory agency's

        i. determination that the rules of such clearing agency as so changed may be inconsistent with the safeguarding of securities or funds in the custody or control of such clearing agency or for which it is responsible and

        ii. reasons for such determination.

5. The Commission shall consult with and consider the views of the Secretary of the Treasury prior to approving a proposed rule filed by a registered securities association that primarily concerns conduct related to transactions in

government securities except where the Commission determines that an emergency exists requiring expeditious or summary action and publishes its reasons therefor. If the Secretary of the Treasury comments in writing to the Commission on a proposed rule that has been published for comment. the Commission shall respond in writing to such written comment before approving the proposed rule. If the Secretary of the Treasury determines. and notifies the Commission that such rule. if implemented, would, or as applied does

    i.   adversely affect the liquidity or efficiency of the market for government securities, or

    ii.   impose any burden on competition not necessary or appropriate in furtherance of the purposes of this section, the Commission shall, prior to adopting the proposed rule, find that such rule is necessary and appropriate in furtherance of the purposes of this section notwithstanding the Secretary's determination.

6.   In approving rules described in paragraph (5), the Commission shall consider the sufficiency and appropriateness of then existing laws and rules applicable to government securities brokers, government securities dealers, and persons associated with government securities brokers and government securities dealers.

c.   The Commission, by rule, may abrogate, add to, and delete from (hereinafter in this subsection collectively referred to as "amend") the rules of a self-regulatory organization (other than a registered clearing agency) as the Commission deems necessary or appropriate to insure the fair administration of the self-regulatory organization, to conform its rules to requirements of this title and the rules and regulations thereunder applicable to such organization, or otherwise in furtherance of the purposes of this title, in the following manner:

1.   The Commission shall notify the self-regulatory organization and publish notice of the proposed rulemaking in the Federal Register. The notice shall include the text of the

proposed amendment to the rules of the self-regulatory organization and a statement of the Commission's reasons, including any pertinent facts, for commencing such proposed rulemaking.

2. The Commission shall give interested persons an opportunity for the oral presentation of data, views, and arguments, in addition to an opportunity to make written submissions. A transcript shall be kept of any oral presentation.

3. A rule adopted pursuant to this subsection shall incorporate the text of the amendment to the rules of the self-regulatory organization and a statement of the Commission's basis for and purpose in so amending such rules. This statement shall include an identification of any facts on which the Commission considers its determination so to amend the rules of the self-regulatory agency to be based, including the reasons for the Commission's conclusions as to any of such facts which were disputed in the rulemaking.

4.

    A. Except as provided in paragraphs (1) through (3) of this subsection, rulemaking under this subsection shall be in accordance with the procedures specified in Section 553 of title 5, United States Code, for rulemaking not on the record.

    B. Nothing in this subsection shall be construed to impair or limit the Commission's power to make, or to modify or alter the procedures the Commission may follow in making rules and regulations pursuant to any other authority under this title.

    C. Any amendment to the rules of a self-regulatory organization made by the Commission pursuant to this subsection shall be considered for all purposes of this title to be part of the rules of such self-regulatory organization and shall not be considered to be a rule of the Commission.

5. With respect to rules described in subsection (b)(5), the Commission shall consult with and consider the views of

the Secretary of the Treasury before abrogating. adding to. and deleting from such rules, except where the Commission determines that an emergency exists requiring expeditious or summary action and publishes its reasons therefor.

d.

1. If any self-regulatory organization imposes any final disciplinary sanction on any member thereof or participant therein, denies membership or participation to any applicant, or prohibits or limits any person in respect to access to services offered by such organization or member thereof or if any self-regulatory organization (other than a registered clearing agency) imposes any final disciplinary sanction on any person associated with a member, or bars any person from becoming associated with a member, the self-regulatory organization shall promptly file notice thereof with the appropriate regulatory agency for the self-regulatory organization and (if other than the appropriate regulatory agency for the self-regulatory organization) the appropriate regulatory agency for such member, participant, applicant, or other person. The notice shall be in such form and contain such information as the appropriate regulatory agency for the self-regulatory organization, by rule, may prescribe as necessary or appropriate in furtherance of the purposes of this title.

2. Any action with respect to which a self-regulatory organization is required by paragraph (1) of this subsection to file notice shall be subject to review by the appropriate regulatory agency for such member, participant, applicant, or other person, on its own motion, or upon application by any person aggrieved thereby filed within thirty days after the date such notice was filed with such appropriate regulatory agency and received by such aggrieved person, or within such longer period as such appropriate regulatory agency may determine. Application to such appropriate regulatory agency for review, or the institution of review by such appropriate regulatory agency on its own motion, shall not operate as a stay of such action unless such appropriate regulatory agency otherwise orders, summarily or after notice

and opportunity for hearing on the question of a stay (which hearing may consist solely of the submission of affidavits or presentation of oral arguments). Each appropriate regulatory agency shall establish for appropriate cases an expedited procedure for consideration and determination of the question of a stay.

e.

1. In any proceeding to review a final disciplinary sanction imposed by a self-regulatory organization on a member thereof or participant therein or a person associated with such a member, after notice and opportunity for hearing (which hearing may consist solely of consideration of the record before the self-regulatory organization and opportunity for the presentation of supporting reasons to affirm, modify, or set aside the sanction)—

    A. if the appropriate regulatory agency for such member, participant, or person associated with a member finds that such member, participant, or person associated with a member has engaged in such acts or practices, or has omitted such acts, as the self-regulatory organization has found him to have engaged in or omitted, that such acts or practices, or omissions to act, are in violation of such provisions of this title, the rules or regulations thereunder, the rules of the self-regulatory organization, or, in the case of a registered securities association, the rules of the Municipal Securities Rulemaking Board as have been specified in the determination of the self-regulatory organization, and that such provisions are, and were applied in a manner, consistent with the purposes of this title, such appropriate regulatory agency, by order, shall so declare and, as appropriate, affirm the sanction imposed by the self-regulatory organization, modify the sanction in accordance with paragraph (2) of this subsection, or remand to the self-regulatory organization for further proceedings; or

        B. if such appropriate regulatory agency does not make any such finding it shall, by order, set aside the sanction imposed by the self-regulatory organization and, if appropriate, remand to the self-regulatory organization for further proceedings.

    2. If the appropriate regulatory agency for a member, participant, or person associated with a member, having due regard for the public interest and the protection of investors, finds after a proceeding in accordance with <u>paragraph (1)</u> of this subsection that a sanction imposed by a self-regulatory organization upon such member, participant, or person associated with a member imposes any burden on competition not necessary or appropriate in furtherance of the purposes of this title or is excessive or oppressive, the appropriate regulatory agency may cancel, reduce, or require the remission of such sanction.

f. In any proceeding to review the denial of membership or participation in a self-regulatory organization to any applicant, the barring of any person from becoming associated with a member of a self-regulatory organization, or the prohibition or limitation by a self-regulatory organization of any person with respect to access to services offered by the self-regulatory organization or any member thereof if the appropriate regulatory agency for such applicant or person, after notice and opportunity for hearing (which hearing may consist solely of consideration of the record before the self-regulatory organization and opportunity for the presentation of supporting reasons to dismiss the proceeding or set aside the action of the self-regulatory organization) finds that the specific grounds on which such denial, bar, or prohibition or limitation is based exist in fact, that such denial, bar, or prohibition or limitation is in accordance with the rules of the self-regulatory organization, and that such rules are, and were applied in a manner, consistent with the purposes of this title, such appropriate regulatory agency, by order, shall dismiss the proceeding. If such appropriate regulatory agency does not make any such finding or if it finds that such denial, bar, or prohibition or limitation imposes any burden on competition not necessary or appropriate in furtherance of the purposes of this title, such appropriate regulatory agency, by order, shall set aside the action of the self-regulatory organization and require it to admit such applicant to membership or participation, permit such person to become associated with a member, or grant such person access to services offered by the self-regulatory organization or member thereof.

g.

    1.   Every self-regulatory organization shall comply with the provisions of this title, the rules and regulations thereunder, and its own rules, and (subject to the provisions of Section 17(d) of this title, paragraph (2) of this subsection, and the rules thereunder) absent reasonable justification or excuse enforce compliance—

        A. in the case of a national securities exchange, with such provisions by its members and persons associated with its members;

        B. in the case of a registered securities association, with such provisions and the provisions of the rules of the Municipal Securities Rulemaking Board by its members and persons associated with its members; and

        C. in the case of a registered clearing agency, with its own rules by its participants.

    2.   The Commission, by rule, consistent with the public interest, the protection of investors, and the other purposes of this title, may relieve any self-regulatory organization of any responsibility under this title to enforce compliance with any specified provision of this title or the rules or regulations thereunder by any member of such organization or person associated with such a member, or any class of such members or persons associated with a member.

h.

    1.   The appropriate regulatory agency for a self-regulatory organization is authorized, by order, if in its opinion such action is necessary or appropriate in the public interest, for the protection of investors, or otherwise in furtherance of the purposes of this title, to suspend for a period not exceeding twelve months or revoke the registration of such

self-regulatory organization, or to censure or impose limitations upon the activities, functions, and operations of such self-regulatory organization, if such appropriate regulatory agency finds, on the record after notice and opportunity for hearing, that such self-regulatory organization has violated or is unable to comply with any provisions of this title, the rules or regulations thereunder, or its own rules or without reasonable justification or excuse has failed to enforce compliance—

    A. in the case of a national securities exchange, with any such provision by a member thereof or a person associated with a member thereof;

    B. in the case of a registered securities association, with any such provision or any provision of the rules of the Municipal Securities Rulemaking Board by a member thereof or a person associated with a member thereof; or

    C. in the case of a registered clearing agency, with any provision of its own rules by a participant therein.

2. The appropriate regulatory agency for a self-regulatory organization is authorized, by order, if in its opinion such action is necessary or appropriate in the public interest, for the protection of investors, or otherwise in furtherance of the purposes of this title, to suspend for a period not exceeding twelve months or expel from such self-regulatory organization any member thereof or participant therein, if such member or participant is subject to an order of the Commission pursuant to Section 15(b)(4) of this title or if such appropriate regulatory agency finds, on the record after notice and opportunity for hearing, that such member or participant has willfully violated or has effected any transaction for any other person who, such member or participant had reason to believe, was violating with respect to such transaction—

    A. in the case of a national securities exchange, any provision of the Securities Act of 1933, the Investment Advisers Act of 1940, the Investment

Company Act of 1940, this title, or the rules or regulations under any of such statutes;

B. in the case of a registered securities association, any provision of the Securities Act of 1933, the Investment Advisers Act of 1940, the Investment Company Act of 1940, this title, or the rules or regulations under any of such statutes, or the rules of the Municipal Securities Rulemaking Board; or

C. in the case of a registered clearing agency, any provision of the rules of the clearing agency.

3. The appropriate regulatory agency for a national securities exchange or registered securities association is authorized, by order, if in its opinion such action is necessary or appropriate in the public interest, for the protection of investors, or otherwise in furtherance of the purposes of this title, to suspend for a period not exceeding twelve months or to bar any person from being associated with a member of such national securities exchange or registered securities association, if such person is subject to an order of the Commission pursuant to Section 15(b)(6) of this title or if such appropriate regulatory agency finds, on the record after notice and opportunity for hearing, that such person has willfully violated or has effected any transaction for any other person who, such person associated with a member had reason to believe, was violating with respect to such transaction—

A. in the case of a national securities exchange, any provision of the Securities Act of 1933, the Investment Advisers Act of 1940, the Investment Company Act of 1940, this title, or the rules or regulations under any of such statutes; or

B. in the case of a registered securities association, any provision of the Securities Act of 1933, the Investment Advisers Act of 1940, the Investment Company Act of 1940, this title, the rules or regulations under any of the statutes, or the rules of the Municipal Securities Rulemaking Board.

4. The appropriate regulatory agency for a self-regulatory organization is authorized by order, if in its opinion such action is necessary or appropriate in the public interest, for the protection of investors, or otherwise in furtherance of the purposes of this title, to remove from office or censure any officer or director of such self-regulatory organization, if such appropriate regulatory agency finds, on the record after notice and opportunity for hearing, that such officer or director has willfully violated any provision of this title, the rules or regulations thereunder, or the rules of such self-regulatory organization, willfully abused his authority, or without reasonable justification or excuse has failed to enforce compliance—

    A. in the case of a national securities exchange, with any such provision by any member or person associated with a member;

    B. in the case of a registered securities association, with any such provision or any provision of the rules of the Municipal Securities Rulemaking Board by any member or person associated with a member; or

    C. in the case of a registered clearing agency, with any provision of the rules of the clearing agency by any participant.

i. If a proceeding under subsection (h)(1) of this section results in the suspension or revocation of the registration of a clearing agency, the appropriate regulatory agency for such clearing agency may, upon notice to such clearing agency, apply to any court of competent jurisdiction specified in Section 21(d) or 27 of this title for the appointment of a trustee. In the event of such an application, the court may, to the extent it deems necessary or appropriate, take exclusive jurisdiction of such clearing agency and the records and assets thereof, wherever located; and the court shall appoint the appropriate regulatory agency for such clearing agency or a person designated by such appropriate regulatory agency as trustee with power to take possession and continue to operate or terminate the operations of such clearing agency in an orderly manner for the protection of participants and investors, subject to such terms and conditions as the court may prescribe.

SECTION 20—LIABILITIES OF CONTROLLING PERSONS AND PERSONS WHO AID AND ABET VIOLATIONS

a. Every person who, directly or indirectly, controls any person liable under any provision of this title or of any rule or regulation thereunder shall also be liable jointly and severally with and to the same extent as such controlled person to any person to whom such controlled person is liable, unless the controlling person acted in good faith and did not directly or indirectly induce the act or acts constituting the violation or cause of action.

b. It shall be unlawful for any person, directly or indirectly, to do any act or thing which it would be unlawful for such person to do under the provisions of this title or any rule or regulation thereunder through or by means of any other person.

c. It shall be unlawful for any director or officer of, or any owner of any securities issued by, any issuer required to file any document, report, or information under this title or any rule or regulation thereunder without just cause to hinder, delay, or obstruct the making or filing of any such document, report, or information.

d. Wherever communicating, or purchasing or selling a security while in possession of, material nonpublic information would violate, or result in liability to any purchaser or seller of the security under any provision of this title, or any rule or regulation thereunder, such conduct in connection with a purchase or sale of a put, call, straddle, option, or privilege with respect to such security or with respect to a group or index of securities including such security, shall also violate and result in comparable liability to any purchaser or seller of that security under such provision, rule, or regulation.

e. **[Reserved]**

f. **Prosecution Of Persons Who Aid And Abet Violations.**—For purposes of any action brought by the Commission under paragraph (1) or (3) of Section 21(d), any person that knowingly provides substantial assistance to another person in violation of a provision of this title, or of any rule or regulation issued under this title, shall be deemed to be in violation of such provision to the same extent as the person to whom such assistance is provided.

SECTION 20A—LIABILITY TO CONTEMPORANEOUS TRADERS FOR INSIDER TRADING

a. **Private Rights Of Action Based On Contemporaneous Trading.** Any person who violates any provision of this title or the rules or regulations thereunder by purchasing or selling a security while in possession of material, nonpublic information shall be liable in an action in any court of competent jurisdiction to any person who, contemporaneously with the purchase or sale of securities that is the subject of such violation, has purchased (where such violation is based on a sale of securities) or sold (where such violation is based on a purchase of securities) securities of the same class.

b. **Limitations On Liability.**

    1. **Contemporaneous Trading Actions Limited to Profit Gained or Loss Avoided.** The total amount of damages imposed under subsection (a) shall not exceed the profit gained or loss avoided in the transaction or transactions that are the subject of the violation.

    2. **Offsetting Disgorgements Against Liability.** The total amount of damages imposed against any person under subsection (a) shall be diminished by the amounts, if any, that such person may be required to disgorge, pursuant to a court order obtained at the instance of the Commission, in a proceeding brought under Section 21(d) of this title relating to the same transaction or transactions.

    3. **Controlling Person Liability.** No person shall be liable under this section solely by reason of employing another person who is liable under this section, but the liability of a controlling person under this section shall be subject to Section 20(a) of this title.

    4. **Statute Of Limitations.** No action may be brought under this section more than 5 years after the date of the last transaction that is the subject of the violation.

c. **Joint And Several Liability For Communicating.** Any person who violates any provision of this title or the rules or regulations thereunder by communicating material, nonpublic information shall be jointly and severally liable under subsection (a) with, and to the same extent as, any person or persons liable under subsection (a) to whom the communication was directed.

d. **Authority Not To Restrict Other Express Or Implied Rights Of Action.** Nothing in this section shall be construed to limit or condition the right of any person to bring an action to enforce a requirement of this title or the availability of any cause of action implied from a provision of this title.

e. **Provisions Not To Affect Public Prosecutions.** This section shall not be construed to bar or limit in any manner any action by the Commission or the Attorney General under any other provision of this title, nor shall it bar or limit in any manner any action to recover penalties, or to seek any other order regarding penalties.

SECTION 21—INVESTIGATIONS, INJUNCTIONS AND PROSECUTION OF OFFENSES

a.

    1. The Commission may, in its discretion, make such investigations as it deems necessary to determine whether any person has violated, is violating, or is about to violate any provision of this title, the rules or regulations thereunder, the rules of a national securities exchange or registered securities association of which such person is a member or a person associated with a member, the rules of a registered clearing agency in which such person is a participant, or the rules of the Municipal Securities Rulemaking Board, and may require or permit any person to file with it a statement in writing, under oath or otherwise as the Commission shall determine, as to all the facts and circumstances concerning the matter to be investigated. The Commission is

authorized, in its discretion, to publish information concerning any such violations, and to investigate any facts, conditions, practices, or matters which it may deem necessary or proper to aid in the enforcement of such provisions, in the prescribing of rules and regulations under this title, or in securing information to serve as a basis for recommending further legislation concerning the matters to which this title relates.

2. On request from a foreign securities authority, the Commission may provide assistance in accordance with this paragraph if the requesting authority states that the requesting authority is conducting an investigation which it deems necessary to determine whether any person has violated, is violating, or is about to violate any laws or rules relating to securities matters that the requesting authority administers or enforces. The Commission may, in its discretion, conduct such investigation as the Commission deems necessary to collect information and evidence pertinent to the request for assistance. Such assistance may be provided without regard to whether the facts stated in the request would also constitute a violation of the laws of the United States. In deciding whether to provide such assistance, the Commission shall consider whether

A. the requesting authority has agreed to provide reciprocal assistance in securities matters to the Commission; and

B. compliance with the request would prejudice the public interest of the United States.

b. For the purpose of any such investigation, or any other proceeding under this title, any member of the Commission or any officer designated by it is empowered to administer oaths and affirmations, subpoena witnesses, compel their attendance, take evidence, and require the production of any books, papers, correspondence, memoranda, or other records which the Commission deems relevant or material to the inquiry. Such attendance of witnesses and the production of any such records may be required from any place in the United States or any State at any designated place of hearing.

c. In case of contumacy by, or refusal to obey a subpoena issued to, any person, the Commission may invoke the aid of any court of the United States within the jurisdiction of which such investigation or proceeding is carried on, or where such person resides or carries on business, in requiring the attendance and testimony of witnesses and the production of books, papers, correspondence, memoranda, and other records. And such court may issue an order requiring such person to appear before the Commission or member or officer designated by the Commission, there to produce records, if so ordered, or to give testimony touching the matter under investigation or in question; and any failure to obey such order of the court may be punished by such court as a contempt thereof. All process in any such case may be served in the judicial district whereof such person is an inhabitant or wherever he may be found. Any person who shall, without just cause, fail or refuse to attend and testify or to answer any lawful inquiry or to produce books, papers, correspondence, memoranda, and other records, if in his power so to do, in obedience to the subpoena of the Commission, shall be guilty of a misdemeanor and, upon conviction, shall be subject to a fine of not more than $1,000 or to imprisonment for a term of not more than one year, or both.

d.

1. Whenever it shall appear to the Commission that any person is engaged or is about to engage in any acts or practices constituting a violation of any provision of this title, the rules or regulations thereunder, the rules of a national securities exchange or registered securities association of which such person is a member or a person associated with a member, the rules of a registered clearing agency in which such person is a participant, or the rules of the Municipal Securities Rulemaking Board, it may in its discretion bring an action in the proper district court of the United States, the United States District Court for the District of Columbia, or the United States courts of any territory or other place subject to the jurisdiction of the United States, to enjoin such acts or practices, and upon a proper showing a permanent or temporary injunction or restraining order shall be granted without bond. The Commission

may transmit such evidence as may be available concerning such acts or practices as may constitute a violation of any provision of this title or the rules or regulations thereunder to the Attorney General, who may, in his discretion, institute the necessary criminal proceedings under this title.

2. **Authority Of A Court To Prohibit Persons From Serving As Officers And Directors.**—In any proceeding under paragraph (1) of this subsection, the court may prohibit, conditionally or unconditionally, and permanently or for such period of time as it shall determine, any person who violated Section 10(b) of this title or the rules or regulations thereunder from acting as an officer or director of any issuer that has a class of securities registered pursuant to Section 12 of this title or that is required to file reports pursuant to Section 15(d) of this title if the person's conduct demonstrates substantial unfitness to serve as an officer or director of any such issuer.

3. **Money Penalties In Civil Actions.**—

    A. **Authority of Commission.**—Whenever it shall appear to the Commission that any person has violated any provision of this title, the rules or regulations thereunder, or a cease-and-desist order entered by the Commission pursuant to Section 21C of this title, other than by committing a violation subject to a penalty pursuant to Section 21A, the Commission may bring an action in the United States district court to seek, and the court shall have jurisdiction to impose, upon a proper showing, a civil penalty to be paid by the person who committed such violation.

    B. **Amount Of Penalty.**—

        i. **First Tier.**—The amount of the penalty shall be determined by the court in light of the facts and circumstances. For each violation, the amount of the penalty shall not exceed the greater of

I. $5,000 for a natural person or $50,000 for any other person, or

II. the gross amount of pecuniary gain to such defendant as a result of the violation.

ii. **Second Tier.**—Notwithstanding clause (i), the amount of penalty for each such violation shall not exceed the greater of

I. $50,000 for a natural person or $250,000 for any other person, or

II. the gross amount of pecuniary gain to such defendant as a result of the violation, if the violation described in subparagraph (A) involved fraud, deceit, manipulation, or deliberate or reckless disregard of a regulatory requirement.

iii. **Third Tier.**—Notwithstanding clauses (i) and (ii), the amount of penalty for each such violation shall not exceed the greater of

I. $100,000 for a natural person or $500,000 for any other person, or

II. the gross amount of pecuniary gain to such defendant as a result of a violation, if—

1. the violation described in subparagraph (A) involved fraud, deceit, manipulation, or deliberate or reckless disregard of a regulatory requirement; and

2. such violation directly or indirectly resulted in substantial losses or created a significant risk of

substantial losses to other persons.

C. **Procedures For Collection.—**

    i. **Payment Of Penalty To Treasury.—**A penalty imposed under this section shall be payable into the Treasury of the United States.

    ii. **Collection Of Penalties.—**If a person upon whom such a penalty is imposed shall fail to pay such penalty within the time prescribed in the court's order, the Commission may refer the matter to the Attorney General who shall recover such penalty by action in the appropriate United States district court.

    iii. **Remedy Not Exclusive.—**The actions authorized by this paragraph may be brought in addition to any other action that the Commission or the Attorney General is entitled to bring.

    iv. **Jurisdiction And Venue.—**For purposes of Section 27 of this title, actions under this paragraph shall be actions to enforce a liability or a duty created by this title.

D. **Special Provisions Relating To A Violation Of A Cease-And-Desist Order.—**In an action to enforce a cease-and-desist order entered by the Commission pursuant to Section 21C, each separate violation of such order shall be a separate offense, except that in the case of a violation through a continuing failure to comply with the order, each day of the failure to comply shall be deemed a separate offense.

4. **Prohibition Of Attorneys' Fees Paid From Commission Disgorgement Funds.—**Except as otherwise ordered by the court upon motion by the Commission, or, in the case of an

administrative action, as otherwise ordered by the Commission, funds disgorged as the result of an action brought by the Commission in Federal court, or as a result of any Commission administrative action, shall not be distributed as payment for attorneys' fees or expenses incurred by private parties seeking distribution of the disgorged funds.

e. Upon application of the Commission the district courts of the United States and the United States courts of any territory or other place subject to the jurisdiction of the United States shall also have jurisdiction to issue writs of mandamus, injunctions, and orders commanding

1. any person to comply with the provisions of this title, the rules, regulations, and orders thereunder, the rules of a national securities exchange or registered securities association of which such person is a member or person associated with a member, the rules of a registered clearing agency in which such person is a participant, and the rules of the Municipal Securities Rulemaking Board, or any undertaking contained in a registration statement as provided in subsection (d) of Section 15 of this title,

2. any national securities exchange or registered securities association to enforce compliance by its members and persons associated with its members with the provisions of this title, the rules, regulations, and orders thereunder, and the rules of such exchange or association, or

3. any registered clearing agency to enforce compliance by its participants with the provisions of the rules of such clearing agency.

f. Notwithstanding any other provision of this title, the Commission shall not bring any action pursuant to subsection (d) or (e) of this section against any person for violation of, or to command compliance with, the rules of a self-regulatory organization unless it appears to the Commission that

1. such self-regulatory organization is unable or unwilling to take appropriate action against such person in the public interest and for the protection of investors, or

    2. such action is otherwise necessary or appropriate in the public interest or for the protection of investors.

g. Notwithstanding the provisions of <u>Section 1407(a) of Title 28, United States Code</u>, or any other provision of law, no action for equitable relief instituted by the Commission pursuant to the securities laws shall be consolidated or coordinated with other actions not brought by the Commission, even though such other actions may involve common questions of fact, unless such consolidation is consented to by the Commission.

h.

    1. <u>The Right to Financial Privacy Act of 1978</u> shall apply with respect to the Commission, except as otherwise provided in this subsection.

    2. Notwithstanding <u>Section 1105</u> or <u>1107</u> of the Right to Financial Privacy Act of 1978, the Commission may have access to and obtain copies of, or the information contained in financial records of a customer from a financial institution without prior notice to the customer upon an ex parte showing to an appropriate United States district court that the Commission seeks such financial records pursuant to a subpoena issued in conformity with the requirements of <u>Section 19(b)</u> of the Securities Act of 1933, <u>Section 21(b)</u> of the Securities Exchange Act of 1934, <u>Section 18(c)</u> of the <u>Public Utility Holding Company Act of 1935</u>, <u>Section 42(b)</u> of the <u>Investment Company Act of 1940</u>, or <u>Section 209(b)</u> of the <u>Investment Advisers Act of 1940</u>, and that the Commission has reason to believe that—

        A. delay in obtaining access to such financial records, or the required notice, will result in—

            i.   flight from prosecution;

            ii. destruction of or tampering with evidence;

            iii. transfer of assets or records outside the territorial limits of the United States;

            iv. improper conversion of investor assets; or

            v. impeding the ability of the Commission to identify or trace the source or disposition of funds involved in any securities transaction;

    B. such financial records are necessary to identify or trace the record or beneficial ownership interest in any security;

    C. the acts, practices or course of conduct under investigation involve—

            i. the dissemination of materially false or misleading information concerning any security, issuer, or market, or the failure to make disclosures required under the securities laws, which remain uncorrected; or

            ii. a financial loss to investors or other persons protected under the securities laws which remains substantially uncompensated; or

    D. the acts, practices or course of conduct under investigation—

            i. involve significant financial speculation in securities; or

            ii. endanger the stability of any financial or investment intermediary.

3. Any application under paragraph (2) for a delay in notice shall be made with reasonable specificity.

4.

    A. Upon a showing described in paragraph (2), the presiding judge or magistrate shall enter an ex parte order granting the requested delay for a period not to exceed ninety days and an order prohibiting the financial institution involved from disclosing that records have been obtained or that a request for records has been made.

    B.   Extensions of the period of delay of notice provided in subparagraph (A) of up to ninety days each may be granted by the court upon application, but only in accordance with this subsection or Section 1109(a), (b)(1), or (b)(2) of the Right to Financial Privacy Act of 1978.

    C.   Upon expiration of the period of delay of notification ordered under subparagraph (A) or (B), the customer shall be served with or mailed a copy of the subpoena insofar as it applies to the customer together with the following notice which shall describe with reasonable specificity the nature of the investigation for which the Commission sought the financial records: "Records or information concerning your transactions which are held by the financial institutions named in the attached subpoena were supplied to the Securities and Exchange Commission on (date), Notification was withheld pursuant to a determination by the (title of court so ordering) under Section 21(h) of the Securities Exchange Act of 1934 that (state reason). The purpose of the investigation or official proceeding was (state purpose)".

5.   Upon application by the Commission, all proceedings pursuant to paragraphs (2) and (4) shall be held in camera and the records thereof sealed until expiration of the period of delay or such other date as the presiding judge or magistrate may permit.

6.   The Commission shall compile an annual tabulation of the occasions on which the Commission used each separate subparagraph or clause of paragraph (2) of this subsection or the provisions of the Right to Financial Privacy Act of 1978 to obtain access to financial records of a customer and include it in its annual report to the Congress. Section 1121(b) of the Right to Financial Privacy Act of 1978 shall not apply with respect to the Commission.

7.

A. Following the expiration of the period of delay of notification ordered by the court pursuant to paragraph (4) of this subsection, the customer may, upon motion, reopen the proceeding in the district court which issued the order. If the presiding judge or magistrate finds that the movant is the customer to whom the records obtained by the Commission pertain, and that the Commission has obtained financial records or information contained therein in violation of this subsection, other than paragraph (1), it may order that the customer be granted civil penalties against the Commission in an amount equal to the sum of—

   i. $100 without regard to the volume of records involved;

   ii. any out-of-pocket damages sustained by the customer as a direct result of the disclosure; and

   iii. if the violation is found to have been willful, intentional, and without good faith, such punitive damages as the court may allow, together with the costs of the action and reasonable attorneys' fees as determined by the court.

B. Upon a finding that the Commission has obtained financial records or information contained therein in violation of this subsection, other than paragraph (1), the court, in its discretion, may also or in the alternative issue injunctive relief to require the Commission to comply with this subsection with respect to any subpoena which the Commission issues in the future for financial records of such customer for purposes of the same investigation.

C. Whenever the court determines that the Commission has failed to comply with this subsection, other than paragraph (1), and the court finds that the circumstances raise questions of whether an officer or employee of the Commission acted in a willful and intentional manner and without good faith with respect to the violation, the Office of Personnel Management shall promptly initiate a proceeding to determine whether disciplinary action is warranted against the agent or employee who was primarily responsible for the violation. After investigating and considering the evidence submitted, the Office of Personnel Management shall submit its findings and recommendations to the Commission and shall send copies of the findings and recommendations to the officer or employee or his representative. The Commission shall take the corrective action that the Office of Personnel Management recommends.

8. The relief described in paragraphs (7) and (10) shall be the only remedies or sanctions available to a customer for a violation of this subsection, other than paragraph (1), and nothing herein or in the Right to Financial Privacy Act of 1978 shall be deemed to prohibit the use in any investigation or proceeding of financial records, or the information contained therein, obtained by a subpoena issued by the Commission. In the case of an unsuccessful action under paragraph (7), the court shall award the costs of the action and attorneys' fees to the Commission if the presiding judge or magistrate finds that the customer's claims were made in bad faith.

9.

 A. The Commission may transfer financial records or the information contained therein to any government authority if the Commission proceeds as a transferring agency in accordance with Section 1112 of the Right to Financial Privacy Act of 1978, except that the customer notice required under Section 1112(b) or (c) of such Act may be delayed upon a showing by the Commission, in accordance with the procedure set forth in paragraphs (4) and (5), that one or more of subparagraphs (A) through (B) of <u>paragraph (2)</u> apply.

B. The Commission may, without notice to the customer pursuant to <u>Section 1112</u> of the Right to Financial Privacy Act of 1978, transfer financial records or the information contained therein to a State securities agency or to the Department of Justice. Financial records or information transferred by the Commission to the Department of Justice or to a State securities agency pursuant to the provisions of this subparagraph may be disclosed or used only in an administrative, civil, or criminal action or investigation by the Department of Justice or the State securities agency which arises out of or relates to the acts, practices, or courses of conduct investigated by the Commission, except that if the Department of Justice or the State securities agency determines that the information should be disclosed or used for any other purpose, it may do so if it notifies the customer, except as otherwise provided in the <u>Right to Financial Privacy Act of 1978</u>, within 30 days of its determination, or complies with the requirements of <u>Section 1109</u> of such Act regarding delay of notice.

10. Any government authority violating <u>paragraph (9)</u> shall be subject to the procedures and penalties applicable to the Commission under <u>paragraph (7)(A)</u> with respect to a violation by the Commission in obtaining financial records.

11. Notwithstanding the provisions of this subsection, the Commission may obtain financial records from a financial institution or transfer such records in accordance with provisions of the <u>Right to Financial Privacy Act of 1978</u>.

12. Nothing in this subsection shall enlarge or restrict any rights of a financial institution to challenge requests for records made by the Commission under existing law. Nothing in this subsection shall entitle a customer to assert any rights of a financial institution.

13. Unless the context otherwise requires, all terms defined in the <u>Right to Financial Privacy Act of 1978</u> which are common to this subsection shall have the same meaning as in such Act.

SECTION 21A—CIVIL PENALTIES FOR INSIDER TRADING

a. **Authority To Impose Civil Penalties.**—

1. **Judicial Actions By Commission Authorized.**—Whenever it shall appear to the Commission that any person has violated any provision of this title or the rules or regulations thereunder by purchasing or selling a security while in possession of material, nonpublic information in, or has violated any such provision by communicating such information in connection with, a transaction on or through the facilities of a national securities exchange or from or through a broker or dealer, and which is not part of a public offering by an issuer of securities other than standardized options, the Commission—

    A. may bring an action in a United States district court to seek, and the court shall have jurisdiction to impose, a civil penalty to be paid by the person who committed such violation; and

    B. may, subject to <u>subsection (b)(1)</u>, bring an action in a United States district court to seek, and the court shall have jurisdiction to impose, a civil penalty to be paid by a person who, at the time of the violation, directly or indirectly controlled the person who committed such violation.

2. **Amount Of Penalty For Person Who Committed Violation.**—The amount of the penalty which may be imposed on the person who committed such violation shall be determined by the court in light of the facts and circumstances, but shall not exceed three times the profit gained or loss avoided as a result of such unlawful purchase, sale, or communication.

3. **Amount Of Penalty For Controlling Person.**—The amount of the penalty which may be imposed on any person who, at the time of the violation, directly or indirectly controlled the person who committed such violation, shall be determined by the court in light of the facts and circumstances, but shall not exceed the greater of $1,000,000, or three times the amount of the profit gained or loss avoided as a result of such controlled person's violation. If such controlled person's violation was a violation by communication, the profit gained or loss avoided as a result of the violation shall, for purposes of this paragraph only, be deemed to be limited to the profit gained or loss avoided by the person or persons to whom the controlled person directed such communication.

b. **Limitations On Liability.**—

1. **Liability Of Controlling Persons.**—No controlling person shall be subject to a penalty under subsection (a)(1)(B) unless the Commission establishes that—

   A. such controlling person knew or recklessly disregarded the fact that such controlled person was likely to engage in the act or acts constituting the violation and failed to take appropriate steps to prevent such act or acts before they occurred; or

   B. such controlling person knowingly or recklessly failed to establish, maintain, or enforce any policy or procedure required under Section 15(f) of this title or Section 204A of the Investment Advisers Act of 1940 and such failure substantially contributed to or permitted the occurrence of the act or acts constituting the violation.

2. **Additional Restrictions On Liability.**—No person shall be subject to a penalty under subsection (a) solely by reason of employing another person who is subject to a penalty under such subsection, unless such employing person is liable as a controlling person under paragraph (1) of this subsection. Section 20(a) of this title shall not apply to actions under subsection (a) of this section.

c. **Authority Of Commission.** The Commission, by such rules, regulations, and orders as it considers necessary or appropriate in the public interest or for the protection of investors, may exempt, in whole or in part, either unconditionally or upon specific terms and conditions, any person or transaction or class of persons or transactions from this section.

d. **Procedures For Collection.—**

    1. **Payment Of Penalty To Treasury.—**A penalty imposed under this section shall (subject to <u>subsection (e)</u>) be payable into the Treasury of the United States.

    2. **Collection Of Penalties.—**If a person upon whom such a penalty is imposed shall fail to pay such penalty within the time prescribed in the court's order, the Commission may refer the matter to the Attorney General who shall recover such penalty by action in the appropriate United States district court.

    3. **Remedy Not Exclusive.—**The actions authorized by this section may be brought in addition to any other actions that the Commission or the Attorney General are entitled to bring.

    4. **Jurisdiction And Venue.—**For purposes of <u>Section 27</u> of this title, actions under this section shall be actions to enforce a liability or a duty created by this title.

    5. **Statute Of Limitations.** No action may be brought under this section more than 5 years after the date of the purchase or sale. This section shall not be construed to bar or limit in any manner any action by the Commission or the Attorney General under any other provision of this title, nor shall it bar or limit in any manner any action to recover penalties, or to seek any other order regarding penalties, imposed in an action commenced within 5 years of such transaction.

e. **Authority To Award Bounties To Informants.** Notwithstanding the provisions of <u>subsection (d)(1)</u>, there shall be paid from amounts imposed as a penalty under this section and recovered by the Commission or the Attorney General, such sums, not to exceed 10 percent of such amounts, as the Commission deems appropriate, to the person or persons who provide information leading to the imposition of such penalty. Any determinations under this subsection including whether, to whom, or in what amount to make payments, shall be in the sole discretion of the Commission, except that no such payment shall be made to any member, officer, or employee of any appropriate regulatory agency, the Department of Justice, or a self-regulatory organization. Any such determination shall be final and not subject to judicial review.

f.   **Definition.**—For purposes of this section, "profit gained" or "loss avoided" is the difference between the purchase or sale price of the security and the value of that security as measured by the trading price of the security a reasonable period after public dissemination of the nonpublic information.

SECTION 21B—CIVIL REMEDIES IN ADMINISTRATIVE PROCEEDINGS

a.   **Commission Authority To Assess Money Penalties.**—In any proceeding instituted pursuant to Sections 15(b)(4), 15(b)(6), 15B, 15C, or 17A of this title against any person, the Commission or the appropriate regulatory agency may impose a civil penalty if it finds, on the record after notice and opportunity for hearing, that such person—

1.   has willfully violated any provision of the Securities Act of 1933, the Investment Company Act of 1940, the Investment Advisers Act of 1940, or this title, or the rules or regulations thereunder, or the rules of the Municipal Securities Rulemaking Board;

2.   has willfully aided, abetted, counseled, commanded, induced, or procured such a violation by any other person;

3.   has willfully made or caused to be made in any application for registration or report required to be filed with the Commission or with any other appropriate regulatory agency under this title, or in any proceeding before the Commission with respect to registration, any statement which was, at the time and in the light of the circumstances under which it was made, false or misleading with respect to any

material fact, or has omitted to state in any such application or report any material fact which is required to be stated therein; or

4. has failed reasonably to supervise, within the meaning of Section 15(b)(4)(E) of this title, with a view to preventing violations of the provisions of such statutes, rules and regulations, another person who commits such a violation, if such other person is subject to his supervision; and that such penalty is in the public interest.

b. **Maximum Amount Of Penalty.—**

1. **First Tier.—**The maximum amount of penalty for each act or omission described in Subsection (a) shall be $5,000 for a natural person or $50,000 for any other person.

2. **Second Tier.—**Notwithstanding paragraph (1), the maximum amount of penalty for each such act or omission shall be $50,000 for a natural person or $250,000 for any other person if the act or omission described in subsection (a) involved fraud, deceit, manipulation, or deliberate or reckless disregard of a regulatory requirement.

3. **Third Tier.—**Notwithstanding paragraphs (1) and (2), the maximum amount of penalty for each such act or omission shall be $100,000 for a natural person or $500,000 for any other person if—

   A. The act or omission described in subsection (a) involved fraud, deceit, manipulation, or deliberate or reckless disregard of a regulatory requirement; and

   B. such act or omission directly or indirectly resulted in substantial losses or created a significant risk of substantial losses to other persons or resulted in substantial pecuniary gain to the person who committed the act or omission.

c. **Determination Of Public Interest.—**In considering under this section whether a penalty is in the public interest, the Commission or the appropriate regulatory agency may consider—

1. whether the act or omission for which such penalty is assessed involved fraud, deceit, manipulation, or deliberate or reckless disregard of a regulatory requirement;

2. the harm to other persons resulting either directly or indirectly from such act or omission;

3. the extent to which any person was unjustly enriched, taking into account any restitution made to persons injured by such behavior;

4. whether such person previously has been found by the Commission, another appropriate regulatory agency, or a self-regulatory organization to have violated the Federal securities laws, State securities laws, or the rules of a self-regulatory organization, has been enjoined by a court of competent jurisdiction from violations of such laws or rules, or has been convicted by a court of competent jurisdiction of violations of such laws or of any felony or misdemeanor described in Section 15(b)(4)(B) of this title;

5. the need to deter such person and other persons from committing such acts or omissions; and

6. such other matters as justice may require.

d. **Evidence Concerning Ability To Pay.**—In any proceeding in which the Commission or the appropriate regulatory agency may impose a penalty under this section, a respondent may present evidence of the respondent's ability to pay such penalty. The Commission or the appropriate regulatory agency may, in its discretion, consider such evidence in determining whether such penalty is in the public interest. Such evidence may relate to the extent of such person's ability to continue in business and the collectability of a penalty, taking into account any other claims of the United States or third parties upon such person's assets and the amount of such person's assets.

e. **Authority To Enter An Order Requiring An Accounting And Disgorgement.**—In any proceeding in which the Commission or the appropriate regulatory agency may impose a penalty under this section, the Commission or the appropriate regulatory agency may enter an order requiring accounting and disgorgement, including reasonable interest. The Commission is authorized to adopt rules, regulations, and orders concerning payments to investors, rates of interest, periods of accrual, and such other matters as it deems appropriate to implement this subsection.

SECTION 21C—CEASE-AND-DESIST PROCEEDINGS

a. **Authority of the Commission.**—If the Commission finds, after notice and opportunity for hearing, that any person is violating, has violated, or is about to violate any provision of this title, or any rule or regulation thereunder, the Commission may publish its findings and enter an order requiring such person, and any other person that is, was, or would be a cause of the violation, due to an act or omission the person knew or should have known would contribute to such violation, to cease and desist from committing or causing such violation and any future violation of the same provision, rule, or regulation. Such order may, in addition to requiring a person to cease and desist from committing or causing a violation, require such person to comply, or to take steps to effect compliance, with such provision, rule, or regulation, upon such terms and conditions and within such time as the Commission may specify in such order. Any such order may, as the Commission deems appropriate, require future compliance or steps to effect future compliance, either permanently or for such period of time as the Commission may specify, with such provision, rule, or regulation with respect to any security, any issuer, or any other person.

b. **Hearing.**—The notice instituting proceedings pursuant to subsection (a) shall fix a hearing date not earlier than 30 days nor later than 60 days after service of the notice unless an earlier date is set by the Commission with the consent of any respondent so served.

c. **Temporary Order.**—

    1. **In General.**—Whenever the Commission determines that the alleged violation or threatened violation specified in the notice instituting proceedings pursuant to subsection (a), or the continuation thereof, is likely to result in significant

dissipation or conversion of assets, significant harm to investors, or substantial harm to the public interest, including, but not limited to, losses to the Securities Investor Protection Corporation, prior to the completion of the proceedings, the Commission may enter a temporary order requiring the respondent to cease and desist from the violation or threatened violation and to take such action to prevent the violation or threatened violation and to prevent dissipation or conversion of assets, significant harm to investors, or substantial harm to the public interest as the Commission deems appropriate pending completion of such proceedings. Such an order shall be entered only after notice and opportunity for a hearing, unless the Commission determines that notice and hearing prior to entry would be impracticable or contrary to the public interest. A temporary order shall become effective upon service upon the respondent and, unless set aside, limited, or suspended by the Commission or a court of competent jurisdiction, shall remain effective and enforceable pending the completion of the proceedings.

2. **Applicability.**—This subsection shall apply only to a respondent that acts, or, at the time of the alleged misconduct acted, as a broker, dealer, investment adviser, investment company, municipal securities dealer, government securities broker, government securities dealer, or transfer agent, or is, or was at the time of the alleged misconduct, an associated person of, or a person seeking to become associated with, any of the foregoing.

d. **Review Of Temporary Orders.**—

1. **Commission Review.**—At any time after the respondent has been served with a temporary cease-and-desist order pursuant to subsection (c), the respondent may apply to the Commission to have the order set aside, limited, or suspended. If the respondent has been served with a temporary cease-and-desist order entered without a prior Commission hearing, the respondent may, within 10 days after the date on which the order was served, request a hearing on such

application and the Commission shall hold a hearing and render a decision on such application at the earliest possible time.

2. **Judicial Review.**—Within—

   A. 10 days after the date the respondent was served with a temporary cease-and-desist order entered with a prior Commission hearing, or

   B. 10 days after the Commission renders a decision on an application and hearing under paragraph (1), with respect to any temporary cease-and-desist order entered without a prior Commission hearing,

   the respondent may apply to the United States district court for the district in which the respondent resides or has its principal place of business, or for the District of Columbia, for an order setting aside, limiting, or suspending the effectiveness or enforcement of the order, and the court shall have jurisdiction to enter such an order. A respondent served with a temporary cease-and-desist order entered without a prior Commission hearing may not apply to the court except after hearing and decision by the Commission on the respondent's application under paragraph (1) of this subsection.

3. **No Automatic Stay Of Temporary Order.**—The commencement of proceedings under paragraph (2) of this subsection shall not, unless specifically ordered by the court, operate as a stay of the Commission's order.

4. **Exclusive Review.**—Section 25 of this title shall not apply to a temporary order entered pursuant to this section.

e. **Authority To Enter An Order Requiring An Accounting And Disgorgement.**—In any cease-and-desist proceeding under subsection (a), the Commission may enter an order requiring accounting and disgorgement, including reasonable interest. The Commission is authorized to adopt rules, regulations, and orders concerning payments to investors, rates of interest, periods of accrual, and such other matters as it deems appropriate to implement this subsection.

SECTION 21D—PRIVATE SECURITIES LITIGATION

a.   **Private Class Actions.—**

1.   **In General**—The provisions of this subsection shall apply in each private action arising under this title that is brought as a plaintiff class action pursuant to the <u>Federal Rules of Civil Procedure</u>.

2.   **Certification Filed With Complaint.—**

A.   **In General.—**Each plaintiff seeking to serve as a representative party on behalf of a class shall provide a sworn certification, which shall be personally signed by such plaintiff and filed with the complaint, that—

i.   states that the plaintiff has reviewed the complaint and authorized its filing;

ii.   states that the plaintiff did not purchase the security that is the subject of the complaint at the direction of plaintiff's counsel or in order to participate in any private action arising under this title;

iii.   states that the plaintiff is willing to serve as a representative party on behalf of a class, including providing testimony at deposition and trial, if necessary;

iv.   sets forth all of the transactions of the plaintiff in the security that is the subject of the complaint during the class period specified it the complaint;

v.   identifies any other action under this title, filed during the 3-year period preceding the date on which the certification is signed by the plaintiff, in which the plaintiff has sought to serve as a representative party on behalf of a class; and

vi. states that the plaintiff will not accept any payment for serving as a representative party on behalf of a class beyond the plaintiff's pro rata share of any recovery, except as ordered or approved by the court in accordance with paragraph (4).

B. **Nonwaiver Of Attorney-Client Privilege.**—The certification filed pursuant to subparagraph (A) shall not be construed to be a waiver of the attorney client privilege.

3. **Appointment Of Lead Plaintiff.**—

A. **Early Notice To Class Members.**—

i. **In General.**—Not later than 20 days after the date on which the complaint is filed, the plaintiff or plaintiffs shall cause to be published, in a widely circulated national business-oriented publication or wire service, a notice advising members of the purported plaintiff class—

I. of the pendency of the action, the claims asserted therein, and the purported class period; and

II. that, not later than 60 days after the date on which the notice is published, any member of the purported class may move the court to serve as lead plaintiff of the purported class.

ii. **Multiple Actions.**—If more than one action on behalf of a class asserting substantially the same claim or claims arising under this title is filed, only the plaintiff or plaintiffs in the first filed action shall be required to cause notice to be published in accordance with clause (i)

      iii. **Additional Notices May Be Required Under Federal Rules.**—Notice required under clause (i) shall be in addition to any notice required pursuant to the Federal Rules of Civil Procedure.

B. Appointment Of Lead Plaintiff.—

      i. **In General.**—Not later than 90 days after the date on which a notice is published under subparagraph (A)(i), the court shall consider any motion made by a purported class member in response to the notice, including any motion by a class member who is not individually named as a plaintiff in the complaint or complaints, and shall appoint as lead plaintiff the member or members of the purported plaintiff class that the court determines to be most capable of adequately representing the interests of class members (hereafter in this paragraph referred to as the "most adequate plaintiff") in accordance with this subparagraph.

      ii. **Consolidated Actions.**—If more than one action on behalf of a class asserting substantially the same claim or claims arising under this title has been filed, and any party has sought to consolidate those actions for pretrial purposes or for trial, the court shall not make the determination required by clause (i) until after the decision on the motion to consolidate is rendered. As soon as practicable after such decision is rendered, the court shall appoint the most adequate plaintiff as lead plaintiff for the consolidated actions in accordance with this paragraph.

      iii. **Rebuttable Presumption.**

          I. **In General.**—Subject to subclause (II), for purposes of clause (I), the court shall adopt a presumption that the most adequate plaintiff in any private action arising under this title is the person or group of persons that—

1. has either filed the complaint or made a motion in response to a notice under subparagraph (A)(i);

2. in the determination of the court, has the largest financial interest in the relief sought by the class, and

3. otherwise satisfies the requirements of Rule 23 of the Federal Rules of Civil Procedure.

II. **Rebuttal Evidence.**—The presumption described in subclause (I) may be rebutted only upon proof by a member of the purported plaintiff class that the presumptively most adequate plaintiff—

1. will not fairly and adequately protect the interests of the class; or

2. is subject to unique defenses that render such plaintiff incapable of adequately representing the class.

iv. **Discovery.**—For purposes of this subparagraph, discovery relating to whether a member or members of the purported plaintiff class is the most adequate plaintiff may be conducted by a plaintiff only if the plaintiff first demonstrates a reasonable basis for a finding that the presumptively most adequate plaintiff is incapable of adequately representing the class.

    v. **Selection Of Lead Counsel.**—The most adequate plaintiff shall, subject to the approval of the court, select and retain counsel to represent the class.

    vi. **Restrictions On Professional Plaintiffs.**—Except as the court may otherwise permit, consistent with the purposes of this section, a person may be a lead plaintiff, or an officer, director, or fiduciary of a lead plaintiff, in no more than 5 securities class actions brought as plaintiff class actions pursuant to the <u>Federal Rules of Civil Procedure</u> during any 3-year period.

4. **Recovery By Plaintiffs.**—The share of any final judgment or of any settlement that is awarded to a representative party serving on behalf of a class shall be equal, on a per share basis, to the portion of the final judgment or settlement awarded to all other members of the class. Nothing in this paragraph shall be construed to limit the award of reasonable costs and expenses (including lost wages) directly relating to the representation of the class to any representative party serving on behalf of a class.

5. **Restrictions On Settlement Under Seal.**—The terms and provisions of any settlement agreement if a class action shall not be filed under seal, except that on motion of any party to the settlement, the court may order filing under seal for those portions of a settlement agreement as to which good cause is shown for such filing under seal. For purposes of this paragraph, good cause shall exist only if publication of a term or provision of a settlement agreement would cause direct and substantial harm to any party.

6. **Restrictions On Payment Of Attorney's Fees And Expenses.**—Total attorneys' fees and expenses awarded by

the court to counsel for the plaintiff class shall not exceed a reasonable percentage of the amount of any damages and prejudgment interest actually paid to the class.

7. **Disclosure Of Settlement Terms To Class Members.**— Any proposed or final settlement agreement that is published or otherwise disseminated to the class shall include each of the following statements, along with a cover page summarizing the information contained in such statements:

   A. **Statement Of Plaintiff Recovery.**—The amount of the settlement proposed to be distributed to the parties to the action, determined in the aggregate and on an average per share basis.

   B. **Statement Of Potential Outcome Of Case.**—

      i. **Agreement On Amount Of Damages.**— If the settling parties agree on the average amount of damages per share that would be recoverable if the plaintiff prevailed on each claim alleged under this title, a statement concerning the average amount of such potential damages per share.

      ii. **Disagreement Of Amount Of Damages.**— If the parties do not agree on the average amount of damages per share that would be recoverable if the plaintiff prevailed on each claim alleged under this title, a statement from each settling party concerning the issue or issues on which the parties disagree.

      iii. **Inadmissibility For Certain Purposes.**— A statement made in accordance with clause (i) or (ii) concerning the amount of damages shall not be admissible in any Federal or State judicial action or administrative proceeding, other than an action or proceeding arising out of such statement.

   C. **Statement Of Attorney's Fees Or Costs Sought.**— If any of the settling parties or their counsel intend to apply to the court for any award of attorney's fees or costs from any fund established as part of the settlement, a statement indicating which parties or counsel intend to make such an application, the amount of fees and costs that will be sought (including the amount of such fees and costs determined on an average per share basis), and a brief explanation supporting the fees and costs sought. Such information shall be clearly summarized on the cover page of any notice to a party of any proposed or final settlement agreement.

D. **Identification Of Lawyer's Representatives.**— The name, telephone number, and address of one or more representatives of counsel for the plaintiff class who will be reasonably available to answer question from class members concerning any matter contained in any notice of settlement published or otherwise disseminated to the class.

E. **Reasons For Settlement.**— A brief statement explaining the reasons why the parties are proposing the settlement.

F. **Other Information.**— Such other information as may be required by the court.

8. **Security For Payment Of Costs In Class Actions.**— In any private action arising under this title that is certified as a class action pursuant to the <u>Federal Rules of Civil Procedure</u>, the court may require an undertaking from the attorneys for the plaintiff class, the plaintiff class, or both, or from the attorneys for the defendant, the defendant, or both, in such proportions and at such times as the court determines are just and equitable, for the payment of fees and expenses that may be awarded under this subsection.

9. **Attorney Conflict Of Interest.**— If a plaintiff class is represented by an attorney who directly owns or otherwise has a beneficial interest in the securities that are the subject of the litigation, the court shall make a determination of whether such ownership or other interest constitutes a

conflict of interest sufficient to disqualify the attorney from representing the plaintiff class.

b. **Requirements For Securities Fraud Actions.**—

1. **Misleading Statements And Omissions**—In any private action arising under this title in which the plaintiff alleges that the defendant—

    A. made an untrue statement of a material fact; or

    B. omitted to state a material fact necessary in order to make the statements made, in the light of the circumstances in which they were made, not misleading;

    the complaint shall specify each statement alleged to have been misleading, the reason or reasons why the statement is misleading, and, if an allegation regarding the statement or omission is made on information and belief, the complaint shall state with particularity all facts on which that belief is formed.

2. **Required State Of Mind.**—In any private action arising under this title in which the plaintiff may recover money damages only on proof that the defendant acted with a particular stale of mind, the complaint shall, with respect to each act or omission alleged to violate this title, state with particularity facts giving rise to a strong inference that the defendant acted with the required state of mind.

3. **Motion To Dismiss; Stay Of Discovery.**—

    A. **Dismissal For Failure To Meet Pleading Requirements.**—In any private action arising under this title, the court shall, on the motion of any defendant, dismiss the complaint if the requirements of paragraphs (1) and (2) are not met.

    B. **Stay Of Discovery.**—In any private action arising under this title, all discovery and other proceedings shall be stayed during the pendency of any motion to dismiss, unless the court finds upon the motion of any party that particularized discovery is necessary to preserve evidence or to prevent undue prejudice to that party.

C.   Preservation Of Evidence.—

    i.   **In General.**—During the pendency of any stay of discovery pursuant too this paragraph, unless otherwise ordered by the court, any party to the action with actual notice of the allegations contained in the complaint shall treat all documents, data compilations (including electronically recorded or stored data), and tangible objects that are in the custody or control of such person and that are relevant to the allegations, as if they were the subject of a continuing request for production of documents from an opposing party under the Federal Rules of Civil Procedure.

    ii.   **Sanction For Willful Violation.**—A party aggrieved by the willful failure of an opposing party to comply with clause (i) may apply to the court for an order awarding appropriate sanctions.

4.   **Loss Causation.**—In any private action arising under this title, the plaintiff shall have the burden of proving that the act or omission of the defendant alleged to violate this title caused the loss for which the plaintiff seeks to recover damages.

c.   Sanctions For Abusive Litigation.—

1.   **Mandatory Review By Court**—In any private action arising under this title, upon final adjudication of the action, the court shall include in the record specific findings regarding compliance by each party and each attorney representing any party with each requirement of Rule 11(b) of the Federal Rules of Civil Procedure as to any complaint, responsive pleading, or dispositive motion.

2.   **Mandatory Sanctions.**—If the court makes a finding under paragraph (1) that a party or attorney violated any

requirement of <u>Rule 11(b) of the Federal Rules of Civil Procedure</u> as to any complaint, responsive pleading, or dispositive motion, the court shall impose sanctions on such party or attorney in accordance with <u>Rule 11 of the Federal Rules of Civil Procedure</u>. Prior to making a finding that any party or attorney has violated <u>Rule 11 of the Federal Rules of Civil Procedure</u>, the court shall give such party or attorney notice and an opportunity to respond.

3. **Presumption In Favor Of Attorneys' Fees And Costs.—**

    A. **In General.**—Subject to <u>subparagraphs (B)</u> and <u>(C)</u>, for purposes of <u>paragraph (2)</u>, the court shall adopt a presumption that the appropriate sanction—

        i.   for failure of any responsive pleading or dispositive motion to comply with any requirement of <u>Rule 11(b) of the Federal Rules of Civil Procedure</u> is an award to the opposing party of the reasonable attorneys' fees and other expenses incurred as a direct result of the violation; and

        ii. for substantial failure of any complaint to comply with any requirement of <u>Rule 11(b) of the Federal Rules of Civil Procedure</u> is an award to the opposing party of the reasonable attorneys' fees and other expenses incurred in the action.

    B. **Rebuttal Evidence.**—The presumption described in <u>subparagraph (A)</u> may be rebutted only upon proof by the party or attorney against whom sanctions are to be imposed that—

        i.   the award of attorneys' fees and other expenses will impose an unreasonable burden on that party or attorney and would be unjust, and the failure to make such an award would not impose a greater burden on the party in whose favor sanctions are to be imposed; or

        ii. the violation of <u>Rule 11(b) of the Federal Rules of Civil Procedure</u> was de minimis.

    C. **Sanctions.**—If the party or attorney against whom sanctions are to be imposed meets its burden under <u>subparagraph (B)</u>, the court shall award the sanctions that the court deems appropriate pursuant to<u>Rule 11 of the Federal Rules of Civil Procedure</u>.

d. **(d) Defendant's right to written interrogatories.**—In any private action arising under this title in which the plaintiff may recover money damages, the court shall, when requested by a defendant, submit to the jury a written interrogatory on the issue of each such defendant's state of mind at the time the alleged violation occurred.

e. **Limitation On Damages.**—

    1. **In General.**—Except as provided in <u>paragraph (2)</u>, in any private action arising under this title in which the plaintiff seeks to establish damages by reference to the market price of a security, the award of damages to the plaintiff shall not exceed the difference between the purchase or sale price paid or received, as appropriate, by the plaintiff for the subject security and the mean trading price of that security during the 90-day period beginning on the date on which the information correcting the misstatement or omission that is the basis for the action is disseminated to the market.

    2. **Exception.**—In any private action arising under this title in which the plaintiff seeks to establish damages by reference to the market price of a security, if the plaintiff sells or repurchases the subject security prior to the expiration of the 90-day period described in <u>paragraph (1)</u>, the plaintiff's damages shall not exceed the difference between the purchase or sale price paid or received, as appropriate, by the plaintiff for the security and the mean trading price of the security during the period beginning immediately after dissemination of information correcting the misstatement or omission and ending on the date on which the plaintiff sells or repurchases the security.

    3. **Definition.**—For purposes of this subsection, the "mean trading price" of a security shall be an average of the daily

trading price of that security, determined as of the close of the market each day during the 90-day period referred to in paragraph (1).

f. **[Reserved]**

g. **Proportionate Liability.—**

1. **Applicability.—**Nothing in this subsection shall be construed to create, affect, or in any manner modify, the standard for liability associated with any action arising under the securities laws.

2. **Liability For Damages.—**

    A. **Joint And Several Liability.—**Any covered person against whom a final judgment is entered in a private action shall be liable for damages jointly and severally only if the trier of fact specifically determines that such covered person knowingly committed a violation of the securities laws.

    B. **Proportionate Liability.—**

        i. **In General.—**Except as provided in paragraph (1), a covered person against whom a final judgment is entered in a private action shall be liable solely for the portion of the judgment that corresponds to the percentage of responsibility of that covered person, as determined under paragraph (3).

        ii. **Recovery by and costs of covered person.—**In any case in which a contractual relationship permits, a covered person that prevails in any private action may recover the attorney's fees and costs of that covered person in connection with the action.

3. **Determination Of Responsibility.—**

    A. **In General.—**In any private action, the court shall instruct the jury to answer special interrogatories, or if there is no jury, shall make findings, with respect to each covered person and each of the other persons claimed by any of the parties to have caused or contributed to the loss incurred by the plaintiff, including persons who have entered into settlements with the plaintiff or plaintiffs, concerning—

1. whether such person violated the securities laws;

2. the percentage of responsibility of such person, measured as a percentage of the total fault of all persons who caused or contributed to the loss incurred by the plaintiff; and

3. whether such person knowingly committed a violation of the securities laws.

B. **Contents Of Special Interrogatories Or Findings.**—The responses to interrogatories, or findings, as appropriate, under subparagraph (A) shall specify the total amount of damages that the plaintiff is entitled to recover and the percentage of responsibility of each covered person found to have caused or contributed to the loss incurred by the plaintiff or plaintiffs.

C. **Factors For Consideration.**—In determining the percentage of responsibility under this paragraph, the trier of fact shall consider—

i. the nature of the conduct of each covered person found to have caused or contributed to the loss incurred by the plaintiff or plaintiffs; and

ii. the nature and extent of the causal relationship between the conduct of each such person and the damages incurred by the plaintiff or plaintiffs.

4. **Uncollectible Share.**—

A. **In General.**—Notwithstanding paragraph (2)(B), upon motion made not later than 6 months after a final judgment is entered in any private action, the court determines that all or part of the share of the judgment of the covered person is not collectible against that covered person, and is also not collectible against a covered person described in paragraph (2)(A), each covered person described in paragraph (2)(B) shall be liable for the uncollectible share as follows:

    i. **Percentage Of Net Worth.**—Each covered person shall be jointly and severally liable for the uncollectible share if the plaintiff establishes that—

        I. the plaintiff is an individual whose recoverable damages under the final judgment are equal to more than 10 percent of the net worth of the plaintiff; and

        II. the net worth of the plaintiff is equal to less than $200,000.

    ii. **Other Plaintiffs.**—With respect to any plaintiff not described in subclauses (I) and (II) of clause (i), each covered person shall be liable for the uncollectible share in proportion to the percentage of responsibility of that covered person, except that the total liability of a covered person under this clause may not exceed 50 percent of the proportionate share of that covered person, as determined under paragraph (3)(B).

    iii. **Net Worth.**—For purposes of this subparagraph, net worth shall be determined as if the date immediately preceding the date of the purchase or sale (as applicable) by the plaintiff of the security that is the subject of the action, and shall be equal to the fair market value of assets, minus liabilities, including the net value of the investments of the plaintiff in real and personal property (including personal residences).

B. **Overall Limit.**—In no case shall the total payments required pursuant to subparagraph (A) exceed the amount of the uncollectible share.

C. **Covered Persons Subject To Contribution.**—A covered person against whom judgment is not collectible shall be subject to contribution and to any continuing liability to the plaintiff on the judgment.

5. **Right Of Contribution.**—To the extent that a covered person is required to make an additional payment pursuant to paragraph (4), that covered person may recover contribution—

A. from the covered person originally liable to make the payment;

B. from any covered person liable jointly and severally pursuant to paragraph (2)(A);

C. from any covered person held proportionately liable pursuant to this paragraph who is liable to make the same payment and has paid less than his or her proportionate share of that payment; or

D. from any other person responsible for the conduct giving rise to the payment that would have been liable to make the same payment.

6. **Nondisclosure To Jury.**—The standard for allocation of damages under paragraphs (2) and (3) and the procedure for reallocation of uncollectible shares under paragraph (4) shall not be disclosed to members of the jury.

7. **Settlement Discharge.**—

A. **In General.**—A covered person who settles any private action at any time before final verdict or judgment shall be discharged from all claims for contribution brought by other persons. Upon entry of the settlement by the court, the court shall enter a bar order constituting the final discharge of all obligations to the plaintiff of the settling covered person arising out of the action. The order shall bar all future claims for contribution arising out of the action—

    i. by any person against the settling covered person; and

    ii. by the settling covered person against any person, other than a person whose liability has been extinguished by the settlement of the settling covered person.

B. **Reduction.**—If a covered person enters into a settlement with the plaintiff prior to final verdict or judgment, the verdict or judgment shall be reduced by the greater of—

    i. an amount that corresponds to the percentage of responsibility of that covered person; or

    ii. the amount paid to the plaintiff by that covered person.

8. **Contribution.**—A covered person who becomes jointly and severally liable for damages in any private action may recover contribution from any other person who, if joined in the original action, would have been liable for the same damages. A claim for contribution shall be determined based on the percentage of responsibility of the claimant and of each person against whom a claim for contribution is made.

9. **Statute Of Limitations For Contribution.**—In any private action determining liability, an action for contribution shall be brought not later than 6 months after the entry of a final, nonappealable judgment in the action, except that an action for contribution brought by a covered person who was required to make an additional payment pursuant to paragraph (4) may be brought not later than 6 months after the date on which such payment was made.

10. **Definitions.**—For purposes of this subsection—

    A. A covered person "knowingly commits a violation of the securities laws"—

        i. with respect to an action that is based on an untrue statement of material fact or omission of a material fact necessary to make the statement not misleading, if—

            I. that covered person makes an untrue statement of a material fact, with actual knowledge that the representation is false, or omits to state a fact necessary in order to make the statement made not misleading, with actual knowledge that, as a result of the omission, one of the material representations of the covered person is false; and

            II. persons are likely to reasonably rely on that misrepresentation or omission; and

        ii. with respect to all action that is based on any conduct that is not described in clause (i), if that covered person engages in that conduct with actual knowledge of the facts and circumstances that make the conduct of that covered person a violation of the securities laws;

    B. reckless conduct by a covered person shall not be construed to constitute a knowing commission of a violation of the securities laws by that covered person;

    C. the term "covered person" means—

        i. a defendant in any private action arising under this title; or

        ii. a defendant in any private action arising under section 11 of the Securities Act of

1933, who is an outside director of the issuer of the securities that are the subject of
the action; and

D. the term "outside director" shall have the meaning
given such term by rule or regulation of the Commission.

SECTION 21E—APPLICATION OF SAFE HARBOR FOR FORWARD-LOOKING STATEMENTS

a. **Applicability.**—This section shall apply only to a forward-looking statement made by—

1. an issuer that, at the time that the statement is made, is subject to the reporting requirements of section 13(a) or section 15(d);

2. a person acting on behalf of such issuer;

3. an outside reviewer retained by such issuer making a statement on behalf of such issuer; or

4. an underwriter, with respect to information provided by
such issuer or information derived from information provided by such issuer.

b. **Exclusions.**—Except to the extent otherwise specifically provided
by rule, regulation, or order of the Commission, this section shall
not apply to a forward looking statement—

1. that is made with respect to the business or operations of
the issuer, if the issuer—

A. during the 3-year period preceding the date on
which the statement was first made—

i. was convicted of any felony or misdemeanor described in clauses (i) through
(iv) of section 15(b)(4)(B); or

ii. has been made the subject of a judicial or
administrative decree or order arising out
of a governmental action that—

          I.   prohibits future violations of the antifraud provisions of the securities laws;

          II. requires that the issuer cease and desist from violating the antifraud provisions of the securities laws; or

          III. determines that the issuer violated the antifraud provisions of the securities laws;

     B. makes the forward-looking statement in connection with an offering of securities by a blank check company;

     C. issues penny stock;

     D. makes the forward-looking statement in connection with a rollup transaction; or

     E. makes the forward-looking statement in connection with a going private transaction; or

2. that is—

     A. included in a financial statement prepared in accordance with generally accepted accounting principles;

     B. contained in a registration statement of, or otherwise issued by, an investment company;

     C. made in connection with a tender offer;

     D. made in connection with an initial public offering;

     E. made in connection with an offering by, or relating to the operations of, a partnership, limited liability company, or a direct participation investment program; or

     F. made in a disclosure of beneficial ownership in a report required to be filed with the Commission pursuant to section 13(d).

c. **Safe harbor.**—

    1. **In General.**—Except as provided in <u>subsection (b)</u>, in any private action arising under this title that is based on an untrue statement of a material fact or omission of a material fact necessary to make the statement not misleading, a person referred to in <u>subsection (a)</u> shall not be liable with respect to any forward-looking statement, whether written or oral, if and to the extent that—

        A. the forward-looking statement is—

            i. identified as a forward-looking statement, and is accompanied by meaningful cautionary statements identifying important factors that could cause actual results to differ materially from those in the forward-looking statement; or

            ii. immaterial; or

        B. the plaintiff fails to prove that the forward-looking statement—

            i. if made by a natural person, was made with actual knowledge by that person that the statement was false or misleading; or

            ii. if made by a business entity; was—

                I. made by or with the approval of an executive officer of that entity; and

                II. made or approved by such officer with actual knowledge by that officer that the statement was false or misleading.

    2. **Oral forward-looking statements.**—In the case of an oral forward-looking statement made by an issuer that is subject to the reporting requirements of <u>section 13(a)</u> or <u>section 15(d)</u>, or by a person acting on behalf of such issuer, the requirement set forth in <u>paragraph (1)(A)</u> shall be deemed to be satisfied—

    A. if the oral forward-looking statement is accompanied by a cautionary statement.—

        i. that the particular oral statement is a forward-looking statement; and

        ii. that the actual results might differ materially from those projected in the forward-looking statement; and

    B. if—

        i. the oral forward-looking statement is accompanied by an oral statement that additional information concerning factors that could cause actual results to materially differ from those in the forward-looking statement is contained in a readily available written document, or portion thereof;

        ii. the accompanying oral statement referred to in clause (i) identifies the document, or portion thereof, that contains the additional information about those factors relating to the forward-looking statement; and

        iii. the information contained in that written document is a cautionary statement that satisfies the standard established in paragraph (1)(A).

3. **Availability.**—Any document filed with the Commission or generally disseminated shall be deemed to be readily available for purposes of paragraph (2).

4. **Effect on other safe harbors.**—The exemption provided for in paragraph (1) shall be in addition to any exemption that the Commission may establish by rule or regulation under subsection (g).

d. **Duty To Update.**—Nothing in this section shall impose upon any person a duty to update a forward-looking statement.

e. **Dispositive Motion.**— On any motion to dismiss based upon subsection (c)(1), the court shall consider any statement cited in the complaint and any cautionary statement accompanying the forward-looking statement, which are not subject to material dispute, cited by the defendant.

f. **Stay Pending Decision on Motion.**—In any private action arising under this title, the court shall stay discovery (other than discovery that is specifically directed to the applicability of the exemption provided for in this section) during the pendency of any motion by a defendant for summary judgment that is based on the grounds that—

   1. the statement or omission upon which the complaint is based is a forward-looking statement within the meaning of this section; and

   2. the exemption provided for in this section precludes a claim for relief.

g. **Exemption Authority.**—In addition to the exemptions provided for in this section, the Commission may, by rule or regulation, provide exemptions from or under any provision of this title, including with respect to liability that is based on a statement or that is based on projections or other forward-looking information, if and to the extent that any such exemption is consistent with the public interest and the protection of investors, as determined by the Commission.

h. **Effect on Other Authority of Commission.**—Nothing in this section limits, either expressly or by implication, the authority of the Commission to exercise similar authority or to adopt similar rules and regulations with respect to forward-looking statements under any other statute under which the Commission exercises rulemaking authority.

i. **Definitions.**—For purposes of this section, the following definitions shall apply:

   1. **Forward-looking statement.**—The term "forward-looking statement" means—

      A. a statement containing a projection of revenues, income (including income loss), earnings (including earnings loss) per share, capital expenditures, dividends, capital structure, or other financial items;

    B. a statement of the plans and objectives of manage-
        ment for future operations, including plans or ob-
        jectives relating to the products or services of the
        issuer;

    C. a statement of future economic performance,
        including any such statement contained in a dis-
        cussion and analysis of financial condition by the
        management or in the results of operations in-
        cluded pursuant to the rules and regulations of the
        Commission;

    D. any statement of the assumptions underlying or re-
        lating to any statement described in subparagraph
        (A), (B), or(C);

    E. any report issued by an outside reviewer retained
        by an issuer, to the extent that the report assesses
        a forward-looking statement made by the issuer; or

    F. a statement containing a projection or estimate of
        such other items as may be specified by rule or reg-
        ulation of the Commission.

2. **Investment Company.**—The term "investment company"
has the same meaning as in section 3(a) of the Investment
Company Act of 1940.

3. **Going private transaction.**—The term "going private transaction" has the meaning given that term under the rules
or regulations of the Commission issued pursuant to section 13(e).

4. **Person acting on behalf of an issuer**—The term "person
acting on behalf of an issuer" means any officer, director,
or employee of such issuer.

5. **Other terms.**—The terms "blank check company", "rollup
transaction", "partnership", "limited liability company",
"executive officer of an entity" and "direct participation
investment program", have the meanings given those terms
by rule or regulation of the Commission.

SECTION 22—HEARINGS BY COMMISSION

Hearings may be public and may be held before the Commission, any member or members thereof, or any officer or officers of the Commission designated by it, and appropriate records thereof shall be kept.

SECTION 23—RULES, REGULATIONS, AND ORDERS; ANNUAL REPORTS

a.

1. The Commission, the Board of Governors of the Federal Reserve System, and the other agencies enumerated in section 3(a)(34) of this title shall each have power to make such rules and regulations as may be necessary or appropriate to implement the provisions of this title for which they are responsible or for the execution of the functions vested in them by this title, and may for such purposes classify persons, securities, transactions, statements, applications, reports, and other matters within their respective jurisdictions, and prescribe greater, lesser, or different requirements for different classes thereof. No provision of this title imposing any liability shall apply to any act done or omitted in good faith in conformity with a rule, regulation, or order of the Commission, the Board of Governors of the Federal Reserve System, other agency enumerated in section 3(a)(34) of this title, or any self-regulatory organization, notwithstanding that such rule, regulation, or order may thereafter be amended or rescinded or determined by judicial or other authority to be invalid for any reason.

2. The Commission and the Secretary of the Treasury, in making rules and regulations pursuant to any provisions of this title, shall consider among other matters the impact any such rule or regulation would have on competition. The Commission and the Secretary of the Treasury shall not adopt any such rule or regulation which would impose a burden on competition not necessary or appropriate in furtherance of the purposes of this title. The Commission and the Secretary of the Treasury shall include in the statement

of basis and purpose incorporated in any rule or regulation adopted under this title, the reasons for the Commission's or the Secretary's determination that any burden on competition imposed by such rule or regulation is necessary or appropriate in furtherance of the purposes of this title.

3. The Commission and the Secretary in making rules and regulations pursuant to any provision of this title, considering any application for registration in accordance with section 19(a) of this title, or reviewing any proposed rule change of a self-regulatory organization in accordance with section 19(b) of this title, shall keep in a public file and make available for copying all written statements filed with the Commission and the Secretary and all written communications between the Commission or the Secretary and any person relating to the proposed rule, regulation, application, or proposed rule change;

Provided, however,

That the Commission and the Secretary shall not be required to keep in a public file or make available for copying any such statement or communication which it may withhold from the public in accordance with the provisions of section 552 of title 5, United States Code.

b.

1. The Commission, the Board of Governors of the Federal Reserve System, and the other agencies enumerated in section 3(a)(34) of this title, shall each make an annual report to the Congress on its work for the preceding year, and shall include in each such report whatever information, data, and recommendations for further legislation it considers advisable with regard to matters within its respective jurisdiction under this title.

2. The appropriate regulatory agency for a self-regulatory organization shall include in its annual report to the Congress for each fiscal year, a summary of its oversight activities under this title with respect to such self-regulatory organization, including a description of any examination conducted as part of such activities of any such organization,

any material recommendation presented as part of such activities to such organization for changes in its organization or rules, and any action by such organization in response to any such recommendation.

3. The appropriate regulatory agency for any class of municipal securities dealers shall include in its annual report to the Congress for each fiscal year a summary of its regulatory activities pursuant to this title with respect to such municipal securities dealers, including the nature of and reason for any sanction imposed pursuant to this title against any such municipal securities dealers.

4. The Commission shall also include in its annual report to the Congress for each fiscal year—

    A. a summary of the Commission's oversight activities with respect to self-regulatory organizations for which it is not the appropriate regulatory agency, including a description of any examination of any such organization, any material recommendation presented to any such organization for changes in its organization or rules, and any action by such organization in response to any such recommendations;

    B. a statement and analysis of the expenses and operations of each self-regulatory organization in connection with the performance of its responsibilities under this title for which purpose data pertaining to such expenses and operations shall be made available by such organization to the Commission at its request;

    C. the steps the Commission has taken and the progress it has made toward ending the physical movement of the securities certificate in connection with the settlement of securities transactions, and its recommendations, if any, for legislation to eliminate the securities certificate;

    D. the number of requests for exemptions from provisions of this title received, the number granted, and the basis upon which any such exemption was granted;

E. a summary of the Commission's regulatory activities with respect to municipal securities dealers for which it is not the appropriate regulatory agency, including the number and nature of, and reason for, any sanction imposed in proceedings against such municipal securities dealers;

F. a statement of the time elapsed between the filing of reports pursuant to <u>section 13(f)</u> of this title and the public availability of the information contained therein, the costs involved in the Commission's processing of such reports and tabulating such information, the manner in which the Commission uses such information, and the steps the Commission has taken and the progress it has made toward requiring such reports to be filed and such information to be made available to the public in machine language;

G. information concerning

i.   the effects its rules and regulations are having on the viability of small brokers and dealers;

ii. its attempts to reduce any unnecessary reporting burden on such brokers and dealers; and

iii. its efforts to help to assure the continued participation of small brokers and dealers in the United States securities markets;

H. a statement detailing its administration of the Freedom of Information Act, <u>section 552</u> of title 5, United States Code, including a copy of the report filed pursuant to subsection (d) of such section; and

I. the steps that have been taken and the progress that has been made in promoting the timely public dissemination and availability for analytical purposes (on a fair, reasonable, and nondiscriminatory basis) of information concerning government securities transactions and quotations, and its recommendations, if any, for legislation to assure timely dissemination of

    i. information on transactions in regularly traded government securities sufficient to permit the determination of the prevailing market price for such securities, and

    ii. reports of the highest published bids and lowest published offers for government securities (including the size at which persons are willing to trade with respect to such bids and offers).

c. The Commission, by rule, shall prescribe the procedure applicable to every case pursuant to this title of adjudication (as defined in section 551 of title 5, United States Code) not required to be determined on the record after notice and opportunity for hearing. Such rules shall, as a minimum, provide that prompt notice shall be given of any adverse action or final disposition and that such notice and the entry of any order shall be accompanied by a statement of written reasons.

d. **Cease-and-Desist Procedures.**—Within 1 year after the date of enactment of this subsection, the Commission shall establish regulations providing for the expeditious conduct of hearings and rendering of decisions under section 21C of this title, section 8A of the Securities Act of 1933, section 9(f) of the Investment Company Act of 1940, and section 203(k) of the Investment Advisers Act of 1940.

SECTION 24—PUBLIC AVAILABILITY OF INFORMATION

a. For purposes of section 552 of title 5, United States Code, the term "records" includes all applications, statements, reports, contracts, correspondence, notices, and other documents filed with or otherwise obtained by the Commission pursuant to this title or otherwise.

b. It shall be unlawful for any member, officer, or employee of the Commission to disclose to any person other than a member, officer, or employee of the Commission, or to use for personal benefit, any information contained in any application, statement, report, contract, correspondence, notice, or other document filed with or otherwise obtained by the Commission

   1. in contravention of the rules and regulations of the Commission under <u>section 552</u> of title 5, United States Code, or

   2. in circumstances where the Commission has determined pursuant to such rules to accord confidential treatment to such information.

c. **Confidential Disclosures**—The Commission may, in its discretion and a showing that such information is needed, provide all "records" (as defined in <u>subsection (a)</u>) and other information in its possession to such persons, both domestic and foreign, as the Commission by rule deems appropriate if the person receiving such records or information provides such assurances of confidentiality as the Commission deems appropriate.

d. **Records Obtained from Foreign Securities Authorities.**— Except as provided in <u>subsection (e)</u>, the Commission shall not be compelled to disclose records obtained from a foreign securities authority if

   1. the foreign securities authority has in good faith determined and represented to the Commission that public disclosure of such records would violate the laws applicable to that foreign securities authority, and

   2. the Commission obtains such records pursuant to

      A. such procedure as the Commission may authorize for use in connection with the administration or enforcement of the securities laws, or

      B. a memorandum of understanding.

For purposes of <u>section 552</u> of title 5, United States Code, this subsection shall be considered a statute described in subsection <u>(b)(3)(B)</u> of such section 552.

e.   **Savings Provisions.**—Nothing in this section shall—

1.   alter the Commission's responsibilities under the <u>Right to Financial Privacy</u>, as limited by <u>section 21(h)</u> of this Act, with respect to transfers of records covered by such statutes, or

2.   authorize the Commission to withhold information from the Congress or prevent the Commission from complying with an order of a court of the United States in an action commenced by the United States or the Commission.

SECTION 25—COURT REVIEW OF ORDERS AND RULES

a.

1.   A person aggrieved by a final order of the Commission entered pursuant to this title may obtain review of the order in the United States Court of Appeals for the circuit in which he resides or has his principal place of business, or for the District of Columbia Circuit, by filing in such court, within sixty days after the entry of the order, a written petition requesting that the order be modified or set aside in whole or in part.

2.   A copy of the petition shall be transmitted forthwith by the clerk of the court to a member of the Commission or an officer designated by the Commission for that purpose. Thereupon the Commission shall file in the court the record on which the order complained of is entered, as provided in <u>section 2112</u> of title 28, United States Code, and the Federal Rules of Appellate Procedure.

3.   On the filing of the petition, the court has jurisdiction, which becomes exclusive on the filing of the record, to affirm or modify and enforce or to set aside the order in whole or in part.

4.   The findings of the Commission as to the facts, if supported by substantial evidence, are conclusive.

5. If either party applies to the court for leave to adduce additional evidence and shows to the satisfaction of the court that the additional evidence is material and that there was reasonable ground for failure to adduce it before the Commission, the court may remand the case to the Commission for further proceedings, in whatever manner and on whatever conditions the court considers appropriate. If the case is remanded to the Commission, it shall file in the court a supplemental record containing any new evidence, any further or modified findings, and any new order.

b.

1. A person adversely affected by a rule of the Commission promulgated pursuant to section 6, 9(h)(2), 11, 11A, 15(c)(5) or (6), 15A, 17, 17A, or 19 of this title may obtain review of this rule in the United States Court of Appeals for the circuit in which he resides or has his principal place of business or for the District of Columbia Circuit, by filing in such court, within sixty days after the promulgation of the rule, a written petition requesting that the rule be set aside.

2. A copy of the petition shall be transmitted forthwith by the clerk of the court to a member of the Commission or an officer designated for that purpose. Thereupon, the Commission shall file in the court the rule under review and any documents referred to therein, the Commission's notice of proposed rulemaking and any documents referred to therein, all written submissions and the transcript of any oral presentations in the rulemaking, factual information not included in the foregoing that was considered by the Commission in the promulgation of the rule or proffered by the Commission as pertinent to the rule, the report of any advisory committee received or considered by the Commission in the rulemaking, and any other materials prescribed by the court.

3. On the filing of the petition, the court has jurisdiction, which becomes exclusive on the filing of the materials set forth in paragraph (2) of this subsection, to affirm and enforce or to set aside the rule.

4. The findings of the Commission as to the facts identified by the Commission as the basis, in whole or in part, of the rule, if supported by substantial evidence, are conclusive. The court shall affirm and enforce the rule unless the Commission's action in promulgating the rule is found to be arbitrary, capricious, an abuse of discretion, or otherwise not in accordance with law; contrary to constitutional right, power, privilege or immunity; in excess of statutory jurisdiction, authority, or limitations, or short of statutory right; or without observance of procedure required by law.

5. If proceedings have been instituted under this subsection in two or more courts of appeals with respect to the same rule, the Commission shall file the materials set forth in paragraph (2) of this subsection in that court in which a proceeding was first instituted. The other courts shall thereupon transfer all such proceedings to the court in which the materials have been filed. For the convenience of the parties in the interest of justice that court may thereafter transfer all the proceedings to any other court of appeals.

c.

1. No objection to an order or rule of the Commission, for which review is sought under this section, may be considered by the court unless it was urged before the Commission or there was reasonable ground for failure to do so.

2. The filing of a petition under this section does not operate as a stay of the Commission's order or rule. Until the court's jurisdiction becomes exclusive, the Commission may stay its order or rule pending judicial review if it finds that justice so requires. After the filing of a petition under this section, the court, on whatever conditions may be required and to the extent necessary to prevent irreparable injury, may issue all necessary and appropriate process to stay the order or rule or to preserve status or rights pending its review; but (notwithstanding section 705 of title 5, United States Code) no such process may be issued by the court before the filing of the record or the materials set forth in subsection (b)(2) of this section unless:

A. the Commission has denied a stay or failed to grant requested relief,

B. a reasonable period has expired since the filing of an application for a stay without a decision by the Commission, or

C. there was reasonable ground for failure to apply to the Commission.

3. When the same order or rule is the subject of one or more petitions for review filed under this section and an action for enforcement filed in a district court of the United States under section 21 (d) or (e) of this title, that court in which the petition or the action is first filed has jurisdiction with respect to the order or rule to the exclusion of any other court, and thereupon all such proceedings shall be transferred to that court; but, for the convenience of the parties in the interest of justice, that court may thereafter transfer all the proceedings to any other court of appeals or district court of the United States, whether or not a petition for review or an action for enforcement was originally filed in the transferee court. The scope of review by a district court under section 21 (d) or (e) of this title is in all cases the same as by a court of appeals under this section.

d.

1. For purposes of the preceding subsections of this section, the term "Commission" includes the agencies enumerated in section 3(a)(34) of this title insofar as such agencies are acting pursuant to this title and the Secretary of the Treasury insofar as he is acting pursuant to section 15C of this title.

2. For purposes of subsection (a)(4) of this section and section 706 of title 5, United States Code, an order of the Commission pursuant to section 19(a) of this title denying registration to a clearing agency for which the Commission is not the appropriate regulatory agency or pursuant to section 19(b) of this title disapproving a proposed rule change by such a clearing agency shall be deemed to be an order

of the appropriate regulatory agency for such clearing agency insofar as such order was entered by reason of a determination by such appropriate regulatory agency pursuant to section 19(a)(2)(C) or 19(b)(4)(C) of this title that such registration or proposed rule change would be inconsistent with the safeguarding of securities or funds.

SECTION 26—UNLAWFUL REPRESENTATIONS

No action or failure to act by the Commission or the Board of Governors of the Federal Reserve System, in the administration of this title shall be construed to mean that the particular authority has in any way passed upon the merits of, or given approval to, any security or any transaction or transactions therein, nor shall such action or failure to act with regard to any statement or report filed with or examined by such authority pursuant to this title or rules and regulations thereunder, be deemed a finding by such authority that such statement or report is true and accurate on its face or that it is not false or misleading. It shall be unlawful to make, or cause to be made, to any prospective purchaser or seller of a security any representation that any such action or failure to act by any such authority is to be so construed or has such effect.

SECTION 27—JURISDICTION OF OFFENSES AND SUITS

The district courts of the United States and the United States courts of any Territory or other place subject to the jurisdiction of the United States shall have exclusive jurisdiction of violations of this title or the rules and regulations thereunder, and of all suits in equity and actions at law brought to enforce any liability or duty created by this title or the rules and regulations thereunder. Any criminal proceeding may be brought in the district wherein any act or transaction constituting the violation occurred. Any suit or action to enforce any liability or duty created by this title or rules and regulations thereunder, or to enjoin any violation of such title or rules and regulations, may be brought in any such district or in the district wherein the defendant is found or is an inhabitant or transacts business, and process in such cases may be served in any other district of which the defendant is an inhabitant or wherever the defendant may be found. Judgments and decrees so rendered shall be subject to review as provided in sections <u>1254</u>, <u>1291</u>, <u>1292</u> and <u>1294</u> of title 28, United States Code. No costs shall be assessed for or against the Commission in any proceeding under this title brought by or against it in the Supreme Court or such other courts.

SECTION 27A—SPECIAL PROVISION RELATING TO STATUTE OF LIMITATIONS ON PRIVATE CAUSES OF ACTION

a. **Effect on Pending Causes of Action.**—The limitation period for any private civil action implied under <u>section 10(b)</u> of this Act that was commenced on or before June 19, 1991, shall be the limitation period provided by the laws applicable in the jurisdiction, including principles of retroactivity, as such laws existed on June 19, 1991.

b. **Effect on Dismissed Causes of Action.**— Any private civil action implied under <u>section 10(b)</u> of this Act that was commenced on or before June 19, 1991—

    1. which was dismissed as time barred subsequent to June 19, 1991, and

    2. which would have been timely filed under the limitation period provided by the laws applicable in the jurisdiction, including principles of retroactivity, as such laws existed on June 19, 1991,

shall be reinstated on motion by the plaintiff not later than 60 days after the date of enactment of this section.

SECTION 28—EFFECT ON EXISTING LAW

a. The rights and remedies provided by this title shall be in addition to any and all other rights and remedies that may exist at law or in equity; but no person permitted to maintain a suit for damages under the provisions of this title shall recover, through satisfaction of judgment in one or more actions, a total amount in excess of his actual damages on account of the act complained of. Nothing in this title shall affect the jurisdiction of the securities commission (or any agency or officer performing like functions) of any State over any security or any person insofar as it does not conflict with the provisions of this title or the rules and regulations thereunder. No State law which prohibits or regulates the making or promoting of wagering or gaming contracts, or the operation of "bucket shops" or other similar or related activities, shall invalidate any put, call, straddle, option, privilege, or other security, or apply to any activity which is incidental or related to the offer, purchase, sale, exercise, settlement, or closeout of any such instrument, if such instrument is traded pursuant to rules and regulations of a self-regulatory organization that are filed with the Commission pursuant to section 19(b) of this Act.

b.   Nothing in this title shall be construed to modify existing law with regard to the binding effect

1.   on any member of or participant in any self-regulatory organization of any action taken by the authorities of such organization to settle disputes between its members or participants,

2.   on any municipal securities dealer or municipal securities broker of any action taken pursuant to a procedure established by the Municipal Securities Rulemaking Board, to settle disputes between municipal securities dealers and municipal securities brokers, or

3.   of any action described in paragraph (1) or (2) on any person who has agreed to be bound thereby.

c.   The stay, setting aside, or modification pursuant to section 19(e) of this title of any disciplinary sanction imposed by a self-regulatory organization on a member thereof, person associated with a member, or participant therein, shall not affect the validity or force of any action taken as a result of such sanction by the self-regulatory organization prior to such stay, setting aside, or modification:

Provided,

That such action is not inconsistent with the provisions of this title or the rules or regulations thereunder. The rights of any person acting in good faith which arise out of any such action shall not be affected in any way by such stay, setting aside, or modification.

d. No State or political subdivision thereof shall impose any tax on any change in beneficial or record ownership of securities effected through the facilities of a registered clearing agency or registered transfer agent or any nominee thereof or custodian therefor or upon the delivery or transfer of securities to or through or receipt from such agency or agent or any nominee thereof or custodian therefor, unless such change in beneficial or record ownership or such transfer or delivery or receipt would otherwise be taxable by such State or political subdivision if the facilities of such registered clearing agency, registered transfer agent, or any nominee thereof or custodian therefor were not physically located in the taxing State or political subdivision. No State or political subdivision thereof shall impose any tax on securities which are deposited in or retained by a registered clearing agency, registered transfer agent, or any nominee thereof or custodian therefor, unless such securities would otherwise be taxable by such State or political subdivision if the facilities of such registered clearing agency, registered transfer agent, or any nominee thereof or custodian therefor were not physically located in the taxing State or political subdivision.

e.

1. No person using the mails, or any means or instrumentality of interstate commerce, in the exercise of investment discretion with respect to an account shall be deemed to have acted unlawfully or to have breached a fiduciary duty under State or Federal law unless expressly provided to the contrary by a law enacted by the Congress or any State subsequent to the date of enactment of the Securities Acts Amendments of 1975 solely by reason of his having caused the account to pay a member of an exchange, broker, or dealer an amount of commission for effecting a securities transaction in excess of the amount of commission another member of an exchange, broker, or dealer would have charged for effecting that transaction, if such person determined in good faith that such amount of commission was reasonable in relation to the value of the brokerage and research services provided by such member, broker, or

dealer, viewed in terms of either that particular transaction or his overall responsibilities with respect to the accounts as to which he exercises investment discretion. This subsection is exclusive and plenary insofar as conduct is covered by the foregoing, unless otherwise expressly provided by contract:

Provided, however,

That nothing in this subsection shall be construed to impair or limit the power of the Commission under any other provision of this title or otherwise.

2. A person exercising investment discretion with respect to an account shall make such disclosure of his policies and practices with respect to commissions that will be paid for effecting securities transactions, at such times and in such manner, as the appropriate regulatory agency, by rule, may prescribe as necessary or appropriate in the public interest or for the protection of investors.

3. For purposes of this subsection a person provides brokerage and research services insofar as he—

    A. furnishes advice, either directly or through publications or writings, as to the value of securities, the advisability of investing in, purchasing, or selling securities, and the availability of securities or purchasers or sellers of securities;

    B. furnishes analyses and reports concerning issuers, industries, securities, economic factors and trends, portfolio strategy, and the performance of accounts; or

    C. effects securities transactions and performs functions incidental thereto (such as clearance, settlement, and custody) or required in connection therewith by rules of the Commission or a self-regulatory organization of which such person is a member or person associated with a member or in which such person is a participant.

SECTION 29—VALIDITY OF CONTRACTS

a. Any condition, stipulation, or provision binding any person to waive compliance with any provision of this title or of any rule or regulation thereunder, or of any rule of an exchange required thereby shall be void.

b. Every contract made in violation of any provision of this title or of any rule or regulation thereunder, and every contract (including any contract for listing a security on an exchange) heretofore or hereafter made the performance of which involves the violation of, or the continuance of any relationship or practice in violation of, any provision of this title or any rule or regulation thereunder, shall be void

   1. as regards the rights of any person who, in violation of any such provision, rule, or regulation, shall have made or engaged in the performance of any such contract, and

   2. as regards the rights of any person who, not being a party to such contract, shall have acquired any right thereunder with actual knowledge of the facts by reason of which the making or performance of such contract was in violation of any such provision, rule or regulation:

   Provided,

      A. That no contract shall be void by reason of this subsection because of any violation of any rule or regulation prescribed pursuant to paragraph (3) of subsection (c) of section 15 of this title, and

      B. that no contract shall be deemed to be void by reason of this subsection in any action maintained in reliance upon this subsection, by any person to or for whom any broker or dealer sells, or from or for whom any broker or dealer purchases, a security in violation of any rule or regulation prescribed pursuant to paragraph (1) or (2) of subsection (c) of section 15 of this title, unless such action is brought within one year after the discovery that such sale or purchase involves such violation and within 3 years after such violation.

The Commission may, in a rule or regulation prescribed pursuant to such paragraph (2), of such section 15(c), designate such rule or regulation, or portion thereof, as a rule or regulation, or portion thereof, a contract in violation of which shall not be void by reason of this subsection.

c. Nothing in this title shall be construed

1. to affect the validity of any loan or extension of credit (or any extension or renewal thereof) made or of any lien created prior or subsequent to the enactment of this title, unless at the time of the making of such loan or extension of credit (or extension or renewal thereof) or the creating of such lien, the person making such loan or extension of credit (or extension or renewal thereof) or acquiring such lien shall have actual knowledge of facts by reason of which the making of such loan or extension of credit (or extension or renewal thereof) or the acquisition of such lien is a violation of the provisions of this title or any rule or regulation thereunder, or

2. to afford a defense to the collection of any debt or obligation or the enforcement of any lien by any person who shall have acquired such debt, obligation, or lien in good faith for value and without actual knowledge of the violation of any provision of this title or any rule or regulation thereunder affecting the legality of such debt, obligation, or lien.

SECTION 30—FOREIGN SECURITIES EXCHANGES

a. It shall be unlawful for any broker or dealer, directly or indirectly, to make use of the mails or of any means or instrumentality of interstate commerce for the purpose of effecting on an exchange not within or subject to the jurisdiction of the United States, any transaction in any security the issuer of which is a resident of, or is organized under the laws of, or has its principal place of business in, a place within or subject to the jurisdiction of the United States, in contravention of such rules and regulations as the Commission may prescribe as necessary or appropriate in the public interest or for the protection of investors or to prevent the evasion of this title.

b. The provisions of this title or of any rule or regulation thereunder shall not apply to any person insofar as he transacts a business in securities without the jurisdiction of the United States, unless he transacts such business in contravention of such rules and regulations as the Commission may prescribe as necessary or appropriate to prevent the evasion of this title.

SECTION 30A—PROHIBITED FOREIGN TRADE PRACTICES BY ISSUERS

a. **Prohibition**—It shall be unlawful for any issuer which has a class of securities registered pursuant to section 12 of this title or which is required to file reports under section 15(d) of this title, or for any officer, director, employee, or agent of such issuer or any stockholder thereof acting on behalf of such issuer, to make use of the mails or any means or instrumentality of interstate commerce corruptly in furtherance of an offer, payment, promise to pay, or authorization of the payment of any money, or offer, gift, promise to give, or authorization of the giving of anything of value to—

   1. any foreign official for purposes of—

      A.

         i. influencing any act or decision of such foreign official in his official capacity, or

         ii. inducing such foreign official to do or omit to do any act in violation of the lawful duty of such official, or

      B. inducing such foreign official to use his influence with a foreign government or instrumentality thereof to affect or influence any act or decision of such government or instrumentality, in order to assist such issuer in obtaining or retaining business for or with, or directing business to, any person;

   2. any foreign political party or official thereof or any candidate for foreign political office for purposes of—

A.

    i. influencing any act or decision of such party, official, or candidate in its or his official capacity, or

    ii. inducing such party, official, or candidate to do or omit to do and act in violation of the lawful duty of such party, official, or candidate,

B. inducing such party, official or candidate to use its or his influence with a foreign government or instrumentality thereof to affect or influence any act or decision of such government or instrumentality, in order to assist such issuer in obtaining or retaining business for or with, or directing business to, any person; or

3. any person, while knowing that all or a portion of such money or thing of value will be offered, given, or promised, directly or indirectly, to any foreign official, to any foreign political party or official thereof, or to any candidate for foreign political office, for purposes of—

A.

    i. influencing any act or decision of such foreign official, political party, party official, or candidate in his or its official capacity, or

    ii. inducing such foreign official, political party, party official, or candidate to do or omit to do any act in violation of the lawful duty of such foreign official, political party, party official or candidate, or

B. inducing such foreign official, political party, party official, or candidate to use his or its influence with a foreign government or instrumentality thereof to affect or influence any act or decision of such government or instrumentality, in order to assist such issuer in obtaining or retaining business for or with, or directing business to, any person.

b. **Exception for Routine Governmental Action**—Subsection (a) shall not apply to any facilitating or expediting payment to a foreign official, political party, or party official the purpose of which is to expedite or to secure the performance of a routine governmental action by a foreign official, political party, or party official.

c. **Affirmative Defenses**—It shall be an affirmative defense to actions under subsection (a) that—

   1. the payment, gift, offer, or promise of anything of value that was made, was lawful under the written laws and regulations of the foreign official's, political party's, party official's, or candidate's country; or

   2. the payment, gift, offer, or promise of anything of value that was made, was a reasonable and bona fide expenditure, such as travel and lodging expenses, incurred by or on behalf of a foreign official, party, party official, or candidate and was directly related to—

      A. the promotion, demonstration, or explanation of products or services; or

      B. the execution or performance of a contract with a foreign government or agency thereof.

d. **Guidelines by the Attorney General**—Not later than one year after the date of the enactment of the Foreign Corrupt Practices Act Amendments of 1988, the Attorney General, after consultation with the Commission, the Secretary of Commerce, the United States Trade Representative, the Secretary of State, and the Secretary of the Treasury, and after obtaining the views of all interested persons through public notice and comment procedures, shall determine to what extent compliance with this section would be enhanced and the business community would be assisted by further clarification of the preceding provisions of this section and may, based on such determination and to the extent necessary and appropriate, issue—

   1. guidelines describing specific types of conduct, associated with common types of export sales arrangements and

business contracts, which for purposes of the Department of Justice's present enforcement policy, the Attorney General determines would be in conformance with the preceding provisions of this section; and

2. general precautionary procedures which issuers may use on a voluntary basis to conform their conduct to the Department of Justice's present enforcement policy regarding the preceding provisions of this section.

The Attorney General shall issue the guidelines and procedures referred to in the preceding sentence in accordance with the provisions of subchapter II of chapter 5 of title 5, United States Code, and those guidelines and procedures shall be subject to the provisions of chapter 7 of that title.

e. **Opinions of the Attorney General**

1. The Attorney General, after consultation with appropriate departments and agencies of the United States and after obtaining the views of all interested persons through public notice and comment procedures, shall establish a procedure to provide responses to specific inquiries by issuers concerning conformance of their conduct with the Department of Justice's present enforcement policy regarding the preceding provisions of this section. The Attorney General shall, within 30 days after receiving such a request, issue an opinion in response to that request. The opinion shall state whether or not certain specified prospective conduct would, for purposes of the Department of Justice's present enforcement policy, violate the preceding provisions of this section. Additional requests for opinions may be filed with the Attorney General regarding other specified prospective conduct that is beyond the scope of conduct specified in previous requests. In any action brought under the applicable provisions of this section, there shall be a rebuttable presumption that conduct, which is specified in a request by an issuer and for which the Attorney General has issued an opinion that such conduct is in conformity with the Department of Justice's present enforcement policy, is in compliance with the preceding provisions of this section.

Such a presumption may be rebutted by a preponderance of the evidence. In considering the presumption for purposes of this paragraph, a court shall weigh all relevant factors, including but not limited to whether the information submitted to the Attorney General was accurate and complete and whether it was within the scope of the conduct specified in any request received by the Attorney General. The Attorney General shall establish the procedures required by this paragraph in accordance with the provisions of subchapter II of chapter 5 of title 5, United States Code, and that procedure shall be subject to the provisions of chapter 7 of that title.

2. Any document or other material which is provided to, received by, or prepared in the Department of Justice or any other department or agency of the United States in connection with a request by an issuer under the procedure established under paragraph (1), shall be exempt from disclosure under section 552 of title 5, United States Code, and shall not, except with the consent of the issuer, be made publicly available, regardless of whether the Attorney General responds to such a request or the issuer withdraws such request before receiving a response.

3. Any issuer who has made a request to the Attorney General under paragraph (1) may withdraw such request prior to the time the Attorney General issues an opinion in response to such request. Any request so withdrawn shall have no force or effect.

4. The Attorney General shall, to the maximum extent practicable, provide timely guidance concerning the Department of Justice's present enforcement policy with respect to the preceding provisions of this section to potential exporters and small businesses that are unable to obtain specialized counsel on issues pertaining to such provisions. Such guidance shall be limited to responses to requests under paragraph (1) concerning conformity of specified prospective conduct with the Department of Justice's present enforcement policy regarding the preceding provisions

of this section and general explanations of compliance responsibilities and of potential liabilities under the preceding provisions of this section.

f. **Definitions**—For purposes of this section:

1. The term "foreign official" means any officer or employee
    of a foreign government or any department, agency, or in-
    strumentality thereof, or any person acting in an official
    capacity for or on behalf of any such government or depart-
    ment, agency, or instrumentality.

2.

   A. A person's state of mind is "knowing" with respect
       to conduct, a circumstance, or a result if—

       i.   such person is aware that such person is
            engaging in such conduct, that such cir-
            cumstance exists, or that such result is sub-
            stantially certain to occur; or

       ii. such person has a firm belief that such cir-
            cumstance exists or that such result is sub-
            stantially certain to occur.

   B. When knowledge of the existence of a particular
       circumstance is required for an offense, such
       knowledge is established if a person is aware of a
       high probability of the existence of such circum-
       stance, unless the person actually believes that such
       circumstance does not exist.

3.

   A. The term "routine governmental action" means
       only an action which is ordinarily and commonly
       performed by a foreign official in—

       i.   obtaining permits, licenses, or other offi-
            cial documents to qualify a person to do
            business in a foreign country;

       ii. processing governmental papers, such as
            visas and work orders;

        iii. providing police protection, mail pick-up and delivery, or scheduling inspections associated with contract performance or inspections related to transit of goods across country;

        iv. providing phone service, power and water supply, loading and unloading cargo, or protecting perishable products or commodities from deterioration; or

        v. actions of a similar nature.

    B. The term "routine governmental action" does not include any decision by a foreign official whether, or on what terms, to award new business to or to continue business with a particular party, or any action taken by a foreign official involved in the decision making process to encourage a decision to award new business to or continue business with a particular party.

SECTION 31—TRANSACTION FEES

a. RECOVERY OF COST OF SERVICES—The Commission shall, in accordance with this subsection, collect transaction fees that are designed to recover the costs to the Government of the supervision and regulation of securities markets and securities professionals, and costs related to such supervision and regulation, including enforcement activities, policy and rulemaking activities, administration, legal services, and international regulatory activities.

b. EXCHANGE-TRADED SECURITIES—Every national securities exchange shall pay to the Commission a fee at a rate equal to 1/300 of one percent of the aggregate dollar amount of sales of securities (other than bonds, debentures, and other evidences of indebtedness) transacted on such national securities exchange, except that for fiscal year 2007 or any succeeding fiscal year such rate shall be equal to 1/800 of one percent of such aggregate dollar amount of sales. Fees collected pursuant to this subsection shall be deposited and collected as general revenue of the Treasury.

c.   OFF-EXCHANGE TRADES OF EXCHANGE REGISTERED SECURITIES—Each national securities association shall pay to the Commission a fee at a rate equal to 1/300 of one percent of the aggregate dollar amount of sales transacted by or through any member of such association otherwise than on a national securities exchange of securities registered on such an exchange (other than bonds, debentures, and other evidences of indebtedness), except that for fiscal year 2007 or any succeeding fiscal year such rate shall be equal to 1/800 of one percent of such aggregate dollar amount of sales. Fees collected pursuant to this subsection shall be deposited and collected as general revenue of the Treasury.

d.   OFF-EXCHANGE TRADES OF LAST-SALE-REPORTED SECURITIES—

     1.   COVERED TRANSACTIONS—Each national securities association shall pay to the Commission a fee at a rate equal to 1/300 of one percent of the aggregate dollar amount of sales transacted by or through any member of such association otherwise than on a national securities exchange of securities (other than bonds, debentures, and other evidences of indebtedness) subject to prompt last sale reporting pursuant to the rules of the Commission or a registered national securities association, excluding any sales for which a fee is paid under subsection (c), except that for fiscal year 2007, or any succeeding fiscal year, such rate shall be equal to 1/800 of one percent of such aggregate dollar amount of sale.

     2.   LIMITATION; DEPOSIT OF FEES—Except as provided in paragraph (3), no amounts shall be collected pursuant to subsection (d) for any fiscal year, except to the extent provided in advance in appropriations Acts. Fees collected during any such fiscal year pursuant to this subsection shall be deposited and credited as offsetting collections to the account providing appropriations to the Commission.

     3.   LAPSE OF APPROPRIATIONS—If on the first day of a fiscal year a regular appropriation to the Commission has not been enacted, the Commission shall continue to collect fees (as offsetting collections) under this subsection at the

rate in effect during the preceding fiscal year, until such a regular appropriation is enacted.

e. DATES FOR PAYMENT OF FEES—The fees required by subsections (b), (c), and (d) of this section shall be paid—

1. on or before March 15, with respect to transactions and sales occurring during the period beginning on the preceding September 1 and ending at the close of the preceding December 31; and

2. on or before September 30, with respect to transactions and sales occurring during the period beginning on the preceding January 1 and ending at the close of the preceding August 31.

SECTION 32—PENALTIES

a. Any person who willfully violates any provision of this title (other than section 30A), or any rule or regulation thereunder the violation of which is made unlawful or the observance of which is required under the terms of this title, or any person who willfully and knowingly makes, or causes to be made, any statement in any application, report, or document required to be filed under this title or any rule or regulation thereunder or any undertaking contained in a registration statement as provided in subsection (d) of section 15 of this title or by any self-regulatory organization in connection with an application for membership or participation therein or to become associated with a member thereof, which statement was false or misleading with respect to any material fact, shall upon conviction be fined not more than $1,000,000 or imprisoned not more than 10 years, or both, except that when such person is a person other than a natural person, a fine not exceeding $2,500,000 may be imposed; but no person shall be subject to imprisonment under this section for the violation of any rule or regulation if he proves that he had no knowledge of such rule or regulation.

b. Any issuer which fails to file information, documents, or reports required to be filed under subsection (d) of section 15 of this title or any rule or regulation thereunder shall forfeit to the United

States the sum of $100 for each and every day such failure to file shall continue. Such forfeiture, which shall be in lieu of any criminal penalty for such failure to file which might be deemed to arise under subsection (a) of this section, shall be payable into the Treasury of the United States and shall be recoverable in a civil suit in the name of the United States.

c.

    1.

        A. Any issuer that violates section 30A(a) shall be fined not more than $2,000,000.

        B. Any issuer that violates section 30A(a) shall be subject to a civil penalty of not more than $10,000 imposed in an action brought by the Commission.

    2.

        A. Any officer or director of an issuer, or stockholder acting on behalf of such issuer, who willfully violates section 30A(a) shall be fined not more than $100,000, or imprisoned not more than 5 years, or both.

        B. Any employee or agent of an issuer who is a United States citizen, national, or resident or is otherwise subject to the jurisdiction of the United States (other than an officer, director, or stockholder acting on behalf of such issuer), and who willfully violates section 30A(a), shall be fined not more than $100,000, or imprisoned not more than 5 years, or both.

        C. Any officer, director, employee, or agent of an issuer, or stockholder acting on behalf of such issuer, who violates section 30A(a) shall be subject to a civil penalty of not more than $10,000 imposed in an action brought by the Commission.

b. Whenever a fine is imposed under paragraph (2) upon any officer, director, employee, agent, or stockholder of an issuer, such fine may not be paid, directly or indirectly, by such issuer.

SECTION 33—SEPARABILITY OF PROVISIONS

If any provision of this Act, or the application of such provision to any person or circumstances, shall be held invalid, the remainder of the Act, and the application of such provision to persons or circumstances other than those as to which it is held invalid, shall not be affected thereby.

SECTION 34—EFFECTIVE DATE

This Act shall become effective on July 1, 1934, except that section 6 and 12(b), (c), (d), and (e) shall become effective on September 1, 1934; and sections 5, 7, 8, 9(a)(6), 10, 11, 12(a), 13, 14, 15, 16, 17, 18, 19, and 30 shall become effective on October 1, 1934.

SECTION 35—AUTHORIZATION OF APPROPRIATIONS

There are authorized to be appropriated to carry out the functions, powers, and duties of the Commission $300,000,000 for fiscal year 1997, in addition to any other funds authorized to be appropriated to the commission.

SECTION 35A—REQUIREMENTS FOR THE EDGAR SYSTEM

a. **Certifications and reports prerequisite to obligation or expenditure of funds; source of funds**

  1. Of the funds appropriated to the Commission pursuant to section 35 of this title for fiscal year 1988 which are available pursuant to section 35(b) of this title for establishment or operation of the electronic data gathering, analysis, and retrieval ('EDGAR') system, the Commission may not obligate or expend more than $5,000,000 for the establishment or operation of the EDGAR system unless the Commission has made the certification required by subsection (c) of this section.

  2. Notwithstanding section 35(b) of this title, no funds appropriated for fiscal year 1989 may be obligated or expended

for the establishment or operation of the EDGAR system, unless the Commission has—

    A. filed each report required during fiscal year 1988 by subsection (b) of this section; and

    B. made the certification required by subsection (c) of this section.

3. Amounts which are available to the Commission under section 35(b) of this title for the EDGAR contract shall be the exclusive source of funds for the procurement and operation of the systems created under that contract by or on behalf of the Securities and Exchange Commission—

    A. for the receipt of filings under Federal securities laws, and

    B. for the automated acceptance and review of the filings and information derived from such filings.

b. **Status and progress reports to Congressional committees.** The Commission shall submit a report to the Committees on Banking, Housing, and Urban Affairs and Governmental Affairs of the Senate and the Committees on Energy and Commerce and Government Operations of the House of Representatives on the status of EDGAR development, implementation, and progress at six-month intervals beginning December 31, 1987, and ending at the close of 1990 (unless otherwise extended by the Congress). Such report shall include the following:

1. The overall progress and status of the project, including achievement of significant milestones and current project schedule.

2. The results of Commission efforts to test new or revised technical solutions for key EDGAR functions. In particular, the following functions shall be addressed and the indicated information provided:

    A. Automating receipt and acceptance processing, including—

        i. development and testing progress and results;

      ii. actual versus estimated development cost; and

      iii. actual effect of this function on Commission staff needs to assist filers.

  B. Data tagging (identifying financial data for analysis by EDGAR), including—

      i. description of the approach selected, identifying the types of financial data to be tagged and the calculations to be performed;

      ii. comments by the filer population on the approach selected;

      iii. the results of testing this approach, including information on the number of filers taking part in the test and their representativeness of the overall filer population;

      iv. actual versus estimated development cost; and

      v. effect of implementing this function on EDGAR benefits.

  C. Searching text for keywords, including—

      i. the technical approach adopted for this function;

      ii. development and testing progress and results;

      iii. data storage requirements and search response times as compared to EDGAR pilot system experience;

      iv. actual versus estimated development cost; and

      v. effect of implementing this function on EDGAR benefits.

3. An update of cost information for the receipt, acceptance and review, and dissemination portions of the system including

a comparison of actual costs with original estimated costs and revised estimates of total system cost and total funding needs for the contract.

4. The status of Commission efforts to obtain and maintain staff with the proper contractual, managerial, and technical expertise to oversee the EDGAR project.

5. The fees, revenues, costs, and profits obtained or incurred by the contractor as a result of the required dissemination of information from the system to the public under the EDGAR contract, except that the information required under this paragraph

   A. need be obtained from the contractor no more frequently than once each year, and

   B. may be submitted to the Congress as a separate confidential document.

6. Such other information or recommendations as the Commission considers appropriate.

c. On or before the date the Commission enters into the contract for the EDGAR system, the Commission shall submit to the Committees on Banking, Housing, and Urban Affairs and Governmental Affairs of the Senate and the Committees on Energy and Commerce and Government Operations of the House of Representatives a certification by the Commission

   1. of the total contract costs to the Federal Government of the EDGAR system for each of the 3 succeeding fiscal years;

   2. that the Commission has analyzed the quantitative and qualitative benefits to be obtained by the establishment and operation of the system and has determined that such benefits justify the costs certified pursuant to paragraph (1);

   3. that (A) the contract requires the contractor to establish a schedule for the implementation of the system; (B) the Commission has reviewed and approved that schedule; and (C) the contract contains adequate assurances of contractor compliance with that schedule;

4. of the capabilities which the system is intended to provide and of the competence of the contractor and of Commission personnel to implement those capabilities; and

5. that mandatory filings from a significant test group of registrants will be received and reviewed by the Commission for a period of at least six months before the adoption of any rule requiring mandatory filing by all registrants.

d. **Rules or regulations.** The Commission, by rule or regulation—

1. shall provide that any information in the EDGAR system that is required to be disseminated by the contractor—

   A. may be sold or disseminated by the contractor only pursuant to a uniform schedule of fees prescribed by the Commission;

   B. may be obtained by a purchaser by direct interconnection with the EDGAR system;

   C. shall be equally available on equal terms to all persons; and

   D. may be used, resold, or redisseminated by any person who has lawfully obtained such information without restriction and without payment of additional fees or royalties; and

2. shall require that persons, or classes of persons, required to make filings with the Commission submit such filings in a form and manner suitable for entry into the EDGAR system and shall specify the date that such requirement is effective with respect to that person or class; except that the Commission may exempt persons or classes of persons, or filings or classes of filings, from such rules or regulations in order to prevent hardships or to avoid imposing unreasonable burdens or as otherwise may be necessary or appropriate; and

3. shall require all persons who make any filing with the Commission, in addition to complying with such other rules concerning the form and manner of filing as the Commission

may prescribe, to submit such filings in written or printed form—

    A. for a period of at least one year after the effective date specified for such person or class under para-graph (2); or

    B. for a shorter period if the Commission determines that the EDGAR system

        i. is reliable,

        ii. provides a suitable alternative to such written and printed filings, and

        iii. assures that the provision of information through the EDGAR system is as effective and efficient for filers, users, and disseminators as provision of such information in written or printed form.

e. **Consultations of Commission with representatives of information interests.** For the purposes of carrying out its responsibilities under subsection (d)(3) of this section, the Commission shall consult with representatives of persons filing, disseminating, and using information contained in filings with the Commission.

SECTION 36—GENERAL EXEMPTIVE AUTHORITY

a. Authority.—

    1. In general.—Except as provided in subsection (b), but notwithstanding any other provision of this title, the Commission, by rule, regulation or order, may conditionally or unconditionally exempt any person, security, or transaction, or any or any class or classes of persons, securities, or transactions, from any provision or provisions of this title or of any rule or regulation thereunder, to the extent that such exemption is necessary or appropriate in the public interest, and is consistent with the protection of investors.

    2. Procedures.—The Commission shall, by rule or regulation, determine the procedures under which an exemptive order

under this section shall be granted and may, in its sole discretion, decline to entertain any application for an order of exemption under this section.

b. Limitation.—The Commission may not, under this section, exempt any person, security, or transaction, or any class or classes of persons, securities, or transactions from section 15C or the rules or regulations issued thereunder or (for purposes of section 15C and the rules and regulations issued thereunder) from any definition in paragraph (42), (43), (44), or (45) of section 3(a).

Appendix 8

GENERAL RULES AND REGULATIONS PROMULGATED UNDER THE SECURITIES ACT OF 1933

RULE 134—COMMUNICATIONS NOT DEEMED A PROSPECTUS

The term *prospectus* as defined in <u>section 2(10)</u> of the Act shall not include a notice, circular, advertisement, letter, or other communication published or transmitted to any person after a registration statement has been filed if it contains only the statements required or permitted to be included therein by the following provisions of this section:

a. Such communication may include any one or more of the following items of information, which need not follow the numerical sequence of this paragraph:

1. The name of the issuer of the security;

2. The full title of the security and the amount being offered;

3. A brief indication of the general type of business of the issuer, limited to the following:

    i. In the case of a manufacturing company, the general type of manufacturing and the principal products or classes of products manufactured;

    ii. In the case of a public utility company, the general type of services rendered and a brief indication of the area served;

iii. In the case of an investment company registered under the <u>Investment Company Act of 1940</u>, the company's classification and subclassification under the Act, whether it is a balanced, specialized, bond, preferred stock or common stock fund and whether in the selection of investments emphasis is placed upon income or growth characteristics, and a general description of an investment company including its general attributes, methods of operation and services offered provided that such description is not inconsistent with the operation of the particular investment company for which more specific information is being given, identification of the company's investment adviser, any logo, corporate symbol or trademark of the company or its investment adviser and any graphic design or device or an attention-getting headline, not involving performance figures, designed to direct the reader's attention to textual material included in the communication pursuant to other provisions of this rule; and, with respect to an investment company issuing redeemable securities:

A. A description of such company's investment objectives and policies, services, and method of operation;

B. Identification of the company's principal officers;

C. The year of incorporation or organization or period of existence of the company, its investment adviser, or both;

D. The company's aggregate net asset value as of the most recent practicable date;

E. The aggregate net asset value as of the most recent practicable date of all registered investment companies under the management of the company's investment adviser;

F. Any pictorial illustration which is appropriate for inclusion in the company's prospectus and not involving performance figures;

G. Descriptive material relating to economic conditions, or to retirement plans or other goals to which an investment in the company could be directed, but not directly or indirectly relating to past performance or implying achievement of investment objectives and

H. Written notice of the terms of an offer made solely to all registered holders of the securities, or of a particular class or series of securities, issued by the company proportate to their holdings, offering to sell additional shares to such holders of securities at prices reflecting a reduction in, or elimination of, the regular sales load charged: *Provided that,*

1. if any printed material permitted by paragraphs (a)(3)(iii)(A) through (H) of this section is included, such communication shall also contain the following legend set in a size type at least as large as and of a style different from, but at least as prominent as, that used in the major portion of the advertisements:

For more complete information about (Name of Company) including charges and expenses (get) (obtain) (send for) a prospectus (from (Name and Address)) (by sending this coupon). Read it carefully before you invest or (pay) (forward funds) (send money). Or,

    2.   if any material permitted by clauses (A) through (G) is used in a radio or television advertisement, such communication shall also contain the following legend given emphasis equal to that used in the major portion of the advertisements:

"For more complete information about (Name of Company) including charges and expenses (get) (obtain) (send for) a prospectus (from (Name and Address)). Read it carefully before you invest or (pay) (forward funds) (send money)." [sic]

For purposes of clauses (B) of this paragraph (a)(3)(iii), *principal officers* means the president in charge of a principal business function and any other person who performs similar policy making functions for the company on a regular basis.

In the case of two or more registered investment companies having the same investment adviser or principal underwriter, the same information described in this paragraph (a)(3)(iii) may be included as to each such company in a joint communication on the same basis as it is permitted in communications dealing with individual companies under this paragraph (a)(3)(iii).

    iv.   In the case of any other type of company, a corresponding statement;

 4.   The price of the security, or if the price is not known, the method of its determination or the probable price range as specified by the issuer or the managing underwriter;

5. In the case of a debt security with a fixed (non-contingent) interest provision, the yield or, if the yield is not known, the probable yield range, as specified by the issuer or the managing underwriter;

6. The name and address of the sender of the communication and the fact that he is participating, or expects to participate, in the distribution of the security;

7. The names of the managing underwriters;

8. The approximate date upon which it is anticipated the proposed sale to the public will commence;

9. Whether, in the opinion of counsel, the security is a legal investment for savings banks, fiduciaries, insurance companies, or similar investors under the laws of any State or Territory or the District of Columbia;

10. Whether, in the opinion of counsel, the security is exempt from specified taxes, or the extent to which the issuer has agreed to pay any tax with respect to the security or measured by the income therefrom;

11. Whether the security is being offered through rights issued to security holders, and, if so, the class of securities the holders of which will be entitled to subscribe, the subscription ratio, the actual or proposed record date, the date upon which the rights were issued or are expected to be issued, the actual or anticipated date upon which they will expire, and the approximate subscription price, or any of the foregoing;

12. Any statement or legend required by any state law or administrative authority; and

13. A communication concerning the securities of a registered investment company may also include any one or more of the following items of information: Offers, descriptions, and explanations of any products and services not constituting securities subject to registration under the Securities Act of 1933, and descriptions of corporations provided that such offers, descriptions and explanations do not relate directly to the desirability of owning or purchasing a security issued

by a registered investment company and that all direct references in such communications to a security issued by a registered investment company contain only the statements required or permitted to be included therein by the other provisions of this rule, and that all such direct references be placed in a separate and enclosed area in the communication.

14.

    i. With respect to any class of debt securities, any class of convertible debt securities or any class of preferred stock, the security rating or ratings assigned to the class of securities by any nationally recognized statistical rating organization and the name or names of the nationally recognized statistical rating organization(s) which assigned such rating(s), and with respect to any class of debt securities, any class of convertible debt securities or any class of preferred stock registered on Form F-9, the security rating or ratings assigned to the class of securities by any other rating organization specified in the Instruction to paragraph (a)2 of General Instruction I of Form F-9 and the name or names of the rating organization or organizations which assigned such rating(s).

    ii. For the purpose of paragraph (a) of this section, the term *nationally recognized statistical rating organization* shall have the same meaning as used in Rule 15c-3-1(c)(2)(vi)(F) under the Securities Exchange Act of 1934.

b. Except as provided in paragraph (c) of this section, every communication used pursuant to this section shall contain the following:

    1. If the registration statement has not yet become effective, the following statement:

"A registration statement relating to these securities has been filed with the Securities and Exchange Commission but has not yet become effective. These securities may not be sold nor may offers to buy be accepted prior to the time the registration statement becomes effective. This (communication) shall not constitute an offer to sell or the solicitation of an offer to buy nor shall there be any sale of these securities in any State in which such offer, solicitation or sale would be unlawful prior to registration or qualification under the securities laws of any such State."

2. A statement whether the security is being offered in connection with a distribution by the issuer or by a security holder, or both, and whether the issue represents new financing or refunding or both; and

3. The name and address of a person or persons from whom a written prospectus meeting the requirements of <u>section 10</u> of the Act may be obtained.

c. Any of the statements or information specified in paragraph (b) of this section may, but need not, be contained in a communication:

1. Which does no more than state from whom a written prospectus meeting the requirements of <u>section 10 of the Act</u> may be obtained, identify the security, state the price thereof and state by whom orders will be executed; or

2. which is accompanied or preceded by a prospectus or a summary prospectus which meets the requirements of <u>section 10 of the Act</u> at the date of such preliminary communication.

d. A communication sent or delivered to any person pursuant to this rule which is accompanied or preceded by a prospectus which meets the requirements of <u>section 10 of the Act</u> at the date of such communication, may solicit from the recipient of the communication an offer to buy the security or request the recipient to indicate, upon an enclosed or attached coupon or card, or in some other manner, whether he might be interested in the security, if the communication contains substantially the following statement:

No offer to buy the securities can be accepted and no part of the purchase price can be received until the registration statement has become effective, and any such offer may be withdrawn or revoked, without obligation or commitment of any kind, at any time prior to notice of its acceptance given after the effective date. An indication of interest in response to this advertisement will involve no obligation or commitment of any kind.

Provided, That such statement need not be included in such a communication to a dealer if the communication refers to a prior communication to the dealer, with respect to the same security, in which the statement was included.

In the case of an investment company registered under the Investment Company Act of 1940 that holds itself out as a "money market fund," a communication used under this section shall contain the disclosure required by Rule 482(a).

RULE 134A—OPTIONS MATERIAL NOT DEEMED A PROSPECTUS

Written materials, including advertisements, relating to standardized options, as that term is defined in Rule 9b-1 under the Securities Exchange Act of 1934, shall not be deemed to be a prospectus for the purposes of Section 2(10) of the Securities Act of 1933; *Provided,* That such materials are limited to explanatory information describing the general nature of the standardized options markets or one or more strategies: *And, Provided Further,* That:

a. The potential risks related to options trading generally and to each strategy addressed are explained;

b. No past or projected performance figures, including annualized rates of return are used;

c. No recommendation to purchase or sell any option contract is made;

d. No specific security is identified, other than

     i. An option or other security exempt from registration under the Act, or

     ii. An index option, including the component securities of the index; and

e. If there is a definitive options disclosure document, as defined in Rule 9b-1 under the Securities Exchange Act of 1934, the materials shall contain the name and address of a person or persons from whom a copy of such document may be obtained.

RULE 135—NOTICE OF PROPOSED REGISTERED OFFERINGS

a. When notice is not an offer. For purposes of <u>section 5</u> of the Act only, an issuer or a selling security holder (and any person acting on behalf of either of them) that publishes through any medium a notice of a proposed offering to be registered under the Act will not be deemed to offer its securities for sale through that notice if:

    1. Legend. The notice includes a statement to the effect that it does not constitute an offer of any securities for sale; and

    2. Limited notice content. The notice otherwise includes no more than the following information:

        i. The name of the issuer;

        ii. The title, amount and basic terms of the securities offered;

        iii. The amount of the offering, if any, to be made by selling security holders;

        iv. The anticipated timing of the offering;

        v. A brief statement of the manner and the purpose of the offering, without naming the underwriters;

        vi. Whether the issuer is directing its offering to only a particular class of purchasers;

        vii. Any statements or legends required by the laws of any state or foreign country or administrative authority; and

        viii. In the following offerings, the notice may contain additional information, as follows:

            A. Rights offering. In a rights offering to existing security holders:

                1. The class of security holders eligible to subscribe;

                2. The subscription ratio and expected subscription price;

    3. The proposed record date;

    4. The anticipated issuance date of the rights; and

    5. The subscription period or expiration date of the rights offering.

B. Offering to employees. In an offering to employees of the issuer or an affiliated company:

    1. The name of the employer;

    2. The class of employees being offered the securities;

    3. The offering price; and

    4. The duration of the offering period.

C. Exchange offer. In an exchange offer:

    1. The basic terms of the exchange offer;

    2. The name of the subject company;

    3. The subject class of securities sought in the exchange offer.

D. Rule 145(a) offering. In a Rule 145(a) offering:

    1. The name of the person whose assets are to be sold in exchange for the securities to be offered;

    2. The names of any other parties to the transaction;

    3. A brief description of the business of the parties to the transaction;

    4. The date, time and place of the meeting of security holders to vote on or consent to the transaction; and

> 5. A brief description of the trans-
> action and the basic terms of the
> transaction.

b. Corrections of misstatements about the offering. A person that publishes a notice in reliance on this section may issue a notice that
contains no more information than is necessary to correct inaccu-
racies published about the proposed offering.

Note to Rule 135:

Communications under this section relating to business combination transactions must be filed as required by Rule 425(b).

RULE 135A—GENERIC ADVERTISING

a. For the purposes only of section 5 of the Act, a notice, circular,
advertisement, letter, sign, or other communication, published or
transmitted to any person which does not specifically refer by name
to the securities of a particular investment company, to the investment company itself, or to any other securities not exempt under
section 3(a) of the Act, will not be deemed to offer any security for
sale, provided:

> 1. Such communication is limited to any one or more of the
> following:
>
> > i. Explanatory information relating to securities of in-
> > vestment companies generally or to the nature of
> > investment companies, or to services offered in con-
> > nection with the ownership of such securities,
> >
> > ii. The mention or explanation of investment compa-
> > nies of different generic types or having various in-
> > vestment objectives, such as *balanced funds, growth
> > funds, income funds, leveraged funds, specialty funds,
> > variable annuities, bond funds,* and *no-load funds,*
> >
> > iii. Offers, descriptions, and explanation of various prod-
> > ucts and services not constituting a security subject
> > to registration under the Act: *Provided,* That such
> > offers, descriptions, and explanations do not relate
> > directly to the desirability of owning or purchasing

> a security issued by a registered investment com-
> pany,
>
> > iv. Invitation to inquire for further information, and
>
> 2. Such communication contains the name and address of a registered broker or dealer or other person sponsoring the communication.

b. If such communication contains a solicitation of inquiries and prospectuses for investment company securities are to be sent or delivered in response to such inquiries, the number of such investment companies and, if applicable, the fact that the sponsor of the communication is the principal underwriter or investment adviser in respect to such investment companies shall be stated.

c. With respect to any communication describing any type of security, service, or product, the broker, dealer, or other person sponsoring such communication must offer for sale a security, service, or product of the type described in such communication.

RULE 135B—MATERIALS NOT DEEMED AN OFFER TO SELL OR OFFER TO BUY

For the purposes only of <u>section 5</u> of the Act, materials meeting the requirements of <u>Rule 9b-1</u> of the Securities Exchange Act of 1934 shall not be deemed to constitute an offer to sell or offer to buy any security.

RULE 135C—NOTICE OF CERTAIN PROPOSED UNREGISTERED OFFERINGS

a. For the purposes only of <u>section 5</u> of the Act, a notice given by an issuer required to file reports pursuant to section <u>13</u> or <u>15(d)</u> of the Securities Exchange Act of 1934 or a foreign issuer that is exempt from registration under the Securities Exchange Act of 1934 pursuant to <u>Rule 12g3-2(b)</u> of this chapter that it proposes to make, is making or has made an offering of securities not registered or required to be registered under the Act shall not be deemed to offer any securities for sale if:

> 1. Such notice is not used for the purpose of conditioning the market in the United States for any of the securities offered;

2.   Such notice states that the securities offered will not be or have not been registered under the Act and may not be offered or sold in the United States absent registration or an applicable exemption from registration requirements; and

3.   Such notice contains no more than the following additional information:

   i.   The name of the issuer;

   ii.   The title, amount and basic terms of the securities offered, the amount of the offering, if any, made by selling security holders, the time of the offering and a brief statement of the manner and purpose of the offering without naming the underwriters;

   iii.   In the case of a rights offering to security holders of the issuer, the class of securities the holders of which will be or were entitled to subscribe to the securities offered, the subscription ratio, the record date, the date upon which the rights are proposed to be or were issued, the term or expiration date of the rights and the subscription price, or any of the foregoing;

   iv.   In the case of an offering of securities in exchange for other securities of the issuer or of another issuer, the name of the issuer and the title of the securities to be surrendered in exchange for the securities offered, the basis upon which the exchange may be made, or any of the foregoing;

   v.   In the case of an offering to employees of the issuer or to employees of any affiliate of the issuer, the name of the employer and class or classes of employees to whom the securities are offered, the offering price or basis of the offering and the period during which the offering is to be or was made or any of the foregoing; and

   vi.   Any statement or legend required by State or foreign law or administrative authority.

b.   Any notice contemplated by this section may take the form of a news release or a written communication directed to security holders or employees, as the case may be, or other published statements.

c. Notwithstanding the provisions of paragraphs (a) and (b) of this section, in the case of a rights offering of a security listed or subject to unlisted trading privileges on a national securities exchange or quoted on the NASDAQ inter-dealer quotation system information with respect to the interest rate, conversion ratio and subscription price may be disseminated through the facilities of the exchange, the consolidated transaction reporting system, the NASDAQ system or the Dow Jones broad tape, provided such information is already disclosed in a Form 8-K on file with the Commission, in a Form 6-K furnished to the Commission or, in the case of an issuer relying on Rule 12g3-2(b) of this chapter, in a submission made pursuant to that Section to the Commission.

d. The issuer shall file any notice contemplated by this section with the Commission under cover of Form 8-K or furnish such notice under Form 6-K, as applicable, and, if relying on Rule 12g3-2(b) of this chapter, shall furnish such notice to the Commission in accordance with the provisions of that exemptive Section.

RULE 137—DEFINITION OF "OFFERS", "PARTICIPATES", OR "PARTICIPATION" IN SECTION 2(11) IN RELATION TO CERTAIN PUBLICATIONS BY PERSONS INDEPENDENT OF PARTICIPANTS IN A DISTRIBUTION

The terms *offers, participates,* or *participation* in section 2(11) of the Act shall not be deemed to apply to the publication or distribution of information, opinions or recommendations with respect to the securities of a registrant which is required to file reports pursuant to section 13 or 15(d) of the Securities Exchange Act of 1934 and proposes to file, has filed or has an effective registration statement under the Securities Act of 1933 if—

a. Such information, opinions, and recommendations are published and distributed in the regular course of its business by a broker or dealer which is not and does not propose to be a participant in the distribution of the security to which the registration statement relates; and

b. Such broker or dealer receives no consideration, directly or indirectly, in connection with the publication and distribution of such information, opinions or recommendations from the registrant, a selling security holder or any participant in the distribution or any other person interested in the securities to which the registration statement relates, and such information, opinions or recommendations are not published or distributed pursuant to any arrangement or understanding, direct or indirect, with such registrant, underwriter, dealer, or selling security holder; *Provided, however,* That nothing herein shall forbid payment of the regular subscription or purchase price of the document or other written communication in which such information, opinions or recommendations appear.

RULE 138—DEFINITION OF "OFFER FOR SALE" AND "OFFER TO SELL" IN SECTIONS 2(10) AND 5(C) IN RELATION TO CERTAIN PUBLICATIONS

a. Where a registrant which meets the requirements of paragraph (c)(1), (c)(2) or (c)(3) of this section proposes to file, has filed or has an effective registration statement under the Act relating solely to a nonconvertible debt security or to a nonconvertible, nonparticipating preferred stock, publication or distribution in the regular course of its business by a broker or dealer of information, opinions or recommendations relating solely to common stock or to debt or preferred stock convertible into common stock of such registrant shall not be deemed to constitute an offer for sale or offer to sell the security to which such registration statement relates for purposes of sections 2(10) and 5(c) of the Act even though such broker or dealer is or will be a participant in the distribution of the security to which such registration statement relates.

b. Where a registrant which meets the requirements of paragraph (c)(1), (c)(2) or (c)(3) of this section proposes to file, has filed or has an effective registration statement under the Act relating solely to common stock or to debt or preferred stock convertible into common stock, the publication or distribution in the regular course of its business by a broker or dealer of information, opinions or recommendations relating solely to a nonconvertible debt security, or to a nonconvertible nonparticipating preferred stock shall not be deemed to constitute an offer for sale or offer to sell the security to which such registration statement relates for purposes of sections 2(10) and 5(c) of the Act, even though such broker or dealer is or will be a participant in the distribution of the security to which such registration statement relates.

c.

1. The registrant meets all of the conditions for the use of Form S-2 or Form F-2;

2. The registrant meets the registrant requirements of Form S-3 or Form F-3; or

3. The registrant is a foreign private issuer which meets all the registrant requirements of Form F-3, other than the reporting history provisions of paragraph A.1. and A.2.(a) of General Instruction I of such form, and meets the minimum float or investment grade securities provisions of either paragraph B.1. or B.2. of General Instruction I. of such form and the registrant's securities have been traded for a period of at least 12 months on a designated offshore securities market, as defined in Rule 902(a).

Instruction to Rule 138

When a registration statement relates to securities which are being registered for an offering to be made on a continuous or delayed basis pursuant to Rule 415(a)1 under the Act and the securities which are being registered include classes of securities which are specified in both paragraphs (a) and (b) of this section on either an allocated or unallocated basis, a broker or dealer may nonetheless rely on:

1. Paragraph (a) of this section when the offering in which such broker or dealer is or will be a participant relates solely to classes of securities specified in paragraph (a) of this section, and

2. Paragraph (b) of this section when the offering in which such broker or dealer is or will be a participant relates solely to classes of securities specified in paragraph (b) of this section.

RULE 139—DEFINITION OF "OFFER FOR SALE" AND "OFFER TO SELL" IN SECTIONS 2(10) AND 5(C) IN RELATION TO CERTAIN PUBLICATIONS

Where a registrant which is required to file reports pursuant to section 13 or 15(d) of the Securities Exchange Act of 1934 or which is a foreign private issuer meeting the conditions of paragraph (a)2 of this section proposes to file, has filed or has an effective registration statement under the Securities Act of 1933 relating to its securities, the publication or distribution by a broker or dealer of information, an opinion or a recommendation with respect to the registrant or any class of its securities shall not be deemed to constitute an offer for sale or offer to sell the securities registered or proposed to be registered for purposes of sections 2(10) and 5(c) of the Act, even though such broker or dealer is or will be a participant in the distribution of such securities, if the conditions of paragraph (a) or (b) of this section have been met:

a.

1. The registrant meets the registrant requirements of Form S-3 or Form F-3 and the minimum float or investment grade securities provisions of either paragraph (B) 1 or 2 of General Instruction I of the respective form and such information, opinion or recommendation is contained in a publication which is distributed with reasonable regularity in the normal course of business; or

2. The registrant is a foreign private issuer that meets all the registrant requirements of Form F-3, other than the reporting history provisions of paragraphs A.1. and A.2.(a) of General Instruction I of such form, and meets the minimum float or investment grade securities provisions of either paragraph B.1. or B.2. of General Instruction I of such form, and the registrant's securities have been traded for a period of at least 12 months on a designated offshore securities market, as defined in Rule 902(a), and such information, opinion or recommendation is contained in a publication which is distributed with reasonable regularity in the normal course of business.

b.

    1. Such information, opinion or recommendation is contained in a publication which:

        i. Is distributed with reasonable regularity in the normal course of business and

        ii. Includes similar information, opinions or recommendations with respect to a substantial number of companies in the registrant's industry, or sub-industry, or contains a comprehensive list of securities currently recommended by such broker or dealer.

    2. Such information, opinion or recommendation is given no materially greater space or prominence in such publication than that given to other securities or registrants; and

    3. An opinion or recommendation as favorable or more favorable as to the registrant or any class of its securities was published by the broker or dealer in the last publication of such broker or dealer addressing the registrant or its securities prior to the commencement of participation in the distribution.

Instructions to Rule 139

1. For purposes of paragraph (a), a research report has not been distributed with *reasonable regularity* if it contains information, an opinion, or a recommendation concerning a company with respect to which a broker or dealer currently is not publishing research.

2. Where projections of a registrant's sales or earnings are included, the publication must comply with the following in order to meet paragraphs (b)(1) and (b)(3).

    A. The projections must have been published previously on a regular basis in order for the publication to meet paragraph (b)(1)(i);

    B. The projections must be included with respect to either a substantial number of companies in the registrant's industry or sub-industry or all companies in a comprehensive list which is contained in the publication, and must cover the same periods with respect to such companies as with respect to the registrant, in order to meet the requirements of paragraph (b)(1)(ii); and

C. Because projections constitute opinions within the meaning of the Rule, they must come within paragraph (b)(3).

RULE 140—DEFINITION OF "DISTRIBUTION" IN SECTION 2(11), FOR CERTAIN TRANSACTIONS

A person, the chief part of whose business consists of the purchase of the securities of one issuer, or of two or more affiliated issuers, and the sale of its own securities, including the levying of assessments on its assessable stock and the resale of such stock upon the failure of the holder thereof to pay any assessment levied thereon, to furnish the proceeds with which to acquire the securities of such issuer or affiliated issuers, is to be regarded as engaged in the distribution of the securities of such issuer or affiliated issuers within the meaning of section 2(11) of the Act.

RULE 141—DEFINITION OF "COMMISSION FROM AN UNDERWRITER OR DEALER NOT IN EXCESS OF THE USUAL AND CUSTOMARY DISTRIBUTORS' OR SELLERS' COMMISSIONS" IN SECTION 2(11), FOR CERTAIN TRANSACTIONS

a. The term *commission* in section 2(11) of the Act shall include such remuneration, commonly known as a spread, as may be received by a distributor or dealer as a consequence of reselling securities bought from an underwriter or dealer at a price below the offering price of such securities, where such resales afford the distributor or dealer a margin of profit not in excess of what is usual and customary in such transactions.

b. The term *commission from an underwriter or dealer* in section 2(11) of the Act shall include commissions paid by an underwriter or dealer directly or indirectly controlling or controlled by, or under direct or indirect common control with the issuer.

c. The term *usual and customary distributors' or sellers' commission* in section 2(11) of the Act shall mean a commission or remuneration, commonly known as a spread, paid to or received by any person selling securities either for his own account or for the account of others, which is not in excess of the amount usual and customary in the distribution and sale of issues of similar type and size; and not in excess of the amount allowed to other persons, if any, for comparable service in the distribution of the particular issue; but such term shall not include amounts paid to any person whose function is the management of the distribution of all or a substantial part of the particular issue, or who performs the functions normally performed by an underwriter or underwriting syndicate.

RULE 142—DEFINITION OF "PARTICIPATES" AND "PARTICIPATION," AS USED IN SECTION 2(11), IN RELATION TO CERTAIN TRANSACTIONS

a. The terms *participates* and *participation* in section 2(11) shall not include the interest of a person

    1. who is not in privity of contract with the issuer nor directly or indirectly controlling, controlled by, or under common control with, the issuer, and

    2. who has no association with any principal underwriter of the securities being distributed, and

    3. whose function in the distribution is confined to an undertaking to purchase all or some specified proportion of the securities remaining unsold after the lapse of some specified period of time, and

    4. who purchases such securities for investment and not with a view to distribution.

b. As used in this section:

    1. The term *issuer* shall have the meaning defined in section 2(4) and in the last sentence of section 2(11).

    2. The term *association* shall include a relationship between two persons under which one:

i.   Is directly or indirectly controlling, controlled by, or under common control with, the other, or

ii. Has, in common with the other, one or more partners, officers, directors, trustees, branch managers, or other persons occupying a similar status or performing similar functions, or

iii. Has a participation, direct or indirect, in the profits of the other, or has a financial stake, by debtor-creditor relationship, stock ownership, contract or otherwise, in the income or business of the other.

3. The term *principal underwriter* shall have the meaning defined in Rule 405.

RULE 143—DEFINITION OF "HAS PURCHASED", "SELLS FOR", "PARTICIPATES", AND "PARTICIPATION", AS USED IN SECTION 2(11), IN RELATION TO CERTAIN TRANSACTIONS OF FOREIGN GOVERNMENTS FOR WAR PURPOSES

The terms *has purchased, sells for, participates,* and *participation,* in section 2(11), shall not be deemed to apply to any action of a foreign government in acquiring, for war purposes and by or in anticipation of the exercise of war powers, from any person subject to its jurisdiction securities of a person organized under the laws of the United States or any State or Territory, or in disposing of such securities with a view to their distribution by underwriters in the United States, notwithstanding the fact that the price to be paid to such foreign government upon the disposition of such securities by it may be measured by or may be in direct or indirect relation to such price as may be realized by the underwriters.

RULE 144—PERSONS DEEMED NOT TO BE ENGAGED IN A DISTRIBUTION AND THEREFORE NOT UNDERWRITERS

Preliminary Note to Rule 144

Rule 144 is designed to implement the fundamental purposes of the Act, as expressed in its preamble, "To provide full and fair disclosure of the character of the securities sold in interstate commerce and through the mails, and to prevent fraud in the sale thereof . . . " The rule is designed to prohibit the creation of public markets in securities of issuers concerning which adequate current information is not available to the public. At the same time, where adequate current information concerning the issuer is available to the public, the rule permits the public sale in ordinary transactions of limited amounts of securities owned by persons controlling, controlled by or under common control with the issuer and by persons who have acquired restricted securities of the issuer.

Certain basic principles are essential to an understanding of the requirement of registration in the Act:

1.   If any person utilizes the jurisdictional means to sell any non-exempt security to any other person, the security must be registered unless a statutory exemption can be found for the transaction.

2.   In addition to the exemptions found in Section 3, four exemptions applicable to transactions in securities are contained in Section 4. Three of these Section 4 exemptions are clearly not available to anyone acting as an "underwriter" of securities. (The fourth, found in Section 4(4), is available only to those who act as brokers under certain limited circumstances.) An understanding of the term "underwriter" is therefore important to anyone who wishes to determine whether or not an exemption from registration is available for his sale of securities.

The term underwriter is broadly defined in Section 2(11) of the Act to mean any person who has purchased from an issuer with a view to, or offers or sells for an issuer in connection with, the distribution of any security, or participates or has a direct or indirect participation in any such undertaking, or participates or has a participation in the direct or indirect underwriting of any such undertaking. The interpretation of this definition has traditionally focused on the words "with a view to" in the phrase "purchased from an issuer with a view to . . . distribution." Thus, an investment banking firm which arranges with an issuer for the public sale of its securities is clearly an "underwriter" under that Section. Individual investors who are not professionals in the securities business may also be "underwriters" within the meaning of that term as used in the Act if they act as links in a chain of transactions through which securities move from an issuer to the public. Since it is difficult to ascertain the mental state of the purchaser at the time of his acquisition, subsequent acts and circumstances have been considered to determine whether such person took with a view to distribution at the time of his acquisition. Emphasis has been placed on factors such as the length of time the person has held the securities and whether there has been an unforeseeable change in circumstances of the holder. Experience has shown, however, that reliance upon such factors as the above has not assured adequate protection of investors through the maintenance of informed trading markets and has led to uncertainty in the application of the registration provisions of the Act.

It should be noted that the statutory language of Section 2(11) is in the disjunctive. Thus, it is insufficient to conclude that a person is not an underwriter solely because he did not purchase securities from an issuer with a view to their distribution. It must also be established that the person is not offering or selling for an issuer in connection with the distribution of the securities, does not participate or have a direct or indirect participation in any such undertaking, and does not participate or have a participation in the direct or indirect underwriting of such an undertaking.

In determining when a person is deemed not to be engaged in a distribution several factors must be considered.

First, the purpose and underlying policy of the Act to protect investors requires that there be adequate current information concerning the issuer, whether the resales of securities by persons result in a distribution or are effected in trading transactions. Accordingly, the availability of the rule is conditioned on the existence of adequate current public information.

Secondly, a holding period prior to resale is essential, among other reasons, to assure that those persons who buy under a claim of a Section 4(2) exemption have assumed the economic risks of investment, and therefore are not acting as conduits for sale to the public of unregistered securities, directly or indirectly, on behalf of an issuer. It should be noted, that there is nothing in Section 2(11) which places a time limit on a person's status as an underwriter. The public has the same need for protection afforded by registration whether the securities are distributed shortly after their purchase or after a considerable length of time.

A third factor, which must be considered in determining what is deemed not to constitute a "distribution," is the impact of the particular transaction or transactions on the trading markets. Section 4(1) was intended to exempt only routine trading transactions between individual investors with respect to securities already issued and not to exempt distributions by issuers or acts of other individuals who engage in steps necessary to such distributions. Therefore, a person reselling securities under Section 4(1) of the Act must sell the securities in such limited quantities and in such a manner as not to disrupt the trading markets. The larger the amount of securities involved, the more likely it is that such resales may involve methods of offering and amounts of compensation usually associated with a distribution rather than routine trading transactions. Thus, solicitation of buy orders or the payment of extra compensation are not permitted by the rule.

In summary, if the sale in question is made in accordance with *all* of the provisions of the rule, as set forth below, any person who sells restricted securities shall be deemed not to be engaged in a distribution of such securities and therefore not an underwriter thereof. The rule also provides that any person who sells restricted or other securities on behalf of a person in a control relationship with the issuer shall be deemed not to be engaged in a distribution of such securities and therefore not to be an underwriter thereof, if the sale is made in accordance with *all* the conditions of the rule.

a. Definitions. The following definitions shall apply for the purposes of this rule.

    1. An "affiliate" of an issuer is a person that directly, or indirectly through one or more intermediaries, controls, or is controlled by, or is under common control with, such issuer.

    2. The term "person" when used with reference to a person for whose account securities are to be sold in reliance upon this rule includes, in addition to such person, all of the following persons:

        i. Any relative or spouse of such person, or any relative of such spouse, any one of whom has the same home as such person;

        ii. Any trust or estate in which such person or any of the persons specified in paragraph (a)(2)(i) of this section collectively own ten percent or more of the total beneficial interest or of which any of such persons serve as trustee, executor or in any similar capacity; and

iii. Any corporation or other organization (other than the issuer) in which such person or any of the persons specified in paragraph (a)(2)(i) of this section are the beneficial owners collectively of ten percent or more of any class of equity securities or ten percent or more of the equity interest.

3. The term restricted securities means:

  i. Securities acquired directly or indirectly from the issuer, or from an affiliate of the issuer, in a transaction or chain of transactions not involving any public offering;

  ii. Securities acquired from the issuer that are subject to the resale limitations of Rule 502(d) under Regulation D or Rule 701(c);

  iii. Securities acquired in a transaction or chain of transactions meeting the requirements of Rule 144A;

  iv. Securities acquired from the issuer in a transaction subject to the conditions of Regulation CE;

  v. Equity securities of domestic issuers acquired in a transaction or chain of transactions subject to the conditions of Rule 901 or Rule 903 under Regulation S;

  vi. Securities acquired in a transaction made under Rule 801 to the same extent and proportion that the securities held by the security holder of the class with respect to which the rights offering was made were as of the record date for the rights offering "restricted securities" within the meaning of this paragraph (a)(3); and

  vii. Securities acquired in a transaction made under Rule 802 to the same extent and proportion that the securities that were tendered or exchanged in the exchange offer or business combination were "restricted securities" within the meaning of this paragraph (a)(3).

b. Conditions to Be Met. Any affiliate or other person who sells restricted securities of an issuer for his own account, or any person who sells restricted or any other securities for the account of an affiliate of the issuer of such securities, shall be deemed not to be engaged in a distribution of such securities and therefore not to be an underwriter thereof within the meaning of Section 2(11) of the Act if all of the conditions of this rule are met.

c. Current Public Information. There shall be available adequate current public information with respect to the issuer of the securities. Such information shall be deemed to be available only if either of the following conditions is met:

1. Filing of Reports. The issuer has securities registered pursuant to Section 12 of the Securities Exchange Act of 1934, has been subject to the reporting requirements of Section 13 of that Act for a period of at least 90 days immediately preceding the sale of the securities and has filed all the reports required to be filed thereunder during the 12 months preceding such sale (or for such shorter period that the issuer was required to file such reports); or has securities registered pursuant to the Securities Act of 1933, has been subject to the reporting requirements of Section 15(d) of the Securities Exchange Act of 1934 for a period of at least 90 days immediately preceding the sale of the securities and has filed all the reports required to be filed thereunder during the 12 months preceding such sale (or for such shorter period that the issuer was required to file such reports). The person for whose account the securities are to be sold shall be entitled to rely upon a statement in whichever is the most recent report, quarterly or annually, required to be filed and filed by the issuer that such issuer has filed all reports required to be filed by Section 13 or 15(d) of the Securities Exchange Act of 1934 during the preceding 12 months (or for such shorter period that the issuer was required to file such reports) and has been subject to such

filing requirements for the past 90 days, unless he knows or has reason to believe that the issuer has not complied with such requirements. Such person shall also be entitled to rely upon a written statement from the issuer that it has complied with such reporting requirements unless he knows or has reason to believe that the issuer has not complied with such requirements.

2. Other Public Information. If the issuer is not subject to Section 13 or 15(d) of the Securities Exchange Act of 1934, there is publicly available the information concerning the issuer specified in paragraphs (a)(5)(i) to (xiv), inclusive, and paragraph (a)(5)(xvi) of Rule 15c2-11 under that Act or, if the issuer is an insurance company, the information specified in Section 12(g)(2)(G)(i) of that Act.

d. Holding Period for Restricted Securities. If the securities sold are restricted securities, the following provisions apply:

1. General Rule. A minimum of one year must elapse between the later of the date of the acquisition of the securities from the issuer or from an affiliate of the issuer, and any resale of such securities in reliance on this section for the account of either the acquiror or any subsequent holder of those securities. If the acquiror takes the securities by purchase, the one-year period shall not begin until the full purchase price or other consideration is paid or given by the person acquiring the securities from the issuer or from an affiliate of the issuer.

2. Promissory Notes, Other Obligations or Installment Contracts. Giving the issuer or affiliate of the issuer from whom the securities were purchased a promissory note or other obligation to pay the purchase price, or entering into an installment purchase contract with such person, shall not be deemed full payment of the purchase price unless the promissory note, obligation or contract:

    i.   provides for full recourse against the purchaser of the securities;

    ii. is secured by collateral, other than the securities purchased, having a fair market value at least equal to the purchase price of the securities purchased; and

   iii. shall have been discharged by payment in full prior to the sale of the securities.

3. Determination of Holding Period. The following provisions shall apply for the purpose of determining the period securities have been held:

   i. Stock Dividends, Splits and Recapitalizations. Securities acquired from the issuer as a dividend or pursuant to a stock split, reverse split or recapitalization shall be deemed to have been acquired at the same time as the securities on which the dividend or, if more than one, the initial dividend was paid, the securities involved in the split or reverse split, or the securities surrendered in connection with the recapitalization;

   ii. Conversions. If the securities sold were acquired from the issuer for a consideration consisting solely of other securities of the same issuer surrendered for conversion, the securities so acquired shall be deemed to have been acquired at the same time as the securities surrendered for conversion;

   iii. Contingent Issuance of Securities. Securities acquired as a contingent payment of the purchase price of an equity interest in a business, or the assets of a business, sold to the issuer or an affiliate of the issuer shall be deemed to have been acquired at the time of such sale if the issuer or affiliate was then committed to issue the securities subject only to conditions other than the payment of further consideration for such securities. An agreement entered into in connection with any such purchase to remain in the employment of, or not to compete with, the issuer or affiliate or the rendering of services pursuant to such agreement shall not be deemed to be the payment of further consideration for such securities.

iv. Pledged Securities. Securities which are bona fide pledged by an affiliate of the issuer when sold by the pledgee, or by a purchaser, after a default in the obligation secured by the pledge, shall be deemed to have been acquired when they were acquired by the pledgor, except that if the securities were pledged without recourse they shall be deemed to have been acquired by the pledgee at the time of the pledge or by the purchaser at the time of purchase.

v. Gifts of Securities. Securities acquired from an affiliate of the issuer by gift shall be deemed to have been acquired by the donee when they were acquired by the donor;

vi. Trusts. Where a trust settlor is an affiliate of the issuer, securities acquired from the settlor by the trust, or acquired from the trust by the beneficiaries thereof, shall be deemed to have been acquired when such securities were acquired by the settlor;

vii. Estates. Where a deceased person was an affiliate of the issuer, securities held by the estate of such person or acquired from such an estate by the beneficiaries thereof shall be deemed to have been acquired when they were acquired by the deceased person, except that no holding period is required if the estate is not an affiliate of the issuer or if the securities are sold by a beneficiary of the estate who is not such an affiliate.

Note. While there is no holding period or amount limitation for estates and beneficiaries thereof which are not affiliates of the issuer, paragraphs (c), (h) and (i) of the rule apply to securities sold by such persons in reliance upon the rule.

viii. Rule 145(a) transactions. The holding period for securities acquired in a transaction specified in Rule 145(a) shall be deemed to commence on the date the securities were acquired by the purchaser in such transaction. This provision shall not apply, however, to a transaction effected solely for the purpose of forming a holding company.

e. Limitation on amount of securities sold. Except as hereinafter provided, the amount of securities which may be sold in reliance upon this rule shall be determined as follows:

1. Sales by affiliates. If restricted or other securities sold for the account of an affiliate of the issuer, the amount of securities sold, together with all sales of restricted and other securities of the same class for the account of such person within the preceding three months, shall not exceed the greater of

    i. one percent of the shares or other units of the class outstanding as shown by the most recent report or statement published by the issuer, or

    ii. the average weekly reported volume of trading in such securities on all national securities exchanges and/or reported through the automated quotation system of a registered securities association during the four calendar weeks preceding the filing of notice required by paragraph (h), or if no such notice is required the date of receipt of the order to execute the transaction by the broker or the date of execution of the transaction directly with a market maker, or

    iii. the average weekly volume of trading in such securities reported through the consolidated transaction reporting system contemplated by Rule 11Aa3-1 under the Securities Exchange Act of 1934 during the four-week period specified in subdivision (ii) of this paragraph.

2. Sales by persons other than affiliates. The amount of restricted securities sold for the account of any person other than an affiliate of the issuer, together with all other sales of restricted securities of the same class for the account of such person within the preceding three months, shall not exceed the amount specified in paragraphs (e)(1)(i), (1)(ii) or (1)(iii) of this section, whichever is applicable, unless the conditions in paragraph (k) of this rule are satisfied.

3. Determination of Amount. For the purpose of determining the amount of securities specified in paragraphs (e)(1) and (2) of this rule, the following provisions shall apply:

    i.   Where both convertible securities and securities of the class into which they are convertible are sold, the amount of convertible securities sold shall be deemed to be the amount of securities of the class into which they are convertible for the purpose of determining the aggregate amount of securities of both classes sold;

    ii.   The amount of securities sold for the account of a pledgee thereof, or for the account of a purchaser of the pledged securities, during any period of three months within one year after a default in the obligation secured by the pledge, and the amount of securities sold during the same three-month period for the account of the pledgor shall not exceed, in the aggregate, the amount specified in paragraph (e)(1) or (2) of this section, whichever is applicable.

    iii.   The amount of securities sold for the account of a donee thereof during any period of three months within one year after the donation, and the amount of securities sold during the same three-month period for the account of the donor, shall not exceed, in the aggregate, the amount specified in paragraph (e)(1) or (2) of this section, whichever is applicable;

    iv.   Where securities were acquired by a trust from the settlor of the trust, the amount of such securities sold for the account of the trust during any period of three months within one year after the acquisition of the securities by the trust, and the amount of securities sold during the same three-month period for the account of the settlor, shall not exceed, in the aggregate, the amount specified in paragraph (e)(1) or (2) of this paragraph, whichever is applicable;

    v.   The amount of securities sold for the account of the estate of a deceased person, or for the account of a beneficiary of such estate, during any period of three months and the amount of securities sold during the same period for the account of the deceased person prior to his death shall not exceed, in the aggregate, the amount specified in subparagraph (1) or (2) of this paragraph, whichever is applicable; *Provided,* That no limitation on amount shall apply if the estate or beneficiary thereof is not an affiliate of the issuer;

    vi. When two or more affiliates or other persons agree to act in concert for the purpose of selling securities of an issuer, all securities of the same class sold for the account of all such persons during any period of three months shall be aggregated for the purpose of determining the limitation on the amount of securities sold;

    vii. The following sales of securities need not be included in determining the amount of securities sold in reliance upon this section: securities sold pursuant to an effective registration statement under the Act; securities sold pursuant to an exemption provided by Regulation A under the Act; securities sold in a transaction exempt pursuant to Section 4 of the Act and not involving any public offering; and securities sold offshore pursuant to Regulation S under the Act.

f.   Manner of sale. The securities shall be sold in "brokers' transactions" within the meaning of section 4(4) of the Act or in transactions directly with a "market maker," as that term is defined in section 3(a)(38) of the Securities Exchange Act of 1934, and the person selling the securities shall not

    1. solicit or arrange for the solicitation of orders to buy the securities in anticipation of or in connection with such transaction, or

2. make any payment in connection with the offer or sale of the securities to any person other than the broker who executes the order to sell the securities. The requirements of this paragraph, however, shall not apply to securities sold for the account of the estate of a deceased person or for the account of a beneficiary of such estate provided the estate or beneficiary thereof is not an affiliate of the issuer; nor shall they apply to securities sold for the account of any person other than an affiliate of the issuer, provided the conditions of paragraph (k) of this rule are satisfied.

g. Brokers' Transactions. The term "brokers' transactions" in Section 4(4) of the Act shall for the purposes of this rule be deemed to include transactions by a broker in which such broker—

1. does no more than execute the order or orders to sell the securities as agent for the person for whose account the securities are sold; and receives no more than the usual and customary broker's commission;

2. neither solicits nor arranges for the solicitation of customers' orders to buy the securities in anticipation of or in connection with the transaction; provided, that the foregoing shall not preclude

    i. inquiries by the broker of other brokers or dealers who have indicated an interest in the securities within the preceding 60 days,

    ii. inquiries by the broker of his customers who have indicated an unsolicited bona fide interest in the securities within the preceding 10 business days; or

    iii. the publication by the broker of bid and ask quotations for the security in an inter-dealer quotation system provided that such quotations are incident to the maintenance of a bona fide inter-dealer market for the security for the broker's own account and that the broker has published bona fide bid and ask quotations for the security in an inter-dealer quotation system on each of at least twelve days within the preceding thirty calendar days with no more than four business days in succession without such two-way quotations;

Note to Subparagraph g(2)(ii): The broker should obtain and retain in his files written evidence of indications of bona fide unsolicited interest by his customers in the securities at the time such indications are received.

3. after reasonable inquiry is not aware of circumstances indicating that the person for whose account the securities are sold is an underwriter with respect to the securities or that the transaction is a part of a distribution of securities of the issuer. Without limiting the foregoing, the broker shall be deemed to be aware of any facts or statements contained in the notice required by paragraph (h) below.

Notes

i. The broker, for his own protection, should obtain and retain in his files a copy of the notice required by paragraph (h).

ii. The reasonable inquiry required by paragraph (g)(3) of this section should include, but not necessarily be limited to, inquiry as to the following matters:

a. The length of time the securities have been held by the person for whose account they are to be sold. If practicable, the inquiry should include physical inspection of the securities;

b. The nature of the transaction in which the securities were acquired by such person;

c. The amount of securities of the same class sold during the past three months by all persons whose sales are required to be taken into consideration pursuant to paragraph (e) of this section;

d.   Whether such person intends to sell additional securities of the same class through any other means;

e.   Whether such person has solicited or made any arrangement for the solicitation of buy orders in connection with the proposed sale of securities;

f.   Whether such person has made any payment to any other person in connection with the proposed sale of the securities; and

g.   The number of shares or other units of the class outstanding, or the relevant trading volume.

h.   Notice of proposed sale. If the amount of securities to be sold in reliance upon the rule during any period of three months exceeds 500 shares or other units or has an aggregate sale price in excess of $10,000, three copies of a notice on Form 144 shall be filed with the Commission at its principal office in Washington, D.C.; and if such securities are admitted to trading on any national securities exchange, one copy of such notice shall also be transmitted to the principal exchange on which such securities are so admitted. The Form 144 shall be signed by the person for whose account the securities are to be sold and shall be transmitted for filing concurrently with either the placing with a broker of an order to execute a sale of securities in reliance upon this rule or the execution directly with a market maker of such a sale. Neither the filing of such notice nor the failure of the Commission to comment thereon shall be deemed to preclude the Commission from taking any action it deems necessary or appropriate with respect to the sale of the securities referred to in such notice. The requirements of this paragraph, however, shall not apply to securities sold for the account of any person other than an affiliate of the issuer, provided the conditions of paragraph (k) of this rule are satisfied.

i.   Bona Fide Intention to Sell. The person filing the notice required by paragraph (h) shall have a bona fide intention to sell the securities referred to therein within a reasonable time after the filing of such notice.

j. Non-exclusive rule. Although this rule provides a means for re-selling restricted securities and securities held by affiliates without registration, it is not the exclusive means for reselling such securities in that manner. Therefore, it does not eliminate or otherwise affect the availability of any exemption for resales under Securities Act that a person or entity may be able to rely upon.

k. Termination of certain restrictions on sales of restricted securities by persons other than affiliates. The requirements of paragraphs (c), (e), (f) and (h) of this rule shall not apply to restricted securities sold for the account of a person who is not an affiliate of the issuer at the time of the sale and has not been an affiliate during the pre-ceding three months, provided a period of at least two years has elapsed since the later of the date the securities were acquired from the issuer or from an affiliate of the issuer. The two-year period shall be calculated as described in paragraph (d) of this section.

RULE 144A—PRIVATE RESALES OF SECURITIES TO INSTITUTIONS

Preliminary Notes

1. This section relates solely to the application of section 5 of the Act and not to antifraud or other provisions of the federal securities laws.

2. Attempted compliance with this section does not act as an exclusive election; any seller hereunder may also claim the availability of any other applicable exemption from the registration requirements of the Act.

3. In view of the objective of this section and the policies underlying the Act, this section is not available with respect to any transaction or series of transactions that, although in technical compliance with this section, is part of a plan or scheme to evade the registration provisions of the Act. In such cases, registration under the Act is required.

4. Nothing in this section obviates the need for any issuer or any other person to comply with the securities registration or broker-dealer reg-istration requirements of the Securities Exchange Act of 1934 (the *Exchange Act),* whenever such requirements are applicable.

5. Nothing in this section obviates the need for any person to comply with any applicable state law relating to the offer or sale of securities.

6. Securities acquired in a transaction made pursuant to the provisions of this section are deemed to be *restricted securities* within the meaning of Rule 144(a)(3) of this chapter.

7. The fact that purchasers of securities from the issuer thereof may purchase such securities with a view to reselling such securities pursuant to this section will not affect the availability to such issuer of an exemption under section 4(2) of the Act, or Regulation D under the Act, from the registration requirements of the Act.

a.   *Definitions.*

    1.   For purposes of this section, *qualified institutional buyer* shall mean:

        i.   Any of the following entities, acting for its own account or the accounts of other qualified institutional buyers, that in the aggregate owns and invests on a discretionary basis at least $100 million in securities of issuers that are not affiliated with the entity:

            A.   Any *insurance company* as defined in section 2(13) of the Act;

            Note: A purchase by an insurance company for one or more of its separate accounts, as defined by section 2(a)(37) of the Investment Company Act of 1940 (the "Investment Company Act"), which are neither registered under section 8 of the Investment Company Act nor required to be so registered, shall be deemed to be a purchase for the account of such insurance company.

            B.   Any *investment company* registered under the Investment Company Act or any *business development company* as defined in section 2(a)(48) of that Act;

C. Any *Small Business Investment Company*
    licensed by the U.S. Small Business Ad-
    ministration under section 301(c) or (d) of
    the Small Business Investment Act of 1958;

D. Any *plan* established and maintained by
    a state, its political subdivisions, or any
    agency or instrumentality of a state or its
    political subdivisions, for the benefit of
    its employees;

E. Any *employee benefit plan* within the mean-
    ing of title I of the Employee Retirement
    Income Security Act of 1974;

F. Any trust fund whose trustee is a bank or
    trust company and whose participants are
    exclusively plans of the types identified in
    paragraph (a)(1)(i)(D) or (E) of this sec-
    tion, except trust funds that include as par-
    ticipants individual retirement accounts or
    H.R. 10 plans.

G. Any *business development company* as de-
    fined in section 202(a)22 of the Investment
    Advisers Act of 1940;

H. Any organization described in section
    501(c)(3) of the Internal Revenue Code,
    corporation (other than a bank as defined
    in section 3(a)(2) of the Act or a savings
    and loan association or other institution
    referenced in section 3(a)(5)(A) of the Act
    or a foreign bank or savings and loan asso-
    ciation or equivalent institution), partner-
    ship, or Massachusetts or similar business
    trust; and

I. Any *investment adviser* registered under
    the Investment Advisers Act.

ii. Any *dealer* registered pursuant to section 15 of the
    Exchange Act, acting for its own account or the

accounts of other qualified institutional buyers, that in the aggregate owns and invests on a discretionary basis at least $10 million of securities of issuers that are not affiliated with the dealer, *Provided,* That securities constituting the whole or a part of an unsold allotment to or subscription by a dealer as a participant in a public offering shall not be deemed to be owned by such dealer;

iii. Any *dealer* registered pursuant to <u>section 15</u> of the Exchange Act acting in a riskless principal transaction on behalf of a qualified institutional buyer;

Note: A registered dealer may act as agent, on a nondiscretionary basis, in a transaction with a qualified institutional buyer without itself having to be a qualified institutional buyer.

iv. Any investment company registered under the Investment Company Act, acting for its own account or for the accounts of other qualified institutional buyers, that is part of a family of investment companies which own in the aggregate at least $100 million in securities of issuers, other than issuers that are affiliated with the investment company or are part of such family of investment companies. *Family of investment companies* means any two or more investment companies registered under the Investment Company Act, except for a unit investment trust whose assets consist solely of shares of one or more registered investment companies, that have the same investment adviser (or, in the case of unit investment trusts, the same depositor), Provided That, for purposes of this section:

A. Each series of a series company (as defined in Rule 18f-2 under the <u>Investment Company Act</u>) shall be deemed to be a separate investment company; and

B. Investment companies shall be deemed to have the same adviser (or depositor) if their advisers (or depositors) are majority-owned subsidiaries of the same parent, or if one investment company's adviser (or depositor) is a majority-owned subsidiary of the other investment company's adviser (or depositor);

v.   Any entity, all of the equity owners of which are qualified institutional buyers, acting for its own account or the accounts of other qualified institutional buyers; and

vi.   Any *bank* as defined in section 3(a)(2) of the Act, any savings and loan association or other institution as referenced in section 3(a)(5)(A) of the Act, or any foreign bank or savings and loan association or equivalent institution, acting for its own account or the accounts of other qualified institutional buyers, that in the aggregate owns and invests on a discretionary basis at least $100 million in securities of issuers that are not affiliated with it and that has an audited net worth of at least $25 million as demonstrated in its latest annual financial statements, as of a date not more than 16 months preceding the date of sale under the Rule in the case of a U.S. bank or savings and loan association, and not more than 18 months preceding such date of sale for a foreign bank or savings and loan association or equivalent institution.

2.   In determining the aggregate amount of securities owned and invested on a discretionary basis by an entity, the following instruments and interests shall be excluded: bank deposit notes and certificates of deposit; loan participations; repurchase agreements; securities owned but subject to a repurchase agreement; and currency, interest rate and commodity swaps.

3.   The aggregate value of securities owned and invested on a discretionary basis by an entity shall be the cost of such securities, except where the entity reports its securities

holdings in its financial statements on the basis of their market value, and no current information with respect to the cost of those securities has been published. In the latter event, the securities may be valued at market for purposes of this section.

4. In determining the aggregate amount of securities owned by an entity and invested on a discretionary basis, securities owned by subsidiaries of the entity that are consolidated with the entity in its financial statements prepared in accordance with generally accepted accounting principles may be included if the investments of such subsidiaries are managed under the direction of the entity, except that, unless the entity is a reporting company under section 13 or 15(d) of the Exchange Act, securities owned by such subsidiaries may not be included if the entity itself is a majority-owned subsidiary that would be included in the consolidated financial statements of another enterprise.

5. For purposes of this section, *riskless principal transaction* means a transaction in which a dealer buys a security from any person and makes a simultaneous offsetting sale of such security to a qualified institutional buyer, including another dealer acting as riskless principal for a qualified institutional buyer.

6. For purposes of this section, *effective conversion premium* means the amount, expressed as a percentage of the security's conversion value, by which the price at issuance of a convertible security exceeds its conversion value.

7. For purposes of this section, *effective exercise premium* means the amount, expressed as a percentage of the warrant's exercise value, by which the sum of the price at issuance and the exercise price of a warrant exceeds its exercise value.

b. *Sales by persons other than issuers or dealers.* Any person, other than the issuer or a dealer, who offers or sells securities in compliance with the conditions set forth in paragraph (d) of this section shall be deemed not to be engaged in a distribution of such securities and therefore not to be an underwriter of such securities within the meaning of sections 2(11) and 4(1) of the Act.

c. *Sales by Dealers.* Any dealer who offers or sells securities in compliance with the conditions set forth in paragraph (d) of this section shall be deemed not to be a participant in a distribution of such securities within the meaning of section 4(3)(C) of the Act and not to be an underwriter of such securities within the meaning of section (11) of the Act, and such securities shall be deemed not to have been offered to the public within the meaning of section (4)(3)(A) of the Act.

d. *Conditions to be met.* To qualify for exemption under this section, an offer or sale must meet the following conditions:

1. The securities are offered or sold only to a qualified institutional buyer or to an offeree or purchaser that the seller and any person acting on behalf of the seller reasonably believe is a qualified institutional buyer. In determining whether a prospective purchaser is a qualified institutional buyer, the seller and any person acting on its behalf shall be entitled to rely upon the following non-exclusive methods of establishing the prospective purchaser's ownership and discretionary investments of securities:

    i. The prospective purchaser's most recent publicly available financial statements, *Provided* That such statements present the information as of a date within 16 months preceding the date of sale of securities under this section in the case of a U.S. purchaser and within 18 months preceding such date of sale for a foreign purchaser;

    ii. The most recent publicly available information appearing in documents filed by the prospective purchaser with the Commission or another United States federal, state, or local governmental agency or self-regulatory organization, or with a foreign governmental agency or self-regulatory organization, *Provided* That any such information is as of a date within 16 months preceding the date of sale of securities under this section in the case of a U.S. purchaser and within 18 months preceding such date of sale for a foreign purchaser;

iii. The most recent publicly available information appearing in a recognized securities manual, *Provided* That such information is as of a date within 16 months preceding the date of sale of securities under this section in the case of a U.S. purchaser and within 18 months preceding such date of sale for a foreign purchaser; or

iv. A certification by the chief financial officer, a person fulfilling an equivalent function, or other executive officer of the purchaser, specifying the amount of securities owned and invested on a discretionary basis by the purchaser as of a specific date on or since the close of the purchaser's most recent fiscal year, or, in the case of a purchaser that is a member of a family of investment companies, a certification by an executive officer of the investment adviser specifying the amount of securities owned by the family of investment companies as of a specific date on or since the close of the purchaser's most recent fiscal year;

2. The seller and any person acting on its behalf takes reasonable steps to ensure that the purchaser is aware that the seller may rely on the exemption from the provisions of section 5 of the Act provided by this section;

3. The securities offered or sold:

i. Were not, when issued, of the same class as securities listed on a national securities exchange registered under section 6 of the Exchange Act or quoted in a U.S. automated inter-dealer quotation system; *Provided,* That securities that are convertible or exchangeable into securities so listed or quoted at the time of issuance and that had an effective conversion premium of less than 10 percent, shall be treated as securities of the class into which they are convertible or exchangeable; and that warrants that may be exercised for securities so listed or quoted at the time of issuance, for a period of less than 3 years from the date of issuance, or that had an effective exercise premium of less than 10 percent, shall be treated as securities of the class to be issued upon exercise; and *Provided further,* That the Commission may from time to time, taking into account then-existing market practices, designate additional securities and classes of securities that will not be deemed of the same class as securities listed on a national securities exchange or quoted in a U.S. automated inter-dealer quotation system; and

ii.　Are not securities of an open-end investment company, unit investment trust or face-amount certificate company that is or is required to be registered under section 8 of the Investment Company Act; and

4.

i.　In the case of securities of an issuer that is neither subject to section 13 or 15(d) of the Exchange Act, nor exempt from reporting pursuant to Rule 12g3-2(b) under the Exchange Act, nor a foreign government as defined in Rule 405 eligible to register securities under Schedule B of the Act, the holder and a prospective purchaser designated by the holder have the right to obtain from the issuer, upon request of the holder, and the prospective purchaser has received from the issuer, the seller, or a person acting on either of their behalf, at or prior to the time of sale, upon such prospective purchaser's request to the holder or the issuer, the following information (which shall be reasonably current in relation to the date of resale under this section): a very brief statement of the nature of the business of the issuer and the products and services it offers; and the issuer's most recent balance sheet and profit and loss and retained earnings statements, and similar financial statements for such part of the two preceding fiscal years as the issuer has been in operation (the financial

statements should be audited to the extent reasonably available).

   ii. The requirement that the information be *reason-
        ably current* will be presumed to be satisfied if:

        A. The balance sheet is as of a date less than
            16 months before the date of resale, the
            statements of profit and loss and retained
            earnings are for the 12 months preceding
            the date of such balance sheet, and if such
            balance sheet is not as of a date less than
            6 months before the date of resale, it shall
            be accompanied by additional statements
            of profit and loss and retained earnings for
            the period from the date of such balance
            sheet to a date less than 6 months before
            the date of resale; and

        B. The statement of the nature of the issuer's
            business and its products and services of-
            fered is as of a date within 12 months prior
            to the date of resale; or

        C. With regard to foreign private issuers, the
            required information meets the timing re-
            quirements of the issuer's home country or
            principal trading markets.

 e. Offers and sales of securities pursuant to this section shall be
     deemed not to affect the availability of any exemption or safe har-
     bor relating to any previous or subsequent offer or sale of such secu-
     rities by the issuer or any prior or subsequent holder thereof.

RULE 145—RECLASSIFICATIONS OF SECURITIES, MERGERS, CONSOLIDATIONS AND ACQUISITIONS OF ASSETS

Preliminary Note to Rule 145

Rule 145 is designed to make available the protection provided by
registration under the Securities Act of 1933, as amended (Act), to

persons who are offered securities in a business combination of the type described in subparagraphs (a)(1), (2), and (3) of the rule. The thrust of the rule is that an "offer", "offer to sell", "offer for sale", or "sale" occurs when there is submitted to security holders a plan or agreement pursuant to which such holders are required to elect, on the basis of what is in substance a new investment decision, whether to accept a new or different security in exchange for their existing security. Rule 145 embodies the Commission's determination that such transactions are subject to the registration requirements of the Act, and that the previously existing "no-sale" theory of Rule 133 is no longer consistent with the statutory purposes of the Act. See Release No. 33-5316 (October 6, 1972). Securities issued in transactions described in paragraph (a) of Rule 145 may be registered on Form S-4 or F-4 or Form N-14 under the Act.

Transactions for which statutory exemptions under the Act, including those contained in sections 3(a)(9), (10), (11), and 4(2), are otherwise available are not affected by Rule 145.

> Note 1: Reference is made to Rule 153a describing the prospectus delivery required in a transaction of the type referred to in Rule 145.

> Note 2: A reclassification of securities covered by Rule 145 would be exempt from registration pursuant to section 3(a)(9) or (11) of the Act if the conditions of either of these sections are satisfied.

a. *Transactions Within the Rule.* An "offer", "offer to sell", "offer for sale" or "sale" shall be deemed to be involved, within the meaning of Section 2(3) of the Act, so far as the security holders of a corporation or other person are concerned where, pursuant to statutory provisions of the jurisdiction under which such corporation or other person is organized, or pursuant to provisions contained in its certificate of incorporation or similar controlling instruments, or otherwise, there is submitted for the vote or consent of such security holders a plan or agreement for

   1. *Reclassifications.* A reclassification of securities of such corporation or other person, other than a stock split, reverse stock split, or change in par value, which involves the substitution of a security for another security;

   2. *Mergers or Consolidations.* A statutory merger or consolidation, or similar plan of acquisition in which securities of

such corporation or other person held by such security holders will become or be exchanged for securities of any other person, unless the sole purpose of the transaction is to change an issuer's domicile solely within the United States; or

3. *Transfers of Assets.* A transfer of assets of such corporation or other person, to another person in consideration of the issuance of securities of such other person or any of its affiliates, if:

   A. such plan or agreement provides for dissolution of the corporation or other person whose security holders are voting or consenting; or

   B. such plan or agreement provides for a pro rata or similar distribution of such securities to the security holders voting or consenting; or

   C. the board of directors or similar representatives of such corporation or other person, adopts resolutions relative to (A) or (B) above within one year after the taking of such vote or consent; or

   D. the transfer of assets is a part of a pre-existing plan for distribution of such securities, notwithstanding (A), (B) or (C), above.

b. *Communications Before a Registration Statement Is Filed.* Communications made in connection with or relating to a transaction described in paragraph (a) of this section that will be registered under the Act may be made under Rule 135, Rule 165 or Rule 166.

c. *Persons and Parties Deemed to Be Underwriters.* For purposes of this rule, any party to any transaction specified in paragraph (a), other than the issuer, or any person who is an affiliate of such party at the time any such transaction is submitted for vote or consent, who publicly offers or sells securities of the issuer acquired in connection with any such transaction, shall be deemed to be engaged in a distribution and therefore to be an underwriter thereof within the meaning of Section 2(11) of the Act. The term "party" as used in this paragraph (c) shall mean the corporations, business entities, or other persons, other than the issuer, whose assets or capital structure are affected by the transactions specified in paragraph (a).

d. *Resale Provisions for Persons and Parties Deemed Underwriters.* Notwithstanding the provisions of paragraph (c), a person or party specified therein shall not be deemed to be engaged in a distribution and therefore not to be an underwriter of registered securities acquired in a transaction specified in paragraph (a) of this section if:

1. such securities are sold by such person or party in accordance with the provisions of paragraphs (c), (e), (f) and (g) of Rule 144;

2. such person or party is not an affiliate of the issuer and a period of at least one year, as determined in accordance with paragraph (d) of Rule 144, has elapsed since the date the securities were acquired from the issuer in such transaction, and the issuer meets the requirements of paragraph (c) of Rule 144; or

3. such person or party is not, and has not been for at least three months, an affiliate of the issuer, and a period of at least two years, as determined in accordance with paragraph (d) of Rule 144, has elapsed since the date the securities were acquired from the issuer in such transaction.

e. *Definition of "Person".* The term "person" as used in paragraphs (c) and (d) of this rule, when used with reference to a person for whose account securities are to be sold, shall have the same meaning as the definition of that term in paragraph (a)(2) of Rule 144 under the Act.

RULE 147—"PART OF AN ISSUE," "PERSON RESIDENT," AND "DOING BUSINESS WITHIN" FOR PURPOSES OF SECTION 3(A)(11)

Preliminary Notes

1. This rule shall not raise any presumption that the exemption provided by Section 3(a)(11) of the Act is not available for transactions by an issuer which do not satisfy all of the provisions of the rule.

2. Nothing in this rule obviates the need for compliance with any state law relating to the offer and sale of the securities.

3. Section 5 of the Act requires that all securities offered by the use of the mails or by any means or instruments of transportation or communication in interstate commerce be registered with the Commission. Congress, however, provided certain exemptions in the Act from such registration provisions where there was no practical need for registration or where the benefits of registration were too remote. Among those exemptions is that provided by Section 3(a)(11) of the Act for transactions in "any security which is a part of an issue offered and sold only to persons resident within a single State or Territory, where the issuer of such security is a person resident and doing business within . . . such State or Territory." The legislative history of that Section suggests that the exemption was intended to apply only to issues genuinely local in character, which in reality represent local financing by local industries, carried out through local investment. Rule 147 is intended to provide more objective standards upon which responsible local businessmen intending to raise capital from local sources may rely in claiming the Section 3(a)(11) exemption.

All of the terms and conditions of the rule must be satisfied in order for the rule to be available. These are:

    i.   that the issuer be a resident of and doing business within the state or territory in which all offers and sales are made; and

    ii. that no part of the issue be offered or sold to nonresidents within the period of time specified in the rule. For purposes of the rule the definition of "issuer" in Section 2(4) of the Act shall apply.

All offers, offers to sell, offers for sale, and sales which are part of the same issue must meet all of the conditions of Rule 147 for the rule to be available. The determination whether offers, offers to sell, offers for sale and sales of securities are part of the same issue (i.e., are deemed to be "integrated") will continue to be a question of fact and will depend on the particular circumstances. See Securities Act of 1933 Release No. 4434 (December 6, 1961). Release 33-4434 indicates that in determining whether offers and sales should be regarded as part of the same issue and thus should be integrated any one or more of the following factors may be determinative:

    iii. Are the offerings part of a single plan of financing;

    iv. Do the offerings involve issuance of the same class of securities;

    v. Are the offerings made at or about the same time;

    vi. Is the same type of consideration to be received; and

    vii. Are the offerings made for the same general purpose.

Subparagraph (b)(2) of the rule, however, is designed to provide certainty to the extent feasible by identifying certain types of offers and sales of securities which will be deemed not part of an issue, for purposes of the rule only.

Persons claiming the availability of the rule have the burden of proving that they have satisfied all of its provisions. However, the rule does not establish exclusive standards for complying with the Section 3(a)(11) exemption. The exemption would also be available if the issuer satisfied the standards set forth in relevant administrative and judicial interpretations at the time of the offering but the issuer would have the burden of proving the availability of the exemption. Rule 147 relates to transactions exempted from the registration requirements of Section 5 of the Act by Section 3(a)(11). Neither the rule nor Section 3(a)(11) provides an exemption from the registration requirements of Section 12(g) of the Securities Exchange Act of 1934, the anti-fraud provisions of the federal securities laws, the civil liability provisions of Section 12(2) of the Act or other provisions of the federal securities laws.

Finally, in view of the objectives of the rule and the purposes and policies underlying the Act, the rule shall not be available to any person with respect to any offering which, although in technical compliance with the rule, is part of a plan or scheme by such person to make interstate offers or sales of securities. In such cases registration pursuant to the Act is required.

4. The rule provides an exemption for offers and sales by the issuer only. It is not available for offers or sales of securities by other persons. Section 3(a)(11) of the Act has been interpreted to permit

offers and sales by persons controlling the issuer, if the exemption provided by that Section would have been available to the issuer at the time of the offering. See Securities Act Release No. 4434 (December 6, 1961). Controlling persons who want to offer or sell securities pursuant to <u>Section 3(a)(11)</u> may continue to do so in accordance with applicable judicial and administrative interpretations.

a.   Transactions Covered.

Offers, offers to sell, offers for sale and sales by an issuer of its securities made in accordance with all of the terms and conditions of this rule shall be deemed to be part of an issue offered and sold only to persons resident and doing business within such state or territory, within the meaning of <u>Section 3(a)(11)</u> of the Act.

b.   Part of an Issue.

1.   For purposes of this rule, all securities of the issuer which are part of an issue shall be offered, offered for sale or sold in accordance with all of the terms and conditions of this rule.

2.   For purposes of this rule only, an issue shall be deemed not to include offers, offers to sell, offers for sale or sales of securities of the issuer pursuant to the exemptions provided by <u>Section 3</u> or <u>Section 4(2)</u> of the Act or pursuant to a registration statement filed under the Act, that take place prior to the six month period immediately preceding or after the six month period immediately following any offers, offers for sale or sales pursuant to this rule, Provided, That, there are during either of said six month periods no offers, offers for sale or sales of securities by or for the issuer of the same or similar class as those offered, offered for sale or sold pursuant to the rule.

Note: In the event that securities of the same or similar class as those offered pursuant to the rule are offered, offered for sale or sold less than six months prior to or subsequent to any offer, offer for sale or sale pursuant to this rule, see <u>Preliminary Note 3</u> hereof, as to which offers, offers to sell, offers for sale, or sales are part of an issue.

c. Nature of the Issuer.

The issuer of the securities shall at the time of any offers and the sales be a person resident and doing business within the state or territory in which all of the offers, offers to sell, offers for sale and sales are made.

1. The issuer shall be deemed to be a resident of the state or territory in which:

    i. it is incorporated or organized, if a corporation, limited partnership, trust or other form of business organization that is organized under state or territorial law;

    ii. its principal office is located, if a general partnership or other form of business organization that is not organized under any state or territorial law;

    iii. his principal residence is located, if an individual.

2. The issuer shall be deemed to be doing business within a state or territory if:

    i. the issuer derived at least 80 percent of its gross revenues and those of its subsidiaries on a consolidated basis

        A. for its most recent fiscal year, if the first offer of any part of the issue is made during the first six months of the issuer's current fiscal year; or

        B. for the first six months of its current fiscal year or during the twelve month fiscal period ending with such six month period, if the first offer of any part of the issue is made during the last six months of the issuer's current fiscal year from the operation of a business or of real property located in or from the rendering of services within such state or territory; provided, however, that this provision does not apply to any issuer which has not had gross revenues in excess of $5,000 from the sale of products or services or other conduct of its business for its most recent twelve month fiscal period;

ii. the issuer had at the end of its most recent semi-annual fiscal period prior to the first offer of any part of the issue, at least 80 percent of its assets and those of its subsidiaries on a consolidated basis located within such state or territory;

iii. the issuer intends to use and uses at least 80 percent of the ne[t] proceeds to the issuer from sales made pursuant to this rule in connection with the operation of a business or of real property, the purchase of real property located in, or the rendering of services within such state or territory; and

iv. the principal office of the issuer is located within such state or territory.

d. Offerees and Purchasers; Person Resident.

Offers, offers to sell, offers for sale and sales of securities that are part of an issue shall be made only to persons resident within the state or territory of which the issuer is a resident. For purposes of determining the residence of offerees and purchasers:

1. A corporation, partnership, trust or other form of business organization shall be deemed to be a resident of a state or territory if, at the time of the offer and sale to it, it has its principal office within such state or territory.

2. An individual shall be deemed to be a resident of a state or territory if such individual has, at the time of the offer and sale to him, his principal residence in the state or territory.

3. A corporation, partnership, trust or other form of business organization which is organized for the specific purpose of acquiring part of an issue offered pursuant to this rule shall be deemed not to be a resident of a state or territory unless all of the beneficial owners of such organization are residents of such state or territory.

e.   Limitation of Resales.

During the period in which securities that are part of an issue are being offered and sold by the issuer, and for a period of nine months from the date of the last sale by the issuer of such securities, all resales of any part of the issue, by any person, shall be made only to persons resident within such state or territory.

Notes:

1.   In the case of convertible securities resales of either the convertible security, or if it is converted, the underlying security, could be made during the period described in paragraph (e) only to persons resident within such state or territory. For purposes of this rule a conversion in reliance on Section 3(a)(9) of the Act does not begin a new period.

2.   Dealers must satisfy the requirements of Rule 15c2-11 under the Securities Exchange Act of 1934 prior to publishing any quotation for a security, or submitting any quotation for publication, in any quotation medium.

f.   Precautions Against Interstate Offers and Sales.

1.   The issuer shall, in connection with any securities sold by it pursuant to this rule:

i.   Place a legend on the certificate or other document evidencing the security stating that the securities have not been registered under the Act and setting forth the limitations on resale contained in paragraph (e);

ii.   Issue stop transfer instructions to the issuer's transfer agent, if any, with respect to the securities, or, if the issuer transfers its own securities, make a notation in the appropriate records of the issuer; and

iii.   Obtain a written representation from each purchaser as to his residence.

2.   The issuer shall, in connection with the issuance of new certificates for any of the securities that are part of the same issue that are presented for transfer during the time period

specified in <u>paragraph (e)</u>, take the steps required by subsections (f)(1)(i) and (ii).

3. The issuer shall, in connection with any offers, offers to sell, offers for sale or sales by it pursuant to this rule, disclose, in writing, the limitations on resale contained in paragraph (e) and the provisions of subsections (f)(1)(i) and (ii) and subparagraph (f)(2).

RULE 148—[RESERVED]

RULE 150—DEFINITION OF "COMMISSION OR OTHER REMUNERATION" IN SECTION 3(A)(9), FOR CERTAIN TRANSACTIONS

The term "commission or other remuneration" in <u>Section 3(a)(9)</u> shall not include payments made by the issuer, directly or indirectly, to its security holders in connection with an exchange of securities for outstanding securities, when such payments are part of the terms of the offer of exchange.

RULE 151—SAFE HARBOR DEFINITION OF CERTAIN "ANNUITY CONTRACTS OR OPTIONAL ANNUITY CONTRACTS" WITHIN THE MEANING OF SECTION 3(A)(8)

a. Any annuity contract or optional annuity contract (a "contract") shall be deemed to be within the provisions of <u>section 3(a)(8)</u> of the Securities Act of 1933, Provided, That

1. The annuity or optional annuity contract is issued by a corporation (the "insurer") subject to the supervision of the insurance commissioner, bank commissioner, or any agency or officer performing like functions, of any State or Territory of the United States or the District of Columbia;

2. The insurer assumes the investment risk under the contract as prescribed in paragraph (b) of this rule; and

3. The contract is not marketed primarily as an investment.

b. The insurer shall be deemed to assume the investment risk under the contract if:

    1. The value of the contract does not vary according to the investment experience of a separate account;

    2. The insurer for the life of the contract

        i. Guarantees the principal amount of purchase payments and interest credited thereto, less any deduction (without regard to its timing) for sales, administrative or other expenses or charges; and

        ii. Credits a specified rate of interest (as defined in paragraph (c) of this rule) to net purchase payments and interest credited thereto; and

    3. The insurer guarantees that the rate of any interest to be credited in excess of that described in paragraph (b)(2)(ii) will not be modified more frequently than once per year.

c. The term "specified rate of interest," as used in paragraph (b)(2)(ii) of this rule, means a rate of interest under the contract that is at least equal to the minimum rate required to be credited by the relevant nonforfeiture law in the jurisdiction in which the contract is issued. If that jurisdiction does not have an applicable nonforfeiture law at the time the contract is issued (or if the minimum rate applicable to an existing contract is no longer mandated in that jurisdiction), the specified rate under the contract must at least be equal to the minimum rate then required for individual annuity contracts by the NAIC Standard Nonforfeiture Law.

RULE 152—DEFINITION OF "TRANSACTIONS BY AN ISSUER NOT INVOLVING ANY PUBLIC OFFERING" IN SECTION 4(2), FOR CERTAIN TRANSACTIONS

The phrase "transactions by an issuer not involving any public offering" in Section 4(2) shall be deemed to apply to transactions not involving any public offering at the time of said transactions although subsequently thereto the issuer decides to make a public offering and/or files a registration statement.

RULE 153A—DEFINITION OF "PRECEDED BY A PROSPECTUS" AS USED IN SECTION 5(B)(2) IN RELATION TO CERTAIN TRANSACTIONS REQUIRING APPROVAL OF SECURITY HOLDERS

The term "preceded by a prospectus", as used in Section 5(b)(2) of the Act with respect to any requirement for the delivery of a prospectus to security holders of a corporation or other person, in connection with transactions of the character specified in paragraph (a) of Rule 145 under the Act, shall mean the delivery of a prospectus:

i.   Prior to the vote of security holders on such transaction; or,

ii.   With respect to actions taken by consent, prior to the earliest date on which the corporate action may be taken; to all security holders of record of such corporation or other person, entitled to vote on or consent to the proposed transaction, at their address of record on the transfer records of the corporation or other person.

RULE 156—INVESTMENT COMPANY SALES LITERATURE

a.   Under the federal securities laws, including section 17(a) of the Securities Act of 1933 and section 10(b) of the Securities Exchange Act of 1934 and Rule 10b-5 thereunder, it is unlawful for any person, directly or indirectly, by the use of any means or instrumentality of interstate commerce or of the mails, to use sales literature which is materially misleading in connection with the offer or sale of securities issued by an investment company. Under these provisions, sales literature is materially misleading if it:

1.   contains an untrue statement of a material fact or

2.   omits to state a material fact necessary in order to make a statement made, in the light of the circumstances of its use, not misleading.

b.   Whether or not a particular description, representation, illustration, or other statement involving a material fact is misleading depends on evaluation of the context in which it is made. In considering whether a particular statement involving a material fact is or might be misleading, weight should be given to all pertinent factors, including, but not limited to, those listed below.

1. A statement could be misleading because of:

    i. Other statements being made in connection with the offer of sale or sale of the securities in question;

    ii. The absence of explanations, qualifications, limitations or other statements necessary or appropriate to make such statement not misleading; or

    iii. General economic or financial conditions or circumstances.

2. Representations about past or future investment performance could be misleading because of statements or omissions made involving a material fact, including situations where:

    i. Portrayals of past income, gain, or growth of assets convey an impression of the net investment results achieved by an actual or hypothetical investment which would not be justified under the circumstances; and

    ii. Representations, whether express or implied, about future investment performance, including:

        A. Representations, as to security of capital, possible future gains or income, or expenses associated with an investment;

        B. Representations implying that future gain or income may be inferred from or predicted based on past investment performance; or

        C. Portrayals of past performance, made in a manner which would imply that gains or income realized in the past would be repeated in the future.

3. A statement involving a material fact about the characteristics or attributes of an investment company could be misleading because of:

    i.   Statements about possible benefits connected with or resulting from services to be provided or methods of operation which do not give equal prominence to discussion of any risks or limitations associated therewith;

    ii.   Exaggerated or unsubstantiated claims about management skill or techniques, characteristics of the investment company or an investment in securities issued by such company, services, security of investment or funds, effects of government supervision, or other attributes; and

    iii.   Unwarranted or incompletely explained comparisons to other investment vehicles or to indexes.

c. For purposes of this section, the term *sales literature* shall be deemed to include any communication (whether in writing, by radio, or by television) used by any person to offer to sell or induce the sale of securities of any investment company. Communications between issuers, underwriters and dealers are included in this definition of sales literature if such communications, or the information contained therein, can be reasonably expected to be communicated to prospective investors in the offer or sale of securities or are designed to be employed in either written or oral form in the offer or sale of securities.

RULE 170—PROHIBITION OF USE OF CERTAIN FINANCIAL STATEMENTS

Financial statements which purport to give effect to the receipt and application of any part of the proceeds from the sale of securities for cash shall not be used unless such securities are to be offered through underwriters and the underwriting arrangements are such that the underwriters are or will be committed to take and pay for all of the securities, if any are taken, prior to or within a reasonable time after the commencement of the public offering, or if the securities are not so taken to refund to all subscribers the full amount of all subscription payments made for the securities. The caption of any such financial statement shall clearly set forth the assumptions upon which such statement is based. The caption shall be in type at least as large as that used generally in the body of the statement.

RULE 174—DELIVERY OF PROSPECTUS BY DEALERS; EXEMPTIONS UNDER SECTION 4(3) OF THE ACT

The obligations of a dealer (including an underwriter no longer acting as an underwriter in respect of the security involved in such transactions) to deliver a prospectus in transactions in a security as to which a registration statement has been filed taking place prior to the expiration of the 40- or 90-day period specified in section 4(3) of the Act after the effective date of such registration statement or prior to the expiration of such period after the first date upon which the security was bona fide offered to the public by the issuer or by or through an underwriter after such effective date, whichever is later, shall be subject to the following provisions:

a. No prospectus need be delivered if the registration statement is on Form F-6.

b. No prospectus need be delivered if the issuer is subject, immediately prior to the time of filing the registration statement, to the reporting requirements of section 13 or 15(d) of the Securities Exchange Act of 1934.

c. Where a registration statement relates to offerings to be made from time to time no prospectus need be delivered after the expiration of the initial prospectus delivery period specified in section 4(3) of the Act following the first bona fide offering of securities under such registration statement.

d. If

   1. the registration statement relates to the security of an issuer that is not subject, immediately prior to the time of filing the registration statement, to the reporting requirements of section 13 or 15(d) of the Securities Exchange Act of 1934, and

   2. as of the offering date, the security is listed on a registered national securities exchange or authorized for inclusion in an electronic inter-dealer quotation system sponsored and

governed by the rules of a registered securities association, no prospectus need be delivered after the expiration of twenty-five calendar days after the offering date. For purposes of this provision, the term *offering date* refers to the later of the effective date of the registration statement or the first date on which the security was bona fide offered to the public.

e.   Notwithstanding the foregoing, the period during which a prospectus must be delivered by a dealer shall be:

   1.   As specified in <u>section 4(3)</u> of the Act if the registration statement was the subject of a stop order issued under <u>section 8</u> of the Act; or

   2.   As the Commission may provide upon application or on its own motion in a particular case.

f.   Nothing in this section shall affect the obligation to deliver a prospectus pursuant to the provisions of <u>section 5</u> of the Act by a dealer who is acting as an underwriter with respect to the securities involved or who is engaged in a transaction as to securities constituting the whole or a part of an unsold allotment to or subscription by such dealer as a participant in the distribution of such securities by the issuer or by or through an underwriter.

g.   If the registration statement relates to an offering of securities of a "blank check company," as defined in <u>Rule 419</u> under the Act, the statutory period for prospectus delivery specified in <u>section 4(3)</u> of the Act shall not terminate until 90 days after the date funds and securities are released from the escrow or trust account pursuant to <u>Rule 419</u> under the Act.

Financial statements which purport to give effect to the receipt and application of any part of the proceeds from the sale of securities for cash shall not be used unless such securities are to be offered through underwriters and the underwriting arrangements are such that the underwriters are or will be committed to take and pay for all of the securities, if any are taken, prior to or within a reasonable time after the commencement of the public offering, or if the securities are not so taken to refund to all subscribers the full amount of all subscription payments made for the securities. The caption of any such financial statement shall clearly set forth the assumptions upon which such statement is based. The caption shall be in type at least as large as that used generally in the body of the statement.

RULE 175—LIABILITY FOR CERTAIN STATEMENTS BY ISSUERS

a. A statement within the coverage of paragraph (b) of this section which is made by or on behalf of an issuer or by an outside reviewer retained by the issuer shall be deemed not to be a fraudulent statement (as defined in paragraph (d) of this section), unless it is shown that such statement was made or reaffirmed without a reasonable basis or was disclosed other than in good faith.

b. This rule applies to the following statements:

1. A forward-looking statement (as defined in paragraph (c) of this section) made in a document filed with the Commission, in Part I of a quarterly report on Form 10-Q and Form 10-QSB, Rule 308a of this chapter, or in an annual report to shareholders meeting the requirements of Rules 14a-3(b) and (c) or 14c-3(a) and (b) under the Securities Exchange Act of 1934, a statement reaffirming such forward-looking statement subsequent to the date the document was filed or the annual report was made publicly available, or a forward-looking statement made prior to the date the document was filed or the date the annual report was publicly available if such statement is reaffirmed in a filed document, in Part I of a quarterly report on Form 10-Q and Form 10-QSB, or in an annual report made publicly available within a reasonable time after the making of such forward-looking statement; *Provided,* That

    i. At the time such statements are made or reaffirmed, either the issuer is subject to the reporting requirements of section 13(a) or 15(d) of the Securities Exchange Act of 1934 and has complied with the requirements of rule 13a-1 or 15d-1 thereunder, if applicable, to file its most recent annual report on Form 10-K and Form 10-KSB, Form 20-F or

Form 40-F; or if the issuer is not subject to the reporting requirements of section 13(a) or 15(d) of the Securities Exchange Act of 1934, the statements are made in a registration statement filed under the Act, offering statement or solicitation of interest written document or broadcast script under Regulation A or pursuant to section 12(b) or (g) of the Securities Exchange Act of 1934, and

    ii. The statements are not made by or on behalf of an issuer that is an investment company registered under the Investment Company Act of 1940; and

2. Information which is disclosed in a document filed with the Commission, in Part I of a quarterly report on Form 10-Q and Form 10-QSB or in an annual report to shareholders meeting the requirements of Rules 14a-3(b) and (c) or 14c-3(a) and (b) under the Securities Exchange Act of 1934 and which relates to

    i. the effects of changing prices on the business enterprise, presented voluntarily or pursuant to Item 303 of Regulation S-K or Regulation S-B or Item 9 of Form 20-F "Management's discussion and analysis of financial condition and results of operations," or Item 302 of Regulation S-K, "Supplementary financial information," or Rule 3-20(c) of Regulation S-X, or

    ii. the value of proved oil and gas reserves (such as a standardized measure of discounted future net cash flows relating to proved oil and gas reserves as set forth in paragraphs 30-34 of Statement of Financial Accounting Standards No. 69) presented voluntarily or pursuant to Item 302 of Regulation S-K.

c. For the purpose of this rule, the term *forward-looking statement* shall mean and shall be limited to:

1. A statement containing a projection of revenues, income (loss), earnings (loss) per share, capital expenditures, dividends, capital structure or other financial items;

2. A statement of management's plans and objectives for future operations;

3. A statement of future economic performance contained in management's discussion and analysis of financial condition and results of operations included pursuant to Item 303 of Regulation S-K or Item 9 of Form 20-F; or

4. Disclosed statements of the assumptions underlying or relating to any of the statements described in paragraphs (c) 1, 2, or 3 of this section.

d. For the purpose of this rule the term *fraudulent statement* shall mean a statement which is an untrue statement of a material fact, a statement false or misleading with respect to any material fact, an omission to state a material fact necessary to make a statement not misleading, or which constitutes the employment of a manipulative, deceptive, or fraudulent device, contrivance, scheme, transaction, act, practice, course of business, or an artifice to defraud, as those terms are used in the Securities Act of 1933 or the rules or regulations promulgated thereunder.

RULE 176—CIRCUMSTANCES AFFECTING THE DETERMINATION OF WHAT CONSTITUTES REASONABLE INVESTIGATION AND REASONABLE GROUNDS FOR BELIEF UNDER SECTION 11 OF THE SECURITIES ACT

In determining whether or not the conduct of a person constitutes a reasonable investigation or a reasonable ground for belief meeting the standard set forth in section 11(c), relevant circumstances include, with respect to a person other than the issuer:

a. The type of issuer;

b. The type of security;

c. The type of person;

d. The office held when the person is an officer;

e. The presence or absence of another relationship to the issuer when the person is a director or proposed director;

f. Reasonable reliance on officers, employees, and others whose duties should have given them knowledge of the particular facts;

g. When the person is an underwriter, the type of underwriting arrangement, the role of the particular person as an underwriter and the availability of information with respect to the registrant; and

h. Whether, with respect to a fact or document incorporated by reference, the particular person had any responsibility for the fact or document at the time of the filing from which it was incorporated.

RULE 215—ACCREDITED INVESTOR

The term *accredited investor* as used in section 2(15)(ii) of the Securities Act of 1933 shall include the following persons:

a. Any savings and loan association or other institution specified in section 3(a)(5)(A) of the Act whether acting in its individual or fiduciary capacity; any broker or dealer registered pursuant to section 15 of the Securities Exchange Act of 1934; any plan established and maintained by a state, its political subdivisions, or any agency or instrumentality of a state or its political subdivisions, for the benefit of its employees, if such plan has total assets in excess of $5,000,000; any employee benefit plan within the meaning of Table I of the Employee Retirement Income Security Act of 1974, if the investment decision is made by a plan fiduciary, as defined in section 3(21) of such Act, which is a savings and loan association, or if the employee benefit plan has total assets in excess of $5,000,000 or, if a self-directed plan, with investment decisions made solely by persons that are accredited investors;

b. Any private business development company as defined in section 202(a)(22) of the Investment Advisers Act of 1940;

c. Any organization described in section 501(c)(3) of the Internal Revenue Code, corporation, Massachusetts or similar business trust, or partnership, not formed for the specific purpose of acquiring the securities offered, with total assets in excess of $5,000,000;

d. Any director, executive officer, or general partner of the issuer of the securities being offered or sold, or any director, executive officer, or general partner of a general partner of that issuer;

e. Any natural person whose individual net worth, or joint net worth with that person's spouse, at the time of his purchase exceeds $1,000,000;

f. Any natural person who had an individual income in excess of $200,000 in each of the two most recent years or joint income with that person's spouse in excess of $300,000 in each of those years and has a reasonable expectation of reaching the same income level in the current year;

g. Any trust, with total assets in excess of $5,000,000, not formed for the specific purpose of acquiring the securities offered, whose purchase is directed by a sophisticated person as described in Rule 506(b)(2)(ii); and

h. Any entity in which all of the equity owners are accredited investors.

Appendix 9

GENERAL RULES AND REGULATIONS PROMULGATED UNDER THE SECURITIES EXCHANGE ACT OF 1934

RULE 10B-1—PROHIBITION OF USE OF MANIPULATIVE OR DECEPTIVE DEVICES OR CONTRIVANCES WITH RESPECT TO CERTAIN SECURITIES EXEMPTED FROM REGISTRATION

The term *manipulative or deceptive device or contrivance,* as used in section 10(b), is hereby defined to include any act or omission to act with respect to any security exempted from the operation of section 12(a) pursuant to any section in this part which specifically provides that this section shall be applicable to such security if such act or omission to act would have been unlawful under section 9(a), or any rule or regulation heretofore or hereafter prescribed thereunder, if done or omitted to be done with respect to a security registered on a national securities exchange, and the use of any means or instrumentality of interstate commerce or of the mails or of any facility of any national securities exchange to use or employ any such device or contrivance in connection with the purchase or sale of any such security is hereby prohibited.

RULE 10B-3—EMPLOYMENT OF MANIPULATIVE AND DECEPTIVE DEVICES BY BROKERS OR DEALERS

a.   It shall be unlawful for any broker or dealer, directly or indirectly, by the use of any means or instrumentality of interstate commerce, or of the mails, or of any facility of any national securities exchange, to use or employ, in connection with the purchase or sale of any security otherwise than on a national securities exchange, any act, practice, or course of business defined by the Commission to be included within the term "manipulative, deceptive, or other fraudulent device or contrivance", as such term is used in section 15(c) of the act.

b. It shall be unlawful for any municipal securities dealer directly or indirectly, by the use of any means or instrumentality of interstate commerce, or of the mails, or of any facility of any national securities exchange, to use or employ, in connection with the purchase or sale of any municipal security, any act, practice, or course of business defined by the Commission to be included within the term "manipulative, deceptive, or other fraudulent device or contrivance," as such term is used in section 15(c)(1) of the act.

RULE 10B-5—EMPLOYMENT OF MANIPULATIVE AND DECEPTIVE DEVICES

It shall be unlawful for any person, directly or indirectly, by the use of any means or instrumentality of interstate commerce, or of the mails or of any facility of any national securities exchange,

a. To employ any device, scheme, or artifice to defraud,

b. To make any untrue statement of a material fact or to omit to state a material fact necessary in order to make the statements made, in the light of the circumstances under which they were made, not misleading, or

c. To engage in any act, practice, or course of business which operates or would operate as a fraud or deceit upon any person, in connection with the purchase or sale of any security.

RULE 10B-6—THROUGH RULE 10B-8 [RESERVED]

[Editors' note: Rule 10B-21 replaced by Regulation M Rule 105; *see* Appendix 10.]

RULE 10B-9—PROHIBITED REPRESENTATIONS IN CONNECTION WITH CERTAIN OFFERINGS

a. It shall constitute a *manipulative or deception device or contrivance,* as used in <u>section 10(b)</u> of the Act, for any person, directly or indirectly, in connection with the offer or sale of any security, to make any representation:

1. To the effect that the security is being offered or sold on an "all-or-none" basis, unless the security is part of an offering or distribution being made on the condition that all or a specified amount of the consideration paid for such security will be promptly refunded to the purchaser unless

    A. all of the securities being offered are sold at a specified price within a specified time, and

    B. the total amount due to the seller is received by him by a specified date; or

2. To the effect that the security is being offered or sold on any other basis whereby all or part of the consideration paid for any such security will be refunded to the purchaser if all or some of the securities are not sold, unless the security is part of an offering or distribution being made on the condition that all or a specified part of the consideration paid for such security will be promptly refunded to the purchaser unless

    A. a specified number of units of the security are sold at a specified price within a specified time, and

    B. the total amount due to the seller is received by him by a specified date.

b. This rule shall not apply to any offer or sale of securities as to which the seller has a firm commitment from underwriters or others (subject only to customary conditions precedent, including "market outs") for the purchase of all the securities being offered.

RULE 10B-10—CONFIRMATION OF TRANSACTIONS

Preliminary Note.

This section requires broker-dealers to disclose specified information in writing to customers at or before completion of a transaction. The requirements under this section that particular information be disclosed is not determinative of a broker-dealer's obligation under the general antifraud provisions of the federal securities laws to disclose additional information to a customer at the time of the customer's investment decision.

a. *Disclosure requirement.* It shall be unlawful for any broker or dealer to effect for or with an account of a customer any transaction in, or to induce the purchase or sale by such customer of, any security (other than U.S. Savings Bonds or municipal securities) unless such broker or dealer, at or before completion of such transaction, gives or sends to such customer written notification disclosing:

   1. The date and time of the transaction (or the fact that the time of the transaction will be furnished upon written request to such customer) and the identity, price, and number of shares or units (or principal amount) of such security purchased or sold by such customer; and

   2. Whether the broker or dealer is acting as agent for such customer, as agent for some other person, as agent for both such customer and some other person, or as principal for its own account; and if the broker or dealer is acting as principal, whether it is a market maker in the security (other than by reason of acting as a block positioner); and

      i. If the broker or dealer is acting as agent for such customer, for some other person, or for both such customer and some other person:

         A. The name of the person from whom the security was purchased, or to whom it was sold, for such customer or the fact that the information will be furnished upon written request of such customer; and

B. The amount of any remuneration received or to be received by the broker from such customer in connection with the transaction unless remuneration paid by such customer is determined pursuant to written agreement with such customer, otherwise than on a transaction basis; and

C. For a transaction in any subject security as defined in Rule 11Ac1-2 or a security authorized for quotation on an automated interdealer quotation system that has the characteristics set forth in Section 17B of this Act, a statement whether payment for order flow is received by the broker or dealer for transactions in such securities and the fact that the source and nature of the compensation received in connection with the particular transaction will be furnished upon written request of the customer; and

D. The source and amount of any other remuneration received or to be received by the broker in connection with the transaction: *Provided, however,* that if, in the case of a purchase, the broker was not participating in a distribution, or in the case of a sale, was not participating in a tender offer, the written notification may state whether any other remuneration has been or will be received and the fact that the source and amount of such other remuneration will be furnished upon written request of such customer; or

ii. If the broker or dealer is acting as principal for its own account:

A. In the case where such broker or dealer is not a market maker in an equity security and, if, after having received an order to buy from a customer, the broker or dealer purchased the equity security from another person to offset a contemporaneous sale to such customer or, after having received an order to sell from a customer, the broker or dealer sold the security to another person to offset a contemporaneous purchase from such customer, the difference between the price to the customer and the dealer's contemporaneous purchase (for customer purchases) or sale price (for customer sales); or

B. In the case of any other transaction in a reported security, or an equity security that is quoted on NASDAQ or traded on a national securities exchange and that is subject to last sale reporting, the reported trade price, the price to the customer in the transaction, and the difference, if any, between the reported trade price and the price to the customer.

3. Whether any odd-lot differential or equivalent fee has been paid by such customer in connection with the execution of an order for an odd-lot number of shares or units (or principal amount) of a security and the fact that the amount of any such differential or fee will be furnished upon oral or written request: *Provided, however,* that such disclosure need not be made if the differential or fee is included in the remuneration disclosure, or exempted from disclosure, pursuant to <u>paragraph (a)(2)(i)(B)</u> of this section; and

4. In the case of any transaction in a debt security subject to redemption before maturity, a statement to the effect that such debt security may be redeemed in whole or in part before maturity, that such a redemption could affect the yield represented and the fact that additional information is available upon request; and

5. In the case of a transaction in a debt security effected exclusively on the basis of a dollar price:

    i. The dollar price at which the transaction was effected, and

    ii. The yield to maturity calculated from the dollar price: *Provided, however,* that this paragraph (a)5(ii) shall not apply to a transaction in a debt security that either:

        A. Has a maturity date that may be extended by the issuer thereof, with a variable interest payable thereon; or

        B. Is an asset-backed security, that represents an interest in or is secured by a pool of receivables or other financial assets that are subject continuously to prepayment; and

6. In the case of a transaction in a debt security effected on the basis of yield:

    i. The yield at which the transaction was effected, including the percentage amount and its characterization (e.g., current yield, yield to maturity, or yield to call) and if effected at yield to call, the type of call, the call date and call price; and

    ii. The dollar price calculated from the yield at which the transaction was effected; and

    iii. If effected on a basis other than yield to maturity and the yield to maturity is lower than the represented yield, the yield to maturity as well as the represented yield; *Provided, however,* that this paragraph (a)6(iii) shall not apply to a transaction in a debt security that either:

        A. Has a maturity date that may be extended by the issuer thereof, with a variable interest rate payable thereon; or

> B. Is an asset-backed security, that represents an interest in or is secured by a pool of receivables or other financial assets that are subject continuously to prepayment; and

7. In the case of a transaction in a debt security that is an asset-backed security, which represents an interest in or is secured by a pool of receivables or other financial assets that are subject continuously to prepayment, a statement indicating that the actual yield of such asset-backed security may vary according to the rate at which the underlying receivables or other financial assets are prepaid and a statement of the fact that information concerning the factors that affect yield (including at a minimum estimated yield, weighted average life, and the prepayment assumptions underlying yield) will be furnished upon written request of such customer; and

   i. [Reserved]

   ii. [Reserved]

   iii. For a transaction in any subject security as defined in Rule 11Ac1-2 or a security authorized for quotation on an automated interdealer quotation system that has the characteristics set forth in Section 17B of the Act, a statement whether payment for order flow is received by the broker or dealer for transactions in such securities and that the source and nature of the compensation received in connection with the particular transaction will be furnished upon written request of the customer; and

   iv. The source and amount of any other remuneration received or to be received by him in connection with the transaction: *Provided, however,* That if, in the case of a purchase, the broker was not participating in a distribution, or in the case of a sale, was not participating in a tender offer, the written notification may state whether any other remuneration has been or will be received and that the source and amount of such other remuneration will be furnished upon written request of such customer; and

8. If he is acting as principal for his own account.

    i.

        A. If he is not a market maker in that security and, if, after having received an order to buy from such customer, he purchased the security from another person to offset a contemporaneous sale to such customer or, after having received an order to sell from such customer, he sold the security to another person to offset a contemporaneous purchase from such a customer, the amount of any mark-up, mark-down, or similar remuneration received in an equity security; or

        B. In any other case of a transaction in a reported security, the trade price reported in accordance with an effective transaction reporting plan, the price to the customer in the transaction, and the difference, if any, between the reported trade price and the price to the customer.

    iii. In the case of a transaction in an equity security, whether he is a market maker in the security (otherwise than by reason of his acting as a block positioner in that security).

9. That the broker or dealer is not a member of the Securities Investor Protection Corporation (SIPC), or that the broker or dealer clearing or carrying the customer account is not a member of SIPC, if such is the case: *Provided, however,* that this paragraph (a)(9) shall not apply in the case of a transaction in shares of a registered open-end investment company or unit investment trust if:

    i. The customer sends funds or securities directly to, or receives funds or securities directly from, the registered open-end investment company or unit investment trust, its transfer agent, its custodian, or other designated agent, and such person is not an associated person of the broker or dealer required by paragraph (a) of this section to send written notification to the customer; and

ii. The written notification required by paragraph (a) of this section is sent on behalf of the broker or dealer to the customer by a person described in paragraph (a)(9)(i) of this section.

b. *Alternative periodic reporting.* A broker or dealer may effect transactions for or with the account of a customer without giving or sending to such customer the written notification described in paragraph (a) of this section if:

1. Such transactions are effected pursuant to a periodic plan or an investment company plan, or effected in shares of any open-end management investment company registered under the Investment Company Act of 1940 that holds itself out as a money market fund and attempts to maintain a stable net asset value per share: *Provided, however,* that no sales load is deducted upon the purchase or redemption of shares in the money market fund; and

2. Such broker or dealer gives or sends to such customer within five business days after the end of each *quarterly* period, for transactions involving investment company and periodic plans, and after the end of each *monthly* period, for other transactions described in paragraph (c)(1) of this section, a written statement disclosing each purchase or redemption, effected for or with, and each dividend or distribution credited to or reinvested for, the account of such customer during the month; the date of such transaction; the identity, number, and price of any securities purchased or redeemed by such customer in each such transaction; the total number of shares of such securities in such customer's account; any remuneration received or to be received by the broker or dealer in connection therewith; and that any other information required by paragraph (a) of this section will be

furnished upon written request: *Provided, however,* that the written statement may be delivered to some other person designated by the customer for distribution to the customer; and

3. Such customer is provided with prior notification in writing disclosing the intention to send the written information referred to in paragraph (c)(1) of this section in lieu of an immediate confirmation.

c. A broker or dealer shall give or send to a customer information requested pursuant to this rule within 5 business days of receipt of the request: *Provided, however,* That in the case of information pertaining to a transaction effected more than 30 days prior to receipt of the request, the information shall be given or sent to the customer within 15 business days.

d. *Definitions.* For the purposes of this section:

1. *Customer* shall not include a broker or dealer;

2. *Completion of the transaction* shall have the meaning provided in Rule 15c1-1 under the Act;

3. *Time of the transaction* means the time of execution, to the extent feasible, of the customer's order;

4. *Debt security* as used in paragraphs (a)(3), (4), and (5) only, means any security, such as a bond, debenture, note, or any other similar instrument which evidences a liability of the issuer (including any such security that is convertible into stock or a similar security) and fractional or participation interests in one or more of any of the foregoing: *Provided, however,* That securities issued by an investment company registered under the Investment Company Act of 1940 shall not be included in this definition;

5. *Periodic plan* means any written authorization for a broker acting as agent to purchase or sell for a customer a specific security or securities (other than securities issued by an open end investment company or unit investment trust registered under the Investment Company Act of 1940), in specific amounts (calculated in security units or dollars), at

specific time intervals and setting forth the commissions or charges to be paid by the customer in connection therewith (or the manner of calculating them); and

6. *Investment company plan* means any plan under which securities issued by an open-end investment company or unit investment trust registered under the Investment Company Act of 1940 are purchased by a customer (the payments being made directly to, or made payable to, the registered investment company, or the principal under-writer, custodian, trustee, or other designated agent of the registered investment company), or sold by a customer pursuant to:

    i. An individual retirement or individual pension plan qualified under the Internal Revenue Code;

    ii. A contractual or systematic agreement under which the customer purchases at the applicable public offering price, or redeems at the applicable redemption price, such securities in specified amounts (calculated in security units or dollars) at specified time intervals and setting forth the commissions or charges to be paid by such customer in connection therewith (or the manner of calculating them; or

    iii. Any other arrangement involving a group of two or more customers and contemplating periodic purchases of such securities by each customer through a person designated by the group: *Provided,* That such arrangement requires the registered investment company or its agent—

        A. To give or send to the designated person, at or before the completion of the transaction for the purchase of such securities, a written notification of the receipt of the total amount paid by the group;

        B. To send to anyone in the group who was a customer in the prior quarter and on whose behalf payment has not been received in the current quarter a quarterly written statement reflecting that a payment was not received on his behalf; and

C. To advise each customer in the group if a payment is not received from the designated person on behalf of the group within 10 days of a date certain specified in the arrangement for delivery of that payment by the designated person and thereafter to send to each such customer the written notification described in paragraph (a) of this section for the next three succeeding payments.

7. *Reported security* shall have the meaning provided in Rule 11Aa3-1 under the Act.

8. *Effective transaction reporting plan* shall have the meaning provided in Rule 11Aa3-1 under the Act.

9. *Payment for order flow* shall mean any monetary payment, service, property, or other benefit that results in remuneration, compensation, or consideration to a broker or dealer from any broker or dealer, national securities exchange, registered securities association, or exchange member in return for the routing of customer orders by such broker or dealer to any broker or dealer, national securities exchange, registered securities association, or exchange member for execution, including but not limited to: research, clearance, custody, products or services; reciprocal agreements for the provision of order flow; adjustment of a broker or dealer's unfavorable trading errors; offers to participate as underwriter in public offerings; stock loans or shared interest accrued thereon; discounts, rebates, or any other reductions of or credits against any fee to, or expense or other financial obligation of, the broker or dealer routing a customer order that exceeds that fee, expense or financial obligation.

10. *Asset-backed security* means a security that is primarily serviced by the cash flows of a discrete pool of receivables or other financial assets, either fixed or revolving, that by their terms convert into cash within a finite time period plus any

rights or other assets designed to assure the servicing or timely distribution of proceeds to the security holders.

e. The Commission may exempt any broker or dealer from the requirements of paragraphs (a) and (b) of this section with regard to specific transactions of specific classes of transactions for which the broker or dealer will provide alternative procedures to effect the purposes of this section; any such exemption may be granted subject to compliance with such alternative procedures and upon such other stated terms and conditions as the Commission may impose.

RULE 10B-13—[RESERVED]

RULE 10B-16—DISCLOSURE OF CREDIT TERMS IN MARGIN TRANSACTIONS

a. It shall be unlawful for any broker or dealer to extend credit, directly or indirectly, to any customer in connection with any securities transaction unless such broker or dealer has established procedures to assure that each customer:

1. Is given or sent at the time of opening the account, a written statement or statements disclosing

   i. the conditions under which an interest charge will be imposed;

   ii. the annual rate or rates of interest that can be imposed;

   iii. the method of computing interest;

   iv. if rates of interest are subject to change without prior notice, the specific conditions under which they can be changed;

   v. the method of determining the debit balance or balances on which interest is to be charged and whether credit is to be given for credit balances in cash accounts;

   vi. what other charges resulting from the extension of credit, if any, will be made and under what conditions; and

vii. the nature of any interest or lien retained by the broker or dealer in the security or other property held as collateral and the conditions under which additional collateral can be required: *Provided, however,* That the requirements of this Paragraph (a)(1) will be met in any case where the account is opened by telephone if the information required to be disclosed is orally communicated to the customer at that time and the required written statement or statements are sent to the customer immediately thereafter: *And provided, further,* That in the case of customers to whom credit is already being extended on the effective date of this section, the written statement or statements required hereunder must be given or sent to said customers within 90 days after the effective date of this Rule; and

2. Is given or sent a written statement or statements, at least quarterly, for each account in which credit was extended, disclosing

   i. the balance at the beginning of the period; the date, amount and a brief description of each debit and credit entered during such period; the closing balance; and, if interest is charged for a period different from the period covered by the statement, the balance as of the last day of the interest period;

   ii. the total interest charge for the period during which interest is charged (or, if interest is charged separately for separate accounts, the total interest charge for each such account), itemized to show the dates on which the interest period began and ended; the annual rate or rates of interest charged and the interest charge for each such different annual rate of interest; and either each different debit balance on which an interest calculation was based or the average debit balance for the interest period, except that if an average debit balance is used, a separate average debit balance must be disclosed for each interest rate applied; and

iii. all other charges resulting from the extension of credit in that account: *Provided, however,* That if the interest charge disclosed on a statement is for a period different from the period covered by the statement, there must be printed on the statement appropriate language to the effect that it should be retained for use in conjunction with the next statement containing the remainder of the required information: *And provided further,* That in the case of "equity funding programs" registered under the Securities Act of 1933, the requirements of this Paragraph (a)(2) will be met if the broker or dealer furnishes to the customer, within 1 month after each extension of credit, a written statement or statements containing the information required to be disclosed under this paragraph.

b. It shall be unlawful for any broker or dealer to make any changes in the terms and conditions under which credit charges will be made (as described in the initial statement made under paragraph (a) of this section), unless the customer shall have been given not less than thirty

1. days written notice of such changes, except that no such prior notice shall be necessary where such changes are required by law: *Provided, however,* That if any change for which prior notice would otherwise be required under this paragraph results in a lower interest charge to the customer than would have been imposed before the change, notice of such change may be given within a reasonable time after the effective date of the change.

RULE 10B-17—UNTIMELY ANNOUNCEMENTS OF RECORD DATES

a. It shall constitute a "manipulative or deceptive device or contrivance" as used in Section 10(b) of the Act for any issuer of a class of securities publicly traded by the use of any means or instrumentality of interstate commerce or of the mails or of any facility of any national securities exchange to fail to give notice in accordance with <u>paragraph (b)</u> hereof of the following actions relating to such class of securities:

1. A dividend or other distribution in cash or in kind, except an ordinary interest payment on a debt security, but including a dividend or distribution of any security of the same or another issuer;

2. A stock split or reverse split; or

3. A rights or other subscription offering.

b. Notice shall be deemed to have been given in accordance with this section only if:

1. Given to the National Association of Securities Dealers, Inc., no later than 10 days prior to the record date involved or, in case of a rights subscription or other offering if such 10 days advance notice is not practical, on or before the record date and in no event later than the effective date of the registration statement to which the offering relates, and such notice includes:

   i. Title of the security to which the declaration relates;

   ii. Date of declaration;

   iii. Date of record for determining holders entitled to receive the dividend or other distribution or to participate in the stock or reverse split;

   iv. Date of payment or distribution or, in the case of a stock or reverse split or rights or other subscription offering, the date of delivery;

   v. For a dividend or other distribution including a stock or reverse split or rights or other subscription offering:

      a. In cash, the amount of cash to be paid or distributed per share, except if exact per share cash distributions cannot be given because of existing conversion rights which may be exercised during the notice period and which may affect the per share cash distribution, then a reasonable approximation of the per share distribution may be provided so long as the actual per share distribution is subsequently provided on the record date,

b. In the same security, the amount of the security outstanding immediately prior to and immediately following the dividend or distribution and the rate of the dividend or distribution,

c. In any other security of the same issuer, the amount to be paid or distributed and the rate of the dividend or distribution,

d. In any security of another issuer, the name of the issuer and title of that security, the amount to be paid or distributed, and the rate of the dividend or distribution and if that security is a right or a warrant, the subscription price,

e. In any other property (including securities not covered under paragraphs (b)(1)(v)(b) through (d) of this section) the identity of the property and its value and basis for assigning that value;

vi. Method of settlement of fractional interests;

vii. Details of any condition which must be satisfied or Government approval which must be secured to enable payment of distribution; and in

viii. The case of stock or reverse split in addition to the aforementioned information;

a. The name and address of the transfer or exchange agent; or

2. The Commission, upon written request or upon its own motion, exempts the issuer from compliance with paragraph

(b)(1) of this section either unconditionally or on specified terms or conditions, as not constituting a manipulative or deceptive device or contrivance comprehended within the purpose of this section; or

3. Given in accordance with procedures of the national securities exchange or exchanges upon which a security of such issuer is registered pursuant to Section 12 of the Act which contain requirements substantially comparable to those set forth in paragraph (b)(1) of this section.

c. The provisions of this rule shall not apply, however, to redeemable securities issued by open-end investment companies and unit investment trusts registered with the Commission under the Investment Company Act of 1940.

RULE 10B-21—[RESERVED]

[Editors' note: Rule 10B-21 replaced by Regulation M Rule 105; *see* Appendix 10.]

RULE 13E-4—TENDER OFFERS BY ISSUERS

a. *Definitions.* Unless the context otherwise requires, all terms used in this section and in Schedule TO shall have the same meaning as in the Act or elsewhere in the General Rules and Regulations thereunder. In addition, the following definitions shall apply:

1. The term *issuer* means any issuer which has a class of equity security registered pursuant to section 12 of the Act, or which is required to file periodic reports pursuant to section 15(d) of the Act, or which is a closed-end investment company registered under the Investment Company Act of 1940.

2. The term *issuer tender offer* refers to a tender offer for, or a request or invitation for tenders of, any class of equity security, made by the issuer of such a class of equity security or by an affiliate of such issuer.

3. As used in this section and in Schedule TO, the term *business day* means any day, other than Saturday, Sunday, or a

Federal holiday, and shall consist of the time period from 12:01 a.m. through 12:00 midnight Eastern Time. In computing any time period under this Rule or Schedule 13E-4, the date of the event that begins the running of such time period shall be included *except that* if such event occurs on other than a business day such period shall begin to run on and shall include the first business day thereafter.

4. The term commencement means 12:01 a.m. on the date that the issuer or affiliate has first published, sent or given the means to tender to security holders. For purposes of this section, the means to tender includes the transmittal form or a statement regarding how the transmittal form may be obtained.

5. The term *termination* means the date after which securities may not be tendered pursuant to an issuer tender offer.

6. The term *security holders* means holders of record and beneficial owners of securities of the class of equity security which is the subject of an issuer tender offer.

7. The term *executive officer* means the president, secretary, treasurer, any vice president in charge of a principal business function (such as sales, administration or finance) or any other person who performs similar policy making functions for a corporation.

8. The term *security position listing* means, with respect to the securities of any issuer held by a registered clearing agency in the name of the clearing agency or its nominee, a list of those participants in the clearing agency on whose behalf the clearing agency holds the issuer's securities and of the participants' respective positions in such securities as of a specified date.

b. Filing, disclosure and dissemination. As soon as practicable on the date of commencement of the issuer tender offer, the issuer or affiliate making the issuer tender offer must comply with:

1. The filing requirements of paragraph (c)(2) of this section;

2. The disclosure requirements of <u>paragraph (d)(1)</u> of this section; and

   3.   The dissemination requirements of <u>paragraph (e)</u> of this section.

c. Material required to be filed. The issuer or affiliate making the issuer tender offer must file with the Commission:

   1.   All written communications made by the issuer or affiliate relating to the issuer tender offer, from and including the first public announcement, as soon as practicable on the date of the communication;

   2.   A <u>Schedule TO</u> (Rule 14d-100), including all exhibits;

   3.   An amendment to Schedule TO (Rule 14d-100) reporting promptly any material changes in the information set forth in the schedule previously filed; and

   4.   A final amendment to Schedule TO (Rule 14d-100) reporting promptly the results of the issuer tender offer.

Instructions to Rule 13e-4(c):

   5.   Pre-commencement communications must be filed under cover of Schedule TO (Rule 14d-100) and the box on the cover page of the schedule must be marked.

   6.   Any communications made in connection with an exchange offer registered under the Securities Act of 1933 need only be filed under <u>Rule 425</u> and will be deemed filed under this section.

   7.   Each pre-commencement written communication must include a prominent legend in clear, plain language advising security holders to read the tender offer statement when it is available because it contains important information. The legend also must advise investors that they can get the tender offer statement and other filed documents for free at the Commission's web site and explain which documents are free from the issuer.

   8.   See <u>Rule 135</u>, <u>Rule 165</u> and <u>Rule 166</u> for pre-commencement communications made in connection with registered exchange offers.

9. "Public announcement" is any oral or written communication by the issuer, affiliate or any person authorized to act on their behalf that is reasonably designed to, or has the effect of, informing the public or security holders in general about the issuer tender offer.

d. Disclosure of tender offer information to security holders.

1. The issuer or affiliate making the issuer tender offer must disclose, in a manner prescribed by paragraph (e)(1) of this section, the following:

   i. The information required by Item 1 of <u>Schedule TO</u> (Rule 14d-100) (summary term sheet); and

   ii. The information required by the remaining items of Schedule TO for issuer tender offers, except for Item 12 (exhibits), or a fair and adequate summary of the information.

2. If there are any material changes in the information previously disclosed to security holders, the issuer or affiliate must disclose the changes promptly to security holders in a manner specified in paragraph (e)(3) of this section.

3. If the issuer or affiliate disseminates the issuer tender offer by means of summary publication as described in paragraph (e)(1)(iii) of this section, the summary advertisement must not include a transmittal letter that would permit security holders to tender securities sought in the offer and must disclose at least the following information:

   i. The identity of the issuer or affiliate making the issuer tender offer;

   ii. The information required by <u>Item 1004(a)(1)</u> and <u>Item 1006(a)</u> of this chapter;

   iii. Instructions on how security holders can obtain promptly a copy of the statement required by paragraph (d)(1) of this section, at the issuer or affiliate's expense; and

iv. A statement that the information contained in the statement required by paragraph (d)(1) of this section is incorporated by reference.

e. Dissemination of tender offers to security holders. An issuer tender offer will be deemed to be published, sent or given to security holders if the issuer or affiliate making the issuer tender offer complies fully with one or more of the methods described in this section.

1. For issuer tender offers in which the consideration offered consists solely of cash and/or securities exempt from registration under <u>section 3</u> of the Securities Act of 1933:

   i. Dissemination of cash issuer tender offers by long-form publication: By making adequate publication of the information required by paragraph (d)(1) of this section in a newspaper or newspapers, on the date of commencement of the issuer tender offer.

   ii. Dissemination of any issuer tender offer by use of stockholder and other lists:

      A. By mailing or otherwise furnishing promptly a statement containing the information required by paragraph (d)(1) of this section to each security holder whose name appears on the most recent stockholder list of the issuer;

      B. By contacting each participant on the most recent security position listing of any clearing agency within the possession or access of the issuer or affiliate making the issuer tender offer, and making inquiry of each participant as to the approximate number of beneficial owners of the securities sought in the offer that are held by the participant;

      C. By furnishing to each participant a sufficient number of copies of the statement required by paragraph (d)(1) of this section for transmittal to the beneficial owners; and

          D. By agreeing to reimburse each participant promptly for its reasonable expenses incurred in forwarding the statement to beneficial owners.

    iii. Dissemination of certain cash issuer tender offers by summary publication:

          A. If the issuer tender offer is not subject to Rule 13e-3, by making adequate publication of a summary advertisement containing the information required by paragraph (d)(3) of this section in a newspaper or newspapers, on the date of commencement of the issuer tender offer; and

          B. By mailing or otherwise furnishing promptly the statement required by paragraph (d)(1) of this section and a transmittal letter to any security holder who requests a copy of the statement or transmittal letter.

Instruction to paragraph (e)(1):

For purposes of paragraphs (e)(1)(i) and (e)(1)(iii) of this section, adequate publication of the issuer tender offer may require publication in a newspaper with a national circulation, a newspaper with metropolitan or regional circulation, or a combination of the two, depending upon the facts and circumstances involved.

2. For tender offers in which the consideration consists solely or partially of securities registered under the Securities Act of 1933, a registration statement containing all of the required information, including pricing information, has been filed and a preliminary prospectus or a prospectus that meets the requirements of Section 10(a) of the Securities Act, including a letter of transmittal, is delivered to security holders. However, for going-private transactions (as defined by Rule 13e-3) and roll-up transactions (as described by Item 901 of Regulation S-K), a registration statement registering the securities to be offered must have become effective

and only a prospectus that meets the requirements of Section 10(a) of the Securities Act may be delivered to security holders on the date of commencement.

Instructions to paragraph (e)(2):

1. If the prospectus is being delivered by mail, mailing on the date of commencement is sufficient.

2. A preliminary prospectus used under this section may not omit information under Rule 430 or Rule 430A.

3. If a preliminary prospectus is used under this section and the issuer must disseminate material changes, the tender offer must remain open for the period specified in paragraph (e)(3) of this section.

4. If a preliminary prospectus is used under this section, tenders may be requested in accordance with Rule 162(a) of this chapter.

3. If a material change occurs in the information published, sent or given to security holders, the issuer or affiliate must disseminate promptly disclosure of the change in a manner reasonably calculated to inform security holders of the change. In a registered securities offer where the issuer or affiliate disseminates the preliminary prospectus as permitted by paragraph (e)(2) of this section, the offer must remain open from the date that material changes to the tender offer materials are disseminated to security holders, as follows:

   i. Five business days for a prospectus supplement containing a material change other than price or share levels;

   ii. Ten business days for a prospectus supplement containing a change in price, the amount of securities sought, the dealer's soliciting fee, or other similarly significant change;

   iii. Ten business days for a prospectus supplement included as part of a post-effective amendment; and

iv. Twenty business days for a revised prospectus when
the initial prospectus was materially deficient.

f. *Manner of making tender offer.*

1. The issuer tender offer, unless withdrawn, shall remain open
until the expiration of:

i.   At least twenty business days from its commencement; and

ii. At least ten business days from the date that notice
of an increase or decrease in the percentage of the
class of securities being sought or the consideration offered or the dealer's soliciting fee to be
given is first published, sent or given to security
holders.

Provided, however, That, for purposes of this paragraph, the
acceptance for payment by the issuer or affiliate of an additional amount of securities not to exceed two percent of the
class of securities that is the subject of the tender offer shall
not be deemed to be an increase. For purposes of this paragraph, the percentage of a class of securities shall be calculated in accordance with <u>section 14(d)(3)</u> of the Act.

2. The issuer or affiliate making the issuer tender offer shall
permit securities tendered pursuant to the issuer tender
offer to be withdrawn:

i.   At any time during the period such issuer tender
offer remains open; and

ii. If not yet accepted for payment, after the expiration
of forty business days from the commencement of
the issuer tender offer.

3. If the issuer or affiliate makes a tender offer for less than
all of the outstanding equity securities of a class, and if a
greater number of securities is tendered pursuant thereto
than the issuer or affiliate is bound or willing to take up and
pay for, the securities taken up and paid for shall be taken
up and paid for as nearly as may be pro rata, disregarding

fractions, according to the number of securities tendered by each security holder during the period such offer remains open; *Provided, however,* That this provision shall not prohibit the issuer or affiliate making the issuer tender offer from:

    i.   Accepting all securities tendered by persons who own, beneficially or of record, an aggregate of not more than a specified number which is less than one hundred shares of such security and who tender all their securities, before prorating securities tendered by others; or

    ii.   Accepting by lot securities tendered by security holders who tender all securities held by them and who, when tendering their securities, elect to have either all or none or at least a minimum amount or none accepted, if the issuer or affiliate first accepts all securities tendered by security holders who do not so elect;

4.   In the event the issuer or affiliate making the issuer tender offer increases the consideration offered after the issuer tender offer has commenced, such issuer or affiliate shall pay such increased consideration to all security holders whose tendered securities are accepted for payment by such issuer or affiliate.

5.   The issuer or affiliate making the tender offer shall either pay the consideration offered, or return the tendered securities, promptly after the termination or withdrawal of the tender offer.

6.   Until the expiration of at least ten business days after the date of termination of the issuer tender offer, neither the issuer nor any affiliate shall make any purchases, otherwise than pursuant to the tender offer, of:

    i.   Any security which is the subject of the issuer tender offer, or any security of the same class and series, or any right to purchase any such securities; and

    ii.   In the case of an issuer tender offer which is an exchange offer, any security being offered pursuant to such exchange offer, or any security of the same class and series, or any right to purchase any such security.

7. The time periods for the minimum offering periods pursuant to this section shall be computed on a concurrent as opposed to a consecutive basis.

8. No issuer or affiliate shall make a tender offer unless:

    i.   The tender offer is open to all security holders of the class of securities subject to the tender offer; and

    ii.   The consideration paid to any security holder pursuant to the tender offer is the highest consideration paid to any other security holder during such tender offer.

9. Paragraph (f)(8)(i) of this section shall not:

    i.   Affect dissemination under paragraph (e) of this section; or

    ii.   Prohibit an issuer or affiliate from making a tender offer excluding all security holders in a state where the issuer or affiliate is prohibited from making the tender offer by administrative or judicial action pursuant to a state statute after a good faith effort by the issuer or affiliate to comply with such statute.

10. Paragraph (f)(8)(ii) of this section shall not prohibit the offer of more than one type of consideration in a tender offer, provided that:

    i.   Security holders are afforded equal right to elect among each of the types of consideration offered; and

    ii.   The highest consideration of each type paid to any security holder is paid to any other security holder receiving that type of consideration.

11. If the offer and sale of securities constituting consideration offered in an issuer tender offer is prohibited by the appropriate authority of a state after a good faith effort by the issuer or affiliate to register or qualify the offer and sale of such securities in such state:

    i.   The issuer or affiliate may offer security holders in such state an alternative form of consideration; and

    ii. Paragraph (f)(10) of this section shall not operate to require the issuer or affiliate to offer or pay the alternative form of consideration to security holders in any other state.

12. *Electronic filings.* If the issuer or affiliate is an electronic filer, the minimum offering periods set forth in paragraph (f)(1) of this section shall be tolled for any period during which it fails to file in electronic format, absent a hardship exemption, the Schedule TO Issuer Tender Offer Statement, the tender offer material specified in Item 1016(a)(1) of Regulation M-A, and any amendments thereto. If such documents were filed in paper pursuant to a hardship exemption (see Rule 201 and Rule 202), the minimum offering periods shall be tolled for any period during which a required confirming electronic copy of such Schedule and tender offer material is delinquent.

g. The requirements of section 13(e)(1) of the Act and Rule 13e-4 and Schedule TO thereunder shall be deemed satisfied with respect to any issuer tender offer, including any exchange offer, where the issuer is incorporated or organized under the laws of Canada or any Canadian province or territory, is a foreign private issuer, and is not an investment company registered or required to be registered under the Investment Company Act of 1940, if less than 40 percent of the class of securities that is the subject of the tender offer is held by U.S. holders, and the tender offer is subject to, and the issuer complies with, the laws, regulations and policies of Canada and/or any of its provinces or territories governing the conduct of the offer (unless the issuer has received an exemption(s) from, and the issuer tender offer does not comply with, requirements that otherwise would be prescribed by this section), *provided that:*

1. Where the consideration for an issuer tender offer subject to this paragraph consists solely of cash, the entire disclosure document or documents required to be furnished to holders of the class of securities to be acquired shall be filed with the Commission on <u>Schedule 13E-4F</u> and disseminated to shareholders residing in the United States in accordance with such Canadian laws, regulations and policies; or

2. Where the consideration for an issuer tender offer subject to this paragraph includes securities to be issued pursuant to the offer, any registration statement and/or prospectus relating thereto shall be filed with the Commission along with the Schedule 13E-4F referred to in paragraph (g)1 of this section, and shall be disseminated, together with the home jurisdiction document(s) accompanying such Schedule, to shareholders of the issuer residing in the United States in accordance with such Canadian laws, regulations and policies.

Note: Notwithstanding the grant of an exemption from one or more of the applicable Canadian regulatory provisions imposing requirements that otherwise would be prescribed by this section, the issuer tender offer will be eligible to proceed in accordance with the requirements of this section if the Commission by order determines that the applicable Canadian regulatory provisions are adequate to protect the interest of investors.

h. This section shall not apply to:

1. Calls or redemptions of any security in accordance with the terms and conditions of its governing instruments;

2. Offers to purchase securities evidenced by a scrip certificate, order form or similar document which represents a fractional interest in a share of stock or similar security;

3. Offers to purchase securities pursuant to a statutory procedure for the purchase of dissenting security holders' securities;

4. Any tender offer which is subject to <u>section 14(d)</u> of the Act;

5. Offers to purchase from security holders who own an aggregate of not more than a specified number of shares that is less than one hundred: *Provided, however,* That:

    i. The offer complies with paragraph (f)(8)(i) of this section with respect to security holders who own a number of shares equal to or less than the specified number of shares, except that an issuer can elect to exclude participants in an issuer's plan as that term is defined in Rule 242.100 of Regulation M, or to exclude security holders who do not own their shares as of a specified date determined by the issuer; and

    ii. The offer complies with paragraph (f)(8)(ii) of this section or the consideration paid pursuant to the offer is determined on the basis of a uniformly applied formula based on the market price of the subject security;

6. An issuer tender offer made solely to effect a rescission offer: *Provided, however,* That the offer is registered under the Securities Act of 1933, and the consideration is equal to the price paid by each security holder, plus legal interest if the issuer elects to or is required to pay legal interest;

7. Offers by closed-end management investment companies to repurchase equity securities pursuant to 270.23c-3 of this chapter;

8. Cross-border tender offers (Tier I). Any issuer tender offer (including any exchange offer) where the issuer is a foreign private issuer as defined in Rule 3b-4 if the following conditions are satisfied.

    i. Except in the case of an issuer tender offer which is commenced during the pendency of a tender offer made by a third party in reliance on Rule 14d-1(c), U.S. holders do not hold more than 10 percent of the class of securities sought in the offer (as determined under Instruction 2 to paragraph (h)(8) and paragraph (i) of this section); and

ii. The issuer or affiliate must permit U.S. holders to participate in the offer on terms at least as favorable as those offered any other holder of the same class of securities that is the subject of the offer; however:

    A. Registered exchange offers. If the issuer or affiliate offers securities registered under the Securities Act of 1933, the issuer or affiliate need not extend the offer to security holders in those states or jurisdictions that prohibit the offer or sale of the securities after the issuer or affiliate has made a good faith effort to register or qualify the offer and sale of securities in that state or jurisdiction, except that the issuer or affiliate must offer the same cash alternative to security holders in any such state or jurisdiction that it has offered to security holders in any other state or jurisdiction.

    B. Exempt exchange offers. If the issuer or affiliate offers securities exempt from registration under Rule 802 of this chapter, the issuer or affiliate need not extend the offer to security holders in those states or jurisdictions that require registration or qualification, except that the issuer or affiliate must offer the same cash alternative to security holders in any such state or jurisdiction that it has offered to security holders in any other state or jurisdiction.

    C. Cash only consideration. The issuer or affiliate may offer U.S. holders cash only consideration for the tender of the subject securities, notwithstanding the fact that the issuer or affiliate is offering security holders outside the United States a consideration that consists in whole or in part of securities of the issuer or affiliate, if the issuer or affiliate has a reasonable basis for believing that the amount of cash is substantially equivalent to the value of the consideration offered to non-U.S. holders, and either of the following conditions are satisfied:

1. The offered security is a "margin security" within the meaning of Regulation T (12 CFR 220.2) and the issuer or affiliate undertakes to provide, upon the request of any U.S. holder or the Commission staff, the closing price and daily trading volume of the security on the principal trading market for the security as of the last trading day of each of the six months preceding the announcement of the offer and each of the trading days thereafter; or

2. If the offered security is not a "margin security" within the meaning of Regulation T (12 CFR 220.2), the issuer or affiliate undertakes to provide, upon the request of any U.S. holder or the Commission staff, an opinion of an independent expert stating that the cash consideration offered to U.S. holders is substantially equivalent to the value of the consideration offered security holders outside the United States.

D. Disparate tax treatment. If the issuer or affiliate offers "loan notes" solely to offer sellers tax advantages not available in the United States and these notes are neither listed on any organized securities market nor registered under the Securities Act of 1933, the loan notes need not be offered to U.S. holders.

  iii. Informational documents.

      A. If the issuer or affiliate publishes or otherwise disseminates an informational document to the holders of the securities in connection with the issuer tender offer (including any exchange offer), the issuer or affiliate must furnish that informational document, including any amendments thereto, in English, to the Commission on Form CB by the first business day after publication or dissemination. If the issuer or affiliate is a foreign company, it must also file a Form F-X with the Commission at the same time as the submission of Form CB to appoint an agent for service in the United States.

      B. The issuer or affiliate must disseminate any informational document to U.S. holders, including any amendments thereto, in English, on a comparable basis to that provided to security holders in the home jurisdiction.

      C. If the issuer or affiliate disseminates by publication in its home jurisdiction, the issuer or affiliate must publish the information in the United States in a manner reasonably calculated to inform U.S. holders of the offer.

  iv. An investment company registered or required to be registered under the Investment Company Act of 1940, other than a registered closed-end investment company, may not use this paragraph (h)(8); or

9. Any other transaction or transactions, if the Commission, upon written request or upon its own motion, exempts such transaction or transactions, either unconditionally, or on specified terms and conditions, as not constituting a fraudulent, deceptive or manipulative act or practice comprehended within the purpose of this section.

i. Cross-border tender offers (Tier II). Any issuer tender offer (including any exchange offer) that meets the conditions in paragraph (i)(1) of this section shall be entitled to the exemptive relief specified in paragraph (i)(2) of this section provided that such issuer tender offer complies with all the requirements of this section other than those for which an exemption has been specifically provided in paragraph (i)(2) of this section:

1. Conditions.

   i. The issuer is a foreign private issuer as defined in Rule 3b-4 and is not an investment company registered or required to be registered under the Investment Company Act of 1940, other than a registered closed-end investment company; and

   ii. Except in the case of an issuer tender offer which is commenced during the pendency of a tender offer made by a third party in reliance on Rule 14d-1(d), U.S. holders do not hold more than 40 percent of the class of securities sought in the offer (as determined under Instruction 2 to paragraphs (h)(8) and (i) of this section).

2. Exemptions. The issuer tender offer shall comply with all requirements of this section other than the following:

   i. Equal treatment—loan notes. If the issuer or affiliate offers loan notes solely to offer sellers tax advantages not available in the United States and these notes are neither listed on any organized securities market nor registered under the Securities Act, the loan notes need not be offered to U.S. holders, notwithstanding paragraph (f)(8) and (h)(9) of this section.

ii. Equal treatment—separate U.S. and foreign offers. Notwithstanding the provisions of paragraph (f)(8) of this section, an issuer or affiliate conducting an issuer tender offer meeting the conditions of paragraph (i)(1) of this section may separate the offer into two offers: One offer made only to U.S. holders and another offer made only to non-U.S. holders. The offer to U.S. holders must be made on terms at least as favorable as those offered any other holder of the same class of securities that is the subject of the tender offer.

iii. Notice of extensions. Notice of extensions made in accordance with the requirements of the home jurisdiction law or practice will satisfy the requirements of <u>Rule 14e-1(d)</u>.

iv. Prompt payment. Payment made in accordance with the requirements of the home jurisdiction law or practice will satisfy the requirements of <u>Rule 14e-1(c)</u>.

Instructions to paragraph (h)(8) and (i) of this section:

3. Home jurisdiction means both the jurisdiction of the issuer's incorporation, organization or chartering and the principal foreign market where the issuer's securities are listed or quoted.

4. U.S. holder means any security holder resident in the United States. To determine the percentage of outstanding securities held by U.S. holders:

   i. Calculate the U.S. ownership as of 30 days before the commencement of the issuer tender offer;

   ii. Include securities underlying American Depositary Shares convertible or exchangeable into the securities that are the subject of the tender offer when calculating the number of subject securities outstanding, as well as the number held by U.S. holders. Exclude from the calculations other types of securities that are convertible or exchangeable into the securities that are the subject of the tender offer, such as warrants, options and convertible securities. Exclude from those calculations securities held by persons who hold more than 10 percent of the subject securities;

iii. Use the method of calculating record ownership in <u>Rule 12g3-2(a)</u>, except that your inquiry as to the amount of securities represented by accounts of customers resident in the United States may be limited to brokers, dealers, banks and other nominees located in the United States, your jurisdiction of incorporation, and the jurisdiction that is the primary trading market for the subject securities, if different than your jurisdiction of incorporation;

iv. If, after reasonable inquiry, you are unable to obtain information about the amount of securities represented by accounts of customers resident in the United States, you may assume, for purposes of this definition, that the customers are residents of the jurisdiction in which the nominee has its principal place of business; and

v. Count securities as beneficially owned by residents of the United States as reported on reports of beneficial ownership that are provided to you or publicly filed and based on information otherwise provided to you.

5. United States. United States means the United States of America, its territories and possessions, any State of the United States, and the District of Columbia.

6. The exemptions provided by paragraphs (h)(8) and (i) of this section are not available for any securities transaction or series of transactions that technically complies with paragraph (h)(8) or (i) of this section but are part of a plan or scheme to evade the provisions of this section.

j.

1. It shall be a fraudulent, deceptive or manipulative act or
    practice, in connection with an issuer tender offer, for an
    issuer or an affiliate of such issuer, in connection with
    an issuer tender offer:

    i.   To employ any device, scheme or artifice to de-
         fraud any person;

    ii. To make any untrue statement of a material fact or
         to omit to state a material fact necessary in order
         to make the statements made, in the light of the cir-
         cumstances under which they were made, not mis-
         leading; or

    iii. To engage in any act, practice or course of business
         which operates or would operate as a fraud or de-
         ceit upon any person.

2. As a means reasonably designed to prevent fraudulent, de-
    ceptive or manipulative acts or practices in connection with
    any issuer tender offer, it shall be unlawful for an issuer or
    an affiliate of such issuer to make an issuer tender offer
    unless:

    i.   Such issuer or affiliate complies with the require-
         ments of paragraphs (b), (c), (d), (e) and (f) of this
         section; and

    ii. The issuer tender offer is not in violation of para-
         graph (j)(1) of this section.

Appendix 10

REGULATION M

INDEX

RULE 100—PRELIMINARY NOTE; DEFINITIONS

a. **Preliminary note:** Any transaction or series of transactions, whether or not effected pursuant to the provisions of Regulation M, remain subject to the antifraud and antimanipulation provisions of the securities laws, including, without limitation, Section 17(a) of the Securities Act of 1933 and Sections 9, 10(b), and 15(c) of the Securities Exchange Act of 1934.

b. For purposes of Regulation M the following definitions shall apply:

ADTV means the worldwide average daily trading volume during the two full calendar months immediately preceding, or any 60 consecutive calendar days ending within the 10 calendar days preceding, the filing of the registration statement; or, if there is no registration statement or if the distribution involves the sale of securities on a delayed basis pursuant to Rule 415 under the Securities Act, two full calendar months immediately preceding, or any consecutive 60 calendar days ending within the 10 calendar days preceding, the determination of the offering price.

Affiliated purchaser means:

1. A person acting, directly or indirectly, in concert with a distribution participant, issuer, or selling security holder in connection with the acquisition or distribution of any covered security; or

2. An affiliate, which may be a separately identifiable department or division of a distribution participant, issuer, or selling security holder, that, directly or indirectly, controls the purchases of any covered security by a distribution participant, issuer, or selling security holder, whose purchases are controlled by any such person, or whose purchases are under common control with any such person; or

3. An affiliate, which may be a separately identifiable department or division of a distribution participant, issuer, or selling security holder, that regularly purchases securities for its own account or for the account of others, or that recommends or exercises investment discretion with respect to the purchase or sale of securities; *Provided, however,* That this paragraph (3) shall not apply to such affiliate if the following conditions are satisfied:

    i.   The distribution participant, issuer, or selling security holder:

         A. Maintains and enforces written policies and procedures reasonably designed to prevent the flow of information to or from the affiliate that might result in a violation of Rules 101, 102, and 104 of Regulation M; and

         B. Obtains an annual, independent assessment of the operation of such policies and procedures; and

    ii. The affiliate has no officers (or persons performing similar functions) or employees (other than clerical, ministerial, or support personnel) in common with the distribution participant, issuer, or selling security holder that direct, effect, or recommend transactions in securities; and

    iii. The affiliate does not, during the applicable restricted period, act as a market maker (other than as a specialist in compliance with the rules of a national securities exchange), or engage, as a broker or a dealer, in solicited transactions or proprietary trading, in covered securities.

Agent independent of the issuer means a trustee or other person who is independent of the issuer. The agent shall be deemed to be independent of the issuer only if:

4. The agent is not an affiliate of the issuer; and

5. Neither the issuer nor any affiliate of the issuer exercises any direct or indirect control or influence over the prices or amounts of the securities to be purchased, the timing of, or the manner in which, the securities are to be purchased, or the selection of a broker or dealer (other than the independent agent itself) through which purchases may be executed; *Provided, however,* That the issuer or its affiliate will not be deemed to have such control or influence solely because it revises not more than once in any three-month period the source of the shares to fund the plan, the basis or determining the amount of its contributions to a plan, or the basis for determining the frequency of its allocations to a plan, or any formula specified in a plan that determines the amount or timing of securities to be purchased by the agent.

Asset-backed security has the meaning contained in General Instruction I.B.5. to Form S-3.

At-the-market offering means an offering of securities at other than a fixed price.

Business day refers to a 24 hour period determined with reference to the principal market for the securities to be distributed, and that includes a complete trading session for that market.

Completion of participation in a distribution. Securities acquired in the distribution for investment by any person participating in a distribution, or any affiliated purchaser of such person, shall be deemed to be distributed. A person shall be deemed to have completed its participation in a distribution as follows:

     6.   An issuer or selling security holder, when the distribution is completed;

     7.   An underwriter, when such person's participation has been distributed, including all other securities of the same class that are acquired in connection with the distribution, and any stabilization arrangements and trading restrictions in connection with the distribution have been terminated; Provided, however, That an underwriter's participation will not be deemed to have been completed if a syndicate over-allotment option is exercised in an amount that exceeds the net syndicate short position at the time of such exercise; and

     8.   Any other person participating in the distribution, when such person's participation has been distributed.

Covered security means any security that is the subject of a distribution, or any reference security.

Current exchange rate means the current rate of exchange between two currencies, which is obtained from at least one independent entity that provides or disseminates foreign exchange quotations in the ordinary course of its business.

Distribution means an offering of securities, whether or not subject to registration under the Securities Act, that is distinguished from ordinary trading transactions by the magnitude of the offering and the presence of special selling efforts and selling methods.

Distribution participant means an underwriter, prospective underwriter, broker, dealer, or other person who has agreed to participate or is participating in a distribution.

Electronic communications network has the meaning contained in Rule 11Ac1-1(a)(8) under the Exchange Act.

Employee has the meaning contained in Form S-8.

Exchange Act means the Securities Exchange Act of 1934.

Independent bid means a bid by a person who is not a distribution participant, issuer, selling security holder, or affiliated purchaser.

NASD means the National Association of Securities Dealers, Inc. or any of its subsidiaries.

Nasdaq means the Nasdaq system as defined in Rule 11Ac1-2(a)(3) under the Exchange Act.

Nasdaq security means a security that is authorized for quotation on Nasdaq, and such authorization is not suspended, terminated, or prohibited.

Net purchases means the amount by which a passive market maker's purchases exceed its sales.

Offering price means the price at which the security is to be or is being distributed.

Passive market maker means a market maker that effects bids or purchases in accordance with the provisions of Rule 103.

Penalty bid means an arrangement that permits the managing underwriter to reclaim a selling concession from a syndicate member in connection with an offering when the securities originally sold by the syndicate member are purchased in syndicate covering transactions.

Plan means any bonus, profit-sharing, pension, retirement, thrift, savings, incentive, stock purchase, stock option, stock ownership, stock appreciation, dividend reinvestment, or similar plan; or any dividend or interest reinvestment plan or employee benefit plan as defined in Rule 405 under the Securities Act.

Principal market means the single securities market with the largest aggregate reported trading volume for the class of securities during the 12 full calendar months immediately preceding the filing of the registration statement; or, if there is no registration statement or if the distribution involves the sale of securities on a delayed basis pursuant to Rule 415, during the 12 full calendar months immediately preceding the determination of the offering price. For the purpose of determining the aggregate trading volume in a security, the trading volume of depositary shares representing such security shall be included, and shall be multiplied by the multiple or fraction of the security represented by the depositary share. For purposes of this paragraph, depositary share means a security, evidenced by a depositary receipt, that represents another security, or a multiple or fraction thereof, deposited with a depositary.

Prospective underwriter means a person:

9. Who has submitted a bid to the issuer or selling security holder, and who knows or is reasonably certain that such bid will be accepted, whether or not the terms and conditions of the underwriting have been agreed upon; or

10. Who has reached, or is reasonably certain to reach, an understanding with the issuer or selling security holder, or managing underwriter that such person will become an underwriter, whether or not the terms and conditions of the underwriting have been agreed upon.

Public float value shall be determined in the manner set forth on the front page of Form 10-K, even if the issuer of such securities is not required to file Form 10-K, relating to the aggregate market value of common equity securities held by non-affiliates of the issuer.

Reference period means the two full calendar months immediately preceding the filing of the registration statement or, if there is no registration statement or if the distribution involves the sale of securities on a delayed basis pursuant to Rule 415, the two full calendar months immediately preceding the determination of the offering price.

Reference security means a security into which a security that is the subject of a distribution ("subject security") may be converted, exchanged, or exercised or which, under the terms of the subject security, may in whole or in significant part determine the value of the subject security.

Restricted period means:

11. For any security with an ADTV value of $100,000 or more of an issuer whose common equity securities have a public float value of $25 million or more, the period beginning on the later of one business day prior to the determination of the offering price or such time that a person becomes a distribution participant, and ending upon such person's completion of participation in the distribution; and

12. For all other securities, the period beginning on the later of five business days prior to the determination of the offering price or such time that a person becomes a distribution participant, and ending upon such person's completion of participation in the distribution.

13. In the case of a distribution involving a merger, acquisition, or exchange offer, the period beginning on the day proxy solicitation or offering materials are first disseminated to security holders, and ending upon the completion of the distribution.

Securities Act means the Securities Act of 1933.

Selling security holder means any person on whose behalf a distribution is made, other than an issuer.

Stabilize or *stabilizing* means the placing of any bid, or the effecting of any purchase, for the purpose of pegging, fixing, or maintaining the price of a security.

Syndicate covering transaction means the placing of any bid or the effecting of any purchase on behalf of the sole distributor or the underwriting syndicate or group to reduce a short position created in connection with the offering.

30% ADTV limitation means 30 percent of the market maker's ADTV in a covered security during the reference period, as obtained from the NASD.

Underwriter means a person who has agreed with an issuer or selling security holder:

14. To purchase securities for distribution; or

15. To distribute securities for or on behalf of such issuer or selling security holder; or

16. To manage or supervise a distribution of securities for or on behalf of such issuer or selling security holder.

RULE 101—ACTIVITIES BY DISTRIBUTION PARTICIPANTS

a. Unlawful Activity. In connection with a distribution of securities, it shall be unlawful for a distribution participant or an affiliated purchaser of such person, directly or indirectly, to bid for, purchase, or attempt to induce any person to bid for or purchase, a covered security during the applicable restricted period; Provided, however, That if a distribution participant or affiliated purchaser is the issuer or selling security holder of the securities subject to the distribution, such person shall be subject to the provisions of Rule 102, rather than this section.

b. Excepted Activity. The following activities shall not be prohibited by paragraph (a) of this section:

1. Research. The publication or dissemination of any information, opinion, or recommendation, if the conditions of Rule 138 or Rule 139 of this chapter are met; or

2. Transactions complying with certain other sections. Transactions complying with Rule 103 or Rule 104; or

3. Odd-lot transactions. Transactions in odd-lots; or transactions to offset odd-lots in connection with an odd-lot tender offer conducted pursuant to Rule 13e-4(h)(5) of this chapter; or

4. Exercises of securities. The exercise of any option, warrant, right, or any conversion privilege set forth in the instrument governing a security; or

5. Unsolicited transactions. Unsolicited brokerage transactions; or unsolicited purchases that are not effected from or through a broker or dealer, on a securities exchange, or through an inter-dealer quotation system or electronic communications network; or

6. Basket transactions.

    i. Bids or purchases, in the ordinary course of business, in connection with a basket of 20 or more securities in which a covered security does not comprise more than 5% of the value of the basket purchased; or

    ii. Adjustments to such a basket in the ordinary course of business as a result of a change in the composition of a standardized index; or

7. De minimis transactions. Purchases during the restricted period, other than by a passive market maker, that total less than 2% of the ADTV of the security being purchased, or unaccepted bids; Provided, however, That the person making such bid or purchase has maintained and enforces written policies and procedures reasonably designed to achieve compliance with the other provisions of this section; or

8. Transactions in connection with a distribution. Transactions among distribution participants in connection with a distribution, and purchases of securities from an issuer or selling security holder in connection with a distribution, that are not effected on a securities exchange, or through an inter-dealer quotation system or electronic communications network; or

9. Offers to sell or the solicitation of offers to buy. Offers to sell or the solicitation of offers to buy the securities being distributed (including securities acquired in stabilizing), or securities offered as principal by the person making such offer or solicitation; or

10. Transactions in Rule 144A securities. Transactions in securities eligible for resale under Rule 144A(d)(3) of this chapter, or any reference security, if the Rule 144A securities are offered or sold in the United States solely to:

    i. Qualified institutional buyers, as defined in Rule 144A(a)(1) of this chapter, or to offerees or purchasers that the seller and any person acting on behalf of the seller reasonably believes are qualified institutional buyers, in transactions exempt from registration under section 4(2) of the Securities Act or Rule 144A or Rule 501 through Rule 508 of this chapter; or

    ii. Persons not deemed to be "U.S. persons" for purposes of Rule 902(o)(2) or Rule 902(o)(7) of this chapter, during a distribution qualifying under paragraph (b)(10)(i) of this section.

c. Excepted Securities. The provisions of this section shall not apply to any of the following securities:

    1. Actively-traded securities. Securities that have an ADTV value of at least $1 million and are issued by an issuer whose common equity securities have a public float value of at least $150 million; Provided, however, That such securities are not issued by the distribution participant or an affiliate of the distribution participant; or

    2. Investment grade nonconvertible and asset-backed securities. Nonconvertible debt securities, nonconvertible preferred securities, and asset-backed securities, that are rated by at least one nationally recognized statistical rating organization, as that term is used in Rule 15c3-1 of this chapter, in one of its generic rating categories that signifies investment grade; or

    3. Exempted securities. "Exempted securities" as defined in section 3(a)(12) of the Exchange Act; or

    4. Face-amount certificates or securities issued by an open-end management investment company or unit investment trust. Face-amount certificates issued by a face-amount certificate company, or redeemable securities issued by an open-end management investment company or a unit investment trust. Any terms used in this paragraph (c)(4) that are defined in the Investment Company Act of 1940 shall have the meanings specified in such Act.

d. Exemptive Authority. Upon written application or upon its own motion, the Commission may grant an exemption from the provisions of this section, either unconditionally or on specified terms and conditions, to any transaction or class of transactions, or to any security or class of securities.

RULE 102—ACTIVITIES BY ISSUERS AND SELLING SECURITY HOLDERS DURING A DISTRIBUTION

a. Unlawful Activity. In connection with a distribution of securities effected by or on behalf of an issuer or selling security holder, it shall be unlawful for such person, or any affiliated purchaser of such person, directly or indirectly, to bid for, purchase, or attempt to induce any person to bid for or purchase, a covered security during the applicable restricted period; Except That if an affiliated purchaser is a distribution participant, such affiliated purchaser may comply with Rule 101, rather than this section.

b. Excepted Activity. The following activities shall not be prohibited by paragraph (a) of this section:

    1. Odd-lot transactions. Transactions in odd-lots, or transactions to offset odd-lots in connection with an odd-lot tender offer conducted pursuant to Rule 13e-4(h)(5) of this chapter; or

    2. Transactions by closed-end investment companies.

        i.   Transactions complying with Rule 23c-3 of this chapter; or

        ii. Periodic tender offers of securities, at net asset value, conducted pursuant to Rule 13e-4 of this chapter by a closed-end investment company that engages in a continuous offering of its securities pursuant to Rule 415 of this chapter; Provided, however, That such securities are not traded on a securities exchange or through an inter-dealer quotation system or electronic communications network; or

    3. Redemptions by commodity pools or limited partnerships. Redemptions by commodity pools or limited partnerships, at a price based on net asset value, which are effected in accordance with the terms and conditions of the

instruments governing the securities; Provided, however, That such securities are not traded on a securities exchange, or through an inter-dealer quotation system or electronic communications network; or

4. Exercises of securities. The exercise of any option, warrant, right, or any conversion privilege set forth in the instrument governing a security; or

5. Offers to sell or the solicitation of offers to buy. Offers to sell or the solicitation of offers to buy the securities being distributed; or

6. Unsolicited purchases. Unsolicited purchases that are not effected from or through a broker or dealer, on a securities exchange, or through an inter-dealer quotation system or electronic communications network; or

7. Transactions in Rule 144A securities. Transactions in securities eligible for resale under Rule 144A(d)(3) of this chapter, or any reference security, if the Rule 144A securities are offered or sold in the United States solely to:

    i.   Qualified institutional buyers, as defined in Rule 144A(a)(1) of this chapter, or to offerees or purchasers that the seller and any person acting on behalf of the seller reasonably believes are qualified institutional buyers, in transactions exempt from registration under section 4(2) of the Securities Act or Rule 144A or Rule 501 through Rule 508 of this chapter; or

    ii. Persons not deemed to be "U.S. persons" for purposes of Rule 902(o)(2) or Rule 902(o)(7) of this chapter, during a distribution qualifying under paragraph (b)(7)(i) of this section.

c. Plans.—

    1. Paragraph (a) of this section shall not apply to distributions of securities pursuant to a plan, which are made:

        i.   Solely to employees or security holders of an issuer or its subsidiaries, or to a trustee or other person acquiring such securities for the accounts of such persons; or

    ii. To persons other than employees or security holders, if bids for or purchases of securities pursuant to the plan are effected solely by an agent independent of the issuer and the securities are from a source other than the issuer or an affiliated purchaser of the issuer.

2. Bids for or purchases of any security made or effected by or for a plan shall be deemed to be a purchase by the issuer unless the bid is made, or the purchase is effected, by an agent independent of the issuer.

d. Excepted Securities. The provisions of this section shall not apply to any of the following securities:

1. Actively-traded reference securities. Reference securities with an ADTV value of at least $1 million that are issued by an issuer whose common equity securities have a public float value of at least $150 million; Provided, however, That such securities are not issued by the issuer, or any affiliate of the issuer, of the security in distribution.

2. Investment grade nonconvertible and asset-backed securities. Nonconvertible debt securities, nonconvertible preferred securities, and asset-backed securities, that are rated by at least one nationally recognized statistical rating organization, as that term is used in Rule 15c3-1 of this chapter, in one of its generic rating categories that signifies investment grade; or

3. Exempted securities. "Exempted securities" as defined in section 3(a)(12) of the Exchange Act; or

4. Face-amount certificates or securities issued by an open-end management investment company or unit investment trust. Face-amount certificates issued by a face-amount certificate company, or redeemable securities issued by an open-end management investment company or a unit investment trust. Any terms used in this paragraph (d)(4) that

are defined in the Investment Company Act of 1940 shall have the meanings specified in such Act.

e. Exemptive Authority. Upon written application or upon its own motion, the Commission may grant an exemption from the provisions of this section, either unconditionally or on specified terms and conditions, to any transaction or class of transactions, or to any security or class of securities.

RULE 103—NASDAQ PASSIVE MARKET MAKING

a. Scope of Section. This section permits broker-dealers to engage in market making transactions in covered securities that are Nasdaq securities without violating the provisions of Rule 101; Except That this section shall not apply to any security for which a stabilizing bid subject to Rule 104 is in effect, or during any at-the-market offering or best efforts offering.

b. Conditions to be Met.

    1. General limitations. A passive market maker must effect all transactions in the capacity of a registered market maker on Nasdaq. A passive market maker shall not bid for or purchase a covered security at a price that exceeds the highest independent bid for the covered security at the time of the transaction, except as permitted by paragraph (b)(3) of this section or required by a rule promulgated by the Commission or the NASD governing the handling of customer orders.

    2. Purchase limitation. On each day of the restricted period, a passive market maker's net purchases shall not exceed the greater of its 30% ADTV limitation or 200 shares (together, "purchase limitation"); Provided, however, That a passive market maker may purchase all of the securities that are part of a single order that, when executed, results in its purchase limitation being equaled or exceeded. If a passive market maker's net purchases equal or exceed its purchase limitation, it shall withdraw promptly its quotations from Nasdaq. If a passive market maker withdraws its quotations pursuant to this paragraph, it may not effect any bid or purchase in the covered security for the remainder of that

day, irrespective of any later sales during that day, unless otherwise permitted by Rule 101.

3. Requirement to lower the bid. If all independent bids for a covered security are reduced to a price below the passive market maker's bid, the passive market maker must lower its bid promptly to a level not higher than the then highest independent bid; Provided, however, That a passive market maker may continue to bid and effect purchases at its bid at a price exceeding the then highest independent bid until the passive market maker purchases an aggregate amount of the covered security that equals or, through the purchase of all securities that are part of a single order, exceeds the lesser of two times the minimum quotation size for the security, as determined by NASD rules, or the passive market maker's remaining purchasing capacity under paragraph (b)(2) of this section.

4. Limitation on displayed size. At all times, the passive market maker's displayed bid size may not exceed the lesser of the minimum quotation size for the covered security, or the passive market maker's remaining purchasing capacity under paragraph (b)(2) of this section; Provided, however, That a passive market maker whose purchasing capacity at any time is between one and 99 shares may display a bid size of 100 shares.

5. Identification of a passive market making bid. The bid displayed by a passive market maker shall be designated as such.

6. Notification and reporting to the NASD. A passive market maker shall notify the NASD in advance of its intention to engage in passive market making, and shall submit to the NASD information regarding passive market making purchases, in such form as the NASD shall prescribe.

7. Prospectus disclosure. The prospectus for any registered offering in which any passive market maker intends to effect transactions in any covered security shall contain the information required in Item 502 (228.502), Item 508 (228.508), Item 502 (229.502), and Item 508 (229.508) of this chapter.

c. Transactions at Prices Resulting from Unlawful Activity. No transaction shall be made at a price that the passive market maker knows or has reason to know is the result of activity that is fraudulent, manipulative, or deceptive under the securities laws, or any rule or regulation thereunder.

RULE 104—STABILIZING AND OTHER ACTIVITIES IN CONNECTION WITH AN OFFERING

a. Unlawful Activity. It shall be unlawful for any person, directly or indirectly, to stabilize, to effect any syndicate covering transaction, or to impose a penalty bid, in connection with an offering of any security, in contravention of the provisions of this section. No stabilizing shall be effected at a price that the person stabilizing knows or has reason to know is in contravention of this section, or is the result of activity that is fraudulent, manipulative, or deceptive under the securities laws, or any rule or regulation thereunder.

b. Purpose. Stabilizing is prohibited except for the purpose of preventing or retarding a decline in the market price of a security.

c. Priority. To the extent permitted or required by the market where stabilizing occurs, any person stabilizing shall grant priority to any independent bid at the same price irrespective of the size of such independent bid at the time that it is entered.

d. Control of Stabilizing. No sole distributor or syndicate or group stabilizing the price of a security or any member or members of such syndicate or group shall maintain more than one stabilizing bid in any one market at the same price at the same time.

e. At-the-Market Offerings. Stabilizing is prohibited in an at-the-market offering.

f. Stabilizing Levels.—

   1. Maximum stabilizing bid. Notwithstanding the other provisions of this paragraph (f), no stabilizing shall be made at a price higher than the lower of the offering price or the stabilizing bid for the security in the principal market (or, if the principal market is closed, the stabilizing bid in the principal market at its previous close).

2. Initiating stabilizing.—

    i. Initiating stabilizing when the principal market is open. After the opening of quotations for the security in the principal market, stabilizing may be initiated in any market at a price no higher than the last independent transaction price for the security in the principal market if the security has traded in the principal market on the day stabilizing is initiated or on the most recent prior day of trading in the principal market and the current asked price in the principal market is equal to or greater than the last independent transaction price. If both conditions of the preceding sentence are not satisfied, stabilizing may be initiated in any market after the opening of quotations in the principal market at a price no higher than the highest current independent bid for the security in the principal market.

    ii. Initiating stabilizing when the principal market is closed.

        A. When the principal market for the security is closed, but immediately before the opening of quotations for the security in the market where stabilizing will be initiated, stabilizing may be initiated at a price no higher than the lower of:

            1. The price at which stabilizing could have been initiated in the principal market for the security at its previous close; or

            2. The most recent price at which an independent transaction in the security has been effected in any market since the close of the principal market, if the person stabilizing knows or has reason to know of such transaction.

B. When the principal market for the security is closed, but after the opening of quotations in the market where stabilizing will be initiated, stabilizing may be initiated at a price no higher than the lower of:

1. The price at which stabilization could have been initiated in the principal market for the security at its previous close; or

2. The last independent transaction price for the security in that market if the security has traded in that market on the day stabilizing is initiated or on the last preceding business day and the current asked price in that market is equal to or greater than the last independent transaction price. If both conditions of the preceding sentence are not satisfied, under this paragraph (f)(2)(ii)(B)(2), stabilizing may be initiated at a price no higher than the highest current independent bid for the security in that market.

iii. Initiating stabilizing when there is no market for the security or before the offering price is determined. If no bona fide market for the security being distributed exists at the time stabilizing is initiated, no stabilizing shall be initiated at a price in excess of the offering price. If stabilizing is initiated before the offering price is determined, then stabilizing may be continued after determination of the offering price at the price at which stabilizing then could be initiated.

3. Maintaining or carrying over a stabilizing bid. A stabilizing bid initiated pursuant to paragraph (f)(2) of this section, which has not been discontinued, may be maintained, or

carried over into another market, irrespective of changes in the independent bids or transaction prices for the security.

4. Increasing or reducing a stabilizing bid. A stabilizing bid may be increased to a price no higher than the highest current independent bid for the security in the principal market if the principal market is open, or, if the principal market is closed, to a price no higher than the highest independent bid in the principal market at the previous close thereof. A stabilizing bid may be reduced, or carried over into another market at a reduced price, irrespective of changes in the independent bids or transaction prices for the security. If stabilizing is discontinued, it shall not be resumed at a price higher than the price at which stabilizing then could be initiated.

5. Initiating, maintaining, or adjusting a stabilizing bid to reflect the current exchange rate. If a stabilizing bid is expressed in a currency other than the currency of the principal market for the security, such bid may be initiated, maintained, or adjusted to reflect the current exchange rate, consistent with the provisions of this section. If, in initiating, maintaining, or adjusting a stabilizing bid pursuant to this paragraph (f)(5), the bid would be at or below the midpoint between two trading differentials, such stabilizing bid shall be adjusted downward to the lower differential.

6. Adjustments to stabilizing bid. If a security goes ex-dividend, ex-rights, or ex-distribution, the stabilizing bid shall be reduced by an amount equal to the value of the dividend, right, or distribution. If, in reducing a stabilizing bid pursuant to this paragraph (f)(6), the bid would be at or below the midpoint between two trading differentials, such stabilizing bid shall be adjusted downward to the lower differential.

7. Stabilizing of components. When two or more securities are being offered as a unit, the component securities shall not be stabilized at prices the sum of which exceeds the then permissible stabilizing price for the unit.

8. Special prices. Any stabilizing price that otherwise meets the requirements of this section need not be adjusted to reflect special prices available to any group or class of persons (including employees or holders of warrants or rights).

g. Offerings with no U.S. Stabilizing Activities—

1. Stabilizing to facilitate an offering of a security in the United States shall not be deemed to be in violation of this section if all of the following conditions are satisfied:

     i.   No stabilizing is made in the United States;

     ii. Stabilizing outside the United States is made in a jurisdiction with statutory or regulatory provisions governing stabilizing that are comparable to the provisions of this section; and

     iii. No stabilizing is made at a price above the offering price in the United States, except as permitted by paragraph (f)(5) of this section.

2. For purposes of this paragraph (g), the Commission by rule, regulation, or order may determine whether a foreign statute or regulation is comparable to this section considering, among other things, whether such foreign statute or regulation: specifies appropriate purposes for which stabilizing is permitted; provides for disclosure and control of stabilizing activities; places limitations on stabilizing levels; requires appropriate recordkeeping; provides other protections comparable to the provisions of this section; and whether procedures exist to enable the Commission to obtain information concerning any foreign stabilizing transactions.

h. Disclosure and Notification—

1. Any person displaying or transmitting a bid that such person knows is for the purpose of stabilizing shall provide prior notice to the market on which such stabilizing will be effected, and shall disclose its purpose to the person with whom the bid is entered.

2. Any person effecting a syndicate covering transaction or imposing a penalty bid shall provide prior notice to the

self-regulatory organization with direct authority over the principal market in the United States for the security for which the syndicate covering transaction is effected or the penalty bid is imposed.

3. Any person subject to this section who sells to, or purchases for the account of, any person any security where the price of such security may be or has been stabilized, shall send to the purchaser at or before the completion of the transaction, a prospectus, offering circular, confirmation, or other document containing a statement similar to that comprising the statement provided for in Item 502(d) of Regulation S-B or Item 502(d) of Regulation S-K.

i. Recordkeeping Requirements. A person subject to this section shall keep the information and make the notification required by Rule 17a-2 of this chapter.

j. Excepted Securities. The provisions of this section shall not apply to:

1. Exempted Securities. "Exempted securities," as defined in section 3(a)(12) of the Exchange Act; or

2. Transactions of Rule 144A securities. Transactions in securities eligible for resale under Rule 144A(d)(3) of this chapter, if such securities are offered or sold in the United States solely to:

    i. Qualified institutional buyers, as defined in Rule 144A(a)(1) of this chapter, or to offerees or purchasers that the seller and any person acting on behalf of the seller reasonably believes are qualified institutional buyers, in a transaction exempt from registration under section 4(2) of the Securities Act or Rule 144A or Rule 501 through Rule 508 of this chapter; or

    ii. Persons not deemed to be "U.S. persons" for purposes of Rule 902(o)(2) or Rule 902(o)(7) of this chapter, during a distribution qualifying under paragraph (j)(2)(i) of this section.

k. Exemptive Authority. Upon written application or upon its own motion, the Commission may grant an exemption from the provisions

of this section, either unconditionally or on specified terms and conditions, to any transaction or class of transactions, or to any security or class of securities.

RULE 105—SHORT SELLING IN CONNECTION WITH A PUBLIC OFFERING

a. Unlawful Activity. In connection with an offering of securities for cash pursuant to a registration statement or a notification on Form 1-A filed under the Securities Act, it shall be unlawful for any person to cover a short sale with offered securities purchased from an underwriter or broker or dealer participating in the offering, if such short sale occurred during the shorter of:

     1. The period beginning five business days before the pricing of the offered securities and ending with such pricing; or

     2. The period beginning with the initial filing of such registration statement or notification on Form 1-A and ending with the pricing.

b. Excepted Offerings. This section shall not apply to offerings filed under Rule 415 of this chapter or to offerings that are not conducted on a firm commitment basis.

c. Exemptive Authority. Upon written application or upon its own motion, the Commission may grant an exemption from the provisions of this section, either unconditionally or on specified terms and conditions, to any transaction or class of transactions, or to any security or class of securities. By the Commission.

Appendix 11

NASD NOTICES TO MEMBERS

95-7 SEC APPROVES NASD PROPOSAL AMENDING FREE-RIDING AND WITHHOLDING INTERPRETATION PROVISIONS*

Executive Summary

On December 7, 1994, in SEC Release No. 34-35059, File No. SR-NASD-94-15, the Securities and Exchange Commission (SEC) approved amendments to the NASD Free-Riding and Withholding Interpretation (Interpretation), an Interpretation of the Board of Governors under Article III, Section 1 of the NASD Rules of Fair Practice. The changes to the Interpretation affect:

- stand-by purchase arrangements by restricted persons;

- the definition of immediate family members, public offerings, and associated persons;

- the use of the "carve out" mechanism for restricted persons in Investment Partnerships and Corporations;

- issuer-directed securities; and
- other provisions of the Interpretation.

The rule change was effective on December 7, 1994.

Background and Description

The Interpretation protects the integrity of the public offering system by ensuring that members make a bona fide public distribution of "hot-issue" securities and do not withhold such securities for their own benefit or use the securities to reward other persons who are in a position to direct future business to the member. Hot issues are defined by the Interpretation as securities of a public offering that trade at a premium in the secondary market whenever such trading commences. The Interpretation prohibits members from retaining the securities of hot issues in their own accounts and prohibits members from using sales of such securities to directors, officers, employees, and associated persons of members and other broker/dealers. It also restricts member sales of hot-issue securities to the accounts of specified categories of persons, including among others, senior officers of banks, insurance companies, registered investment companies, registered investment advisory firms, and any other persons within such organizations whose activities influence or include the buying or selling of securities. These basic prohibitions and restrictions are also made applicable to sales by members of hot-issue securities to accounts in which any such persons may have a beneficial interest and, with limited exceptions, to members of the immediate family of those persons restricted by the Interpretation.

The substantive amendments to the Interpretation are as follows.

Stand-By Arrangements

Before the amendments, the Interpretation prohibited the sale of a hot issue to a group of stand-by purchasers if any purchaser is restricted under the Interpretation and has a beneficial interest in the stand-by account. This prohibition could affect the successful completion of an offering in which some of the offered securities are not otherwise purchased during the offering period. The Interpretation has been amended to permit restricted accounts to purchase hot-issue securities pursuant to a stand-by arrangement (*i.e.*, an agreement to purchase securities not purchased during the offering period) under certain conditions:

- disclosure of the arrangement in the prospectus;
- the arrangement is the subject of a formal written agreement;
- the managing underwriter represents in writing no other purchases were available;
- three-month holding period.

Members are reminded that when the securities are sold by the stand-by purchasers, such purchases would need to comply with all applicable regulatory requirements including prospectus delivery pursuant to Section 5 of the Securities Act of 1933 and Rule 10b-6 under the Securities Exchange Act of 1934.

Definition of Immediate Family

The Interpretation previously restricted immediate family members of persons enumerated in Paragraph 2 (persons associated with broker/dealers), and Paragraphs 3 and 4 (persons having a connection to the offering and individuals related to banks, insurance companies, and other institutional type accounts) of the Interpretation from participating in hot-issue distributions. The Interpretation defined immediate family members very broadly and included such persons as father-, mother-, brother-, and sister-in-law. The NASD determined that the immediate family member provisions often placed inequitable restrictions on a person with a fairly remote connection to a restricted person named in the Interpretation (*e.g.,* the sister-in-law of a bank vice president), and often resulted in unduly burdensome compliance difficulties for members monitoring whether such persons are restricted or become restricted. The amendments to the immediate family member provisions will ensure that those persons with a substantial nexus to a restricted person will be similarly restricted under the Interpretation, provide a clearer test for NASD members in determining whether such persons are restricted, and eliminate the Interpretation's application to persons for whom the restriction did not serve an important regulatory purpose.

The amendments do the following:

- retain the investment history exemption, and expand it to include the use of investment history at firms other than the member making the allocation. The burden of obtaining such information would remain with the firm making the sale;

- the immediate family restrictions on persons enumerated in paragraphs 3 and 4 of the Interpretation are eliminated and the Interpretation only applies to the enumerated individuals in those categories and to persons who are supported directly or indirectly to a material extent by the restricted person;

- the immediate family restrictions on persons associated with broker/dealers continue to apply to persons supported by the restricted individual and to allocations by the restricted individual's firm, but no longer prohibit sales to non-supported family members of a person associated with a broker/dealer by a broker/dealer that does not employ the restricted person, where the restricted person has no ability to control the allocation of the hot issue.

It will continue to be a violation if it can be determined that the restricted person has a beneficial interest in the account to which an allocation is made.

Venture Capital Investors

The NASD concluded that bona fide venture-capital investors should be allowed to purchase a hot issue to maintain their percentage ownership in an entity, notwithstanding that the venture-capital investor may be a restricted person, or that such person may have a beneficial interest in the venture-capital account. Venture-capital investors often play a pivotal role in the continued viability of an entity before its public offering, and such an investor should be allowed to maintain his or her ownership interest after the entity completes its public offering.

The venture capital investor, to purchase the hot issue without implicating the Interpretation's restrictions, will have to meet these conditions:

- one year of pre-existing ownership in the entity;

- no increase in the investor's percentage ownership above that held for the three months before the filing of a registration statement in connection with the initial public offering;

- a lack of special terms connection with the purchase; and

- the venture-capital investor will not sell, pledge, hypothecate, or otherwise dispose of the securities for three months after the effective date of the registration statement in connection with the offering.

The NASD believes that the conditions imposed on the venture-capital investor ensure that the securities may be purchased by a bona fide venture-capital investor who has had an on-going interest in an entity, yet protects against any attempt to circumvent the Interpretation's restrictions by investing in an entity shortly before its public offering.

Investment Partnerships and Corporations

Before the amendments, the Interpretation, under Investment Partnerships and Corporations, generally disallowed sales of a hot issue to an investment partnership or corporation, or similar account (investment partnership) if a restricted person has a beneficial interest in the entity. In August 1992 and October 1993 *Notices to Members,* the NASD announced it was going to allow investment partnerships, on an interim basis, to use a carve-out mechanism to prevent restricted persons with an interest in an investment partnership from participating in hot-issue allocations. This carve-out mechanism required the NASD member making such allocation to set up a separate account for these transactions and obtain from the investment partnership and its accountant's documentation that indicates that the restricted persons are prevented from participating in a hot-issue allocation.

The NASD concluded that the carve-out methodology was the most equitable and appropriate approach for investment partnerships in which restricted persons have a beneficial interest, and the carve-out procedure has been codified under the Beneficial Interest section of the Interpretation. The carve-out procedure will not allow a person restricted under the Interpretation to receive a hot-issue allocation inconsistent with the Interpretation's provisions, but will not inequitably penalize persons not restricted under the Interpretation due to their interest in an investment partnership in which a restricted person also has an interest. A typical scenario is where a limited partnership with many limited partners is restricted under the Interpretation because one of the limited partners is an officer of an insurance company, and therefore restricted under Paragraph 4 of the Interpretation. Rather than restricting the whole limited partnership, the carve-out procedure would allow the limited partnership to purchase the hot issue by properly allocating the hot issue away from the restricted limited partner according to the specified requirements proposed.

In addition, the NASD believes that a beneficial interest, as defined under the previous Interpretation, should not be created by the receipt of a management fee based on the performance of an account. The NASD believes that investment partnerships and other similar accounts require that the management fee structure of such accounts include a performance-based component. Thus, an investment advisor restricted under Paragraph 4 of the Interpretation could restrict an entire investment partnership, in which no restricted persons have an interest, based solely on the investment advisor receiving a fee based on the performance of the securities in the investment partnership account. The NASD believes that the receipt of a performance-based fee, without the existence of any other beneficial interest, should not create such an interest.

Definition of Public Offering

Under the previous Interpretation, the definition of a public offering included all distributions of securities, whether registered or unregistered under the Securities Act of 1933. The NASD concluded that the definition had the unintended effect of implicating the Interpretation's restrictions for bona fide private placements of securities that do not present the potential abuses that the Interpretation is intended to guard against. The amendment to the definition, which will not apply the Interpretation to a traditional private placement of securities, is appropriate because such distributions generally are limited in scope and have holding periods placed on the placed securities. Thus, such placements will not be within the purview of the Interpretation in that distribution is limited and that the potential for restricted persons to purchase the securities and resell or "flip" them in a short period of time is limited due to the resale restrictions associated with such offerings.

Associated Person Definition

Article I, Section (m) of the NASD By-Laws defines a "person associated with a member" to include a partner of a broker/dealer and any person who is directly or indirectly controlling or controlled by such member, whether or not such person is registered with the Association. The NASD has found that a certain degree of confusion exists as to the status of passive investors in broker/dealers, such as broker/dealer limited partners, equity owners, or subordinated lenders.

The NASD believes that, under certain circumstances, such persons should not be restricted as persons associated with a broker/dealer for purposes of the Interpretation due to their limited, passive investment in a broker/dealer. Thus, the NASD has determined that if a person owns or has contributed 10 percent or less to a broker/dealer's capital, such person should not be construed to be an associated person; provided that such ownership interest is a passive investment, the person does not receive hot issues from the member in which he or she has the ownership interest, and that the broker/dealer is not in a position to direct hot issues to the person. The NASD believes that the limitations placed on such persons not to be considered associated persons will prevent the same from attempting to use their ownership interests in a broker/dealer to effect the purchase of hot issues, and circumvent the Interpretation's objective of a bona fide distribution of a hot issue. This definition is being used only to determine restriction under the Interpretation and should not be construed as determinative of whether a person is associated with a broker/dealer for other purposes.

Persons Associated with Limited Business Broker/Dealers

Similar to the status of persons with a limited ownership interest in a broker/dealer, the NASD concluded that persons associated with certain broker/dealers that transact a limited securities business should also not be restricted as associated persons under Paragraph 2 of the Interpretation. Specifically, the Interpretation has been amended so that persons associated with broker/dealers whose business is limited to direct participation programs or investment company/variable product securities will not be restricted under the Interpretation to the same extent as those persons associated with broker/dealers with a more comprehensive securities business. It should be noted, however, that the amendment applies only to a person associated with such a limited broker/dealer, and not to the broker/dealer itself. The NASD does not believe that it is appropriate for any NASD member to purchase a hot-issue security for its own account, regardless of the scope of its securities business.

Issuer-Directed Securities

Previously, an employee of an issuer, who also was restricted under the Interpretation, had to receive permission from the NASD Board of Governors to purchase hot-issue securities of its employer, if the employee did not have the requisite investment history with the NASD member making the securities distribution.

The NASD concluded that it was inequitable to impose such restrictions on employees of issuers who are in most cases tangentially restricted under the Interpretation, in connection with their purchase of securities issued by their employer. Issuer-directed share programs are viewed as a valuable tool in employee development and retention, and the NASD does not believe that the objectives of the Interpretation are furthered by imposing essentially the same restrictions on such purchases as those not involving an employer/employee relationship. Thus, the amendment to the Issuer Directed Securities section of the Interpretation will allow employees of issuers to purchase hot-issue securities of the employer under the same terms and conditions as persons associated with NASD members are permitted to purchase securities issued by the member, pursuant to an exemption provided in Section 13 of Schedule E to the NASD By-Laws.

Under the changes to the issuer-directed provision of the Interpretation, the employee will still be restricted if the restricted person directly or indirectly materially supports the employee. If permission is granted by the Board of Governors, the employee is allowed to purchase the securities of the employer without meeting the investment history requirement, but the amount purchased would still have to meet the insubstantial and not disproportionate tests described above.

Cancellation Provision

The NASD determined to clarify in the Interpretation that it will not be a violation if an NASD member makes an allocation of a hot issue to a restricted person or account, so long as the member canceled the trade and reallocated the security at the public offering price to a unrestricted account, prior to the end of the first business day after the date on which secondary market trading begins. The NASD believes that the clarification will remedy any concerns caused by inadvertent violations of the Interpretation that are corrected by the NASD member making the distribution.

To help members meet their responsibilities under this cancellation provision, the NASD will provide notification on the Nasdaq News Frame of the name of those new issues that the NASD has determined to have traded at a premium in the secondary market and therefore will be subject to regulatory review by the NASD under its Free-Riding Interpretation. This notification on the News Frame will take place by no later than after the close of business on the first day of trading and will continue to be displayed on the next business day as well. This will allow members adequate time to cancel trades made to restricted accounts and to reallocate those shares.

Members are reminded that cancellation and reallocation may raise issues under Rule 10b-6. Members are directed to the SEC Release approving these rule changes where this issue is discussed.

Other Considerations

The amendments to the Interpretation clarify the NASD's position that unregistered investment advisors (persons who manage hedge funds, investment partnerships or corporations, investment clubs, or similar entities) are considered Paragraph 4 restricted persons. The amendments also make clear that if investment partnerships and corporations accept investment funds from other investment entities, the investing entities must provide the partnership or corporation with documentation and assurances as outlined in the Rule that restricted persons, if any, are not participating in the purchase of hot issues. The NASD would also point out that shares purchased in the hot-issue account for investment partnerships and corporations must remain in that account until they are sold.

Questions regarding this Notice should be directed to the NASD Office of General Counsel at (202) 728-8294.

Text of Amendments to the NASD's Free-Riding and Withholding Interpretation Under Article III, Section 1 of the NASD Rules of Fair Practice

(**Note:** New language is underlined; deletions are in [brackets].)

Introduction

The following Interpretation of Article III, Section 1 of the Association's Rules of Fair Practice is adopted by the Board of Governors of the Association pursuant to the provisions of Article VII, Section 3(a) of the Association's By-Laws and Article I, Section 3 of the Rules of Fair Practice.

This Interpretation is based upon the premise that members have an obligation to make a bona fide public distribution at the public offering price of securities of a public offering which trade at a premium in the secondary market whenever such secondary market begins (a "hot issue") regardless of whether such securities are acquired by the member as an underwriter, as a selling group member, or from a member participating in the distribution as an underwriter or a selling group member, or otherwise. The failure to make a bona fide public distribution when there is a demand for an issue can be a factor in artificially raising the price. Thus, the failure to do so, especially when the member may have information relating to the demand for the securities or other factors not generally known to the public, is inconsistent with high standards of commercial honor and just and equitable principles of trade and leads to an impairment of public confidence in the fairness of the investment banking and securities business. Such conduct is, therefore, in violation of Article III, Section 1 of the Association's Rules of Fair Practice and this Interpretation thereof which establishes guidelines in respect to such activity.

As in the case of any other Interpretation issued by the Board of Governors of the Association, the implementation thereof is a function of the District Business Conduct Committees and the Board of Governors. Thus, the Interpretation will be applied to a given factual situation by individuals active in the investment banking and securities business who are serving on these committees or on the Board. They will construe this Interpretation to effectuate its overall purpose to assure a public distribution of securities for which there is a public demand.

The Board of Governors has determined that it shall not be considered a violation of this Interpretation if a member which makes an allocation to a restricted person or account of an offering that trades at a premium in the secondary market, cancels the trade for such restricted person or account, prior to the end of the first business day following the date on which secondary market trading commences and reallocates such security at the public offering price to a non-restricted person or account.

Interpretation

Except as provided herein, it shall be inconsistent with high standards of commercial honor and just and equitable principles of trade and a violation of Article III, Section 1 of the Association's Rules of Fair Practice for a member, or a person associated with a member, to fail to make a bona fide public distribution at the public offering price of securities of a public offering which trade at a premium in the secondary market whenever such secondary market begins regardless of whether such securities are acquired by the member as an underwriter, a selling group member or from a member participating in the distribution as an underwriter or selling group member, or otherwise. Therefore, it shall be a violation of Article III, Section 1 for a member, or a person associated with a member, to:

1. Continue to hold any of the securities so acquired in any of the member's accounts;

2. Sell any of the securities to any officer, director, general partner, employee or agent of the member or of any other broker/dealer, or to a person associated with the member or with any other broker/dealer, or to a member of the immediate family of any such person; provided however, that:

    (a) This prohibition shall not apply to a person in a limited registration category as that term is defined below;

    (b) The prohibition shall not apply to sales to a member of the immediate family of a person associated with a member who is not supported directly or indirectly to a material extent by such person if the sale is by a broker/dealer other than that employing the restricted person and the restricted person has no ability to control the allocation of the hot issue.

3. Sell any of the securities to a person who is a finder in respect to the public offering or to any person acting in a fiduciary capacity to the managing underwriter, including, among others, attorneys, accountants and financial consultants, or to [a member of the immediate family of any such

person;] <u>any other person who is supported directly or indirectly, to a material extent, by any person specified in this paragraph.</u>

4. Sell any securities to any senior officer of a bank, savings and loan institution, insurance company, [registered] investment company, [registered] investment advisory firm or any other institutional type account <u>(including, but not limited to, hedge funds, investment partnerships, investment corporations, or investment clubs),</u> domestic or foreign, or to any person in the securities department of, or to any employee or any other person who may influence or whose activities directly or indirectly involve or are related to the function of buying or selling securities for any bank, savings and loan institution, insurance company, [registered] investment company, [registered] investment advisory firm, or other institutional type account, domestic or foreign, or to [a member of the immediate family of any such person;] <u>any other person who is supported directly or indirectly, to a material extent, by any person specified in this paragraph.</u>

5. Sell any securities to any account in which any person specified under paragraphs (1), (2), (3) or (4) hereof has a beneficial interest;

   Provided, however, a member may sell part of its securities acquired as described above to:

   (a) persons enumerated in paragraphs (3) or (4) hereof; and

   (b) members of the immediate family of persons enumerated in paragraph (2) hereof provided that such person enumerated in paragraph (2) does not contribute directly or indirectly to the support of such member of the immediate family; and

   (c) any account in which any person specified under paragraph (3) or (4) or subparagraph (b) of this paragraph has a beneficial interest; if the member is prepared to demonstrate that the securities were sold to such persons in accordance with their normal investment practice [with the member], that the aggregate of the securities so sold is insubstantial and not disproportionate in amount as compared to sales to members of the public and that the amount sold to any one of such persons is insubstantial in amount.

6. Sell any of the securities, at or above the public offering price, to any other broker/dealer; provided, however, a member may sell all or part of the securities acquired as described above to another member broker/dealer upon receipt from the latter in writing assurance that such purchase would be made to fill orders for bona fide public customers, other than those enumerated in paragraphs (1), (2), (3), (4) or above, at the public offering price as an accommodation to them and without compensation for such.

7. Sell any of the securities to any domestic bank, domestic branch of a foreign bank, trust company or other conduit for an undisclosed principal unless:

   (a) An affirmative inquiry is made of such bank, trust company or other conduit as to whether the ultimate purchasers would be persons enumerated in paragraphs (1) through (5) hereof and receives satisfactory assurance that the ultimate purchases would not be such persons, and that the securities would not be sold in a manner inconsistent with the provisions of paragraph (6) hereof; otherwise, there shall be a rebuttable presumption that the ultimate purchasers were persons enumerated in paragraphs (1) through (5) hereof or that the securities were sold in a manner inconsistent with the provisions of paragraph (6) hereof;

   (b) A recording is made on the order ticket, or its equivalent, or on some other supporting document, of the name of the person to whom the inquiry was made at the bank, trust company or other conduit as well as the substance of what was said by that person and what was done as a result thereof;

    (c) The order ticket, or its equivalent, is initialed by a registered principal of the member; and

    (d) Normal supervisory procedures of the member provide for a close follow-up and review of all transactions entered into with the referred to domestic bank, trust companies or other conduits for undisclosed principals to assure that the ultimate recipients of securities so sold are not persons enumerated in paragraphs (1) through (6) hereof.

8. Sell any of the securities to a foreign broker/dealer or bank unless:

    (a) In the case of a foreign broker/dealer or bank which is participating in the distribution as an underwriter, the agreement among underwriters contains a provision which obligates the said foreign broker/dealer or bank not to sell any of the securities which it receives as a participant in the distribution to persons enumerated in paragraphs (1) through (5) above, or in a manner inconsistent with the provisions of paragraph (6) hereof; or

    (b) In the case of sales to a foreign broker/dealer or bank which is not participating in the distribution as an underwriter, the selling member:

        (i) makes an affirmative inquiry of such foreign broker/dealer or bank as to whether the ultimate purchasers would be persons enumerated in paragraphs (1) through (5) hereof and receives satisfactory assurance that the ultimate purchasers of the securities so purchased would not be such persons, and that the securities would not be sold in a manner inconsistent with the provisions of paragraph (6) hereof;

        (ii) a recording is made on the order ticket, or its equivalent, or upon some other supporting document, of the name of the person to whom the inquiry was made at the foreign broker/dealer or bank as well as the substance of what was said by that person and what was done as a result thereof; and

(iii) the order ticket, or its equivalent, is initialed by a registered principal of the member.

The obligations imposed upon members in their dealings with foreign broker/dealers or banks by this paragraph 8(b) can be fulfilled by having the foreign broker/dealer or bank to which sales falling within the scope of this Interpretation are made execute Form FR-1, or a reasonable facsimile thereof. This form, which gives a blanket assurance from the foreign broker/dealer or bank that no sales will be made in contravention of the provisions of this Interpretation, can be obtained at any District Office of the Association or at the Executive Office. The acceptance of an executed Form FR-1, or other written assurance, by a member must in all instances be made in good faith. Thus, if a member knows or should have known of facts which are inconsistent with the representations received, such will not operate to satisfy the obligations imposed upon him by this paragraph.

Scope and Intent of Interpretation

In addition to the obvious scope and intent of the above provisions, the intent of the Board of Governors in the following specific situations is outlined for the guidance of members.

Limited Business Broker/Dealer

The restrictions placed on associated persons pursuant to Paragraph 2 of the Interpretations shall not apply to persons associated with NASD members engaged solely in the purchase or sale of either investment company/variable contracts securities or direct participation program securities.

Issuer Directed Securities

This Interpretation shall apply to securities which are part of a public offering notwithstanding that some or all of those securities are specifically directed by the issuer to accounts which are included within the scope of paragraphs (3) through (8) above. Therefore, if a person within the scope of those paragraphs to whom securities were directed did not have the required [an] investment history [with the member or registered representative from whom they were to be purchased], the member would not be permitted to sell him such securities. Also, the "disproportionate" and "insubstantial" tests would apply as in all other situations. Thus, the directing of a substantial number of securities to any one person would be prohibited as would the directing of securities to such accounts in amounts which would be disproportionate as compared to sales to members of the public. If such issuer-directed securities are sold to the issuer's employees or directors or potential employees or directors resulting from an intended merger, acquisition, or other business combination, such securities may be sold without limitation as to amount and regardless of whether such employees have an investment history as required by the Interpretation; provided, however, that in the case of an offering of securities for which a bona fide independent market does not exist, such securities shall not be sold, transferred, assigned, pledged, or hypothecated for a period of three months following the effective date of the offering. This Interpretation shall also apply to securities which are part of a public offering notwithstanding that some of those securities are specifically directed by the issuer on a non-underwritten basis. In such cases, the managing underwriter of the offering shall be responsible for insuring compliance with this Interpretation in respect to those securities.

Notwithstanding the above, sales of issuer directed securities may be made to non-employee/director restricted persons without the required investment history after receiving permission from the Board of Governors. Permission will be given only if there is a demonstration of valid business reasons for such sales (such as sales to distributors and suppliers [or key employees], who are in each case incidentally restricted persons), and the member seeking permission is prepared to demonstrate that the aggregate amount of securities so sold is insubstantial and not disproportionate as compared to sales to members of the public, and that the amount sold to any one of such persons is insubstantial in amount; provided, however, that such securities shall not be sold, transferred, assigned, pledged, or hypothecated for a period of three months following the effective date of the offering.

Stand-By Purchasers

Securities purchased pursuant to a stand-by arrangement shall not be subject to the provisions of the Interpretation if the following conditions are met:

1. The stand-by agreement is disclosed in the prospectus.

2. The stand-by arrangement is the subject of a formal written agreement.

3. The managing underwriter represents in writing that it was unable to find any other purchasers for the securities.

4. The securities purchased shall be restricted from sale or transfer for a period of three months.

Investment Partnerships and Corporations

A member may not sell [securities of a public offering which trade at a premium in the secondary market whenever such secondary market begins ("hot issue"),] a hot issue to the account of any investment partnership or corporation, domestic or foreign (except companies registered under the Investment Company Act of 1940) including but not limited to, hedge funds, investment clubs, and other like accounts unless the member complies with either of the following alternatives:

(A) prior to the execution of the transaction, the member has received from the account a current list of the names and business connections of all persons having any beneficial interest in the account, and if such information discloses that any person [enumerated in paragraphs (1) through (4) hereof] restricted under this Interpretation has a beneficial interest in such account, any sale of securities to such account must be consistent with the provisions of this Interpretation, or

(B) prior to the execution of the transaction, the member has obtained a copy of a written representation [current opinion] from counsel admitted to practice law before the highest court of any state or the account's independent certified public accountant stating that such counsel or accountant reasonably believes that no person with a beneficial interest in the account is a restricted person under this Interpretation and stating that, in providing such [opinion] representation, counsel or accountant:

(1) has reviewed and is familiar with this Interpretation;

(2) has reviewed a current list of all persons with a beneficial interest in the account supplied by the account manager;

(3) has reviewed information supplied by the account manager with respect to each person with a beneficial interest in the account, including the identity, the nature of employment, and any other business connections of such persons; and

(4) has requested and reviewed other documents and other pertinent information and made inquiries of the account manager and received responses thereto, if counsel or the accountant determines that such further review and inquiry are necessary and relevant to determine the correct status of such persons under the Interpretation.

The member shall maintain a copy of the names and business connections of all persons having any beneficial interest in the account or a copy of the current [opinion of counsel] written representation in its files for at least three years following the member's last sale of a new issue to the account, depending upon which of the above requirements the member elects to follow. For purposes of this section, a list or [opinion] written representation shall be deemed to be current if it is based upon the status of the account as of a date not more than 18 months prior to the date of the transaction.

Beneficial Interest

The term beneficial interest means not only ownership interests, but every type of direct financial interest of any persons enumerated in paragraphs (1) through (4) hereof in such account [, including, without limitation, management fees based on the performance of the account].

Provided, however, that no restricted person shall be deemed to have a beneficial interest in an account receiving a hot issue as a result of ownership of an interest in an investment partnership or corporation, or similar type account ("investment entity"), if the following conditions are met.

1. The investment entity establishes a separate brokerage account, with a separate identification number, for its new-issue purchases. At the end of each fiscal year, the general partner, or similarly situated party, will certify in writing to its independent certified public accountants that: (a) all hot issues purchased by the investment entity were placed in this new-issue account; and (b) that the participants in the new-issue account are not restricted persons under this Interpretation.

2. Prior to the execution of the initial hot-issue transaction, the investment entity's accountant or attorney will provide a written representation that complies with paragraph B of the section of this Interpretation entitled "Investment Partnerships and Corporations."

3. As part of its audit procedure for the investment entity, the independent certified public accountant will confirm in writing to the investment entity that all allocations for the new-issue account were made in accordance with the provisions of the applicable investment entity agreement that restricts participation in hot-issue purchases.

4. The investment entity will maintain in its files copies of the certifications, representations, and confirmations referred to in paragraphs (1)–(3) above for at least three years following the last purchase of a hot issue for the new-issue account.

5. The investment entity will accept investment funds from other investment entities if such other accounts provide the same documentation and assurances described in paragraphs (1)–(4) above that restricted persons will not participate in the purchase of hot issues.

6. The certifications and documents required in paragraphs (1)–(3) above shall be provided to the member holding such account at such time as these certifications and documents are filed with the investment entity and its independent certified public accountant and, the member shall make such documentation available to the NASD upon request.

Venture Capital Investors

This Interpretation shall not prohibit the sale of hot issues in an initial public offering to a person restricted under the Interpretation or to an account in which such restricted person has a beneficial interest (a "Venture Capital Investor") if the following conditions are met:

1. The Venture Capital Investor has held an ownership interest in the company issuing the hot issue securities for a period of one year prior to the effective date of the public offering;

2. The acquisition of the hot issue securities in the public offering does not increase the percentage equity ownership of the Venture Capital Investor in the company above that held three months prior to the filing of the registration statement in connection with the offering;

3. The Venture Capital Investor received no special terms in connection with the purchase; and

4. The securities purchased shall be restricted from sale or transfer for a period of three months following the conclusion of the offering.

Violations by Recipient

In those cases where a member or person associated with a member has been the recipient of securities of a public offering to the extent that such violated the Interpretation, the member or person associated with a member shall be deemed to be in violation of Article III, Section 1 of the Rules of Fair Practice and this Interpretation as well as the member who sold the securities since their responsibility in relation to the public distribution is equally as great as that of the member selling them. In those cases where a member or a person associated with a member has caused, directly or indirectly, the distribution of securities to a person falling within the restrictive provisions of this

Interpretation the member or person associated with a member shall also be deemed to be in violation of Article III, Section 1 of the Rules of Fair Practice and this Interpretation. Receipt by a member or a person associated with a member of securities of a hot issue which is being distributed by an issuer itself without the assistance of an underwriter and/or selling group is also intended to be subject to the provisions of this Interpretation.

Violations by Registered Representative Executing Transaction

The obligation which members have to make a bona fide public distribution at the public offering price of securities of a hot issue is also an obligation of every person associated with a member who causes a transaction to be executed. Therefore, where sales are made by such persons in a manner inconsistent with the provisions of this Interpretation, such persons associated with a member will be considered equally culpable with the member for the violations found taking into consideration the facts and circumstances of the particular case under consideration.

Disclosure

The fact that a disclosure is made in the prospectus or offering circular that a sale of securities would be made in a manner inconsistent with this Interpretation does not take the matter out of its scope. In sum, therefore, disclosure does not affect the proscriptions of this Interpretation.

Explanation of Terms

The following explanation of terms is provided for the assistance of members. Other words which are defined in the By-Laws and Rules of Fair Practice shall, unless the context otherwise requires, have the meaning as defined therein.

Associated Person

A person associated with a member or any other broker/dealer, as defined in Article I, paragraph (m) of the NASD's By-Laws, shall not include a person whose association with the member is limited to a passive ownership interest in the member of ten percent or less, and who does not receive hot issues from the member in which he or she has the ownership interest; and that such member is not in a position to direct hot issues to such person.

Public Offering

The term public offering shall mean any primary or secondary distribution of securities made pursuant to a registration statement or offering circular including exchange offers, rights offerings, offerings made pursuant to a merger or acquisition, straight debt offerings and all other securities distributions of any kind whatsoever except any offering made pursuant to an exemption under Section 4(1), 4(2) or 4(6) of the Securities Act of 1933, as amended, or pursuant to Rule 504 (unless considered a public offering in the states where offered), Rule 505 or Rule 506 adopted under the Securities Act of 1933, as amended [all distributions of securities whether underwritten or not; whether registered, unregistered or exempt from registration under the Securities Act of 1933, and whether they are primary or secondary distributions, including intrastate distributions and Regulation A issues, which sell at an immediate premium, in the secondary market]. It shall not mean exempted securities as defined in Section 3(a)(12) of the Securities Exchange Act of 1934.

Immediate Family

The term immediate family shall include parents, mother-in-law or father-in-law, husband or wife, brother or sister, brother-in-law or sister-in-law, son-in-law or daughter-in-law, and children. In addition, the term shall include any other person who is supported, directly or indirectly, to a material extent by the member, person associated with the member or other person specified in paragraph[s] (2)[, (3), or (4)] above.

Normal Investment Practice

Normal investment practice shall mean the history of investment of a restricted person in an account or accounts maintained by the restricted person. [maintained with the member making the allocation. In cases where an account was previously maintained with another member, but serviced by the same registered representative as the one currently servicing the account for the member making the allocation, such earlier investment activity may be included in the restricted person's investment history.]

Usually the previous one-year period of securities activity is the basis for determining the adequacy of a restricted person's investment history. Where warranted, however, a longer or shorter period may be reviewed. It is the responsibility of the registered representative effecting the allocation, as well as the member, to demonstrate that the restricted person's investment history justifies the allocation of hot issues. Copies of customer account statements or other records maintained by the registered representative or the member may be utilized to demonstrate prior investment activity. In analyzing a restricted person's investment history the Association believes the following factors should be considered:

(1) The frequency of transactions in the account or accounts during that period of time. Relevant in this respect are the nature and size of investments.

(2) A comparison of the dollar amount of previous transactions with the dollar amount of the hot issue purchase. If a restricted person purchases $1,000 of a hot issue and his account revealed a series of purchases and sales in $100 amounts, the $1,000 purchase would not appear to be consistent with the restricted person's normal investment practice.

(3) The practice of purchasing mainly hot issues would not constitute a normal investment practice. The Association does, however, consider as contributing to the establishment of a normal investment practice, the purchase of new issues which are not hot issues as well as secondary market transactions.

Disproportionate

In respect to the determination of what constitutes a disproportionate allocation, the Association uses a guideline of 10% of the member's participation in the issue, however acquired. It should be noted, however, that the 10% factor is merely a guideline and is one of a number of factors which are considered in reaching determinations of violations of the Interpretation on the basis of disproportionate allocations. These other factors include, among other things:

- the size of the participation;
- the offering price of the issue;
- the amount of securities sold to restricted accounts; and,
- the price of the securities in the aftermarket.

It should be noted that disciplinary action has been taken against members for violations of the Interpretation where the allocations made to restricted accounts were less than 10% of the member's participation. The 10% guideline is applied as to the aggregate of the allocations.

Notwithstanding the above, a normal unit of trading (100 shares or 10 bonds) will in most cases not be considered a disproportionate allocation regardless of the amount of the member's participation. This means that if the aggregate number of shares of a member's participation which is allocated to restricted accounts does not exceed a normal unit of trading, such allocation will in most cases not be considered disproportionate. For example, if a member receives 500 shares of a hot issue, he may allocate 100 shares to a restricted account even though such allocation represents 20% of that member's participation. Of course, all of the remaining shares would have to be allocated to unrestricted accounts and all other provisions of the Interpretation would have to be satisfied. Specifically, the allocation would have to be consistent with the normal investment practice of the account to which it was allocated and the member would not be permitted to sell to restricted persons who were totally prohibited from receiving hot issues.

Insubstantiality

This requirement is separate and distinct from the requirements relating to disproportionate allocations and normal investment practice. In addition, this term applies both to the aggregate of the securities sold to restricted accounts and to each individual allocation. In other words, there could be a substantial allocation to an individual account in violation of the Interpretation and yet be no violation on that ground as to the total number of shares allocated to all accounts. The determination of whether an allocation to a restricted account or accounts is substantial is based upon, among other things, the number of shares allocated and/or the dollar amount of the purchase.

SALES BY ISSUERS IN CONVERSION OFFERINGS

(a) *Definitions*

For purposes of this Subsection, the following terms shall have the meanings stated:

(1) "Conversion offering" shall mean any offering of securities made as part of a plan by which a savings and loan association or other organization converts from a mutual to a stock form of ownership.

(2) "Eligible purchaser" shall mean a person who is eligible to purchase securities pursuant to the rules of the Federal Home Loan Bank Board or other governmental agency or instrumentality having authority to regulate conversion offerings.

(b) *Conditions for Exemption*

This Interpretation shall not apply to a sale of securities by the issuer on a non-underwritten basis to any person who would otherwise be prohibited or restricted from purchasing a hot issue security if all of the conditions of this Subsection (b) are satisfied.

(1) *Sales to Members, Associated Persons of Members and Certain Related Persons*

If the purchaser is a member, person associated with a member, member of the immediate family of any such person to whose support such person contributes, directly or indirectly, or an account in which a member or person associated with a member has a beneficial interest:

(A) the purchaser shall be an eligible purchaser;

(B) the securities purchased shall be restricted from sale or transfer for a period of [150 days] three months following the conclusion of the offering; and

(C) the fact of purchase shall be reported in writing to the member where the person is associated within one day of payment.

(2) *Sales to Other Restricted Persons*

If the purchaser is not a person specified in Subsection (b)(1) above, and is [the purchaser shall be] an eligible purchaser pursuant to Subsection (a)(2), the conditions of Subsection (b)(1) shall not apply to such purchaser.

95-27 NASD INTRODUCES REVISED FREE-RIDING QUESTIONNAIRE AND FORM FR-1*

Executive Summary

As a result of recent amendments to the Free-Riding and Withholding Interpretation of the NASD Board of Governors under Article III, Section 1 of the NASD Rules of Fair Practice, the NASD revised the questionnaire that is used to review whether an offering was distributed according to the Interpretation. Revisions also were made to NASD Form FR-1, which may be used by members in their dealings with non-U.S. broker/dealers or banks. Copies of the revised forms follow this Notice.

Background

The NASD adopted the Interpretation based on the premise that members are obligated to make a bona fide public distribution at the public offering price of securities of a public offering that trade at a premium in the secondary market whenever such secondary market begins (a hot issue), regardless of whether such securities are acquired by the member as an underwriter, as a selling group member, from a member participating in the distribution as an underwriter or a selling group member, or otherwise. The Interpretation includes specific prohibitions and restrictions as a guide for members participating in an offering of hot-issue securities.

On December 7, 1994, the Securities and Exchange Commission (SEC) approved several amendments to the Interpretation. _Notices to Members 95-7_ describes the amendments in detail. These changes necessitated revisions to the questionnaire used by the NASD in reviewing offerings for compliance with the Interpretation and to NASD Form FR-1, which may be used by members to obtain assurances from non-U.S. broker/dealers or banks that no sales will be made by them in contravention of the Interpretation.

Free-Riding Questionnaire

In its review for compliance with the Interpretation, the NASD issued a questionnaire to the managing underwriter and to members participating in the distribution of the hot issues. Members must complete the questionnaire and forward it to the appropriate NASD District Office. The revised questionnaire is divided into four sections:

- Section I, overall figure from the managing underwriter;

- Section II, overall figures from all other underwriters, selling group members, and participants in the distribution;

- Section III, breakdown of the distribution by the participant; and

- Section IV, detailed information on sales to restricted accounts.

Sections I and II

In the first two sections, a member must indicate the total number of securities that have been confirmed by the firm. For this questionnaire, "confirmed" means the number of hot-issue securities allocated to the firm for distribution and for which the firm has issued a confirmation/comparison reflecting the full details of such sales to retail customers, institutional accounts, or other broker/dealers. When participating in a distribution of hot-issue securities, broker/dealers are responsible for ensuring compliance with the Free-Riding and Withholding Interpretation for all securities allocated and confirmed by that broker/dealer, including shares billed and delivered on behalf of others, such as designated orders, group sales, and directed sales.

A member completes Section I **or** Section II of the questionnaire. Section I is completed by the managing underwriter **only**. Section II is completed by all underwriters, selling group members, and other participants in the distribution, except for the managing underwriter.

Section III

All members must complete Section III. In this section, a member indicates the total number of securities distributed in each of 10 categories. The categories are addressed in the questionnaire in the same basic order in which they are addressed in the Interpretation. Unless otherwise noted, a member must provide detailed information on these sales in Section IV.

The figures reported in Section III are final figures after a member makes any cancellations and reallocations. Members should note that the total figure in Section III should equal the total number of securities confirmed in Section I or Section II.

Section IV

Section IV requires a member to provide detailed information on sales that were made to restricted accounts. The Interpretation includes specific circumstances in which it is permissible to sell to a restricted account, provided the member demonstrates compliance with the applicable provisions of the Interpretation.

NASD Form FR-1

For sales to a non-U.S. broker/dealer or bank, which is not participating in the distribution as an underwriter, the selling member must make an affirmative inquiry regarding the ultimate purchasers and comply with certain recordkeeping requirements. However, the Interpretation provides that a member may fulfill these obligations by having the non-U.S. broker/dealer or bank execute Form FR-1, or a reasonable facsimile of it.

In completing Form FR-1, the non-U.S. broker/dealer or bank gives the selling member a blanket assurance that no sales will be made in contravention of the provisions of the Interpretation. This form, which also was revised to conform with the recent amendments, is reprinted following this Notice. Members may reproduce copies of it or, as provided in the Interpretation, obtain other written assurance from the non-U.S. broker/dealer or bank.

* * *

Questions about the amendments to, or other provisions of, the Interpretation, should be directed to the NASD Office of General Counsel at (202) 728-8953. Questions regarding the Free-Riding Questionnaire or NASD Form FR-1 may be directed to Erin Gilligan, District Coordinator, Compliance Department, at (202) 728-8946.

Free-Riding Questionnaire

1 of 5 Pages

3/95

NATIONAL ASSOCIATION OF SECURITIES DEALERS, INC.

DATE

KEYBOARD ()

RE: KEYBOARD () **Offering Date:** KEYBOARD ()

INSTRUCTIONS: *Each member is required to complete either Section I or Section II based upon the capacity in which they acted in the distribution of the new issue. Sections III and IV must be completed by all firms for their "confirmed"* securities. It is the executing broker/ dealer's responsibility to ensure that securities were distributed in compliance with the Free-Riding and Withholding Interpretation.*

SECTION I.   TO BE COMPLETED BY THE MANAGING UNDERWRITER ONLY

A. Total number of securities offered for public distribution:

(Include any additional shares received from the issuer as part of any over-allotment provision.)

B. Total number of securities allocated to other underwriters and selling group members:

C. Total number of securities confirmed* by your firm to retail and institutional customers, including all shares billed and delivered on behalf of others, designated orders, group sales, directed sales, etc.:

---

*For purposes of this questionnaire, "confirmed" means the number of new issue securities allocated to the firm for distribution purposes and for which the firm has issued a confirmation/comparison reflecting the full details of such sale to retail customers, institutional accounts or other broker/ dealers. When participating in a distribution of new issue securities, broker/ dealers are responsible for ensuring compliance with the Free-Riding and Withholding Interpretation for all securities allocated and confirmed by that broker/dealer.

SECTION II. TO BE COMPLETED BY ALL UNDERWRITERS, SELLING GROUP MEMBERS AND OTHER PARTICIPANTS IN THE DISTRIBUTION

A. Total number of securities confirmed* by your firm to retail and institutional customers. (Do not include shares billed and delivered on your behalf by the managing underwriter, designated orders, group sales, directed sales, etc.):

B. Indicate capacity in which your firm participated in the offering:

Underwriter

Selling group

Other (define) _____

SECTION III. BREAKDOWN OF SECURITIES DISTRIBUTED BY YOUR FIRM

INSTRUCTIONS: *Indicate total number of securities distributed in each category and, unless otherwise noted, provide detailed information in Section IV, "Sales to Restricted Accounts." This breakdown should contain the final figures after giving effect to all cancellations and reallocations. For additional information regarding categories, please refer to the Board of Governors Interpretation "Free-Riding and Withholding" under Article III, Section 1, of the Rules of Fair Practice.*

1. Securities held in a firm account.

2. Sales to any officer, director, general partner, employee or agent of the member or any other broker/dealer, or to persons associated with the member or with any other broker/dealer, or to a member of the immediate family of such person.

---

*For purposes of this questionnaire, "confirmed" means the number of new issue securities allocated to the firm for distribution purposes and for which the firm has issued a confirmation/comparison reflecting the full details of such sale to retail customers, institutional accounts or other broker/dealers. When participating in a distribution of new issue securities, broker/dealers are responsible for ensuring compliance with the Free-Riding and Withholding Interpretation for all securities allocated and confirmed by that broker/dealer.

Indicate the number of shares/units that were sold pursuant to the following provisions:

(A) Sales to persons associated with broker/dealers whose business is limited to investment company/variable contract securities or direct participation programs.

Number of shares/units

(B) Sales to a member of the immediate family of a person associated with a member who is not supported directly or indirectly by that person if the sale is by a broker/dealer other than that employing the restricted person and the restricted person has no ability to control the allocation of the hot issue.

Number of shares/units

It is not necessary to complete Section IV for items 2(A) and (B).

3. Sales to a person who is a finder with respect to the public offering or to any person acting in a fiduciary capacity to the managing underwriter, including among others, attorneys, accountants and financial consultants, or to any other person who is supported directly or indirectly, to a material extent, by any person specified in this paragraph.

4. Sales to any senior officer of a bank, savings and loan institution, insurance company, investment company, investment advisory firm or any other institutional type account, (including, but not limited to hedge funds, investment partnerships, investment corporations, or investment clubs) domestic or foreign, or to any person in the securities department of, or to any employee or any other person who may influence or whose activities directly or indirectly involve or are related to the function of buying and selling securities for any bank, savings and loan institution, insurance company, investment company, investment advisory firm, or other institutional type account, domestic or foreign, or to any other person who is supported directly or indirectly, to a material extent, by any person specified in this paragraph.

5. Sales to any account in which any person specified under paragraphs (1), (2), (3), or (4) has a beneficial interest.

6. Sales to other domestic broker/dealers for bona fide public customers, other than those enumerated in paragraphs (1)(2)(3)(4) or (5) above.

Name of Broker/Dealer	No. of Shares/Units	Written Representation Received (pursuant to paragraph 6)
		Yes_____ No_____
		Yes_____ No_____
		Yes_____ No_____

It is not necessary to complete Section IV for item 6.

7. Sales to any domestic bank, domestic branch of a foreign bank, trust company or other conduit for an undisclosed principal.

    (A) Indicate the number of shares/units that were sold based upon assurances obtained that ultimate purchasers were not restricted persons.

    Number of shares/units

It is not necessary to complete Section IV for item 7(A).

8. Sales to a foreign broker/dealer or bank.

    Indicate the number of shares/units that were sold pursuant to the following conditions:

    (A) Sales by a foreign broker/dealer or bank participating in the distribution as an underwriter were made in accordance with provisions of underwriting agreement.

    Number of shares/units

    (B) Affirmative inquiry was obtained that ultimate purchasers were not restricted persons.

    Number of shares/units

It is not necessary to complete Section IV for items 8(A) and (B).

9. Sales to an investment partnership or corporation, domestic or foreign (except companies registered under the Investment Company Act of 1940) including but not limited to hedge funds, investment clubs, and other like accounts.

Indicate the number of shares/units that were sold pursuant to the following conditions:

(A) "Carve out" mechanism was utilized.

Number of shares/units

(B) Determination was made based upon file containing information on all persons having a beneficial interest or the opinion of counsel or accountant was obtained.

Number of shares/units

It is not necessary to complete Section IV for items 9 (A) and (B).

10. Sales to public customers.

It is not necessary to complete Section IV for item 10.

TOTAL (1 through 10) =

Please note that the total should be equal to total securities confirmed by your firm as noted in Section I or II.

Indicate the number of shares/units that were originally sold to a restricted account and were subsequently cancelled prior to the end of the first business day after the date on which secondary market trading begins and were reallocated to an unrestricted account. Not applicable.

Signature of Principal Title

NOTE: *Questionnaires should be returned to your District Office by the date specified.*

SECTION IV.   SALES TO RESTRICTED ACCOUNTS

PLEASE NOTE THAT IN CERTAIN CIRCUMSTANCES AS SET FORTH IN THE INTERPRETATION, IT IS PERMISSIBLE TO SELL TO A RESTRICTED ACCOUNT. HOWEVER, IT IS THE OBLIGATION OF THE MEMBER TO DEMONSTRATE COMPLIANCE WITH THE APPLICABLE PROVISIONS OF THE INTERPRETATION.

REPORTING MEMBER _____

ISSUE _____

DATE OF PUBLIC OFFERING _____

Number of Shares/Units	Name of Purchaser	Name of Registered Representative (Handling A/C)	Category Reported in Section III	Indicate Employment Classification, Family Member Relationship, etc. of Purchaser*	Indicate Whether Issuer-Directed Sales, Stand-by Arrangement Sales, or Sales to Venture Capital Investors**

*Sales are permitted to members of the immediate family provided that such persons do not contribute directly or indirectly to the support of such member of the immediate family; securities were sold to such persons in accordance with their normal investment practice and that the aggregate of the securities so sold is insubstantial and not disproportionate. To demonstrate investment history at your firm or another broker/dealer, please submit a transcript or other evidence for each account. Transcript should include account's practice prior to offering (*i.e.,* 1 year).

**Sales of issuer-directed securities, sales purchased pursuant to a stand-by arrangement and sales to venture capital investors, are not subject to provisions of the interpretation provided the conditions stipulated in the interpretations are met.

NASD FORM FR-1

Representation from Non-United States Broker/Dealers or Banks regarding NASD Board of Governors Interpretation with respect to "Free-Riding and Withholding" under Article III, Section I, of the Rules of Fair Practice.

Date

Name of Non-United States Broker/Dealer or Bank

Address

Pursuant to the obligations imposed upon members in their dealings with Non-United States broker/dealers or banks under paragraph 8(b) of the Interpretation, this form gives assurances to (selling member name) that no sales will be made in contravention of the provisions of this Interpretation.

It is our understanding that the securities falling within the scope of the Interpretation are those of an issue which trade at a premium in the secondary market whenever such secondary market begins. We further understand that the Interpretation prohibits:

1. Sales to any broker/dealer, including a member of the National Association of Securities Dealers, Inc. (NASD); provided, however, a purchasing firm may sell all or part of the securities acquired as described above to another member broker/dealer upon receipt from the latter, written assurance that such a purchase would be made to fill orders from bona fide public customers, other than those enumerated in paragraphs (2), (3), (4) or (5) below, at the public offering as an accommodation to them and without compensation for such.

2. Sales to any officer, director, general partner, employee or agent of the member or any other broker/dealer, or to persons associated with the member or with any other broker/dealer, or to a member of the immediate family* of any such person. This provision does not apply to:

    1. Sales to persons associated with broker/dealers whose business is limited to the purchase or sale of either investment

*The term immediate family shall include parents, mother-in-law or father-in-law, husband or wife, brother or sister, brother-in-law or sister-in-law,

company/variable contract securities or direct participation programs.

2. Sales to a member of the immediate family of a person associated with a member who is not supported directly or indirectly to a material extent by such person if the sale is by the broker/dealer other than that employing the restricted person and the restricted person has no ability to control the allocation of the hot issue.

3. Sales to a person who is a finder with respect to the public offering or to any person acting in a fiduciary capacity to the managing underwriter, including among others, attorneys, accountants and financial consultants, or to any other person who is supported directly or indirectly, to a material extent, by any person specified in this paragraph.

4. Sales to any senior officer of a bank, savings and loan institution, insurance company, investment company, investment advisory firm or any other institutional type account, (including, but not limited to hedge funds, investment partnerships, investment corporations, or investment clubs) domestic or foreign, or to any person in the securities department of, or to any employee or any other person who may influence or whose activities directly or indirectly involve or are related to the function of buying and selling securities for any bank, savings and loan institution, insurance company, investment company, investment advisory firm, or other institutional type account, domestic or foreign, or to any other person who is supported directly or indirectly, to a material extent, by any person specified in this paragraph.

5. Sales to any account in which any person specified under paragraphs (1), (2), (3), or (4) has a beneficial interest provided that:

1. Sales to members of the immediate family of persons enumerated above in paragraph (2), may be made if such persons do not contribute directly or indirectly to the support of such member of the immediate family; and

son-in-law or daughter-in-law, children, and any other person who is supported directly or indirectly, to a material extent by the member or other person specified above.

2. Sales may be made to persons specified under paragraphs (3) and (4), if the firm is prepared to demonstrate that the securities were sold to such persons in accordance with their normal investment practice, that the aggregate of the securities so sold is insubstantial and not disproportionate in amount as compared to the sales to members of the public and that the amount sold to any one of such persons is insubstantial in amount.

We understand that by providing Form FR-1 to the aforementioned NASD member we are asserting that no sales were made in contravention of the provisions of the Interpretation.

Signature of Executive Title

95-42 SEC APPROVES AMENDMENTS
TO PROSPECTUS DELIVERY REQUIREMENTS
TO ACCOMMODATE T+3 SETTLEMENT*

Executive Summary

On May 11, 1995, the Securities and Exchange Commission (SEC or Commission) approved amendments to its rules that would implement two alternative methodologies proposed by the securities industry to expedite the delivery of final prospectuses on public offerings of securities to accommodate the T+3 settlement cycle under SEC Rule 15c6-1. The new amendments will become effective on June 7, 1995, simultaneously with the effective date of Rule 15c6-1.

Discussion

The SEC adopted on May 11, 1995, a number of amendments to its rules that will permit members to more quickly deliver a prospectus in new offerings of securities after June 7, 1995, when the new T+3 settlement cycle goes into effect pursuant to Rule 15c6-1. The amendments address industry concerns regarding an exemption that was adopted in Rule 15c6-1 to permit new offerings to be settled on a T+5 cycle, while secondary trading in the same securities will be settled in a T+3 cycle. The securities industry expressed concern that a disparate settlement cycle for primary offerings and secondary trading results in operational issues, increased settlement risk, systemic credit risk to members, and market risk as a result of secondary market volatility. The primary reason given by the SEC when it adopted Rule 15c6-1 as to why settlement of primary offerings within the T+3 settlement cycle has not been feasible for many issues was the amount of time it takes to print and deliver prospectuses.

The SEC has approved two approaches proposed by the Securities Industry Association and by a group of four firms: CS First Boston

Corporation; Goldman, Sachs & Co.; Lehman Brothers, Inc.; and Morgan Stanley Co. A copy of the descriptive part of the SEC release without the final pages describing the rule language changes is attached to this Notice. The main features of the amendments approved by the SEC are:

- Amendments to Rule 15c6-1 to require that most offerings underwritten on a firm-commitment basis settle on a T+3 cycle. The Rule also permits offerings underwritten on a firm-commitment basis that are priced after the close of the market to settle on a T+4 cycle and permits the managing underwriter to establish an alternative settlement cycle for an entire offering where appropriate.

- Adoption of new Rule 434 under the Securities Act that permits all required prospectus information to be delivered to investors in the preliminary prospectus traditionally disseminated and a "term sheet" delivered after effectiveness of the offering. The amendments require that the term sheet be clearly marked as a supplement to the preliminary prospectus and that copies of the preliminary prospectus be available to investors upon request when the term sheet is distributed. Closed-end investment companies and unit investment trusts also can rely on the new rule.

- Amendment to Rule 430A to extend the time period from five to 15 business days in which a prospectus supplement containing pricing and other related information omitted from the registration statement must be filed.

- Amendments to the SEC's disclosure rules to permit the disclosure items that are subject to change at the time of the offering to be placed at the front or back of the prospectus so that the main part of the final prospectus can be printed in advance of effectiveness of the offering.

- Amendments to the SEC's filing requirements to permit, for all registered offerings:

  —the registration of only the title of the securities to be registered, without designation of the number of securities, and the proposed maximum offering price;

—the registration after effectiveness of an increase in the size and price of an offering that together represent no more than a 20 percent increase in the maximum aggregate offering price by using an abbreviated registration statement that will become effective upon filing;

—the filing of size or price changes by fax or EDGAR copy between 5:30 P.M. and 10 P.M. and payment of the filing fee; and

—fax or telephone requests for acceleration of a registration statement.

The SEC also announced that it is making available an information brochure for investors that answers many of the common questions raised by retail investors concerning T+3. Members are encouraged to provide copies of this information brochure to their customers. The brochure can be obtained through the SEC's consumer information telephone line at (800) SEC-0330.

Questions regarding this Notice may be directed to Thomas R. Cassella, Vice President, Compliance, (202) 728-8237.

SECURITIES AND EXCHANGE COMMISSION

17 CFR PARTS 202, 228, 229, 230, 232, 239, 240, 270 and 274

RELEASE NO. 33-7168; 34-35705; IC-21061

FILE NO. S7-7-95

RIN 3235-AG40

PROSPECTUS DELIVERY; SECURITIES TRANSACTIONS SETTLEMENT

AGENCY: Security and Exchange Commission.

ACTION: Final rules.

SUMMARY: The Commission is adopting revisions to its rules and forms and a new rule in order to implement two solutions to prospectus delivery issues arising in connection with the change to T+3 securities transaction settlement. These revisions, among other things, include changes that highlight the location of the risk factor disclosure within the prospectus. In addition, the Commission is eliminating an exemption from T+3 settlement for purchases and sales of securities pursuant to a firm commitment offering, providing a T+4 time frame to firm commitment offerings under certain conditions, and adopting a modified procedure whereby participants in firm commitment offerings may agree to an extended settlement time frame.

EFFECTIVE DATE: The new rule and the revisions to rules and forms are effective June 7, 1995.

FOR FURTHER INFORMATION CONTACT: Anita Klein, Joseph Babits or Michael Mitchell (202) 942-2900, Division of Corporation Finance; and, with regard to questions concerning revisions to the T+3 settlement rule, Jerry W. Carpenter or Christine Sibille, (202) 942-4187, Division of Market Regulation; and, with regard to questions concerning Rule 15c2-8 revisions, Alexander Dill, (202) 942-4892, Division of Market Regulation; and, with regard to questions concerning the application to investment companies, Kathleen Clarke, (202) 942-0721, Division of Investment Management, U.S. Securities and Exchange Commission, Washington, D.C. 20549.

SUPPLEMENTARY INFORMATION:

INTRODUCTION AND BACKGROUND

On October 6, 1993, the Commission adopted Rule 15c6-1[1] under the Securities Exchange Act of 1934 (the "Exchange Act").[2] That rule is scheduled to become effective on June 7, 1995.[3] Rule 15c6-1 requires that the standard settlement time frame for most broker-dealer trades be three business days after the trade (hereinafter "T+3"). Rule 15c6-1 provides a limited exemption from T+3 for the sale of securities for cash pursuant to a firm commitment offering registered under the Securities Act of 1933 (the "Securities Act").[4] Resales of such securities, however, remain within T+3.

Since the adoption of Rule 15c6-1, members of the brokerage community have suggested that the Commission eliminate this exemption

---

1. 17 CFR 240.15c6-1. *See* Exchange Act Release No. 33023 (Oct. 6, 1993) [58 FR 52891].

2. 15 U.S.C. 78a *et seq.*

3. *See* Exchange Act Release No. 34952 (Nov. 9, 1994) [59 FR 59137].

4. 15 U.S.C. 77a *et seq.*

because, among other reasons, the bifurcated settlement cycle created for initial sales and resales of new issues[5] would be disruptive to broker-dealer operations and to the clearance and settlement system. According to the brokerage community, the primary reason that settlement with T+3 is not feasible for many new issues is the amount of time it takes to print and deliver prospectuses.[6]

Two proposals to ease prospectus delivery within T+3 were submitted for Commission consideration. One was submitted by the Securities Industry Association ("SIA") and one was submitted by a group of four investment firms: CS First Boston Corporation, Goldman, Sachs & Co., Lehman Brothers Inc. and Morgan Stanley & Co. Incorporated (the "Four Firms").[7] These proposals recommended markedly different solutions to accomplishing prospectus delivery within T+3.

On February 21, 1995, the Commission proposed new Rule 434 and amendments to existing rules and forms based upon these two

---

5. The term "new issues" as used herein refers to both initial public offerings and offerings of additional securities by companies.

6. Some of these timing difficulties can be expected to be alleviated as markets increasingly rely on non-paper delivery media. In recognition of that development, the staff issued an interpretive letter to facilitate the use of electronic transmission to satisfy prospectus delivery requirements. *Brown & Wood* (Feb. 17, 1995). The Division of Corporation Finance staff, in addition to issuing the *Brown & Wood* letter, is considering generally delivery under the Securities Act of prospectuses through other non-paper media (*e.g.,* audiotapes, videotapes, facsimile, directed electronic mail, and CD ROMs). The staff anticipates submitting to the Commission in the near future recommendations intended both to facilitate compliance with the Securities Act's prospectus delivery requirements and to encourage continued technological developments of non-paper delivery media.

7. *See* letter from Robin Shelby, CS First Boston Corporation; Goldman Sachs & Co.; Steven Barkenfield, Lehman Brothers Inc.; and John Ander, Morgan Stanley Co. Inc. to Anita Klein, Securities and Exchange Commission, dated Jan. 24, 1995 and letter from Goldman Sachs to Anita Klein, Securities and Exchange Commission, dated Feb. 3, 1995. *See also* letter from Joseph McLaughlin, Brown & Wood, on behalf of the Securities Industry Association, to Anita Klein, Securities and Exchange Commission, dated Feb. 1, 1995. Copies of these proposals are available for inspection and duplication at the Commission's Public Reference Room, 450 Fifth St. N.W., Washington, D.C. 20549, File Number S7-7-95.

proposals.[8] The Commission sought comment regarding which approach should be implemented, or whether the Commission should implement both approaches and thereby allow market participants a choice as to which to use in any given offering. Twenty-nine comment letters were received in response to the Proposing Release.[9] Most commenters addressing the questions of whether to adopt one or both approaches favored the adoption of both of the Commission's approaches.

As described in greater detail below, the Commission is adopting both approaches, largely as proposed, to provide market participants with the flexibility of selecting between alternative methods to expedite prospectus delivery under a T+3 clearance and settlement system.[10] Because of the concerns expressed by some commenters with respect to the potential for investor confusion, however, the Commission intends to monitor closely disclosure practices that develop under the new rules and will undertake revisions to the rules if necessary to address investor problems.

On February 21, 1995, the Commission also proposed amendments to Rule 15c6-1 to eliminate the current exemption for firm commitment offerings except offerings of asset-backed securities and structured securities, to provide for a T+4 standard settlement period for offerings priced after the close of the markets ("after-market pricings"), and to permit the managing underwriter to establish T+3, T+4, or T+5 as the standard settlement period for an entire offering if certain conditions were met. In general, commenters favored the proposed amendments to Rule 15c6-1. Many commenters, however, objected to the requirements and limitations contained in the T+3, T+4, or T+5 proposal. As described below, the Commission is eliminating the blanket exemption from Rule 15c6-1 for firm commitment offerings, is adopting the T+4 standard for after-market pricings, and is adopting a revised

---

8. *See* Securities Act Release No. 7141 (Feb. 21, 1995) [60 FR 10724] (hereinafter, the "Proposing Release").

9. These letters of comment and a summary thereof are available for inspection and duplication at the Commission's Public Reference Room, 450 Fifth Street N.W., Washington, D.C. 20549, File No. S7-7-95.

10. As adopted, the approaches will apply specifically to certain investment companies registered under the Investment Company Act of 1940 (15 U.S.C. 80a-1 *et seq.*) (hereinafter, the "Investment Company Act") (*i.e.,* closed-end investment companies and unit investment trusts ("UITs")). *See infra* Sections II.A.8 and II.B.3.d.

provision authorizing exceptions from T+3 settlement for certain firm commitment offerings.[11]

PROSPECTUS DELIVERY APPROACHES

A. The Four Firms Approach

The Four Firms proposal was premised on the view that the process of preparing and delivering prospectuses in new issues could be accelerated sufficiently to comply with T+3 if six steps were taken by the Commission to facilitate the printing of a significant portion of the final prospectus prior to pricing. Those six steps, noted below, are being adopted substantially as proposed.[12] Except as otherwise noted, these steps are applicable to any offering.

1. Re-ordering of Prospectuses

As was proposed, the Commission is adopting rule revisions enabling the contents of prospectuses to be re-ordered to expedite the printing process.[13] All portions likely to be subject to change at the

---

11. With the help of staff of the Commission's Division of Corporation Finance and Office of General Counsel, the Commission's Advisory Committee on the Capital Formation and Regulatory Processes is examining the relative costs and benefits of the Securities Act's transactional registration scheme, including the prospectus delivery requirements. *See* Commission File No. 265-20.

12. For a discussion of the application of the Four Firms approach to investment companies, *see infra* Section II.A.8.

13. Certain Commission rules that specify the location of information in the forepart of the prospectus, or in a specified order within the prospectus, are being revised to eliminate certain requirements regarding location. *See* revisions to Items 503(b) and 503(c) of Regulation S-K, 17 CFR 229.503(b) and 229.503(c); Items 503(b) and 503(c) of Regulation S-B, 17 CFR 228.503(b) and 228.503(c); and Securities Industry Guide 4, 17 CFR 229.801(d). Consistent with the proposal, no revision has been made to order and location rules that relate to specific and limited classes of transactions. *See* Items 903(a) and 904(a) of Regulation S-K, 17 CFR 229.903(a) and 229.904(a) summary of a roll-up transaction, reasonably detailed description of each material risk and effect of the roll-up transaction); Securities Act Industry Guide 5, 17 CFR 229.801(e), (real estate limited partnerships suitability standards). In addition, issuers of limited partnership interests and other real estate investment vehicles must continue to comply with the

time of pricing may be placed together in the beginning of the prospectus after the front cover page in a "pricing-related information" section, or may be wrapped around the remainder of the prospectus just inside the front and back cover pages.[14] While summary and risk factors sections must remain in the forepart of the prospectus, those sections may immediately follow the "pricing-related information" section rather than preceding it. To ensure that investors continue to be able to locate the risk factors section in all offerings with ease, however, rule revisions also provide that the currently required cross reference to that section on the cover page of the prospectus now identify with specificity (*e.g.* by page number) the location of that section within the prospectus.[15] In addition, rule revisions require that the risk factors section be captioned within the prospectus as "Risk Factors" and clarify that the table of contents required on the back cover of the prospectus must include a reference to the risk factors section and specify the page number on which it begins.[16]

---

disclosure guidance set forth in Securities Act Release No. 6900 (June 17, 1991) [56 FR 28979].

14. Commenters noted that, if prospectuses are printed in a folio manner, moving pricing-related information to the front of the prospectus may not result in earlier printing of the remainder of the prospectus. Thus, the Commission is providing the flexibility to "wrap" the "pricing-related information" section. Of course, whether the price-related information is set forth in the front or wrapped, the information set forth in the prospectus must be presented in a clear, concise and understandable fashion, as required by Rule 421(b) under the Securities Act, 17 CFR 230.421(b). *See also* Rule 421(a) under the Securities Act, 17 CFR 230.421(a), which requires that information in a prospectus be set forth in a fashion so as not to obscure any of the required information necessary to keep the required information from being incomplete or misleading; and Securities Act Release No. 6900 (June 17, 1991) [56 FR 28979].

15. *See* revisions to Regulation S-K Item 501(c)(4), 17 CFR 229.501(c)(4), and Regulation S-B Item 501(a)(4), 17 CFR 228.501(a)(4). As revised, the rules also require that the cross reference be printed in bold-face roman type at least as high as twelve-point modern type and at least two points leaded.

16. *See* revisions to Item 503(c)(1), 17 CFR 229.503(c)(1) and 17 CFR 228.503(c)(1); Item 502(g), 17 CFR 229.502(g); Item 502(f), 17 CFR 228.502(f).

Further, rule revisions provide that specific information currently required on the prospectus cover pages may be placed under an appropriate caption elsewhere in the prospectus.[17] Otherwise, the prospectus cover pages must continue to contain information currently specified by Commission rules.[18]

The "pricing-related information" section may include those portions of a prospectus that may change as a result of pricing, such as use of proceeds, capitalization, pro forma financial information, dilution, selling shareholder information and shares eligible for future sale.[19] The pricing information portion itself may be included in the price-related information section. These adopted rule revisions which allow re-ordering of information within a prospectus for convenience in printing do not alter existing requirements with respect to the filing of post-effective amendments or supplements with the Commission when material changes or additions affect information set forth in the prospectus contained in an effective registration statement. However, other rule revisions discussed below do alter existing requirements.

2. Changes in Offering Size and Estimated Price Range

To prevent delays in printing prospectuses that arise when the size of an offering is changed after the effective date of the registration statement, or the pricing of the securities falls outside the estimated

---

17. *See* revisions to Item 502(a), (b), (c) and (f) of Regulation S-K, 17 CFR 229.502(a), 229.502(b), 229.502(c) and 229.502(f); revisions to Item 502(a), (b) and (c) of Regulation S-B, 17 CFR 228.502(a), 228.502(b) and 228.502(c); and revisions to the Instruction following Item 502(f) of Regulation S-B, 17 CFR 228.502(f). These revisions relate to disclosure regarding: the availability of Exchange Act information about the registrant, the nature of reports to be given to security holders, undertakings with respect to information incorporated by reference, and the enforceability of civil liabilities against certain foreign persons.

18. *See* Item 501(c) of Regulation S-K, 17 CFR 229.501(c) (outside front cover page); Item 502(d), (e) and (g) of Regulation S-K, 17 CFR 229.502(d), 229.502(e), and 229.502(g) (inside front cover page and outside back cover page); Item 501 of Regulation S-B, 17 CFR 228.501 (outside front cover page); and Item 502(d), (e) and (f) of Regulation S-B, 17 CFR 228.502(d), 228.502(e) and 228.502(f) (inside front cover page and outside back cover page).

19. *See* Instruction to Item 503(c) of Regulations S-K and S-B, 17 CFR 229.503(c) and 228.503(c).

range, the Commission under specified conditions is eliminating or streamlining the filings that result. Although originally contemplated only for Rule 430A offerings, the adopted revisions provide the same flexibility for all registered offerings.

a.   Registration of Classes of Securities

In order to minimize the instances in which an increase in the offering size would result in the need to file a new registration statement, rule revisions are being adopted to increase registrants' flexibility with respect to the amount of securities being registered in an offering. Under the revised rules, an issuer is permitted to register securities in an offering by specifying only the title of the class of securities to be registered and the proposed maximum aggregate offering price.[20] Except in the case of the unallocated shelf procedure available to Form S-3 eligible companies, the aggregate dollar amount associated with each class of securities offered must be disclosed in the "Calculation of Registration Fee" table. Where issuers registered a greater amount of securities than needed in the offering, such additional securities may be carried forward to a subsequent registration statement without incurring an additional registration fee.[21]

---

20. *See* revisions to Rule 457(o) under the Securities Act, 17 CFR 230.457(o). The amount of securities to be registered and the proposed maximum offering price per unit are no longer required to be set forth in the "Calculation of Registration Fee" table. Of course, an issuer may continue to specify such information therein if it so chooses and relies upon Rule 457(a). Regardless of the method chosen for the "Calculation of Registration Fee" table, however, the registrant continues to be required to specify in the prospectus the amount of securities being offered, and where the registrant is not a reporting company, a bona fide estimate of the range of the maximum offering price. *See* Rule 501(c)(6) of Regulation S-K, 17 CFR 229.501(c)(6) and Rule 501(6) of Regulation S-B, 17 CFR 228.501(6).

21. *See* revisions to Rule 429, 17 CFR 230.429. Under Rule 429, in a new registration statement filed in the future for another offering of that class of securities, the registrant would indicate in a footnote to the "Calculation of Registration Fee" table that part of the registration fee had been paid previously in connection with an earlier registration statement. The footnote must specify the exact dollar amount of the fee being carried over and the related registration statement file number.

b.   Increases in Offering Size—Registration of Additional Securities

When the pricing terms of an offering are finalized, it is not unusual for changes to be made in the offering size through adjustments to both price and volume.[22] Where this process requires registration of additional securities, the revised rules and forms permit the filing of an abbreviated registration statement to register the additional amount of securities to be offered and sold.[23] Such an abbreviated registration is available to an issuer that is registering additional securities in an amount and at a price that together represent no more than a 20% increase in the maximum aggregate offering price set forth in the "Calculation of Registration Fee" table in the earlier effective registration statement.[24] Such registration would consist of: the facing page, a statement incorporating by reference the contents of the earlier registration statement relating to the offering, all required consents and opinions, and the signature page. While not required by the rule, the registrant also may include in the new registration statement, instead of in a filing under Rule 424, any price-related information with respect to the offering that was omitted from the earlier registration statement pursuant to Rule 430A.[25] The abbreviated registration statement must be filed prior to the time sales are made and confirmations are sent or

---

22. While participants in a registered distribution may only offer the amount of securities registered to be offered, it is possible that indications of interest received in response to such offers may exceed the amount registered to be offered. Sales of securities in excess of the volume initially registered will not result in Section 5 liability if the participants in the distribution did not solicit indications of interest in an amount in excess of that registered and the procedures discussed in this section are followed.

23. *See* revisions to General Instructions of Forms SB-1, SB-2, S-1, S-2, S-3, S-11, F-1, F-2 and F-3.

24. In the context of an offering from a shelf registration statement, the 20% increase would be measured based upon the amount of securities on the shelf.

25. Consistent with offerings where a new registration statement is not required to be filed as a result of a change of no more than 20% in the size of the offering, information necessary to update disclosure contained in the earlier registration statement as a result of the increase may be reflected in a form of prospectus filed under Rule 424(b), 17 CFR 230.424(b). *See infra* Section II.A.2.c.

given, and will become effective automatically upon filing.[26] As adopted, this abbreviated registration format is available regardless of whether the earlier registration statement was prepared in reliance upon Rule 430A.

In addition to providing an abbreviated registration format for such increases in offering size, rule revisions allow such registration statements to be filed promptly even when pricing occurs after the Commissions business hours.[27] Such a registration statement may be filed with the Commission by persons other than mandated electronic filers by transmitting a single copy of it via facsimile to the Commission's principal office from 5:30 P.M. to 10:00 P.M.[28] Electronic filers may file such a registration statement from 5:30 P.M. to 10:00 P.M. by transmitting it through EDGAR.[29] Such filings become automatically effective upon receipt by the Commission of the complete facsimile or EDGAR copy and payment of the filing fee.

To accommodate payment of the filing fee after the close of banking hours, rule revisions provide that payment with respect to such registration statements may be made by: (i) instructing a bank or wire

---

26. *See* Rule 462(b), 17 CFR 230.462(b). The registration statement is deemed to be a part of the earlier registration statement relating to the offering. *See, e.g.,* General Instruction V. to Form S-1.

27. *See* revisions to Rule 110, 17 CFR 230.110; Rule 402, 17 CFR 230.402; Rule 455, 17 CFR 230.455; and Rule 472, 17 CFR 230.472; Rule 13, 17 CFR 232.13 and Rule 3a, 17 CFR 202.3a.

28. Effective June 7, 1995, the telephone number for that facsimile machine is (202) 942-7333 and the telephone number for the staff person that can answer questions regarding such facsimiles between the hours of 5:30 P.M. and 10:00 P.M. (Eastern Standard Time or Eastern Daylight Savings Time, whichever is currently in effect) is (202) 942-8900. Filings (other than electronic filings through EDGAR) between 5:30 P.M. and 10:00 P.M. on Forms SB-1 and SB-2 for this purpose must be sent via this facsimile system to the Commission's principal office rather than to the regional or district offices of the Commission.

29. The new EDGAR form types for purposes of registration statements under Rule 462 are S-1MEF, S-2MEF, S-3MEF, F-1MEF, F-2MEF, F-3MEF, SB-1MEF and SB-2MEF. A post-effective amendment to any of these new form types should be designated as form type POS462B. With respect to other aspects of the adopted proposals and electronic filers, *see also infra* Section IV.

transfer service to transmit a wire transfer to the Commission of the requisite amount as soon as practicable (but in any event no later than the close of the next business day following the date the registration statement is faxed to the Commission); and (ii) providing specific certifications to the Commission with the abbreviated registration statement.[30] Specifically, the registrant must certify to the Commission that: the registrant (or its agent) has so instructed its bank or a wire transfer service to pay the Commission; that it will not revoke such instructions; and that it has sufficient funds in the relevant account to cover the amount of the filing fee. These instructions may be transmitted on the day of filing the registration statement after the close of business of such bank or wire transfer service, provided that the registrant undertakes to confirm receipt of such instructions by the bank or wire transfer service the following business day.

c.   Changes in Offering Size; Deviation from Price Range

Currently, a post-effective amendment is not required to be filed where there is a decrease in volume of securities offered or the actual offering price is outside the disclosed estimated price range, unless such decrease or change would change materially the disclosure included in the registration statement at the time of effectiveness.[31] Under the revised rules, a post-effective amendment does not have to be filed in connection with any registered offering if there is a decrease or increase in the offering size (if such an increase would not require additional securities to be registered) and/or the actual price is outside the estimated price range if, in the aggregate, the new size and price represent no more than a 20% change in the maximum aggregate offering price set forth in the "Calculation of Registration Fee" table in the effective registration statement.[32]

_____

30. *See* revisions to Rule 111, 17 CFR 230.111. This payment certification document accompanying an abbreviated registration statement should be transmitted by electronic filers under EDGAR form type CORRESP.

31. *See* Securities Act Release No. 6964 (Oct. 22, 1992) [57 FR 48970] for a discussion of the materiality standard as it applies to these changes.

32. *See* revision to Instruction to Paragraph (a) of Rule 430A, 17 CFR 230.430A and revisions to Item 512(a)(1)(ii) of Regulations S-K and S-B, 17 CFR 229.512(a)(1)(ii) and 228.512(a)(1)(ii). This revision pertains to changes in offering size that occur at pricing and does not extend to changes

3. Manual Signatures and Incorporation by Reference of Opinions and Consents

Under the proposals, rule revisions would have provided that duplicated or facsimile versions of manual signatures could be included on the signature page in place of the manual signatures currently required in a registration statement to increase the size of the offering. In response to comment, the rule revisions being adopted have been expanded to permit duplicated or facsimile versions of manual signatures in any registration statement or post-effective amendment filed under the Securities Act and any reports filed under the Exchange Act.[33] These revisions will provide the same flexibility to all paper filers that is accorded EDGAR filers. In addition, under the revised rules, signatures on required opinions and consents in such filings also may be duplicated or facsimile versions of manual signatures.[34] In all cases where duplicated or facsimile versions of manual signatures are used, the registrant must maintain the manually signed version in its files for five years after the filing of the related document and provide it to the Commission or the staff upon request.

Rule revisions also allow opinions and consents required in abbreviated registration statements registering an additional 20% to be incorporated by reference to the extent that the opinions and consents contained in the earlier effective registration statement were drafted to apply to any subsequent registration statement filed solely to increase

---

made after that time. While no post-effective amendment is required to be filed, issuers continue to be responsible for evaluating the effect of a volume change or price deviation on the accuracy and completeness of disclosure made to investors. When there is a change in offering size or deviation from the price range beyond the 20% threshold, a post-effective amendment would continue to be required only if such change or deviation materially changes the previous disclosure. Of course, if an increase beyond the 20% threshold requires registration of additional securities, a new registration statement updated in all respects must be filed.

33. *See* revisions to Rule 402, 17 CFR 230.402; Rule 12b-11, 17 CFR 240.12b-11; Rule 14d-1, 17 CFR 240.14d-1; and Rule 16a-3, 17 CFR 240.16a-3.

34. *See* revisions to Rule 402, 17 CFR 230.402; Rule 439, 17 CFR 230.439; Rule 12b-11, 17 CFR 240.12b-11; Rule 14d-1, 17 CFR 240.14d-1; and Rule 16a-3, 17 CFR 240.16a-3.

the offering up to a 20% threshold.[35] Where opinions and consents cannot be incorporated, duplicated or facsimile versions of manual signatures may be included in the new opinion or consent required to be filed in the abbreviated registration statement.

4. Rule 430A Pricing Period

As was proposed, the Commission is extending the period during which a prospectus supplement containing pricing and other related information omitted from a registration statement may be filed pursuant to Rule 430A under the Securities Act.[36] The "pricing" period is extended from five to fifteen business days after the effective date of the registration statement or any post-effective amendment thereto. Although originally proposed as an extended ten-business-day period, the adopted fifteen-business-day period should provide additional flexibility for purposes of complying with T+3, without defeating the purpose of that limitation.[37]

Where a Rule 430A offering is not priced within the fifteen-day period, a post-effective amendment updated in all respects that either restarts the pricing period or contains the Rule 430A pricing information (*i.e.* similar to a traditional pricing amendment) must be filed and effective prior to sales. While no changes to this requirement are being made, other rule revisions are being adopted to minimize the delay that could result. Such a post-effective amendment, which must be filed prior to the time sales are made and confirmations are sent, will become effective upon filing if the prospectus contained therein contains

---

35. *See* Rule 411(c) under the Securities Act, 17 CFR 230.411(c), new Rule 439(b) under the Securities Act, 17 CFR 230.439(b), and changes to General Instructions of Forms SB-1, SB-2, S-1, S-2, S-3, S-11, F-1, F-2 and F-3. In addition, Items 601(b)(24) of Regulations S-K and S-B, 17 CFR 229.601(b)(24) and 17 CFR 228.601(b)(24), are revised so that a power of attorney included in the earlier registration statement relating to the offering also may relate to the short-form registration statement filed to register the additional securities.

36. *See* revisions to Rule 430A(a)(3), 17 CFR 230.430A(a)(3).

37. The principal purpose of the original five-day limitation was to prevent delayed offerings being made under Rule 430A by persons that do not meet the criteria for use of shelf registration. *See* Securities Act Release No. 6714 (May 27, 1987) [52 FR 21252].

no material changes from, or additions to, the prospectus previously filed as part of the effective registration statement other than the price-related information omitted from the registration statement in reliance on Rule 430A.[38] A Company filing a post-effective amendment that reflects other material prospectus changes or additions (other than the "20% increase in offering size" changes) would follow current procedures under which the post-effective amendment is subject to selective review and is declared effective.

5.   Immediate Takedowns from a Shelf Registration

The Four Firms proposal requested that the Commission permit immediate takedowns after a shelf registration statement becomes effective. As indicated in the Proposing release, immediate offerings from an effective shelf registration statement currently are permitted. At the time of effectiveness, information in the shelf registration statement is required to the extent it is known or reasonably available to the registrant.[39] Accordingly, if an offering of securities is certain at the time the shelf registration statement becomes effective, the relevant information (*e.g.,* description of securities, plan of distribution and use of proceeds) must be disclosed with respect to the securities subject to the immediate takedown and the Rule 430A undertakings should be included (if the issuer wants Rule 430A pricing flexibility).

6.   Acceleration of Effectiveness

As was proposed, adopted rule revisions allow requests to accelerate effectiveness of registration statements to be transmitted to the Commission by fax transmission. In addition, rule revisions permit oral requests for acceleration to be made,[40] provided that the Commission previously receives a letter indicating that the registrant and the

---

38. *See* Rule 462(c), 17 CFR 230.462(c).

39. *See* Rule 409, 17 CFR 230.409.

40. *See* Securities Act Rule 461(a), 17 CFR 230.461(a). Both an authorized representative of the registrant and an authorized representative of the managing underwriter will be required to make such request orally. The rule revisions do not adopt a requirement suggested by some commenters that an oral request be followed by transmission to the Commission of a written request, nor are facsimile or duplicate versions required to be followed by transmission to the Commission of the manually signed versions.

managing underwriter may make oral requests for acceleration and that they are aware of their obligations under the Securities Act.[41]

In order to facilitate the ability of the Commission staff, pursuant to delegated authority, to reach a determination and other factors set forth in Section 8(a) of the Securities Act,[42] persons making oral acceleration requests should be prepared to provide orally the prospectus dissemination information that typically is set forth in a written acceleration request. Such information generally includes: the date of the preliminary prospectus distributed, the approximate dates of distribution, the number of prospective underwriters and dealers to whom the preliminary prospectus was furnished, the number of prospectuses so distributed, and the number of prospectuses distributed to others, identifying them in general terms.[43] In addition, in the case of non-reporting companies, an affirmative statement from the managing underwriter may be requested with regard to whether it has been informed by participating underwriters and dealers that copies of the preliminary prospectus have been or are being distributed to all persons to whom it is then expected to mail confirmations not less than 48 hours prior to the time it is expected to mail such confirmations.[44]

7. T+4 Settlement for Firm Commitment Offerings Priced After the Close of the Market

As discussed elsewhere in this release, the Commission is eliminating the current exemption contained in Rule 15c6-1 for firm commitment offerings, thus bringing those transactions under a T+3 settlement standard. In response to the Four Firms proposal, the Commission proposed an amendment to Rule 15c6-1 that would establish four business days after the trade date ("T+4") as the standard settlement cycle for firm commitment offerings priced after 4:30 P.M. The

---

41. *See* Securities Act Rule 461(a), 17 CFR 230.461(a). The liability of persons who sign the registration statement, the underwriters and others under Section 11(a) of the Securities Act, 15 U.S.C. §77k(a), is based upon the registration statement at the time it becomes effective.

42. 15 U.S.C. §77h(a).

43. *See* Rule 418(a)(7), 17 CFR 230.418(a)(7). *See also* Rule 460, 17 CFR 230.460.

44. *See* Rule 418(a)(7)(vi), 17 CFR 230.418(a)(7)(vi) and Securities Act Release No. 4968 (Apr. 24, 1969) [34 FR 7235]. Of course, this information is not applicable to delayed shelf offerings.

vast majority of commenters who addressed this proposal expressed support for settlement on a T+4 basis.[45] Several of these commenters reasoned that it is difficult to print and deliver the final prospectus within a T+3 settlement time frame when the securities are priced late in the day. These commenters also opined that the potential systemic and market risks associated with the T+4 provision should be limited because most of the secondary trading in the subject securities will not begin until the opening of the market on the next business day and, therefore, the primary issuance of securities will be available to settle secondary trading in the security.

The T+4 provision in the Four Firms proposal was intended to provide time to deliver prospectuses by settlement. Establishing T+4 as the standard for this category of offerings also will provide certainty and reduce confusion as to the appropriate settlement cycle. Accordingly, the Commission is adopting the amendment for settlement of specific offerings on a T+4 basis with only minor technical corrections.[46]

8.   Investment Companies

The Commission requested comment on whether the Four Firms proposal should apply to investment companies. Commenters did not believe that open-end investment companies would require any special provisions to facilitate T+3 settlement because they are engaged in the continuous offerings of securities with pre-printed prospectuses, but endorsed the application of the Four Firms proposal to closed-end investment companies and unit investment trusts ("UITs"). The revisions to Rule 430A (the extension of the pricing period and changes to offering

---

45. One commenter argued that a T+4 standard was unnecessary because the override provision in paragraph of (a) of Rule 15c6-1, if broadly interpreted, would provide sufficient flexibility to after-market offerings. *See* letter from John Brandow, Davis Polk & Wardwell to Jonathan Katz, Securities and Exchange Commission, dated April 3, 1995. As discussed elsewhere in this release, the Commission is instead adopting a specific override provision for firm commitment offerings.

46. *See* Rule 15c6-1(c), 17 CFR 15c6-1(c). As proposed, this paragraph provided an exemption for securities sold pursuant to a firm commitment offering. This language has been amended to clarify that the exemption applies to contracts for the sale of such securities and that the exemption only applies to sales from the issuer to the underwriter and initial sales by broker-dealers participating in the offering.

size and price range), to Rule 461(a) (facsimile or oral accelerations of effective dates), and to Rule 15c6-1 (T+4 settlement for firm commitment offerings priced after 4:30 P.M.) by their terms apply to the registration statements of closed-end investment companies and UITs.[47] The Investment Company Act permits UITs, but not closed-end investment companies, to increase the size of an offering by post-effective amendment.[48] Therefore, the Commission is adopting rule and form revisions that will permit closed-end investment companies to take advantage of the short-form registration statement that permits an increase in offering size.[49] Under the rule and form amendments, as adopted, company prospectuses because the current prospectus requirements appear to provide sufficient flexibility to accommodate expedited printing of prospectuses.

B. The SIA Approach

The second part of the Commission's proposal was based on the proposal submitted by the SIA. The SIA proposal was predicated on the premise that prospectus delivery could be accomplished much more

---

47. As noted previously, the revised rules permit duplicated or facsimile versions of manual signatures in all reports filed under the Exchange Act, as well as registration statements filed under the Securities Act. The Commission is adopting similar revisions for investment companies. *See* revisions to Rule 8b-11, 17 CFR 270.8b-11.

48. *See* Section 24(e)(1) of the Investment Company Act, 15 U.S.C. 80a-24(e)(1); *see also* Rule 485(b)(1)(i), 17 CFR 270.485(b)(1)(i), which provides for the immediate effectiveness of a post-effective amendment filed by a UIT for the purpose of increasing the amount of securities proposed to be offered under Section 24(e)(1).

49. Modifications to the registration statement form for closed-end investment companies, Form N-2 (17 CFR 274.11a), provide for the registration of additional securities pursuant to new Rule 462(b). Revisions to (i) paragraph (b) of Rule 483, which sets forth the exhibit requirements for investment company registration statement forms, provide that a power of attorney filed for a registration statement form also relates to a related registration statement form filed pursuant to Rule 462(b), and (ii) paragraph (c) of Rule 483 provide that a consent may be incorporated by reference into a registration statement form filed pursuant to Rule 462(b) from a related registration statement form.

quickly if issuers could convey the Section 10(a) prospectus information in multiple documents delivered to investors at different times, rather than in a traditional, integrated final prospectus prepared through last-minute mass printing, shipping and mailing.

Rule 434 under the Securities Act,[50] which is based upon the SIA approach, is being adopted largely as proposed. Rule 434 permits participants in registered firm commitment underwritten offerings of securities for cash and specified registered offerings for cash made on an agency basis (hereinafter, "eligible offerings") to convey prospectus information in more than one document and allows such documents to be delivered to investors at separate intervals and in varying manners. Rule 434 does not require that a final, integrated prospectus be delivered to investors. In the aggregate, however, all required information will still be disclosed to investors prior to or at the same time as a confirmation is sent, either through physical delivery or, in the case of short-form registered offerings,[51] through physical delivery and delivery by publication.

1.   Non-Short-Form Registered Offerings

As adopted, in eligible offerings not using short-form registration, persons may comply with their prospectus delivery obligations by delivering a preliminary prospectus,[52] a term sheet, if necessary[53] and

---

50. 17 CFR 230.434.

51. "Short-form" registration is used herein to refer to registration on Commission Forms S-3 or F-3. To be eligible to use short-form registration for a primary offering, an issuer must have a public float of $75 million and must have been reporting with the Commission for one year. *See* General Instructions I.A.3. and I.B.1. to Form S-3 and General Instructions I.A.1. and I.B.1. to Form F-3.

52. "Preliminary prospectus" is used herein to refer to either a preliminary prospectus used in reliance on Rule 430, 17 CFR 230.430, or a prospectus omitting information in reliance on Rule 430A(a), 17 CFR 230.430A(a).

53. In order to reflect industry nomenclature, "term sheet" is used in this release to refer to the document called a "supplementing memorandum" in the Proposing Release. In addition, "abbreviated term sheet" is now used in place of "abbreviated supplementing memorandum." Regardless of the nomenclature used, these documents constitute supplements to prospectuses subject to completion.

a confirmation.[54] The term sheet is required to include all information material to investors with respect to the offering that is not disclosed in the delivered preliminary prospectus or the confirmation.[55]

Neither the process of filing registration statements and amendments thereto, nor the Commission's registration statement review process, is intended to be altered in connection with the adoption of Rule 434.[56] Rule 434 requires that the preliminary prospectus and the term sheet, taken together, not materially differ from the disclosure included in the effective registration statement.[57] The term sheet must be filed with the Commission within two business days after the earlier of pricing or first use.[58] Thus, term sheets generally will not be reviewed prior

---

54. The preliminary prospectus, the term sheet and the confirmation may be delivered together or separately under Rule 434, provided that the former two are sent or given prior to or with the confirmation. *See* Rule 434(b)(1), 17 CFR 230.434(b)(1). *See also* Rule 434(c)(1), 17 CFR 230.434(c)(1) with respect to the preliminary or base prospectus, the abbreviated term sheet and the confirmation. Note that the prospectus delivery obligations pursuant to Rule 15c2-8 under the Exchange Act are independent of those discussed in this section. A term sheet or abbreviated term sheet generally may not be sent or given prior to the preliminary or base prospectus given the limitations set by Section 5(b)(1) of the Securities Act and the definition of "prospectus" set forth in Section 2(10) of the Securities Act. The Commission will raise no objection where a preliminary or base prospectus being delivered separately is sent or given in a manner reasonably calculated to arrive prior to or at the same time with the term sheet or abbreviated term sheet but the term sheet or abbreviated term sheet nevertheless precedes the preliminary or base prospectus.

55. *See* Rule 434(b)(3), 17 CFR 230.434(b)(3).

56. As under current practice, the staff will continue to consider whether recirculation of a prospectus is needed when there are material changes in disclosure arising after the prospectus subject to completion has been given to investors. *See* Rules 460 and 461(b), 17 CFR 230.460 and 230.461(b).

57. *See* Rule 434(b)(2), 17 CFR 230.434(b)(2). The disclosure in the preliminary prospectus and term sheet would be measured against the disclosure set forth in the registration statement as of its effective date, including omitted Rule 430A price-related information deemed a part thereof by virtue of Rule 430A(b), 17 CFR 230.430A(b).

58. *See* Rule 424(b)(7), 17 CFR 230.424(b)(7). Each filed copy of a term sheet or abbreviated terms sheet, like other filings under Rule 424, must

to use. Except in the case of delayed shelf offerings, the term sheet is deemed to be a part of the registration statement as of the time such registration statement was declared effective.[59] In the case of such delayed offerings, the term sheet is deemed to be a part of the registration statement as of the time the term sheet is filed with the Commission.[60]

Several commenters on the Proposing Release suggested that the Commission require that a secondary preliminary prospectus (either an updated version or another copy of the version previously circulated) be circulated to investors either with the term sheet or shortly before the term sheet is delivered.[61] Circulation of a second preliminary prospectus is not required by Rule 434 as adopted, but nothing in the Rule precludes offering participants from doing so.

As adopted, rule 434 is not limited with respect to the amount of time that could elapse between delivery of the preliminary prospectus and the term sheet. Further, the Rule does not contain any limitation on the magnitude of changes from the disclosure set forth in the circulated preliminary prospectus that the term sheet may contain. As noted above, however, the rule is not available for non-short-form registered offerings if the disclosure in the preliminary prospectus and term sheet materially differ from the disclosure contained in the prospectus filed as a part of the effective registration statement.

2. Short-Form Registered Offerings

In Rule 434 eligible offerings using short-form registration, persons may comply with their prospectus delivery obligations by delivering a

---

contain in the upper right corner of its cover page a reference to the part of Rule 424 under which the filing is made (*i.e.* Rule 424(b)(7)) and the file number of the registration statement to which the prospectus relates. *See* Rule 424(e), 17 CFR 230.424(e).

59. *See* Rule 434(d), 17 CFR 230.434(d).

60. *Id.*

61. *See, e.g.,* letter from John Olson et al., American Bar Association to Jonathan Katz, Securities and Exchange Commission, dated April 14, 1995; letter from Edward Adams, Fredrikson & Byron to Jonathan Katz, Securities and Exchange Commission, dated March 31, 1995; and letter from Steven Machov, Merrill Corporation to Jonathan Katz, Securities and Exchange Commission, dated April 3, 1995.

preliminary or base prospectus,[62] an abbreviated term sheet[63] and a confirmation. An abbreviated term sheet must contain, unless previously disclosed in the circulated preliminary or base prospectus or in the registrant's Exchange Act filings incorporated by reference into the prospectus: (i) the description of securities required by Item 202 of Regulation S-K, or a fair and accurate summary thereof;[64] and (ii) information regarding material changes required by Item 11 of Form S-3 or Form F-3.[65] Under new Rule 434, certain offering-specific disclosure included in a traditional final prospectus[66] will be required only in the prospectus supplement filed with the Commission.[67] This information could include, for example, use of proceeds and syndicate and specific plan of distribution information.

Registrants will be required to indicate on the cover page of their registration statement, by checking a box, that reliance on Rule 434 for prospectus delivery is intended. Persons checking the box, however,

---

62. "Base prospectus" is used herein to refer to a prospectus contained in a registration statement at the time of effectiveness (or as subsequently revised) that omits information that is not yet known concerning an offering pursuant to Rule 415, 17 CFR 230.415.

63. The abbreviated term sheet is filed with the Commission in accordance with Rule 424(b)(7), 17 CFR 230.424(b)(7). *See* Rule 434(d), 17 CFR 230.434(d), with respect to abbreviated term sheets being deemed a part of the registration statement.

64. 17 CFR 229.202.

65. *See* Rule 434(c)(3), 17 CFR 230.434(c)(3).

66. Offering-specific information required to be filed but permitted not to be delivered physically under Rule 434 short-form registered offerings is set forth in Items 501-510 of Regulation S-K, 17 CFR 229.502-229.510. In addition, a summarized version of the description of securities set forth in Item 202 of Regulation S-K, 17 CFR 229.202, may be delivered physically rather than the full description filed with the Commission.

67. *See* Rule 434(c)(2), 17 CFR 230.434(c)(2). For example, the final prospectus traditionally delivered to investors in shelf offerings has included information set forth in both the base prospectus and a prospectus supplement. In shelf offerings relying on Rule 434, information in the prospectus supplement will not be delivered physically to investors, except to the extent it is disclosed pursuant to the abbreviated term sheet. The prospectus supplement in such offerings, however, must be filed with the Commission by the time any confirmation is sent or given to investors. *See* Rule 434(c)(2)(ii), 17 CFR 230.434(c)(2)(ii).

would not be required to rely on Rule 434 if they later determined to deliver prospectus information otherwise in connection with the offering.

Any term sheet or abbreviated term sheet sent or given in reliance upon Rule 434 must state on the top center of the front cover page that it is a supplement to a prospectus and identify that prospectus by issuer name and date. The term sheet or abbreviated term sheet also, in that location, must clearly identify that it is a term sheet or abbreviated term sheet used in reliance on Rule 434, must clearly identify the documents that, when taken together, constitute the Section 10(a) prospectus, and must be dated as of the approximate date of its first use.[68]

3. Scope of the Proposed Rule

a.   Underwritten Offerings for Cash

Rule 434, as adopted, extends only to offerings where the sole consideration given in exchange for securities is cash. Offerings such as exchange offers and business combinations are not included. As noted in the Proposing Release, in those offerings, the final prospectus is traditionally used to begin the process of soliciting votes or consents to a transaction. Thus, the logistical difficulties of prospectus delivery are not associated with those offerings.

The adopted Rule also does not extend to offerings that are made other than on a firm commitment basis with underwriters, except for offerings of investment grade debt made in connection with a medium-term note ("MTN") program registered with the Commission on either a continuous or delayed shelf basis.[69] Concern has been expressed that exclusion of these MTN securities from the Rule would unnecessarily push such transactions out of the T+3 settlement cycle.[70] Further, while these MTN securities typically are sold through an underwriter on an agency rather than a firm commitment basis, assurance has been given that, once an agreement has been reached between the investor and the MTN program agent, the preparation and delivery of a prospectus occurs in a manner identical to that in a principal transaction.[71]

---

68. *See* Rule 434(e), 17 CFR 230.434(e).

69. *See* Rule 434(a), 17 CFR 230.434(a). These MTN offerings rely on Rule 415(a)(1)(ix) or (x), respectively.

70. *See* letter from Kevin Moynihan, Merrill Lynch to Jonathan Katz, Securities and Exchange Commission, dated April 7, 1995.

71. *Id.*

b.   Offerings of Asset-Backed Securities

As adopted, Rule 434 excludes offerings of asset-backed securities ("ABS").[72] Settlement in connection with ABS offerings currently takes place outside of the T+3 time frame, on approximately a T+10 cycle, and is likely to continue to do so. As noted in the Proposing Release, the existing settlement schedule is the result primarily of factors unique to these offerings, which are the same factors that result in such offerings not lending themselves to use of incremental disclosure. These factors include: (i) the distinctive structuring process for most ABS offerings, which typically extends almost to the time when the security is priced, whereby a variety of structures may be considered as the sponsor attempts to meet investors' needs; (ii) the time needed for identification of the specific pool of collateral which will support the ABS; and (iii) the necessity of creating shortly before sale of the ABS a prospectus supplement of significant length and complexity that details the characteristics of specific pool assets and the transaction's structure, the summarization of which would not serve as an adequate substitute for the complete description in the prospectus supplement.

c.   Offerings of Structured Securities

As adopted, Rule 434 also excludes offerings of structured securities.[73] "Structured securities," for purposes of Rule 434, are defined to mean securities whose cash flow characteristics depend upon one or more indices or that have imbedded forwards or options or securities where an investor's investment return and the issuer's payment obligations are contingent on, or highly sensitive to, changes in the value of underlying assets, indices, interest rates or cash flows.[74] This definition was proposed to be included in Rule 15c6-1 but is set forth in Rule 434 instead since Rule 15c6-1 as adopted makes no reference to

---

72. "Asset-backed security" is defined for purposes of Rule 434 the same way it is defined in General Instruction I.B.5. of Form S-3: a security that is primarily serviced by the cashflows of a discrete pool of receivables or other financial assets, either fixed or revolving, that by their terms convert into cash within a finite time period plus any rights or other assets designed to assure the servicing or timely distribution or proceeds to the securityholders. *See* Rule 434(f), 17 CFR 230.434(f).

73. *See* Rule 434(a), 17 CFR 230.434(a).

74. *See* Rule 434(h), 17 CFR 230.434(h).

such securities. As noted in the Proposing Release, these securities usually have terms that are highly complex, with many employing one or more indices as a basis for determining the issuer's payment obligations (*e.g.,* coupon, principal, redemption payments). A structured security's value is derived not only from the creditworthiness of its issuer, but also from any underlying assets, indices, interest rates or cash flow upon which the security is predicated. Because of the complexities associated with these securities, investors may not fully understand the investment risks when purchasing structured securities, especially those with complicated structures. A complete description of offering-specific information therefore is of particular importance to investors in making an investment decision, given the market risks resulting from the structure of these securities. Otherwise, as noted in the Proposing Release, the incremental distribution of information under the Rule, when combined with the complex nature of these securities, could result in material disclosure not being readily accessible to investors.

   d.   Investment Companies

As proposed, Rule 434 would have provided that it would not apply to the offering of any security of any company registered under the Investment Company Act. The Commission requested comment on whether the prospectus delivery modifications in the SIA proposal also should apply to closed-end investment companies and UITs. Commenters endorsed the proposed prospectus delivery method for closed-end investment companies and UITs, and the Commission is adopting revisions that apply new Rule 434 to these investment companies.[75]

4.   Conforming Amendments to Rule 15c2-8

   a.   Rule 15c2-8 Amendments

The Commission is adopting the amendments to rule 15c2-8[76] as proposed. The amendments expand the use of the terms "preliminary prospectus" and "final prospectus," as currently used in the Rule, to

---

75. *See* revisions to Rule 497, 17 CFR 230.497, which sets forth fund prospectus filing requirements with the Commission, that require, parallel to the changes to the general prospectus filing requirements in Rule 424, 17 CFR 230.424(b), the filing of prospectuses allowed under Rule 434 on or prior to the date a confirmation is sent or given to an investor.

76. 17 CFR 240.15c2-8.

include the terms "prospectus subject to completion" and "Section 10(a) prospectus," respectively, to reflect the terminology of Rule 434. Additionally, the term "sending" is substituted for the term "mailing" to accommodate prospectus delivery by means other than traditional mailing.

Six commenters addressed Rule 15c2-8. None of these commenters objected to the proposed changes, although several of them raised other issues regarding Rule 15c2-8, which are discussed below. The Commission may propose further amendments to Rule 15c2-8 based on its experience with Rule 434, or more generally, to reflect market developments and staff interpretations that have occurred since the Rule was last amended.[77]

b. Rule 15c2-8 Issues Raised by Commenters

In the case of an offering of securities of an issuer that previously has not been required to file reports under Section 13(a) and 15(d) of the Exchange Act, Rule 15c2-8(b)[78] requires that a preliminary prospectus be delivered to any person who is expected to receive a confirmation of sale at least 48 hours prior to sending such confirmation.[79] Two commenters noted that because preliminary prospectuses generally are not used in offerings of asset-backed securities, some broker-dealers have adopted the practice of delivering the final prospectus to purchasers at least 48 hours prior to mailing the confirmation of an asset-backed security. These commenters urged the Commission either to modify Rule 15c2-8 to acknowledge this industry practice or to except asset-backed securities from Rule 15c2-8(b). In the Commission's view, delivery of the final prospectus at least 48 hours prior to sending the confirmation will satisfy the requirement of Rule 15c2-8(b) in the case of offerings of asset-backed securities where no preliminary prospectus is used.[80]

---

77. Rule 15c2-8(d) was last amended in Exchange Act Release No. 25546 (Apr. 4, 1988) [53 FR 11841].

78. 17 CFR 240.15c2-8(b).

79. This requirement is satisfied by delivering a preliminary prospectus that is current at the time of its delivery.

80. This interpretation of paragraph (b) is consistent with the longstanding staff position that delivery of a final prospectus at least 48 hours prior to sending the confirmation is required in cases where no preliminary prospectus is circulated and the offering is sold solely on the basis of a final prospectus.

With respect to the obligations of a managing underwriter to provide copies of the prospectus to participating broker-dealers, two commenters sought interpretive guidance with respect to the terms "sufficient copies" and "reasonable quantities," as used in Rule 15c2-8(g) and (h),[81] respectively, in light of the recently issued Brown & Wood letter,[82] which permits electronic delivery of prospectuses in certain circumstances.[83] The Brown and Wood letter was not intended to modify any obligation that a managing underwriter currently has pursuant to paragraphs (g) or (h) of Rule 15c2-8 to produce, reproduce, or deliver, in such quantities as requested, a preliminary, amended, or final prospectus to broker-dealers participating in the offering. Accordingly, a managing underwriter may discharge its obligations pursuant to Rule 15c2-8(g) or (h) by delivering a prospectus (or any portion thereof) electronically to a participating broker-dealer, if the recipient broker-dealer expressly consents to delivery in such form.

One commenter suggested revising Rule 15c2-8(b) to require delivery of the preliminary prospectus at least 48 hours, but not more than 60 days, prior to sending the confirmation. Another commenter suggested that the Commission require the managing underwriter to deliver the final prospectus to offering participants by the close of business

---

81. 17 CFR 240.15c2-8(g) and (h). Paragraph (g) requires a managing underwriter to take reasonable steps to ensure that all broker-dealers participating in an offering are promptly furnished with "sufficient copies, as requested by them" of each preliminary, amended, or final prospectus to enable such participating brokers-dealers to comply with their obligations under Rule 15c2-8(b), (c), (d), and (e). Similarly, paragraph (h) requires a managing underwriter to take reasonable steps to ensure that any broker-dealer participating in an offering or trading in the registered security is furnished "reasonable quantities of the final prospectus . . . as requested by him" in order to enable the broker-dealer to comply with Section 5(b)(1) and (2) of the Securities Act.

82. *See supra* footnote 6.

83. These commenters inquired whether Rule 15c2-8(g) and (h) would permit a managing underwriter to deliver the pre-printed portion of the prospectus by traditional methods, followed by the remainder (or "wrap" portion), containing only the pricing and other "last minute" disclosure, by electronic transmission. These commenters advised that the recipient broker-dealers would be expected to duplicate the remainder (or "wrap" portion) and assemble the two parts for delivery to investors.

on T+2, so that such participants may send the prospectus to investors no later than T+3. Consistent with the adoption of both the SIA proposal and the Four Firms proposal, the Commission believes that offering participants should have as much flexibility as possible to determine how to comply with their prospectus delivery obligations within T+3, without the burden of additional restrictions, and therefore has determined not to amend the Rule as suggested at this time. As noted, however, the Commission may propose additional amendments to Rule 15c2-8 based on its experience with Rule 434.

III.   REVISION OF THE RULE 15c6-1 EXEMPTION

In the Proposing Release, the Commission proposed to establish T+3 as the presumptive settlement date for firm commitment offerings by eliminating the exemption from T+3 settlement for sales for cash in connection with firm commitment offerings.[84] However, the Commission proposed to allow managing underwriters flexibility to choose T+3, T+4, or T+5 settlement under specific conditions, including written notice to prospective purchasers and the exchanges prior to pricing.[85] The Commission also proposed exemptions from T+3 settlement for firm commitment offerings of asset-backed and structured securities. These amendments were proposed to reduce the confusion caused by different settlement cycles for new issue and secondary market trades, while also providing flexibility to settle certain firm commitment offerings beyond T+3 when the standard settlement cycle cannot be met.

Most commenters supported elimination of the general exclusion for firm commitment offerings. As one commenter noted, establishing a T+3 settlement standard for these transactions will reduce risk, provide certainty in the form of a written standard, and avoid bifurcation of the settlement cycle.[86] Several commenters cited specific categories

---

84. *See* 17 CFR 240.15c6-1(b)(2).

85. Rule 15c6-1(a) contains a general override provision that permits the parties to a contract to specify an alternate settlement cycle if the agreement is made at the time of the trade. Complying with this provision in the context of a firm commitment offering may be difficult because of the need to obtain the express agreement of all parties participating in the offering.

86. *See* letter from Brent Taylor, J.P. Morgan Securities, Inc. to Jonathan Katz, Securities and Exchange Commission, dated March 30, 1995.

of securities requiring settlement cycles longer than T+3.[87] Most commenters, however, preferred to resolve difficulties in settling offerings through a general override provision rather than specific exemptions of classes of securities.

The majority of commenters that addressed the merits of the proposed override provision expressed support for a specific override provision for firm commitment offerings but objected to the terms of Rule 15c6-1(e) as proposed. Several commenters asserted that the T+5 maximum settlement period did not provide adequate flexibility for settlement of certain firm commitment offerings. Furthermore, many of the commenters argued that the requirement of written notice to all prospective purchasers on or before pricing was burdensome and should be eliminated.[88] Commenters disagreed over the manner in which an alternate settlement date should be established, though most commenters concurred that such authority should not be granted solely to the managing underwriter.

To address the various issues raised by the commenters in connection with the proposed modifications of the exemption for firm commitment offerings, the Commission is amending Rule 15c6-1 to eliminate the exemption for firm commitment offerings and to include a specific override provision[89] which will permit the establishment of an alternate settlement date for the sale of all securities subject to a firm commitment offering upon agreement by the managing underwriter and the issuer of the securities. This override provision does not contain the

---

87. In addition to asset-backed securities and structured securities, commenters raised settlement concerns in connection with medium term note programs registered under short-form shelf registration, capital market debt transactions, securities exempt from registration under Section 3(a)(4) or 3(a)(11) of the Securities Act, and certain transactions involving swaps.

88. Specifically, several commenters asserted that the settlement period may not be known sufficiently in advance of pricing to provide written notice and that such notice is duplicative of the information provided orally and in the confirmation.

89. *See* Rule 15c6-1(d), 17 CFR 15c6-1(d). This specific override provision would not extend to offerings of investment grade debt made in connection with a medium-term note program sold though an underwriter on an agency basis. Such transactions may, however, be accomplished in accordance with the general override provision set forth in Rule 15c6-1(a), 17 CFR 240.15c6-1(a).

notice requirements in the proposed override provision and does not limit the settlement period to a maximum of T+5. The Commission has decided not to adopt a provision exempting offerings of particular classes of securities. Instead, the Commission believes that an alternate settlement cycle can be established for these offerings through the override provision for firm commitment offerings.

In adopting the proposed amendments to Rule 15c6-1, the Commission seeks to provide flexibility for settlement beyond T+3 for certain firm commitment offerings that require such treatment in light of the special characteristics of the subject securities. The Commission is mindful of the concern that lack of certainty in settlement standards may create confusion in the market place. Accordingly, the Commission stresses that the override provision is not intended to dilute the presumption in favor of application of the T+3 settlement cycle in connection with firm commitment offerings. Instead, the override provision is intended to be used only in those circumstances when T+3 settlement is not feasible.

Furthermore, the Commission recognizes that it is important that the registered clearing agencies, through which settlement of firm commitment offerings and secondary market trades will occur, receive notice of non-standard settlement dates. The Commission encourages issuers and underwriters to notify promptly the registered clearing agencies of the settlement period of an offering. It may be appropriate for the clearing agencies as self-regulatory organizations under the Exchange Act to modify their rules to require such notice at such times and in such manners as the clearing agencies need to make provision for non-standard settlement cycles. The Commission will monitor the use of the override provision on an ongoing basis.

IV.   EDGAR USAGE

After the effective date of these proposals and until the necessary form types are available through the EDGAR system, registrants that are mandated electronic filers should file in paper format those documents relating to the proposals being adopted other than the abbreviated registration form filed pursuant to Rule 462(b).[90] All other

---

90. Only those documents that are filed pursuant to Rule 424(b)(7), Rule 462(c) and Rule 497(h)(2) may be filed in paper format. *See supra* footnotes 29 and 30 and accompanying text.

documents unrelated to the proposals being adopted must continue to be filed electronically by mandated electronic filers. The necessary form types are expected to be available with the release of a new version of the EDGARLink software in Autumn 1995. Notice will be provided in the SEC Digest, the *Federal Register* and on the EDGAR Bulletin Board when the new EDGAR form types are available.

V. COST-BENEFIT ANALYSIS

Five commenters responded to the Commission's request for comments regarding the costs and benefits of the proposed rules. Four of the five commenters expected the cost of printing and shipping of prospectuses to decline as a result of the proposed rules.[91] The other commenter stated that the increased administrative burdens and costs that may be imposed on dealers as a result of multiple or duplicate mailings of various documents could negate the intended benefit of the SIA approach.[92] One commenter, a financial printer, provided empirical data on the proposals. The printer concluded that, in three basic scenarios regarding the printing and delivery of a Form S-1, a reduction in costs ranging from 8% to 88% would be obtainable as a result of the new delivery alternatives under the proposed rules.[93] The Commission believes the new rule and amendments provide market participants with additional flexibility that should result in lower transaction costs, while not diminishing investor protection.

---

91. *See* letter from Karl Barnickol, American Society of Corporate Secretaries to Jonathan Katz, Securities and Exchange Commission, dated Aril 10, 1995; Joel Brenner, Storch & Brenner (on behalf of R.R. Donnelley Financial), to Jonathan G. Katz, Secretary, Securities and Exchange Commission, dated March 31, 1995; W. Scott Jardine, Nike Securities L.P., to Jonathan Katz, Securities and Exchange Commission, dated March 31, 1995; Larry W. Martin, John Nuveen & Co. Incorporated, to Jonathan Katz, Securities and Exchange Commission, dated March 30, 1995.

92. *See* Letter from George Miller, Public Securities Association to Jonathan Katz, Securities and Exchange Commission, dated April 10, 1995.

93. *See* letter from Joel Brenner, Storch & Brenner (on behalf of R.R. Donnelley Financial), to Jonathan G. Katz, Secretary, Securities and Exchange Commission, dated March 31, 1995.

VI. SUMMARY OF FINAL REGULATORY FLEXIBILITY ANALYSIS

The Commission has prepared a Final Regulatory Flexibility Analysis ("FRFA"), pursuant to the requirements of the Regulatory Flexibility Act,[94] regarding the rule and amendments to existing regulations being adopted. The FRFA notes that the new rule and amendments will provide entities with greater flexibility and efficiency with respect to the timing of printing and delivery of prospectus information, thereby facilitating compliance with Rule 15c6-1 under the Exchange Act and access to the public securities markets. As discussed more fully in the analysis, the new rule and amendments to Securities Act regulations should decrease the costs associated with fulfilling entities' prospectus delivery obligations under the Securities Act. The amendments to Exchange Act rules and forms are not anticipated to have any significant economic impact on entities. The new rule may impose minimal additional reporting, recordkeeping or compliance requirements, while the amendments do not impose any new reporting, recordkeeping or compliance requirements on any entities. No alternatives to the new rule and amendments consistent with their objectives and the Commission's statutory mandate were found.

The overall effect of the new rule and amendments is to provide entities increased efficiency in raising capital from the public securities markets. The aspects that provide for the incremental delivery of prospectus information will apply to any entity engaged in a public distribution with respect to an eligible offering. The amendments to Securities Act regulations should streamline the registration process and thereby facilitate compliance with prospectus delivery within T+3. The new rule and amendments to Securities Act regulations also will apply to certain investment companies registered under the Investment Company Act, *i.e.* closed-end investment companies and unit investment trusts. The amendments to regulations under Section 15(c) of the Exchange Act will reflect the availability of expedited delivery of prospectus information provided by the new rule and amendments to the Securities Act regulations.

A copy of the FRFA may be obtained from Michael Mitchell, Division of Corporation Finance, Securities and Exchange Commission,

---

94. 5 U.S.C. §604 (1988).

450 Fifth Street, N.W., Mail Stop 3-3, Washington, D.C. 20549, (202) 942-2900.

VII. EFFECTIVE DATE

The new rule and the revisions to rules and forms are effective June 7, 1995, in accordance with the Administrative Procedures Act, which allows for effectiveness in less than 30 days after publication, inter alia, for "a substantive rule which grants or recognizes an exemption or relieves a restriction" and "as provided by the agency for good cause found and published with the rule." 5 U.S.C. 553(d)(1) and (d)(3). The adopted rule and revisions primarily lessen restrictions of existing rules in that they either provide a more efficient way for offering participants to accomplish prospectus delivery or they streamline the registration and prospectus preparation and printing processes. In addition, the Commission finds there is good cause for the adopted rule and revisions to become effective on June 7, 1995 since they are designed to allow market participants to accomplish prospectus delivery in eligible offerings in a T+3 settlement cycle. Since the T+3 settlement cycle will become effective on June 7, 1995, the adoption of the rule and revisions on that date will ensure that potential market disruption relating to prospectus delivery prior to settlement of such offerings would be avoided. The exemption from Rule 15c6-1 for certain firm commitment offerings also is being eliminated in this time frame because of its potential for market disruption if allowed to go into effect. Any possible negative effect of eliminating that exemption is offset by the adoption of an expanded provision allowing such offerings to settle outside of the Rule 15c6-1 mandated time frame if the participants in the offering so elect.

SPECIAL NASD NOTICE TO MEMBERS

JUNE 5, 1995

97-10 SEC TO APPROVE AMENDMENTS TO NASD RULES TO FACILITATE COMPLIANCE WITH SEC REGULATION M*

Executive Summary

The Securities and Exchange Commission's (SEC) Regulation M, which regulates the market activities of persons with an interest in the outcome of an offering of securities, became effective on March 4, 1997. The new Rule replaced SEC Rules 10b-6, 10b-6A, 10b-7, 10b-8, and 10b-21. The NASD has filed with the SEC proposed amendments, to be effective March 4, 1997, to NASD rules regarding corporate financing, The Nasdaq Stock Market, Inc. (Nasdaq), and the OTC Bulletin Board (OTCBB) that are designed to assist members in complying with Regulation M. In general, the amendments to NASD rules establish a new requirement for members to obtain an Underwriting Activity Report from the Corporate Financing Department of NASD Regulation, Inc. (NASD Regulation) with respect to a proposed distribution subject to SEC Rule 101; modify current Nasdaq requirements with respect to the entry of a stabilizing or penalty bid and requests for excused withdrawal of quotations or designation of quotations as those of a passive market maker; and establish new requirements for notification with respect to penalty bids and syndicate covering transactions for Nasdaq and OTCBB securities. It is anticipated the amendments will be effective March 4, 1997.

Introduction

On December 20, 1996, the SEC approved new Regulation M to replace Rules 10b-6, 10b-6A, 10b-7, 10b-8, and 10b-21 (the trading practice rules) under the Securities Exchange Act of 1934,[1] which were

---

*Copyright 1998 National Association of Securities Dealers, Inc. All rights reserved. [NASD Manual & Notices to Members] — NASD MANUAL & NOTICES TO MEMBERS — NOTICES TO MEMBERS — 1997 Notices to Members — 97-10 SEC To Approve Amendments To NASD Rules To Facilitate Compliance With SEC Regulation M — http://secure.nasdr.com/wbs/NETbos.dll?RefShow?ref=NASD4;&xinfo=goodbye.htm.

1. Securities Act Release No. 7375 (December 20, 1996); 62 FR 520 (January 3, 1997).

rescinded. New Regulation M, which consists of Rules 100 through 105, governs the activities of underwriters, issuers, selling security-holders, and others that have an interest in the outcome of an offering of securities. Regulation M became effective March 4, 1997.

This Notice provides a summary of the provisions of Regulation M and describes the amendments to the NASD rules to be approved by the SEC effective March 4, 1997 that are intended to facilitate compliance by members with the new requirements of Regulation M. The text of the amendments are attached to this Notice. Also attached are copies of notification forms to be used by members to submit required notifications by fax or by electronic communication to the NASD. Members should only rely on the text published by the SEC in the Federal Register as the final version of the amendments.

Background

Regulation M represents the culmination of more than a two-year effort by the SEC to review and modernize the trading practice rules, which had been in effect for over 40 years. In recent years, the trading practice rules have come under attack from many market participants for the limitations they place on distribution and ordinary market-making activities of underwriters and others and the increased costs that are imposed as a result. Particular concern has been directed at the effect of the trading practice rules on international offerings. Because foreign markets generally do not have comparable rules, and because the trading practice rules are deemed to apply to foreign distributions that occur only in part in the U.S., the rules have potentially serious international competitive consequences that have necessitated a series of interpretations and amendments designed to improve the effect of the rules in the context of international offerings.

Rule 101—Distribution Participant Restrictions

The SEC has divided <u>Rule 10b-6</u> into two rules, <u>Rules 101</u> and <u>102</u>, which cover the activities of (i) distribution participants and their affiliated purchasers and (ii) issuers and selling shareholders and their affiliated purchasers, respectively. <u>Rule 101</u> of Regulation M applies trading restrictions to underwriters, prospective underwriters, syndicate members and their affiliated purchasers. The most significant change from <u>Rule 10b-6</u> is that the restrictions of <u>Rule 101</u> on bids for, purchases of, or attempts to induce a bid or purchase by a restricted person, do not apply to certain securities (e.g., investment grade rated debt) that presently are subject to regulation by Rule 10b-6.

The "cooling-off" periods of Rule 10b-6 that were triggered by the anticipated commencement of the distribution have been replaced with a three-tier "restricted period" that is calculated from the date on which the subject security is priced. Under Regulation M, the SEC has adopted a dual standard of world-wide average daily trading volume and public float value. Actively traded securities, *i.e.,* securities with an average daily trading volume (ADTV) of at least $1 million and a public float value of at least $150 million, are no longer subject to any restricted period, although trading in such actively traded securities remains subject to the anti-fraud and anti-manipulation provisions of the federal securities laws.

Securities with an ADTV of at least $100,000, with a public float value of at least $25 million, are subject to a restricted period of one day prior to the date on which the subject security's price is determined and all other securities that do not meet the ADTV or public float value tests are subject to a restricted period of five days. The SEC determined that the thrust of the restricted period should focus on daily trading activity since higher-priced securities that trade more frequently are more difficult to manipulate. Also, the public float volume test is intended to capture within Rule 101 those securities that experience unusual trading volume relative to their public float.[2]

In calculating the ADTV, distribution participants may use either a two-calendar month period or a 60-day rolling period, to be calculated within 10 days of the filing of the offering. Moreover, the SEC is not designating acceptable information sources for determining ADTV, so long as the participant has a reasonable basis for believing that the information is reliable. As set forth below, NASD Regulation will issue an Underwriting Activity Report to the manager of the underwriting syndicate that provides the domestic ADTV and public float value for a security that is subject to SEC Rule 101 to assist members' compliance with SEC Rule 101.

Rule 101 also includes exemptions from the imposition of the "restricted period" for: (i) exempted securities; (ii) exercises of options and other securities, including rights received in connection with a

---

2. The public float is the aggregate amount of common equity securities held by non-affiliates as would be reported by an issuer on SEC Form 10-K.

rights offering; (iii) transactions in the ordinary course of business in baskets of securities involving the offered security; (iv) transactions involving sales of Rule 144A securities of foreign and domestic issuers to qualified institutional buyers or persons deemed not to be U.S. persons; and (v) redeemable securities issued by an open-end investment company or unit investment trust. The restrictions on other debt securities are substantially narrowed.

The trading restrictions of Rule 101 are only applicable to a "covered security," defined to include the security that is the subject of a distribution and "reference securities." The SEC defines "reference security" to include a security into which a subject security may be converted, exchanged, or exercised, or which, under the terms of the subject security, may in whole or in significant part determine the value of the subject security. This new focus on subject and reference securities narrows the potential universe of securities in which trading must be restricted during a distribution in comparison to the securities covered under Rule 10b-6, which included any security of the "same class or series" as the security being distributed and any "right to purchase" such security. As a result, trading in derivative securities (*e.g.,* convertible securities, options, and warrants) during the distribution of an underlying security and of "rights to purchase" the securities of a target company in a merger or exchange offer is no longer restricted by Rule 101.

Bids for and purchases of outstanding nonconvertible debt securities are not restricted by Rule 101 unless the security being purchased is identical in all of its terms to the security being distributed. Further, investment grade nonconvertible debt securities, nonconvertible preferred securities, and asset-backed securities are specifically excluded from coverage by the Rule. In the situation where Rule 101 is applicable to outstanding debt, the restricted period will generally be less than five days. In addition, an existing exclusion for research reports has been expanded to allow the dissemination of information in the ordinary course of business during the restricted period.

Rule 101 includes an important new exception for "inadvertent" violations of de minimis size, including bids that are not accepted, and one or more purchases that in the aggregate over the restricted period total less than 2 percent of the security's ADTV, provided that the distribution participant had in place policies and procedures reasonably designed to achieve compliance with the Rule.

Rule 102—Issuer and Selling Securityholder Restrictions

Rule 102 limits bids and purchases by issuers, selling security-holders, and their affiliated purchasers during the applicable restricted period in a manner similar to Rule 101. Unlike Rule 101, however, Rule 102 does not provide an exemption for actively traded subject securities (although an exemption is available for actively traded reference securities) or for transactions in investment grade debt and preferred stock. Although transactions under employee benefit or dividend reinvestment plans generally are exempt, this exemption does not extend to plans that are open to persons other than employees and securityholders and that involve direct distributions from the issuer or an affiliate.

Rules 101 and 102 permit a member affiliated with an issuer or selling securityholder to comply with the provisions of Rule 101, rather than Rule 102, provided that the member is not itself the issuer or selling shareholder.

Rule 103—Passive Market Making in Nasdaq Stocks

Rule 103 of Regulation M, which replaces Rule 10-6A, permits "passive" market-making activity in Nasdaq stocks in connection with distributions during the restricted periods to alleviate liquidity problems that may exist in the market during those periods. The new Rule permits passive market making for any Nasdaq-listed security distribution that is conducted as a fixed-price offering underwritten on a firm-commitment basis. Rule 103 generally limits a market maker's bids and purchases to the highest current independent bid (a bid from a market maker that is not participating in the distribution).

Rule 103 allows passive market making throughout the restricted period, in contrast to Rule 10b-6A, which prohibited passive market making upon the commencement of offers and sales. Although Rule 103 retains the core provisions of Rule 10b-6A in a number of respects, the SEC eliminated the requirement in Rule 10b-6A that limited availability of the Rule to Nasdaq stocks that meet minimum share price and public float criteria, where Nasdaq market makers that are participating in the distribution account for at least 30 percent of the total trading volume in the security. Rule 103 continues to generally limit a passive market maker's bids and purchases to the highest current independent bid and limit the amount of net purchases a passive market maker can make on any day to 30 percent of its ADTV, although an initial ADTV limit of 200 shares in now available for less active market makers. The bid display size limitation has also been retained.

In connection with the initial ADTV limit of 200 shares, Rule 103 also provides that all passive market makers whose initial ADTV limit is between 1 and 199 shares are allowed a net purchasing capacity of 200 shares. The new Rule allows passive market makers to make bids or purchases at a price above the highest independent bid where necessary to comply with any SEC or NASD rule relating to the execution of customer orders, such as the order handling rules. The SEC also permits a passive market maker that is involved in a contemporaneous purchase and sale of a security to "net" the transactions for purposes of the ADTV calculation as long as the two transactions are reported within 30 seconds of each other.

Rule 104—Stabilizing Transactions/Syndicate Covering Transactions/Penalty Bids/Recordkeeping

Rule 104 replaces Rule 10b-7 to regulate stabilization activities during a distribution. The new Rule retains the requirement that only one stabilizing bid is permitted in any market at the same price at the same time. The new Rule permits a stabilizing bid to be initiated, maintained, reduced, or raised based on the current price in the principal market for the security (domestic or foreign), as long as the bid does not exceed the offering price of the security or the stabilizing bid in the principal market. The Rule provides that the appropriate price level for initiating a stabilizing bid is the security's principal market, with certain variations for different market situations. Thus, the most significant change from Rule 10b-7 is the ability under Rule 104 to increase a stabilizing bid to the level of the highest independent bid in the principal market.

For the first time, the SEC has imposed disclosure and recordkeeping requirements in connection with syndicate short-covering transactions and the enforcement of "penalty bids." Rule 104 requires any person effecting a syndicate covering transaction or intending to enforce a penalty bid to disclose that fact to the self-regulatory organization with direct oversight over the principal market in the U.S. for the security. Moreover, Rule 104 requires a new legend in the offering document referencing disclosures to a discussion in the "plan of distribution" section of the prospectus regarding stabilization activities and aftermarket activities and their potential effects on the market price. Similar disclosure is required in a document sent to a purchaser regarding stabilizing transactions in connection with the offering. It is anticipated that the SEC will delay implementation of the new notification requirements (but not the disclosure requirements) until April 1, 1997.

Managing underwriters will be required by amendments to SEC Rule 17a-2 to keep records of syndicate covering transactions and penalty bids, as well as stabilizing information. The information will be required to be retained for three years. These recordkeeping requirements are effective April 1, 1997.

Rule 105—Short Sales

Rule 105 has been adopted to replace Rule 10b-21 to limit short selling prior to a public offering by sellers who cover their short positions by purchasing securities in the offering. Rule 105 reduces the period of coverage to five business days prior to pricing, instead of the current period, which extends from the date of the filing of the registration statement until the commencement of offers and sales. Moreover, Rule 105 does not apply to short sales of derivative securities.

Amendments to NASD Rules

General

The amendments to the Nasdaq rules eliminate the requirement that members' submit their request to enter a stabilizing or penalty bid, on the day prior to the requested action. Furthermore, in connection with stabilizing and penalty bids, the amendments replace the current requirement for written notification with a requirement for notification followed by written confirmation. These changes are made to permit the NASD to respond to the quicker timetable that is increasingly characteristic of securities distributions and, particularly, to provide members the maximum flexibility required for shelf offerings.

In addition, the amendments to the Nasdaq and OTCBB rules distinguish between the obligations of members that are distribution participants and members that are affiliated purchasers (as those terms are defined in SEC Rule 100 adopted under Regulation M). While a member that is a distribution participant may stabilize the price of a security and engage in passive market making, a member that is considered an affiliated purchaser is not permitted to conduct these market-related activities during a distribution.

The amendments also clarify that the requirements for stabilizing, excused withdrawal, passive market making, penalty bids, and syndicate covering transactions in a Nasdaq or OTCBB security apply regardless of whether a Nasdaq or OTCBB security is the subject of the distribution or is a reference security (as those terms are defined in SEC Rule 100 adopted under Regulation M). Similarly, the requirement that a member request an Underwriting Activity Report, as discussed below, from the NASD Regulation Corporate Financing Department applies regardless of whether a publicly traded security is a subject or reference security under SEC Rule 101.

Nasdaq Rules

NASD Rule 4200—Definitions

Amendments are adopted to Rule 4200 of the Nasdaq rules to: (1) delete the definition of "penalty bid" because SEC Rule 100 contains a definition of penalty bid; (2) amend the definition of "stabilizing bid" to refer to the definition of "stabilizing" in SEC Rule 100; (3) delete the definition of "pre-effective stabilizing bid" as unnecessary and confusing; and (4) adopt new paragraph (b) Rule 4200 to incorporate the definitions of important terms from SEC Rule 100 adopted under Regulation M for purposes of the Nasdaq rules. Moreover, for purposes of the Nasdaq rules, the NASD has adopted a definition of the term "Underwriting Activity Report" to reference the report that will be provided by the Corporate Financing Department to the managing underwriter of a distribution of a publicly traded subject or reference security that is subject to SEC Rule 101 and includes forms that are to be used by members to comply with their notification obligations under Nasdaq rules. The requirement that members obtain the Report is adopted in Rule 2710(b)(11), discussed below.

NASD Rule 4614—Stabilizing Bids

Rule 4614 of the Nasdaq rules has been amended to add new paragraph (a) that requires a market maker that intends to stabilize the price of a Nasdaq security in compliance with SEC Rule 104 to submit a request to Nasdaq Market Operations to enter a one-sided bid identified on Nasdaq as a stabilizing bid. Paragraph (b) retains the requirement that only one market maker in an issue may enter a stabilizing bid. Several provisions that impose limitations on stabilizing bids have been organized under a new heading in paragraph (c).

The notice provisions in renumbered subparagraph (d)(1) have been revised to permit submission to Nasdaq Market Operations of a market maker's request to enter a stabilizing bid at any time. Currently, <u>Rule 4614</u> requires that Nasdaq Market Operations be notified on the day prior to the first day on which the stabilizing bid is to appear. This requirement is no longer necessary. It is, however, the obligation of the member to provide the staff sufficient time to enter its one-sided stabilizing bid on Nasdaq and the staff of Nasdaq Market Operations will enter a member's stabilizing bid as soon as possible after receipt of the request from the member.

The requirement in subparagraph (d)(1) that the request for entry of a stabilizing bid be in writing has been deleted and is replaced by a requirement that the request be confirmed in writing by the end of the day on which the stabilizing bid is entered. In light of the speed at which many secondary offerings and shelf distributions are priced and distributed and the volatility of the market, the NASD believes it is important that members be provided the ability to move quickly in response to changing market conditions and the requirements of such offerings. The provision permits a member to submit its written request on an Underwriting Activity Report provided by the Corporate Financing Department or to provide another form of written notice to Nasdaq Market Operations that contains the information related to its request to stabilize the price of a security.

[A market maker may enter a stabilizing bid in Nasdaq, which bid will be identified with the appropriate identifier on the Nasdaq quotation display.]

<u>Market Maker Obligation/Identifier</u>

<u>A market maker that intends to stabilize the price of a Nasdaq security that is a subject or reference security under SEC Rule 101 shall submit a request to Nasdaq Market Operations for the entry of a one-sided bid that is identified on Nasdaq as a stabilizing bid in compliance with the standards set forth in this Rule and SEC Rules 101 and 104.</u>

<u>(b) Eligibility</u>

Only one market maker in an issue may enter a stabilizing bid.

<u>(c) Limitations on Stabilizing Bids</u>

      <u>(1)</u> A stabilizing bid [will] <u>shall</u> not be [displayed] <u>entered in Nasdaq</u> unless <u>at least</u> one <u>other</u> market maker in addition

to the market maker entering the stabilizing bid is registered <u>as a market maker</u> in the [issue] <u>security</u> and enter[s]<u>ing</u> quotations <u>that are considered an independent bid under SEC Rule 104</u>.

([b]<u>2</u>) [Character]

[A stabilizing bid, pre-effective stabilizing bid, or a penalty bid may be entered in Nasdaq.] A stabilizing bid must be available for all freely tradable outstanding securities of the same class being offered.

<u>(3) A market maker shall not enter a stabilizing bid at the same time that it is quoting any other bid or offer in the security.</u>

([c] <u>d</u>) [Notice] <u>Submission of Request</u> to Association

(1) A market maker that wishes to enter a stabilizing bid shall [so notify the] <u>submit a request to</u> Nasdaq Market Operations [in writing prior to the first day on which the stabilizing bid is to appear in Nasdaq] <u>for the entry in the Nasdaq quotation display of a one-sided bid identified as a stabilizing bid. The market maker shall confirm its request in writing no later than the end of the day on which the stabilizing bid is entered by submitting an Underwriting Activity Report to Nasdaq Market Operations that includes the information required by subparagraph (d)(2).</u> [and the fact that the market maker is a manager of the distribution]

<u>(2) In lieu of submitting the Underwriting Activity Report as set forth in subparagraph (d)(1),</u> [T]the <u>market maker may provide written</u> [notice] <u>confirmation to Nasdaq Market Operations that</u> shall include<u>:</u>

(A) the [name] <u>identity</u> of the security and its Nasdaq symbol;

(B) [the date on which the security's registration will become effective, if it is already included in Nasdaq] <u>the contemplated effective date of the offering and the date when the offering will be priced;</u>

[(C) whether the stabilizing bid will be a penalty bid or a penalty-free bid]

(C) the date and time that an identifier should be included on the Nasdaq quotation display; and

(D) a copy of the cover page of the preliminary or final prospectus [or shelf registration statement] or similar offering document, unless the Association determines otherwise.

[(2) In the case of a pre-effective stabilizing bid, the notice shall include (A) the name of the security and its Nasdaq symbol; (B) the contemplated effective date of the offering; (C) whether it is contemplated that the pre-effective stabilizing bid will be converted to a stabilizing bid and, if so, whether the stabilizing bid will be a penalty bid or a penalty-free bid; and (D) a copy of the preliminary prospectus, unless the Association determines otherwise.]

[(3) A market maker that has provided the written notice prescribed above shall also contact Nasdaq Market Operations for authorization on the day the market maker wishes to enter the stabilizing bid.]

[(d) Dual Bids in the Same Issue. A market maker shall not enter a stabilizing bid at the same time that it is quoting any other bid or offer in the issue.]

[(e) Volume Reporting for Stabilizing Bids. A market maker entering a stabilizing bid shall report all purchases made on the stabilizing bid and enter "zero volume" for sales during the period in which the stabilizing bid is in effect.]

4619. Withdrawal of Quotations and Passive Market Making

(a)–(c) No change.

(d) Excused withdrawal status or passive market maker status may be granted to a market maker that is a distribution participant (or, in the case of excused withdrawal status, an affiliated purchaser) in order to comply with SEC Rules [10b-6] 101, [or Rule 10b-6A(T)] 103, or 104 under the Act on the following conditions:

(1) A [market maker] member acting as a manager (or in a similar capacity) of a distribution of a Nasdaq security that is a subject or reference security under SEC Rule 101 and any

<u>member that is a distribution participant or that is an affil-
iated purchaser in such a distribution that does not have a
manager</u> shall [: (A)] provide written notice to Nasdaq Market Operations [of the prospective distribution] <u>no later than
the business day prior to the first entire trading session of
the one-day or five-day restricted period under SEC Rule
101, unless later notification is necessary under the specific
circumstances.</u> [and the fact that the market maker is a manager of the distribution, the Nasdaq security or securities
that are subject to <u>SEC Rule 10b-6</u> no later than 5 business
days following the filing of a registration statement with the
Association pursuant to <u>Rule 2710</u>, or, if the member is not
required to file the registration statement with the Association, no later than 5 business days following the filing of
offering documents with the appropriate regulatory authority; and, (B) no later than noon Eastern Time on the business day prior to the beginning of the cooling off period:]

[(i)] <u>(A)</u> [request] <u>The notice required by subparagraph
(d)(1) of this Rule shall be provided by sub-
mitting a completed Underwriting Activity
Report that includes a request on behalf of
each market maker that is a distribution participant or an affiliated purchaser to</u> withdraw[al of] the market maker[s']<u>'s</u> quotations<u>,</u>
or [identification of] <u>that includes a request on
behalf of each market maker that is a distribution participant that its</u> [the market makers']
quotations <u>be identified</u> as those of a passive
market maker [by providing written notice to
Nasdaq Market Operations of the identity of
the market makers that are distribution par-
ticipants], <u>and includes</u> the contemplated date
and time of the commencement of the [cool-
ing off period] <u>restricted period</u>. [and the identity of the market makers that intend to act as
passive market makers; and]

[(ii)] <u>(B)</u> <u>The managing underwriter shall</u> advise [the]
<u>each</u> market maker that [they have] <u>it has</u> been

identified as a distribution participant[s] or an affiliated purchaser to Nasdaq Market Operations and that [their] its quotations will be automatically withdrawn or identified as passive market maker quotations, [upon the request made by the manager] unless [they submit to] a market maker that is a distribution participant notifies [the Association the notice specified in] Nasdaq Market Operations as required by subparagraph [(3)] (d)(2), below.

[(2) If the security is being distributed pursuant to an offering for which no registration statement or offering document is required to be filed, each market maker that is a distribution participant shall, no later than noon Eastern Time on the business day prior to the beginning of the cooling off period, provide written notice to Nasdaq Market Operations of its participation in the distribution, the contemplated date and time of the commencement of the cooling off period, the Nasdaq security or securities that are subject to SEC Rule 10b-6, and request withdrawal of its quotations or identification as a passive market maker.]

([3]2) A market maker that has been identified to Nasdaq Market Operations as a distribution participant shall [provide written notice to] promptly notify Nasdaq Market Operations and the manager of its intention not to participate in the prospective distribution or not to act as a passive market maker [no later than 4:00 P.M. Eastern Time on the business day prior to the beginning of the cooling off period] in order to avoid having its quotations withdrawn or identified as the quotations of a passive market maker, or in order to have its excused withdrawal status rescinded.

(3) If a market maker that is a distribution participant withdraws its quotations in a Nasdaq security in order to comply with the net purchases limitation of SEC Rule 103 or with any other provision of SEC Rules 101, 103, or 104 and promptly notifies Nasdaq Market Operations of its action, the withdrawal shall be deemed an excused withdrawal.

Nothing in this subparagraph shall prohibit the Association from taking such action as is necessary under the circumstances against a member and its associated persons for failure to contact Nasdaq Market Operations to obtain an excused withdrawal as required by subparagraphs (a) and (d) of this Rule.

(4) [In the event the manager of a distribution is not a market maker, each market maker that is a distribution participant shall comply with paragraph (d)(1) unless another market maker has assumed responsibility for compliance.] The quotations of a passive market maker shall be identified on Nasdaq as those of a passive market maker.

[For purposes of this Rule, the term "cooling off period" refers to the periods specified in SEC Rule 10b-6(a)(4)(xi), the terms "distribution" and "distribution participant" refers to these terms as defined in SEC Rule 10b-6(c)(5) and (c)(6) and the term "passive market maker" refers to this term as defined in SEC Rule 10b-6A(T).]

4623. Penalty Bids and Syndicate Covering Transactions

(a) A market maker acting as a manager (or in a similar capacity) of a distribution of a Nasdaq security that is a subject or reference security under SEC Rule 101 shall provide written notice to the Corporate Financing Department of NASD Regulation, Inc. of its intention to impose a penalty bid on syndicate members or to conduct syndicate covering transactions pursuant to SEC Rule 104 prior to imposing the penalty bid or engaging in the first syndicate covering transaction. A market maker that intends to impose a penalty bid on syndicate members may request that its quotation be identified as a penalty bid on Nasdaq pursuant to paragraph (c) below.

(b) The notice required by paragraph (a) shall include:

(1) the identity of the security and its Nasdaq symbol;

(2) the date the member is intending to impose the penalty bid and/or conduct syndicate covering transactions; and

(3) the amount of the syndicate short position, in the case of syndicate covering transactions.

(c) Notwithstanding paragraph (a), a market maker may request that its quotation identified as a penalty bid on Nasdaq display by providing notice to Nasdaq Market Operations, which notice shall include the date and time that the penalty bid identifier should be entered on Nasdaq and, if not in writing, shall be confirmed in writing no later than the end of the day on which the penalty bid identifier is entered on Nasdaq.

(d) The written notice required by paragraphs (a) and (c) of this Rule may be submitted on the Underwriting Activity Report by including the information required by subparagraphs (b)(1) and (b)(2) or paragraph (c).

6500. OTC BULLETIN BOARD SERVICE

6540. Requirements Applicable to Market Makers

(a) No change.

(b) No change.

    (1) Permissible Quotation Entries

        (A)–(C) No change.

        (D) Any member that intends to be a distribution participant in a distribution of securities subject to SEC Rule 101, or is an affiliated purchaser in such distribution, and is entering quotations in an OTCBB-eligible security that is the subject or reference security of such distribution shall (unless another member has assumed responsibility for compliance with this paragraph):

            (i) provide written notice to Nasdaq Market Operations prior to the pricing of the distribution that includes the intended date and time of the pricing of the offering;

            (ii) withdraw all quotations in the OTCBB-eligible security to comply with the applicable restricted period under SEC Rule 101 and not enter a stabilizing bid pursuant to SEC Rule 104 in the OTCBB; and

(iii) provide written notice to the Corporate Financing Department of NASD Regulation, Inc. of its intention to impose a penalty bid or to conduct syndicate covering transactions pursuant to SEC Rule 104 prior to imposing the penalty bid or engaging in the first syndicate covering transaction. Such notice shall include information as to the date the penalty bid or first syndicate covering transaction will occur and the amount of the syndicate short position.

(E) The written notice required by subparagraphs (b)(1)(D)(i) and (iii) of this rule may be submitted on the Underwriting Activity Report provided by the Corporate Financing Department of NASD Regulation, Inc. by including the information required by those subparagraphs.

(F) For purposes of subparagraph (D), SEC Rules 100, 101, 103 and 104 are rules of the Commission adopted under Regulation M and the following terms shall have the meanings as defined in SEC Rule 100: "affiliated purchaser," "distribution," "distribution participant," "penalty bid," "reference security," "restricted period," "stabilizing," "subject security," and "syndicate covering transaction."

UNDERWRITING ACTIVITY REPORT
REQUEST FORM

ATTENTION: NASD REGULATION CORPORATE FINANCING
              DEPARTMENT

CITY, STATE
DATE
BK: GSC-3335

—REQUEST FOR UNDERWRITING ACTIVITY REPORT—

RE: # OF SHARES

     ISSUER

     TYPE OF SECURITY

     SYMBOL

PURSUANT TO FILING REQUIREMENTS OF NASD CONDUCT RULE 2710(B)(11), AND ACTING, IN OUR CAPACITY AS MANAGER WE REQUEST AN UNDERWRITING ACTIVITY REPORT ON THE ABOVE SUBJECT/REFERENCED SECURITY:

FILING DATE: XXXXXXXXXX

ANTICIPATED TAKEDOWN: XXXXXXXXXX

ANTICIPATED PRICING DATE: XXXXXXXXXX

SIGNATURE: XXXXXXXXXX

TITLE: XXXXXXXXXX

CONTACT (IF DIFFERENT FROM ABOVE):   XXXXXXXXXX

MEMBER NAME

Via CommScan, L.L.C.

REGULATION M RESTRICTED PERIOD COMMENCEMENT FORM

ATTENTION: NASDAQ MARKET OPERATIONS

CITY, STATE
DATE
BK: GSC-3333

—REGULATION M RESTRICTED PERIOD COMMENCEMENT—

RE: # OF SHARES

    ISSUER

    TYPE OF SECURITY

    SYMBOL

PURSUANT TO THE PROVISIONS OF SEC RULES 101 AND 103 UNDER REGULATION M, YOU ARE ADVISED OF OUR INTENTION TO COMMENCE THERESTRICTED PERIOD ON 00/00/00 AT XX:XX XX.

PURSUANT TO RULE 4619(D) WE ADVISE YOU THAT THE FOLLOWING DEALERS ARE DISTRIBUTION PARTICIPANTS OR AFFILIATED PURCHASERS AND THEIR QUOTES SHOULD BE WITHDRAWN FROM THE MARKET OR DESIGNATED AS PASSIVE MARKET MAKING QUOTES AS INDICATED:

MEMBERS   PASSIVE OR EXCUSED

MEMBER 1   XXXXXXX

MEMBER 2   XXXXXXX

MEMBER 3   XXXXXXX

MEMBER N   XXXXXXX

SIGNATURE: XXXXXXXXX

TITLE: XXXXXXXXX

CONTACT (IF DIFFERENT FROM ABOVE):   XXXXXXXXX

MEMBER NAME

Via CommScan, L.L.C.

REGULATION M TRADING NOTIFICATION FORM

ATTENTION: NASD REGULATION CORPORATE FINANCING
DEPARTMENT NASDAQ MARKET OPERATIONS
DEPARTMENT

CITY, STATE
DATE
BK: GSC-3334

—REGULATION M TRADING NOTIFICATION—

RE: # OF SHARES

ISSUER

TYPE OF SECURITY

SYMBOL

OFFER PRICE: XXXXXXXXX

LAST TRADE BEFORE OFFER: XXXXXXXXX

EFFECTIVE DATE: XXXXXXXXX

EFFECTIVE TIME: XXXXXXXXX

TRADE DATE: XXXXXXXXX

PURSUANT TO THE PROVISIONS OF SEC RULE 104 UNDER REGU-
LATION M, YOU ARE ADVISED OF OUR INTENTION TO ENGAGE IN
THE BELOW LISTED ACTIVITY ON THE DATE SHOWN:

ACTIVITY	DATE	TIME
FIRST STABILIZING TRANSACTION:	XXXXXXX	XXXXX
FIRST COVERING TRANSACTION:	XXXXXXX	
FIRST PENALTY BID TRANSACTION:	XXXXXXX	XXXXX (OPTIONAL)

SIGNATURE: XXXXXXXXXX

TITLE: XXXXXXXXXX

CONTACT (IF DIFFERENT FROM ABOVE): XXXXXXXXXX

TELEPHONE NUMBER   XXX-XXX-XXXX

MEMBER NAME

Via CommScan, L.L.C.

97-91 NASD REMINDS MEMBERS OF OBLIGATIONS UNDER FREE-RIDING AND WITHHOLDING INTERPRETATION*

Executive Summary

NASD Regulation, Inc., reminds members of their obligations under the Free-Riding and Withholding Interpretation (IM-2110-1) with respect to venture capitalists and the cancellation safe harbor provisions. This information was previously provided to members through Compliance Desk in a Member Alert dated November 21, 1997.

Questions concerning this *Notice* should be directed to Gary L. Goldsholle, Senior Attorney, Office of General Counsel, NASD Regulation[SM], at (202) 728-8104.

Background

Venture Capital Investors

NASD Regulation is reminding members of their obligations under the Free-Riding and Withholding Interpretation, IM-2110-1 (Interpretation), with respect to allocations of hot issues to venture capitalists. Paragraph (b)(4) of the Interpretation restricts sales of hot issues to certain persons affiliated with "a bank, savings and loan institution, insurance company, investment company, investment advisory firm or any other institutional type account (including, but not limited to, hedge funds, investment partnerships, investment corporations, or investment clubs)." [1] A venture capitalist falls within the scope of paragraph (b)(4) when he or she is a senior officer of an "institutional type account" or otherwise is a person who may influence or whose activities directly or indirectly involve or are related to the function of buying or selling securities of an "institutional type account." This type of account includes, among others, investment partnerships and investment

---

*Copyright 1998 National Association of Securities Dealers, Inc. All rights reserved. [NASD Manual & Notices to Members]— NASD MANUAL & NOTICES TO MEMBERS—NOTICES TO MEMBERS—1997 Notices to Members—97-91 NASD Reminds Members Of Obligations Under Free-Riding And Withholding Interpretation—http://secure.nasdr.com/wbs/NETbos.dll?RefShow?ref=NASD4;&xinfo=goodbye.htm.

1. IM-2110-1(b)(4).

corporations, which are frequently used by venture capitalists. Members should ensure, therefore, that sales of hot issues to venture capitalists who are restricted under the Interpretation are made consistent with the Interpretation.

Persons restricted under paragraph (b)(4) are generally referred to as conditionally restricted persons. As such, they may purchase hot issues from a member only if the member is "prepared to demonstrate that the securities were sold to such persons in accordance with their normal investment practice, that the aggregate of the securities so sold is insubstantial and not disproportionate in amount as compared to sales to members of the public and that the amount sold to any one of such persons is insubstantial in amount."[2]

In 1994, the Securities and Exchange Commission (SEC) approved amendments to the Interpretation which, among other things, included an exemption for venture capital investors who meet certain enumerated criteria. The venture capital provisions of paragraph (h) of the Interpretation are not a general exemptive provision for venture capital investors. In fact, these narrow exemptive provisions were adopted because, under most circumstances, members otherwise would be prohibited from selling hot issues to venture capitalists. The venture capital investor provisions included in paragraph (h) of the Interpretation allow venture capital investors to purchase a hot issue security to maintain their percentage ownership interest in an entity, notwithstanding that such venture capital investor may be restricted under the Interpretation.

Cancellation Safe Harbor

NASD Regulation is also reminding members of the scope of the cancellation safe harbor provisions of paragraph (a)(3). Specifically, paragraph (a)(3) provides that it shall not be "a violation of the interpretation if a member which makes an allocation to a restricted person or account of an offering that trades at a premium in the secondary market, cancels the trade for such restricted person or account, prior to the end of the first business day following the date on which secondary market trading commences and reallocates such security at the public offering price to a non-restricted person or account."[3] The SEC

2. IM-2110-1(b)(5).
3. IM-2110-1(a)(3).

order adopting the cancellation safe harbor[4] and the related *NASD Notice to Members*[5] both stated that the cancellation provisions were intended to remedy concerns caused by inadvertent violations of the Interpretation that are corrected by the member making the distribution. Thus, paragraph (a)(3) permits members to allocate securities to restricted persons and subsequently reallocate such hot issue securities to other accounts within the time limits prescribed by the safe harbor only to the extent that such reallocation is to remedy an inadvertent violation of the Interpretation.[6]

---

4. 59 F. R. 64455, 64458 (December 14, 1994).

5. *NASD Notice to Members 95-7* (February 1995).

6. This sentence has been modified from the Member Alert dated November 21, 1997, to more clearly define the scope of paragraph (a)(3).

98-48 SEC APPROVES AMENDMENTS TO FREE-RIDING AND WITHHOLDING INTERPRETATION; EFFECTIVE AUGUST 17, 1998*

Executive Summary

On May 18, 1998, the Securities and Exchange Commission (SEC) approved amendments to National Association of Securities Dealers, Inc. (NASD®) Interpretive Material 2110-1 (IM-2110-1) and Rule 2720, revising certain provisions of the Free-Riding and Withholding Interpretation (Interpretation). These amendments address direct and indirect owners of broker/dealers, investment grade debt offerings, foreign investment companies, secondary offerings, issuer directed share programs, and accounts under the Employment Retirement Income Security Act. The amendments also provide NASD Regulation, Inc., staff with general exemptive authority. These rule amendments will be effective on August 17, 1998. The text of the amended rules and the *Federal Register* version of the SEC approval order are attached. This *Notice* is being issued to alert members of their revised compliance responsibilities under the Interpretation.

Questions concerning this Notice should be directed to Gary L. Goldsholle, Assistant General Counsel, Office of General Counsel, NASD Regulation℠, at (202) 728-8104.

Background

The purpose of the Interpretation is to protect the integrity of the public offering system by ensuring that members make a bona fide public distribution of "hot issue" securities and do not withhold such securities for their own benefit or use such securities to reward persons who are in a position to direct future business to the member. Hot issue securities are defined by the Interpretation as securities of a public offering that trade at a premium in the secondary market whenever such

---

trading commences. The Interpretation also assures that members and participants in the securities industry do not take unfair advantage of their "insider position" in the industry to the detriment of public investors.

The Interpretation prohibits members from retaining the securities of hot issues in their own accounts and prohibits members from allocating such securities to directors, officers, employees, and associated persons of such members and other broker/dealers. It also restricts member sales of hot issue securities to the accounts of specified categories of persons, including, among others, senior officers of banks, insurance companies, investment companies, investment advisory firms, or any other institutional type account, and any other person with such organizations whose activities influence or include the buying and selling of securities. These basic prohibitions and restrictions are also made applicable to sales by members to accounts in which any such persons may have a beneficial interest and, with some exceptions, to members of the immediate family of those persons restricted by the Interpretation.

Amended Rules

NASD Regulation has received SEC approval of amendments to IM-2110-1 and Rule 2720. *See* 63 FR 28535 (May 26, 1998). These amendments provide for the following:

Exemptive Authority

New paragraph (a)(5) of the Interpretation provides NASD Regulation staff with general exemptive authority. As revised, the Interpretation authorizes NASD Regulation staff, upon written request made by a member, pursuant to the Rule 9600 Series, to provide an exemption unconditionally or on specified terms from any or all provisions, consistent with the purposes of the Interpretation, the protection of investors, and the public interest. Persons requesting an exemption from the Interpretation should submit a detailed written statement of the grounds for granting the exemption to: NASD Regulation, Inc., Attn: Office of General Counsel, 1735 K Street, N.W., Washington, DC 20006.

Treatment of Direct and Indirect Owners of Broker/Dealers

New paragraph (b)(9) addresses persons who directly or indirectly have an ownership interest in a broker/dealer, other than a limited business broker/dealer as defined in paragraph (c) of the Interpretation. The sub-paragraph creates a new category of restricted person, providing generally that members shall not sell hot issue securities to a person, or a member of the immediate family of such person who is supported directly or indirectly to a material extent by such person, who has contributed capital to a broker/dealer, other than solely a limited business broker/dealer, or the account in which any such person has a beneficial interest. The amendments provide an exemption from this new category for persons whose ownership interest is passive and less than 10 percent, and where either: (1) such person purchases hot issues from a person other than the member in which it has a passive ownership and such person is not in a position to direct the allocation of hot issues; or (2) the member in which such person has a passive ownership interest or the parent of such member is publicly traded on an exchange or The Nasdaq Stock Market℠ (Nasdaq®).

The provisions in new paragraph (b)(9) also provide an exemption for sales to the account of any person restricted under subparagraph (b)(9) that is established for the benefit of bona fide public customers, including, among others, insurance company general, separate, and investment accounts, and bank trust accounts. Members should be aware that this exemption applies solely to the accounts of persons restricted pursuant to paragraph (b)(9). It should be noted that paragraph (b)(9) does not restrict purchases of hot issues by any entity owned in part or whole by the person restricted by paragraph (b)(9), but instead reaches only the "accounts" in which restricted owners have a beneficial interest.

Rated Investment Grade Debt

The amendments to the Interpretation exempt certain classes of debt securities. Specifically, the amendments exempt debt securities (other than debt securities convertible into common or preferred stock) and financing instrument-backed securities that are rated by a nationally recognized statistical rating organization in one of its four highest generic rating categories. Members should be aware that debt securities and financing instrument-backed securities must *both* be rated by a nationally recognized statistical rating organization in one of its four highest generic rating categories. NASD Regulation reminds members that the Interpretation will continue to apply to all other types of debt instruments, except those expressly excluded.

Foreign Investment Companies

The amendments to paragraphs (f) and (l)(6) of the Interpretation exempt sales of hot issues to foreign investment companies that meet the following criteria: (1) the fund has 100 or more investors; (2) the fund is listed on a foreign exchange or authorized for sale to the public by a foreign regulatory authority; (3) no more than 5 percent of the fund assets are to be invested in the hot issue securities being offered; and (4) any person owning more than 5 percent of the shares of the fund is not a restricted person as described in paragraph (b)(1), (2), (3), (4), or (9) of the Interpretation. In order for a member to sell hot issues to a foreign investment company, as defined above, the member must receive a written certification prepared by counsel admitted to practice law before the highest court of any state of the United States or the foreign jurisdiction where the investment company is organized, or by an independent certified public accountant licensed in any state of the United States or the foreign jurisdiction where the investment company is organized.

The written certification made pursuant to paragraph (l)(6) shall be deemed current for the same period as certifications furnished pursuant to paragraph (f)(1)(B). Specifically, a written certification by counsel or an independent certified public accountant shall be deemed current if it is based upon the status of the account as of a date not more than 18 months prior to the date of the hot issue transaction.

For purposes of paragraph (l)(6), NASD Regulation interprets the provision that there be 100 or more investors to require that 100 or more persons have direct investments in the foreign investment company. NASD Regulation would not permit investors of an entity that in turn invests in the foreign investment company to be included in the total number of investors for purposes of paragraph (l)(6).

Secondary Distributions

The amendments also exempt certain secondary offerings from the Interpretation. The amendments to the definition of the term "public offering"[1] in paragraph (l)(1) exempt hot issues in a secondary

---

1. The amendments to the definition of "public offering" apply only to the Interpretation and do not affect any other NASD rule, including Rules 2710, 2810, and 2720.

distribution by an issuer, or any security holder of the issuer, of "actively-traded securities." New paragraph (l)(7)(A) defines "actively-traded securities" as securities that have an average daily trading volume (ADTV) of at least $1 million and are issued by an issuer whose common equity securities have a public float of at least $150 million. New paragraph (l)(7)(B) defines the term "ADTV." The definitions of "actively-traded securities" and "ADTV" were modeled after the SEC's Regulation M. 62 FR 520 (January 3, 1997).

Issuer-Directed Share Exemptions

Issuer-directed share programs have become an increasingly valuable and popular tool for employee development and retention. The amendments to paragraph (d) of the Interpretation are designed to simplify the application of the issuer-directed share exemption to employees and directors of an issuer. The amendments permit an issuer specifically to direct its own shares to employees and directors, or employees and directors of a parent or subsidiary of the issuer, or any other entity which controls or is controlled by the issuer, or potential employees and directors resulting from an intended merger, acquisition, or other business combination of the issuer. For purposes of this paragraph, a parent-subsidiary or other control relationship would be deemed to include an entity that holds 50 percent or more of any class of equity securities of another entity. Employees and directors of sister corporations to the issuer are not subject to an exemption for issuer-directed securities, however, members may request an exemption for such persons under paragraph (a)(5) as discussed above.

Members should note that the issuer-directed share program is no longer limited to persons restricted in paragraphs (b)(3) through (8) of the Interpretation. NASD Regulation's amendments permit employees and directors of an issuer to purchase hot issues from such issuer's directed share program even if such employees and directors are materially supported by persons associated with a member restricted under paragraph (b)(2) of the Interpretation.

The amendments also consolidate the issuer-directed share provisions in paragraph (d). Separate provisions addressing issuer-directed share programs of members and parents of members were contained in Rule 2720(m). The new provisions standardize the "lock-up" period for issuer-directed securities to three months.

NASD Regulation reminds members that the Interpretation is designed to ensure that members make a bona fide public distribution of hot issue securities of a public offering that trade at a premium in the secondary market regardless of whether such securities are acquired by the member as an underwriter, as a selling group member, or from a member participating in the distribution as an underwriter or a selling group member, or otherwise. These provisions ensure that the Interpretation applies to securities that are part of a public offering notwithstanding that some of those securities are specifically directed by the issuer on a non-underwritten basis. NASD Regulation will continue its practice of requiring the managing underwriter of the offering to be responsible for ensuring that the distribution of non-underwritten securities is made in compliance with the Interpretation.

As a result of the plenary exemptive authority granted in new paragraph (a)(5), NASD Regulation has eliminated paragraph (d)(2) from the Interpretation. Members may request an exemption for the sale of issuer-directed securities to a restricted person who is neither an employee nor director of the issuer under the general exemptive procedures described above. While NASD Regulation staff will be able to exercise greater flexibility than currently permitted under the Interpretation, members should articulate a valid business reason for such sales. In addition, members should represent that such securities shall not be subject to the same "lock-up" provisions as securities directed by an issuer pursuant to paragraph (d).

Accounts for Qualified Plans Under the Employment Retirement Income Security Act (ERISA)

New paragraph (f)(3) addresses the status of qualified employee benefit plans under ERISA. Generally, the amendments provide that an employee benefits plan qualified under ERISA shall not be deemed restricted. The amendments in new paragraph (b)(3) provide guidance in determining the factual circumstances in which a qualified ERISA plan would be deemed restricted.

Questionnaire

In its review for compliance with the Interpretation, NASD Regulation regularly issues a Free-Riding Questionnaire through the Compliance Desk software service to the managing underwriter and other

members participating in the distribution of hot issue securities.
NASD Regulation has revised the questionnaire to reflect the amendments to the Interpretation. A copy of the new Questionnaire follows
this *Notice*. Additional information about the Compliance Desk and the
Questionnaire is contained in *Notice to Members 96-18*.

Text of Rule Amendments

(*Note: New text is <u>underlined</u>; deletions are [bracketed]*.)

IM-2110-1. Free-Riding and Withholding

(a) Introduction

> (1) No change.
>
> (2) As in the case of any other interpretation issued by the
> [Board of Governors of the] Association, the implementa-
> tion thereof is a function of the NASD Regulation staff
> [District Business Conduct Committee] and the [Board of
> Governors] NASD Regulation Board of Directors. Thus,
> the interpretation will be applied to a given factual situation
> by NASD Regulation staff, subject to oversight by the
> Board, with staff soliciting input from individuals active in
> the investment banking and securities business [who are
> serving on these committees or on the Board. They]. In
> making such interpretations, staff and the Board will con-
> strue this interpretation to effectuate its overall purpose to
> assure a public distribution of securities for which there is
> a public demand.
>
> (3)–(4) No change.
>
> (5) The NASD Regulation staff, upon written request, may,
> taking into consideration all relevant factors, provide an
> exemption either unconditionally or on specified terms
> from any or all of the provisions of this interpretation upon
> a determination that such exemption is consistent with the
> purposes of the interpretation, the protection of investors,
> and the public interest. A member may appeal a decision
> issued by NASD Regulation staff to the National Adjudi-
> catory Council pursuant to the Code of Procedure.

(b) Violations of Rule 2110

    (1)–(8) No Change

    (9) Sell any of the securities to any person, or to a member of the immediate family of such person who is supported directly or indirectly to a material extent by such person, who owns or has contributed capital to a broker/dealer, other than solely a limited business broker/dealer as defined in paragraph (c) of this interpretation, or the account in which any such person has a beneficial interest, provided, however, that:

        (A) The prohibition shall not apply to any person who directly or indirectly owns any class of equity securities of, or who has made a contribution of capital to, a member, and whose ownership or capital interest is passive and is less than 10% of the equity or capital of a member, as long as:

            (i) such person purchases hot issues from a person other than the member in which it has such passive ownership and such person is not in a position by virtue of its passive ownership interest to direct the allocation of hot issues, or

            (ii) such member's shares or shares of a parent of such member are publicly traded on an exchange or Nasdaq.

        (B) This prohibition shall not apply to sales to the account of any person restricted under this subparagraph (9) established for the benefit of bona fide public customers, including insurance company general, separate and investment accounts, and bank trust accounts.

        (C) For purposes of this subparagraph (9), any person with an equity ownership or capital interest in an entity that maintains an investment in a member shall be deemed to have a percentage interest in the member equal to the percentage interest of the

<u>entity in the member multiplied by the percentage interest of such person in such entity.</u>

(c) No Change

(d) Issuer-Directed Securities

[(1) This interpretation shall apply to securities which are part of a public offering notwithstanding that some or all of those securities are specifically directed by the issuer to accounts which are included within the scope of paragraph (b)(3) through (8) above. Therefore, if a person within the scope of those subparagraphs to whom securities were directed did not have the required investment history, the member would not be permitted to sell him such securities. Also, the "disproportionate" and "insubstantial" tests would apply as in all other situations. Thus, the directing of a substantial number of securities to any one person would be prohibited as would the directing of securities to such accounts in amounts which would be disproportionate as compared to sales to members of the public. If such issuer-directed securities are sold to the issuer's employees or directors or potential employees or directors resulting from an intended merger, acquisition, or other business combination, such securities may be sold without limitation as to amount and regardless of whether such employees have an investment history as required by the interpretation; provided, however, that in the case of an offering of securities for which a bona fide independent market does not exist, such securities shall not be sold, transferred, assigned, pledged, or hypothecated for a period of three months following the effective date of the offering. This interpretation shall also apply to securities which are part of a public offering notwithstanding that some of those securities are specifically directed by the issuer on a non-underwritten basis. In such cases, the managing underwriter of the offering shall be responsible for insuring compliance with this interpretation in respect to those securities.]

[(2) Notwithstanding the above, sales of issuer-directed securities may be made to non-employee/director restricted persons without the required investment history after receiving permission from the Board of Governors. Permission will be given only if there is a demonstration of valid business reasons for such sales (such as sales to distributors and suppliers, who are in each case incidentally restricted persons), and the member seeking permission is prepared to demonstrate that the aggregate amount of securities so sold is insubstantial and not disproportionate as compared to sales to members of the public, and that the amount sold to any one of such persons is insubstantial in amount; provided, however, that such securities shall not be sold, transferred, assigned, pledged, or hypothecated for a period of three months following the effective date of the offering.]

Employees and directors of an issuer, a parent of an issuer, a subsidiary of an issuer, or any other entity which controls or is controlled by an issuer, or potential employees and directors resulting from an intended merger, acquisition, or other business combination of an issuer otherwise subject to this interpretation in paragraphs (b)(2) through (9) may purchase securities that are part of a public offering that are specifically directed by the issuer to such persons; provided, however, that in the case of an offering of securities for which a bona fide independent market does not exist, such securities shall not be sold, transferred, assigned, pledged, or hypothecated for a period of three months following the effective date of the offering.

(e) No Change

(f) Investment Partnerships and Corporations

   (1) A member may not sell a hot issue to the account of any investment partnership or corporation, domestic or foreign (except companies registered under the Investment Company Act of 1940 or foreign investment companies as defined herein) including but not limited to hedge funds, investment clubs, and other like accounts unless the member complies with either of the following alternatives:

      (A)–(B) No Change

(2) The member shall maintain a copy of the names and business connections of all persons having any beneficial interest in the account or a copy of the current written representation in its files for at least three years following the member's last sale of a new issue to the account, depending upon which of the above requirements the member elects to follow. For purposes of this paragraph (f) and the certification required pursuant to paragraph (l)(6), a list or written representation shall be deemed to be current if it is based upon the status of the account as of a date not more than 18 months prior to the date of the transaction.

(3) An employee benefits plan qualified under the Employee Retirement Income Security Act shall be deemed restricted under this interpretation in accordance with the following provisions:

   (A) Any plan sponsored by a broker/dealer is restricted;

   (B) Any plan sponsored by an entity that is not involved in financial services activities is not restricted whether or not any plan participants may be restricted;

   (C) Any plan sponsored by an entity that is engaged in financial services activities, including but not limited to, banks, insurance companies, investment advisers, or other money managers, is not restricted, provided that the plan permits participation by a broad class of participants and is not designed primarily for the benefit of restricted persons.

(g)–(k) No Change

(l) Explanation of Terms

The following explanation of terms is provided for the assistance of members. Other words which are defined in the By-Laws and Rules shall, unless the context otherwise requires, have the meaning as defined therein.

[(1) Associated Person

A person associated with a member or any other broker/dealer, as defined in Article I of the Association's By-Laws, shall not include a person whose association with the member is limited to a passive ownership interest in the member of 10% or less, and who does not receive hot issues from the member in which he or she has the ownership interest; and that such member is not in a position to direct hot issues to such person.]

[(2)]

(1) Public Offering

The term public offering shall mean any primary or secondary distribution of securities made pursuant to a registration statement or offering circular including exchange offers, rights offerings, offerings made pursuant to a merger or acquisition, straight debt offerings, and all other securities distributions of any kind whatsoever except any offering made pursuant to an exemption under Section 4(1), 4(2) or 4(6) of the Securities Act of 1933, as amended. The term public offering shall exclude exempted securities as defined in Section 3(a)(12) of the Act, and debt securities (other than debt securities convertible into common or preferred stock) and financing instrument-backed securities that are rated by a nationally recognized statistical rating organization in one of its four highest generic rating categories. The term public offering shall exclude secondary offerings by an issuer, or any security holder of the issuer, of actively-traded securities.

[(3)]

(2) Immediate Family

The term immediate family shall include parents, mother-in-law or father-in-law, husband or wife, brother or sister, brother-in-law or sister-in-law, son-in-law or daughter-in-law, and children. In addition, the term shall include any other person who is supported, directly or indirectly, to a material extent by the member, person associated with the member or other person specified in paragraph (b)(2) above.

[(4)]

(3) Normal Investment Practice

Normal investment practice shall mean the history of investment of a restricted person in an account or accounts maintained by the restricted person. Usually the previous one-year period of securities activity is the basis for determining the adequacy of a restricted person's investment history. Where warranted, however, a longer or shorter period may be reviewed. It is the responsibility of the registered representative effecting the allocation, as well as the member, to demonstrate that the restricted person's investment history justifies the allocation of hot issues. Copies of customer account statements or other records maintained by the registered representative or the member may be utilized to demonstrate prior investment activity. In analyzing a restricted person's investment history the Association believes the following factors should be considered:

(A) The frequency of transactions in the account or accounts during that period of time. Relevant in this respect are the nature and size of investments.

(B) A comparison of the dollar amount of previous transactions with the dollar amount of the hot-issue purchase. If a restricted person purchases $1,000 of a hot issue and his account revealed a series of purchases and sales in $100 amounts, the $1,000 purchase would not appear to be consistent with the restricted person's normal investment practice.

(C) The practice of purchasing mainly hot issues would not constitute a normal investment practice. The Association does, however, consider as contributing to the establishment of a normal investment practice, the purchase of new issues which are not hot issues as well as secondary market transactions.

[(5)]

(4) Disproportionate

(A) In respect to the determination of what constitutes a disproportionate allocation, the Association uses a guideline of 10% of the member's participation in the issue, however acquired. It should be noted, however, that the 10% factor is merely a guideline and is one of a number of factors which are considered in reaching determinations of violations of the interpretation on the basis of disproportionate allocations. These other factors include, among other things:

> (i)   the size of the participation;
>
> (ii) the offering price of the issue;
>
> (iii) the amount of securities sold to restricted accounts; and
>
> (iv) the price of the securities in the after-market.

(B) It should be noted that disciplinary action has been taken against members for violations of the interpretation where the allocations made to restricted accounts were less than 10% of the member's participation. The 10% guideline is applied as to the aggregate of the allocations.

(C) Notwithstanding the above, a normal unit of trading (100 shares or 10 bonds) will in most cases not be considered a disproportionate allocation regardless of the amount of the member's participation. This means that if the aggregate number of shares of a member's participation which is allocated to restricted accounts does not exceed a normal unit of trading, such allocation will in most cases not be considered disproportionate. For example, if a member receives 500 shares of a hot issue, he may allocate 100 shares to a restricted account even though such allocation represents 20% of the member's participation. Of course, all of the remaining shares would have to be allocated to unrestricted accounts and all other provisions of the interpretation would have to be satisfied. Specifically, the allocation would have to be consistent with the normal investment practice of the account to which it was allocated and the member would not be permitted to sell to restricted persons who were totally prohibited from receiving hot issues.

[(6)]

(5) Insubstantiality

This requirement is separate and distinct from the requirements relating to disproportionate allocations and normal investment practice. In addition, this term applies both to the aggregate of the securities sold to restricted accounts and to each individual allocation. In other words, there could be a substantial allocation to an individual account in violation of the interpretation and yet be no violation on that ground as to the total number of shares allocated to all accounts. The determination of whether an allocation to a restricted account or accounts is substantial is based upon, among other things, the number of shares allocated and/or the dollar amount of the purchase.

(6) Foreign Investment Company

The term foreign investment company shall include any fund company organized under the laws of a foreign jurisdiction, which has provided to the member a written certification prepared by counsel admitted to practice law before the highest court of any state of the United States or such foreign jurisdiction, or by an independent certified public accountant licensed to practice in any state of the United States or such foreign jurisdiction, that states that:

(A) the fund has 100 or more investors;

(B) the fund is listed on a foreign exchange or authorized for sale to the public by a foreign regulatory authority;

        (C) no more than 5% of the fund assets are to be invested in the securities being offered; and,

        (D) any person owning more than 5% of the shares of the fund is not a restricted person as described in paragraphs (b)(1), (2), (3), (4) or (9) of this interpretation.

    (7) Actively-traded securities

        (A) Actively-traded securities means securities that have an ADTV value of at least $1 million and are issued by an issuer whose common equity securities have a public float value of at least $150 million.

        (B) "ADTV" means the worldwide average daily trading volume, during the two full calendar months immediately preceding, or any 60 consecutive calendar days ending within the 10 calendar days preceding, the filing of the registration statement; or, if there is no registration statement or if the distribution involves the sale of securities on a delayed basis pursuant to Securities Act Rule 415, two full calendar months immediately preceding, or any consecutive 60 calendar days ending within the 10 calendar days preceding, the determination of the offering price.

(m) No Change

2720. Distribution of Securities of Members and Affiliates— Conflicts of Interest

(a)–(l) No Change

[(m)   Sales to Employees—No Limitations

Notwithstanding the provisions of IM-2110-1, "Free-Riding and Withholding," a member may sell securities issued by a member, a parent of a member, an entity which wholly owns a member, an entity which owns (alone or in the aggregate with any wholly-owned, non-public subsidiary) at least 51% of the outstanding voting stock of a member or by an issuer treated as a member or parent of a member under paragraph (i) hereof to the member's employees; potential employees resulting from an intended merger, acquisition, or other business combination of members resulting in one public successor corporation; persons associated with the member; and the immediate family of such employees or associated persons without limitation as to amount and regardless of whether such persons have an investment history with the member as required by IM-2110-1; provided, however, that in the case of an offering of equity securities for which a bona fide independent market does not exist, such securities shall not be sold, transferred, assigned, pledged, or hypothecated for a period of five months following the effective date of the offering.]

(n)–(q) are redesignated as (m)–(p)

Attachments

Free-Riding Questionnaire

6/98

NATIONAL ASSOCIATION OF SECURITIES DEALERS, INC.

Firm:

Address:

Re: Offering Date:

INSTRUCTIONS. Each member is required to complete either Section I or Section II based upon the capacity In which they acted in the distribution of the new issue. Sections III and IV must be completed by all firms for their "confirmed"* securities. It is the executing broker/dealer's

---

*For purposes of this questionnaire, "confirmed" means the number of new issue securities allocated to the firm for distribution purposes and for which the firm has issued a confirmation/comparison reflecting the full detail of such sale to retail customers, institutional accounts, or other broker/dealers. When participating in a distribution of new issue securities, broker/dealers are responsible for ensuring compliance with the Free-Riding and Withholding Interpretation for all securities allocated and confirmed by that broker/dealer.

responsibility to ensure that securities were distributed in compliance with the Free-Riding and Withholding Interpretation, IM-2110-1.

SECTION I.   TO BE COMPLETED BY THE MANAGING
             UNDERWRITER ONLY

A. Total number of securities offered for public distribution: (Include any additional shares sold as part of any over-allotment provision and any shares sold short for the account of the syndicate.)

B. Total number of securities allocated for sale to other underwriters and selling group members:

C. Total number of securities confirmed* by your firm to retail and institutional customers, including all shares billed and delivered on behalf of others, designated orders, group sales, directed sales, etc.:

SECTION II.   TO BE COMPLETED BY ALL UNDERWRITERS,
              SELLING GROUP MEMBERS AND OTHER
              PARTICIPANTS IN THE DISTRIBUTION

A. Total number of securities confirmed* by your firm to retail and institutional customers. (Do not include shares billed and delivered on your behalf by the managing underwriter, designated orders, group sales, directed sales, etc.):

B. Indicate capacity in which your firm participated in the offering:

- Underwriter

- Selling Group

- Other (define)

---

*For purposes of this questionnaire, "confirmed" means the number of new issue securities allocated to the firm for distribution purposes and for which the firm has issued a confirmation/comparison reflecting the full detail of such sale to retail customers, institutional accounts, or other broker/dealers. When participating in a distribution of new issue securities, broker/dealers are responsible for ensuring compliance with the Free-Riding and Withholding Interpretation for all securities allocated and confirmed by that broker/dealer.

SECTION III. BREAKDOWN OF SECURITIES DISTRIBUTED BY YOUR FIRM

INSTRUCTIONS. Indicate total number of securities distributed in each category and, unless otherwise noted, provide detailed information in Section IV, "Sales to Restricted Accounts." This breakdown should contain the final figures after giving effect to all cancellations and reallocations. For additional information regarding categories, please refer to the Free-Riding and Withholding Interpretation, IM 2110-1.

1. Securities held in a firm account.

2. Sales to any officer, director, general partner, employee or agent of the member or any other broker/dealer, or to person associated with the member or with any other broker/dealer, or to a member of the immediate family of such a person.

   Indicate the number of shares/units that were sold pursuant to the following provisions:

   (A) Sales to persons associated with broker/dealers whose business is limited to investment company/variable contract securities or direct participation programs.

   Number of shares/units

   (B) Sales to a member of the immediate family of a person associated with a member who is not supported directly or indirectly by that person if the sale is by a broker/dealer other than that employing the restricted person and the restricted person has no ability to control the allocation of the hot issue.

   Number of shares/units

   It is not necessary to complete Section IV for items 2 (A) and (B).

3. Sales to a person who is a finder with respect to the public offering or to any person acting in a fiduciary capacity to the managing underwriter, including among others, attorneys, accountants and financial consultants, or to any other person who is supported directly or indirectly, to a material extent, by any person specified in this paragraph.

4. Sales to any senior officer of a bank, savings and loan institution, insurance company, investment company, investment advisory firm,

or any other institutional type account, (including, but not limited to hedge funds, investment partnerships, investment corporations, or investment clubs) domestic or foreign, or to any person in the securities department of, or to any employee or any other person who may influence or whose activities directly or indirectly involve or are related to the function of buying and selling securities for any bank, savings and loan institution, insurance company, investment company, investment advisory firm, or other institutional type account, domestic or foreign, or to any other person who is supported directly or indirectly, to a material extent, by any person specified in this paragraph.

5. Sales to any account in which any person specified under paragraphs (2), (3), or (4) has a beneficial interest.

6. Sales to other domestic broker/dealers for bona fide public customers, other than those enumerated in paragraphs (2), (3), (4), or (5) above.

Name of Broker/Dealer	No. of Shares/Units	Written Representation Received (pursuant to paragraph 6)	
		Yes_____	No_____
		Yes_____	No_____
		Yes_____	No_____

It is not necessary to complete Section IV for item 6.

7. Sales to any domestic bank, domestic branch of a foreign bank, trust company or other conduit for an undisclosed principal.

    (A) Indicate the number of shares/units that were sold based upon assurances obtained that ultimate purchasers were not restricted persons.

    Number of shares/units

It is not necessary to complete Section IV for item 7(A).

8. Sales to a foreign broker/dealer or bank.

    Indicate the number of shares/units that were sold pursuant to the following conditions.

(A) Sales by a foreign broker/dealer or bank participating in the distribution as an underwriter that were made in accordance with provisions of underwriting agreement.

Number of shares/units

(B) Affirmative inquiry was obtained that ultimate purchasers were not restricted persons.

Number of shares/units

It is not necessary to complete Section IV for items 8(A) and (B).

9. Sales to direct and indirect owners of a broker/dealer.

Indicate the number of shares/units that were sold pursuant to the following provisions.

(A) Sales to direct and indirect owners whose passive ownership interest amounts to less than 10% of the broker/dealer, and:

(1) the owner purchases hot issues from a person other than the member in which it has a passive ownership interest, and such owner is not in a position to direct the allocation of hot issues, or

Number of shares/units

(2) the shares of the member or parent of the member in which the passive owner has an ownership interest are traded on an exchange or Nasdaq.

Number of shares/units

(B) Sales to the account of any person restricted under paragraph (b)(9) of the Interpretation established for the benefit of bona fide public customers.

Number of shares/units

It is not necessary to complete Section IV for items 9(A) and (B).

10. Sales to an investment partnership or corporation, domestic or foreign (except companies registered under the Investment Company Act of 1940 or exempt foreign investment company as defined in the Free-Riding and Withholding Interpretation) including but not limited to hedge funds, investment clubs, and other like accounts.

Indicate the number of shares/units that were sold pursuant to the following conditions:

(A) "Carve out" mechanism was utilized.

Number of shares/units

(B) Determination was made based upon file containing information on all persons having a beneficial interest, or the opinion of counsel or accountants was obtained.

Number of shares/units

It is not necessary to complete Section IV for items 10(A) and (B).

11. Sales to public customers.

It is not necessary to complete Section IV for item 11.

TOTAL (1 through 11)

Please note that the total should be equal to total securities confirmed by your firm as noted in Section I or II.

Indicate the number of shares/units that were originally sold to a restricted account and were subsequently canceled prior to the end of the first business day after the date on which secondary market trading begins and were reallocated to an unrestricted account.

	*	Not Applicable

Signature of Principal		Title

NOTE. Questionnaires should be returned to the Corporate Financing Department by the date specified.

SECURITIES AND EXCHANGE COMMISSION

[Release No. 34-40001; File No. SR-NASD-97-95]

Self-Regulatory Organizations; Order Granting Approval of Proposed Rule Change By the National Association of Securities Dealers, Inc. Relating to Amendments to the Free-Riding and Withholding Interpretation

May 18, 1998.

I. Introduction

On December 23, 1997,[1] the National Association of Securities Dealers Regulation, Inc. ("NASD Regulation") filed with the Securities and Exchange Commission ("SEC" or "Commission") a proposed rule change pursuant to Section 19(b)(1) of the Securities Exchange Act of 1934 ("Act"),[2] and Rule 194-b thereunder.[3] Notice of the proposal appeared in the *Federal Register* on February 11, 1998.[4] The Commission received one comment letter regarding the proposal.[5] The

---

1. On March 12, 1998, NASD Regulation filed Amendment No. 1 to the proposal. Amendment No. 1 revised Paragraph (b)(9)(A)(ii) to include the shares of a member's parent that are publicly traded on an exchange or Nasdaq in the exemption granted for shares of members traded on an exchange or Nasdaq. Section III of this approval order contains a further discussion of this amendment. In brief, the technical amendment was necessary to reflect the fact that members are often part of a holding company structure wherein the parent of the member is the entity that actually trades on an exchange or Nasdaq. Amendment No. 1 also corrected a drafting error in the original proposal's Paragraph (d) of IM-2110-1 to clarify that both employees and directors may take advantage of an exemption for issuer directed securities programs. Because this amendment is technical the statute does not require that it be published for comment.

2. 15 U.S.C. 78s(b)(1).

3. 17 CFR 240-19b-4.

4. Securities Exchange Act Release No. 39620 (February 4, 1998), 63 FR 7026 (February 11, 1998).

5. *See* letter from Sullivan & Cromwell to Jonathan G. Katz, Secretary, SEC, dated March 13, 1998.

commenter generally supported the proposed rule change with some modifications.[6]

The proposal amends Interpretative Material IM-2110-1 and <u>Rule 2720</u> to revise certain aspects of the Free-Riding and Withholding Interpretation ("Interpretation"). The purpose of the Interpretation is to protect the integrity of the public offering system by ensuring that members make a bona fide public distribution of "hot issue" securities and do not withhold such securities for their own benefit or use the securities to reward other persons who are in a position to direct future business to the member. Hot issues are defined by the Interpretation as securities of a public offering that trade at a premium in the secondary market whenever such trading commences.

The Interpretation prohibits members from retaining the securities of hot issues in their own accounts and prohibits members from allocating such securities to directors, officers, employees and associated persons of such members and other broker-dealers. It also restricts member sales of hot issue securities to the accounts of specified categories of persons, including, among others, senior officers of banks, insurance companies, registered investment companies, registered investment advisory firms and any other person with such organizations whose activities influence or include the buying and selling of securities. These basic prohibitions and restrictions are also made applicable to sales by members of hot issue securities to accounts in which any such persons may have a beneficial interest and, with some exceptions, to members of the immediate family of those persons restricted by the Interpretation.

In March 1997, the NASD Regulation Board of Directors ("Board"), acting upon recommendation from the National Business Conduct Committee ("NBCC")[7] considered various amendments to the

---

6. On April 9, 1998, NASD Regulation filed Amendment No. 2 to the proposal. See letter to Katherine A. England, Assistant Director, Division of Market Regulation. Amendment No. 2 responds to the comment letter submitted by Sullivan and Cromwell regarding the proposed rule change. NASD Regulation's response to the comment letter is discussed in detail in Section III of this approval order. Because this amendment is technical the statute does not require that it be published for comment.

7. The name of this committee has been changed to National Adjudicatory Council. *See* Securities Exchange Act Release No. 39470 (December 19, 1997), 62 FR 67927 (December 30, 1997).

Interpretation. The Board submitted a series of proposed rule amendments to the membership for comment in Notice to Members 97-30. NASD Regulation received 22 comment letters in response to Notice to Members 97-30. As described below, the proposal has been amended in response to these comments.

II. Summary Description of the Proposed Rule Change

A. Exemptive Authority

Previously, there has not been a provision in the Interpretation itself to allow the NBCC, the Board, or NASD Regulation staff to grant exemptive relief. In the past, the NBCC, relying on the NASD By-Law's grant of authority to the Board and its Committees, granted exemptions in certain unique circumstances. NASD Rule 9600 delegates exemptive authority in the Interpretation to the Office of General Counsel. The Interpretation previously provided for exemption relief solely in cases involving sales of issuer-directed securities to non-employee-director restricted persons pursuant to Paragraph (d)(2) of the Interpretation.

As revised, the Interpretation authorizes NASD Regulation staff, upon written request and taking into consideration all relevant factors, to provide an exemption either unconditionally or on specified terms from any or all of the provisions of the Interpretation, consistent with the purposes of the Interpretation, the protection of investors and the public interest. The proposed rule revisions also provide that persons may appeal decisions of NASD Regulation staff to the National Adjudicatory Council.

B. Treatment of Direct and Indirect Owner of Broker-Dealers

In 1994, the Interpretation's definition of "associated person" was amended to exempt certain passive investors in broker-dealers.[8] Among other things, the rule amendments approved in the instant filing address two limitations from the previous amendments. First, the definition of associated person as previously provided in the Interpretation did not include non-natural persons that have an ownership interest in or have contributed capital to a broker-dealer. Secondly, the Interpretation did

---

8. Securities Exchange Act Release No. 35059 (December 7, 1994), 59 FR 64455, 64457 (December 14, 1994).

not affirmatively specify any ownership levels at which a natural person becomes an associated person by reason of his or her ownership interest in a broker-dealer. Rather, the Interpretation only specified when a natural person is not an associated person.

In Notice to Members 97-30, NASD Regulation proposed creating a new definition of "restricted person." Among other things, commenters advised the NASD that this approach would result in confusion because the term "restricted person" was already used throughout the Interpretation. Commenters also observed that when the proposed restricted persons provisions were read with other sections of the Interpretation, the Interpretation would appear to be so broad as to preclude purchases by any entity that owns 10 percent or more of a broker-dealer or any account in which such entity has a beneficial interest.

Having considered the potential problems with creating a new definition of "restricted person," to clarify the application of the Interpretation to natural and non-natural persons, the Interpretation has been revised by NASD Regulation to create a new Paragraph (b)(9) of IM 2110-1. Paragraph (b)(9)(A) would exempt from the Interpretation's prohibitions purchases by any person who directly or indirectly owns any class of equity securities of, or who has made a contribution of capital to, a member, and whose ownership or capital interest is passive and is less than 10 percent of the equity or capital of a member, as long as such person purchases hot issues from a person other than the member in which it has such passive ownership and such person is not in a position by virtue of its passive ownership interest to direct the allocation of hot issues.

Alternatively, a second exemption embodied in Paragraph (b)(9)(A) would exclude purchases by any person who directly or indirectly owns any class of equity securities of, or who has made a contribution of capital to, a member, and whose ownership or capital interest is passive and is less than 10 percent of the equity or capital of a member, as long as such member's shares, or shares of a parent of such member, are traded on an exchange or Nasdaq.

In response to commenters' concerns that the rule revisions proposed in Notice to Members 97-30 would prohibit sales of hot issues to all entities within many insurance companies that own a broker-dealer, Paragraph (b)(9)(B) of the proposal exempts sales of hot issues to any account established for the benefit of bona fide public customers of a person restricted pursuant to Paragraph (b)(9). This exception expressly notes that such accounts would include, but are not limited to, an insurance company's general or separate accounts.

Finally, Paragraph (b)(9)(C) retains the indirect ownership provisions originally proposed in Notice to Members 97-30. Specifically, it provides that any person with an equity ownership or capital interest in an entity that maintains an investment in a member shall be deemed to have a percentage interest of the entity of the member multiplied by the percentage interest of such person in such entity.

C. Exception to the Public Offering Definition

Heretofore, debt offerings have been included in the Interpretation's definition of "public offering." The proposed rule change would provide an exception from the Interpretation for debt securities other than debt securities convertible into common or preferred stock. This exclusion is based upon the rationale that such offerings do not raise the same issues as equity offerings inasmuch as the price for a particular debt security generally fluctuates based on interest rate movements rather than demand factors. The definition of public offering also would except financing instrument-backed securities that are rated by a nationally recognized statistical rating organization in one of the four highest generic rating categories. Lastly, NASD Regulation has reconsidered its earlier position and, in response to comment letters received regarding Notice to Members 97-30, revised the term public offering so as to exclude secondary offerings by an issuer whose securities are actively traded securities. The modified Interpretation defines actively traded securities to include securities that have a worldwide average daily trading volume value of at least $1 million and are issued by an issuer whose common equity securities have a public float value of at least $150 million.

D. Foreign Mutual Funds

Purchases of shares of investment companies registered under the Investment Company Act of 1940 were previously exempt from the Interpretation based upon the rationale that the interest of any one restricted person in an investment company ordinarily is de minimis and because ownership of investment company shares generally is subject to frequent turnover. The proposed rule revisions would extend this rationale to the purchase of shares of foreign investment companies and thus exempt such shares from the Interpretation, subject to verification procedures designed, among other things, to ensure that the company is listed on a foreign exchange or authorized for sale to the policy by a foreign regulatory authority.

E. Issuer-Directed Share Exemption

In Notice to Members 97-30, NASD Regulation stated that persons have requested that the language of Paragraph (d) of the Interpretation be modified to clarify that the exemption is available to employees of the issuer who are materially supported by a restricted person and both employees and non-employee directors. Based upon the comments received and its own initiative to clarify and streamline the issuer-directed securities provisions more generally, the proposed rule change modifies Paragraph (d) of the Interpretation to permit persons associated with a member and their immediate family members to purchase hot issues. The amendments clarify that the exemptions apply to employees and directors of a parent or subsidiary of the issuer, consistent with NASD Regulation's past practice.

F. Accounts for Qualified Plans Under the Employment Retirement Income Security Act ("ERISA")

The Interpretation has not previously expressly addressed the status of qualified employee benefit plans under ERISA. In direct response to the requests of commenters, the proposed rule change clarifies the status of such accounts. To that end, the proposal incorporates within the Interpretation itself a prior NBCC interpretation governing the matter. As a general rule, NASD Regulation believes qualified ERISA plans should not be deemed an "investment partnership or corporation" and should not be considered a "restricted account" for purposes of the Interpretation. The proposed amendments to the Interpretation provide guidance, however, in determining the factual circumstances wherein a qualified ERISA plan could be deemed restricted.

III.   Comments Letters Received and Amendment No. 2 to the Proposal

As noted above, the Commission received one comment letter from Sullivan and Cromwell. Amendment No. 2 to the filing responds to the comment letter and, as discussed below, amends the proposal to address issues raised by the Sullivan and Cromwell letter.

A. Investment Grade Securities

The proposed rule change exempts from the Interpretation debt securities (other than debt securities convertible into common or preferred stock) and financing instrument backed-securities that are rated by a nationally recognized statistical rating organization in one of its four highest generic rating categories. Sullivan and Cromwell recommends that NASD Regulation exempt "investment grade preferred securities," (*i.e.,* preferred equities) from the Interpretation based upon its understanding that prices for such securities are principally based on prevailing interest rates and that many investors view investment grade preferred securities of different issuers as being largely fungible.

NASD Regulation does not agree with Sullivan and Cromwell that "investment grade preferred securities" should be excluded from the Interpretation, because NASD Regulation does not believe that the prices of investment grade preferred securities are based on interest rate movements to the same extent as investment grade debt. NASD Regulation believes that demand-side factors play an important role in the price of many preferred securities. In addition, preferred securities generally differ from investment grade debt in that they are rarely collateralized. Moreover, purchasers of preferred securities often look to the issuer's business and management in determining whether to purchase the security. For these reasons, NASD Regulation believes that "investment grade preferred securities" should not be excluded from the Interpretation. Amendment No. 2 to the filing states, however, that NASD Regulation will evaluate the impact of excluding investment grade debt and investment grade financing-backed securities from the Interpretation and will consider in the future whether preferred equities should also be excluded.

B. Paragraph (b)(9) and Direct/Indirect Owners of Broker-Dealers

In Paragraph (b)(9) of the proposed rule change, NASD Regulation prohibits members from selling hot issues to any person or to a member of the immediate family of such person who owns or has contributed capital to a broker-dealer, other than solely a limited business broker-dealer as defined in Paragraph (c) of the Interpretation, or the account in which any such person has a beneficial interest, with certain exceptions for ownership interest of less than 10%. Importantly, however, Paragraph (b)(9) exempts sales to the account of a restricted person that is established for the benefit of bona fide public customers.

The Sullivan & Cromwell letter makes a number of particularized comments, which are discussed in detail below. The thrust of Sullivan & Cromwell comments is that Paragraph (b)(9) should be revised to apply only to institutions that are "principally engaged in the broker-dealer business." In responding to the suggestion, NASD Regulation notes that it has rejected this argument many times and continues to believe that such a narrow approach is inconsistent with the scope and intent of the Interpretation. As reiterated in Amendment No. 2 to the filing, NASD Regulation is of the opinion that the proposed revisions by Sullivan and Cromwell would leave open a substantial possibility of reciprocal self-dealing among broker-dealer and owners of broker-dealers.

NASD Regulation notes that the Interpretation protects the integrity of the public offering process by ensuring that members make a bona fide public distribution at the public offering price of hot issue securities and do not withhold such securities for their own benefit or use such securities to reward other persons in the financial services business who are in a position to direct future business to the member. NASD Regulation believes the Interpretation also ensures that members of the securities industry do not take advantage of their inside position in the industry to the detriment of public investors. In light of the foregoing rationales, NASD Regulation believes that persons who own a significant percentage of a broker-dealer, *i.e.,* 10% or more, should be restricted under the Interpretation.

NASD Regulation notes that it has provided an exemption from the interpretation for persons that own 10% or more of a broker-dealer by permitting such persons to purchase hot issues for the benefit of bona fide public customers, or for an ERISA account pursuant to Paragraph (f)(3). NASD Regulation does not believe that permitting such persons to purchase hot issues for proprietary accounts, even if such hot issues directly or indirectly benefit some public shareholder, is consistent with the purposes of the Interpretation.

    1.   Banks and Industrial Companies with Broker-Dealer
        Subsidiaries and Affiliates

Sullivan and Cromwell states in its letter that it is concerned that the proposed rule change would affect the public offering market by making hot issues unavailable to many institutional customers, and in particular, banks with broker-dealer subsidiaries and affiliates. Sullivan and Cromwell observes that proposed Paragraph (b)(9) generally would prohibit the sale of hot issues to banks with broker-dealer subsidiaries and affiliates. To the extent that these banks purchase hot issues on a proprietary basis, NASD Regulation believes that the Interpretation should apply. NASD Regulation notes, however, that banks with broker-dealer subsidiaries and affiliates may purchase hot issues on behalf of bona fide public customers, pursuant to the exemption set forth in Paragraph (b)(9).

The proposed rule change also would prohibit industrial companies that own broker-dealers, such as General Electric Company ("GE") and Ford Motor Company ("Ford") from purchasing hot issues for their own account. Here again, NASD Regulation believes that this is the correct result. However, companies such as GE and Ford would be able to purchase hot issues for an account in which they have a beneficial interest, provided that such account is established for the benefit of bona fide public customers.

2. Accounts Established for the Benefit of Bona Fide Public Customers

As stated above, Paragraph (b)(a) of the proposed rule change contains an exemption for sales to the account of any person restricted under this subparagraph that is established for the benefit of bona fide public customer. Specifically, Paragraph (b)(9) states that such accounts would include "insurance company general and separate accounts." NASD Regulation included these examples because it understood that investments from such accounts are passed on directly to policy holders, *i.e.*, bona fide public customers.

The Sullivan and Cromwell letter suggests that the exemption for accounts established for the benefit of bona fide public customers applies solely to life insurance companies. As explained by NASD Regulation, it was not intended that the exemption described in Paragraph (b)(9) apply solely to life insurance companies. NASD Regulation intended that the exemption apply across all industries. Accordingly, Paragraph (b)(9)(B) of the proposed rule change has been amended. The revised language is set forth below. Additions to the provision are italicized. Language to be deleted appears in brackets.

This prohibition shall not apply to sales to the account of any person restricted under this paragraph established for the benefit of bona fide public customers, including [an] insurance company general [or], *separate and investment accounts and bank trust accounts.*

3.   Shares of a Member Traded as Part of a Holding Company

As originally proposed, Paragraph (b)(9) of the proposed rule change would exempt any person who owns any class of equity securities of, or who has made a contribution of capital to, a member, and whose ownership or capital interest is passive and is less than 10% of the equity or capital of a member, so long as such member's shares are publicly traded on an exchange or Nasdaq. Sullivan & Cromwell states that this exemption does not properly reflect the fact that many of the largest broker-dealers are subsidiaries of publicly traded holding companies and are not themselves publicly traded. NASD Regulation previously addressed this issue in Amendment No. 1 to the filing. Amendment No. 1 revises paragraph (b)(9)(A)(ii) to include within the exemption shares of a parent of a member firm that are publicly traded on an exchange or Nasdaq.

4.   Immediate Family Members

Paragraph (b)(9) applies to "any person, or to a member of the immediate family of such person." Sullivan and Cromwell states that Paragraph (b)(9) would require a member, for example Merrill Lynch, to confirm not only that its customer does not own any Merrill Lynch Parent stock, but also that none of his or her immediate family members owns any such stock. Sullivan and Cromwell also states that Paragraph (b)(9) does not exempt immediate family members who are not materially supported by the restricted person, as does Paragraph (b)(2) of the Interpretation. Sullivan and Cromwell maintains that it would be almost impossible for a broker-dealer owned by a publicly traded holding company to comply with Paragraph (b)(9) since, on its face, it would require the broker-dealer to obtain complete information regarding the securities portfolios of each of its customers' immediate family members. Proposed Paragraph (b)(9), however, is implicated only by persons who own 10% or more of a member. Nevertheless, NASD Regulation believes that the provisions regarding the immediate family members of restricted persons under proposed Paragraph (b)(9) should not be more restrictive than the provisions in Paragraph (b)(2), which pertain to associated persons of a member. NASD Regulation has therefore amended Paragraph (b)(9) so as to exclude immediate family members who are not materially supported by restricted persons. Revised Paragraph (b)(9) is set forth below. New language is italicized.

Sell any of the securities to any person, or to a member of the immediate family of such person *who is supported directly or indirectly to a material extent by such person, * * *.*

5. Miscellaneous Changes to Paragraph (b)(9)

Pursuant to Amendment No. 2, NASD Regulation also corrected an inadvertent clerical error in Paragraph (b)(9)(C) of the proposed rule change that was identified by the Sullivan and Cromwell comment later. The missing language set forth below was contained in the proposed rule change as published in NASD Notice to Members 97-30, but was omitted from the rule filing. New language is italicized. Revised Paragraph (b)(9)(C) has been amended to read as follows:

For purposes of this paragraph, any person with an equity ownership or capital interest in an entity that maintains an investment in a member shall be deemed to have a percentage interest in the member equal to the percentage interest of the entity *in the member multiplied by the percentage interest* of such person in such entity.

C. Foreign Investment Companies

Paragraphs (f) and (1)(6) of the proposed rule change would exempt foreign investment companies *i.e.,* foreign mutual funds, organized under the laws of the foreign jurisdiction, that have provided to the member a written certification prepared by counsel or an independent certified public accountant, which states that: (1) The fund has 100 or more investors; (2) the fund is listed on a foreign exchange or authorized for sale to the public by a foreign regulatory authority, (3) no more than 5% of the fund assets are to be invested in the hot issue securities being offered, and (4) any person owning more than 5% of the shares of the fund is not a restricted person.

Sullivan and Cromwell states that while it agrees that an exemption should be provided for foreign investment companies, it opposes any requirement that NASD members obtain written certification from an attorney or accountant. Sullivan and Cromwell proposes instead that NASD Regulation exempt foreign investment companies based upon their "status" under foreign regulatory regimes, for example, any fund qualified for sale under the European Union's Directive on Undertakings for Collective Investment in Transferable Securities.

In response to comments received regarding <u>Notice to Members 97-30</u>, and to alleviate the burdens associated with the written certification requirement, NASD Regulation modified proposed Paragraph (1)(6) to permit foreign, and not just U.S., attorneys and accountants to provide written certifications. NASD Regulation continues to believe, however, that written certifications are an appropriate method of determining whether a particular foreign investment company meets the criteria for exemption from the Interpretation and does not agree that this requirement should be eliminated.

Sullivan and Cromwell states in its comment letter that if written certifications are to be required, it recommends two changes. First Sullivan and Cromwell states that foreign investment companies, like registered investment companies, do not investigate the status of their shareholders and thus will be unable to comply with the requirement to certify that "any person owning more than 5% of the shares of the fund is not a person described in Paragraphs (b)(1), (2), (3), or (4) of the Rule."

NASD Regulation considered this issue in proposing the exemption for foreign investment companies but concluded that the concerns of the Interpretation that restricted persons do not indirectly purchase hot issues through foreign investment companies were paramount. Accordingly, if a foreign investment company is owned more than 5% by a person, an attorney or accountant must certify that such person is not a restricted person under the Interpretation. The attorney or accountant providing the written certification required pursuant to paragraph (1)(6) may rely upon information supplied by the foreign investment company and any shareholder that owns more than 5% of the foreign investment company. NASD Regulation is of the opinion that the shareholder is likely to cooperate with any request by the foreign investment company, or its counsel or accountant, regarding the shareholder's status under the Interpretation since the shareholder's cooperation may enhance the foreign investment company's investment opportunities by permitting it to invest in hot issues. As a practical matter, however, the requirement to determine whether a more than 5% shareholder is a restricted person is unlikely to affect many foreign investment companies because, as Sullivan and Cromwell concedes in its comment letter, each foreign investment company must have at least 100 shareholders and, consequently, it is unlikely that the interest of any one person will exceed the 5% threshold.

Second, Sullivan and Cromwell states that, as drafted, Paragraph (1)(6) of the Interpretation would require a member firm to obtain a written certification prior to each hot issue sale to a foreign investment company. Sullivan and Cromwell views this as unduly burdensome and recommends that NASD Regulation revise Paragraph (1)(6) to be consistent with Paragraph (f)(2), which states that "a written representation shall be deemed to be current if it is based upon the status of the account as of a date more than 18 months prior to the date of the transaction." NASD Regulation agrees that members should not be required to obtain a written certification before each transaction and will adopt the same standard in effect for certifications made pursuant to Paragraph (f)(2). Accordingly, the final sentence of Paragraph (f)(2) of the Interpretation shall be amended as set forth below. New language is italicized.

For purposes of this paragraph (f) *and the certification required pursuant to paragraph (1)(6)* a list or written representation shall be deemed to be current if it is based upon the status of the account as of a date not more than 18 months prior to the date of the transaction.

In addition to responding to the Sullivan and Cromwell observations, Amendment No. 2 corrected proposed Paragraph (1)(6)(D) to make the paragraph clearer and more consistent with other parts of the Interpretation. The revised paragraph is set forth below. New language is italicized. Language to be deleted from the paragraph appears in brackets.

Any person owning more than 5% of the share of the fund is not a restricted person as described in paragraph (b)(1), (2), (3), [or] (4) or (9) of the [Rule] interpretation.

D. Secondary Distributions

The proposed rule change exempts from the Interpretation secondary distributions by an issuer whose securities are actively-traded securities. Sullivan and Cromwell supports the decision to exempt secondary offerings but objects to the provision in the definition of "actively-traded securities" that excludes securities issued by the distribution participant or an affiliate of the distribution participant. NASD Regulation's proposed rule change to exempt secondary offerings was drafted to track the exemption for actively-traded securities set forth in the SEC's Regulation M. In adopting the exemption for secondary distributions, NASD Regulation was focusing on the average daily trading value and public float value provisions of Regulation M exempt securities. NASD Regulation agrees with Sullivan and Cromwell concerning secondary offerings of members or affiliates of members and proposes revising the definition of "actively-traded securities" to extend the exemption to securities issued by a distribution participant or an affiliate of the distribution participant. Paragraph (1)(7)(A), as amended, is set forth below. Language to be deleted from the paragraph appears in brackets.

Actively-traded securities means securities that have an ADTV value of at least $1 million and are issued by an issuer whose common equity securities have a public float value of at least $150 million[; provided, however, that such securities are not issued by the distribution participant or an affiliate of the distribution participant].

Finally, Sullivan Cromwell notes that Paragraph (l)(1) refers to secondary distributions "by an issuer." Sullivan and Cromwell asks whether secondary distributions by an existing security holder are subject to the Interpretation. If not, Sullivan and Cromwell recommends amending the text of proposed Paragraph (l)(1) to extend the exemption to such distributions. NASD Regulation did not intend to exclude from the exemption secondary offerings by security holders. Accordingly, it has revised Paragraph (l)(1) as set forth below. New language is italicized. Language to be deleted from the paragraph appears in brackets.

The term public offering shall exclude secondary distributions by an issuer *or any security holder of the issuer, of* [whose securities are] actively-traded securities.

IV. Conclusion

The Commission has carefully considered the comments set forth in the Sullivan and Cromwell letter. As discussed in detail above, the NASD Regulation has made a number of technical amendments to the proposal in response to the Sullivan and Cromwell letter, which the Commission believes are consistent with the spirit of the Interpretation. Indeed, the Commission believes the changes to the proposal which were made pursuant to Amendment No. 1 and No. 2 will facilitate the ability of NASD member firms to comply with the Interpretation, because the amendments further clarify the intent of the proposed rule change. For example, in response to the Sullivan and Cromwell letter, the Interpretation was amended to clarify that the exemption in paragraph (b)(9)(B) for sales to the accounts of restricted persons established for the benefit of bona fide public customers was intended to apply across all industries, as opposed to life insurance companies exclusively. Similarly, Amendment No. 1 to the proposal facilitates member firm compliance by amending the paragraph (b)(9)(A)(ii) exemption for shares of a member traded on an exchange or Nasdaq to include an exemption for shares of a member traded as a part of a holding company. This amendment fosters member firm compliance with the Interpretation by recognizing that many of the largest broker-dealers are subsidiaries of publicly traded holding companies and are not themselves publicly traded.

NASD Regulation has determined not to revise the proposal in response to Sullivan and Cromwell's suggestion that paragraph (b)(9) of the Interpretation, which with certain exceptions, prohibits sales of hit issue securities to any person who owns or has contributed capital to a broker-dealer, be revised such that it only applies to institutions engaged "principally in the broker-dealer business." The Commission agrees with NASD Regulation that such an amendment is inconsistent with the scope and intent of the proposal, because the modification would leave open a substantial possibility of self-dealing between broker-dealers and owners of broker-dealers. Accordingly, the Commission believes NASD Regulation has a sound investor protection basis for its decision not to narrow the scope of paragraph (b)(9) of the Interpretation as requested by Sullivan and Cromwell.

The Commission believes the proposed rule change, as amended, is consistent with the provisions of section 15(A)(b)(6) of the Act,[9] which provides in pertinent part that the rules of a national securities association be designed to prevent fraudulent and manipulative acts, promote just and equitable principles of trade and protect investors and the public interest. Specifically, the proposal preserves public confidence in the fairness of the investment banking and securities business by ensuring that members of the investment banking community do not unfairly benefit from public offerings by virtue of their positions as insiders, to the detriment of public investors. Preservation of investor confidence in the fairness of the markets is critical to the continued participation of all classes of securities marked participants. The Commission believes, moreover, that the proposed rule change is consistent

---

9. 15 U.S.C. 78o-3.

with section 15A(b)((9)[10] in that it will alleviate certain inequities caused by the Interpretation, which imposed burdens on competition not necessary or appropriate in furtherance of the purposes of the Act.

In approving this proposal, the Commission notes that it is has considered the proposal's impact on efficiency, competition, and capital formation.[11] The Commission believes the proposal will facilitate the capital raising process by removing restrictions and compliance burdens imposed by the Interpretation with respect to certain transactions where application of the Interpretation does not enhance investor protection or the public interest. For example, the proposal excludes from the definition of public offering secondary offerings by an issuer whose securities are actively traded securities. At the same time, the Interpretation continues to apply to those securities allocations that pose a risk of undercutting the Interpretation's objective of ensuring a bona fide distribution of hot issue securities to the public.

It is therefore ordered, pursuant to Section 19(b)(2)[12] of the Act, that the proposed rule change SR-NASD-97-95 be and hereby is approved.

For the Commission, by the Division of Market Regulation, pursuant to delegated authority.[13]

Margaret H. McFarland,
Deputy Secretary.
[FR Doc. 98-13850 Filed 5-22-98; 8:45 A.M.]
BILLING CODE 8010-01-M

---

10. 15 U.S.C. 78o-3.
11. 15 U.S.C. 78c(f).
12. 15 U.S.C. 78s(b)(2).
13. 17 CFR 200.30-3(a)(12).

98-88 UNDERWRITING COMPENSATION IN PUBLIC OFFERINGS*

Executive Summary

NASD Regulation, Inc. (NASD Regulation^{SM}) is issuing this *Notice to Members* to remind members that compensation received by members in public offerings of securities is to be determined through negotiation with the issuer offering the securities. Consistent with long-standing policy, it is conduct inconsistent with just and equitable principles of trade for any member or person associated with a member to engage, directly or indirectly, in any conduct that discourages the competitive activities of other member firms. This includes, but is not limited to, directly or indirectly engaging in any conduct that inhibits competition in the pricing of services offered by members including conduct that threatens, harasses, coerces, intimidates, or otherwise attempts improperly to influence, constrain, or inhibit the freedom of a member or person associated with a member to price its services competitively.

Questions regarding this *Notice* may be directed to Gary Goldsholle, Assistant General Counsel, Office of General Counsel, NASD Regulation, at (202) 728-8104.

Discussion

The National Association of Securities Dealers, Inc. (NASD®) Rule 2710(c) prohibits a member or person associated with a member from receiving compensation or participating in a public offering of securities if the underwriting compensation in connection with the public offering is unfair or unreasonable. NASD Regulation's Corporate Financing Department (Department) has direct responsibility for the review of underwriting compensation. The Department reviews public offerings before their effective dates and aggregates all items of value proposed to be received by underwriters and related persons. Total compensation is then reviewed and a determination is made as to whether the compensation is fair and reasonable.

The pricing of underwriting compensation, including the gross spread on offerings, is determined by the issuer and the underwriter through negotiation, subject to NASD Regulation's review to ensure that it is fair and reasonable. NASD Regulation has noted a high degree of price uniformity in gross spreads charged by underwriters in initial public offerings of corporate equity securities. NASD Regulation considers it important to remind members that there is no standard level of underwriting compensation. Prices should be determined through competition and the level of underwriter compensation on a given transaction should be the product of negotiation between the issuer and the underwriter. The exchange of current price information among competitors in this context may raise serious anti-competitive concerns. Any attempt improperly to influence another member in its pricing is a violation of NASD Rule 2110.

As set forth in IM-2110-5, it is NASD Regulation's long-standing policy that it is conduct inconsistent with just and equitable principles of trade for any member or person associated with a member to coordinate the prices of such member with any other member or associated person; to direct or request another member to alter a price; or to engage, directly or indirectly, in any conduct that threatens, harasses, coerces, intimidates, or otherwise attempts improperly to influence another member or person associated with a member. This includes, but is not limited to, any attempt to influence another member or person associated with a member to adjust or maintain a price or other conduct that retaliates against or discourages the competitive activities of another market participant. While IM-2110-5(5) specifically permits member firms to engage in any underwriting (or any syndicate for the underwriting) of securities to the extent permitted by the federal securities laws, this exclusion does not permit member firms to engage in conduct that discourages the competitive activities of other firms.

Member firms should review their practices and procedures regarding the pricing of their services in public offerings to ensure that such pricing results from appropriate negotiation with the issuer, and that conduct of the type noted above is prohibited. A finding of such conduct will result in disciplinary action. Member firms should also review their supervisory procedures regarding underwriting compensation to ensure that the requirement for free negotiation of fees is emphasized to all relevant employees and that procedures exist to identify any questionable activity.

Appendix 12

NATIONAL SECURITIES MARKETS IMPROVEMENT ACT OF 1996

AN ACT

To amend the Federal securities laws in order to promote efficiency and capital formation in the financial markets, and to amend the Investment Company Act of 1940 to promote more efficient management of mutual funds, protect investors, and provide more effective and less burdensome regulation.

Be it enacted by the Senate and House of Representatives of the United States of America in Congress assembled,

SECTION 1. SHORT TITLE; TABLE OF CONTENTS.

(a) SHORT TITLE.—This Act may be cited as the "National Securities Markets Improvement Act of 1996".

(b) TABLE OF CONTENTS.—The table of contents of this Act is as follows:

SEC. 2. DEFINITIONS.

For purposes of this Act—
(1) the term "Commission" means the Securities and Exchange Commission; and
(2) the term "State" has the same meaning as in section 3 of the Securities Exchange Act of 1934.

SEC. 3. SEVERABILITY.

If any provision of this Act, an amendment made by this Act, or the application of such provision or amendment to any person or circumstance is held to be unconstitutional, the remainder of this Act, the amendments made by this Act, and the application of the provisions of such to any person or circumstance shall not be affected thereby.

TITLE I—CAPITAL MARKETS

SEC. 101. SHORT TITLE.

This title may be cited as the "Capital Markets Efficiency Act of 1996".

SEC. 102. CREATION OF NATIONAL SECURITIES MARKETS.

(a) IN GENERAL.—Section 18 of the Securities Act of 1933 (15 U.S.C. 77r) is amended to read as follows:

"SEC. 18. EXEMPTION FROM STATE REGULATION OF SECURITIES OFFERINGS.

(a) SCOPE OF EXEMPTION. —Except as otherwise provided in this section, no law, rule, regulation, or order, or other administrative action of any State or any political subdivision thereof—

(1) requiring, or with respect to registration or qualification of securities, or registration or qualification of securities transactions, shall directly or indirectly apply to a security that—

(A) is a covered security; or

(B) will be a covered security upon completion of the transaction;

(2) shall directly or indirectly prohibit, limit, or impose any conditions upon the use of—

(A) with respect to a covered security described in subsection (b), any offering document that is prepared by or an behalf of the issuer; or

(B) any proxy statement, report to shareholders, or other disclosure document relating to a covered security or the issuer thereof that is required to be and is filed with the Commission or any national securities organization registered under section 15A of the Securities Exchange Act of 1934, except that this subparagraph does not apply to the laws, rules, regulations, or orders, or other administrative actions of the State of incorporation of the issuer; or

(3) shall directly or indirectly prohibit, limit, or impose conditions, based on the merits of such offering or issuer, upon the offer or sale of any security described in paragraph (1).

(b) COVERED SECURITIES.—For purposes of this section, the following are covered securities:

(1) EXCLUSIVE FEDERAL REGISTRATION OF NATIONALLY TRADED SECURITIES.—A security is a covered security if such security is—

(A) listed, or authorized for listing, on the New York Stock Exchange or the American Stock Exchange, or listed on the National Market System of the Nasdaq Stock Market (or any successor to such entities);

(B) listed, or authorized for listing, on a national securities exchange (or tier or segment thereof) that has listing standards that the Commission determines by rule (on its own initiative or on the basis of a petition) are substantially similar to the listing standards applicable to securities described in subparagraph (A); or

(C) is a security of the same issuer that is equal in seniority or that is a senior security to a security described in subparagraph (A) or (B).

(2) EXCLUSIVE FEDERAL REGISTRATION OF INVESTMENT COMPANIES.— A security is a covered security if such security is a security issued by an investment company that is registered, or that has filed a registration statement, under the Investment Company Act of 1940.

(3) SALES TO QUALIFIED PURCHASERS.— A security is a covered security with respect to the offer or sale of the security to qualified purchasers, as defined by the Commission by rule. In prescribing such rule, the Commission may define the term qualified purchaser' differently with respect to different categories of securities, consistent with the public interest and the protection of investors.

(4) EXEMPTION IN CONNECTION WITH CERTAIN EXEMPT OFFERINGS.— A security is a covered security with respect to a transaction that is exempt from registration under this title pursuant to—

(A) paragraph (1) or (3) of section 4, and the issuer of such security files reports with the Commission pursuant to section 13 or 15(d) of the Securities Exchange Act of 1934;

(B) section 4(4);

(C) section 3(a), other than the offer or sale of a security that is exempt from such registration pursuant to paragraph (4) or (11) of such section, except that a municipal security that is exempt from such registration pursuant to paragraph (2) of such section is not a covered security with respect to the offer or sale of such security in the State in which the issuer of such security is located; or

(D) Commission rules or regulations issued under section 4(2), except that this subparagraph does not prohibit a State from imposing notice filing requirements that are substantially similar to those required by rule or regulation under section 4(2) that are in effect on September 1, 1996.

(c) PRESERVATION OF AUTHORITY.—

(1) FRAUD AUTHORITY.—Consistent with this section, the securities commission (or any agency or office performing like functions) of any State shall retain jurisdiction under the laws of such State to investigate and bring enforcement actions with respect to fraud or deceit, or unlawful conduct by a broker or dealer, in connection with securities or securities transactions.

(2) PRESERVATION OF FILING REQUIREMENTS.—

(A) NOTICE FILINGS PERMITTED.—Nothing in this section prohibits the securities commission (or any agency or office performing like functions) of any State from requiring the filing of any document filed with the Commission pursuant to this title, together with annual or periodic reports of the value of securities sold or offered to be sold to persons located in the State (if such sales data is not included in documents filed with the Commission), solely for notice purposes and the assessment of any fee, together with a consent to service of process and any required fee.

(B) PRESERVATION OF FEES.—

(i) IN GENERAL.—Until otherwise provided by law, rule, regulation, or order, or other administrative action of any State, or any political subdivision thereof, adopted after the date of enactment of the Capital Markets Efficiency Act of 1996, filing or registration fees with respect to securities or securities transactions shall continue to be collected in amounts determined pursuant to State law as in effect on the day before such date.

(ii) SCHEDULE.—The fees required by this subparagraph shall be paid, and all necessary supporting data on sales or offers for sales required under subparagraph (A), shall be reported on the same schedule as would have been applicable had the issuer not relied on the exemption provided in subsection (a).

(C) AVAILABILITY OF PREEMPTION CONTINGENT ON PAYMENT OF FEES.—

(i) IN GENERAL.—During the period beginning on the date of enactment of the National Securities Market

Improvement Act of 1996 and ending 3 years after that date of enactment, the securities commission (or any agency or office performing like functions) of any State may require the registration of securities issued by any issuer who refuses to pay the fees required by subparagraph (B).

(ii) DELAYS.—For purposes of this subparagraph, delays in payment of fees or underpayments of fees that are promptly remedied shall not constitute a refusal to pay fees.

(D) FEES NOT PERMITTED ON LISTED SECURITIES.—Notwithstanding subparagraphs (A), (B), and (C), no filing or fee may be required with respect to any security that is a covered security pursuant to subsection (b)(1), or will be such a covered security upon completion of the transaction, or is a security of the same issuer that is equal in seniority or that is a senior security to a security that is a covered security pursuant to subsection (b)(1).

(3) ENFORCEMENT OF REQUIREMENTS.—Nothing in this section shall prohibit the securities commission (or any agency or office performing like functions) of any State from suspending the offer or sale of securities within such State as a result of the failure to submit any filing or fee required under law and permitted under this section.

(d) DEFINITIONS.—For purposes of this section, the following definitions shall apply:

(1) OFFERING DOCUMENT.—The term 'offering document'—

(A) has the meaning given the term 'prospectus' in section 2(10), but without regard to the provisions of subparagraphs (A) and (B) of that section; and

(B) includes a communication that is not deemed to offer a security pursuant to a rule of the Commission.

(2) PREPARED BY OR ON BEHALF OF THE ISSUER.—Not later than 6 months after the date of enactment of the Securities Amendments Act of 1996, the Commission shall, by rule, define the term 'prepared by or on behalf of the issuer' for purposes of this section.

(3) STATE.—The term 'State' has the same meaning as in section 3 of the Securities Exchange Act of 1934.

(4) SENIOR SECURITY.—For purposes of this paragraph, the term 'senior security' means any bond, debenture, note, or similar

obligation or instrument constituting a security and evidencing indebtedness, and any stock of a class having priority over any other class as to distribution of assets or payment of dividends."

(b) STUDY AND REPORT ON UNIFORMITY.—The Commission shall conduct a study, after consultation with States, issuers, brokers, and dealers, on the extent to which uniformity of State regulatory requirements for securities or securities transactions has been achieved for securities that are not covered securities (within the meaning of section 18 of the Securities Act of 1933, as amended by paragraph (1) of this subsection). Not later than 1 year after the date of enactment of this Act, the Commission shall submit a report to the Congress on the results of such study.

SEC. 103. BROKER-DEALER EXEMPTIONS FROM STATE LAW.

(a) IN GENERAL.—Section 15 of the Securities Exchange Act of 1934 (15 U.S.C. 78o) is amended by adding at the end the following new subsection:

(h) LIMITATIONS ON STATE LAW.—

(1) CAPITAL, MARGIN, BOOKS AND RECORDS, BONDING, AND REPORTS.—No law, rule, regulation, or order, or other administrative action of any State or political subdivision thereof shall establish capital, custody, margin, financial responsibility, making and keeping records, bonding, or financial or operational reporting requirements for brokers, dealers, municipal securities dealers, government securities brokers, or government securities dealers that differ from, or are in addition to, the requirements in those areas established under this title. The Commission shall consult periodically the securities commissions (or any agency or office performing like functions) of the States concerning the adequacy of such requirements as established under this title.

(2) DE MINIMIS TRANSACTIONS BY ASSOCIATED PERSONS.—No law, rule, regulation, or order, or other administrative action of any State or political subdivision thereof may prohibit an associated person of a broker or dealer from affecting a transaction described in paragraph (3) for a customer in such State if—

(A) such associated person is not ineligible to register with such State for any reason other than such a transaction;

(B) such associated person is registered with a registered securities association and at least one State; and

(C) the broker or dealer with which such person is associated is registered with such State.

(3) DESCRIBED TRANSACTIONS.—

(A) IN GENERAL.—A transaction is described in this paragraph if—

(i) such transaction is effected—

(I) on behalf of a customer that, for 30 days prior to the day of the transaction, maintained an account with the broker or dealer; and

(II) by an associated person of the broker or dealer—

(aa) to which the customer was assigned for 14 days prior to the day of the transaction; and

(bb) who is registered with a State in which the customer was a resident or was present for at least 30 consecutive days during the 1-year period prior to the day of the transaction;

(ii) the transaction is effected—

(I) on behalf of a customer that, for 30 days prior to the day of the transaction, maintains an account with the broker or dealer; and

(II) during the period beginning on the date on which such associated person files an application for registration with the State in which the transaction is effected and ending on the earlier of—

(aa) 60 days after the date on which the application is filed; or

(bb) the date on which such State notifies the associated person that it has denied the application for registration or has stayed the pendency of the application for cause.

(B) RULES OF CONSTRUCTION.—For purposes of subparagraph (A)(i)(II)—

(i) each of up to 3 associated persons of a broker or dealer who are designated to effect transactions during the absence or unavailability of the principal associated person for a customer may be treated as an associated person to which such customer is assigned; and

(ii) if the customer is present in another State for 30 or more consecutive days or has permanently changed his or her residence to another State, a transaction is not described in this paragraph, unless the association person of the broker or dealer files an application for registration with such State not later than 10 business days after the later of the date of the transaction, or the date of the discovery of the presence of the customer in the other State for 30 or more consecutive days or the change in the customer's residence."

(b) TECHNICAL AMENDMENT.—Section 28(a) of the Securities Exchange Act of 1934 (15 U.S.C. 78bb(a)) is amended by striking "Nothing" and inserting "Except as otherwise specifically provided in this title, nothing".

SEC. 104. BROKER-DEALER FUNDING.

(a) MARGIN REQUIREMENTS.—

(1) EXTENSIONS OF CREDIT BY BROKER-DEALERS.—Section 7(c) of the Securities Exchange Act of 1934 (15 U.S.C. 78g(c)) is amended to read as follows:

(c) UNLAWFUL CREDIT EXTENSION TO CUSTOMERS.—

(1) PROHIBITION.—It shall be unlawful for any member of a national securities exchange or any broker or dealer, directly or indirectly, to extend or maintain credit or arrange for the extension or maintenance of credit to or for any customer—

(A) on any security (other than an exempted security), in contravention of the rules and regulations which the Board of Governors of the Federal Reserve System (hereafter in this section referred to as the 'Board') shall prescribe under subsections (a) and (b); and

(B) without collateral or on any collateral other than securities, except in accordance with such rules and regulations as the Board may prescribe—

(i) to permit under specified conditions and for a limited period any such member, broker, or dealer to maintain a credit initially extended in conformity with the rules and regulations of the Board; and

> (ii) to permit the extension or maintenance of credit in cases where the extension or maintenance of credit is not for the purpose of purchasing or carrying securities or of evading or circumventing the provisions of subparagraph (A).

(2) EXCEPTION.—This subsection and the rules and regulations issued under this subsection shall not apply to any credit extended, maintained, or arranged by a member of a national securities exchange or a broker or dealer to or for a member of a national securities exchange or a registered broker or dealer—

> (A) a substantial portion of whose business consists of transactions with persons other than brokers or dealers; or

> (B) to finance its activities as a market maker or an underwriter;

except that the Board may impose such rules and regulations, in whole or in part, on any credit otherwise exempted by this paragraph if the Board determines that such action is necessary or appropriate in the public interest or for the protection of investors."

(2) EXTENSIONS OF CREDIT BY OTHER LENDERS.—Section 7(d) of the Securities Exchange Act of 1934 (78 U.S.C. 78g(d)) is amended to read as follows:

(d) UNLAWFUL CREDIT EXTENSION IN VIOLATION OF RULES AND REGULATIONS; EXCEPTION TO APPLICATION OF RULES, ETC.—

> (1) PROHIBITION.—It shall be unlawful for any person not subject to subsection (c) to extend or maintain credit or to arrange for the extension or maintenance of credit for the purpose of purchasing or carrying any security, in contravention of such rules and regulations as the Board shall prescribe to prevent the excessive use of credit for the purchasing or carrying of or trading in securities in circumvention of the other provisions of this section. Such rules and regulations may impose upon all loans made for the purpose of purchasing or carrying securities limitations similar to those imposed upon members, brokers, or dealers by subsection (c) and the rules and regulations thereunder.

> (2) EXCEPTIONS.—This subsection and the rules and regulations issued under this subsection shall not apply to any credit extended, maintained, or arranged—

(A) by a person not in the ordinary course of business;

(B) on an exempted security;

(C) to or for a member of a national securities exchange or a registered broker or dealer—

(i) a substantial portion of whose business consists of transactions with persons other than brokers or dealers; or

(ii) to finance its activities as a market maker or an underwriter;

(D) by a bank on a security other than an equity security; or

(E) as the Board shall, by such rules, regulations, or orders as it may deem necessary or appropriate in the public interest or for the protection of investors, exempt, either unconditionally or upon specified terms and conditions or for stated periods, from the operation of this subsection and the rules and regulations thereunder.

(3) BOARD AUTHORITY.—The Board may impose such rules and regulations, in whole or in part, on any credit otherwise exempted by subparagraph (C) if it determines that such action is necessary or appropriate in the public interest or for the protection of investors.".

(b) BORROWING BY MEMBERS, BROKERS, AND DEALERS.— Section 8 of the Securities Exchange Act of 1934 (15 U.S.C. 78h) is amended—

(1) by striking subsection (a); and

(2) by redesignating subsections (b) and (c) as subsections (a) and (b), respectively.

SEC. 105. EXEMPTIVE AUTHORITY.

(a) GENERAL EXEMPTIVE AUTHORITY UNDER THE SECURITIES ACT OF 1933.—Title I of the Securities Act of 1933 (15 U.S.C. 77a et seq.) is amended by adding at the end the following new section:

SEC. 28. GENERAL EXEMPTIVE AUTHORITY.

"The Commission, by rule or regulation, may conditionally or unconditionally exempt any person, security, or transaction, or any class or classes of persons, securities, or transactions, from any provision or provisions of this title or of any rule or regulation issued under this title, to the extent that such exemption is necessary or appropriate in the public interest, and is consistent with the protection of investors.

(b) GENERAL EXEMPTIVE AUTHORITY UNDER THE SECURITIES EXCHANGE ACT OF 1934.—Title I of the Securities Exchange Act of 1934 (15 U.S.C. 78a et seq.) is amended by adding at the end the following new section:

SEC. 36. GENERAL EXEMPTIVE AUTHORITY.

(a) AUTHORITY.—

(1) IN GENERAL.—Except as provided in subsection (b), but notwithstanding any other provision of this title, the Commission, by rule, regulation, or order, may conditionally or unconditionally exempt any person, security, or transaction, or any class or classes of persons, securities, or transactions, from any provision or provisions of this title or of any rule or regulation thereunder, to the extent that such exemption is necessary or appropriate in the public interest, and is consistent with the protection of investors.

(2) PROCEDURES.—The Commission shall, by rule or regulation, determine the procedures under which an exemptive order under this section shall be granted and may, in its sole discretion, decline to entertain any application for an order of exemption under this section.

(b) LIMITATION.—The Commission may not, under this section, exempt any person, security, or transaction, or any class or classes of persons, securities, or transactions from section 15C or the rules or regulations issued thereunder or (for purposes of section 15C and the rules and regulations issued thereunder) from any definition in paragraph (42), (43), (44), or (45) of section 3(a).".

SEC. 106. PROMOTION OF EFFICIENCY, COMPETITION, AND CAPITAL FORMATION.

(a) SECURITIES ACT OF 1933.—Section 2 of the Securities Act of 1933 (15 U.S.C. 77b) is amended—

(1) by inserting "(a) DEFINITIONS.—" after "Sec. 2."; and

(2) by adding at the end the following new subsection:

(b) CONSIDERATION OF PROMOTION OF EFFICIENCY, COMPETITION, AND CAPITAL FORMATION.—Whenever pursuant to this title the Commission is engaged in rulemaking and is required to consider or determine whether an action is necessary or appropriate in the public interest, the Commission shall also consider, in addition to the protection of investors, whether the action win promote efficiency, competition, and capital formation.".

(b) SECURITIES EXCHANGE ACT OF 1934.—Section 3 of the Securities Exchange Act of 1934 (15 U.S.C. 78c) is amended by adding at the end the following new subsection:

(f) CONSIDERATION OF PROMOTION OF EFFICIENCY, COMPETITION, AND CAPITAL FORMATION.—Whenever pursuant to this title the Commission is engaged in rulemaking, or in the review of a rule of a self-regulatory organization, and is required to consider or determine whether an action is necessary or appropriate in the public interest, the Commission shall also consider, in addition to the protection of investors, whether the action will promote efficiency, competition, and capital formation.".

(c) INVESTMENT COMPANY ACT OF 1940.—Section 2 of the Investment Company Act of 1940 (15 U.S.C. 80a-2) is amended by adding at the end the following new subsection:

(c) CONSIDERATION OF PROMOTION OF EFFICIENCY, COMPETITION, AND CAPITAL FORMATION.—Whenever pursuant to this title the Commission is engaged in rulemaking and is required to consider or determine whether an action is consistent with the public interest, the Commission shall also consider, in addition to the protection of investors, whether the action will promote efficiency, competition, and capital formation.".

SEC. 107. PRIVATIZATION OF EDGAR

(a) EXAMINATION.—The Commission shall examine proposals for the privatization of the EDGAR system. Such examination shall promote competition in the automation and rapid collection and dissemination of information required to be disclosed. Such examination shall include proposals that maintain free public access to data filings in the EDGAR system.

(b) REPORT.—Not later than 180 days after the date of enactment of this Act, the Commission shall submit to the Congress a report on the examination under subsection (a). Such report shall include such recommendations for such legislative action as may be necessary to implement the proposal that the Commission determines most effectively achieves the objectives described in subsection (a).

SEC. 108. IMPROVING COORDINATION OF SUPERVISION.

Section 17 of the Securities Exchange Act of 1934 (15 U.S.C, 78q) is amended by adding at the end the following new subsection:

(i) COORDINATION OF EXAMINING AUTHORITIES.—

(1) ELIMINATION OF DUPLICATION.—The Commission and the examining authorities, through cooperation and coordination of examination and oversight activities, shall eliminate any unnecessary and burdensome duplication in the examination process.

(2) COORDINATION OF EXAMINATIONS.—The Commission and the examining authorities shall share such information, including reports of examinations customer complaint information, and other nonpublic regulatory information, as appropriate to foster a coordinated approach to regulatory oversight of brokers and dealers that are subject to examination by more than one examining authority.

(3) EXAMINATIONS FOR CAUSE.—At any time, any examining authority may conduct an examination for cause of any broker or dealer subject to its jurisdiction.

(4) CONFIDENTIALITY.—

(A) IN GENERAL.—Section 24 shall apply to the sharing of information in accordance with this subsection. The Commission shall take appropriate action under section 24(c) to ensure that such information is not inappropriately disclosed.

(B) APPROPRIATE DISCLOSURE NOT PROHIBITED.—Nothing in this paragraph authorizes the Commission or any examining authority to withhold information from the Congress, or prevent the Commission or any examining authority from complying with a request for information from any other Federal department or agency requesting the information for purposes within the scope of its jurisdiction, or complying with an order of a court of the United States in an action brought by the United States or the Commission.

(5) DEFINITION.—For purposes of this subsection, the term 'examining authority' means a self-regulatory organization registered with the Commission under this title (other than a registered clearing agency) with the authority to examine, inspect, and otherwise oversee the activities of a registered broker or dealer.".

SEC. 109. INCREASED ACCESS TO FOREIGN BUSINESS INFORMATION.

Not later than 1 year after the date of enactment of this Act, the Commission shall adopt rules under the Securities Act of 1933 concerning the status under the registration provisions of the Securities Act of 1933 of foreign press conferences and foreign press releases by persons engaged in the offer and sale of securities.

TITLE II—INVESTMENT COMPANY ACT AMENDMENTS

SEC. 201. SHORT TITLE.

This title may be cited as the "Investment Company Act Amendments of 1996".

SEC. 202. FUNDS OF FUNDS.

Section 12(d)(1) of the Investment Company Act of 1940 (15 U.S.C. 80a-12(d)(1)) is amended—

(1) in subparagraph (E)(iii)—

(A) by striking "in the event such investment company is not a registered investment company,"; and

(B) by inserting "in the event that such investment company is not a registered investment company," after

(2) by redesignating subparagraphs (G) and (H) as subparagraphs (H) and (I), respectively;

(3) by striking "this paragraph (1)" each place that term appears and inserting "this paragraph";

(4) by inserting after subparagraph (F) the following new subparagraph:

"(G)(i) paragraph does not apply to securities of a registered open-end investment company or a registered unit investment trust (hereafter in this subparagraph referred to as the 'acquired company') purchased or otherwise acquired by a registered open-end investment company or a registered unit investment trust (hereafter in this subparagraph referred to as the 'acquiring company') if—

(I) the acquired company and the acquiring company are part of the same group of investment companies;

(II) the securities of the acquired company, securities of other registered open-end investment companies and registered unit investment trusts that are part of the same group of investment companies, Government securities, and short-term paper are the only investments held by the acquiring company;

(III) with respect to—

(aa) securities of the acquired company, the acquiring company does not pay and is not assessed any charges or fees for distribution-related activities, unless the acquiring company does not charge a sales load or other fees or charges for distribution-related activities; or

(bb) securities of the acquiring company, any sales loads and other distribution-related fees charged, when aggregated with any sales load and distribution-related fees paid by the acquiring company with respect to securities of the acquired fund, are not excessive under rules adopted pursuant to section 22(b) or section 22(c) by a securities association registered under section 15A of the Securities Exchange Act of 1934, or the Commission;

(IV) the acquired company has a policy that prohibits it from acquiring any securities of registered open-end investment companies or registered unit investment trusts in reliance on this subparagraph or subparagraph (F); and

(V) such acquisition is not in contravention of such rules and regulations as the Commission may from time to time prescribe with respect to acquisitions in accordance with this subparagraph, as necessary and appropriate for the protection of investors.

(ii) For purposes of this subparagraph, the term 'group of investment companies' means any 2 or more registered investment companies that hold themselves out to investors as related companies for purposes of investment and investor services."; and

(5) by adding at the end the following new subparagraph:

(J) The Commission, by rule or regulation, upon its own motion or by order upon application, may conditionally or unconditionally exempt any person, security, or transaction, or any class or classes of persons, securities, or transactions from any provision of this subsection, if and to the extent that such exemption is consistent with the public interest and the protection of investors."

SEC. 203. FLEXIBLE REGISTRATION OF SECURITIES.

(a) AMENDMENTS TO REGISTRATION STATEMENTS.—Section 24(e) of the Investment Company Act of 1940 (15 U.S.C. 80a-24(e)) is amended—

(1) by striking paragraphs (1) and (2);

(2) by striking "(3) For" and inserting "For"; and

(3) by striking "pursuant to this subsection or otherwise".

(b) REGISTRATION OF INDEFINITE AMOUNT OF SECURITIES.—Section 24(f) of the Investment Company Act of 1940 (15 U.S.C. 80a-24(f)) is amended to read as follows:

(f) REGISTRATION OF INDEFINITE AMOUNT OF SECURITIES.—

(1) REGISTRATION OF SECURITIES.—Upon the effective date of its registration statement, as provided by section 8 of the Securities Act of 1933, a face-amount certificate company, open-end management company, or unit investment trust, shall be deemed to have registered an indefinite amount of securities.

(2) PAYMENT OF REGISTRATION FEES.—Not later than 90 days after the end of the fiscal year of a company or trust referred to in paragraph (1), the company or trust, as applicable, shall pay a registration fee to the Commission, calculated in the manner specified in section 6(b) of the Securities Act of 1933, based on the aggregate sales price for which its securities (including, for purposes of this paragraph, all securities issued pursuant to a dividend reinvestment plan) were sold pursuant to a registration of an indefinite amount of securities under this subsection during the previous fiscal year of the company or trust, reduced by—

(A) the aggregate redemption or repurchase price of the securities of the company or trust during that year; and

(B) the aggregate redemption or repurchase price of the securities of the company or trust during any prior fiscal year ending not more than 1 year before the date of enactment of the Investment Company Act Amendments of 1996, that were not used previously by the company or trust to reduce fees payable under this section.

(3) INTEREST DUE ON LATE PAYMENT.—A company or trust paying the fee required by this subsection or any portion thereof more than 90 days after the end of the fiscal year of the company or trust shall pay to the Commission interest on unpaid amounts, at the average investment rate for Treasury tax and loan accounts published by the Secretary of the Treasury pursuant to section 3717(a) of title 31, United States Code. The payment of interest pursuant to this paragraph shall not preclude the Commission from bringing an action to enforce the requirements of paragraph (2).

(4) RULEMAKING AUTHORITY.—The Commission may adopt rules and regulations to implement this subsection."

(c) EFFECTIVE DATE.—The amendments made by this section shall become effective on the earlier of—

(1) 1 year after the date of enactment of this Act; or

(2) the effective date of final rules or regulations issued in accordance with section 24(f) of the Investment Company Act of 1940, as amended by this section.

SEC. 204. FACILITATING USE OF CURRENT INFORMATION IN ADVERTISING.

Section 24 of the Investment Company Act of 1940 (15 U.S.C. 80a-24) is amended by adding at the end the following new subsection:

"(g) ADDITIONAL PROSPECTUSES.—In addition to any prospectus permitted or required by section 10(a) of the Securities Act of 1933, the Commission shall permit, by rules or regulations deemed necessary or appropriate in the public interest or for the protection of investors, the use of a prospectus for purposes of section 5(b)(1) of that Act with respect to securities issued by a registered investment company. Such a prospectus, which may include information the substance of which is not included in the prospectus specified in section 10(a) of the Securities Act of 1933, shall be deemed to be permitted by section 10(b) of that Act."

SEC. 205. VARIABLE INSURANCE CONTRACTS.

(a) UNIT INVESTMENT TRUST TREATMENT.—Section 26 of the Investment Company Act of 1940 (15 U.S.C. 80a-26) is amended by adding at the end the following new subsection:

"(e) EXEMPTION.—

(1) IN GENERAL.—Subsection (a) does not apply to any registered separate account funding variable insurance contracts, or to the sponsoring insurance company and principal underwriter of such account.

(2) LIMITATION ON SALES.—It shall be unlawful for any registered separate account funding variable insurance contracts, or for the sponsoring insurance company of such account, to sell any such contract—

(A) unless the fees and charges deducted under the contract, in the aggregate, are reasonable in relation to the services rendered, the expenses expected to be incurred, and the risks assumed by the insurance company, and, beginning on the earlier of August 1, 1997, or the earliest effective date of any registration statement or amendment thereto for such contract following the date of enactment of this subsection, the insurance company so represents in the registration statement for the contract; and

(B) unless the insurance company—

(i) complies with all other applicable provisions of this section, as if it were a trustee or custodian of the registered separate account;

(ii) files with the insurance regulatory authority of the State which is the domiciliary State of the insurance company, an annual statement of its financial condition, which most recent statement indicates that the insurance company has a combined capital and surplus, if a stock company, or an unassigned surplus, if a mutual company, of not less than $1,000,000, or such other amount as the Commission may from time to time prescribe by rule, as necessary or appropriate in the public interest or for the protection of investors; and

(iii) together with its registered separate accounts, is supervised and examined periodically by the insurance authority of such State.

(3) FEES AND CHARGES.—For purposes of paragraph (2), the fees and charges deducted under the contract shall include all fees and charges imposed for any purpose and in any manner.

(4) REGULATORY AUTHORITY.—The Commission may issue such rules and regulations to carry out paragraph (2)(A) as it determines are necessary or appropriate in the public interest or for the protection of investors."

(b) PERIODIC PAYMENT PLAN TREATMENT.—Section 27 of the Investment Company Act of 1940 (15 U.S.C. 80a-27) is amended by adding at the end the following new subsection:

"(i)(1) This section does not apply to any registered separate account funding variable insurance contracts, or to the sponsoring insurance company and principal underwriter of such account, except as provided in paragraph (2).

(2) It shall be unlawful for any registered separate account funding variable insurance contracts, or for the sponsoring insurance company of such account, to sell any such contract unless—

(A) such contract is a redeemable security; and

(B) the insurance company complies with section 26(e)

and any rules or regulations issued by the Commission under section 26(e)."

SEC. 206. REPORTS TO THE COMMISSION AND SHAREHOLDERS.

Section 30 of the Investment Company Act of 1940 (15 U.S.C. 80a-29) is amended—

(1) in subsection (b), by striking paragraph (1) and inserting the following:

"(1) such information, documents, and reports (other than financial statements), as the Commission may require to keep reasonably current the information and documents contained in the registration statement of such company filed under this title;"

(2) by redesignating subsections (c), (d), (e), and (f) as subsections (d), (e), (g), and (h), respectively;

(3) by inserting after subsection (b) the following new subsection:

"(c)(1) The Commission shall take such action as it deems necessary or appropriate, consistent with the public interest and the protection of investors, to avoid unnecessary reporting by, and minimize the compliance burdens on, registered investment companies and their affiliated persons in exercising its authority—

      (A) under subsection (f); and

      (B) under subsection (b)(1), if the Commission requires the filing of information, documents, and reports under that subsection on a basis more frequently than semiannually.

    (2) Action taken by the Commission under paragraph (1) shall include considering, and requesting public comment on—

      (A) feasible alternatives that minimize the reporting burdens on registered investment companies; and

      (B) the utility of such information, documents, and reports to the Commission in relation to the costs to registered investment companies and their affiliated persons of providing such information, documents, and reports.";

    (4) by inserting after subsection (e) (as redesignated by paragraph (2) of this section), the following new subsection:

"(f) The Commission may, by rule, require that semiannual reports containing the information set forth in subsection (e) include such other information as the Commission deems necessary or appropriate in the public interest or for the protection of investors."; and

    (5) in subsection (g) (as redesignated by paragraph (2) of this section), by striking "subsections (a) and (d) and inserting "subsections (a) and (e)."

SEC. 207. BOOKS, RECORDS, AND INSPECTIONS.

    Section 31 of the Investment Company Act of 1940 (15 U.S.C. 80a-30) is amended—

    (1) by striking subsections (a) and (b) and inserting the following:

"(a) MAINTENANCE OF RECORDS.

    (1) IN GENERAL.—Each registered investment company, and each underwriter, broker, dealer, or investment adviser that is a majority-owned subsidiary of such a company, shall maintain and preserve such records (as defined in section 3(a)(37) of the Securities Exchange Act of 1934) for such period or periods as the Commission, by rules and regulations, may prescribe as necessary or appropriate in the public interest or for the protection of investors.

Each investment adviser that is not a majority-owned subsidiary of, and each depositor of any registered investment company, and each principal underwriter for any registered investment company other than a closed-end company, shall maintain and preserve for such period or periods as the Commission shall prescribe by rules and regulations, such records as are necessary or appropriate to record such person's transactions with such registered company.

(2) MINIMIZING COMPLIANCE BURDEN.—In exercising its authority under this subsection, the Commission shall take such steps as it deems necessary or appropriate, consistent with the public interest and for the protection of investors, to avoid unnecessary recordkeeping by, and minimize the compliance burden on, persons required to maintain records under this subsection (hereafter in this section referred to as 'subject persons'). Such steps shall include considering, and requesting public comment on—

(A) feasible alternatives that minimize the recordkeeping burdens on subject persons;

(B) the necessity of such records in view of the public benefits derived from the independent scrutiny of such records through Commission examination;

(C) the costs associated with maintaining the information that would be required to be reflected in such records; and

(D) the effects that a proposed recordkeeping requirement would have on internal compliance policies and procedures.

(b) EXAMINATIONS OF RECORDS.—

(1) IN GENERAL.—All records required to be maintained and preserved in accordance with subsection (a) shall be subject at any time and from time to time to such reasonable periodic, special, and other examinations by the Commission, or any member or representative thereof, as the Commission may prescribe.

(2) AVAILABILITY.—For purposes of examinations referred to in paragraph (1), any subject person shall make available to the Commission or its representatives any copies or extracts from such records as may be prepared without undue effort, expense, or delay as the Commission or its representatives may reasonably request.

(3) COMMISSION ACTION.—The Commission shall exercise its authority under this subsection with due regard for the benefits of internal compliance policies and procedures and the effective implementation and operation thereof";

(2) by redesignating subsections (c) and (d) as subsections (e) and (f), respectively;

(3) by inserting after subsection (b) the following new subsections:

"(c) LIMITATIONS ON DISCLOSURE BY COMMISSION.—Notwithstanding any other provision of law, the Commission shall not be compelled to disclose any internal compliance or audit records, or information contained therein, provided to the Commission under this section. Nothing in this subsection shall authorize the Commission to withhold information from the Congress or prevent the Commission from complying with a request for information from any other Federal department or agency requesting the information for purposes within the scope of the jurisdiction of that department or agency, or complying with an order of a court of the United States in an action brought by the United States or the Commission. For purposes of section 552 of title 5, United States Code, this section shall be considered a statute described in subsection (b)(3)(B) of such section 552.

(d) DEFINITIONS.—For purposes of this section—

(1) the term 'internal compliance policies and procedures' means policies and procedures designed by subject persons to promote compliance with the Federal securities laws; and

(2) the term 'internal compliance and audit record' means any record prepared by a subject person in accordance with internal compliance policies and procedures.";

(4) in subsection (e), as redesignated, by inserting "Regulatory Authority.—" before "The Commission"; and

(5) in subsection (f), as redesignated, by inserting "Exemption Authority.—" before 'The Commission".

SEC. 208. PROHIBITION ON DECEPTIVE INVESTMENT COMPANY NAMES.

Section 35(d) of the Investment Company Act of 1940 (15 U.S.C. 80a-34(d)) is amended to read as follows:

"(d) DECEPTIVE OR MISLEADING NAMES.—It shall be unlawful for any registered investment company to adopt as a part of the name or title of such company, or of any securities of which it is the issuer, any word or words that the Commission finds are materially deceptive or misleading. The Commission is authorized, by rule, regulation, or order, to define such names or titles as are materially deceptive or misleading."

SEC. 209. AMENDMENTS TO DEFINITIONS.

(a) EXCEPTED INVESTMENT COMPANIES.—Section 3(c) of the Investment Company Act of 1940 (15 U.S.C. 80a-3(c)) is amended—

(1) In paragraph (1), by inserting after the first sentence the following: "Such issuer shall be deemed to be an investment company for purposes of the limitations set forth in subparagraphs (A)(i) and (B)(i) of section 12(d)(1) governing the purchase or other acquisition by such issuer of any security issued by any registered investment company and the sale of any security issued by any registered open-end investment company to any such issuer.";

(2) in subparagraph (A) of paragraph (1)—

(A) by inserting after "issuer," the first place that term appears, the following: "and is or, but for the exception provided for in this paragraph or paragraph (7), would be an investment company, and

(B) by striking "unless, as of" and all that follows through the end of the subparagraph and inserting a period;

(3) in paragraph (2)—

(A) by striking "and acting as broker," and inserting acting as broker, and acting as market intermediary,";

(B) by inserting "A" after "(2)"; and

(C) by adding at the end the following new subparagraph: "(B) For purposes of this paragraph—

(i) the term 'market intermediary' means any person that regularly holds itself out as being willing contemporaneously to engage in, and that is regularly engaged in, the business of entering into transactions on both sides of the market for a financial contract or one or more such financial contracts; and

(ii) the term 'financial contract' means any arrangement that—

(I) takes the form of an individually negotiated contract, agreement, or option to buy, sell, lend, swap, or repurchase, or other similar individually negotiated transaction commonly entered into by participants in the financial markets;

(II) is in respect of securities, commodities, currencies, interest or other rates, other measures of value, or any other financial or economic interest similar in purpose or function to any of the foregoing, and

(III) is entered into in response to a request from a counter party for a quotation, or is otherwise entered into and structured to accommodate the objectives of the counter party to such arrangement."; and

(4) by striking paragraph (7) and inserting the following:

"(7)(A) Any issuer, the outstanding securities of which are owned exclusively by persons who, at the time of acquisition of such securities, are qualified purchasers, and which is not making and does not at that time propose to make a public offering of such securities. Securities that are owned by persons who received the securities from a qualified purchaser as a gift or bequest, or in a case in which the transfer was caused by legal separation, divorce, death, or other involuntary event, shall be deemed to be owned by a qualified purchaser, subject to such rules, regulations, and orders as the Commission may prescribe as necessary or appropriate in the public interest or for the protection of investors.

(B) Notwithstanding subparagraph (A), an issuer is within the exception provided by this paragraph if—

(i) in addition to qualified purchasers, outstanding securities of that issuer are beneficially owned by not more than 100 persons who are not qualified purchasers, if—

(I) such persons acquired any portion of the securities of such issuer on or before September 1, 1996; and

(II) at the time at which such persons initially acquired the securities of such issuer, the issuer was excepted by paragraph (1); and

(ii) prior to availing itself of the exception provided by this paragraph—

(I) such issuer has disclosed to each beneficial owner, as determined under paragraph (1), that future investors will be limited to qualified purchasers, and that ownership in such issuer is no longer limited to not more than 100 persons; and

(II) concurrently with or after such disclosure, such issuer has provided each beneficial owner, as determined under paragraph (1), with a reasonable opportunity to redeem any part or all of their interests in the issuer, notwithstanding any agreement to the contrary between the issuer and such persons, for that person's proportionate share of the issuer's net assets.

(C) Each person that elects to redeem under subparagraph (B)(ii)(II) shall receive an amount in cash equal to that person's proportionate share of the issuer's net assets, unless the issuer elects to provide such person with the option of receiving, and such person agrees to receive, all or a portion of such person's share in assets of the issuer. If the issuer elects to provide such persons with such an opportunity, disclosure concerning such an opportunity shall be made in the disclosure required by subparagraph (B)(ii)(I).

(D) An issuer that is excepted under this paragraph shall nonetheless be deemed to be an investment company for purposes of the limitations set forth in subparagraphs (A)(i) and (B)(i) of section 12(d)(1) relating to the purchase or other acquisition by such issuer of any security issued by any registered investment company and the sale of any security issued by any registered open-end investment company to any such issuer.

(E) For purposes of determining compliance with this paragraph and paragraph (1), an issuer that is otherwise excepted under this paragraph and an issuer that is otherwise excepted under paragraph (1) shall not be treated by the Commission as being a single issuer for purposes of determining whether the outstanding securities of the issuer excepted under paragraph (1) are beneficially owned by not more than 100 persons or whether the outstanding securities of the issuer excepted under this paragraph are owned by persons that are not qualified purchasers. Nothing in this subparagraph shall be construed to establish that a person is a bona fide qualified purchaser for purposes of this paragraph or a bona fide beneficial owner for purposes of paragraph (1)."

(b) QUALIFIED PURCHASER.—Section 2(a) of the Investment Company Act of 1940 (15 U.S.C. 80a2(a)) is amended by adding at the end the following new paragraph:

"(51)(A) 'Qualified purchaser' means—

(i) any natural person (including any person who holds a joint, community property, or other similar shared ownership interest in an issuer that is excepted under section 3(c)(7) with that person's qualified purchaser spouse) who owns not less than $5,000,000 in investments, as defined by the Commission;

(ii) any company that owns not less than $5,000,000 in investments and that is owned directly or indirectly by or for 2 or more natural persons who are related as siblings or spouse (including former spouses), or direct lineal descendants by birth or adoption, spouses of such persons, the estates of such persons, or foundations, charitable organizations, or trusts established by or for the benefit of such persons;

(iii) any trust that is not covered by clause (ii) and that was not formed for the specific purpose of acquiring the securities offered, as to which the trustee or other person authorized to make decisions with respect to the trust, and each settlor or other person who has contributed assets to the trust, is a person described in clause (i), (ii), or (iv); or

(iv) any person, acting for its own account or the accounts of other qualified purchasers, who in the aggregate owns and invests on a discretionary basis, not less than $25,000,000 in investments.

(B) The Commission may adopt such rules and regulations applicable to the persons and trusts specified in clauses (i) through (iv) of subparagraph (A) as it determines are necessary or appropriate in the public interest or for the protection of investors.

(C) The term 'qualified purchaser' does not include a company that, but for the exceptions provided for in paragraph (1) or (7) of section 3(c), would be an investment company (hereafter in this paragraph referred to as an 'excepted investment company'), unless all beneficial owners of its outstanding securities (other than short-term paper), determined in accordance with section 3(c)(1)(A), that acquired such securities on or before April 30, 1996 (hereafter in this paragraph referred to as 'pre-amendment beneficial owners'), and all pre-amendment beneficial owners of the outstanding securities (other than short-term paper) of any excepted investment company that, directly or indirectly, owns any outstanding securities of such excepted investment company, have consented to its treatment as a qualified purchaser. Unanimous consent of all trustees, directors, or general partners of a company or trust referred to in clause (h) or (iii) of subparagraph (A) shall constitute consent for purposes of this subparagraph."

(c) CONFORMING AMENDMENTS.—Section 3(a) of The Investment Company Act of 1940 (15 U.S.C. 80a3(a)) is amended—

(1) by striking "(1)" and inserting "(A)";

(2) by striking "(2)" and inserting "(B)";

(3) by striking "(3)" and inserting "(C)";

(4) by inserting "(1)" after "(a)";

(5) by striking "As used" and inserting "(2) As used"; and

(6) in paragraph (2)(C), as designated by paragraph (5) of this subsection—

(A) by striking "which are" and inserting the following: "which (i) are"; and

(B) by inserting before the period at the end, the following: ", and (ii) are not relying on the exception from the definition of investment company in paragraph (1) or (7) of subsection (c)".

(d) RULEMAKING REQUIRED.—

(1) IMPLEMENTATION OF SECTION 3(C)(1)(B).—Not later than 1 year after the date of enactment of this Act, the Commission shall prescribe rules to implement the requirements of section 3(c)(1)(13) of the Investment Company Act of 1940 (15 U.S.C. 80a–3(c)(1) (B)), as amended by this section.

(2) IDENTIFICATION OF INVESTMENTS.—Not later than 180 days after the date of enactment of this Act, the Commission shall prescribe rules defining the term, or otherwise identifying, "investments" for purposes of section 2(a)(51) of the Investment Company Act of 1940, as added by this Act.

SEC. 302. FUNDING FOR ENHANCED ENFORCEMENT PRIORITY.

There are authorized to be appropriated to the Commission, for the enforcement of the Investment Advisers Act of 1940, not more than $20,000,000 in each of fiscal years 1997 and 1998, in addition to any funds authorized to be appropriated to the Commission for this or other purposes.

SEC. 303. IMPROVED SUPERVISION THROUGH STATE AND FEDERAL COOPERATION.

(a) STATE AND FEDERAL RESPONSIBILITIES.—The Investment Advisers Act of 1940 (15 U.S.C. 80b–1 et seq.) is amended by inserting after section 203 the following new section:

SEC. 203A. STATE AND FEDERAL RESPONSIBILITIES.

(a) ADVISERS SUBJECT TO STATE AUTHORITIES.—

(1) IN GENERAL.—No investment adviser that is regulated or required to be regulated as an investment adviser in the State in which it maintains its principal office and place of business shall register under section 203, unless the investment adviser—

(A) has assets under management of not less than $25,000,000, or such higher amount as the Commission may, by rule, deem appropriate in accordance with the purposes of this title; or

(B) is an adviser to an investment company registered under title I of this Act.

(2) DEFINITION.—For purposes of this subsection, the term assets under management means the securities portfolios with respect to which an investment adviser provides continuous an regular supervisory or management services.

(b) ADVISERS SUBJECT TO COMMISSION AUTHORITY.—

(1) IN GENERAL.—No law of any State or political subdivision thereof requiring the registration, licensing, or qualification as an investment adviser or supervised person of an investment adviser shall apply to any person—

(A) that is registered under section 203 as an investment adviser, or that is a supervised person of such person, except that a State may license, register, or otherwise qualify any investment adviser representative who has a place of business located within that State; or

(B) that is not registered under section 203 because that person is excepted from the definition of an investment adviser under section 202(a)(11).

(2) LIMITATION.—Nothing in this subsection shall prohibit the securities commission (or any agency or office performing like

functions) of any State from investigating and bringing enforcement actions with respect to fraud or deceit against an investment adviser or person associated with an investment adviser.

(c) EXEMPTIONS.—Notwithstanding subsection (a), the Commission, by rule or regulation upon its own motion, or by order upon application, may permit the registration with the Commission of any person or class of persons to which the application of subsection (a) would be unfair, a burden on interstate commerce, or otherwise inconsistent with the purposes of this section.

(d) FILING DEPOSITORIES.—The Commission may, by rule, require an investment adviser—

(3) EMPLOYEE EXCEPTION.—Not later than 1 year after the date of enactment of this Act, the Commission shall prescribe rules pursuant to its authority under section 6 of the Investment Company Act of 1940 to permit the ownership of securities by knowledgeable employees of the issuer of the securities or an affiliated person without loss of the exception of the issuer under paragraph (1) or (7) of section 3(c) of that Act from treatment as an investment company under that Act.

(4) BENEFICIAL OWNERSHIP.—Not later than 180 days after the date of enactment of this Act, the Commission shall prescribe rules defining the term "beneficial owner" for purposes of section 3(c)(7)(B) of the Investment Company Act of 1940, as amended by this Act.

(e) EFFECTIVE DATE.—The amendments made by this section shall take effect on the earlier of—

(1) 180 days after the date of enactment of this Act; or

(2) the date on which the rulemaking required under subsection (d)(2) is completed.

SEC. 210. PERFORMANCE FEES EXEMPTIONS.

Section 205 of the Investment Advisers Act of 1940 (15 U.S.C. 80b-5) is amended—

(1) in subsection (b)—

(A) in paragraph (2), by striking "or" at the end;

(B) in paragraph (3), by striking the period at the end and inserting a semicolon; and

(C) by adding at the end the following new paragraphs:

"(4) apply to an investment advisory contract with a company excepted from the definition of an investment company under section 3(c)(7) of title I of this Act; or

(5) apply to an investment advisory contract with a person who is not a resident of the United States."; and

(2) by adding at the end the following new subsection:

"(e) The Commission, by rule or regulation, upon its own motion, or by order upon application, may conditionally or unconditionally exempt any person or transaction, or any class or classes of persons or transactions, from subsection (a)(1), if and to the extent that the exemption relates to an investment advisory contract with any person that the Commission determines does not need the protections of subsection (a)(1), on the basis of such factors as financial sophistication, net worth, knowledge of and experience in financial matters, amount of assets under management, relationship with a registered investment adviser, and such other factors as the Commission determines are consistent with this section."

TITLE III—INVESTMENT ADVISERS SUPERVISION COORDINATION ACT

SEC. 301. SHORT TITLE.

This title may be cited as the "Investment Advisers Supervision Coordination Act."

"(1) to file with the Commission any fee, application, report, or notice required by this title or by the rules issued under this title through any entity designated by the Commission for that purpose; and

(2) to pay the reasonable costs associated with such filing.

(e) STATE ASSISTANCE.—Upon request of the securities commissioner (or any agency or officer performing like functions) of any State, the Commission may provide such training, technical assistance, or other reasonable assistance in connection with the regulation of investment advisers by the State."

(b) ADVISERS NOT ELIGIBLE TO REGISTER.—Section 203 of the Investment Advisers Act of 1940 (15 U.S.C. 80b-3) is amended—

(1) in subsection (c), in the matter immediately following paragraph (2), by inserting "and that the applicant is not prohibited from

registering as an investment adviser under section 203A" after "satisfied"; and

    (2) in subsection (h), in the second sentence—

        (A) by striking "existence or" and inserting "existence,"; and

        (B) by inserting "or is prohibited from registering as an investment adviser under section 203A," after "adviser,".

    (c) DEFINITION OF "SUPERVISED PERSON".—Section 202(a) of the Investment Advisers Act of 1940 (15 U.S.C. 80b-2(a)) is amended—

    (1) by striking "requires—" and inserting "requires, the following definitions shall apply:"; and

    (2) by adding at the end the following new paragraph:

    "(25) 'Supervised person' means any partner, officer, director (or other person occupying a similar status or performing similar functions), or employee of an investment adviser, or other person who provides investment advice on behalf of the investment adviser and is subject to the supervision and control of the investment adviser."

    (d) CONFORMING AMENDMENT.—Section 203(a) of the Investment Advisers Act of 1940 (15 U.S.C. 80b-3(a)) is amended by striking "subsection (b) of this section" and inserting "subsection (b) and section 203A."

SEC. 304. INTERSTATE COOPERATION.

Section 222 of the Investment Advisers Act of 1940 (15 U.S.C. 80b–18a) is amended to read as follows:

SEC. 222. STATE REGULATION OF INVESTMENT ADVISERS.

"(a) JURISDICTION OF STATE REGULATORS.—Nothing in this title shall affect the jurisdiction of the securities commissioner (or any agency or officer performing like functions) of any State over any security or any person insofar as it does not conflict with the provisions of this title or the rules and regulations thereunder.

    (b) DUAL COMPLIANCE PURPOSES.—No State may enforce any law or regulation that would require an investment adviser to maintain any books or records in addition to those required under the laws of the

State in which it maintains its principal place of business, if the investment adviser—

    (1) is registered or licensed as such in the State in which it maintains its principal place of business; and

    (2) is in compliance with the applicable books and records requirements of the State in which it maintains its principle place of business.

    (c) LIMITATION ON CAPITAL AND BOND REQUIREMENTS.—No State may enforce any law or regulation that would require an investment adviser to maintain a higher minimum net capital or to post any bond in addition to any that is required under the laws of the State in which it maintains its principal place of business, if the investment adviser—

    (1) is registered or licensed as such in the State in which it maintains its principal place of business; and

    (2) is in compliance with the applicable net capital or bonding requirements of the State in which it maintains its principal place of business.

    (d) NATIONAL DE MINIMIS STANDARD.—No law of any State or political subdivision thereof requiring the registration, licensing, or qualification as an investment adviser shall require an investment adviser to register with the securities commissioner of the State (or any agency or officer performing like functions) or to comply with such law (other than any provision thereof prohibiting fraudulent conduct) if the investment adviser—

    (1) does not have a place of business located within the State; and

    (2) during the preceding 12-month period, has had fewer than 6 clients who are residents of that State."

SEC. 305. DISQUALIFICATION OF CONVICTED FELONS.

    (a) AMENDMENT.—Section 203(e) of the Investment Advisers Act of 1940 (15 U.S.C. 80b-3(e)) is amended—

    (1) by redesignating paragraphs (3) through (7) as paragraphs (4) through (8), respectively; and

    (2) by inserting after paragraph (2) the following new paragraph:

"(3) has been convicted during the 10-year period preceding the date of filing of any application for registration, or at any time thereafter, of—

(A) any crime that is punishable by imprisonment for 1 or more years, and that is not described in paragraph (2); or

(B) a substantially equivalent crime by a foreign court of competent jurisdiction."

(b) CONFORMING AMENDMENTS.—Section 203 of the Investment Advisers Act of 1940 (15 U.S.C. 80b3) is amended—

(1) in subsection (e)(6) (as redesignated by subsection (a) of this section), by striking "this paragraph (5)" and inserting "this paragraph";

(2) in subsection (f)—

(A) by striking "paragraph (1), (4), (5), or (7) of subsection (e) of this section" and inserting "paragraph (1), (5), (6), or (8) of subsection (e)";

(B) by striking "paragraph (3)" and inserting "paragraph (4)"; and

(C) by striking "said subsection" each place that term appears and inserting "subsection"; and

(3) in subsection (i)(1)(D), by striking "section 203(e)(5) of this title" and inserting "subsection (e)(6)."

SEC. 306. INVESTOR ACCESS TO INFORMATION.

The Commission shall—

(1) provide for the establishment and maintenance of a readily accessible telephonic or other electronic process to receive inquiries regarding disciplinary actions and proceedings involving investment advisers and persons associated with investment advisers; and

(2) provide for prompt response to any inquiry described in paragraph (3).

SEC. 307. CONTINUED STATE AUTHORITY.

(a) PRESERVATION OF FILING REQUIREMENTS.—Nothing in this title or any amendment made by this title prohibits the securities commission (or any agency or office performing like functions) of any State from requiring the filing of any documents filed with the Commission pursuant to the securities laws solely for notice purposes, together with a consent to service of process and any required fee.

(b) PRESERVATION OF FEES.—Until otherwise provided by law, rule, regulation, or order, or other administrative action of any State, or any political subdivision thereof, adopted after the date of enactment of this Act, filing, registration, or licensing fees shall, notwithstanding the amendments made by this title, continue to be paid in amounts determined pursuant to the law, rule, regulation, or order, or other administrative action as in effect on the day before such date of enactment.

(c) AVAILABILITY OF PREEMPTION CONTINGENT ON PAYMENT OF FEES.—

(1) IN GENERAL.—During the period beginning on the date of enactment of this Act and ending 3 years after that date of enactment, the securities commission (or any agency or office performing like functions) of any State may require registration of any investment adviser that fails or refuses to pay the fees required by subsection (b) in or to such State, notwithstanding the limitations on the laws, rules, regulations, or orders, or other administrative actions of any State, or any political subdivision thereof, contained in subsection (a), if the laws of such State require registration of investment advisers.

(2) DELAYS.—For purposes of this subsection, delays in payment of fees or underpayments of fees that are promptly remedied in accordance with the applicable laws, rules, regulations, or orders, or other administrative actions of the relevant State shall not constitute a failure or refusal to pay fees.

SEC. 308. EFFECTIVE DATE.

(a) IN GENERAL.—This title and the amendments made by this title shall take effect 180 days after the date of enactment of this Act.

(b) CONFORMING AMENDMENT.—

(1) IN GENERAL.—Section 3(38)(B) of the Employee Retirement Income Security Act of 1974 (29 U.S.C. 1002(38)(B)) is amended by inserting "or under the laws of any State" after "1940".

(2) SUNSET.—The amendment made by paragraph (1) shall cease to be effective 2 years after the date of enactment of this Act.

TITLE IV—SECURITIES AND EXCHANGE COMMISSION AUTHORIZATION

SEC. 401. SHORT TITLE.

This title may be cited as the "Securities and Exchange Commission Authorization Act of 1996".

SEC. 402. PURPOSES.

The purposes of this title are—
(1) to authorize appropriations for the Commission for fiscal year 1997; and
(2) to reduce over time the rates of fees charged under the Federal securities laws.

SEC. 403. AUTHORIZATION OF APPROPRIATIONS.

Section 35 of the Securities Exchange Act of 1934 is amended to read as follows:

SEC. 35. AUTHORIZATION OF APPROPRIATIONS.

"There are authorized to be appropriated to carry out the functions, powers, and duties of the Commission $300,000,000 for fiscal year 1997, in addition to any other funds authorized to be appropriated to the Commission.".

SEC. 404. REGISTRATION FEES.

Section 6(b) of the Securities Act of 1933 (15 U.S.C. 779b)) is amended to read as follows:
"(b) REGISTRATION FEE.—
(1) RECOVERY OF COST OF SERVICES.—The Commission shall, in accordance with this subsection, collect registration fees that are designed to recover the costs to the government of the securities registration process, and costs related to such process, including

enforcement activities, policy and rulemaking activities, administration, legal services, and international regulatory activities.

(2) FEE PAYMENT REQUIRED.—At the time of filing a registration statement, the applicant shall pay to the Commission a fee that shall be equal to the sum of the amounts (if any) determined under the rates established by paragraphs (3) and (4). The Commission shall publish in the Federal Register notices of the fee rates applicable under this section for each fiscal year.

(3) GENERAL REVENUE FEES.—The rate determined under this paragraph is a rate equal to $200 per $1,000,000 of the maximum aggregate price at which such securities are proposed to be offered, except that during fiscal year 2007 and any succeeding fiscal year such rate is equal to $67 per $1,000,000 of the maximum aggregate price at which such securities are proposed to be offered. Fees collected during any fiscal year pursuant to this paragraph shall be deposited and credited as general revenues of the Treasury.

(4) OFFSETTING COLLECTION FEES.—

(A) IN GENERAL.—Except as provided in subparagraphs (B) and (C), the rate determined under this paragraph is a rate equal to the following amount per $1,000,000 of the maximum aggregate price at which such securities are proposed to be offered:

(i) $95 during fiscal year 1998;
(ii) $78 during fiscal year 1999;
(iii) $64 during fiscal year 2000;
(iv) $50 during fiscal year 2001;
(v) $39 during fiscal year 2002;
(vi) $28 during fiscal year 2003;
(vii) $9 during fiscal year 2004;
(viii) $5 during fiscal year 2005; and
(ix) $0 during fiscal year 2006 or any succeeding fiscal year.

(B) LIMITATION; DEPOSIT.—Except as provided in subparagraph (C), no amounts shall be collected pursuant to this paragraph (4) for any fiscal year except to the extent provided in advance in appropriations Acts. Fees collected during any fiscal year pursuant to this paragraph shall be deposited and credited as offsetting collections in accordance with appropriations Acts.

(C) LAPSE OF APPROPRIATIONS.—If on the first day of a fiscal year a regular appropriation to the Commission has not been enacted, the Commission shall continue to collect fees (as offsetting collections) under this paragraph at the rate in effect during the preceding fiscal year, until such a regular appropriation is enacted.

(5) PRO RATA APPLICATION OF RATES.—The rates required by this subsection shall be applied pro rata, to amounts and balances equal to less than $1,000,000."

SEC. 405. TRANSACTION FEES.

(a) AMENDMENT.—Section 31 of the Securities Exchange Act of 1934 (15 U.S.C. 78ee) is amended to read as follows:

SEC. 31. TRANSACTION FEES.

"(a) RECOVERY OF COST OF SERVICES.—The Commission shall, in accordance with this subsection, collect transaction fees that are designed to recover the costs to the Government of the supervision and regulation of securities markets and securities professionals, and costs related to such supervision and regulation, including enforcement activities, policy and rulemaking activities, administration, legal services, and international regulatory activities.

(b) EXCHANGE-TRADED SECURITIES.—Every national securities exchange shall pay to the Commission a fee at a rate equal to $1/300$ of one percent of the aggregate dollar amount of sales of securities (other than bonds, debentures, and other evidences of indebtedness) transacted on such national securities exchange, except that for fiscal year 2007 or any succeeding fiscal year such rate shall be equal to $1/800$ of one percent of aggregate dollar amount of sales. Fees collected pursuant to this subsection shall be deposited and collected as general revenue of the Treasury.

(c) OFF-EXCHANGE TRADES OF EXCHANGE REGISTERED SECURITIES.—Each national securities association shall pay to the Commission a fee at a rate equal to $1/300$ of one percent of the aggregate dollar amount of sales transacted by or through any member of such association otherwise than on a national securities exchange of securities registered on such an exchange (other than bonds, debentures, and other evidences of indebtedness), except that for fiscal year 2007 or any succeeding fiscal year such rate shall be equal to $1/_{800}$ of one percent of such aggregate dollar amount of sales. Fees collected pursuant to this subsection shall be deposited and collected as general revenue of the Treasury.

(d) OFF-EXCHANGE TRADES OF LAST-SALE-REPORTED SECURITIES.—

(1) COVERED TRANSACTIONS.—Each national securities association shall pay to the Commission a fee at a rate equal to $1/_{300}$ of one percent of the aggregate dollar amount of sales transacted by or through any member of such association otherwise than on a national securities exchange of securities (other than bonds, debentures, and other evidences of indebtedness) subject to prompt last sale reporting pursuant to the rules of the Commission or a registered national securities association, excluding any sales for which a fee is paid under subsection (c), except that for fiscal year 2007, or any succeeding fiscal year, such rate shall be equal to $1/_{800}$ of one percent of such aggregate dollar amount of sale.

(2) LIMITATION; DEPOSIT OF FEES.—Except as provided in paragraph (3), no amounts shall be collected pursuant to subsection (d) for any fiscal year, except to the extent provided in advance in appropriations Acts. Fees collected during any such fiscal year pursuant to this subsection shall be deposited and credited as offsetting collections to the account providing appropriations to the Commission.

(3) LAPSE OF APPROPRIATIONS.—If on the first day of a fiscal year a regular appropriation to the Commission has not been enacted, the Commission shall continue to collect fees (as offsetting collections) under this subsection at the rate in effect during the preceding fiscal year, until such a regular appropriation is enacted.

(e) DATES FOR PAYMENT OF FEES.—The fees required by subsections (b), (c), and (d) of this section shall be paid—

(1) on or before March 15, with respect to transactions and sales occurring during the period beginning on the preceding September 1 and ending at the close of the preceding December 31; and

(2) on or before September 30, with respect to transactions and sales occurring during the period beginning on the preceding January 1 and ending at the close of the preceding August 31.

(f) EXEMPTIONS.—The Commission, by rule, may exempt any sale of securities or any class of sales of securities from any fee imposed by this section, if the Commission finds that such exemption is consistent with the public interest, the equal regulation of markets and brokers and dealers, and the development of a national market system.

(g) PUBLICATION.—The Commission shall publish in the Federal Register notices of the fee rates applicable under this section for each fiscal year."

(b) EFFECTIVE, DATES; TRANSITION.—

(1) IN GENERAL.—Except as provided in paragraph (2), the amendment made by subsection (a) shall apply with respect to transactions in securities that occur on or after October 1,1997.

(2) OFF-EXCHANGE TRADES OF LAST SALE REPORTED TRANSACTIONS.—The amendment made by subsection (a) shall apply with respect to transactions described in section 31(d)(1) of the Securities Exchange Act of 1934 (as amended by subsection (a) of this section) that occur on or after September 1, 1997.

SEC. 406. TIME FOR PAYMENT.

Section 4(e) of the Securities Exchange Act of 1934 (15 U.S.C. 78d(e)) is amended by inserting before the period at the end thereof the following: "and the Commission may also specify the time that such fee shall be determined and paid relative to the filing of any statement or document with the Commission".

SEC. 407. SENSE OF THE CONGRESS CONCERNING FEES.

It is the sense of the Congress that, in order to maintain the competitiveness of United States securities markets relative to foreign markets, no fee should be assessed on transactions involving portfolios of equity securities taking place at times of day characterized by low volume and during nontraditional trading hours.

TITLE V—REDUCING THE COST OF SAVING AND INVESTMENT

SEC. 501. EXEMPTION FOR ECONOMIC, BUSINESS, AND INDUSTRIAL DEVELOPMENT COMPANIES.

Section 6(a) of the Investment Company Act of 1940 (15 U.S.C. 80a-6(a)) is amended by adding at the end the following new paragraph:

"5(A) Any company that is not engaged in the business of issuing redeemable securities, the operations of which are subject to regulation by the State in which the company is organized under a statute governing entities that provide financial or managerial assistance to enterprises doing business, or proposing to do business, in that State if—

(i) the organizational documents of the company state that the activities of the company are limited to the promotion of economic, business, or industrial development in the State through the provision of financial or managerial assistance to enterprises doing business, or proposing to do business, in that State, and such other activities that are incidental or necessary to carry out that purpose;

(ii) immediately following each sale of the securities of the company by the company or any underwriter for the company, not less than 80 percent of the securities of the company being offered in such sale, on a class-by-class basis, are held by persons who reside or who have a substantial business presence in that State;

(iii) the securities of the company are sold, or proposed to be sold, by the company or by any underwriter for the company, solely to accredited investors, as that term is defined in section 2(a)(15) of the Securities Act of 1933, or to such other persons that the Commission, as necessary or appropriate in the public interest and consistent with the protection of investors, may permit by rule, regulation, or order; and

(iv) the company does not purchase any security issued by an investment company or by any company that would be an investment company except for the exclusions from the definition of the term 'investment company' under paragraph (1) or (7) of section 3(c), other than

(I) any debt security that is rated investment grade by not less than 1 nationally recognized statistical rating organization; or

(II) any security issued by a registered open-end investment company that is required by its investment policies to invest not less than 65 percent of its total assets in securities described in subclause (1) or securities that are determined by such registered open-end investment company to be comparable in quality to securities described in subclause (I).

(B) Notwithstanding the exemption provided by this paragraph, section 9 (and, to the extent necessary, enforce section 9, sections 38 through 51) shall apply to a company described in this paragraph as if the company were an investment company registered under this title.

(C) Any company proposing to rely on the exemption provided by this paragraph shall file with the Commission a notification stating that the company intends to do so, in such form and manner as the Commission may prescribe by rule.

(D) Any company meeting the requirements of this paragraph may rely on the exemption provided by this paragraph upon filing with the Commission the notification required by subparagraph (C), until such time as the Commission determines by order that such reliance is not in the public interest or is not consistent with the protection of investors.

(E) The exemption provided by this paragraph may be subject to such additional terms and conditions as the Commission may by rule, regulation, or order determine are necessary or appropriate in the public interest or for the protection of investors."

SEC. 502. INTRASTATE CLOSED-END INVESTMENT COMPANY EXEMPTION.

Section 6(d)(1) of the Investment Company Act of 1940 (15 U.S.C. 80a-6(d)(1)) is amended by striking "$100,000" and inserting "$10,000,000, or such other amount as the Commission may set by rule, regulation, or order."

SEC. 503. DEFINITION OF ELIGIBLE PORTFOLIO COMPANY.

Section 2(a)(46)(C) of the Investment Company Act of 1940 (15 U.S.C. 80a-2(a)(46)(C)) is amended—
    (1) in clause (ii), by striking "or" at the end;
    (2) by redesignating clause (iii) as clause (iv); and
    (3) by inserting after clause (ii) the following:
        "(iii) it has total assets of not more than $4,000,000, and capital and surplus (shareholders' equity less retained earnings) of not less than $2,000,000, except that the Commission may adjust such amounts by rule, regulation, or order to reflect changes in 1 or more generally accepted indices or other indicators for small businesses; or."

SEC. 504. DEFINITION OF BUSINESS DEVELOPMENT COMPANY.

Section 2(a)(48)(B) of the Investment Company Act of 1940 (15 U.S.C. 80a-2(a)(48)(B)) is amended by adding at the end the following: "provided further that a business development company need not make available significant managerial assistance with respect to any company described in paragraph (46)(C)(iii), or with respect to any other company that meets such criteria as the Commission may by rule, regulation, or order permit, as consistent with the public interest, the protection of investors, and the purposes of this title; and."

SEC. 505. ACQUISITION OF ASSETS BY BUSINESS DEVELOPMENT COMPANIES.

Section 55(a)(1)(A) of the Investment Company Act of 1940 (15 U.S.C. 80a-54(a)(1)(A)) is amended—
    (1) by striking "or from any person" and inserting "from any person"; and
    (2) by inserting before the semicolon ", or from any other person, subject to such rules and regulations as the Commission may prescribe as necessary or appropriate in the public interest or for the protection of investors."

SEC. 506. CAPITAL STRUCTURE AMENDMENTS.

Section 61(a) of the Investment Company Act of 1940 (15 U.S.C. 80a-60(a)) is amended—

(1) in paragraph (2), by striking "if such business development company" and all that follows through the end of the paragraph inserting a period;

(2) in paragraph (3)(A)—

(A) by striking "senior securities representing indebtedness accompanied by";

(B) by inserting "accompanied by securities," after "of such company,"; and

(C) in clause (ii), by striking "senior"; and

(3) in paragraph (3)—

(A) in subparagraph (A), by striking "and" at the end;

(B) in subparagraph (B), by striking the period at the end of clause (iv) and inserting "; and"; and

(C) by inserting immediately after subparagraph (B) the following new subparagraph:

"(C) a business development company may issue warrants, options, or rights to subscribe to, convert to, or purchase voting securities not accompanied by securities, if—

(i) such warrants, options, or rights satisfy the conditions in clauses (i) and (iii) of subparagraph (A); and

(ii) the proposal to issue such warrants, options, or rights is authorized by the shareholders or partners of such business development company, and such issuance is approved by the required majority (as defined in section 57(o)) of the directors of or general partners in such company on the basis that such issuance is in the best interests of the company and its shareholders or partners."

SEC. 507. FILING OF WRITTEN STATEMENTS.

Section 64(b)(1) of the Investment Company Act of 1940 (15 U.S.C. 80a-63(b)(1)) is amended by inserting "and capital structure" after "portfolio."

SEC. 508. CHURCH EMPLOYEE PENSION PLANS.

(a) AMENDMENT TO THE INVESTMENT COMPANY ACT OF 1940.—
Section 3(c) of the Investment Company Act of 1940 (15 U.S.C. 80a-
3(c)) is amended by adding at the end the following new paragraph:

"(14) Any church plan described in section 414(e) of the Internal Revenue Code of 1986, if, under any such plan, no part of the assets may be used for, or diverted to, purposes other than the exclusive benefit of plan participants or beneficiaries, or any company or account that is—

(A) established by a person that is eligible to establish and maintain such a plan under section 414(e) of the Internal Revenue Code of 1986; and

(B) substantially all of the activities of which consist of—

(i) managing or holding assets contributed to such church plans or other assets which are permitted to be commingled with the assets of church plans under the Internal Revenue Code of 1986; or

(ii) administering or providing benefits pursuant to church plans."

(b) AMENDMENT TO THE SECURITIES ACT OF 1933.—Section 3(a) of the Securities Act of 1933 (15 U.S.C. 77c(a)) is amended by adding at the end the following new paragraph:

"(13) Any security issued by or any interest or participation in any church plan, company or account that is excluded from the definition of an investment company under section 3(c)(14) of the Investment Company Act of 1940."

(c) AMENDMENTS TO THE SECURITIES EXCHANGE ACT OF 1934.—

(1) EXEMPTED SECURITIES.—Section 3(a)(12)(A) of the Securities Exchange Act of 1934 (15 U.S.C. 78c(a)(12)(A)) is amended—

(A) in clause (v), by striking "and" at the end;

(B) by redesignating clause (vi) as clause (vii); and

(C) by inserting after clause (v) the following new clause:

"(vi) solely for purposes of sections 12, 13, 14, and 16 of this title, any security issued by or any interest or participation in any church plan, company, or account that is excluded from the definition of an investment company under section 3(c)(14) of the Investment Company Act of 1940; and".

(2) EXEMPTION FROM BROKER-DEALER PROVISIONS.—Section 3 of the Securities Exchange Act of 1934 (15 U.S.C. 78c) is amended by adding at the end the following new subsection:

"(g) CHURCH PLANS.—No church plan described in section 414(e) of the Internal Revenue Code of 1986, no person or entity eligible to establish and maintain such a plan under the Internal Revenue Code of 1986, no company or account that is excluded from the definition of an investment company under section 3(c)(14) of the Investment Company Act of 1940, and no trustee, director, officer or employee of or volunteer for such plan, company, account person, or entity, acting within the scope of that person's employment or activities with respect to such plan, shall be deemed to be a 'broker', 'dealer', 'municipal securities broker', 'municipal securities dealer', 'government securities broker', 'government securities dealer', 'clearing agency, or 'transfer agent' for purposes of this title—

(1) solely because such plan, company, person, or entity buys, holds, sells, trades in, or transfers securities or acts as an intermediary in making payments in connection with transactions in securities for its own account in its capacity as trustee or administrator of, or otherwise on behalf of, or for the account of, any church plan, company, or account that is excluded from the definition of an investment company under section 3(c)(14) of the Investment Company Act of 1940; and

(2) if no such person or entity receives a commission or other transaction-related sales compensation in connection with any activities conducted in reliance on the exemption provided by this subsection."

(d) AMENDMENT TO THE INVESTMENT ADVISERS ACT OF 1940.—Section 203(b) of the Investment Advisers Act of 1940 (15 U.S.C. 80b-3(b)) is amended—

(1) in paragraph (3), by striking "or" at the end;

(2) in paragraph (4), by striking the period at the end and inserting "; or"; and

(3) by adding at the end the following new paragraph:

"(5) any plan described in section 414(e) of the Internal Revenue Code of 1986, any person or entity eligible to establish and maintain such a plan under the Internal Revenue Code of 1986, or any trustee, director, officer, or employee of or volunteer for any such plan or person, if such person or entity acting in such capacity, provides investment advice exclusively to, or with respect to, any plan, person, or entity or any company, account, or fund that is excluded from the definition of an investment company under section 3(c)(14) of the Investment Company Act of 1940."

(e) AMENDMENT TO THE TRUST INDENTURE ACT OF 1939.—Section 304(a)(4)(A) of the Trust Indenture Act of 1939 (15 U.S.C. 77ddd(4) (A)) is amended by striking "or (11)" and inserting "(11), or (14)".

(F) PROTECTION OF CHURCH EMPLOYEE BENEFIT PLANS UNDER STATE LAW.—

(1) REGISTRATION REQUIREMENTS.—Any security issued by or any interest or participation in any church plan, company, or account that is excluded from the definition of an investment company under section 3(c)(14) of the Investment Company Act of 1940, as added by subsection (a) of this section, and any offer, sale, or purchase thereof, shall be exempt from any law of a State that requires registration or qualification of securities.

(2) TREATMENT OF CHURCH PLANS.—No church plan described in section 414(e) of the Internal Revenue Code of 1986, no person or entity eligible to establish and maintain such a plan under the Internal Revenue Code of 1986, no company or account that is excluded from the definition of an investment company under section 3(c)(14) of the Investment Company Act of 1940, as added by subsection (a) of this section, and no trustee, director, officer, or employee of or volunteer for any such plan, person, entity, company, or account shall be required to qualify, register, or be subject to regulation as an investment company or as a broker, dealer, investment adviser, or agent under the laws of any State solely because such plan, person, entity, company, or account buys, holds, sells, or trades in securities for its own account or in its capacity as a trustee or administrator of or otherwise on behalf of, or for the account of, or provides investment advice to, for, or on behalf of, any such plan, person, or entity or any company or account that is excluded from the definition of an investment company under section 3(c)(14) of the Investment Company Act of 1940, as added by subsection (a) of this section.

(g) AMENDMENT TO THE INVESTMENT COMPANY ACT OF 1940.—
Section 30 of the Investment Company Act of 1940 (15 U.S.C. 80a-29)
is amended by adding at the end the following new subsections:

"(g) DISCLOSURE TO CHURCH PLAN PARTICIPANTS.—A person that
maintains a church plan that is excluded from the definition of an
investment company solely by reason of section 3(c)(14) shall provide
disclosure to plan participants, in writing, and not less frequently than
annually, and for new participants joining such a plan after May 31,
1996, as soon as is practicable after joining such plan, that—

(1) the plan, or any company or account maintained to manage
or hold plan assets and interests in such plan, company, or account,
are not subject to registration, regulation, or reporting under this
title, the Securities Act of 1933, the Securities Exchange Act of
1934, or State securities laws; and

(2) plan participants and beneficiaries therefore will not be
afforded the protections of those provisions.

(h) NOTICE TO COMMISSION.—The Commission may issue rules
and regulations to require any person that maintains a church plan that
is excluded from the definition of an investment company solely by reason of section 3(c)(14) to file a notice with the Commission containing such information and in such form as the Commission may
prescribe as necessary or appropriate in the public interest or consistent with the protection of investors."

SEC. 509. PROMOTING GLOBAL PREEMINENCE OF AMERICAN SECURITIES MARKETS.

It is the sense of the Congress that—

(1) the United States and foreign securities markets are increasingly becoming international securities markets, as issuers and
investors seek the benefits of new capital and secondary market
opportunities without regard to national borders;

(2) as issuers seek to raise capital across national borders, they
confront differing accounting requirements in the various regulatory jurisdictions;

(3) the establishment of a high-quality comprehensive set of
generally accepted international accounting standards in cross-
border securities offerings would greatly facilitate international

financing activities and, most significantly, would enhance the ability of foreign corporations to access and list in United States markets;

(4) in addition to the efforts made before the date of enactment of this Act by the Commission to respond to the growing internationalization of securities markets, the Commission should enhance its vigorous support for the development of high-quality international accounting standards as soon as practicable; and

(5) the Commission, in view of its clear authority under law to facilitate the access of foreign corporations to list their securities in United States markets, should report to the Congress, not later than 1 year after the date of enactment of this Act, on progress in the development of international accounting standards and the outlook for successful completion of a set of international standards that would be acceptable to the Commission for offerings and listings by foreign corporations in United States markets.

SEC. 510. STUDIES AND REPORTS.

(a) IMPACT OF TECHNOLOGICAL ADVANCES.—
  (1) STUDY.—
    (A) IN GENERAL.—The Commission shall conduct a study of—
      (i) the impact of technological advances and the use of on-line information systems on the securities markets, including steps that the Commission has taken to facilitate the electronic delivery of prospectuses to institutional and other investors;
      (ii) how such technologies have changed the way in which the securities markets operate; and
      (iii) any steps taken by the Commission to address such changes.
    (B) CONSIDERATIONS.—In conducting the study under subparagraph (A), the Commission shall consider how the Commission has adapted its enforcement policies and practices in response to technological developments with regard to—
      (i) disclosure, prospectus delivery, and other customer protection regulations;

(ii) intermediaries and exchanges in the domestic and international financial services industry;

(iii) reporting by issuers, including communications with holders of securities;

(iv) the relationship of the Commission with other national regulatory authorities and organizations to improve coordination and cooperation; and

(v) the relationship of the Commission with State regulatory authorities and organizations to improve coordination and cooperation.

(2) REPORT.—Not later than 1 year after the date of enactment of this Act, the Commission shall submit a report to the Congress on the results of the study conducted under paragraph (1).

(b) SHAREHOLDER PROPOSALS.—

(1) STUDY.—The Commission shall conduct a study of—

(A) whether shareholder access to proxy statements pursuant to section 14 of the Securities Exchange Act of 1934 has been impaired by recent statutory, judicial, or regulatory changes; and

(B) the ability of shareholders to have proposals relating to corporate practices and social issues included as part of proxy statements.

(2) REPORT.—Not later than 1 year after the date of enactment of this Act, the Commission shall submit a report to the Congress on the results of the study conducted under paragraph (1), together with any recommendations for regulatory or legislative changes that it considers necessary to improve shareholder access to proxy statements.

(c) PREFERENCING.—

(1) STUDY.—The Commission shall conduct a study of the impact on investors and the national market system of the practice known as "preferencing" on one or more registered securities exchanges, including consideration of—

(A) how preferencing impacts—

(i) the execution prices received by retail securities customers whose orders are preferenced; and

(ii) the ability of retail securities customers in all markets to obtain executions of their limit orders in preferenced securities; and

(B) the costs of preferencing to such customers.

(2) REPORT.—Not later than 6 months after the date of enactment of this Act, the Commission shall submit a report to the Congress on the results of the study conducted under paragraph (1).

(3) DEFINITION.—For purposes of this subsection, the term "preferencing" refers to the practice of a broker acting as a dealer on a national securities exchange, directing the orders of customers to buy or sell securities to itself for execution under rules that permit the broker to take priority in execution over same-priced orders or quotations entered prior in time.

(d) BROKER-DEALER UNIFORMITY.—

(1) STUDY.—The Commission, after consultation with registered securities associations, national securities exchanges, and States, shall conduct a study of the impact of disparate State licensing requirements on associated persons of registered brokers or dealers and methods for States to attain uniform licensing requirements for such persons.

(2) REPORT.—Not later than 1 year after the date of enactment of this Act, the Commission shall submit to the Congress a report on the study conducted under paragraph (1). Such report shall include recommendations concerning appropriate methods described in paragraph (1)(B), including any necessary legislative changes to implement such recommendations.

Approved October 11, 1996.

Appendix 13

ELECTRONIC COMMUNICATIONS NETWORKS

Archipelago Holdings
100 South Wacker Drive,
  Suite 2000
Chicago, IL 60606
Ph: 312-960-1696
Fx: 312-960-1369
www.tradearcho.com

Arizona Stock Exchange
20 Exchange Place, 31st Floor
New York, NY 10005
Ph: 212-514-8890
www.azx.com

Ashton Technology Group, Inc.
11 Penn Center
1835 Market Street, Suite 420
Philadelphia, PA 19103
Ph: 215-751-1900
Fx: 215-636-3560
www.ashtontecgroup.com

ATTAIN
160 Summit Avenue
Montvale, NJ 07645
Ph: 201-782-0110/877-432-9872
Fx: 201-782-9681
www.traintotrade.com

BRUT ECN, LLC
55 Broadway, 7th Floor
New York, NY 10006
Ph: 212-952-0280
Fx: 212-651-0898
www.ebrut.com

Instinet
875 Third Avenue
New York, NY 10022
Ph: 212-310-9500
www.instinet.com

The Island ECN
50 Broad Street, 6th Floor
New York, NY 10004
Ph: 212-231-5000
Fx: 212-487-2983
www.islandecn.com

Investment Technology Group
Executive Offices
380 Madison Avenue
New York, New York 10017
212-588-4000
www.itginc.com

ITG POSIT
380 Madison Avenue
New York, NY 10017
Ph: 212-444-6300
Fx 212-444-6295
www.itginc.com

Lattice Trading
State Street Brokerage
225 Franklin Street, 19th Floor
Boston, MA 02110
Ph: 617-664-1814
Fx: 617-664-8069
www.statestreet.com

MarketXT, Inc.
100 Broadway
New York, NY 10005
Fx: 212-777-7676
www.marketxt.com

Match Plus
Michelle Radcliffe
Ph: 415-537-8600

NexTrade
301 S. Missouri Avenue
Clearwater, FL 33756
Ph: 727-446-0823
Fx: 727-443-1102
www.nextrade.org

NYFIX Millennium
100 Wall Street, 21st Floor
New York, NY 10005
Ph: 212-809-3542
Fx: 212-809-1013
www.nyfix.com

OptiMark, Inc.
10 Exchange Place, 24th Floor
Jersey City, NJ 07302
Ph. 201-536-7000
Fx: 201-435-3123
www.optimark.com

PRIMEX Trading
885 Third Avenue
New York, NY 10022
Ph: 212-230-2475
Fx: 212-755-9723
www.primextrading.com

REDIBook ECN LLC
10 Exchange Place, 9th Floor
Jersey City, NJ 07302
Ph: 201-309-4594
Fx: 201-434-5048
www.redibook.com

Terra Nova Trading
100 South Wacker Drive,
  Suite 1550
Chicago, IL 60606
Ph: 800-228-4216
Fx: 312-960-0723
www.terranovatrading.com

Tradebook and **Global
  Tradebook**
Bloomberg
499 Park Avenue, 10th Floor
New York, NY 10022
Ph: 212-318-2780
Fx: 917-369-6206
www.bloomberg.com

**Tradepoint Financial
  Networks, plc**
35 King Street
London, United Kingdom
WC2E 8JD
Ph: 171-240-5000
Fx: 171-240-5300

Tradeweb
1 World Trade Center,
  Suite 5149
New York, NY 10048
Ph: 800-541-2263
Fx: 212-775-1003
www.tradeweb.com

Appendix 14

INVESTMENT BANK SERVICE MARKED DERIVATIVE SECURITIES

Individual firm service marked derivative securities started to appear as proprietary products in the early 1980s with the creation of PRIMES and SCORES (Alex, Brown), CATS (Salomon Brothers) and TIGERS and LYONS (Merrill Lynch). Since then, such securities have proliferated. A current list of acronyms (including their definition and sponsor) known to the editors as of October 1998 follows.[1]

ACES	Automatically convertible equity securities	Goldman Sachs
CHIPS	Common-linked higher income participation securities	Bear Stearns
CRESTS	Convertible redeemable equity structured trust security	Montgomery (B of A)
CUBS	Customized upside basket securities	Bear Stearns
DARTS	Derivative adjustable securities	Raymond James
DECS	Debt exchangeable for common stock	Salomon Brothers
DECSV	Dividend enhanced convertible stock	N/A

---

1. The editors thank CommScan LLC for its help in compiling this list.

ELKS	Equity linked securities	Salomon Brothers
EPICS	Exchange preferred income cumulative shares	N/A
EPPICS	Equity providing preferred income convertible note securities	N/A
EPIPS	Enhanced perpetual income preferred securities	Everen
HIGH TIDES	Remarketable term income deferrable equity securities	CSFB
HOLDRS	Holding company depository receipts	Merrill Lynch
ICONS	Investment common convertible notes	Merrill Lynch/ Salomon
IQ Notes	Insured quarterly notes	Edward Jones
LYONS	Liquid yield option notes	Merrill Lynch
MARCS	Mandatory adjustable redeemable convertible securities	UBS
MEDS	Monthly exchangeable debt securities	JP Morgan
METS	Mandatory exchangeable trust securities	N/A
MIPS	Monthly income preferred shares	Goldman Sachs
PACERS	Principal accruing enhanced return securities	Lehman
PARCKS	Premium accelerable redemptive convertible knockout securities	Deutsche Bank
PEACS	Preferred equity redemption cumulative stock	Morgan Stanley/ Merrill Lynch

PEACS	Premium adjustable convertible securities	Morgan Stanley
PEEQS	Protected exchangeable equity linked securities	Morgan Stanley
PENS	Privatization exchangeable notes	Goldman Sachs
PEPS	Premium exchangeable participating shares	Morgan Stanley
PEARS	Preferred equity redemption cumulative stock	Merrill Lynch/ Morgan Stanley
PERQS	Preferred equity linked redemption cumulative stock	Morgan Stanley
PIERS	Preferred income equity redeemable securities	Lehman Brothers
PIES	Premium income exchangeable securities	Lehman Brothers
PRIDES	Preferred redeemable increased dividend equity securities	Merrill Lynch
PRIZES	Participating redeemable indexed zero-premium exchangeable shares	CSFB/Merrill Lynch
QUIDS	Quarterly income debt securities	Goldman Sachs
QUINTS	Quarterly income tiered securities	Edward Jones
QUIPS	Quarterly income preferred securities	Goldman Sachs
ROARS	Remarketable or redeemable securities	Montgomery
SAILS	Stock appreciation income linked securities	CSFB

SEALS	Securities enhancing aftermarket liquidity	Prudential Securities
SIRENS	Step-up income redeemable equity notes	CSFB
SPURS	Shared preference redeemable securities	Warburg Dillon Read
STRYPES	Structured yield product exchangeable for stock	Merrill Lynch
SUNS	Stock upside note securities	Lehman Brothers
TAPS	Threshold appreciation price securities	Salomon Smith Barney
TECONS	Team convertible securities	JP Morgan
TEES	Trust equity enhanced securities	Sutro
TIDES	Term income deferrable equity securities	CSFB
TIMES	Trust issued mandatory exchange securities	Bear Stearns
TIPS	Trust issued preferred securities	N/A
TOPRS	Trust originated preferred securities	Morgan/Merrill/ Lehman
TRACES	Trust automatic common exchange securities	Goldman Sachs
TRENDS	Trust enhanced distribution security	Donaldson Lufkin Jenrette
TREX	Trust issued required equity exchange securities trust	Warburg Dillon Read
YEELDS	Yield enhanced equity linked debt securities	Lehman Brothers
YES	Yield enhanced securities	Goldman Sachs
ZENS	Zero premium exchangeable subordinated notes	Goldman Sachs

GLOSSARY

The securities industry in general and investment banking in particular are heavily dependent on often colorful terms, phrases, and abbreviations unique to the conduct of this business—the vernacular of the Street. The aim of this chapter is to focus on terms used in the investment banking, underwriting, distribution, and aftermarket trading aspects of the business. The glossary also includes some general industry terms to assist the newcomer/trainee to ramp up his or her learning curve as quickly as possible. The editor and SIA welcome any and all additions and modifications to this (or any other) section of the Handbook. Many glossary items contain a Handbook chapter number for ease of cross reference should the user desire a more detailed explanation of the particular term.

While there are many financial glossaries available, the one included in John Downes' and John Elliot Goodman's *Finance & Investment Handbook, Fourth Edition,* contains a very thorough assemblage of over 5,000 basic securities industry terms and covers a whole host of investment issues and other useful information.[1] No serious industry practitioner should be without this tool![2] Wherever possible, this glossary defers to and attempts not to duplicate the Downes/Goodman efforts in keeping with established SIA policy. For example, where this Handbook glossary gives only the full name to an acronym or an abbreviation, the user should go to Downes and Goodman's work for

---

1. Downes, John and John Elliot Goodman. *Finance & Investment Handbook,* Fourth Edition, Hauppauge, NY: Barron's Educational Series Inc. 1995.

2. For a glossary alone, *see* Downes, John and John Elliot Goodman, *Dictionary of Finance and Investment Terms,* Fourth Edition, Hauppauge, NY: Barron's Educational Series Inc., 1995.

the actual definition. The reason for keeping acronyms and abbreviations in this glossary is simple, the acronym or abbreviation does not appear in Downes/Goodman in that form, and the user's first introduction to the term may in fact be in such form.

The derivatives business has steadily become a more and more significant part of new issue activity since the early- to mid-1980s. The section of this chapter appearing after the Glossary identifies derivative acronyms currently in use. For a first-rate and comprehensive explanation of derivative terms, the editor recommends *The Dictionary of Financial Risk Management.*[3]

The glossary that follows is a compilation of terms, some of which were sourced from:

> J.E. Liss & Co., Inc.
> Prudential Securities, Inc.
> Securities Industry Association
> SunTrust Equitable Securities
> Trenam, Kemker, Scharf, Barkin, Frye, O'Neill & Mullis

The editors hereby thank each of these organizations for their gracious permission to adapt certain items from publications or manuals made available to them.

AAU   *See* **Agreement Among Underwriters.**

Acceleration Request   Formal request by a registrant/issuer to the SEC to speed up ("accelerate") the automatic declaration of "effectiveness" of its registration statement, which would occur 20 days after filing in the normal course of business.

Account   Commonly used abbreviation for Underwriting Account. *See* **Underwriting Account.**

Accredited Investor   Defined in Rule 501(a) of Regulation D under the 33 Act, as amended, to identify eight separate categories of individuals and artificial entities who, by virtue of their close relationship with an issuer, their wealth or other salient factors,

---

3. Gastineau, Gary L. and Mark P. Kritzman. *The Dictionary of Financial Risk Management,* New York, NY. Frank J. Fabozzi Associates, 1996.

have been accorded special treatment by the SEC. Such treatment includes exclusion from the "counting" of permissible purchasers in a Regulation D offering and, where an offering is limited solely to accredited investors, removes the necessity for complying with the mandated narrative disclosure requirements otherwise applicable to such offerings. Accredited investors include natural persons who are executive officers or directors of the issuer, any general partner (or executive officer or director or general partner of the general partner) of the issuer, millionaires, and persons whose annual income exceeds $200,000 ($300,000 for individuals and their spouses) in each of the most recent two years and who have a reasonable expectation of reaching that same level in the current year; entities include banks, savings and loan associations, registered broker-dealers, insurance companies, corporations, trusts, partnerships or organizations described under Section 501(c)(3) of the Internal Revenue Code, in each case, not formed solely for the purpose of making the investment and with total assets in excess of $5,000,000; and certain pension and profit sharing trusts with more than $5,000,000 in assets. Private placement and high risk investments may be sold only to accredited investors. *See* **Regulation D.**

Adjustable Rate Security   Security whose interest or dividend rate adjusts or resets periodically according to a predetermined formula.

ADR   American Depositary Receipt.

ADTV   *See* **Average Daily Trading Volume.**

Affiliate   Person standing in a control relationship with another person. The relationship may arise in one of several situations including: (i) control of an affiliate by another person; (ii) control by an affiliate of another person; and (iii) common control of an affiliate and another person by a different party. In each case, control may be direct or indirect. The formal SEC definition is set forth in a number of places, including Rule 405 of the 33 Act. For example, and as a general rule, executive officers, directors and stockholders owning 10 percent or more of the equity securities of a corporation are affiliates of the corporation and, depending on the facts, affiliates of one another. Affiliates are sometimes referred to as "control persons." General partners in a limited partnership are affiliates of the partnership and vice versa. *See* **Control/Control Person.**

Aftermarket   Trading that takes place in the securities of an underwritten public offering after termination of price and trading restrictions governing that offering.

Aftermarket Performance   Price action of an underwritten security in the aftermarket measured against its initial offering price.

Agent   Entity or person acting in a non-risk capacity and charging a commission to arrange a transaction between two parties. *See* **Broker.**

Agreement Among Underwriters (AAU)   Document that empowers lead manager to act on behalf of other underwriters in a public offering. *See* **Chapter 3.**

AIBD   *See* **Association of International Bond Dealers.**

Aircraft Carrier Release   The November 3, 1998, SEC release proposing fundamental and comprehensive changes to portions of the 33 Act relating to securities offerings and to portions of the 34 Act relating to periodic reporting and disclosure requirements. *See* **Chapter 1.**

All Hands Meeting   Any meeting attended by representatives of all the various parties to an underwritten transaction, *i.e.,* issuer, issuer's counsel, issuer's auditor, the lead and all co-managing underwriters and underwriters' counsel. The venue is often an office of issuer's counsel but can be anywhere.

All Sold   Representation by an underwriter/distributor or a selected dealer to the book running manager that the subject firm's allocated securities have all been placed with end investors.

All Sold Request   Portion of the lead manager's release wire which requires underwriters and selected dealers to advise the manager of any unsold portion of their allotment.

Allocation   Amount of securities that a firm or individual salesperson has been given ("allocated") to sell, or the amount of securities an end investor receives from a salesperson. Also, the process of allotting (also referred to as "circling") securities.

Amendment   In regards to a registration statement, a formal filing with the SEC of changes to the original document and identified using Arabic numerals.

AMEX   American Stock Exchange.

Antifraud Provisions   Referring generally to all of the bases under statute, rule, or court created causes of action under which liability may be asserted for failure to tell "the truth, the whole truth and nothing but the truth" in connection with a securities transaction. A violation may occur not only for misstatement or half-truth but also for omission. Sources of antifraud liability include, but are not limited to, Sections 11, 12(2), and 17 of the 33 Act; Sections 10(b), 14(a), and 14(e) of the 34 Act, as amended; and the series of rules promulgated under such statutes, including the most well-known of the antifraud provisions, SEC Rule 10b-5. State securities laws contain similar provisions. *See* **Material Information.**

Ask   Price at which a dealer offers securities. *See* **Bid.**

Associated Person   Sales person or employee under the control of a broker-dealer. Such persons cannot buy Hot Issue securities. *See* **Chapter 7.**

Association of International Bond Dealers (AIBD)   Forerunner of the International Securities Markets Association (ISMA).

At the Market Re-Offering   Seldom used technique of re-offering underwritten securities at various prices and at various times as opposed to a traditional fixed price reoffering.

Average Daily Trading Volume (ADTV)   Calculation used to help determine Passive Market Making parameters for an underwriter. *See* **Chapter 5.**

Banking Act of 1933   Also known as the Glass-Steagall Act. Legislation that formally separated deposit taking (commercial banking) and risk taking (investment banking and insurance underwriting). *See* **Chapter 1.**

Banque d'Affaires   Continental European equivalent of a merchant bank with a traditionally heavier concentration of industrial holdings than its English or American counterparts.

Beauty Contest   Review process conducted by an issuer to identify the lead and any co-managers for an underwritten public offering. For IPOs, the process is usually long in duration, often involving written questionnaires and a final meeting where each investment banking firm makes a formal presentation of its capabilities, usually summarized in a binder carrying the firm's logo and called a "pitchbook."

Benchmark   A touchstone or comparison against which value or performance may be measured.

Beneficial Owner   Person(s) or entity(ies) deemed by SEC rules to have beneficial ownership of securities, *i.e.,* the power to vote or sell them. Not necessarily the actual owner of record. Beneficial ownership is used to trigger the requirement to file and report such ownership with the SEC. *See* **Beneficial Ownership Reports** and **Record Owner.**

Beneficial Ownership Reports   (Forms 3, 4 and 5; Schedules 13D, 13G, 14D-1, and 14D-9). Required to be filed with the SEC by persons, entities and persons and entities deemed under SEC rules to be acting in concert (called a "Group") with respect to the beneficial ownership of securities of a public company (copies of the reports are also sent to the company). Forms 3, 4, and 5 are filed by persons who are executive officers, directors, or beneficial owners of 10 percent or more of the outstanding voting securities of a public company; reports are required to be filed with respect to initial ownership and subsequent transactions in the security. These reports may provide the facts on which to establish a violation of short swing trading prohibitions (*see* **Short Swing Trading**). Persons, entities, and any Group beneficially owning five percent or more of the voting securities of a public company must file Schedules 13D and 13G. Schedule 13D requires detailed information about the Group's background and intentions with respect to the company (act as an investor, buy the whole company, seek to discharge management, etc.), financing of the acquisition of company securities, and requires prompt amendment if substantial additional securities are acquired or if any prior disclosure is no longer correct. Schedules 14D-1 and 14D-9 are filed by participants in tender offers and include information similar to that on Schedule 13D, tailored to the context of a tender offer.

Best Execution   SEC concept requiring a fiduciary to pay close attention to the quality of securities transactions it executes on behalf of customers. Originally, an execution occurring at the National

Best Bid or Best Offer (NBBO) was thought to be sufficient to achieve "best execution," but fiduciaries are now charged with taking into consideration such other factors as timing, size, and overall market conditions and must review their trade execution activity on a periodic basis.

Bid Price at which a dealer will purchase securities. *See* **Ask.**

Bid and Ask Quote or quotation for a security or a market. The high bid and low offer in a Nasdaq security is known as the "inside" market.

Big Bang October 27, 1986—date marking the end of trading cartels on the London Stock Exchange. April 1, 1998—deregulation of Japanese domestic financial system begins.

Black Tuesday October 29, 1929—date of the infamous U.S. stock market crash.

Blotter Any compilation of underwriting or trading activity, such as a list of underwriters in bracket order or selling group in alphabetical order, and noting commitments, retention, give-ups, payments, designations, and MBD's.

Blue Sky Law Popular name for law that each of the 50 states enacted, Kansas being the first in 1911, to protect residents against securities fraud. So named after a Kansas Supreme Court Justice who, in reaction to an egregious scheme by which promoters were trying to sell unsuspecting investors securities, observed that such securities had no more value than ". . . so many feet of 'blue sky.'" In addition to SEC registration, an issuer must register or file with the state securities commission in each state in which any stock is to be sold—the summary of such activity is the so-called "preliminary blue sky survey."[4] This filing must be made prior to pricing and confirmation of sales to individual investors (institutional investors are exempt) as securities may not be sold to a retail client in a state where the issue is not "blue skied" or where the selling securities firm or broker is not licensed. Prior to actual SEC effectiveness, pricing and release for sale of an offering, the lead manager must

---

4. *See* Downes and Goodman, *Finance & Investment Handbook,* Fourth Edition, for listing of U.S. state securities regulators, pp. 710-712.

notify all participants of any states which have not granted the offering "final blue sky clearance."

Book   Compilation of all committed purchasers of an underwritten transaction. *See* **Shadow Book.**

Book Building   Originally an English/Euro term describing the U.S. process/style of assembling pre-price indications of interest in an underwritten transaction.

Book Entry   Process of automated securities settlement in a certificateless environment. Transactions that used to require issuance of engraved certificates to represent ownership are now just electronic "book entries" in a central securities custodian depository, and evidence of ownership is an entry on a month end customer statement issued by the order executing broker-dealer. Culmination of an industry wide effort that began in the wake of the back office paperwork nightmare of the late 1960s.

Book of Business   An investment bank's backlog of unpriced deals.

Bookie   *See* **Broker's Broker.**

Borrower   Euro term for an issuer of new debt securities.

Bought Deal   Offering purchased from an issuer by an underwriter(s) prior to the underwriter having a book for the transaction. Originally a Eurobond market activity that started to occur more frequently in the U.S. in the late 1970s.

Bound Volume   Collection of all relevant correspondence, filing documents, and contracts related to a specific underwritten or merger/acquisition or divestiture transaction. Takes its name from the time honored custom of tabulating all papers chronologically and binding them together in an embossed (sometimes leather bound) volume.

bp or "beep"   A basis point or one hundredth of one percent.

Bracket   Grouping of dealers subscribing to equal underwriting commitments as listed in the "underwriting" section of a prospectus or as grouped ("bracketed") in a tombstone advertisement. *See* **Commitment** and **Chapter 3.**

Bracketing (Syndicate) List   List of participants in a new issue compiled by the lead manager. Each bracket contains the names of underwriters grouped by equal commitments. The placement of underwriters into brackets is based on historical tradition, general firm size and capital position, past distribution performance, issuer/seller request, and syndicate manager discretion. Types of bracket lists include preliminary draft(s), invitation list and final underwriting. *See* **Final Underwriting Account** and **Chapter 3.**

Breakeven   Length of time an investor has to own a convertible to earn back the premium of the conversion price over the last sale of the underlying security by collecting its coupon or dividend income.

Breakdown   Individual elements of the gross spread, *i.e.,* management fee, underwriting fee, selling concession, and dealer re-allowance. *See* **Gross Spread** and **Chapter 4.**

Broker   *See* **Agent.**

Broker-Dealer   Entity that receives compensation for assisting in or effecting the sale or purchase of underwritten securities. Compensation may be direct or indirect and need not be paid out of the proceeds of the offering in question. Characterization as a broker-dealer is different and distinct from the statutory requirements for such persons to be registered with appropriate regulatory authorities. As a further distinction, brokers receive compensation for effecting sales or purchases on behalf of others who are the owners of the securities; a broker does not own the security. Dealers receive compensation for effecting sales or purchases of securities made on behalf of their own account; the dealer actually owns the security. Frequently, the distinction between the two types of transactions is blurred. Formal definitions are set forth in Section 2 of the 33 Act and Section 3 of the 34 Act.

Broker's Broker (Bookie)   Specialized, focused securities firm that deals only, and only on an anonymous basis, with other brokers and/or dealers conducting a public business. Most commonly found in the secondary fixed income market place.

Bulge Bracket   Originally an underwriting bracket larger in dollar commitment than the major bracket, and normally the largest bracket beneath the manager and/or co-managers. In effect, the inclusion of a special bracket creates a "bulge" between the two underwriting brackets both in the final prospectus underwriting table and in the tombstone announcing the issue. The term has come to denote a firm that occupies a position of special prominence or prestige in investment banking circles. (Editor's note—for a complete discussion of the evolution of underwriting procedures and practices, see the two Samuel L. Hayes III articles noted in the Bibliography.) *See also* **Special Bracket** and **Chapter 3.**

Bull Dog   English pound sterling denominated bond offered in the London market by an offshore issuer.

Bullet (or Bullet Maturity)   A bond carrying no sinking fund or call provision.

Bulletin Board (OTC)   NASD supervised dealer market for very small market capitalization companies where bids and offers are posted by dealers but do not represent affirmative obligations to purchase or sell shares. In essence, the NASD has modernized the old pink sheet market.

Busted Deal   An underwriting that is not completed.

Buy Side   Colloquial term for an investor, particularly institutional. *See* **Sell Side.**

Canadian Wrapper   Minor addendum to a prospectus to permit sales to qualified Canadian investors. *See* **Chapter 2** and **Wrapper.**

Cap Table   Section in a prospectus that describes the capitalization of the issuer.

Capital Markets   Collectively, the markets for all securities. **Primary**—where new issue securities are marketed, priced, and initially distributed. **Secondary**—where new issue securities are traded once their initial price and trading restrictions have been removed. Also, the location or department on a trading floor that handles new issue origination—the focal point of coordination of investment banking with sales, trading, and research.

Cede & Co.   Nominee name for the Depository Trust Company (**DTC**).

Certain Transactions Prospectus section describing any and all relationships between a control person and the company itself (*e.g.,* a company leases facilities from its founder or a large shareholder).

Certificate Actual piece of paper evidencing ownership of a security. At one time widely used, usually on watermarked paper, finely engraved with delicate etchings to discourage forgery. Almost extinct today as most publicly traded companies have long since deposited their certificates with the Depository Trust Company where ownership exists via electronic book entry. However, investors may still ask for ("order out") a physical certificate.

Check-Off Sheet Useful way for capital markets personnel to ensure that all procedures deemed necessary by his/her firm for the proper handling of an underwritten offering are in fact completed in a timely manner.

Circle Verbal commitment by the managing underwriter or syndicate manager to allocate a certain number of an underwritten transaction's securities to a firm or to a salesperson(s) within a firm. This term prohibits others from claiming these securities. A circle becomes an order after the registration statement has been declared effective, the offering has been released for sale and the account "circled" acknowledges receipt of the offering terms and confirms its intention to purchase.

(The) City Financial district of London.

Clean Up Transaction undertaken to re-distribute (almost always at a lower price) a block of unsold securities remaining from a less than fully distributed underwritten public offering.

Clearance and Settlement Process whereby securities transactions are handled between two contra-party brokers or dealers after the actual trade occurs. The processing of trade documentation and comparison is the "clearance," and the exchange of securities and monies is the "settlement."

Clearing Correspondent Firm that has its securities transactions processed by another firm that handles such business for a number of firms. *See* **Fully Disclosed Clearing Arrangement, Omnibus Clearing Arrangement,** and **Correspondent Relationship.**

Closing   Formal process of completing/exchanging/verifying all documentation relating to an underwritten transaction and the actual exchange of monies ("net proceeds") for securities.

Closing Dinner   Traditional celebration of the completion of an investment banking transaction. Attendees usually include only those intimately involved with the deal from the issuer, both sets of attorneys, the accounting firm and the lead manager and any co-manager(s).

Cold Deal   Slow selling underwritten offering. *See* **Hot Deal.**

Cold Issue   Official NASD term describing an offering that does not trade at an immediate premium in the aftermarket. *See* **Hot Issue.**

Comment Letter (Comments)   Formal written response summarizing the SEC's required-by-law review of an issuer's registration statement to ensure full disclosure. Prior to declaring the registration statement "effective," the SEC reviewing staff must receive issuer responses satisfactory to the staff to each item in the comment letter. Such responses often require issuer revision of various aspects of the prospectus. In some cases, the SEC may even require a "recirculation" of the preliminary prospectus because it deems the required changes to be material or significant. *See* **Recirculation.**

Commitment (Underwriting or Participation)   Amount of securities for which a participating underwriter is contractually responsible to purchase from the issuer. The actual amount is determined by the lead manager, and all firms underwriting the same amounts are collectively referred to as a "bracket." *See* **Bracket** and **Chapter 3.**

Commitment Committee   Ad hoc group of experienced senior people charged with reviewing whether or not their firm should enter into an issuer client relationship. Most firms exclude investment banking personnel from membership on this committee to insure independent thinking.

Company Request   Inclusion of an underwriter in a syndicate specifically at the issuer's request.

Comparables (Comps) Group of similar or comparable already public companies and/or certain ratio(s) of such companies used by the lead manager to help determine the filing price range of an initial public offering. The comparison usually receiving the most emphasis is the price earnings ratio.

Compensation Bid Little used variation of competitive bidding, whereby the issuer specifies that the winning bidder must re-offer the securities at a specified price (normally par). Thus, the size of the underwriting discount, or compensation, becomes the determining factor in a common stock offering or a determining factor (along with coupon) in a fixed income offering. *See* **Chapter 2.**

Competitive Bid Procedure for offering securities for sale through a bidding process that has its antecedents in the Public Utility Holding Company Act of 1935 requirement (repealed in 1994) that securities of companies coming under the Act access public capital via open competition. *See* **Chapter 2.**

(CommScan) Compliance Desk Electronic link between The National Association of Securities Dealers Regulation, Inc. (NASDR) and underwriters that permits rapid dissemination of compliance issues, releases, alerts, etc.

Comps *See* **Comparables.**

Conduct Rules Established by the Board of Governors of the National Association of Securities Dealers (NASD) to foster just and equitable principles of trade and business: maintenance of high standards of commercial honor and integrity among members; prevention of fraud and manipulative practices; establishment of safeguards against unreasonable profits, commissions and other charges; and collaboration with governmental and other agencies to protect investors and the public interest in accordance with Section 15A of the Maloney Act, which provides for the regulation of the over-the-counter market through national securities associations registered with the SEC.

Consensus Estimate Arithmetic average of all publicly published securities analysts' earnings per share estimates for a company.

Control/Control Person Formally defined by the SEC as the power to direct or cause the direction of the management and policies of a person. Control may exist through direct or indirect means, including stock ownership, official position as an officer or director, contracts, personal relationships, long standing behavior patterns, etc. Insofar as stock or other equity securities ownership is concerned, control will generally exist with ownership of far less than a numerical majority of the outstanding stock or securities. The concept of control relates to the existence of an affiliation relationship and affiliates are frequently referred to as "control" persons. Determination as to whether a control relationship exists, and therefore whether a person is an affiliate, always depends on all the facts and circumstances. However, as a general rule of thumb, executive officers, directors, and persons owning 10 percent or more of the equity securities of a corporation, and the general partner(s) of a limited partnership will each be deemed to be an affiliate of or control person of the entity in question. In addition, each person ordinarily will be deemed to control members of his or her family living in their home. Only a very careful exploration of the relationships among controlling, controlled and commonly controlled parties will provide an understanding of what persons are part of a control group and, therefore, affiliates of one another. *See* Section 15 of the 33 Act and Section 20 of the 34 Act, both of which provide joint and several liability for controlling persons of issuers in the case of securities laws violations. The determination of control person status and whether an affiliation relationship exists are also important in determining the availability of certain securities registration resale exemptions under both federal and many state laws. *See* **Affiliate.**

Convertible Arbitrage   Simultaneous long purchase of a convertible security and short sale of the convertible's underlying common stock according to a predetermined ratio.

Correspondent Relationship   Where one securities firm depends upon another securities firm to perform one or more functions. Most often used in execution, clearing and/or settlement.

Cover   Colloquial term for the front page of a prospectus or short for "cover bid."

Cover Bid   Runner-up in a competitive bid—second best proposal received by the issuer.

Covered Securities   Several classes of securities denominated under Section 18 of the 33 Act as to which federal law has preempted any state securities law registration requirements (generally those traded on the NYSE, AMEX, or Nasdaq National Market; registered investment companies; sales to "qualified purchasers" as that term is defined by the SEC and certain private placements made under Section 4(2) of the 33 Act, *i.e.,* Rule 506 transactions but not Rule 504 or 505 transactions). *See* **National Securities Markets Improvements Act of 1996** and **Chapter 1.**

Cross Border   Securities transaction occurring across the boundary of two different nations.

Cube (Lucite)   Colloquial term for a deal/transaction memento or souvenir. Derived from 1960s technology that encased a miniature copy of a prospectus in a lucite cube for desktop display. *See* **Deal Toy, Lucite,** and **Memento.**

The Curb   Colloquial term for the American Stock Exchange (AMEX) which traces its roots to merchants and auctioneers trading securities at the docksides of lower New York City sometime before 1793. Outdoor trading of unlisted securities, facilitated by hand signals from on-street brokers to their upstairs colleagues sitting in often open office windows, began at Wall and Hanover Streets and later moved south to Broad Street in the 1840s. Trading came indoors to its current location in 1921. Its name was modified often, becoming the New York Curb Agency in 1908, then . . . Association in 1911 . . . Market in 1921 . . . Exchange in 1929 and American Stock Exchange in 1953. The Exchange became a wholly owned subsidiary of the NASD on November 2, 1998.

Cursory Review   Quick completion of the required SEC review of a registration statement, usually accomplished in considerably less than the maximum time period and carrying few if any comments. *See* **Comments.**

Deal Economics   *See* **Fee Split.**

Deal Expenses   All legitimate expenses incurred in the execution of an investment banking transaction. There are usually two categories—issuer and underwriter. *See* **Chapter 4.**

Deal Toy   1970s evolution of a deal cube whereby miniature reproductions of an issuing company's product are crafted into a memento of the transaction. *See* **Cube, Lucite,** and **Memento.**

Dealer   Individual or firm acting as principal rather than as agent. Typically, a dealer buys for its own account and sells to a customer from its own inventory. A dealer's profit or loss is the difference between the price paid and the price received for the same security. The dealer's confirmation to the customer must disclose it has acted as principal. A firm may function, at different times, either as broker (agent) or dealer (principal). For example, a specialist on the floor of an exchange acts as a dealer when it buys or sells stock for its own account to maintain a market (affirmative obligation) and acts as a broker when it executes a limit order left with it by a floor broker.

Dealer Agreement   Contract between a selling group member (selected dealer) and the syndicate manager defining terms of the offering and binding the dealer to NASD conformity and SEC trading restrictions. *See* **Selected Dealer Agreement** and **Chapter 2.**

Dealer Re-allowance   Largest discount from the offering price of a new issue security at which two securities dealers may trade as principal with each other.

Dealing Room   Euro term for a securities firm's trading floor.

Delayed Delivery   An issuer option (to institutions or in rare cases to individuals) to extend settlement(s) beyond the original closing date. A Delayed Delivery Contract is drawn between the purchaser and the issuing company. Underwriters' commitments and the overall size of the offering are reduced by the amount of participation in a Delayed Delivery sale. (Editor's note—Delayed Delivery Contracts generally require a minimum of $250,000 principal amount of investment.) *See* **Chapter 2.**

Delivery Date   *See* **Settlement Date.**

Depository Trust Company (DTC)   Established in its present form on May 11, 1973, having evolved from the old Central Certificate Service—an exchange clearing and settlement mechanism. It is the result of an industry-wide effort to deal with the paperwork crisis of the late 1960s. In an ironic twist, surging volume resulting from the bull market of that era choked the street's antiquated trade processing facilities. In an extraordinary move, secondary markets were closed on Wednesdays from June 12 to December 31, 1968, to enable firms to clear up their unprocessed trade backlogs and install more modern data processing equipment and procedures. In addition, four-day settlement was extended to five-day and NYSE trading hours were shortened to 9:30 A.M. to 2:30 P.M. Today, DTC is both a limited purpose trust company (with membership in the Federal Reserve System) and a clearing agency registered with the SEC as an SRO. It is the world's largest central securities depository through which members effect securities deliveries and payment between each other via computerized electronic bookkeeping entries, thereby eliminating the physical movement of securities certificates.[5]

Derivative (Investment Bank Service-Marked) Security
See separate listing at end of Glossary.

Designated Order   *See* **Directed Order.**

Designated Security   Regulatory designation for penny stock, for most purposes describing an issue of securities selling at less than $5 per share, with less than $2 million in balance sheet assets and not traded on Nasdaq or a bona fide national securities exchange.

Direct Public Offering (DPO)   Offering of new securities handled by the issuing company without assistance of an underwriter or soliciting dealer.

Directed Order   Institutions may request protection for a large order of an underwritten issue through the syndicate manager, directly from a "pot" of securities (Institutional Pot) set aside for this purpose. Through the manager, the institution may designate ("direct") the sales credits attached to these securities to certain underwriters or selected dealers. Such securities are confirmed and delivered by the lead manager, with sales credits paid out as part of final underwriter settlement. *See* **Manager Bill Deliver** and **Chapters 5** and **6.**

------

5. The editors thank Edward J. McGuire, Jr., Anthony Reres and Stephen Wheeler for their help in explaining the raison d'être and genesis of DTC.

Distribution   Crucial to several key provisions of, but not specifically defined in, the 33 Act. Process by which securities find their way from private hands (the issuer or its stockholders) into public hands. Frequently, a distribution may take the form of a public offering, but it may also refer to a series of one or more private sales (and resales) that ultimately come to rest in the hands of the investing public. Also, indicating the act of sending something to an investor, *e.g.,* cash dividend, additional shares, etc.

Distribution Report   Sales report compiled to show sales by state and by type of account, and often used as a marketing tool by investment bankers to demonstrate distribution prowess.

Dividend Policy   Statement by a company's board of directors as to its longer term intent as to payment of dividends, *e.g.,* as a minimum percentage of earnings or at a low quarterly amount with a year end extra or special dividend that varies, based on operating results.

Dog and Pony Show   Company or investment bank sponsored trip to visit investors that is not related to an underwritten transaction.

Done Deal   Previously rumored and now announced deal that has not yet formally closed.

Down Grade   Reduction in the credit rating of a company by a recognized rating agency. *See* **Up Grade.**

DPO   *See* **Direct Public Offering.**

DRIP   Dividend Reinvestment Plan.

Drop   Declination of an underwriting invitation by a dealer.

DTC   Depository Trust Company.

Due Diligence   Pursuant to preparation for a transaction, the formal procedure whereby an investment bank(s) and its (their) counsel perform all necessary inspection and examination of a company's operations, books and records in order to satisfy it (themselves) as to the accuracy and legitimacy of the company's statements and representations with regard to past history, current operations and future prospects. Investment banks acting in an underwriting or advisory capacity are of necessity exposed to potential claims that may be made against them under certain provisions of the 33 Act, 34

Act or 40 Act should the transaction go awry. Their standard defense is demonstration of performance of due diligence. *See* **Chapter 2.**

Due Diligence Meeting   Historically, an informational meeting involving all parties associated with the underwriting of a new issue. The meeting allowed participating underwriters to meet management and ask questions pertaining to the preliminary prospectus and the disclosure contained therein. As the pace of underwriting activity accelerated in the 1980s and 1990s, this type of meeting has fallen into disuse as participating underwriters increasingly rely totally on the lead manager to perform the due diligence function.

Earnings Comparison   Examination of the relationship of a company's current quarterly earnings with its prior quarter in the same year or the same quarter of the prior year.

Earnings to Fixed Charges Coverage   Number of times an issuer's earnings cover its fixed charges. Usually expressed to one decimal point and an important ratio used in determining a fixed income security's rating.

EBITDA   Earnings before interest, taxes, depreciation, and amortization.

EASDAQ   European Association of Securities Dealers Automated Quotation.

e-Dealer   Selling group participant in an electronic distribution of an underwriting.

EDGAR   (SEC's) Electronic Data Gathering and Retrieval (System).

Effective   Declaration by the SEC that its review of a registration statement is complete. After the SEC declares a registration statement effective, the lead manager may release the securities for sale, commence the offering, and confirm indications of interest into orders.

Effective date   Date on which the SEC declares a registration statement to be in effect; generally no earlier than the 20th calendar day after filing the registration statement.

Electronic Data Gathering and Retrieval (EDGAR) System
SEC's automated system under which public companies and other

reporting companies who must comply with responsibilities to file documents under the federal securities laws effect such filings electronically. As of May 16, 1996, all public and reporting companies were required to file via EDGAR. The original idea behind EDGAR was to make data immediately available to the investment community under the efficient market theory, and it was hoped by some that eventually EDGAR or its successor would permit immediate, real-time, electronic dissemination of prospectuses and other information about public offerings and public companies. The intended result would be to level substantially the information playing field between analysts and other information insiders and the general public. In September 1995 the SEC opened a Web site on the Internet <http://www.sec.gov>, making all EDGAR entries available free of charge 24 hours after filing.

e-Manager　　Lead manager of an e-Syndicate.

Employee Retirement Income Security Act (ERISA)　　1974 Act, as amended, which, along with regulations promulgated thereunder by the Internal Revenue Service and the Department of Labor, comprise the regulatory environment for tax-favored retirement and other employee benefit plans.

Enterprise Value　　Sum of public company's market capitalization plus its total debt outstanding.

ERISA　　Employee Retirement Income Security Act of 1974.

ESOP　　Employee Stock Ownership Plan.

e-Syndicate　　Sub-syndicate comprised exclusively of dealers intending to distribute an underwritten issue electronically.

European Association of Securities Dealers Automated Quotation (EASDAQ)　　Brussels-based European equity market equivalent of the U.S. Nasdaq.

Exchange　　Self-Regulatory Organization (SRO) registered with and regulated by the SEC, under the auspices of which listed securities are traded. Exchanges may be national (*e.g.,* New York and American) or regional (*e.g.,* Boston, Chicago, Chicago Board Options, Pacific, and Philadelphia) or electronic (*e.g.,* Arizona and Cincinnati) or international.

Exchange Distribution   Rarely used technique whereby a seller of a large block of stock arranges to have a brokerage firm (for an agency fee) or an underwriter (for an underwriting fee) distribute the shares. The purchase is executed, an announcement appears on the relevant exchange tape that the block crossed was an "exchange distribution" (in an agency arrangement) or that the distribution is on-going (in an underwritten arrangement). Different from a "spot secondary" in that, in an exchange distribution, individual transactions are executed on the exchange floor and reported on the tape individually.

Fallen Angel   Once high-flying public company whose stock price has fallen dramatically.

FCS   *See* **Financial Communications Society.**

(The) Fed   United States Federal Reserve System. *See* **Chapter 1.**

Fed Watcher   Securities analyst who devotes his/her time to analyzing the activities of the Fed.

Federal Energy Regulatory Commission (FERC)   Oversees public utility companies. *See* **35 Act** and **Chapter 1.**

Fee Split or Split   Pre-arranged basis upon which co-managers divide the management fee, underwriting fee, free retentions, and institutional pot sales credits. Often very contentious and nowhere disclosed to the public in writing. Also known as "deal economics."

FERC   *See* **Federal Energy Regulatory Commission.**

Filing   Actual filing of a registration statement by an issuer with the Securities and Exchange Commission. From 1933 until 1996, a physical event but now electronic via EDGAR.

Filing Fee(s)   Payable by a registrant upon filing of a registration statement. *See* **Chapter 1** for description and calculation.

Filing Range   Price range, usually a $2 spread (but sometimes $3), appearing on the cover of a preliminary prospectus and used by underwriters as the initial starting point for valuation and by issuers as the basis for calculation of the SEC filing fee.

Final Prospectus   Widely distributed portion of a company's registration statement. The formal written document that sets forth the facts concerning an existing business enterprise that an investor needs to make an informed decision. It also includes all the information which the preliminary prospectus contains plus the price at which the security was offered to the public, the underwriting discount, the sales concession allowed to the members of the underwriting group and selected dealers, the maximum reallowance discount for interdealer trading and the breakdown of amounts underwritten by syndicate members (bracketing).

Final Settlement   The closing accounting and exchange of monies between the lead manager and all underwriters, requiring documentation of all expenses incurred in bringing the issue to market. Under NASD rules, this event must occur no later than 90 days after the transaction itself closes or the lead manager becomes subject to NASD sanction (popularly known as the "Blum-Cashman Rule" named after its long-time proponents). *See* **Chapter 6.**

Final Underwriting Account   List of underwriters and their statutory commitments which appears in a final prospectus in the "underwriting" section. *See* **Bracketing.**

Financial Communications Society (FCS)   Not-for-profit organization dedicated to improvement of professional standards in financial communications. *See* **Chapter 8.**

Financial Services Act (FSA)   Enacted November 6, 1986, to create a regulatory oversight structure for the London financial markets.

Firm   Ready to effect a transaction as opposed to "subject" to one or more conditions that must be met prior to execution of a transaction. *See* **Subject.**

Fixed Price Reoffering   For almost all underwritten issues, the negotiated price at which the underwriter(s) and dealers, if any, reoffer the securities to the public. Under NASD Rules of Fair Practice, a dealer cannot sell shares of an underwritten offering at a price higher than that set forth in the prospectus. SEC rules allow the lead manager to "peg" the issue price, if necessary, through the use of a syndicate stabilizing bid to maintain an orderly secondary market until the distribution is deemed complete and syndicate price and trading restrictions have been removed. *See* **Chapter 5.**

Flat Description of an underwriting account that is neither long nor short—zero inventory.

Follow-on Offering Underwritten new issue of shares that already have an existing public market.

Force Majeure Unexpected or disruptive event that may excuse a party from a contract. *See* **Chapter 6.**

Form S-1 Used for registration under the 33 Act for securities of a registrant for which no other form is authorized. IPOs are typically filed on Form S-1.

Form S-2 Used for registration under the 33 Act for companies already subject to SEC filing for a period of 12 months. Incorporates by reference the company's public documents already on file with the SEC.

Form S-3 Used for registration under the 33 Act for companies already subject to SEC filing for a period of 12 months that have at least $75 million in market capitalization. Incorporates by reference all public documents filed and to be filed by an issuer with the SEC in the next year or until the next Form 10-k is filed.

Formula Pricing Used on follow-on or secondary offerings only. Such an issue is typically priced according to a pre-determined "formula"—on the closing bid (for a Nasdaq listed issue) or at the last sale (for an exchange listed issue) and re-offered to the public concurrent with pricing. A precursor to 430-A offerings.

Forward Calendar Industry's or individual firm's backlog of publicly disclosed new business.

Forward Looking Statement Safe Harbor Enacted as a part of the Private Securities Litigation Reform Act of 1995 (Rule 175). The Safe Harbor is intended to encourage public companies to make predictive or forward looking statements by providing protection from liability if actual events do not occur as predicted and if Safe Harbor procedures were followed at the time such forward looking statements were written or made. To qualify for the Safe Harbor, among other things, the predictive statements must be reasonable based upon the information and assumptions known to the company at the time the statements are made, and the investing public must have been told or had access to what the company views are the

principal risks and uncertainties that will impact its ability to achieve
the future event or goal. The quality of disclosures made in attempts
to navigate into the Safe Harbor have varied greatly, ranging from
candid assessment of a company's future that the framers of the
statute and the SEC had hoped for to boilerplate lists of generic risk
factors that have done little to enhance the quality of disclosure to
investors. This formal focus on future events marked a sharp break
with past SEC practice which at one time had rules absolutely
prohibiting use of forward looking or predictive information. SEC
policy and party line for many years was simply that investors could
only receive historical information because predictive information
was inherently unreliable. The specific provisions of the Safe Harbor
apply only to 34 Act reports and liabilities; however, it is common
to see Safe Harbor cautionary statements in 33 Act documents.

Fourth Market   Unofficial off-exchange forum whereby buyers
and sellers (usually institutional investors) conduct transactions
without benefit of a securities firm agent/dealer intermediary but
often facilitated by Instinet.

Free Retention   Securities that an underwriter may distribute in
any manner it so chooses without disclosing the precise nature
of that distribution to any other party (including the lead manager).
See **Retention.**

Free-Riding and With-Holding   Free-Riding is either the
prohibited practice whereby an investor buys and sells a new issue
security so rapidly as to avoid actually putting up any money, or the
prohibited practice of an NASD member firm selling securities to
preferred individuals while unfilled orders from the public still exist.
With-Holding is the prohibited practice wherein a syndicate member
withholds a portion of newly issued securities from the public in
anticipation of selling them at a price higher than the initial public
offering price. *See* **Chapter 7.**

Freed-Up or Free to Trade   Termination of a syndicate.
Underwriting and selling group members are no longer held to the
Agreement Among Underwriters provision to sell only at the fixed
offering price but may buy and sell the issue at market prices.

FSA   *See* **Financial Services Act.**

Fully Disclosed Clearing Arrangement Where a clearing firm knows the name and identification of its client firms' investor customers. It processes ("clears") the client firms' transactions, carries the client firms' investor customer accounts (and any margin balances) on its books and generates the client firms' month-end investor customer statements. *See* **Omnibus Clearing Arrangements.**

General Corporate Purposes Catch-all phrase used in "Use of Proceeds" section of a prospectus to describe all other uses for monies raised in a new issue of securities not already specifically described.

Give-Up Portion of an underwriter's commitment which the lead manager withholds for sales to institutions (via the institutional pot) and Selected Dealers (via the selling group pot). Calculated as the difference between underwriting commitment and final retention. *See* **Retention.**

Glass-Steagall Act *See* **Banking Act of 1933.**

Global Offering An underwriting with tranches offered in more than one country and in more than one continent.

Good Faith Deposit Dollar amount (usually three percent of the face amount of the securities offered for sale) that must be in the hands of an issuer before a bidder's proposal receives consideration. Once common in competitive bidding, this practice is seldom used today.

Green Shoe (The Shoe) Another term for the over-allotment option granted to underwriters in the Underwriting Agreement. It was first used in an offering for the Green Shoe Company in 1963. *See also* **Over-Allotment** and **Chapter 5.**

Greenwich Research Survey Third-party survey that ranks subscribing client securities firms by a number of subjective criteria within that firm's peer group. The individual names of its peers are not disclosed to the subscriber.

Gross Spread In an underwritten transaction, the difference between the price paid to an issuer by the underwriter(s) and the reoffering price that purchasers must pay. The gross spread is the pre-expense fee earned by underwriters and has traditionally been broken down into a management fee (approximately 20 percent), an underwriting fee (20 to 30 percent) and a selling concession (50 to 60 percent), but there are no hard and fast rules covering this breakdown. *See* **Chapter 4.**

Group Sale   Originally used to describe a procedure whereby institutional purchases from the pot carry no designation for credit to specific underwriters. Purchase is made out of the "institutional pot," and each underwriter receives sales credits based on the percentage its underwriting commitment bears to the entire offering. In current practice, an offering subject to group sale usually means that the lead manager will not allocate any free retention shares to underwriters. Rather, the lead manager, possibly co-managers, and perhaps a select number of firms who are "friends of the company," will place all shares on behalf of the entire syndicate. The lead manager then compensates each underwriter not allocated shares with a dollar amount equal to the sales credits that would have been earned on a normal free retention (*e.g.,* 10 percent of its underwriting commitment). *See* **Chapter 5.**

Gun Jumping   Any activity that may be deemed to violate the strict limits on publicity imposed by the 33 Act on any company planning a federally registered public offering. Such limits apply commencing with the decision to make a public offering and last until after distribution of the securities is complete. Designed to insure that the selling of securities in a public offering occurs principally via the formal documents filed with the SEC (the prospectus and other documents comprising the registration statement). Limited communications are permitted by certain rules of the 33 Act, the best known of which cover tombstone advertisements seen in the financial press that simply give bare bones, purely factual information about an offering.

Hedge Fund   Non-SEC registered investment partnership with wide investment latitude. Often erroneously used as a description of an investor that purchases new issues with a view to immediate resale; more accurately known as a "flipper."

Hot Deal   Street term for an in demand issue. *See* **Cold Deal.**

Hot Issue   Official NASD term describing an offering where demand exceeds supply such that the issue trades at a premium above its initial offering price in the aftermarket. Special NASD restrictions apply to Hot Issues which necessitate completion of a Hot Issue Questionnaire. The NASD prohibits purchase of shares of a Hot Issue by employees of securities firms, their immediate families and certain other individuals. *See* **Cold Issue** and **Free-Riding** and **With-Holding** and **Chapter 7.**

House of Issue   An investment bank with a long record of originating/lead managing new issues.

I|B|E|S, Inc.   Institutional Brokers Estimate System.

Illiquidity/Illiquid Market   *See* **Thin Market.**

In Principle   In theory—without regard to an actual situation. As used in an underwriting invitation—morally but not legally binding.

Indication of Interest   Dealer's or investor's non-binding interest in purchasing securities that are in registration. Indications of interest are not firm commitments to buy a security and should be solicited only with information obtained from a preliminary prospectus. Each prospective purchaser must receive a preliminary prospectus. Indications of interest are meant to be an accurate reflection of investor interest in an offering, and the sum total of such indications of interest is the pre-price book in a deal. *See* **Book.**

Information Agent   Company dedicated to distributing information regarding a transaction to the owners of (shareholders) or lenders to (bond holders) one of the businesses involved in a transaction. *See* **Proxy Solicitor.**

Initial Offering Price   Fixed price shown on the cover of the final prospectus, as contrasted with the expected offering price (or price range) indicated on the preliminary prospectus (red herring) and the aftermarket price(s) once the security is free to trade.

Initial Public Offering (IPO)   Company's first offering of stock to the public which may be all primary (new), all secondary (already issued and outstanding), or a combination of primary and secondary.

Inside Market   High bid and low offer in a Nasdaq or other dealer market. *See* **Bid** and **Ask.**

Insider Trading Sanctions Acts (the Insider Trading Sanctions Acts of 1984, ITSA, and the **Insider Trading and Securities Fraud Enforcement Act of 1988, ITSFEA)**   Popular names given to statutes adopted in the mid- and late-1980s amending the 34 Act to impose civil, monetary, and criminal penalties (in addition to those arising under general anti-fraud provisions) for the misuse of inside information. ITSFEA replaced and expanded upon the now repealed ITSA. Passed by Congress partly in response to the highly publicized insider trading abuses of senior executives of both the securities and business communities. Civil fines may be the greater of three times the profit made or loss avoided or $1 million per violation. Persons deemed to have controlled the violator (*e.g.,* the violator's employer) are subject to the same fines, if the control person knew or recklessly disregarded the fact that the controlled person was likely to engage in a violation and failed to take appropriate action. Additionally, if the control person is a registered broker dealer or investment advisor, it is subject to such fines if it knowingly or recklessly failed to establish, maintain or enforce any policy or procedure required by any applicable statute or regulation to prevent insider trading abuses. *See* **Chapter 1.**

Institutional Investor Magazine All-Star Poll   Annual poll started in 1972. Taken of unnamed buy side investors that rank sell side securities research analysts and published in the October edition of the magazine. Analysts named in this poll are referred to as "II All-Stars."

Institutional Pot/Institutional Pot Orders   Managing underwriters often establish a "pot" which will "protect" stock for institutional clients. Institutions are theoretically able to designate the sales credits attached to portions of their total order to any member(s) of the underwriting account or other selected dealers. In practice, the lead manager normally obtains the lion's share. Designated (or directed) orders are typically treated as "Manager Bill and Deliver" (MBDs) with all of the order processing and settling handled directly between the institutional investors and the bookrunning manager. *See* **Chapter 5.**

Integrated Disclosure System   Refers to the SEC's formal adoption in 1982 of coordinated disclosure requirements and forms for 33 Act and 34 Act obligations, requiring disclosure of substantially identical information in substantially identical format, in connection with the initial issuance and registration of securities and for companies subject to the periodic reporting and other requirements imposed under Section 12 of the 34 Act. Although long sought after, adoption of an integrated disclosure system represented a significant lessening of the disclosure burden on issuers who had previously been required to compile and report different information on different SEC forms. At the same time, adoption of this system was intended to enhance investor protection by providing uniform information to investors regardless of whether such investors purchased securities directly from issuers in a registered offering or in the secondary marketplace from third persons.

International Primary Markets Association (IPMA)   Dealer group formed in the mid-1980s to codify new issue underwriting practices in the Eurobond Market.

International Securities Markets Association (ISMA)   Successor organization to the Association of International Bond Dealers (AIBD). Founded in 1968 as a Swiss organization, headquartered in Zurich but with most of its market making member firms operating out of London, to establish rules for and oversee the conduct of the Eurobond Market. ISMA affiliation satisfies an international securities firm's requirement to attain membership in an offshore exchange.

IPMA   *See* **International Primary Markets Association.**

IPO   Initial Public Offering.

ISMA   *See* **International Securities Markets Association.**

ITS   Intermarket Trading System.

ITSA   *See* **Insider Trading Sanctions Act.**

ITSFEA   *See* **Insider Trading and Securities Fraud Enforcement Act.**

Issuer Request   *See* **Company Request.**

Jump Ball Pot   With regard to institutional pot sales credits, this arrangement theoretically puts all co-managers and underwriters on equal footing in competing for orders. In reality, the book running manager almost always has a distinct edge, and issuers sometimes elect to limit or "cap" the lead manager's portion of sales credits. *See* **Chapter 5.**

Kicker   Special feature(s) added to a security to increase its marketability by offering the prospect of additional price appreciation; or to the terms of purchase (*e.g.,* timing of an offering of a yield security to give the purchaser five dividends in just over 12 months). Also called "sweetener," "bell & whistle," or "wrinkle."

Know Your Customer   Article 3 of the NASD Rules of Fair Practice and NYSE Rule 405.

Lead Manager/Underwriter   Investment bank selected by the issuer/seller of an underwritten offering to act as the leader of the offering, *i.e.,* "run the books." Until the 1970s, most underwritten issues had only one sole manager. Today, most issues have co-managers with one designated as the "lead"—the firm in over-all charge. In the mid-1990s a trend naming "co-lead" managers started to develop. While the term "co-lead" is an oxymoron, it is also reflective of both the competitiveness that has developed among underwriters seeking "the books" and the growing reluctance on the part of issuer clients to make a difficult choice.

League Tables   Quarterly and annual tables published by third-party statistical services to rank investment banking activity by a variety of measures, *e.g.,* total dollar volume, number of deals lead-managed or co-managed, etc. Used by firms in their pitch books to indicate investment banking prowess.

Leaves   A trade report. Unexecuted portion of an order that remains after part of the order has been completed (*e.g.,* an order to sell 10,000 shares at 20 has 5,000 shares trade — the report back to the executing broker/dealer is "sold 5,000 at 20; leaves 5,000; last $19^7/_8$ bid for 1,000—1,000 offered at $20^1/_8$.")

Legend Stock/Lettered Stock   Popular way of referring to stock or other securities received in a private placement. The terms probably arose because of the practice of putting a legend on such securities referring to their limited transferability; and/or the requirement for the execution of an investment letter in which the purchaser acknowledges the limited transferability and represents that the securities are being acquired for investment and without a view to, or in connection with, any distribution in violation of applicable securities registration provisions. Technically, the terms were superseded by the SEC's adoption in the early 1970s of the term "restricted securities."

(Nasdaq) Level I, II, III Service   The Nasdaq stock market offers three types ("levels") of service: Level I—inside quote for individual securities and available globally on salespersons' desktops; Level II—quotations of all market makers for a security and available only to trading departments of both sell side brokers and buy side institutional investors; Level III—quotations of all market makers for a security but available only to registered Nasdaq market makers (who are able to update/change their markets via desktop terminals).

Liability   There are three types of liabilities relating to underwriting syndicates. Pot Liability—each underwriter is responsible for a percentage of any unsold long position in the "pot" based on its underwriting as a percentage of the total underwriting commitment; however, underwriters who have taken down (retained) their entire underwriting commitment escape this liability. Stabilization Liability—each underwriter is responsible pro rata for its percentage of any loss incurred on disposition of securities purchased in stabilization regardless of its retention, and the percentage is based on its underwriting as a percentage of the total underwriting commitment. Loss on Oversale—each underwriter is responsible, pro rata, for its percentage of any loss incurred in covering a naked short position in the pot. Again, the percentage is as calculated in the prior two examples.

The List   Entire roster of companies whose shares trade (are "listed") on an exchange.

Loaded   Refers to a preferred stock nearing its dividend declaration date. Since preferred stock dividends do not officially accrue (like bond interest), the "loaded" description is an informal market technique for approximating the accrual process.

Lock-Up Agreement   Formal restriction(s) on re-sale of securities owned by insider(s)/control person(s).

Long Position   In reference to an underwriting, the total of all undistributed securities. In reference to the pot, the total amount of undistributed securities in the pot.

Lucite (Cube or **Deal Toy)**   *See* **Memento.**

M & A   Merger and Acquisition.

MAC   *See* **Material Adverse Change.**

Major Firm   Firm regularly appearing in the first underwriting bracket below the manager(s). Normally second highest status in the underwriting social pecking order, but below bulge (or special) bracket if one exists. *See* **Bracketing** and **Chapter 3.**

Maloney Act   1938 legislation creating the National Association of Securities Dealers (NASD).

Managed Business   An offering for which a firm is acting either as lead manager (running the books) or as co-manager and evidenced by the appearance of its name on the cover of the prospectus.

Manager Bill & Deliver Order (Manager B&D or MBD) Occurs when an institution purchases securities directly from an underwriter(s) (away from the institutional pot) and later requests that the lead manager withhold the securities from such underwriter(s) and deliver them directly to the purchasing institution—in effect, a bookkeeping device. *See* **Chapter 5.**

Management Fee   Portion of the gross spread in an underwriting that goes only to the lead manager and any co-manager(s). Currently it is approximately 20 percent in a negotiated transaction and five percent in a competitive transaction, although no hard and fast rules exist. Its actual amount is not disclosed to the public nor is the split of this fee between managers (if there is more than one) disclosed— a split that may be even or uneven. *See* **Chapter 4.**

Management's Discussion and Analysis (MD&A)   Section of a prospectus where company management discusses its views on the reasons for its operational and financial performance.

Managing Underwriter   Lead investment banking firm of a syndicate formed for the purchase and distribution of a new issue of securities. The Agreement Among Underwriters authorizes the managing underwriter, or syndicate manager, broad and sweeping powers to act as leader for the group in structuring, marketing, pricing, purchasing, distributing and trading the issue in the immediate aftermarket. The firm "running the books".

Marginable Offerings   A stock may be eligible for purchase on margin on underwritten offering terms if it is being offered from selling shareholders covered under the registration statement. If the underwritten stock is listed on an exchange or Nasdaq but is a primary offering, then there is a thirty day waiting period before it is eligible for margin. Such determination is made by The Board of the Federal Reserve. IPOs are never marginable on initial offering terms.

Mark Up Session   A meeting held to revise, rewrite, or edit an underwriting document.

Market Out Clause   Provision(s) under which an underwriting syndicate may not honor its underwriting agreement commitment. *See* **Chapters 2** and **4.**

Market Return   Return provided by an index measuring a specific market activity or sector. Often used as a benchmark against which to measure performance.

Material Adverse Change (MAC)   An event, as relates to the financial condition of a SEC reporting company, deemed significant enough to cause breach of an underwriting agreement. *See* **Chapter 2.**

Material Information   Concept describing information which a typical investor would reasonably consider important in making an investment decision concerning a security (buy, sell, or hold). The information must be considered in light of the total mix of all other information available to the investor and, according to some courts, may be material even if it would not have changed the ultimate decision to buy, sell or hold. Material misstatements or omissions of material information form the basis for violation of numerous securities laws. *See* **Antifraud Provisions.**

Maximum Filing Price (MFP)   Upper end of the filing range of an offering. Used strictly to calculate SEC and NASD filing fees. *See* **Chapter 1.**

MBD *See* **Manager Bill & Deliver Order.**

McLagen Survey   Third-party survey ranking subscribing client securities firms by any number of subjective criteria within a firm's peer group, such as commissions, lead managed offerings, etc. The names of peers are not disclosed to the subscriber. Know colloquially as the "McLagen numbers."

MD&A   *See* **Management's Discussion** and **Analysis.**

Memento   Ad hoc creation to memorialize an underwritten offering or other investment banking transaction. Usually a document, prospectus or tombstone, framed, or encased in lucite. Traditionally handed out at the closing dinner. *See* **Cube, Lucite,** and **Deal Toy.**

Mezzanine Bracket   Underwriting bracket whose participation commitment is less than the major firms but greater than any regional firms. *See* **Bracketing** and **Chapter 3.**

MFP   *See* **Maximum Filing Price.**

Morning Call   Formal, firm-wide, daily, trading floor originated conference call held to allow dissemination of research, secondary market, and new issue information to all sales and trading personnel.

Naked Short   Oversold syndicate short position that exceeds the amount that may be purchased (covered) from the issuer/seller as part of any over-allotment option. *See* **Chapter 5.**

NASAA   *See* **North American Securities Administrators Association.**

NASD   National Association of Securities Dealers, Inc.

National Best Bid or Best Offer (NBBO)   At an instant in time, the highest bid for and lowest offer of a particular exchange listed security. Comparable to Nasdaq's inside market.

National Securities Markets Improvements Act of 1996 (NSMIA)
Crafted at the behest of an alliance of securities industry interest groups and strongly opposed by state securities regulators. NSMIA was intended to modernize securities regulation by eliminating certain federal and state regulatory overlaps through Congressional preemption of state powers. Included are preemption of certain state powers to regulate investment companies (mutual funds), investment

advisors, broker-dealers, and securities sales. *See* **Covered Securities** and **Chapter 1.**

Nationally Recognized Statistical Rating Organization (NRSRO)
SEC's formal designation for a securities rating agency, thereby qualifying its ratings for legal and technical use.

NBBO   *See* **National Best Bid** or **Best Offer.**

Negotiated Deal   Underwritten offering where the non-money terms and the public offering price are determined through discussion ("negotiation") between the managing underwriter and the issuer rather than through a competitive bidding process.

Net Interest Cost (NIC)   Determinant of high or "winning" proposal in a competitive bid for fixed income securities. Calculated by dividing the proposed interest rate for a bond coupon (dividend for a preferred stock) by the bid ("price to be paid to the issuer"). The low NIC is the high bid. *See* **Chapter 2.**

(The) New York Society of Security Analysts, Inc. (NYSSA)
Founded in 1937 as a public financial forum and avenue for professional development. Today, it offers a wide menu of activities, services conferences, events and educational courses. *See* **Chapter 7.**

NIC   *See* **Net Interest Cost.**

Nifty-Fifty   List of 50 growth stocks developed by Morgan Guaranty Trust Company in the early 1970s—at the time, so called "one-decision" stocks in which the purchase price was not deemed critical to the investment decision-making process under the assumption that underlying earnings growth would eventually justify the price paid. Morgan Stanley revived and revised the list in 1995.

Non-Money Terms   Details of an underwritten security that are not price or gross-spread related (*e.g.,* dividend or coupon dates, maturity, call, and sinking fund provisions, etc.).

(NASD) No Objections Letter   An opinion rendered by the staff of the NASD's Corporate Financing Department, on behalf of the NASD's Corporate Financing Committee, in which the staff states that it has "no objections" to the underwriting compensation and other distribution terms and arrangements of the issue under review.

North American Securities Administrators Association (NASAA)
Association of state and/or provincial securities administrators from
the United States and Canada that provides a central clearinghouse
for efforts to combat securities fraud, develops uniform (or at least
compatible) regulatory schemes and works with the SEC and the
private bar to coordinate changes in securities law and regulations.
NASAA is a very powerful lobbying body in both Congress and in
individual states.

NRSRO *See* **Nationally Recognized Statistical Rating
Organization.**

NSCC National Securities Clearing Corporation.

NSMIA *See* **National Securities Markets Improvement Act of
1996.**

NYSE New York Stock Exchange.

NYSSA *See* **The New York Society of Security Analysts, Inc.**

Off-Board Trading Transactions in exchange listed shares
occurring off the floor of such exchange.

Off-Board Trading Privilege Automatically granted to any
underwriter that is long securities after termination of offering price
and trading restrictions. Permits the underwriter(s) to dispose of such
securities in a net price/off-board transaction(s). *See* **Chapter 5.**

Off-the-Run Securities Noncurrent coupon U.S. Government and
Agency fixed income securities. *See* **On-the Run Securities.**

Offering

Primary	Securities are sold and proceeds received by the issuing company.
Secondary	Securities are sold and proceeds received by a selling stock holder(s).
Tender Offer	When Company *A* wants to acquire Company *B,* it issues a notice called a Tender Offer to acquire most or all of the outstanding common stock of Company *B* from Company *B*'s shareholders for a price usually higher

	(but not necessarily so) than the market price of the stock.
Exchange	Company wants to retire an outstanding issue of securities. It issues new securities at terms presumably slightly better (from the investor's eyes) to replace ("exchange") the ones it wants to retire.
Forced Conversion	Company calls for redemption of a convertible security at a price which makes it profitable for the holder to convert into the underlying common stock.

(The) Old Lady of Threadneedle Street   The Bank of England.

Old Rate   Number in the last published New York Stock Exchange minimum fixed rate commission schedule. (Editor's note—NYSE member firms were always permitted to charge more than this rate, but few in fact did.)

Omnibus Clearing Arrangement   Where a clearing firm does not know the name and identification of its client firms' investor customers. The clearing firm processes ("clears") the client firms' transactions but does not carry the client firms' investor customer accounts (or margin balances) on its books nor generate month-end investor customer statements. *See* **Clearing Correspondent** and **Fully Disclosed Clearing Arrangement.**

On-the-Run Securities   Current coupon U.S. Government and Agency securities. The term is derived from a no-longer-published daily list ("run") of all such securities produced for many years by Morgan Guaranty Trust Company.

One-on-One Meeting (One-on-One)   As relates to pre-price marketing of a new issue via a roadshow, a meeting between an institutional investor and senior officials of the issuer (most commonly the CEO and CFO), accompanied by a representative of the lead manager and usually held on the premises of the potential investor.

Open Ticketing   Procedure within a firm participating in an underwritten offering whereby any and all branches may take down securities on an equal access basis without going through indication of interest or allocation phases. In an "open ticketing" situation, brokers may take down an unlimited amount of securities until the ticketing status changes to "subject."

Ordinary Share (Ord)   Actual security underlying an American Depositary Receipt.

Out-of-Town Bracket   Now seldom used term analogous to regional bracket.

Over-Allotment Option (Green Shoe)   A technique of selling a greater number of securities than the issuer is offering for the purpose of creating buying power in the aftermarket to support the price of the offered securities if necessary. The Underwriting Agreement grants the underwriters an option to purchase additional shares from the issuer or selling shareholder only for the purpose of covering over-allotments. *See* **Chapter 5.**

Overnight Offering   Underwritten offering priced after the close of trading in a security's "home" market and offered globally with price and trading restrictions removed pre-opening in the home market the next day.

Papers   Commonly used term to describe the formal documents that accompany an underwriting invitation.

Par Value   In the case of common stock, the dollar amount assigned to each share by the issuing company's charter or articles of incorporation. At one time, par value represented the original investment in the company or the cash, goods or services that stood behind each share. Today, par value has little or no significance with regard to common stock, and shares often are labeled "no par" or "without par value." However, in the case of preferred stock or bonds, it has significance since it represents the value per individual security off which the preferred dividend or bond interest is calculated, and also represents the liquidation or redemption value (ignoring any cumulative dividends or accrued interest).

Participant   Underwriter or selling group member in an underwritten offering.

Participation   Level of activity or commitment when a firm acts as an underwriter or a selected dealer but not as a lead or co-manager. *See* **Commitment.**

Passive Market Making   Technique permitting an underwriter(s) to continue to make a secondary market in the underwritten security until the deal has been priced. *See* **Chapter 5.**

Penalty Bid   Technique to discourage flippers from operating in the immediate after market of an underwritten offering. The lead manager may place a penalty bid on its stabilizing or short-covering of an IPO and enforce the penalty by charging back the sales credits attached to repurchased shares to the underwriting member or selling group participant who originally distributed such stock. DTC facilitates this process by disclosing the seller's identity to the lead manager through DTC's electronic tracking process. *See* **Chapter 5.**

Penalty Charges and Physical Delivery of Shares   *See* **Chapter 6.**

Performance Report   Report prepared by the syndicate department showing commitments, free retentions, directed orders and total sales (retention) for each underwriter. It also lists selling group members and their takedowns, names and sizes of directed orders and any manager bills and delivers. Often used as a marketing tool in a beauty contest presentation.

PERP   Perpetual bond; one with no maturity date.

PHLX   Philadelphia Stock Exchange.

Physical Delivery   Long-time practice of actually sending ("delivering") securities to a purchaser. With the establishment of DTC, a practice now mostly restricted to evidence ownership in a privately held company.

Pink Herring   Unofficial reference to the documents permitted to be used to "test the waters" in accordance with SEC Rule 254.

Pitchbook   *See* **Beauty Contest.**

Pot   Amount of securities withheld by the manager for directed orders, group sales or selling group sales. *See* **Give-Up** and **Chapter 5.**

Pot Liability   Term describing an individual underwriter's contractual obligation to purchase its proportionate share of any unsold balance of an underwriting. Usually distributed to underwriters by the lead manager after termination of price and trading restrictions.

PPM   *See* **Private Placement Memorandum.**

Praecipium   Originally developed and widely used in eurobond offerings. So-called "super" management fee usually taken only by a global coordinator(s) in a multi-tranche, global offering. The carve out of a piece (normally 25 to 50 basis points—but no hard and fast rule exists) of the traditional management fee and payable only to the global coordinator(s) *e.g.,* a three percent gross spread produces a management fee of 60 basis points—the praecipium might range from 25 to 50 of this 60.

Preliminary Prospectus   Also known as a red herring and used to solicit pre-price interest in an underwritten offering. Gives preliminary information about the financial status of the registrant company, background of management, risk(s) of the offering, use of proceeds, etc. A preliminary prospectus is distinguishable from the final prospectus by the SEC-mandated red ink disclaimer strip printed on the left hand side of the cover page of the document indicating that the information contained therein is subject to completion or amendment; that a registration statement has been filed, but the SEC has not yet declared it effective; and that individual state securities laws govern distribution of the document. *See* **Final Prospectus.**

Pricing Meeting/Call   Meeting in which a deal is formally priced.

Price Talk   Pre-price indication of price and/or yield used in marketing a new issue. It can and often does change before actual terms are set.

Principal   Person for whom a broker executes an order; or, a dealer buying or selling for its own account; or, the amount of an individual's capital; or, the face amount of a bond ("face value").

Principal Transaction   One in which a dealer commits capital.

Private Placement   Section 4(2) of the 33 Act exempts certain transactions not involving "public offerings" of securities from the registration requirements of that Act. The term probably developed as a shorthand way of referring to transactions satisfying the statutory exemption. Ordinarily, the general term private placement encompasses not only a transaction satisfying the statutory private placement for an issuer of securities, but also a transaction satisfying one of the safe harbors set forth in Regulation D. There is no specific listing of the conditions to satisfy in order to qualify for a statutory private placement. A statutory private placement relies on a collection of SEC releases, administrative pronouncements, SEC litigation positions and court cases on the subject. Taken together, all of these authorities are not consistent with one another, so it is difficult to produce a coherent picture of what is required for a statutory private placement in all but the most certain of circumstances (*e.g.,* a private sale of securities to a single insurance company). In addition, reference to a private placement may also extend to an isolated sale or private transaction exemption provided for in various state securities laws. *See also* Section $4(1^1/_2)$ of the 33 Act.

Private Placement Memorandum (PPM)   Written document(s) providing narrative and financial disclosure for a private placement.

Prospectus   Specific portion of a registration statement filed with the SEC in a registered public offering, including the bulk of mandated narrative and financial disclosures. The prospectus is the portion of the registration statement distributed to the public. More generically, the term refers to any written offering document used in any offering (public or private). The issuing company, its legal counsel, the underwriter(s) and its(their) legal counsel all work together to prepare this document. It describes the company and the offering terms. A preliminary prospectus (red herring), issued prior to SEC effectiveness, contains sections which describe the use of proceeds; financial data; investment policies; description of company; description of offering and plan of distribution. The final prospectus, issued after effectiveness, also includes a list of underwriters, the price paid to the company, the gross spread or underwriter's compensation and other non-money terms, as well as any material change(s) which may have taken place between original filing and effectiveness. *See* **Preliminary Prospectus.**

Prospectus Delivery Requirement   Each prospective purchaser must receive a preliminary prospectus, and any and all amended preliminary prospectus(es). Each purchaser must receive a final prospectus accompanying its order confirmation. The requirement for ensuring compliance rests with the soliciting and/or order confirming underwriter or selected dealer.

Protection   Practice whereby an underwriting participant supplies ("protects") securities from its own free retention against a directed order.

Proxy Solicitor   Firm retained to assist in contacting investors to raise their response rate to the document in their possession. Works on behalf of shareholders or on behalf of a third party seeking to acquire control. *See* **Information Agent.**

Public Company   One whose stock has a quoted trading market.

Purchase Agreement   *See* **Underwriting Agreement.**

QIB   *See* **Qualified Institutional Buyer.**

QIU   *See* **Qualified Independent Underwriter.**

Qualified Independent Underwriter (QIU)   Independent pricer for certain underwritten offerings as per NASD schedule E. *See* **Chapters 7** and **8.**

Qualified Institutional Buyer (QIB)   Member of a class of institutional purchasers of securities (such as banks, insurance companies, broker-dealers or companies meeting certain minimum financial asset size standards) accorded special status under Rule 144A *See* **Rule 144A.**

Quiet Period   Period during which research, sales, and trading must operate under certain restrictions as relate to the secondary market securities of a company with a filed registration statement. *See* **Chapter 3.**

Quote and Size   Highest bid (to buy) and lowest offer (to sell) in a given market at a specified time accompanied by the size of each. When stated verbally, the bid price comes first followed by its size, then the offer size followed by its price—*e.g.,* 15 bid for a 1,000 (shares), 1,000 (shares) offered at $15^1/_4$. The numerical difference between the two numbers is called the spread, and the actual size of the spread is called its width.

Rating Service (Agency)   *See* **Nationally Recognized Statistical Rating Organization.**

Ratio of Earnings to Fixed Charges   *See* **Earnings to Fixed Charges Coverage.**

Re-allowance   Largest discount from the offering price at which trading between dealers may take place in a new issue security prior to the termination of its price and trading restrictions.

Recirculation   SEC requirement for underwriter(s) to redistribute ("recirculate") an amended preliminary prospectus 48 hours prior to pricing; the result of material change(s) to the original document.

Record Owner   In the case of ownership of securities, refers to the person or entity actually entered on the official records of the issuer or its transfer agent as the owner of such securities and used to determine the owner's entitlement to have notice of and vote on matters at a meeting of stockholders (bondholders) and to receive dividends (interest). May be a bank, securities firm, clearing house (such as Depository Trust Company—DTC or Cede—its nominee name) whose business it is to serve as a record owner for banks, brokers and others. SEC rules impose certain duties on record owners to communicate all formal issuer news releases with the actual beneficial owners of the securities for which these entities serve. *See* **Beneficial Owner** and **Beneficial Ownership Reports.**

Red Herring   *See* **Preliminary Prospectus.**

Regional Firm   Underwriter/broker-dealer headquartered outside of New York City. *See* **Chapter 3.**

Regional Investment Bankers Association (RIBA)   Charleston S.C. headquartered trade association of NASD member firms primarily focused on raising capital for so-called micro- or small-cap issuers.

Registrant   Company filing a registration statement with the SEC.

Registration Statement   Formal name given to the document filed with the SEC containing mandatory disclosure of a company's business and financial prospects in order to effect registration of securities under the 33 Act or state securities law. Registration statements filed with the SEC are made on different forms depending on the SEC rules applicable to the issuer, the type of transaction in which the securities will be issued and other factors. These SEC forms are designated with the letter "S" followed by a hyphen and the number of the form. Part I of the document is the prospectus distributed to the public. Part II, containing additional and more detailed information such as the company's certificate of incorporation, its bylaws, the underwriting agreement, etc., is not widely distributed (circulated) but is available upon order from the SEC.

Regulation A   An exemption from the registration requirements of the 33 Act promulgated under Section 3(b) of the 33 Act which is less like a traditional private offering exemption and more akin to a mini-public offering filed with and reviewed by the SEC. Permits an issuer to sell securities in an unregistered public offering, up to an aggregate amount of $5 million in any one year, provided that the issuer satisfies all conditions of the Regulation.

Regulation D   SEC Rules 501 through 508 promulgated under Section 3(b) and Section 4(2) of the 33 Act describing different types of limited offerings exempt from the securities registration requirements of the 33 Act. Substantive exempt transactions are described in Rule 504 covering offerings not in excess of $1,000,000; Rule 505 covering offerings not in excess of $5,000,000; and Rule 506 for offerings of unlimited dollar amount. Although not an absolute condition to claiming the exemptions made available under Regulation D, the rules do call for filing with the SEC of at least one Form D. *See* **Accredited Investor.**

Regulation S   Rules 901 through 906, promulgated under the 33 Act, provide exemption from the securities registration requirements of the 33 Act for securities issued and resold in foreign or offshore transactions.

Regulation S-B   SEC regulations promulgated in 1992 (under the 33 and 34 Acts) in connection with adoption of a series of modifications to the law intended to assist smaller companies in the capital formation process. Similar in content to Regulation S-K but intended to be written in more easily understood prose. Principal omissions are those regarding extensive disclosure of executive compensation and stock performance that are in Regulation S-K. *See* **Regulation S-K** and **Small Business Issuer.**

Regulation S-K   SEC regulations promulgated under the 33 and 34 Acts, including the narrative disclosure (non-financial statement) requirements used to comply with substantially all registration statements filed under the 33 Act, and used in annual and other periodic reports filed pursuant to the 34 Act. Consists of Items 101 through 802. Disclosure requirements are centralized in Regulation S-K in order to avoid the need to refer to multiple sources for document content requirements.

Regulation S-X   SEC regulations promulgated under the 33 and 34 Acts providing the substantive financial statement and accounting data requirements used to comply with substantially all registration statements filed under the 33 Act and used in annual and other periodic reports filed pursuant to the 34 Act.

Release for Sale   Commencement of the formal offering of an underwriting by the lead manager.

Release Wire   Formal telegraphic/electronic announcement to underwriters and selected dealers, if any, by the lead manager announcing that the sale of a new issue may commence.

Reopen   Process of underwriting and distributing an additional amount of bonds for an issuer carrying the same coupon, maturity date and all other non-money terms as an existing issue already trading in the secondary market.

Reporting Company   Any company, public or private, that must file periodic reports with the SEC.

Representations (Reps) and Warranties   Formal acknowledgment of one party's disclosure(s) of and commitment to upholding/ performing certain mutually agreed upon actions to a contra party. *See* **Chapter 2.**

Restricted List   Compilation of securities in which an individual firm is involved as an underwriter. The firm may accept non-deal related orders in the same or similar classes of securities on this list only on an unsolicited basis and must mark any such tickets accordingly. The restriction period of any individual stock lasts from filing date until termination of price and trading restrictions.

Restricted Securities   First defined under SEC Rule 144 as securities issued in a transaction, or chain of transactions, not involving any public offering (*i.e.,* a private placement), or issued in a transaction complying with Section 4(6), Section 4(2) of Regulation D. Since adoption of this formal definition, "restricted securities" is the technically correct way to refer to legend or lettered stock (named after the letter which the purchaser must sign, agreeing not to attempt to resell the securities publicly except by registration or exemption). The definition is important because of the responsibilities it imposes upon issuers (and indirectly their advisers), in transactions resulting in issuance of restricted securities, to explain the restriction(s) on resale of such securities.

Retention   Amount of an underwriter's statutory underwriting commitment which the lead manager allows the underwriter to keep for the underwriter's own sales effort. Initial retention is usually a fixed percentage of the underwriter's total underwriting commitment, while final retention includes any give-up's, additional takedown(s) and directed orders. *See* **Free Retention, Give-Up, Takedown, Directed Order,** and **Chapter 5.**

Reverse Inquiry   Process initiated by an investment bank whereby an investor's portfolio need or requirement leads to creation of an ad hoc underwritten transaction designed to fill the so-identified need or requirement.

RIBA   *See* **Regional Investment Bankers Association.**

Right of First Refusal   Contractual agreement that, if found in an underwriting agreement, obligates the issuer to give the lead-manager the right to manage any future financings for a defined period of time after the current offering is priced and distributed.

Roadshow   Process whereby the book running manager arranges and then accompanies issuer senior management (customarily the Chief Executive Officer and the Chief Financial Officer) on a one- to three-week trip to major money center cities both in the United States and abroad to meet potential investors. The story told must be consistent with and stay inside of the four corners of the prospectus. Most of these meetings occur with institutional investors. *See* **One-on-One Meeting.**

Rule 144   Promulgated under the 33 Act by the SEC, providing exemption from the securities registration requirements of the 33 Act for resale(s) of securities held by control persons and affiliates and of restricted securities, regardless of their owners, provided that such restricted securities have been held for a minimum amount of time (generally at least one year). Sales exempted under Rule 144 may generally be made only in limited amounts and require adherence to certain procedures specified in the Rule.

Rule 144A   Promulgated under the 33 Act, providing a private placement exemption from the securities registration requirements of the 33 Act for resale(s) of securities by certain institutional owners (known as Qualified Institutional Buyers or "QIBs") under far fewer restrictions than imposed on sellers under Rule 144 and normally carrying registration rights for the purchasers. *See* **Rule 144** and **Qualified Institutional Buyer.**

Rule 405   New York Stock Exchange "know your customer rule," stating what is suitable for one investor may be less appropriate for another. *See* Article 3 of the NASD Rules of Fair Practice for an extensive definition/discussion.

Rule 415   Permits a company to register an amount of securities ". . . it might reasonably expect to sell within a two year period . . ." for an offering(s) to be conducted on a continuous or delayed basis more than 30 days into the future. Codifies the so-called shelf registration process whereby securities already registered under this rule can be "taken down off the shelf" and reoffered to the public.

Rule 430A   Permits the SEC to declare a registration statement effective without having actual pricing information. The issuer must supply such information by filing an ex-post-facto amendment.

Rule 701   Promulgated under the 33 Act as Rules 701, 702, and 703. Provides exemption from the securities registration requirements of the 33 Act to nonpublic companies for the offer, sale, and issuance of securities to employees, officers, directors, and certain consultants and independent contractors, provided the principal purpose of the transaction is compensatory (for services rendered) rather than for the purpose of raising new capital for the issuer.

Sales Credit (Selling Concession)   Portion of the underwriting gross spread that rewards the actual sale of a security—the sales incentive to distribute a security. Credited to the firm or salesperson responsible for making such sale.

Schedule E   *See* **Qualified Independent Underwriter** and **Chapter 7.**

SEAQ   *See* **Stock Exchange Automated Quotation.**

Seasoning   Period after the offering of a new issue, wherein a company's securities start to develop a research following and a broader investor base, thereby gradually building secondary market liquidity.

Secondary Offering/Distribution   Public sale of a large block of already issued and outstanding securities held by investors, usually corporations, institutions or other affiliated persons, with the proceeds from such offering going to the selling shareholder(s) rather than the issuer. Such a sale is handled in the over-the-counter market, usually underwritten and executed at a fixed price with the seller(s) obtaining permission from the applicable SRO. A term often but erroneously used to denote a follow-on public offering of primary shares for an already listed company.

Securities and Investment Board (SIB)   Body set up under the Financial Services Act to police both London's self regulatory organizations and its financial markets but without the power of the U.S. Securities and Exchange Commission.

Securities Industry Association (SIA)   The United States' securities industry's trade group/lobby. Result of a 1971 amalgamation of the Association of Stock Exchange Firms (ASEF) and the Investment Bankers Association (IBA), the two then existing trade groups representing retail firms (ASEF) and investment banking firms (IBA) respectively.

Security   Statutory definition in Section 2(1) of the 33 Act defines a security broadly: "Unless the context otherwise requires . . . the term 'security' means any note, stock, treasury stock, bond, debenture, evidence of indebtedness, certificate of interest or participation in any profit sharing agreement, collateral trust certificate, preorganization certificate or subscription, transferable share, investment contract, voting trust certificate, certificate of deposit for a security, fractional undivided interest in oil, gas or other mineral rights; any put, call, straddle, option or privilege on any security, certificate of deposit, or group or index of securities (including any interest therein or based on the value thereof), or any put, call, straddle, option or privilege entered into on a national securities exchange relating to foreign currency; or, in general, any interest or instrument commonly known as a 'security' or any certificate of interest or participation in, temporary or interim certificate for, receipt for, guaranty of or warrant or right to subscribe to or purchase any of the foregoing." The risk of liability and the costs and burdens of complying with the securities laws have been a constant source of inspiration for entrepreneurs who have sought to avoid the impact of such laws by selling something that was not a security but just as a good as a security insofar as the investor is concerned. Court tests determining when a security exists have concentrated on substance rather than form. The current state of the law for analyzing unusual investment or financing schemes to determine if they are indeed securities is a test that must satisfy the following six factors: (1) Investment of money. (2) In a common enterprise. (3) With the expectation of profit. (4) Profit to be derived from efforts of someone other than the investor. (5) Marketed in the manner of a traditional security or investment. (6) Economic realities of the transaction are those present in a sale(s) of traditional securities.

Selected Dealer   Non-underwriter distributor of a new issue, earning only the sales credit portion of the gross spread and only on the securities it actually distributes. *See* **Selling Group.**

Selling Concession   The discount, or difference between the price at which underwriter and selected dealer participants make purchases from the lead manager, and the public offering price at which such participants make sales to the public.

Selling Group   Composed of two groups: (1) an underwriter participates in selling group to the extent that its net take down exceeds its underwriting commitment; and (2) a non-underwriter participates in selling group when it takes down underwritten securities for re-sale to an investor(s). *See* **Selected Dealer.**

Selling Shareholder(s)   Owner(s) of shares who is(are) selling as part of a registered (or non-registered) underwritten public offering.

Sell Side   Colloquial term for a securities firm/broker-dealer. *See* **Buy Side.**

Session   One day of trading from the opening to the closing.

Shadow Book   Compilation of all suspected or would-be
purchasers of an underwritten transaction that have not yet actually
committed. *See* **Book.**

Short List   Originally a Euro term—indicates finalists in an
investment banking selection process. *See* **Beauty Contest.**

Short Swing Trading   Section 16(b) of the 34 Act prohibits the
purchase and sale of publicly traded securities within a six-month
period by executive officers, directors, and 10 percent or greater
beneficial owners of securities of that company. If such trading
activity occurs, the violator may be compelled to return any profit
from such trades to the company. The prohibition against short swing
trading may be enforced by any shareholder and is sometimes
confused with insider trading. *See* **Beneficial Ownership Reports.**

SIB   *See* **Securities and Investment Board.**

SIPC   Securities Investor Protection Corporation.

Small Business Issuer   Issuer class created by the SEC and
afforded the opportunity to take advantage of certain reductions in
both the amount and type of disclosures required in public offerings
by use of Forms SB-1 and SB-2, as described in the initial phases of
the 34 Act obligations pursuant to Regulation SB. Generally defined
as a company meeting the following criteria: (1) U.S. or Canadian
domicile. (2) Not a mutual fund. (3) Annual revenues of less than
US $25,000,000. (4) If public, the aggregate value of shares held by
non-affiliates must not exceed US $25,000,000.

SOES   Small Order Execution System.

Soft Dollar Arrangement   Agreement between an asset
manager/money manager and a broker-dealer whereby the money
manager will receive securities research and/or non-execution
services in exchange for brokerage commissions paid to that broker-
dealer from the execution of buy and/or sell transactions generated
on behalf of investor client accounts. Under the safe harbor provided
by Section 28(e) of the 34 Act, when an asset manager causes clients
to pay a commission that is higher than the lowest rate generally
available, that manager is "paying up" for research or other services
with "soft dollars." The term has also been applied to allocation of

sales credits generated in an underwritten transaction. Since the issuer/seller of an underwritten deal is, in effect, "paying" the sales credit (commission) because it is part of the gross spread, institutional purchasers have learned to apportion pieces of a large purchase order of the underwritten deal to various underwriters and selected dealers to "pay" for other services through the vehicle of the syndicate sales credit.

Solicited Transaction One initiated by a broker or dealer call ("solicitation") to an investor customer.

SPAC *See* **Special Purpose Acquisition Corporation.**

Special Bracket Formerly synonymous with bulge bracket, but today more indicative of a one-time or ad hoc bracket created to accommodate a firm or a small group of firms in a position (bracket), almost always higher, in which it(they) world normally not appear. *See* **Bulge Bracket** and **Chapter 3.**

Special Bracket Firm *See* **Bulge Bracket Firm** and **Chapter 3.**

Special Purpose Acquisition Corporation (SPAC) Company formed to acquire a business(es) with cash or securities created by the IPO of the SPAC—a so-called blind pool.

Spinning Controversial allocation of Hot Issue IPO shares to a senior executive(s) of a potential underwriting client company. *See* **Chapter 7.**

Spot Secondary Non-registered sale of exchange or Nasdaq listed, already issued and outstanding shares of a company being re-distributed from one seller to one or many new buyers. It takes place in the over-the-counter market, usually on a firm underwritten basis. *See* **Underwritten Block Trade.**

Spread *See* **Gross Spread.**

Spread Sheet Fact sheet containing the terms negotiated at a final price meeting, including the offering price, the gross spread and its breakdown, the terms relating to dividend payment or interest accrual, the day and date and place of settlement and delivery and all other information pertinent to the transaction.

SRO **Self-Regulatory Organization.**

Stabilization   The placement by the lead manager of orders to buy, or in NASDAQ of a syndicate bid, for the purpose of preventing the fall in price of the offered security during the offering period. This is a form of temporary manipulation permitted by Regulation M. *See* **Chapter 5.**

Stale Date   Date after which a registrant must update the contents of a filing with the SEC.

Step Up Privilege   Over-allotment option in an underwritten standby of a pre-emptive rights offering, permitting dealer takedown of an incremental percentage of securities beyond its underwriting amount.

Sticker   With regard to a prospectus, a post-effective/post-pricing addendum to the document that contains additional information deemed not material enough to require recirculation. Takes its name from the less-than-full-page size of its printed content that is affixed to the prospectus cover with a gummed "sticker."

Stock Exchange Automated Quotation (SEAQ)   Computerized upstairs telephonic dealer market that replaced physical on-floor trading on the London Stock Exchange at the inception of Big Bang in October 1986.

Sub-Major Bracket   Underwriting bracket appearing between the mezzanine and the first regional bracket of an underwriting account. *See* **Chapter 3.**

Subject   Syndicate term indicating the book-running manager is no longer allocating shares of an issue. *See* **Firm.**

Subject to Prior Sale and/or Change in Price   Traditional qualifying phrase appended to an offer of secondary market securities.

Supply   With reference to a directed order, the act by the lead manager of allocating additional securities from the pot to an underwriting participant or selected dealer stemming from the decision of the purchaser of such securities to direct a portion of the sales credits attached to those securities for the credit of an individual firm (thereby increasing that firm's retention). *See* **Protection.**

Syndicate   Ad hoc group of underwriters (dealers) who band together to underwrite (purchase from the issuer/seller), almost always at a fixed price less an underwriting discount (gross spread), and to distribute a new issue of securities or a block (usually large) of already issued and outstanding securities at a stated fixed price to investors.

Syndicate Invitation   Formal offer by the lead manager to participate in an underwriting and detailing the non-money terms and other specifics of the transaction.

Syndicate Settlement   Also known as the closing date. Day on which the lead manager pays for and receives the underwritten securities from the company/issuer/seller. In turn, underwriters and selling group members pick up and pay for their take-down from the lead manager. Usually conforms to three-day secondary market settlement requirements but may be longer.

Syndicate Short   Amount of underwritten securities offered in excess of the offering's actual size that have been intentionally over-allotted by the lead manager.

Tag   As in "price" tag—synonymous with price and usually relating to a secondary market security.

Tag Ends   As in "down to . . .", a phrase usually indicating an unsold balance of 10 percent or less of an underwritten offering.

Take Back   Recapture of securities by the lead manager that had been allotted to an underwriter(s) and/or selected dealer(s). The lead manager has the contractual right (but not the obligation), under the AAU, to recapture ("take back") unsold (long) positions solely at its discretion.

Take Down (Retention)   The act of "taking down" underwritten securities from the lead manager for distribution to an investor(s).

T & R Table   *See* **Time and Responsibility Table.**

Targeted Stock (Tracking Stock)   Assignment of a portion of a conglomerate's business(es) via an underwritten offering to the public. Distinguished from a spin-off in that, here, the parent retains ownership of the targeted/tracked division while investors are able to "target" or "track" that portion of the overall company's activities for investment. Often used as an attempt to enhance shareholder value.

Taxable Fixed Income (TFI)   The trading floor(s) or portion thereof where a firm conducts its sales and trading of corporate bonds and preferred stocks.

Ten Percent Order (Ten Percenter)   Order from one buyer for 10 percent of the total size of an underwritten offering.

Termination   Removal of formal price and trading restrictions of a new issue, indicating that the securities are free to trade in the open (secondary) market. The lead manager issues formal notice of this event, most often after determination that the issue is "all sold." If there is a penalty bid in effect, it may remain so.

TFI   *See* **Taxable Fixed Income.**

Time and Responsibility (T&R) Table   Compilation of the sequence of events, and primary responsibility assignment for ensuring completion of such events, for an underwritten public offering. Prepared by the lead manager and a primary focus of the first "all hands meeting." *See* **All Hands Meeting.**

Timing   Estimated date of offering for an underwritten issue, expressed in terms of year, quarter, month, week (or variation of any of the preceding periods, *e.g.,* "early to mid . . ."), or actual day.

Tire Kicker   Potential purchaser of securities who never declares him/herself by actually purchasing.

Tombstone   Advertisement announcing an underwritten offering, or other investment banking transaction, that may include, but is not limited to, the name of the issuing company, amount and description of securities, offering price, trading symbol, location of secondary trading and name(s) of underwriter(s). So-called because of its formal, stilted appearance. *See* **Appendix 3.**

Trading Suspension   Temporary halt in the secondary market for a security. Usually occurs due to a large order imbalance on either the sell or (less often) the buy side stemming from the announcement of an unexpected event.

Tranche   A discrete portion of an underwritten offering, *i.e.,* an offering may have a United States or North American tranche, a

European or Asian tranche or a single country tranche, often with separate underwriting syndicates for each.

UA   Underwriting Agreement.

Underwriter's Purchase Price   Price paid to the issuer/seller(s) by the underwriters. Calculated by deducting the gross spread from the offering price.

Underwriting Account (Account)   Entire list of dealers committed to purchase an issue.

Underwriting Activity Report   A NASD requirement if the lead manager elects to employ Passive Market Making. *See* **Chapter 5.**

Underwriting Commitment   Quantity of securities a firm commits to purchase from the issuer/seller. Such commitment is important as it relates to a firm's conformance with SEC/NASD net capital rules. Importantly, this quantity is not necessarily the amount ("retention") of securities a firm will have available for actual re-sale to its investor clients. A firm's underwriting commitment represents the maximum number of securities for which it is liable to purchase should the lead manager choose to purchase securities from the issuer/seller in a less-than-fully distributed deal. On such an occasion, where the lead manager requires underwriters to take down their respective unsold underwriting commitments (pot liability), it indicates that demand for the securities is soft. The underwriting commitment percentage is also the basis for any future contribution by participating firms to any litigation expense, and it also determines each firm's final share of the net underwriting fee. Mathematically, it is a firm's underwriting commitment divided by the total size of the deal.

Underwritten Block Trade   The purchase, with a view to immediate resale, of a large amount of new issue or secondary securities by a single firm, or small syndicate of firms, and eschewing the traditional marketing period associated with a new issue. Normally occurs only in extremely liquid, seasoned securities.

Unsold Balance   Undistributed securities remaining in a syndicate account at the actual moment of inquiry.

Unsolicited Transaction   One initiated by an investor or customer call to a broker or dealer. *See* **Solicited Transaction.**

Upstairs   Off of an exchange trading floor, as in "upstairs" firm— *e.g.,* a broker/dealer conducting a sales, trading and research business with buy side investors—as opposed to a dealer firm operating as a specialist "downstairs" on an exchange floor.

Use of Proceeds   Use(s) to which an issuing company plans for the monies raised by selling a new issue of securities. Becomes particularly important if a reduction in either the size or price (or both) of an issue alters significantly such use—a potential cause for recirculation.

Whisper Number   Unofficial, non-company sanctioned earnings per share estimate that begins to circulate among investors and dealers between two regularly scheduled earnings reporting periods for the company in question.

Wire   A formal communication between the lead manager and any participant(s) (and vice versa) of an underwriten transaction and customarily sent through a third-party service provider.

Working Party List   Compilation of senior people from each entity/firm involved in an investment banking transaction. It usually includes individual's names with their firm name, addresses (work and home) and all voice and data communication numbers (work and home, including summer and/or weekend). Normally put together at the first all hands meeting.

Wrapper   Addendum to a final prospectus, usually in the form of a two page (four side) printed document "wrapped" around the outside of the prospectus itself.

INVESTMENT BANK SERVICE
MARKED DERIVATIVE SECURITIES

Individual firm service marked derivative securities started to appear as proprietary products in the early 1980s with the creation of PRIMES and SCORES (Alex, Brown), CATS (Salomon Brothers) and TIGERS and LYONS (Merrill Lynch). Since then, such securities have proliferated. A current list of acronyms (including their definition and sponsor) known to the Editor as of October 1998 follows.[6]

ACES	Automatically convertible equity securities	Goldman Sachs
CHIPS	Common-linked higher income participation securities	Bear Stearns
CUBS	Customized upside basket securities	Bear Stearns
DECS	Debt exchangeable for common stock	Salomon Brothers
ELKS	Equity linked securities	Salomon Brothers
EPIPS	Enhanced perpetual income preferred securities	Everen
EPPICS	Equity providing preferred income convertible note securities	Merrill Lynch
ICONS	Investment common convertible notes	Merrill Lynch/ Salomon

---

6. The editors thank CommScan LLC for its help in compiling this list.

IQ Notes	Insured quarterly notes	Edward Jones
LYONS	Liquid yield option notes	Merrill Lynch
MARCS	Mandatory adjustable redeemable convertible securities	UBS
MEDS	Monthly exchangeable debt securities	JP Morgan
MIPS	Monthly income preferred shares	Goldman Sachs
PARCKS	Premium accelerable redemptive convertible knockout securities	Deutsche Bank
PEEQS	Protected exchangeable equity linked securities	Morgan Stanley
PENS	Privatization exchangeable notes	Goldman Sachs
PEPS	Premium exchangeable participating shares	Morgan Stanley
PEARS	Preferred equity redemption cumulative stock	Merrill Lynch/ Morgan
PERQS	Preferred equity linked redemption quarterly pay securities	Morgan Stanley
PIERS	Preferred income equity redeemable securities	Lehman Brothers
PIES	Premium income exchangeable securities	Lehman Brothers
PRIDES	Preferred redeemable increased dividend equity securities	Merrill Lynch
QUIDS	Quarterly income debt securities	Goldman Sachs

QUIPS	Quarterly income preferred securities	Goldman Sachs
ROARS	Remarketable or redeemable securities	Montgomery
SAILS	Stock appreciation income linked securities	CSFB
SEALS	Securities enhancing aftermarket liquidity	Prudential Securities
SIRENS	Step-up income redeemable equity notes	CSFB
SPURS	Shared preference redeemable securities	Warburg Dillon Read
STRYPES	Structured yield product exchangeable for stock	Merrill Lynch
SUNS	Stock upside note securities	Lehman Brothers
TAPS	Threshold appreciation price securities	Salomon Smith Barney
TECONS	Team convertible securities	JP Morgan
TEES	Trust equity enhanced securities	Sutro
TIDES	Term income deferrable equity securities	CSFB
TIMES	Trust issued mandatory exchange securities	Bear Stearns
TOPRS	Trust originated preferred securities	Morgan/Merrill/ Lehman
TRACES	Trust automatic common exchange securities	Goldman Sachs
YEELDS	Yield enhanced equity linked debt securities	Lehman Brothers
YES	Yield enhanced securities	Goldman Sachs

BIBLIOGRAPHY/SUGGESTED REFERENCE SOURCES

Allen, Samuel N. *"A Lawyer's Guide to the Operation of Underwriting Syndicates,"* 26 *New England Law Review* 319, Winter 1991.

American Stock Exchange 1994 Fact Book. New York, 1994.

Auerbach, Joseph and Samuel L. Hayes III. *Investment Banking and Diligence—What Price Deregulation?* Boston: Harvard Business School Press, 1986.

A.G. Becker Paribas Incorporated. *Commercial Paper Issuer Reports, Basic Series 1984/1.* Chicago, 1984.

The Best in Securities Offerings: The Full Text of Insightful Articles to Help You Raise Capital Successfully. New York: Bowne & Co. Inc., 1998.

Bloomenthal, Harold S. *Going Public and the Public Corporation,* Securities Law Series Volume 1A. New York: Clark Boardman Callaghan, 1997.

Bloomenthal, Harold S. and Holme, Roberts & Owen L.L.P. *Going Public Handbook.* Volume 1. St. Paul, MN: West Group, 1998.

Bochner, Steven E. and Priest, Gregory M. *Guide to the Initial Public Offering,* Second Edition. Merrill Corporation, 1993.

Carosso, Vincent P. *Investment Banking in America—A History.* Cambridge, MA: Harvard University Press, 1970.

Chen, Hsuan-Chi and Jay R. Ritter. "The Seven Percent Solution." *Journal of Finance* 55, no. 3 (June 2000).

Childs, C.F. *Concerning United States Government Securities.* Chicago: RR Donnelley & Sons Company, 1947.

Cook, Timothy Q. and Robert K. LaRoche. *Instruments of the Money Market,* Seventh Edition. Richmond, VA: Federal Reserve Bank of Richmond, 1993.

Downes, John, ed. *Dictionary of Finance and Investment Terms,* Fourth Edition. Hauppauge, NY: Barron's Educational Series Inc., 1995.

Downes, John, and Jordan Elliot Goodman. *Finance & Investment Handbook,* Fourth Edition. Hauppauge, NY: Barron's Educational Series Inc., 1995.

The Federal Reserve System—Purposes and Functions, Fifth Edition. Washington D.C.: Board of Governors of The Federal Reserve System, 1963.

The Federal Reserve System—Purposes and Functions, Eighth Edition. Washington D.C.: Board of Governors of The Federal Reserve System, 1994.

Fennelly, John F. and Robert W. Clark, Jr., eds. *Fundamentals of Investment Banking.* Englewood Cliffs, NJ: Prentice-Hall, Inc., 1949.

Financial Management Division, Securities Industry Association, *FMD Newsbriefs.* New York, 1997.

Fishman, James J. *The Transformation of Threadneedle Street—the Deregulation of Britain's Financial Services.* Durham, NC: Carolina Academic Press, 1993.

Friedman, Stanley J. and Donald E. Schwartz. *How to Go Public,* Corporate Law and Practice Transcript Series No. 17. New York: Practising Law Institute, 1971.

Gastineau, Gary L. and Mark P. Kritzman. *The Dictionary of Financial Risk Management* Frank J. Fabozzi Associates, 1996.

Going Public. New York: The Nasdaq Stock Market, Inc., 1998 (Revised 2000).

Grant, Jr., William J. *"Overview of the Underwriting Process." Securities Underwriting: A Practitioner's Guide.* pp. 25-45. Edited by Kenneth J. Bialkin and William J. Grant, Jr. New York City: Practising Law Institute, 1985.

Halle, John J., Ronald J. Lone and Yingxi Fu. *Going Public*, Fourth Edition. Stoel Rives Boley Jones & Grey, RR Donnelley Financial, International Printing & Information Management Services, RR Donnelley & Sons Company.

Harper, Victor L., *"Second Edition—Handbook of Investment Products and Services,"* New York: New York Institute of Finance, 1986.

Hayes III, Samuel L., ed. *Wall Street and Regulation.* Boston, MA: Harvard Business School Press, 1987.

Hayes III, Samuel L., A. Michael Spence and David Van Praag Marks. *Competition in the Investment Banking Industry.* Cambridge and London: Harvard University Press, 1983.

Hayes III, Samuel L. and Philip M. Hubbard. *Investment Banking.* Boston: Harvard Business School Press, 1990.

Hayes, III, Samuel L., *"Investment Banking: power structure in flux,"* pp. 136-152, Harvard Business Review, Boston, March–April 1971.

Hayes, III, Samuel L., *"The Transformation of Investment Banking,"* pp. 152-170, Harvard Business Review, Boston, January–February 1979.

Israels, Carlos L. and George M. Duff, Jr. *When Corporations Go Public.* New York: Practising Law Institute, 1962.

Jennings, Richard W., Harold Marsh Jr., John C. Coffee, Jr. and Joel Seligman. *Federal Securities Laws—Selected Statues, Rules and Forms,* 1995 Edition. New York: The Foundation Press, Inc., 1995.

Johnson, Jr., Charles J. *Corporate Finance and the Securities Laws.* Prentice Hall Law & Business, Englewood Cliffs NJ, 1991.

Johnson, Jr., Charles J. and Joseph McLaughlin. *Corporate Finance and the Securities Laws, Second Edition.* Englewood Cliffs, NJ: Aspen Law & Business, 1997.

Kerr, Ian M. *Big Bang.* London: Euromoney Publications, 1986.

Lehmann, Michael B. *The Irwin Guide to Using The Wall Street Journal,* 5th Edition. New York: McGraw-Hill, 1996.

Leisner, Richard M. *An Introduction to Basic Federal Securities Laws Applicable to Certain Capital Formation Techniques.* Tampa, FL: Trenam, Kemker, Scharf, Barkin, Frye, O'Neill & Mullis, P.A., 1997, 1998, and 1999.

Little, Jeffrey B. and Lucien Rhodes. *Understanding Wall Street,* Second Edition. Blue Ridge Summit, PA: Tab Books Inc., 1987.

Loss, Louis. *Fundamentals of Securities Regulation.* Boston and Toronto: Little, Brown and Company, 1983.

Mackay, Charles. *Extraordinary Popular Delusions and the Madness of Crowds.* New York: The Noonday Press, 1932 (written in 1835).

Medina, Harold R. Corrected opinion of, in *United States v. Morgan Stanley et. al.* filed February 4, 1954 as 118 F. Supp. 621 (S.D.N.Y. 1953).

Millard, Andrew, ed. *SBC Warburg Euromoney Directory 1996.* London: Euromoney Publications PLC, 1996.

Neumark, John Arthur, ed. *Wall Street 20th Century.* Yale Daily News, New Haven, 1960.

O'Connor, J.F.T. *Banks Under Roosevelt.* Chicago: Callaghan and Company, 1938.

Quarter Century of Trust, A Short History of The Depository Trust Company, pamphlet.

Rea, David B. and William J. Grant, Jr. "The Syndication and Marketing Process." *Securities Underwriting: A Practitioner's Guide.* pp. 277-291. Edited by Kenneth J. Bialkin and William J. Grant, Jr. New York City: Practising Law Institute, 1985.

Report of Special Study of Securities Markets of the Securities and Exchange Commission—Part I. 88th Congress, 1st sess, H. Doc. 95. Washington: U.S. Government Printing Office, 1963.

Schnelder, Carl W., Manko, Joseph M. and Kant, Robert S. *Going Public: Practice, Procedure and Consequences.* New York: Bowne & Co., Inc., supplement to the Bowne Red Box subscription service, 1996.

Sherwood, Hugh C. *How Corporate and Municipal Debt is Rated—An Inside Look at Standard & Poor's Rating System.* New York: John Wiley & Sons, 1976.

Sobel, Robert. *The Big Board—A History of the New York Stock Market.* New York and London: The Free Press, 1965.

Still, Elizabeth L. and Strongin, David G., eds. *The Securities Industry Briefing Book—A Partnership with America.* New York and Washington: Securities Industry Association, 1994.

United States Securities and Exchange Commission. *The Work of the SEC.* http://www.sec.gov/asec/wot.htm. Washington, 1997.

United States Securities and Exchange Commission. *About the SEC.* http://www.sec.gov/about sec.htm. Washington, 1997.

Urdang, Laurence, Editor, *"The Random House Dictionary of the English Language."* New York: Random House, 1968.

Winter, Elmer L. *A Complete Guide to Making A Public Stock Offering.* Englewood Cliffs, NJ: Prentice-Hall, Inc., 1962.

BIBLIOGRAPHY

[faded, illegible bibliographic entries]

INDEX

[References are to sections.]